Developmental Variation and Learning Disorders

Developmental Variation and Learning Disorders

SECOND EDITION

Melvin D. Levine, M.D.

Professor of Pediatrics,
The University of North Carolina School of Medicine

Director, The Clinical Center for the Study of
Development and Learning, The University
of North Carolina, Chapel Hill, A University-Affiliated Program

Cochair, All Kinds of Minds, A Nonprofit Institute
Dedicated to the Understanding of Differences in Learning

With
Martha Reed, M.Ed.

Psychoeducational Specialist
Faculty, All Kinds of Minds

Educators Publishing Service, Inc.
Cambridge and Toronto

ISBN 0-8388-1992-3

Educators Publishing Service, Inc., 31 Smith Place, Cambridge, MA 02138-1089

For Bambi,
whose energizing encouragement, understanding,
and perspective permeate these chapters

and

For Mark,
whose dedication to teaching and learning,
encouragement, and patience have contributed
inspiration and courage to this endeavor

Contents

Preface to the Second Edition

It has been more than ten years since the publication of the first edition of *Developmental Variation and Learning Disorders.* During that period the status of children with differences in learning has been affected by some far-reaching advancements and some devastating setbacks.

On the notably positive side have been the dramatic revelations brought about by neuroscientific and educational research. A multitude of exacting studies have enabled us to pinpoint more accurately the mechanisms and even the micro-neuroanatomical lesions that underlie certain patterns of disordered learning. Ample research funding, along with neuroimaging techniques and increasingly rigorous investigative methodologies, have stimulated this growth spurt in our knowledge. Using this new knowledge, we have developed some highly promising modes of intervention that have the potential for facilitating the learning and development of many struggling children.

The dark side of the past ten years can be seen in our growing inability to provide targeted services to affected children. First, we lack cost-effective service delivery models. In both education and medicine, we have failed to develop validated multidisciplinary systems for the evaluation and long-term management of students with learning disorders. Consequently, we have not translated our increasingly sophisticated knowledge into more and better help for faltering young people. Many school systems, extolling the virtues of "inclusionism" (in some cases as a rationalization for insufficient funding) have neglected the highly individualized needs of countless educationally thwarted yet salvageable children and adolescents. These include students who would benefit immeasurably from language therapy, social skills training, assistance with written output, help with mathematical concept formation, or other forms of support.

A second problem exists in the domain of educational policy formulation. In their zeal to elevate academic standards, many politicians have made the assumption that "one size fits all," that all children and adolescents require identical educational experiences, that they must meet common educational standards, and that their educational accomplishments must be assessed by one test or a uniform series of tests. Such policy often dictates that teachers and schools be judged by the test scores of their students rather than the care they provide to growing children. The result is a trend toward "teaching to the test." This blatantly discriminates against children with learning disorders and/or unique talents, many of whom are unable to reveal their strengths on traditional tests. To treat (or test) all students in the same manner is to treat them unequally.

A third negative tendency during the last decade has been the creation, propagation, and canonization of yet more diagnostic labels, and more ways of lumping children together under these labels, thereby neglecting their salient individual differences and quite often stigmatizing them. The labels ostensibly help access funding and establish an individual's eligibility for services. At the same time, however, these too simplistic categories justify the overuse of medication and other potential therapeutic shortcuts and Band-Aids. Most importantly, these labels are often intrinsically pessimistic and reductionist. It is regrettable that we have been unable to offer, in a nonstigmatizing way, unqualified help to children who so desperately need assistance. Like the first edition, this revised version of *Developmental Variation and Learning Disorders* shuns labeling entirely in favor of informed observation, an understanding of the phenomena that impede learning, and management that is based on a child's unique profile of strengths, affinities, and dysfunctions.

In the second edition of this book, we have updated each chapter while preserving the original organization of the text. The chapter on attention has been extensively rewritten to represent this fundamental construct as a fragile network of basic brain controls. Substantial revisions have also been made in the chapters covering the other seven neurodevelopmental constructs.

Martha Reed, a talented educational diagnostician, has collaborated actively in the writing of this edition. In particular, she has revised the chapters on educational subskills and skills, while infusing many other chapters with practical insights into assessment and management.

We hope that educators, clinicians, and policy makers will value the second edition of *Developmental Variation and Learning Disorders* not only as a source of abundant information about children and adolescents but also as a volume with a mission and a distinct humanitarian philosophy. We want these pages to empower and energize our readers to redeem children who are innocent victims of their own misinterpreted neurodevelopmental profiles—children who are a disappointment to the adults in their lives and, more importantly, a disappointment to themselves.

Preface to the First Edition

I have written *Developmental Variation and Learning Disorders* to help those who are helping school children who are not succeeding. This book strives to meet that goal by drawing together a vast and decidedly fragmented body of theoretical and scientific knowledge against a backdrop of clinical realism. It reflects my perspective as a developmental-behavioral pediatrician, who during two decades has evaluated and collaborated with several thousand children whose faltering and suffering have deterred their education. This book is also the product of my long-standing immersion in a steadily evolving literature that concerns itself with learning disorders and with the normal development and developmental expectations of school children. Moreover, my own research questions and findings have exerted their influence on the content of these pages. From my studies and observations, a distinct point of view has emerged and given special impetus to the creation of *Developmental Variation and Learning Disorders.* It is a point of view solidly grounded in a fervent belief in, respect for, and celebration of individual variation during childhood.

Perhaps in the same way that the early lives of some novelists may influence their works, a succession of formative life experiences has left a firm imprint on me and thus on the pages of *Developmental Variation and Learning Disorders.* Perhaps the reader's understanding of this book will be enhanced by knowledge of some of these experiences.

As a school-age child, I contended (not always successfully) with my own developmental variations; I experienced my share of failure and embarrassment, which was understandably painful. But in retrospect, what was injurious was that neither I nor any of the adults in my life were capable of seeing and describing the factors contributing to or complicating my struggles, so I was not soothed by the benefit of insight.

Throughout elementary and junior high school, I was infatuated with biographies and spent long hours reading about the tortured early lives of ultimately successful people. The epigraphs for each chapter in this book testify to the continuing influence of this inclination.

In high school I became interested in writing and struggled intently with my own stylistic limitations and creative bottlenecks. In college, studying philosophy and literature triggered my interest in epistemology and ethics. During the summers I worked as a camp counselor, teaching mountain climbing to school-age boys and girls who astonished me with their varied responses to the challenge of striving toward a summit. For some, inordinate effort exacted anguish, while for others, who sought the heaviest backpacks and savored the most hostile weather conditions, it produced satisfaction. The ultimate exhilaration of the view from the top and the varied reactions to personal mastery made a lasting impression on me during these early observations of differences in childhood performance.

Graduate study and medical school, internship, and residency solidified my earlier interest in theories of knowledge and school-age children. As a pediatrician, I came to realize that I was far more interested in outpatients than in inpatients; the physical and functional health of active children in a social context offered an important and intellectually exciting challenge.

Two years as the school physician and a general pediatrician on an overseas military base taught me an appreciation for the many ways in which collaboration between pediatricians and schools could have a powerful impact on the lives of children. The child in the school environment came to symbolize the ultimate integration of physical health, mental health, and neurodevelopmental function. I knew then that I would always want to work closely with children, teachers, administrators, and educational policy makers.

After my military service, I became director of the outpatient department at The Children's Hospital in Boston. Initially I expected that much of my responsibility would revolve around fevers, chronic illnesses, and other traditional pediatric problems. Instead, it turned out that most children referred to the general outpatient clinics were manifesting disorders of function rather than conditions of physical ill health. Not only that, most were of school age. It was during these first years as director of an outpatient department that I became concerned about the ethics and epistemology of diagnostic evaluations of children. I found that the assessment and treatment of a child with learning difficulties all too often reflected the professional training of the person to whom that child was referred (often arbitrarily). If children saw a psychiatrist, there was a strong chance that their problems would be perceived as psychiatric. If children were referred to a speech and language pathologist, linguistic aspects might be thought to constitute all or a large part of their difficulties. A neurologist would promulgate a neurological formulation, and those of us in pediatrics had our own diagnostic biases, too. In fact, it became quite clear that the evaluation of children with school difficulties and other functional problems was far too dependent on the specialized training of the individuals they consulted.

At the same time, I discovered that children were not always fairly evaluated in their schools. Although Public Law 94-142 became important legislation, its implementation was frequently compromised by fiscal considerations, political conflicts of interest, disciplinary biases, rigidly enforced regulations, and a lack of consistent quality control over the assessment process. I felt that parents and children were being victimized. To deal with these concerns, my colleagues and I set up multidisciplinary clinics for the independent evaluation of children with learning problems. Our need to *describe* rather than label such children led us to compile a series of neurodevelopmental examinations and standardized questionnaires. Our goal was to identify strengths, styles, and weaknesses unique to each child to allow for a more balanced view. These questionnaires and examinations— *The ANSER System, the PEER, the PEEX*, and the *PEERAMID*—are cited frequently throughout *Developmental Variation and Learning Disorders*, not because they are ideal or the best of available instruments, but because they are the procedures with which I am most familiar and comfortable. Similar instruments, used in an empirical manner, are apt to be equally effective.

At the same time that I have been striving to become a competent developmentalist, I have been building skills in my avocational pursuit as a farmer of geese. Over many years, I have managed to accumulate and observe a rather substantial collection of many varieties of domestic and wild geese. The developmental variation within the gaggle has been as striking as it would be in any seventh grade classroom. The cover of this book depicts that diversity.

As I continue to evaluate children with school problems, I am struck by the endless patterns of learning styles and strengths and weaknesses that I have not yet encountered in any textbook or review article. New issues, novel clusters of neurodevelopmental and educational findings, highly individualized feelings, and unique environmental circumstances invariably come into view. All too often, it is the uniqueness of children that contributes to their learning problems. Interestingly, it is often that same uniqueness that suggests the answers to habilitation. Consequently, when I decided to write this book, I hoped that it would enable readers who participate in the care of children with school problems to broaden their vision of these children and to be able to describe what it is that they have seen. This approach is staunchly empirical and phenomenological; the aim is to look for individual differences rather than to find likenesses in developing children.

The discrepancies in academic and clinical ways of thinking about disappointing children have disturbed me. I have read countless articles about "L.D. students," "dyslexics," or "ADDs," and although I have usually learned from such studies, I have often found myself needing to modify research findings for myself so that they might pertain to the children with whom I have been involved. These children are simply too complex to be characterized by simplistic labels, tidy systems of subtyping, or statistically generated syndromes.

The time is right for fresh efforts at integrating what we have learned about normal development in school-age children and what we are discovering about problematic learning and difficult life adjustment during childhood. I am firmly convinced that we need to regard children with learning problems as functioning along a dynamic continuum of normal developmental variation while struggling to satisfy constantly evolving expectations.

The autobiographical themes and personal convictions elucidated above insinuate themselves throughout this volume. They contribute to an eclecticism that I hope transcends traditional disciplinary borders. I hope that *Developmental Variation and Learning Disorders* will serve to facilitate communication among professionals while encouraging more sensitive collaborative observation and formulation. Furthermore, this book should serve to demonstrate the ease with which creative and effective *prescription* can emerge from careful *description*. Ultimately, I hope that adults who find themselves immersed in the lives of struggling children will accept and respect developmental variations, trying to change only what *must* be changed, recognizing that in dealing with such children, we ourselves intrude upon the pages of the biographies of a new generation.

Acknowledgments

The authors would like to offer their appreciation to the many thoughtful and dedicated individuals who have helped make this second edition a reality. We are especially appreciative of the creative talent of Pamela Levine, who created the striking cover of this edition. Missy Wakely played a major and indispensable role in updating the references for the book. We are also grateful for the administrative support of Pamela McBain and the heroic and totally competent editing efforts of Joy Sobeck. In addition, a number of individuals and foundations have been exceptionally supportive of our work to help children with differences in learning. Charles and Helen Schwab have been especially helpful. Alexa Culwell, of the Charles and Helen Schwab Foundation, has remained a strong advocate and constant source of productive advice. The generosity of the Emily Hall Tremaine Foundation is also acknowledged. Sally Bowles has inspired us with her wisdom and has done wonders to enhance public awareness of the plight of children with learning disorders. We would also like to acknowledge the remarkable support of the Olin Foundation and, especially, the commitment of Mary Dell Pritzlaff. In addition, it is essential to recognize the ongoing interest and support of the Geraldine R. Dodge Foundation. We are grateful, too, to the federal Bureau of Maternal and Child Health Care, as well as the Administration on Developmental Disabilities, for their generous funding of the Clinical Center for the Study of Development and Learning. Finally, a strong expression of gratitude is extended to the entire staff, faculty, and board of All Kinds of Minds, a nonprofit institute dedicated to the understanding of differences in learning.

Chapter 1

The Disappointing Child

Mrs. Fahy took three of my best friends . . . and skipped them to the sixth grade, but she didn't skip me. I really didn't care that much, but as soon as my mother heard about it, she rushed down to the schoolhouse to find out what was wrong with little Melvin and how come he got passed over. I could have told her if she'd asked me. I had a mind of my own and I didn't cotton to parroting stuff back to the teacher. That was all. But to hear my mother at that time you'd have thought she'd just gotten the news that I had just been pronounced the village idiot.
— Melvin Belli, *My Life on Trial*

Despite the level of teaching and the principal's special interest, the painter-to-be would not study. He fought every morning against going to school; a sturdy servant, Carmen Mendoza, was entrusted with the job and often had to resort to force. Pablo refused to go unless he was allowed to take along one of the pigeons his father used as models: in school the teacher let him raise the lid of his desk and set the bird behind it, to draw peacefully, shielded from the others. But even this was not enough to keep him quiet: he would go over to the window and knock on it to attract the attention of passersby.
— Pierre Cabanne, *Pablo Picasso: His Life and Times*

Developmental Variation and Learning Disorders is about disappointing children, school-age persons whose life performances fall short. They disappoint their families, their teachers, and themselves. Performance failure can perturb their early years in many ways. This book explores the various pathways that lead to disappointing early-life adjustment and performance. It examines some of the complex factors that perpetuate failure to meet expectations as well as those that help generate resiliency and, ultimately, life fulfillment.

In recent years considerable interest in the field of learning disorders has developed. Affected children are believed to have discrete central nervous system mediated problems that compromise academic proficiency and sometimes behavior and social interaction as well. These problems have been referred to as the *low-severity–high-prevalence* dysfunctions of childhood: *high-prevalence* because

1

they affect a large number of schoolchildren—perhaps as many as 15 to 20 percent of students—and *low-severity* in comparison with more serious handicapping conditions, such as mental retardation or multiple handicaps. Despite the relatively low severity of these conditions, most investigators, clinicians, teachers, and parents agree that they have a powerful impact on the lives of affected children and their families. Most important, however, such central nervous system problems contribute substantially to the plight of the disappointing child.

There is considerable disagreement about the causes, the treatments, and even the precise nature of the dysfunctions that impede learning. The following chapters construct a way of thinking about disappointing children that accounts for current observations while providing a basis for future research and constant refinement of our understanding. This chapter reviews some important features in the life of the school-age child and the multiple forces—both destructive and constructive—that influence development, shape experience, and result either in fulfillment or disappointment. It ponders some questions that have plagued the fields of psychology, education, pediatrics, neurology, and child development in their many attempts to explain childhood failure and maladaptation. Then follows a model for understanding, diagnosing, and managing these problems. This particular approach forms the basis for the remaining chapters of the book.

THE LIFE CIRCUMSTANCES OF THE SCHOOLCHILD

Any understanding of the impacts of developmental variation requires appreciation of the milieus in which we place schoolchildren and of the expectations that steadily evolve during their lives. From the moment school-age children emerge from the bed covers each day until their safe return to that security, they are preoccupied with the avoidance of humiliation at all cost. They have a constant need to look good, sidestep embarrassment, and gain respect, especially from their peers. School-age children must struggle to reconcile personal standards and expectations with those of the school, the family, and other children. These demands are by no means static. Expectations and development evolve, and qualitative changes occur in the child's central nervous system function, encompassing metamorphoses of abilities, inabilities, gains, losses, and trade-offs.

The functional development of the schoolchild is neither uniform nor linear, but is punctuated by hesitations, false starts, trial and error, regressions, and progressions. Many psychologists and child development specialists have postulated various stages, which have been called into question repeatedly because they suggest general propensities of human development rather than uniformly applicable and predictable stages. In fact, researchers increasingly recognize that children at times must regress or unlearn certain beliefs and concepts before they can master new skills or acquire more effective perspectives and strategies (Kessen and Scott 1992). Furthermore, the precise routes of development vary considerably from child to child, from culture to culture, and from community to community. There may be even more variation in development than there is in expectation. That is, children are expected to acquire certain skills and degrees of autonomy at particular ages or stages. In reality, they experience substantial variety in their readiness to acquire skills and in the learning styles and levels of enthusiasm they have available for these acquisitions. Consequently, schoolchildren must reconcile their personal sets of unique capabilities and shortcomings with constantly evolving mandates from the adult world and the peer group. All the while, they seek to avoid humiliation, to please, and to sustain feelings of worthiness—to satisfy both self and an ever present audience.

This book was written with this backdrop in mind. The child with a learning disorder faces an especially daunting challenge in the quest to feel respected among peers, admired by parents, and reasonably satisfied with the track record achieved by his steadily evolving mind.

VARIATION, DYSFUNCTION, DISABILITY, AND HANDICAP

Problems of definition inevitably complicate any discussion of the low-severity–high-prevalence dysfunctions of childhood. Issues of normality plague the investigator, the clinician, and the philosopher. Because brain functioning varies tremendously from person to person, we need a way of describing that functioning along a continuum. At what point do variations constitute dysfunctions? When should an unusual pattern of development be construed as a dysfunction? When is dysfunction a disability? When is a disability a handicap? The continuum from variation to dysfunction to disability and then to handicap is germane to the subject matter and philosophical stance of this book and to the manner in which we conceptualize the disappointing child (see table 1-1).

Variation becomes most significant when it impedes development, at which point we are dealing with *dysfunction*, as one or more discrete developmental functions are clearly weak or delayed. Thus, a child with deficiencies in critical aspects of memory might be considered to have a memory dysfunction. When these deficiencies interfere with the performance of tasks, the child is said to be *disabled* for those particular tasks. When those tasks, in turn, are of importance, the child is *handicapped,* particularly if there is no way she or he can overcome or bypass the disability. Therefore, it is essential to recognize that a variation in development need not be a dysfunction, a dysfunction need not create disability, and a disability may never become a handicap.

To illustrate these concepts, let us imagine a boy who is unable to find precise words quickly. He is quite proficient in other developmental functions. He reveals developmental variation, or a profile of strengths and weaknesses that is simply one way to be. In terms of language production, however, this boy exhibits dysfunction. As he goes through school, he starts to have trouble participating actively in class discussions and expressing ideas on paper. In debates and book reports, his performance indicates disability. However, over time he finds ways to compensate for his language dysfunction so that it does not become a handicap.

Table 1-1. The variation-to-handicap continuum

VARIATION

    Definition: An unusual pattern of style, strength, and/or weakness in one or more components of a developmental function

    Example: A strong vocabulary, very good verbal reasoning, but some weakness in processing lengthy complex sentences

    Effects: Usually of little or no impact unless complicated by other factors or unusual expectations

DYSFUNCTION

    Definition: A pattern of developmental variation that significantly impairs performance in a particular developmental function

    Example: A poor vocabulary, trouble finding words, and weakness of verbal memory—together thwarting overall linguistic skills

    Effects: Variable, depending on severity, expectations, employment of compensatory strengths, and presence of other dysfunctions

DISABILITY

    Definition: One or more dysfunctions that result in poor performance on a particular type of task

    Example: A language dysfunction associated with a reading disability

    Effects: Variable, depending on the importance of the affected task, and the age and social and/or educational setting of the child (e.g., a reading disability has more impact than a dancing disability)

HANDICAP

    Definition: A disability that is uncompensated for and that compromises a critical area of performance

    Example: A reading disability

    Effects: Of high impact

What handicaps a person at one age may not do so at another. For example, a developmental dysfunction may thwart learning during early elementary school. But as expectations change, as maturation occurs, and as the student learns to employ strengths effectively, that dysfunction may become insignificant and not in the least disabling or handicapping. On the other hand, a child may have from birth underlying dysfunctions that do not become disabilities until they start to be academically relevant. Children with developmental output failure (see chapter 6) may experience no difficulties academically until they confront the demand for large amounts of writing. They may be good at reading and mathematics but have disheartening difficulty transmitting complex ideas on paper. Thus, they have developmental dysfunctions with the potential for disability from an early age, but it is not until expectations evolve to the point where essay writing is demanded that their dysfunctions disable them. If writing is of great importance, the disability becomes a distinct handicap.

    A major difference between childhood and adulthood resides in the intersection between dysfunction and handicap. Adults are able to practice specialties and avoid their areas of weakness while children are required to be generalists. Adults who were relatively nonverbal children, whose language skills were clearly dysfunctional, may perform extremely well as architects, engineers, physicists, or artists, orchestrating vocational and avocational pursuits to minimize requirements for linguistic facility. Such options are not available to children, who are expected to read poetry, write book reports, and take vocabulary tests just like everyone else. Therefore more of their disabilities have the potential to become handicaps.

Cultural factors are important. A young child may have trouble coordinating his eyes and hands effectively. Living in a North American suburb, this may create no problems at all. Yet if that child had grown up in eighteenth-century America, ineptitude with a rifle may well have rendered him handicapped. Thus, the "handicaps" that we encounter in children are sometimes artifacts—byproducts of our insistence that children be at least fairly good at everything. Ultimately, well-differentiated, highly specialized children who do not easily meet traditional educational expectations may, with their assets and deficits, achieve substantially as adults if they can survive with sufficient self-esteem. Sometimes dysfunctions may even delineate areas of talent and enhance strengths. It is worth asking whether twelve years of education requiring the practice of a poorly fitting specialty endanger the mental health and self-esteem of some students. Conversely, some students who function well during school years because they are generalists possessing a broad range of capabilities may have difficulties finding their niches as adults.

These considerations require judicious and moderate use of the terms *disability* and *handicap*. This book espouses a nonlabeling approach. Labels have the potential for oversimplification of human developmental dysfunction and the more lethal potential for self-fulfilling prophecy. They are reductionist, sometimes forcing us to make artificial distinctions. In labeling a child "emotionally disturbed" or "learning disabled," for example, we imply mutually exclusive categories. In fact, a child who is having difficulty with learning is likely also to be enduring emotional turmoil. A child with festering anxiety, one who is sad or depressed, is more likely to have associated developmental dysfunctions that interfere with school performance. In this way, labeling creates false dichotomies that can seriously misrepresent and oversimplify a child's problems and needs.

The compulsion to label disappointing children is an outgrowth of two controversies that have been the subject of great debate. Perhaps the most commonly contested of these is the balance between nature and nurture, the disagreement over whether the major determinants of outcome reside in the child's own biological makeup, constitution, or genetic endowment or whether a child's difficulties or strengths result from factors in the environment and family. In a provocative review, Kessen and Scott (1992) present two quotations that typify opposite ends of the spectrum. From the behaviorist John Watson:

> Give me a dozen healthy infants, well formed, and my own specified world to bring them up in and I'll guarantee to take any one at random and train him to become any type of specialist I might select—doctor, lawyer, merchant, chief, and yes, even

beggar-man and thief, regardless of his talents, penchants, tendencies, abilities, vocations, and race of his ancestors (p. 32).

Watson's statement is an extreme example. His belief that skill levels are determined largely by the environment and experience is implicit. The position articulated by Gesell and quoted by Kessen and Scott (1992) is a direct contrast:

It is doubtful whether the basic temperamental qualities of infants can be measurably altered by environmental influence. Training in hygiene may exert a very palpable and important influence on the organization of the personality without necessarily altering the underlying nature or habitude.

The controversy over the nature-nurture and organic-emotional dichotomies is by no means clinically trivial. Major therapeutic implications as well as standards of accountability evolve naturally from one's stance on these issues. For example, if a child's difficulties are primarily emotional, should the school be held relatively less accountable and responsible for remediation, with the burden falling mainly on the parents? If, on the other hand, a truly endogenous dysfunction is recognized, is the educational system then expected to bear the primary responsibility for any remediation? What about those cases in which the problem seems to worsen over time, with the child becoming increasingly delayed in acquiring skill or maladaptive in behavior? The failure to progress is often assessed in terms of nature and nurture. Is the school doing an inadequate job of helping this student with his or her intrinsic dysfunctions? Or is the home environment such that resulting behavior and effective problems are impeding learning?

A second dualistic controversy relates to the separateness of cognitive and emotional development. Are behavior and adaptation primarily dependent on cognitive development or on emotional growth? The studies of Piaget (1952) typify a cognitive deterministic approach. Many twentieth-century development specialists and cognitive psychologists have subscribed to his observations and theories in their views of child development as a series of distinct stages of conceptual growth (see chapter 7). Piaget's concepts allow for interactions within the nature-nurture polarity (Piaget and Inhelder 1968). In contrast, Freud (1965) and his followers and disciples proposed stages tied to emotional development during childhood. Their stages were less related to inborn characteristics, placing more emphasis on critical life events as they occur during periods of special vulnerability. Much of the psychoanalytic movement has stressed nurture over nature.

Dualisms serve a purpose, allowing for the careful elucidation of factors that influence the developing human. However, what we have gained by refining these concepts we may have paid for in overly narrow research and clinical activity that has tended to reflect the training and biases of the investigator or clinician more than the complexity of the child or children under scrutiny. Research efforts ought to be aimed at enhancing our capacity to describe and/or identify relevant functional elements while de-emphasizing their rank ordering.

The confluence of multiple influences at any given point in a child's development is a central theme of this book. Any child has a highly complex, inborn circuitry—a central nervous system and, in fact, an entire mind and body—replete

with possibilities, limitations, and preferred pathways or styles. Within limits, there is great potential for change, generated by an almost infinite range of forces, including experience during infancy (such as parenting or bonding), the effects of illnesses or other health stresses, critical life events, encounters with the educational system and with peers, modifications imposed by sociocultural values, constraints of socioeconomic status, and the impacts of various role models.

At any point, the child represents the product of diverse constitutional predispositions interacting with multiple exogenous factors. The range and number of influences is so great that any single factor is apt to be relatively weak when viewed in the context of an entire child during his or her lifespan. Therefore, narrow notions of etiology, or cause, are hard to substantiate. A discrete reason for a child's difficulty is unlikely. Children are highly resilient: they withstand substantial stress from without as well as from within. Thus, the research investigator, educator, and clinician who wish to understand the disappointing child must seek to describe the numerous influences that together impair resiliency and cause a child to become disappointing.

It is sometimes difficult to determine which factors came first, and which are primary and which are secondary. Is an adolescent doing poorly on homework because she is simply not motivated, or has she lost all motivation because she has performed so poorly on previous homework? Is this girl depressed primarily because of the family turmoil she experiences at home, or is her depression secondary to her academic failure in school? Is a student not learning because of his disruptive behavior, or is the latter merely a strategy employed to divert attention from his embarrassment over not learning?

Because these questions are extremely difficult, and fallacious reasoning can plague the responder, this book advocates a phenomenological, eclectic perspective. Clinicians, educators, and research scientists should strive to become the best possible describers of children. In other words, when studying a child or a group of children, we should attempt to depict essential elements of developmental function and performance. The best description leads to the best prescription. The description is an account not only of problems and weaknesses but also (perhaps more important) of talents and advantages, the exploitation of which may go a long way toward alleviating the burdens imposed by dysfunction. This volume stresses primarily the developmental functions and their contributions to behavioral adjustment and academic success. Such phenomena are this book's primary subject matter, inspired by a need in the literature for this emphasis.

A CONCEPTUAL MODEL

This text will adhere to a model of school learning and productivity that helps elucidate the ways in which children succeed or fail in different aspects of the academic curriculum. Within this model four hierarchical levels of performance are considered (fig. 1-1).

These levels of performance are of course highly interdependent. Basic neurodevelopmental functions come together and synchronize to allow for the acqui-

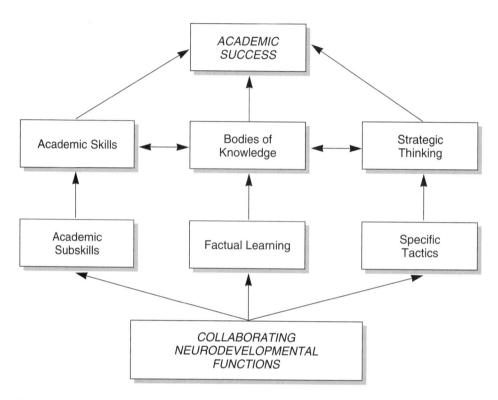

Figure 1-1.   A hierarchy leading to academic success

Academic success ultimately depends on interactions of neurodevelopmental functions that promote subskill acquisition to converge as skills, factual learning to form bodies of knowledge, and a range of tactics that allow for strategic approaches to challenges.

sition of subskills and fundamental knowledge. The subskills (of a particular skill, such as those needed for writing) converge to form specific skills, while units of fundamental knowledge coalesce to create a body of interconnected facts and procedures. Ultimately, a child's cumulative skills and knowledge interact with a host of environmental and psychological factors to generate various school-related outcomes (such as an interest in learning, preparedness for a career, and intact self-esteem). The pages that follow will examine these four levels in more detail.

Neurodevelopmental Functions

Neurodevelopmental functions are basic abilities of the human mind. They represent neurological capacities in that they are mediated by the brain. They are developmental in that they are expected to become increasingly effective over time and with experience (i.e., practice). A vast multitude of neurodevelopmental functions exist and operate throughout our lives. A subgroup of these functions is germane to learning and to academic performance. For example, phonological awareness (chapter 5) is a neurodevelopmental function that is critical for learning how to decode individual words during reading. It is also necessary for learning a foreign language. Word retrieval is a neurodevelopmental function that is critical for participation in class discussions, and is also important for transcribing ideas in writing.

Neurodevelopmental *dysfunctions* are weaknesses in specific brain abilities. Examples include a dysfunction in some component of short-term memory, difficulty keeping track of finger positions, or trouble with self-monitoring. Since there is no such thing as a flawless or perfect brain, it is likely that all children harbor some specific neurodevelopmental dysfunctions which may or may not be sufficiently severe and relevant to academic performance to interfere with learning in school. When we say that a student has a neurodevelopmental dysfunction, we are not actually taking any particular position on how that dysfunction came to be. The weakness may be genetic in origin, it may relate to some medical condition the child endured earlier in life, or it may be the result of environmental stress, deprivation, or various cultural influences. Frequently, neurodevelopmental dysfunctions are the product of multiple factors. In most cases, we simply do not know why a child harbors a dysfunction. Fortunately, in most instances, we need not ascertain the source of a dysfunction in order to help a child overcome its negative effects.

Children proceed through their school years with changing neurodevelopmental profiles. These profiles are sets of strengths and weaknesses that characterize individual students. Over time, a child may improve in an area of weak function and/or decline in a previously strong domain. Thus profiles are considerably plastic. As a result of their ongoing educational experience and any specific interventions, children show remarkable malleability with respect to the dysfunctions that impede them. Additionally, some children are especially resilient; they have certain compensatory strengths or life circumstances that enable them to minimize the academic and psychological impacts of their dysfunctions. Such protective factors may include effective and supportive adults in their lives, strong language abilities, or highly effective teaching.

Neurodevelopmental functions can be grouped into eight *constructs,* abstract categories of function that facilitate our thinking about neurodevelopmental functions and dysfunctions. The constructs are not meant to be thought of as isolated areas of function; on the contrary, functions within constructs overlap and transact extensively. Because we speak of constructs rather than real entities, we always have the option of modifying these categories, i.e., adding others, deleting, merging two of them, etc. The eight constructs are represented in figure 1-2. These constructs will comprise the basis for the next seven chapters of this book.

Uncovering and understanding a child's neurodevelopmental profile is an essential part of the evaluation process for a student who is experiencing academic difficulty. It is equally important to analyze carefully the precise expectations that are being imposed. As they proceed through their school years, children must con-

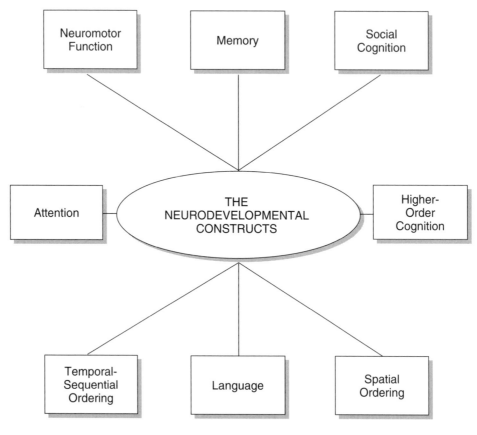

Figure 1-2. Neurodevelopmental constructs

The diagram depicts the eight neurodevelopmental constructs that will be examined in this book. Although the constructs can be studied individually, within the human brain they are highly interactive, as they collaborate in all behavioral and cognitive activities. Highly specific neurodevelopmental functions are contained within each construct.

tend with evolving expectations, steady changes in the curriculum and academic workload that require the use of different functions in different ways at different grade levels. Thus, the language functions needed for success in kindergarten and first grade differ from those required for mastery of content in middle school. Similarly, different memory functions come into play at successive grade levels. Thus, during a child's education a steady "competition" takes place between a changing neurodevelopmental profile and evolving expectations. Consequently, a student can develop the onset of learning problems at any point. Likewise, expectations may at any time begin to tap the strengths within a child's profile, thereby enabling her or him to savor success in school for the first time.

Subskills, Knowledge, and Strategies

Neurodevelopmental functions come together to form academic subskills. A subskill is one component of an overall skill. For example, the subskills subsumed under writing skill include: letter formation (i.e., legibility), spelling, mechanics (such as punctuation and capitalization), written language, use of prior knowledge, brainstorming (to generate ideas), and organization. Each subskill is the product of collaboration between a specific group of neurodevelopmental functions. Therefore, it is possible to analyze any academic subskill to determine which neurodevelopmental functions are most commonly required for that subskill to be mastered. This book will examine the many interactions between neurodevelopmental functions and the subskills that they generate.

When a child exhibits a weak subskill, it is important to seek the one or more weak neurodevelopmental functions that are impeding its acquisition. Two possibilities are common. A child may exhibit a dysfunction in one or more of the requisite neurodevelopmental functions. Alternatively, she or he may harbor a dysfunction at the junction between two functions. In the latter instance, two neurodevelopmental functions are adequate when operating independently of each other but have difficulty functioning collaboratively. For example, a child may display strong access to information in long-term memory as well as good manual dexterity (fine motor ability or eye-hand coordination.) But he is unable to get the fingers to work in concert with long-term memory, as a result of which no one can read his handwriting. His memory works well when there is no motor function involved, and his fingers operate dexterously when there is no memory involved. He simply cannot base a motor output on a memory input. Consequently, he shows poor memory for letter forms while writing. Such a dysfunction at the junction between two functions is a very common cause of poor legibility in writing (see chapter 10).

It is important to recognize that subskills sometimes demand different functions for their ongoing utilization than those required for their initial acquisition. Over time, with practice, subskills can become increasingly automatic and demand much less voluntary memory and attentional strength than were needed during earlier stages of learning.

In addition to academic subskills, neurodevelopmental functions and dysfunctions permit knowledge acquisition and shape the way a child approaches tasks and challenges (i.e., his or her efficiency, organization, problem solving and use of strategies).

Skills, Sophisticated Knowledge, and Approach to Learning

We have noted that neurodevelopmental functions interact to enable the formation of subskills, while subskills come together to create skills. The actual application of a skill demands that the subskills operate in reasonable synchrony. Thus, if the recall of facts in arithmetic is a longer and more laborious process than the recall of procedures, this dys-synchrony of subskills can easily thwart the development of mathematical efficiency and accuracy.

It is important to emphasize that not all school-related skills are strictly academic. Included in a child's repertoire of skills are athletic abilities, overall social skills, and technical capacities in art, music, and other such pursuits. Success in these domains also depends on the mobilization of specific neurodevelopmental functions to form and apply subskills which then become integrated and synchronized to generate the needed overall skill.

assessm̄t̄

If a child appears to be deficient in a particular academic or nonacademic skill, it is appropriate to identify any underlying subskill weaknesses. Once this assessment is completed, one can look for the relevant dysfunctions or dysfunctions at the junctions between functions that are causing the problem. Remediation can then try to strengthen the weak functions(s) and reconstruct the lagging subskill. These processes will be dealt with in substantial detail in later chapters.

School-Related Outcomes

A child or adolescent's academic skills come together with a host of temperamental, environmental, and additional psychological factors to yield school-related outcomes. At any point in a child's school career, a series of (tentative) outcomes can be discerned. They may include such parameters as self-esteem, motivation to keep learning, grades, special affinities and talents, emotional health, behavior, moral values, popularity with peers, and ambition. While all of these outcomes also depend on influences outside of school, they are certainly significantly affected by a child's experience as a student. Neurodevelopmental functional profiles and their adequacy in the face of evolving expectations, as well as the status of a child's subskills and skills, play a pivotal role in promoting positive school-related outcomes. On the other hand, neurodevelopmental dysfunctions that lead to misunderstandings and to repeated failure and frustration strongly predispose a child to negative school-related outcomes.

With school-related problems, it is important to survey the child's performance for possible gaps or breakdowns in neurodevelopmental functions that may be creating subskill deficiencies which, in turn, thwart skill development, and thereby contribute to the negative outcomes, such as behavior problems, low self-esteem, and/or a lack of motivation.

I will apply the model I have described throughout this book, as I elaborate on an approach that stresses functional observation and management based on the close observation and vivid description of children rather than on diagnostic labels.

THE FRAMEWORK OF *DEVELOPMENTAL VARIATION AND LEARNING DISORDERS*

Part 1 of this book surveys the eight neurodevelopmental constructs and their constituent functions as they affect the lives of the young schoolchild and adolescent. An implicit conceptual model governed the selection and division of subject matter. What unfolds here is not intended to be a wiring diagram of the central nervous system or a comprehensive directory of neurological functions. Instead, this book studies phenomena of childhood information processing and production that are most relevant to achieving success in school. The specific functions chosen for scrutiny have been associated with disordered learning and reduced productivity among disappointing children in the research literature, in my own investigations, and in overall diagnostic experience. By elucidating the problems of these children, this volume also develops a way of looking at common patterns of neurodevelopmental function and variation.

To appreciate fully the constructs covered in chapters 2 through 8, the reader must recognize the following critical points:

- Each of the eight constructs consists of many discrete but related elements, with the result that a child may manifest uneven abilities within a developmental function. For example, in the area of language, a child's verbal reasoning abilities may progress faster than expressive language fluency. Therefore, this book examines the range of developmental variations occurring both within and between functions.

- The eight constructs do not represent self-contained systems, but are influenced by, and themselves influence, various constitutional and environmental forces, among which we can include the child's affect, temperament, physical health, self-esteem, cultural background, and motivation. No description of a child is complete without an account of these endogenous and exogenous factors. In particular, it is relevant to estimate how such factors have affected the developmental functions and areas of academic performance.

- The description of development and variation in each construct is not based on a rigid, inevitable progression of states. Although each chapter describes such progressions, individuals vary considerably both in the rate at which they develop and the degree of competency they attain during school years. The evolution of these functions need not occur in a straight line or incline steadily upward. In fact, for most children it is likely that development charts a circuitous path, one characterized by progressions and regressions, gains and losses, and learning and unlearning.

- The operations of the eight constructs overlap and interact. There are strong ties between attention and memory, between auditory attention and language proficiency, between attention to sequences and sequential processing skill, and between attention to social feedback cues and social ability. In fact, we can examine any two developmental functions and discern their discrete properties as well as their robust interactions.

- Our ability to identify and describe neurodevelopmental functions does not necessarily endorse a rigid or highly modular model of information processing or production. In particular, there is no fixed chronological order or invariant mechanism of thinking or remembering. However, we can view the constructs in a diagrammatic representation. Figure 1-3 shows information processing initiated through selective attention. Incoming data are sorted into their sequential and/or simultaneous components, held in memory and associated with previously stored information, given some language attributes (named), reasoned in higher-order cognition, and finally comprehended and assimilated. As can be seen in figure 1-3, an analogous process, involving multiple developmental functions, culminates in motor implementation and a product.

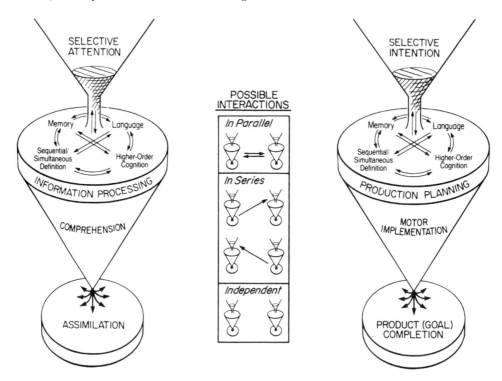

Figure 1-3. Schematic representation of processing and production subsystems as sources of developmental variation

This diagram offers a basis for thinking about the interactions between developmental functions. Two similar systems are depicted: on the left are the mechanisms through which data are chosen for consideration, interpreted, and retained; on the right are the mechanisms through which output, or productivity, occurs. For information processing and production planning the various developmental functions interact and equilibrate: The two systems may be used in series (as in reading a passage and *then* writing about it), in parallel (as in reading the instructions *while* assembling a model airplane), or independently (as in concentrating on the radio *and* driving a car). Developmental variation and dysfunctions may occur at any point(s) on this diagram, thereby potentially thwarting the child's performance. Additionally, individual strengths or talents may be present at any point(s), thereby facilitating these systems and even allowing the child to compensate for dysfunctions. The systems are driven by multiple factors, including motivation, the specific content they are addressing, and the amount of effort and time demanded. The components of this model and their interactions will be described in detail in the chapters that follow.

- We can document variations in neurodevelopmental functions without clearly understanding why they exist. Although we may harbor suspicions, it is seldom possible to prove, for example, that language delays were definitely caused by multiple ear infections. As we describe developmental functions in a particular child, we must be careful not to emphasize etiology. We are more interested in knowing *that* the child has a language delay than why. Such an approach facilitates nonaccusatory description.

- This book's examination of the neurodevelopmental constructs focuses almost exclusively on the school years. This focus is not meant to imply that what precedes the school years is in any way irrelevant. Any good development specialist must have a grasp on the antecedents of these functions insofar as they are observable during infancy, the toddler years, and the period immediately before preschool. It is equally germane to complete the life cycle perspective by studying the effects of the relevant functions on adult life.

Part 2 of this volume consists of four chapters devoted to academic areas. Each chapter discusses the normal progression of students' abilities and expectations and considers disabilities and the ways in which students are predisposed to the dysfunctions described in part 1. Part 2 stresses that no single entities called reading disability, dyscalculia (mathematics disability), or dysgraphia exist. It emphasizes the ways in which multiple patterns of dysfunction impede the acquisition of skill and day-to-day performance. It also discusses methods of assessment and management, although detailed evaluation of error patterns and gaps in skills mastery are covered more comprehensively in education texts. The emphasis in this volume is on the relationship between academic skill delays and developmental dysfunction, and on the diagnostic and therapeutic implications of such relationships.

The final four chapters, which comprise part 3, offer a longitudinal perspective. Chapter 13 surveys current knowledge of the many factors that predispose children to dysfunction and disability. Chapters 14 and 15, which offer general guidelines for the assessment and management of disappointing schoolchildren, are intended to help the reader integrate and organize the kinds of diagnostic and therapeutic recommendations set forth in parts 1 and 2. Finally, chapter 15 looks at the future, analyzing outcomes and factors that promote resiliency in disappointing children.

HOPE

This book is the result of recognizing that the more we involve ourselves with disappointing children, the more we understand the risks they must take during childhood. As students, they suffer for their variations. They are at risk not just for prolonged suffering during years that should be marked by the gratifying pleasures of discovery and growth, but for more long-standing loss of self-esteem and identity. The resources of education may be wasted on these children. Their lives may bear the scars of unjust accusation, chronic feelings of inadequacy, and shamefully untapped talent. Understanding developmental variation, characterizing it without oversimplifying it, and intervening vigorously on behalf of developing humans experiencing inordinate failure—these are urgent needs. In trying to help, we must also strive not to harm. This volume is therefore offered with the belief that it can inform and energize our responses to a disappointing child's concealed cry for help. That continues to be the hope.

Part 1

Exploring Developmental Functions

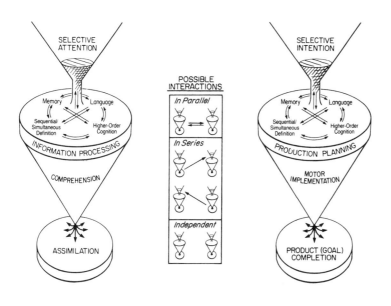

Chapter 2

Attention

Malcolm's grades suffered. It was not because he lacked intellectual curiosity; on the contrary, he'd go to the rear of the classroom, select a book from the library shelf, and eagerly absorb its contents. But when work was assigned, he'd drag his feet. He'd doodle, daydream, and stare out the window. When teachers called on him, he frequently had no idea what the class was doing. . . . If the teacher called on someone else when he had his hand raised, he'd make a scene. He was the first inside the school building in the morning, the first outside at recess time, and the first to leave when school was dismissed in the afternoon.
— Bruce Perry, *Malcolm: The Life of a Man Who Changed Black America*

She was never so happy as when as when copying flowers, designing fairies, or illustrating stories with queer specimens of art. Her teacher complained that instead of doing her sums she covered her slate with animals; the blank pages of her atlas were used to copy maps on, and caricatures of the most ludicrous description came fluttering out of her books at unlucky moments.
— Caroline Ticknor, *May Alcott: A Memoir*

Attention, Attention Deficits, and "Attention Deficit Disorder" (ADD)

Most people are very familiar with the term *attention deficit disorder* (ADD). In recent years it has been used to characterize a presumed syndrome in which affected individuals harbor a group of traits, including distractibility, hyperactivity, impulsivity, and deficient concentration. Serious issues have arisen in conceptualizing ADD as a distinct clinical entity. First, it tends to neglect the extreme heterogeneity of individuals who are having problems with attention. Second, it tends to separate attention from other relevant areas of developmental function (such as language, memory, and social cognition) rather than perceiving the quality of a person's attention as part of an overall broad developmental profile. This failure has prevented people from considering the powerful effects of other areas of neurodevelopmental function on attentional processes. Third, adherents to the notion of ADD as a syndrome have tended to neglect the normal functions that comprise attention; rather than examining how those functions operate and, in some instances, break down, they have allowed the condition to be defined by a list of traits. In keeping with the nonlabeling philosophy of this book, problems with attention are not viewed as a distinct and uniform diagnostic category or syndrome. Rather, weaknesses of attentional function (i.e., attention deficits) will be conceptualized as nonspecific breakdowns or developmental delays in certain key regulatory brain processes. Attention as a category will be viewed as one neurodevelopmental construct.

The poet Emily Dickinson once wrote, "I dwell in possibilities. . . . " The human central nervous system could easily echo that sentiment. Our brains are constantly sorting through the possibilities for further thinking, for reacting, for behaving, and for creating. The possibilities are seemingly endless. Fortunately, a series of delicately calibrated controls governs conscious encounters with possibilities. These controls simultaneously energize and regulate selectivity, monitoring, and the goal-directed flow of output from the central nervous system. The controls are subsumed under the neurodevelopmental construct of *attention.*

Attention can be conceptualized as a network of highly interactive controls over conscious mental functioning. Problems with attention—attention deficits—represent breakdowns in one or more of these controls. The attention controls play a strictly managerial role in the human mind. That is, they do not actually interpret incoming information or implement actions and reactions; rather, the attention controls activate, regulate, and monitor those parts of the brain that are more directly involved in performance. For example, the attention controls do not enable one to understand language, but instead regulate the intensity and selectivity of listening, which secondarily has an impact on comprehension.

The attention controls can be grouped into three systems: *mental energy control, processing control,* and *production control* (see fig. 2-1). The next section will explore these three control systems and the individual controls that comprise them. It will describe the normal functioning of each control and the phenomena that are observable when that control chronically breaks down.

THE CONTROL SYSTEMS AND THEIR BREAKDOWN POINTS

The three control systems are highly interactive. *Mental energy controls* regulate the initial flow, allocation, and maintenance of an energy supply necessary to foster alertness and facilitate the exertion of effort. *Processing controls* regulate the intake of information as well as its further interpretation. *Production controls* oversee the mind's output. It should be obvious that a reasonable flow of mental energy is needed for optimal processing and production. It is also the case that efficiency and selectivity of intake and output can "conserve fuel."

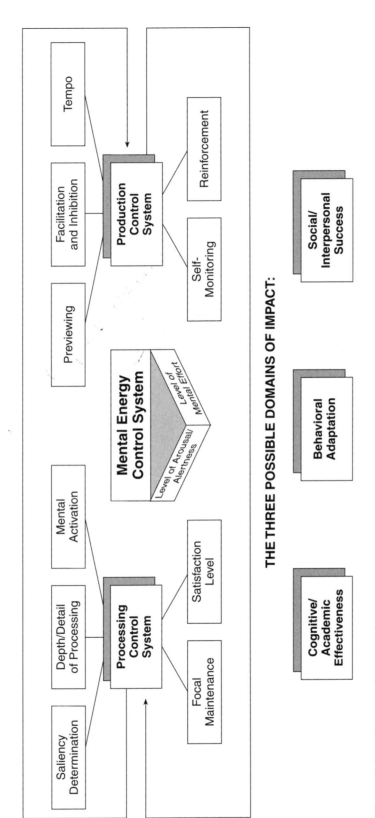

THE THREE POSSIBLE DOMAINS OF IMPACT:

Figure 2-1. The attention controls

The three control systems each have three principal domains of impact, namely, cognition and academic performance, behavioral adaptation, and interpersonal (social) effectiveness. Thus, problems with specific attention controls may negatively affect one or more of these domains.

We can now look closely at the three control systems and their constituent individual controls. In each case normal function will be described along with the phenomena observed when dysfunction exists.

The Mental Energy Control System

In recent years there has been considerable interest in the ways in which the mind acquires and utilizes the energy needed for thinking and for intellectual productivity (Sergeant 1996). The term *cognitive energetics* is often applied to the study of such processes. Evidence suggests that the central nervous system has finite energy resources that must be properly mobilized and allocated to meet task demands (Gopher and Navon 1980). As Sergeant notes, "The resource model of selective attention conceives attention as a general pool of energy that is limited but can be distributed over simultaneous demands" (p. 61).

Mental energy controls regulate the distribution of resources needed for concentration and goal-directed action. The control system can be divided into two components: arousal and alertness control, and mental effort control.

Arousal and Alertness Control. The ability to initiate and maintain concentration is essential for success in schoolwork as well as in most other pursuits (see table 2-1). The *arousal and alertness control* function includes the capacity to fend off the ever present threat of mental fatigue, and to remain focused without experiencing excessive tiredness, which in turn may lead to a loss of concentration. This function also involves the capacity to regulate the flow of mental energy so that a heightened state of arousal can be attained under circumstances that demand particularly intense concentration or vigilance.

Arousal and alertness control is closely tied to the regulation of sleep and the maintenance of appropriate daily rhythms of sleep and wakefulness. In other

Table 2-1. Alertness and arousal control

FORM	EXPLANATION	EXAMPLES
Alertness	Maintaining sufficient energy for concentration	Listening to instructions in a classroom setting
Sleep-arousal balance	Sleeping adequately at night, feeling alert during the day	Being sufficiently well rested to focus effectively in school
Arousal regulation	Being able to increase level of arousal when needed	Increasing level of attention when heeding a warning

words, this control assures that an individual is sleeping adequately at night and feeling sufficiently awake during the day. Sleep and arousal are regulated within the reticular activating system and the locus coeruleus, two areas within the brain stem. Variations in neurotransmitter metabolism and release during the day and night are associated with patterns of sleep and wakefulness.

Dysfunctions of arousal and alertness control. Children with dysfunctions of arousal and alertness control endure excessive mental fatigue in the classroom. They experience intermittent difficulty with concentration and therefore have problems sustaining their focus on relevant information. The manifestations of their mental fatigue are sometimes misleading or even paradoxical. They may fidget, squirm, and become hyperactive, seeming attempts to combat the uncomfortable feeling of fatigue. Rather than acknowledging explicitly that their minds feel tired in school, they are apt to lament that "school is too boring." Many such children can be observed to yawn and stretch in class more often than their peers.

A subgroup of children with attention deficits manifests a sleep-arousal imbalance. They fail to sleep adequately at night and have trouble sustaining their alertness during the school day. Often it is hard for them to fall asleep at night; they may be wide awake at midnight. It may be equally difficult for them to separate from a bed in the morning. Once at school they may display varying patterns of insufficient alertness, such as trouble getting started on school activities in the morning, difficulty focusing after lunch, or a tendency to tune in and out.

Children with weaknesses of alertness and arousal may also have trouble regulating and modulating their level of alertness. They may not become sufficiently aroused during important events (such as studying for a major examination) or they may become overaroused (too excited and invested) at unimportant moments (while watching TV). Thus, they are unable to match the intensity of the mental energy flow to the particular context or circumstances in which they find themselves at the moment.

Mental Effort Control. The ability to exert mental effort when called for is critical as children develop a cognitive working capacity during their school years (see table 2-2). They need to be able to delay gratification, struggle through sometimes frustrating intellectual challenges, and create academic products that demand considerable energy. Their effort needs to be sustained and goal directed. The ability to initiate, allocate, maintain, and terminate (at the right time) a flow of mental effort is closely linked to academic productivity and success. Often mental effort entails the ability and willingness to do "things you don't feel like doing," presumably to satisfy some greater and often delayed good that will result from the effort, or to avoid negative consequences, such as punishment. In scientific terms, mental effort has been conceptualized as the energy demanded of an individual when its current state of energy is not sufficient to perform a task (Sanders 1983).

There is a reciprocal relationship between mental effort and motivation. When an individual feels highly motivated to undertake and complete an activity, rela-

Table 2-2. Mental effort control

FORM	EXPLANATION	EXAMPLES
Working capacity	Ability to engage in activities requiring effort	Completing homework, studying for tests
Behavior	Capacity to exert effort needed to comply/adapt	Accepting limits in school
Consistent output	Mainenance of a steady level of performance	Revealing a steady level of effort and quality in schoolwork

tively little mental effort is required. If motivation is low, far greater mental effort is demanded. When a child perceives a task as difficult and unexciting, she may need great mental effort to complete it. Motivation may dwindle in part because the effort required is so great (see pp. 497–500 for a more detailed discussion of motivation).

Dysfunctions of mental effort control. For some children work is too much work. They have a great deal of trouble exerting mental effort, accomplishing assignments, or fulfilling responsibilities that are not particularly entertaining or immediately motivating. They may appear lazy or oppositional. They are apt to be negligent in completing assignments. They often require heavy prodding and coercion of various types to accomplish work. Battles over homework completion commonly disrupt their families, especially as these children pass through the middle grades. Feelings of fatigue and boredom seriously compromise their productivity in school and elsewhere.

Some students with weak mental energy control have trouble getting started with tasks or activities; they seem to require excessive coercion or a "jump start" to begin doing homework or fulfilling domestic responsibilities. At other times, they may be able to begin an activity but are unable to sustain the effort or finish what they start.

Poor control over mental effort may also be associated with behavior problems. An affected child may seem to lack the energy needed to control behavior. His or her fatigue may actually lead to a loss of behavioral control with a resultant outpouring of negative actions.

The Enigma of Performance Inconsistency

Children who experience problems with mental energy control do not endure these problems all of the time; they manifest these deficiencies much of the time and often during moments when alertness of mental effort is needed. Because of the intermittence of their inattention, affected children exhibit considerable performance inconsistency. They can be alert and productive on some days or during some hours but at other times display mental fatigue and a lack of effort. This inconsistency is most often highly erratic. Some children tune in and tune out for periods of seconds or minutes during much of the school day. Or, they may function well during certain hours, days, or weeks, only to disappoint the adult world with their seeming inability to perform during other hours, days, or weeks. Such patterns of inconsistency may be reflected in inconsistent test scores over a semester or, alternatively, in inconstant error patterns within tests. For example, a student may succeed on two questions, then miss the next three, then do well on the subsequent three. That same student may answer some difficult questions accurately and then show poor performance on easier ones, the random error pattern suggesting variable attention.

Not surprisingly, the adult world frequently misinterprets performance inconsistency. The fact that a child can succeed admirably some of the time often elevates general expectations, so that when the child is out of focus she or he may seem to be "not really trying." Such children grow up with the constant refrain, "We know she can do it when she sets her mind to it," with the misguided implication that consistency of performance is totally within the child's control.

Now that we have examined the mental energy controls and their dysfunctions, we can turn our attention to the processing controls, a set of regulatory functions that depend heavily on the controls of energy distribution and maintenance that I have described.

The Processing Controls

The processing controls regulate information intake and utilization. The information may be used as a basis for learning, as guidance for behavior or compliance, or as input needed for relating reciprocally to others (as occurs during the processing of conversation). The processing control system contains five basic controls: saliency determination, processing depth and detail, cognitive activation, focal maintenance, and satisfaction control.

Saliency Determination. Discrimination between important and unimportant information is essential. Our processing systems simply cannot handle the information overload that would flood our consciousness if there were no control over what gets interpreted, stored, and/or utilized from moment to moment. That control is· what is meant by *saliency determination,* sometimes also referred to as *selective attention.* The concept of selectivity is a critical component of most scientific models of attention (Mirsky 1996).

Table 2-3 shows that saliency determination involves the constant review of available stimuli and the rejection of those stimuli that are not sufficiently relevant or necessary to accomplish a goal. At the same time, data which are deemed important are selected or highlighted for further processing and utilization. Using

Table 2-3. Saliency determination

FORM	EXPLANATION	EXAMPLES
Distraction filtration	Focusing on a purposeful information source or currently meaningful sensory pathway	Listening to the teacher instead of looking out the window; ignoring irrelevant background noises
Task analysis	Focusing on relevant data to meet current expectation	Following directions so as to complete an assignment
Rank ordering	Determining relative levels of importance, prioritizing	Knowing what to study for a test
Main points identification	Deciding what is most significant in a message	Summarizing, paraphrasing, underlining
Vigilance	Being alert to important, rarely occurring stimuli	Proofreading
Divided attention	Being able to focus on multiple important "targets" simultaneously	Listening to the teacher in geography while at the same time looking at a map on the wall
Experience analysis	Knowing what was relevant or important in an occurrence (post hoc)	Learning from experiences

the term *focus-execute,* Mirsky et al. (1991) characterize the process as the capacity to select target stimuli from an array for enhanced processing."

Saliency determination, like other processing controls, must interact with other neurodevelopmental functions. Thus, making rational determinations of saliency requires some preliminary interpretation. For instance, to know what is important in a paragraph, one must possess some understanding of its content. It is also the case, however, that the ability to identify a main point greatly enhances comprehension of that paragraph. Thus saliency determination, like all of the attention controls, works reciprocally with other neurodevelopmental functions.

Dysfunctions of saliency determination. Children with weakness of saliency determination often show signs of overt distractibility. In addition or instead, they may reveal less obvious difficulties related to rank-ordering stimuli, identifying main points, dividing their attention effectively, and analyzing tasks and experiences.

Many children with attention deficits are described as "distractible." That is, they focus on seemingly irrelevant stimuli. Within a population of children with

Table 2-4. Common forms of distractibility

FORM	MANIFESTATIONS
Visual	Tendency to focus on irrelevant sights or trivial visual details
Auditory	Tendency to focus on background sounds; trouble with sustained listening
Tactile	Tendency to touch and handle objects instead of attending
Temporal	Tendency to focus on the future or the past rather than present activities
Somatic	Tendency to focus on body feelings, trivial pains, discomforts, scabs, scars
Social	Tendency to focus on peers, ignoring other stimuli

attention deficits, different patterns of distractibility are found. Table 2-4 describes some common patterns.

The individual forms of distractibility listed in table 2-4 may be more or less prominent in individual children. The inability to filter out totally irrelevant stimuli may seriously impede learning and day-to-day classroom engagement and participation. On the other hand, in some cases distractibility and creativity may go hand in hand. Some distractible children are capable of making observations and sensing similarities that would elude other children. They can be highly observant, noticing things that others might miss.

As noted, children with weaknesses of saliency determination may also manifest more subtle problems, sometimes referred to as difficulties with *significance determination*. It may be hard for them to identify main ideas in a story or paragraph. When confronting a word problem in arithmetic, they may struggle to determine what information is needed to solve the problem and what is irrelevant. Older students may have great difficulty studying for a test—reading a text and deciding what's most important or relevant and therefore most likely to be asked on the examination. History textbooks are often the downfall of students with saliency determination problems; they have great trouble deciding what's most important amid the plethora of information. Note taking and underlining or highlighting may also challenge these individuals. Problems with vigilance may make it hard for them to proofread (especially if they also have difficulty with self-monitoring; see pp. 38–40).

Students with weak saliency determination may show unorthodox patterns of memory. They may manifest a tendency to remember trivial details better than they recall critical details, a phenomenon often referred to as *incidental learning* (see p. 70).

Depth and Detail of Processing.   If a student is to understand and utilize salient information fully, she must register it in consciousness with adequate depth. That is, she must concentrate hard enough on the incoming stimuli. Such in-depth concentration helps her hold incoming information in place, enter it in short-term memory, and begin to interpret it (see table 2-5).

Depth of processing strongly influences the appreciation of internal detail, i.e., the fine-grained information contained within an array of data. The more deeply a person is concentrating, the more effectively he or she will assimilate fine detail. As processing depth diminishes, internal detail becomes increasingly vague. An analogy is the use of a postmark on an envelope; if it has not been stamped hard enough, much of the fine detail of the imprint may not be discernible; only its rough outline is visible. We could determine that the letter had been canceled, but not be able to read the date or originating post office.

Dysfunctions of processing depth and detail. It is common for children with attention deficits to show shallow processing and a lack of focus on detail. Shallow processing creates situations in which information "goes in one ear and out the other." These children are likely to need instructions and explanations repeated. They may not fully process the instructions for a homework assignment. Much of their listening and watching is likely to be superficial.

Children so affected may reveal a lack of awareness of fine detail, along with a much greater appreciation of the "big picture." Their minds are apt to be more like a wide-angle than a telephoto lens. In solving a series of arithmetic problems, such a student may demonstrate a good understanding of the concepts and processes but have trouble dealing with small details, such as the difference between a plus sign and a minus sign or between the numbers 23 and 32. As a result he is prone to commit careless errors even in the face of strong understanding.

As depth and detail of processing is a control, it can be turned up too high or down too low. Consequently, there are some children with attention deficits who are said to *overattend.* They become bogged down in fine detail and have trouble perceiving the great significance or "big picture." They may function slowly, spending too much time on small details. Interestingly, some students seem to alternate between being too attentive to detail and being highly superficial and

Table 2-5. Depth and detail of processing

FORM	EXPLANATION	EXAMPLES
Concentration depth	Processing with sufficient intensity	Listening carefully to directions
Concentration balance	Seeing the big picture without losing the internal detail	Reading for meaning
Registration in short-term memory	Processing with enough depth to retain information	Remembering material while studying
Attention to detail	Focusing enough to appreciate fine detail	Attending to operational signs in arithmetic

"wide-angle" at other times. They simply have trouble regulating the depth and detail of their processing.

Shallow processing also takes a toll on short-term memory function. This phenomenon is often seen in children with attentional dysfunction who, as a result, may have trouble responding to recently delivered directions. Their short-term memory deficits may also make it hard for them to study. They may review material repeatedly and still not register it with sufficient depth in short-term memory. This frustrating predicament becomes conspicuously evident when one tries to quiz that student on information she is studying at the moment.

Shallow processing may sometimes lead to apparent noncompliant behavior. A student may violate limits in school because he never fully processes the rules, warnings, and admonitions articulated by the teacher. The resulting transgressions may be misinterpreted as intentional violations rather than unintended failure to appreciate the described behavioral limitations.

Cognitive Activation. When new information enters the mind, it should activate and connect to prior knowledge and experience. An actively engaged mind takes in new material and allows it call up relevant preexisting facts and ideas, often using the new input to reconstruct somewhat related prior knowledge. This form of cognition is known as *active learning* or *active processing*. It involves complex interactions between processing control and memory. An active processor keeps on connecting and associating. Cognitive activation helps a student form connections between bits or areas of knowledge. The control over this activity is an essential part of attention, for it is important that cognitive activation not be calibrated at a level that is either too high (overactive) or excessively low or passive. Optimal active processing adds to the enjoyment of intellectual content, enabling students to formulate interesting contrasts and comparisons as they learn. However, overly active processing (see next section) may actually distract a student or distort the intended meaning of incoming information. The inhibition of such "free flights of ideas" is another responsibility subsumed under cognitive activation control (see table 2-6).

Dysfunctions of cognitive activation. Some students with attention deficits tend to be passive processors. When new knowledge is imparted, not much occurs within the student's mind. She forges few if any associations and connections. Such a child may seldom elaborate on knowledge, failing therefore to mingle her own perspectives with new inputs. Showing a marked overreliance on rote memory in school, these students often seem to regurgitate knowledge on tests or when called on in class, without fully understanding or integrating it. They have a tendency to be nonelaborative and they are likely to feel understimulated and unfulfilled in school.

The opposite phenomenon also commonly occurs in students with attention deficits, namely a tendency to overactivate their minds, to experience the free flight of ideas in school and elsewhere. When some new bit of data enters their minds, it automatically elicits an extended chain of associations which can be

Table 2-6. Cognitive activation control

FORM	EXPLANATION	EXAMPLES
Association	Actively linking new inputs to prior knowledge	Associating something in class with a recent TV show
Connection	Thinking about relationships between areas of learning	Connecting fractions with decimals
Elaboration	Interpreting actively, relating inputs to personal ideas/values	Forming an opinion about something the teacher communicates
Free flight inhibition	Preventing excessive activation	Recognizing that an idea has triggered daydreaming and then refocusing

quite irrelevant to the topic at hand. The teacher may say something about a bird which reminds the child of a duck which, in turn, leads to thoughts about Donald Duck, which reminds him of his trip to Disneyworld, which makes him think of the vacation he will be taking next summer to the Grand Canyon where he will ride a mule into the canyon, which makes him wonder how big mules are. In a short period thoughts of birds have been transformed into mule speculations.

Children who have trouble inhibiting such free flight are often highly imaginative and fanciful. They frequently make comments in class that seem to have little or nothing to do with current topics or activities. They may gravitate toward the back of the room, where they create surrealistic drawings or pursue their rich fantasy lives in other ways.

Some children with dysfunctions of cognitive activation actually harbor manifestations at both extremes: at times their minds are passive and, at other times, far too active. It seems hard for them to match the level of mental activity with current circumstances or demands.

Focal Maintenance Control. The ability to match the duration of focus to the demands posed by incoming information is another parameter of optimal attention. Many investigators have studied the processes involved in sustained attention. There is widespread agreement that the ability to sustain a focus is an important and distinct component of attention (Halperin 1996). Clearly, certain forms of input demand extended concentration if they are to be processed with accuracy, while other circumstances call for briefer attention with more frequent changing of focus. Thus a child must tailor the length of concentration (sometimes known as *attention span*) to task demands and the nature of the subject matter. Focal maintenance also entails the ongoing monitoring of attention, so that it continues when it is yielding useful information and terminates when that is no longer the case. Table 2-7 summarizes the forms of focal maintenance control necessary for effective attention.

Table 2-7. Focal maintenance control

FORM	EXPLANATION	EXAMPLES
Sustained attention	Focusing long enough to process fully	Listening to entire set of instructions from the teacher
Shifts of attention	Changing focus when mission is completed; not perseverating	Shifting from reading a story to listening to directions for next activity
Set maintenance	Continuing foci that are working well, discontinuing those no longer leading to a set goal	Focusing on dictionary long enough to find word or shifting to other source when word cannot be located

Dysfunctions of focal maintenance control. It is common to describe children with attention deficits as having "short attention spans." Many of them do manifest this trait. However, it is also true that such children may *perseverate,* that is, concentrate too long on certain kinds of stimuli and not long enough on other (perhaps more worthwhile) inputs. They may show evidence of perseveration some of the time. They are likely to have trouble with *set maintenance,* losing focus too soon when needed information is continuing to arrive and/or concentrating too long when there is no longer a flow of useful data. It may be hard for them to shift attention smoothly from one target to the next.

Satisfaction Control. Children are likely to vary in what it takes to satisfy their attention. The processing controls operate best under conditions that their user feels are fulfilling or gratifying in some way. It is obvious that not all information input and daily experience is exciting and fun. It is possible and common for incoming data to be important but not entertaining or especially alluring to the processor. Nevertheless, it is worthy of attention. Satisfaction control enables an individual to exercise good processing control even when the inputs are not immediately exciting. As such, it becomes an important ingredient of intrinsic motivation. Further, it allows for delay of gratification, for the dampening of immediate wants and appetites, and for the allocation of mental energy to the processing of relatively low-interest information or stimuli. In other words, this control facilitates a sense of satisfaction and fulfillment that can occur under conditions of attention without high excitation (see table 2-8).

Dysfunctions of satisfaction control. Many children with attention deficits have been described as *insatiable.* They are exceedingly hard to satisfy. They crave intensity and feel unfulfilled and restless unless their surrounding conditions are conducive to high levels of fun and immediate gratification. Their insatiability can impede the function of their processing controls, as they are unable to attend effectively in a classroom setting unless the subject matter is particularly entertaining.

Table 2-8. Satisfaction control

FORM	EXPLANATION	EXAMPLES
Gratification delay	Being able to postpone rewards	Studying for test to get pleasure from good grades
Appetite dampening	Reducing intensity of material/ experiential wants	Doing homework while wanting to go shopping
Appetite termination	Being able to cease or curtail gratification	Being able to stop playing and start other activity
Motivation	Feeling motivated to focus	Wanting to study
Focus under moderate-low excitation conditions	Being able to feel satisfied in the absence of high levels of excitement	Behaving well under peaceful conditions in the current environment

There are two common forms of insatiability: material and experiential. Children harboring *material insatiability* want *things* much of the time. When they want something, they crave it. They may have great difficulty postponing gratification, needing to have the object of their yearning immediately, if not sooner. Yet, almost as soon as they get what they want, they start the quest for another material acquisition. They have trouble functioning when they want something; they can wear out their parents until they receive what they have been seeking. They are often accumulators and collectors, as they appear to lust after and hoard material possessions.

Children with *experiential insatiability* seem to hunger for intensity of experience. They want excitement and, when none is available, they are likely to create the excitement, often by committing provocative acts just "to stir things up." This phenomenon is, of course, associated with some loss of behavioral control. Their need for excitement also impairs concentration in school. In a sense, they are distracted by their own appetites. They are able to concentrate, but only when the material is sufficiently compelling or overtly attractive to them. Unfortunately, no educational system can sustain this high level of attractiveness throughout the school day. There is a great deal of material that is simply not exciting but needs to be learned nonetheless. These children experience their greatest difficulty with such less motivating content.

As insatiable children reach adolescence, they are likely to engage in risk-taking behaviors, which may help satisfy their hunger for excitement. This trait also places them at risk for substance abuse and some antisocial behaviors. Interestingly, insatiability during childhood and adolescence may ultimately evolve into productive drive and ambition in an adult. Thus, the trait is not necessarily negative, but it carries substantial risk.

Having explored processing controls, we will now delineate the functions and dysfunctions associated with the control over output, the regulatory effects of *pro-*

duction controls. These two types of controls are highly interdependent in that effective output often depends on accurate and efficient interpretation of information. Likewise, production is a way of learning. We are constantly processing or interpreting for ourselves and others what we are doing. Thus, processing and production enhance each other's roles.

The Production Controls

Production controls govern the multiple pathways of output. They regulate the creation of products (such as writing reports for school), the implementation of behaviors (such as acting appropriately in class), and the formation and nurture of relationships (such as maintaining a close friendship). In general, production controls allow the mind to operate slowly and deliberatively. Much of what falls under the category of production controls coincides with what are currently called *executive functions.* However, it should be stressed that there is considerable disagreement among investigators and clinicians regarding the components of these varied managerial functions of the mind. Denckla (1996) provides a good review of the issues. This section describes five production controls: previewing control, facilitation and inhibition control, tempo control, self-monitoring control, and reinforcement control.

Previewing Control. Previewing control is a function that helps us to predict the outcomes of our planned actions. It represents the mind's facility with forethought and foresight. Denckla (1996) refers to this form of control as "attention to the future." It enables us to anticipate an occurrence or event in order to plan a response likely to engender a positive outcome. Thus, through previewing, an individual is able to look ahead, estimate outcomes, and be prepared for upcoming circumstances and challenges.

Good previewing helps a student in many ways (table 2-9). She or he can have an idea of what a report will be like once the topic is selected. A student uses previewing to study for a test, to estimate answers in mathematics, and to decide what books and papers to bring home to accomplish various assignments. In the latter case, the student forms a picture of the evening "study scene" and fills in the materials needed.

Previewing helps with transitions. By picturing what is coming next, a student can be better prepared to move smoothly into a new activity.

Previewing plays a significant role in behavioral adaptation as well. It enables children to consider the "What if I . . . " question: "What if I say this, will I get into trouble?" "What if I fail to hand in this assignment, what will happen to me?" "How will my parents react when they find out?" These kinds of questions also relate closely to social skill. To relate effectively to others, it is necessary to keep predicting with accuracy others' reactions to things you are about to say or do in their presence: "What if I tell my friends that I caught a huge fish last weekend? Will they think I'm excellent or will they think I boast too much?"

Table 2-9. Previewing control

FORM	EXPLANATION	EXAMPLES
Quantitative prediction	Estimating final numbers in calculations	Knowing roughly the answer to a math problem
Social prediction	Foreseeing effects of one's actions on relationships	Predicting whether others will laugh at your joke
Behavioral prediction	Foreseeing the consequences of an action	Realizing you'll get punished if you cheat
Anticipation	Having an awareness of what might come next	Recognizing that someone is about to tease you
Product outcome vision	Having an idea of what a product will be like when finished	Picturing what your art project will look like when it is completed
Transition readiness	Looking ahead to prepare for a new activity/challenge	Knowing what you'll need to take to your next class

Dysfunctions of previewing. Children with poor previewing may endure considerable academic trouble. They may have no idea of how a report or project is going to turn out. This can lead to disorganized output that strays from the topic and has poorly defined goals. Some of these children have trouble estimating answers in mathematics, so that their responses on assignments and quizzes can be bizarre and nowhere near the correct answers.

Weak previewing also engenders behavioral maladaptation in some children. They commit aggressive or antisocial acts without first predicting the responses of others. In other words, they get into trouble because they did not foresee the consequences of their actions. They may also have trouble with anticipation, so that it may be hard for them to prepare an appropriate behavior in advance of an occurrence. They may not be able to think, for example, "I heard my new science teacher is very strict, so I better not fool around much in his class." Social anticipation may be impaired as well, preventing a child from thinking, "I bet she's going to invite me to her party, but I don't want to go. What should I say when she asks me?" Because of their weak previewing, such children seem to be taken by surprise; they are unready to respond in the most appropriate manner.

Many children with previewing problems have trouble with transitions. Because they fail to foresee next events, they are apt to lack the materials or preparation needed to deal with them. They may arrive in class without a pencil, come home with the wrong books, and be reluctant to move from one activity to another because they have not thought about what the transition might entail. Sometimes their lack of readiness creates in them a high level of anxiety at times of transition.

Table 2-10. Facilitation and inhibition control

FORM	EXPLANATION	EXAMPLES
Response inhibition	Delaying a response long enough to review additional options	Not reacting immediately when insulted by a peer
Temptation resistance	Avoiding seductive but ill-advised activities	Refraining from smoking in early adolescence
Stress management	Reviewing possible solutions when feeling sad or apprehensive; developing frustration tolerance	Thinking of various ways to catch up with overdue work
Strategy development and problem solving	Considering various approaches before undertaking task/project	Figuring out how to study for a particular test in school
Verbal regulation	Thinking about how and whether to communicate a message	Modifying or canceling a statement to avoid hurting someone's feelings
Voice control	Adjusting the loudness of one's voice	Not yelling or shouting needlessly
Behavioral regulation	Canceling or curtailing an inappropriate/ineffective behavior	Reducing one's aggression on the playground
Active control	Separating an emotional response from the immediate emotional content of the stimulus	Trying not to get too angry at a person for doing someting that irritates you
Motor regulation	Control over the level and efficiency of motor output	Slowing down when starting to become hyperactive

Facilitation and Inhibition Control. Just as saliency determination control facilitates the sorting out of possibilities for the intake of information, facilitation and inhibition control allows one to review possibilities for output or action, facilitating the best possibility while inhibiting the others. While saliency determination control allows for *selective attention,* facilitation and inhibition control promotes *selective intention.*

Facilitation and inhibition control enables an individual to review options for behavior, for verbal communication, for undertaking a task, or for various forms of problem solving, and then facilitates the possibility that is most likely to succeed while inhibiting (i.e., eliminating or postponing) the other choices. The related concept of *response inhibition* involves the capacity to delay or abort first reactions to stimuli, at least long enough to consider other possible responses (see table 2-10). For example, when solving a word problem in arithmetic, instead of using the first method that comes to mind, it might be wise to wonder, "What are the ways I could solve this problem and what is the very best way?" If a child pushes and shoves a fellow student, the victim may react immediately and aggressively, or may make use of facilitation and inhibition control to review quickly the behavioral options of the moment and select the best one for implementation.

The review of options and selection of best choices can be important for problem solving (see pp. 222–26), for coping with stress, and for thinking through various study skills and learning strategies (i.e., "Let's see, what's the best way to remember these French vocabulary words?").

Facilitation and inhibition control also relates to the level and efficiency of motor activity. When operating well, this control inhibits excessive motor activity, thereby conserving physical energy. It also serves to inhibit muscle groups that need not participate in a particular action, while simultaneously activating those muscle groups that are critical to performance. Such neuromotor facilitation and inhibition potentiates smooth and efficient motor output.

Dysfunctions of facilitation and inhibition control. Various forms of disinhibition can be especially problematic during childhood. Children may exhibit verbal, behavioral, effective, and/or motor control weaknesses. Thus, they may get into difficulty for saying things they should not have said (and would not have said had they thought about them). Analogously, they may transgress in school and at home because they act without sufficient premeditation. They may also reveal a lack of response inhibition and temptation resistance, tending to act and react in a way that reflects the first possibility that comes to mind, rather than engaging in a review of behavioral options.

Some students with weak facilitation and inhibition functions may reveal a low frustration tolerance. They may "fly off the handle" or lose interest when things are not going their way. In some cases this is a direct result of actually not having alternatives or strategies to think about to deal with setbacks or frustration.

Weak facilitation and inhibition control can also exact an academic toll. A child may solve a mathematics problem or meet some other scholastic challenge by doing the first thing that comes to mind rather than surveying the possible problem-solving routes and selecting the best one. Poor study skills may be a result of a chronic inability to seek best methods before engaging in an academic pursuit.

A lack of sufficient motor inhibition may result in hyperactivity or a tendency to move around too quickly and without purpose. It should be emphasized, however, that not all children with attention deficits display this phenomenon. Some children with attention deficits are indeed hyperactive, while others are normally active or even, in some cases, underactive. Of interest is the fact that the population of normally active and underactive children with attention deficits includes a higher proportion of females than is seen in the hyperactive group. Also, older adolescents (of both genders) with attention deficits often do not show signs of hyperactivity.

Weak motor facilitation and inhibition can also result in motor inefficiency. Overflow movements, a tendency to engage in a motor act and mirror it in the mouth or opposite limb (see p. 195), may be a manifestation of deficient facilitation and inhibition. That is, instead of activating only the specific muscle groups needed to accomplish a task, the central nervous system induces movement in superfluous muscle groups. Sometimes it is possible to observe an affected child playing a sport, riding a bicycle, or running, and detect the extraneous movement that is occurring due to weak motor inhibition.

Other possible signs of poor facilitation and inhibition include loud speech, emotional overreaction to stimuli, and generally deficient problem-solving skills.

Barkley (in press) has developed an encompassing theoretical basis for attentional difficulty. Limiting his discussion to the label "ADHD" (applied to children who have attention deficits plus hyperactivity), he cites a fundamental deficiency in inhibitory functions as a central mechanism. Barkley's formulation bears considerable resemblance to some aspects of what I here call problems with production controls.

Tempo Control. In general, production controls enable a person to function slowly and deliberatively. They decelerate responses to allow for more thought-out actions. Tempo control involves several closely related forms of regulation. First, it selects and applies the appropriate rate for completing a task or engaging in an activity. The pace should not be excessively fast or too slow; it should match task demands and available time.

Second, tempo control relates to the synchronization of multiple functions. This control is essential, since virtually all activities require the collaborative participation of multiple neurodevelopmental functions. These functions need to operate together at the same or compatible rates. For example, the flow of ideas while speaking needs to be synchronized with the encoding of those ideas in language (which, in turn, demands the synchronization of word finding with sentence formulation with narrative organization).

Finally, tempo control is associated with an appreciation of time in general. It helps regulate the allocation of time to tasks at hand, the prediction of time required, and the ability to use time as a medium to facilitate productivity (i.e., time management). Tempo control also instills a sense of *stepwisdom,* the idea that many activities need to be undertaken in a series of steps or stages rather than all at once. Stepwisdom greatly enhances productivity and makes sizable tasks more manageable. See table 2-11 for examples of the functions of tempo control.

Dysfunctions of tempo control. Tempo control difficulties are a frequent concomitant of attentional dysfunction. Children with this dysfunction may do many things much too quickly, thereby committing careless errors and performing at a level inferior to what would be seen with more deliberative pacing. Frequently, they may appear to be in a hurry to get things over with. At other times, they may operate too slowly, seldom functioning at a rate that matches current conditions and needs.

Table 2-11. Tempo control

FORM	EXPLANATION	EXAMPLES
Pacing	Performing at a rate appropriate to the task and available time	Using the right amount of time on a test
Synchronization of functions	Inducing functions to operate at same rate during a task	Synchronizing motor function, language, ideation, and memory while writing
Stepwisdom	Being able to break down and perform tasks in stages	Doing a project in manageable steps over time
Time management	Appreciating and working with time intervals	Meeting deadlines, allocating time for homework

Many children with tempo control problems have a diminished appreciation of time and its optimal utilization. They may have trouble staging tasks, difficulty meeting deadlines (procrastinating endlessly), and problems scheduling or allocating time to meet demands. They may be said, in fact, to be in a "time warp." Frequently, these children falter when undertaking tasks that require the synchronization of multiple functions, at which times they are likely to feel overwhelmed and discouraged. Most commonly this is manifest when they are expected to write large amounts. They may encounter problems trying to synchronize the multiple subskills and functions needed for efficient and satisfying written output (see chapter 10).

Hyperactivity and Impulsivity

It is common for children with attention deficits to be described as *hyperactive* and/or *impulsive.* These terms correspond to some of the control problems described here. A child may be hyperactive because of several control weaknesses. Hyperactive behavior may sometimes stem from a child's need to "wake himself up," to become more aroused and alert through physical activity. Hyperactivity may also represent a form of motor disinhibition, or it can be a manifestation of poor tempo control. Impulsivity is likely to represent an amalgam of poor previewing, weak facilitation and inhibition, and problems with tempo control. Thus, an impulsive child is apt to have trouble looking ahead and predicting an outcome prior to acting; difficulty inhibiting first responses; and problems slowing down his current tempo sufficiently to reflect before undertaking a cognitive/academic task, responding with a behavior, and/or putting forth a social initiative. Hence, he is perceived (correctly) as impulsive.

Self-Monitoring Control.   Self-monitoring serves as a quality control mechanism by enabling an individual to know how she is performing *while* doing something, and how she just performed immediately *after* doing something. Self-monitoring permits self-regulation. It affords the opportunity to get back on course when one finds oneself straying from the accomplishment of a goal. For example, while writing a report, a child may notice that she is no longer on the topic she set out to pursue. While driving a car, one might notice that one is slightly out of one's lane and then make a precise correction. A child may be talking out in class and recognize that he is beginning to irritate the teacher—so he stops. Self-monitoring constitutes a feedback loop, a mechanism that fosters ongoing evaluation (i.e., "How am I doing?") during and right after various activities and the creation of products.

There are many forms of self-monitoring that are needed for optimal behavior, interpersonal relationships, and school performance. The ability to detect one's own errors plays an indispensable academic role in all subject areas. Behavioral and social self-monitoring are needed to comply with rules of discipline and to relate effectively to others. Our neuromotor systems require constant feedback; while playing a sport or writing, the involved muscle groups need to report back to the brain on their current locations, so that they can be "told" where to go next (see chapter 6). These self-monitoring activities need to occur "on line" and post hoc. That is, one needs to know how a task or activity is proceeding while undertaking it, and one needs to evaluate its degree of success or failure after completing it. Self-monitoring control, when working properly, serves these purposes, as outlined in table 2-12.

Dysfunctions of self-monitoring. Poor or absent self-monitoring can have a range of effects on behavior and academic performance. Affected students are prone to make frequent careless errors when they work. They have difficulty with proofreading, a process they often studiously avoid. They may diverge markedly from the directions for an assignment without realizing that they are no longer doing what they were instructed to do. Their lack of awareness prevents them from self-righting while performing. Some students are chronically unable to evaluate their own performance; after taking a test in school such a student may report to have done extremely well, while he has actually failed the examination. Their

Table 2-12. Self-monitoring control

FORM	EXPLANATION	EXAMPLES
Social feedback reception	Reading cues that indicate social success or failure	Noticing when anyone laughs when one is acting silly
Academic error detection	Detecting work errors/ proofreading	Recognizing a spelling error while/after writing
Behavioral regulation	Noting the effects of one's behaviors	Realizing you are getting into trouble on playground
Motor feedback	Sensing the location and activity of one's muscles	Localizing fingers during writing (see chapter 6)

inability to know how they are doing over time can make it difficult for such students to allocate effort—to know, for example, that they will need to study harder for the next test because they are getting further and further behind in a course.

Behavioral and social difficulties can result from poor self-monitoring. A child may keep repeating an action that was initially amusing without detecting the anguish of those around him. Some of these children seem oblivious to social feedback cues, such as those that can be read in the facial expressions, vocal inflections, and body movements of those with whom one is interacting.

Poor feedback from muscles can result in writing difficulties (*finger agnosia*), while diminished body position sense can be one source of gross motor dysfunction in some children with attention deficits.

Reinforcement Control. The extent to which a child uses previous experience to guide current output is within the domain of reinforcement control. Just as previewing control represents foresight, reinforcement control makes use of hindsight. It enables one to base current responses and actions on previous (negative and positive) experience. This regulatory component enables an individual to learn from punishment and reward, to be sensitive to positive and negative reinforcement. Such sensitivity facilitates the use of previous outcomes of one's actions to influence current or anticipated actions (see table 2-13). If a child behaved in a way that got her into trouble yesterday, she should not repeat that pattern of behavior this afternoon. If a student found an excellent way to solve a particular math problem last week, he should use that method to solve a similar arithmetic challenge he now faces. That is, the new method that led to success and gratification should be reinforcing enough for the student to include it in his future repertoire of strategies. If a particular experience has occurred repeatedly, the child might even derive a rule from such past experience (e.g., "Whenever mom's in a bad mood, hold off on telling her you lost something on the way to school"). (Chapter 7 contains further information on rule acquisition.) Through good reinforcement control, past experiences connect to current decision making. In this way, precedents and learned rules can help steer behavior and academic output.

Table 2-13. Reinforcement control

FORM	EXPLANATION	EXAMPLES
Sensitivity to reward and punishment	Tendency of an individual to respond adequately to reward and/or punishment	Not repeating an action for which you were disciplined yesterday
Rule guidance	Ability to use experience to form rules to guide output	Using the fact that certain behaviors inevitably lead to certain positive or negative reactions from others
Academic outcome use	Incorporation of academic methods that have worked	Using a study technique that worked well on last quiz

Dysfunctions of reinforcement control. There are many children with attention deficits who are described as *weakly reinforceable*. They get into trouble one day and then re-enact like violations shortly thereafter. At times, they seem not to react to punishment. They may also show a diminished response to praise or rewards. Organized reward systems for good behavior or academic productivity may be short-lived in these cases, as the children reveal their underresponsiveness to them. Their actions often seem disconnected from previous experience. They simply do not make sufficient use of the outcomes of past behaviors to determine current behavioral output. In a sense, reinforcement control can be thought of as hindsight, while previewing control comprises foresight. Well-regulated output demands both.

Many children with weak reinforcement control encounter learning difficulties that are based, in part, on their inadequate use of past successes and failures to shape their approaches to learning. They often appear unable to assimilate new techniques or strategic approaches that have facilitated work when they have tried them in the past. As a result, they do too many things the hard way. They do not acquire a rapidly growing repertoire of academic output tactics that should emerge from direct experience. Such children may also reveal a reduced appreciation of rules that govern behavior. They may have trouble generalizing from one situation to another, a process that is greatly facilitated by the child's development of rules and application of them in relevant contexts or circumstances.

Now that we have examined the attention controls and described their commonly encountered dysfunctions, we can now explore a series of key issues related to these critical areas. First, we will offer some further general ideas that refine the concepts presented above. Then we will look at what is known about the representation of the attention controls in specific anatomical parts of the human brain. After that we will review some of what is known about the life histories of individuals who experience significant problems with the attention controls.

The Attention Controls: Some General Considerations

Some general points should help refine one's thinking about the attention controls and their breakdowns:

- The individual attention controls are highly interdependent. Thus, effective previewing enhances facilitation and inhibition, good self-monitoring makes an individual more reinforceable, and well-regulated mental energy control helps establish optimal levels of cognitive activation. Consequently, the attention controls comprise an overall system rather than a set of isolated regulatory functions. This is analogous to other systems in the human body. For example, in the cardiovascular system, the heart and the aorta are distinct entities, but their functions are tightly interdependent, so that a problem in one can cause damage to the other, and a strength in one can help compensate for a problem in the other.

- An individual attention control, such as saliency determination, may be weak while others appear to function adequately. In such cases, one should consider sources of difficulty aside from generalized attention deficits. For example, saliency determination may be weak because a child has a language disorder and reduced understanding of certain subject matter; it is impossible to make good determinations of saliency when understanding is very poor.

- The attention controls may work under certain conditions but not under others. A child may have problems with attention at school but not at home. In part, this too may result from problems processing information and meeting expectations in school. A child's attention controls are apt to reveal higher than usual effectiveness under high-interest conditions (e.g., while working on a hobby); when utilizing strengths (e.g., while a highly skilled athlete plays a sport); and when motivation levels are elevated (e.g., while seeking a short-term reward). A child's attention controls may deteriorate when he or she is placed in a setting that is ill matched to the child's personality, current neurodevelopmental profile, or cultural background. Breakdowns in attention controls can result when a teacher's teaching style is disparate from a child's manner of learning. This is especially common in those cases in which attention was somewhat weak to begin with.

- The attention controls collaborate closely with other neurodevelopmental functions in all activities. Sometimes there are distinct breakdowns in the relationships between attention and other functions. For example, attention and memory may not interact properly. At times it can be hard to decide if a child is not remembering because she is not concentrating or if she is not concentrating because she is having trouble stabilizing information in short-term memory. Similarly, interactions and potential breakdowns at the junctions exist between attention and all of the other neurodevelopmental functions. Production controls relate constantly to higher-order cognitive functions in the generation of rules, the application of strategies, the use of problem-solving skills, and the development of metacognition.

- Acute or chronic anxiety can interfere significantly with the attention controls. For instance, mental energy may be diverted or exhausted when a child is worried or intensely preoccupied with personal problems or fears. It can sometimes be difficult to differentiate between attention deficits and affective disorders during childhood.

- When assessing a child's attention controls, it is critical to ask the question that stems from these general principles: Does this child have a breakdown in one, several, or most of the attention controls? The more controls affected the more likely it is that the child has primary attention deficits (as opposed to attention deficits mainly as a result of a processing problem or anxiety). Are there indications that this child's attentional problems only manifest themselves in certain contexts or situations? Are there contexts in which the attention controls work especially well? Are there any forms of processing (e.g., language or visual-spatial) that either bring out or minimize that child's problems with attention? To what extent is anxiety impairing the operation of the attention controls? These and other questions form the basis for assessment of a child with signs of attentional difficulty.

ATTENTION CONTROLS AND THEIR BRAIN LOCATIONS

There is still much to be learned regarding the neuroanatomy of attention. However, in recent years, a growing body of knowledge has helped us understand which parts of the human brain take responsibility (or, more often, partial responsibility) for each control.

The mental energy controls are largely under the influence of nuclei located in the brain stem. Specifically, the reticular activating system and the locus coeruleus are centers of activity that contain nerve cells rich in the neurotransmitter dopamine. These cells play a significant role in promoting *nonspecific arousal.* That is, they activate higher cortical cells with no specific target in mind; they simply wake up consciousness. Interestingly, these brain stem cells have rich connections with the prefrontal cortex (Pennington et al. 1996), which, as we shall see, governs production controls.

Processing controls are the most diffuse in their localization, which is to say that their functions are carried out in various remote brain sites. The controls pertaining to specific modalities (such as visual or verbal processing) are located in association areas adjacent to the parts of the brain responsible for perceiving those specific forms of input. Mirsky (1996) describes components of attention and has investigated their neuroanatomical connections. Table 2-14 summarizes some of his findings.

The functional localization noted in table 2-14 is not hard and fast. As Mirsky (1996) notes, "the system organization allows for shared responsibility for attentional function, which implies that the specialization is not absolute and that some structures may substitute for others in the event of injury."

The production controls are more centrally located than the processing controls. For the most part, these controls have their headquarters in the prefrontal cortex.

Table 2-14. Anatomical sites of some processing controls

FUNCTION (MIRSKY'S TERMS)	RELATED ATTENTION CONTROLS	NEUROANATOMICAL SITES
Focusing on environmental events	Saliency determination, depth of processing	Superior temporal and inferior parietal cortices, plus structures in the corpus striatum
Sustaining focus	Focal maintenance	Rostral midbrain structures, as well as other thalamic and brain stem areas
Shifting focus	Focal maintenance	Prefrontal cortex, including the anterior cingulate gyrus
Encoding or *stabilizing* incoming data	Processing depth and cognitive activation	Hippocampus and amygdala

The production controls closely parallel what are now sometimes called the *executive functions*. There have been many studies documenting problems with these controls in patients who have had damage to this part of the brain. As Tranel, Anderson, and Benton (1995) note, "There is rarely a discussion of disturbances of executive functions that does not make reference to dysfunction of prefrontal brain regions."

ONSETS AND LIFE HISTORIES OF INDIVIDUALS WITH ATTENTION DEFICITS

Investigations of the life histories of children with attention deficits that have been undertaken in various disciplines have suffered from confusion over precisely who is being studied. Once again, assuming homogeneity oversimplifies our knowledge of these children. Most studies in the research literature focus primarily on the symptom of hyperactivity and its evolution. However, a broader view, such as that presented in this chapter, reveals that research on life history is sparse. At best we can piece together some fragments of knowledge to provide hints about how and when attention deficits emerge and insights into their manifestations over time.

Onsets

Mothers of children with attention deficits often tell their pediatrician, "This baby has always been different, even in the womb." Reports of inordinate kicking, of a frenzied fetus, are not unusual. Indeed, it may be that neurologically based disorganization exists prenatally in some children.

During a child's first five years, the development and persistence of signs of attention deficit appear to be in a state of flux (Campbell, Schleifer, and Weiss 1978). In one study, children were followed longitudinally and monitored for traits such as excessive distractibility, impulsiveness, and uncontrolled activity (Palfrey et al. 1985). By examining children when they reached specific ages and systematically questioning their parents, the researchers discovered that many children displayed these characteristic traits periodically. Moreover, it was not unusual for some children to display these traits at one age and subsequently manage to overcome them. In another group these traits persisted throughout the early years of life. However, the onsets of this latter group varied considerably—for some, symptoms began when they were infants; for others, when they were toddlers; and for still others, when they entered kindergarten. Clinical experience with schoolchildren suggests strongly that this flux persists into the middle school years.

Some children experience attention deficits for the first time when they enter school. In other children, symptoms appear to subside or diminish significantly during early elementary school. However, some children begin to show significant attention deficits in late elementary and junior high school, seemingly for the first time. Children in this group may reach a point at which educational and social demands exceed their capacities for attention to detail, and adults' expectations and reactions elicit latent symptoms (Chess 1979). Or an increasing level of potential distraction may confront youngsters at puberty and soon overwhelm those who are predisposed to weakness of attention. Frequently, an investigation of their histories will reveal that they had mild manifestations of these deficits earlier in life, but that the traits were not severe enough to interfere with function in any sphere. A final group of children seems to improve significantly at onset of puberty. In fact, hyperkinesis, the symptom of overactivity, very frequently lessens at this time. In the past, this led to the assumption that the problem stops at puberty. In many cases, the hyperkinesis does indeed diminish, but the other symptoms (such as insatiability, restlessness, inappropriate tempo, and easy fatigability) persist and frequently worsen.

This variation in ages of onset is difficult to account for. In the future, determining whether children who show a particular age-related history share other features in common will be important. Does the child with early onset and persistent symptoms have a totally different disorder from the child whose initial onset is in first grade or even junior high school? Is the difference between them simply a matter of degree, or are there different biochemical, neurophysiological, or environmental causes of their dysfunctions? Finally, there is the issue of reciprocity— how parents, teachers, and other adults handle the problem of disorganized behavior, and how their responses affect the child's actions and reactions.

Life Histories

Like other developmental dysfunctions, attention deficits are not static in their symptomatology, but change depending on the child's maturation, cognitive development, and the evolving expectations of adults. Some of this phenomenology is described below, although children vary considerably.

Infancy. Wender (1971) described infants possibly destined to show manifestations of "minimal cerebral dysfunction" at school age. Wender characterized these infants as often "insatiable, unpredictable, and irritable." Interestingly, insatiability and unpredictability are cardinal features described in older children with attention deficits. Researchers have described infants predisposed to attention deficits as overactive, constantly twisting, squirming, and arching their backs in a manner that makes it difficult for a mother to interact reciprocally with them. These infants may climb out of their cribs in the first year, wear out mattresses, and damage toys. They may display what seems to be an overabundance of exploratory behavior, but it is not clear just how purposeful or goal-directed this behavior is. Others have described unusual vocalization in these infants, in particular a high-pitched crying that approximates a piercing, shrill scream. This crying may become quite excessive, severely taxing the patience of the parents and engendering profound feelings of inadequacy that may cause them to withdraw from the relationship with the infant in various unconscious ways. This frequent distress and crying may interfere with the infant's exploration of her or his external environment and create an "experiential deficit" that may impede cognitive development (Schaffer 1977).

Unusual sleep patterns may also be early precursors of attention deficits. In particular, a less than appropriate amount of quiet sleep, as described in "the hyperactive infant" (Barnard and Collar 1973), may be an early manifestation of reticular activating system dysfunction or sleep-arousal imbalance. Often the infant has a history of failing to follow any kind of regular sleep pattern and of having a great deal of difficulty falling asleep. The irregular sleep periods may be brief (Campbell 1976).

Feeding difficulty can also be an early indicator of attention problems. Unpredictable feeding habits, a tendency to be finicky, and stubbornness about food may lead to considerable strife between mother and infant (Campbell 1976). In many cases, the infant becomes hungry at odd times and seems not to be fully satisfied after feedings. This might be an early indicator of what is to become chronic insatiability.

Many of these sets of traits constitute risk factors for interactional problems between mother and infant. In some instances, these traits may be antecedents of poor social reciprocity with peers and siblings in later life.

Infant temperament has generated interest over the years. Chess and Thomas (1983) described a series of temperamental characteristics that comprise an infant's style of behavior. Different qualities in these characteristics account for variation in the behavior and personality of babies. Constellations of these temperamental characteristics include the "easy" child, the "slow-to-warm-up" child, and the "difficult" child. The "difficult" child has frequently been associated with the clinical picture of attention deficits. Thomas and Chess (1977) describe these children as manifesting irregularity in biological functions, negative withdrawal responses to new stimuli, nonadaptability or slow adaptability to change, and intense mood expressions that are frequently negative. These children show irregular sleep and feeding schedules; slow acceptance of new foods; prolonged adjustment periods to new routines, people, or situations; and relatively frequent and loud periods of crying. Laughter is also characteristically loud. Frustration typically produces a violent tantrum (p. 23).

Carey (1982a) and others have produced parent questionnaires that document these traits effectively and may predict attention deficits. However, not all children with attention deficits manifest early-life temperamental dysfunctions; nor do all "difficult" infants become schoolchildren with attention deficits.

Toddler and Preschool. The classic picture of the two to four year old with attention deficits is a toddler who is noncompliant, fearless, unresponsive to discipline, generally driven, and out of control (Drash 1975). This pertains, however, in only the most extreme cases and in those who have a high loading of hyperkinesis as part of their symptom complex. Their impulsiveness makes them accident prone as well as susceptible to childhood poisoning and other forms of trauma. Parents may be afraid to turn their backs on such children, fearing the destruction of property or self-inflicted harm that may ensue. Toddlers or preschool children with attention deficits may or may not have delays in cognitive development. In some instances, they may be slow in acquiring language or in developing self-help or motor skills. Because many of the traits of attention deficits in older children are in fact part of the normal behavior of many two year olds, diagnosis can be elusive. Therefore, a parent's question about whether the frenetic behavior of a two year old is "normal" or not is a challenge for the clinician. Frequently a wait-and-see stance is advocated, since two year olds are often restless, egocentric, active, impersistent, unpredictable, and distractible. In the most extreme cases, those in which a toddler is clearly out of control, intervention is warranted, especially when a parent is totally exhausted by the interaction. A substantial proportion of children with these extreme behaviors will likely continue to have difficulties with the selection and regulation of attention into the school years.

School Entry.   The first indications of attention deficits may surface in kindergarten and first grade. The transition from home to school may bring forth children who have difficulty remaining in their seats, staying attentive, and interacting effectively in the social arena (Wender 1971). They may be overly egocentric and restless as well as unable to share and finish tasks. In some cases, these are the children who had temperamental dysfunction during infancy and the toddler years. On the other hand, newly evident cases are sometimes discovered in the early grades (Palfrey et al. 1985). These children may manifest milder symptoms or show the delayed appearance of attention deficit. Incidentally, these children may or may not be delayed in the acquisition of skills. Those who have good language abilities, effective visual processing, adequate memory, and higher-order cognition despite their attention deficits may well acquire academic skills in the early grades. A portion of them will experience difficulty later, and have serious problems as the volume of detail grows in middle or late elementary school.

Elementary School.   Children with strong receptive language skills may not need to listen very intently in the early grades, being able to understand what the teacher says while processing relatively few words. Their good sense of language enables them to generalize from context or from very few cues with great ease. As the requirements for precise language increase in later elementary school, more sustained auditory attention is demanded. At this point the student may show significant academic deterioration. Typical findings in children with attention deficits during elementary school were described earlier in this chapter.

Secondary School.   The hyperkinesis of many children who also have attention deficits lessens as they approach and go through puberty (Routh 1978). However, many of the subtler features of attention deficits often persist.

Secondary school increasingly demands longer and more intense periods of concentration, finer discriminations among minor details, and a general need to assimilate and remember far more specific material. In other words, it becomes more difficult to survive academically solely on the basis of appreciating broad concepts. Those students with attention deficits who are adept at seeing the whole picture but who have great difficulty with internal detail may actually deteriorate significantly in secondary school (Cohen, Weiss, and Minde 1972). Many of them develop problems with saliency determination which can have a major negative impact on performance in heavily detailed subjects, such as history and biology. Many of these students also exhibit signs of passive processing (see p. 29), showing little propensity to form rich associations and activate relevant prior knowledge during classes in school. Significant difficulties with the production controls in this age group can have behavioral, academic, or social impacts, as affected students may show high levels of impulsivity, problems with planning, difficulties with self-monitoring, and trouble learning from experience (i.e., reduced reinforceability). They are often assumed to be suffering from, and are often unjustly accused of, poor motivation, laziness, or some other form of moral turpitude. Since they are living up neither to their own expectations nor to those of their parents and teachers, these adolescents may become increasingly depressed, suffering from low self-esteem and chronic deprivation of success (Cantwell 1979). Their anxiety may further erode or displace attention. The adolescent's incessant need to look good in front of peers aggravates the condition. She or he may not wish to acknowledge that there is a problem and thus may refuse help or insist that everything is going to work out. Such a student may be reluctant to take medication, get help from a tutor, or even undergo an evaluation.

Additionally, adolescence introduces a host of new potential distractors: the adolescent's own rapidly changing body, sexuality, and a range of other temptations (such as alcohol and drugs). The adolescent with attention deficits is likely to be exquisitely vulnerable.

Middle school and high school may tend to bring out associated dysfunctions in a student with attention deficits. Thus, a teenager who has problems with attention plus memory plus language may deteriorate as the demands for effective language and memory function grow exponentially during these years. When a student with attention deficits appears to worsen during adolescence, therefore, it is extremely important to consider the possible role of her or his other forms of dysfunction.

Unlike hyperkinesis, the trait of insatiability may become more pronounced in adolescence. Affected teenagers may become chronically restless, perpetually feeling that whatever they are doing now isn't quite right, that there are better things ahead. At the same time, these teens gain in their ability to concentrate on highly motivating tasks while lagging in their capacity to concentrate on less exciting activities (such as schoolwork). For example, a compelling interest in cars or the opposite sex may elicit such intensive selective attention that other stimuli meet increasing interference in competing for attention. Academically, this often creates a discrepancy between demonstrated capacity and day-to-day performance.

The teenager's self-esteem can be damaged when resultant underachievement is misconstrued as a *voluntary* phenomenon. Teachers' comments that they need to "try harder" may reflect this perspective. In reality, these teenagers probably have no idea how to overcome their distractibility, restlessness, fatigue, and inattention to detail (Levine and Zallen 1984).

Some children with attention deficits show resiliency in adolescence, seeming in some cases to "find themselves." These fortunate survivors discover some captivating interests that happen to coincide with academic and/or other expectations of adults. During the period that Piaget calls "formal operations," some adolescents emerge as excellent conceptualizers. They are able to employ abstract thinking effectively and strong "top-down" thinking to compensate for their relative inattention to detail. Some adolescents develop specialized interests such as computers, artistic pursuits, or work with engines, that can be pursued as life work. Such focused pursuits can have a remarkably beneficial effect; some students with rather specialized minds can find their niche and thrive once they do so.

Thus, the phenomenon of attention deficits seems to reach an important transition point during adolescence: some victims make a remarkable recovery from their troublesome selective attention while others persist or even deteriorate. Solid family and educational support systems, high IQ, and relative affluence are possible factors likely to improve prognosis in this age group. However, we do not yet clearly understand what makes the difference.

Early Adult Life. A number of longitudinal prospective studies of attention problems have focused primarily on "hyperactivity," possibly limiting their value with regard to contemporary concepts of attention deficits. Nevertheless, there are indications that young people with attention problems are a group that is at high risk. Weiss et al. (1979) followed seventy-five such youths into early adult life and found that many of their problems persisted—in particular, a wide range of impulsive behaviors. Those with attention problems had a higher prevalence of illicit drug use than their matched controls. A noteworthy finding is that many of the youths with attention problems have been involved in serious automobile accidents. This should not be surprising, especially if we consider what it must be like to drive an automobile when one is insatiable, impulsive, distractible, perhaps overactive, and relatively impervious to feedback. Moreover, children with attention deficits (especially boys) have a peculiar tendency to become infatuated with wheels. Beginning with wheeled or winged toys, and progressing to bicycles, dirt bikes, motorcycles, and fast cars, these youths are often obsessed by fast-moving vehicles—as if these were the first bodies they have ever been able to control and steer. Thus, despite their constellation of maladaptive driving traits, this particular segment of the population likely puts an enormous amount of mileage on cars, a prime example of developmental dysfunctions of childhood that have long-lasting effects, constitute health and safety risks, and go well beyond a simple impact on school performance. Young adults with attention deficits may be predisposed to a number of other unfortunate outcomes. Crime and delinquency, divorce and general instability of relationships, as well as chronic depression and other forms of mental illness have been reported (Bellak 1979).

There is also a bright side. Weiss et al. (1979) found that many young people with attention problems were doing well in their jobs and that their employers were satisfied with their work. This suggests that when young people with attention deficits are allowed to find their areas of specialization or preferred pursuit, they are more likely to perform with greater consistency and dependability. As we scrutinize carefully the range of traits seen in youngsters with attention deficits, we develop a strong sense that at least some of the traits have the potential to evolve into strengths or talents. Insatiability in childhood may ultimately be transformed into ambition during adult life. How many millionaires have been satisfied after earning their first million? Distractibility and the free flight of ideas may develop into creativity and inventiveness. In fact, it is not at all unusual to hear parents remark that their children with attention deficits are incredibly creative or have fantastic imaginations. Clearly, children predisposed to distraction and incidental learning are apt to notice relationships in their environments or in their past experiences that would elude other, more disciplined minds. At least some of these relationships, if carried to some logical conclusion, may contain viable ingredients for new concepts, new products, and new solutions to problems. The highly impulsive child may become an admirably decisive adult, one who is highly productive. It is tempting to consider whether children with attention deficits would struggle less in school if an administrative assistant could accompany them to class and help with their homework. In other words, they may understand and generate ideas without difficulty, while their detail work is disastrous. The adult world clearly has abundant opportunity for big thinkers, conceptualizers, and entrepreneurs who may not be very good at day-to-day housekeeping, bookkeeping, or management of details; these individuals can collaborate with colleagues who thrive on such details.

Children who have many traits of attention deficit probably grow up to be vulnerable even as adults (Huessy, Metoyer, and Townsend 1974). The manifestations and complications are quite varied (Hallowell and Ratey 1994). However, it may be possible to contain these tendencies—indeed, to convert some of them to assets, to circumvent weaknesses, and to mobilize their many compensatory strengths effectively. Furthermore, more options are available to young adults than to children. Adults can pursue highly motivating areas of vocation and avocation with much greater freedom than they could earlier in life. Such opportunity in itself may be most therapeutic.

In contemplating the potential negative consequences of attention deficits, it is important to distinguish between a child's life history of attention deficits and the outcome of chronic deprivation of success, persistent feelings of worthlessness, and a sense that one is a loser at an early age. Children who grow up overcriticized, who are deprived of a sense of mastery, and who become increasingly anxious about their own worthiness may, in fact, be the ones that experience adversity in adult life.

ASSESSMENT OF ATTENTION

There are many different ways to assess the attention controls and uncover attention deficits in children. Each has its distinct advantages and disadvantages. The following list summarizes and comments on these forms of assessment.

- *Retrospectively completed questionnaires.* These are usually behavioral check-lists that are filled out by parents and teachers. In general, they correspond to the symptoms of "ADD" as delineated in the *Diagnostic and Statistical Manual* of the American Psychiatric Association (DSM-IV; see pp. 19–20). The *Conner's Questionnaire* (short and long forms) is the most commonly used. *The ANSER System* questionnaires contain separate forms that are completed by a child's teachers and parents as well as a form on which children age nine and above rate their own attention.

Conner's questionnaire

- *Direct measures of attention.* These direct methods are now often computerized and tend to detect weaknesses of vigilance, impulsivity, deterioration of attention over time, and weak focus on detail. Examples include the *Gordon Diagnostic Test* and the *TOVA*. The vigilance tests on *PEEX 2* and *PEERAMID 2* (see fig. 2-2) are less extensive direct tests of attention. There exists a multitude of tests, largely for research purposes, that relate to the specific attention controls. These include tests of vigilance or continuous performance, assessments of impulsivity vs. reflectivity, and a range of tests for cognitive flexibility, strategy use, and other dimensions of production control. These tests have been extensively reviewed by Barkley (1994).

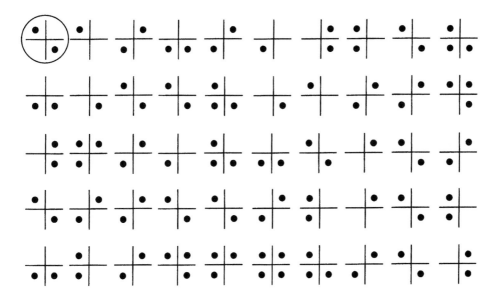

Figure 2-2. Vigilance test on *PEEX 2*

- *Guided observations of attention.* These techniques stress the prospective inspection of attention over time. During the pediatric neurodevelopmental examinations (*PEEX 2* and *PEERAMID 2*) the examiner systematically observes attention during the performance of specific tasks. Figure 2-3 shows the observation grid that is used.

Considerable caution is necessary when interpreting the results of assessments of attention. Many biases can distort the findings. Some precautions are listed in the box below.

Precautions Regarding the Assessment of Attention

- Some questionnaires may be more calibrated to detect behavior problems and less sensitive to the cognitive/academic manifestations of attentional dysfunction. These questionnaires may tend to identify all children with serious behavior problems as having "ADD." After all, it is hard even to imagine a child with serious misbehavior who is seldom impulsive, who concentrates well, and does not talk out of turn.

- Questionnaire scoring systems may not be valid. Many questionnaires are based on the underlying (questionable) assumption that the number of traits manifested determines whether or not a child has an attention deficit. However, a child may have relatively few incapacitating symptoms and not "qualify" as having attention deficits. Cutoff points may be arbitrary and not clinically valid or helpful.

- The validation of attention questionnaires makes use of imperfect methods. There is no gold standard against which to establish their accuracy.

- The agreement between observers is often poor. A school questionnaire may suggest the presence of attentional difficulty, while the parent questionnaire paints a very different picture of the child. Even individual teachers may reveal disagreement; similar disparities may be found between parents.

- Direct tests of attention may depend too much on the current state of the child. Since attention deficits represent a chronic problem and since performance inconsistency is the rule, an isolated test of attention may not detect the problem. Also, such tests assess only a few of the attention controls; manifestations such as weak reinforceability and poor previewing are not included. Furthermore, some children may find the testing situation especially interesting and challenging, which obscures their attentional difficulties. In general, children with attention deficits perform much better on a one-to-one encounter than they do in a group; this too can distort the results of direct testing.

- Direct observations can also be problematic. They may be highly subjective and depend too much on the observer's tolerance, astuteness, and level of experience. Attention can be affected by the complexity and level of interest a child derives from the content and expectations he confronts. Some children, for example, may exhibit attentional difficulty in settings that are highly verbal and detail laden but not in other environments. During testing or direct observations the evaluator must always take into consideration the particular characteristics of the setting that may be influencing attentional function.

ATTENTION CHECKPOINT ONE (Fine Motor/Graphomotor)

OBSERVATION	SCORE			DESCRIPTION
Impulsivity	0	1	2	Started task in an unplanned manner or answered too quickly—compromising quality
Frenetic tempo	0	1	2	Paced task too quickly
Poor attention to detail	0	1	2	Missed relevant detail during task
Distractibility	0	1	2	Became distracted during task or seemed not to listen
Mental fatigue	0	1	2	Yawned, stretched, otherwise showed fatigue during task
Deterioration over time	0	1	2	Lost focus as task progressed or had difficulty sustaining attention
Performance inconsistency	0	1	2	Showed erratic error pattern during task
Poor monitoring	0	1	2	Performance impaired by poor monitoring or made careless errors
Gross overactivity	0	1	2	Displayed extraneous large muscle motion during task, e.g., appeared restless, left seat
Fidgetiness	0	1	2	Displayed extraneous small muscle motion during task, e.g., appeared fidgety, squirmy

Total	
6	16–20
7	19–20
8	19–20
9	

Total for Checkpoint One   (0–20) ___ ___

```
                        Key
    0=Observed on >1 task          1=Observed on 1 task
                2=Never observed
```

Comments:

Figure 2-3.   Observation grid used in *PEEX 2* and *PEERAMID 2*

The most valid and reliable assessments of attention are likely to be those that combine several methods, such as the use of questionnaires (completed by more than one source) plus direct observations.

Assessment should focus on evaluating the status of the specific attention controls as they affect academic performance, behavioral adaptation, and social interaction. An accurate description of strengths and weaknesses in the specific controls is likely to be far more helpful than a score or a label. This description of attention controls can then be integrated with descriptions of the child's strengths and weaknesses in other domains to formulate a comprehensive management plan (see chapter 15). Figure 2-4 from *The ANSER System* is one method for assessing and documenting the adequacy of individual attention controls. Several observers can complete the form (either prospectively or retrospectively).

The end product of an assessment of attention should be a descriptive profile of the child's attention controls, their strengths, and their deficiencies. In most

ATTENTION CONTROL INVENTORY

Directions: The tables below (Parts I, II, and III) include a series of traits that are found commonly among children and adolescents who are having problems with attention. The traits are grouped in three parts, Mental Energy Controls (needed to maintain alertness and exert effort), Processing Controls (needed to focus properly on incoming information), and Production Controls (needed to regulate work output and behavior). Each part lists traits that may be seen in children who have problems with attention. In some instances, the individual traits may affect school work or behavior or the ability to relate to other children. Please use the rating key to show which of these traits are found in this student. You can indicate whether the trait is affecting the student's school work, behavior, and/or social life. Squares that are shaded need not be marked. The Abbreviation Keys show how each trait is a weakness in a particular kind of attention control.

RATING KEY

3 = Never or Almost Never Evident
2 = Occasionally Evident
1 = Evident Often
0 = Evident All or Almost All the Time

PART I - MENTAL ENERGY CONTROLS

(Alertness, Arousal, Mental Effort)

	Con	Trait	Effects on School Work				Effects on Behavior				Effects on Peers			
			0	1	2	3	0	1	2	3	0	1	2	3
AC01	AL	Has trouble staying alert												
AC02	AL	Attention hard to attract												
AC03	AL	Loses focus unless very interested												
AC04	CO	Has unpredictable behavior/school work												
AC05	CO	Has excellent days and poor days												
AC06	CO	Keeps "tuning in and tuning out"												
AC07	ME	Has trouble finishing things he/she starts												
AC08	ME	Has difficulty getting started with homework												
AC09	ME	Has a hard time exerting effort/doing work												
AC10	SL	Has trouble falling/staying asleep at night												
AC11	SL	Has trouble getting up in the morning												
AC12	SL	Looks tired												

Abbreviation Key
Mental Energy Controls

CON	Attention Controls	Forms of mental regulation
AL	Alertness Control	Being able to become and remain alert
CO	Consistency Control	Performing and behaving in a consistent manner
ME	Mental Effort Control	Working, putting forth effort
SL	Sleep Control	Sleeping well at night, awake enough during day

- 12 -

Figure 2-4. Attention Control Inventory from *The ANSER System* questionnaires

PART II - PROCESSING CONTROLS

	Con	Trait	Effects on School Work				Effects on Behavior				Effects on Peers			
			0	1	2	3	0	1	2	3	0	1	2	3
AC13	SD	Is easily distracted by sounds												
AC14	SD	Focuses on unimportant details												
AC15	SD	Is easily distracted by visual things												
AC16	PD	Forgets what he/she just heard												
AC17	PD	Focuses too deeply at times												
AC18	PD	Misses important information												
AC19	CA	Mind is not active while learning												
AC20	CA	Has unusual ideas or thoughts												
AC21	CA	Daydreams, free associates easily												
AC22	FM	Doesn't concentrate long enough												
AC23	FM	Shows uneven concentration												
AC24	FM	Has trouble shifting attention												
AC25	SC	Craves excitement												
AC26	SC	Has trouble delaying gratification												
AC27	SC	Gets bored easily												

ABBREVIATION KEY*

CON	Attention Controls	Forms of mental regulation
SD	Saliency Determination	Focusing on important information
PD	Processing Depth	Concentrating with the right strength
CA	Cognitive Activation	Regulating the mind's level of activity
FM	Focal Maintenance	Focusing for the best amount of time
SC	Satisfaction Control	Feeling content while focusing

Figure 2-4. *(Continued)*

PART III - PRODUCTION CONTROLS

Con		Trait	Effects on Learning				Effects on Behavior				Effects on Peers			
			0	1	2	3	0	1	2	3	0	1	2	3
AC28	PC	Doesn't think ahead before acting												
AC29	PC	Has trouble planning work												
AC30	PC	Is not prepared for what's coming next												
AC31	FI	Often does first thing that comes to mind												
AC32	FI	Does not use strategies												
AC33	FI	Doesn't predict effects of acts or words												
AC34	TC	Is overactive/fidgety												
AC35	TC	Is disorganized with time												
AC36	TC	Does many things too quickly												
AC37	SM	Makes many careless errors												
AC38	SM	Fails to notice when bothering others												
AC39	SM	Has trouble knowing how he/she's doing												
AC40	RE	Punishment doesn't make a difference												
AC41	RE	Seems not to learn from experience												
AC42	RE	Keeps making same kinds of mistakes												

ABBREVIATION KEY*

CON	Attention Control	Forms of mental regulation
PC	Previewing Control	Looking ahead/anticipating
FI	Facilitation & Inhibition	Picking the best possible actions
TC	Tempo Control	Acting/doing things at the best rate
SM	Self-monitoring	Watching what you're doing to assure quality
RE	Reinforceability	Use of prior experience to guide actions

*Detailed explanations of these terms and their implications can be found in Dr. Mel Levine's book, *Educational Care* (Cambridge, MA: Educators Publishing Service, Inc., 1994).

Figure 2-4. *(Continued)*

cases it is not possible to decide on a cause or an etiology for the child's attention deficits. Nevertheless, it is important to seek possible causes or closely associated conditions which may be present.

THE MANAGEMENT OF ATTENTION DEFICITS

The management of weak attention controls must be one part of the management of a child's overall neurodevelopmental profile. This section, however, contains suggestions specifically for the management of attention issues.

Demystification

Children with attention deficits can benefit from a substantial emphasis on learning about the attention controls. They need to understand the workings of normal attention as well as the specific breakdowns that are causing them difficulty in life. They should acquire a vocabulary regarding attention. The concepts and terminology they learn should also be used by their teachers and parents.

Demystification can be achieved by having the child read relevant information about attention. My children's books, *Keeping a Head in School* (1990; for middle and high school students) and *All Kinds of Minds* (1993; for elementary schoolchildren) may be helpful. The Concentration Cockpit (fig. 2-5) helps children conceptualize the attention controls by likening them to the controls in an airplane cockpit. The child rates himself on each of the controls by marking his pointer with a magic marker in each meter. The adult explaining the controls can document the child's responses in an administration booklet, which can augment assessment as well as demystification. For older adolescents and young adults, I use a more straightforward explanation with graphic representation (fig. 2-6).

A clinician, parent, and/or teacher should periodically review demystification with the child. The child should feel comfortable reporting specific examples of times when his attention controls have worked well, as well as instances of breakdowns. Having provided demystification, the clinician or teacher is in a much better position to enact bypass strategies and interventions at the breakdown points. It must be stressed that such management techniques are likely to be most effective when the child understands the reasons they are being used. Thus, demystification strongly fortifies other forms of intervention. Chapter 15 provides further information regarding the process of demystification.

Managing the Specific Controls: Bypass Strategies and Interventions at the Breakdown Points

Once one has identified the attention controls that a child most needs to work on, it is possible to devise specific strategies. Some of these are methods of bypassing weak attention controls, while others are direct interventions to help strengthen the attention controls. The suggestions contained in the following pages are not meant to be exhaustive. They are intended as first steps, with the expectation that

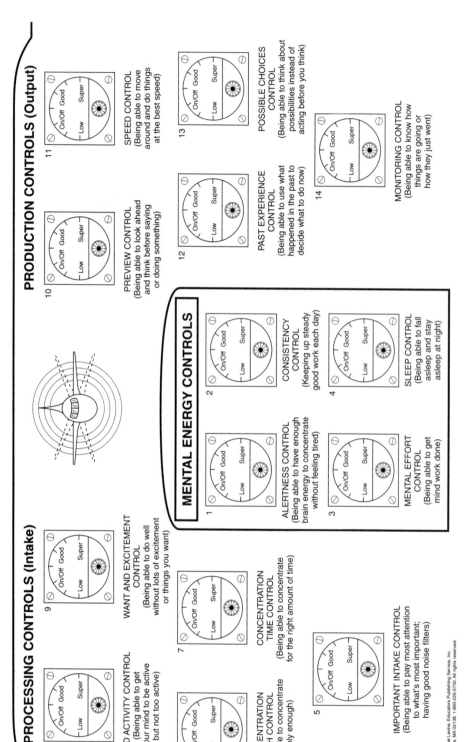

PROCESSING CONTROLS (Intake)

8 MIND ACTIVITY CONTROL (Being able to get your mind to be active but not too active)

9 WANT AND EXCITEMENT CONTROL (Being able to do well without lots of excitement or things you want)

6 CONCENTRATION DEPTH CONTROL (Being able to concentrate deeply enough)

7 CONCENTRATION TIME CONTROL (Being able to concentrate for the right amount of time)

5 IMPORTANT INTAKE CONTROL (Being able to pay most attention to what's most important; having good noise filters)

PRODUCTION CONTROLS (Output)

10 PREVIEW CONTROL (Being able to look ahead and think before saying or doing something)

11 SPEED CONTROL (Being able to move around and do things at the best speed)

12 PAST EXPERIENCE CONTROL (Being able to use what happened in the past to decide what to do now)

13 POSSIBLE CHOICES CONTROL (Being able to think about possibilities instead of acting before you think)

14 MONITORING CONTROL (Being able to know how things are going or how they just went)

MENTAL ENERGY CONTROLS

1 ALERTNESS CONTROL (Being able to have enough brain energy to concentrate without feeling tired)

2 CONSISTENCY CONTROL (Keeping up steady good work each day)

3 MENTAL EFFORT CONTROL (Being able to get mind work done)

4 SLEEP CONTROL (Being able to fall asleep and stay asleep at night)

Figure 2-5. The Concentration Cockpit: attention controls for behavior, learning, and getting along with people

This diagram is used to inform young children about attention deficits.

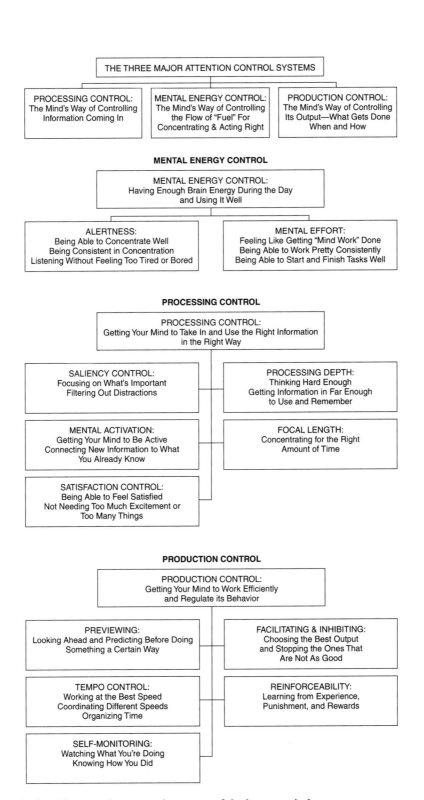

Figure 2-6. The attention control systems of the human mind

This diagram is one of a series of aids used to help adolescents understand attention and attention deficits.

teachers and clinicians will supplement the list with techniques that work particularly well for them in the settings in which they work. It should be emphasized that the measures outlined in this section will be most effective if the child understands what each applied intervention intends to accomplish. In other words, demystification is an essential accompaniment of each management strategy.

Dysfunctions of Mental Energy Control

Inconsistent alertness

- A child may benefit from preferential seating in class. Being close to the teacher may help a student sustain alertness.

- Carefully manage any sleep-arousal imbalance, including consistent bedtimes, the use of white background noise for sleep, reassuring the child to alleviate anxiety over sleep, and in some cases medication to facilitate falling asleep (Catapres in small doses at bedtime has been recommended for this purpose; see p. 583).

- Reduce "chunk size": institute frequent breaks for homework and, in class, shorten assignments.

- Encourage the use of hands for physical activity (ball of clay, doodling) while concentrating; moving feet or tapping them rhythmically may also help.

- Stimulant medication may significantly increase alertness (see p. 65).

- Exploit strong modalities/affinities in school to strengthen foci.

Inconsistent effort

- Avoid using inconsistency as a "moral" issue (i.e., "We know you can do better; we've seen you do it when you really want to").

- Encourage staged approaches to task completion, with scheduled work breaks, following which effort may be fortified.

- Document graphically on a calendar or in a diary "on times" and "off times" for effort.

- Ask students to describe—verbally and/or in writing—exactly what it feels like to be running out of mental effort.

- Search for tactics to make effort increasingly less effortful (i.e., ask, "What can you do to make work easier for yourself?").

- Rotate work sites at home; a child should try studying for 10 minutes in the bedroom, 15 minutes on the living room floor, 10 minutes in the kitchen, etc.

- A child may benefit from nonaccusatory assistance at work initiation ("a jump-start"; i.e., parent may need to write the first line of a report or help with first math problem).

- Stimulant medication may help improve mental effort.

Dysfunctions of Processing Control

Poor saliency determination

- Stress development of paraphrasing and summarization skills.

- Encourage a child to play video games that emphasize vigilance and attention to relevant detail.

- Encourage underlining and circling skills during reading.

- Help a child practice crossing out superfluous information (e.g., devise word problems containing too much information).

- Minimize specific vulnerable pathways of distraction in work settings at home and at school.

- Use consistent background sounds (e.g., music) for study.

- Arrange breaks during which the child can consciously pursue the facilitated distraction pathway (e.g., give a visually distractible child the chance to look out the window during a work break).

- Give a child the chance subtle/inconspicuous reminders to tune back in during periods of high distraction; a tap on the shoulder may work.

Superficial or excessively deep processing

- Teach the child to apply rehearsal strategies (see pp. 68–69): subvocalization, visual "scratch pad" use, and note taking (even primitive forms thereof).

- Encourage self-testing techniques as part of studying.

- Paraphrasing what's heard or read can increase the depth of processing.

- The child may need repetition of instructions or explanations.

- Encourage the child to make good eye contact while listening.

- When processing is too deep, encourage the student to read or work at a more rapid pace. When necessary, impose time limits.

Passive or extremely active processing

- Attach reminder cards to desk or notebook ("Am I being passive or is my mind active or maybe *too active?*").

- Develop disciplined elaboration activities to make the mind a more active processor ("What are the things you already know that this new stuff reminds you of?" "How is it pretty much like it?" "How is it new and different?").

- The acquisition and longitudinal (long-term) pursuit of expertise may encourage active processing; the child starts by processing actively in an area about which he knows a great deal and in which he has strong interest.

- Have the child keep score of "canceled mind trips" and/or "wake-up calls" (attempts to get his mind back on track).

- Create opportunities for a child to use the creative/imaginary propensities inherent in "free flight" tendencies; these children desperately need creative outlets.

- Encourage high-quality "top-down" processing (i.e., free associating and infusing one's own ideas, values, perceptions into what is being read or listened to).

Focal maintenance problems

- Praise the child whenever she sustains attention appropriately.

- If necessary, give a very explicit reminder when it is time to change focus.

- Use computer software for learning to extend attention.

- The suggestions under "Inconsistent Alertness" (above) also pertain to focal maintenance problems.

Insatiability

- Use high motivational content to bolster learning.

- Emphasize the "ethics" of sharing and taking the perspective of others.

- Be explicit about delays of gratification (i.e., "You will be able to play football in forty minutes—not before then").

- Help the child identify and acknowledge low motivational processing tasks (things that make her feel a little bored when she listens to or reads about them).

- At home, designate specific times as "getting satisfied times," and other times as periods of gratification delay.

- Use the word *insatiability* every day with minimal moralization (e.g., "How has your insatiability been going today? Do you think it's a little out of control?").

Dysfunctions of Production Control

Poor previewing

- Institute "what if?" exercises in behavioral, social, and/or cognitive-academic domains (e.g., "What if you call your friend a 'dummy'? How will that make him feel about you?").

- Stress articulating and describing final products (i.e., "What do you want this to look like when it's finished?" "What is it you want to say in this report?" "What do you want this girl to think about you?" "How would you like your behavior to be in the lunch room?").

- Help the child practice writing or telling stories that end with a particular sentence (e.g., "George's gerbil will never eat that again!") or write reports creating the last paragraph first.

- Have the a student practice estimating answers to quantitative questions.

Weak facilitation and inhibition

- The child is likely to benefit from specific training in problem-solving skills (see pp. 254–57) applied across social, behavioral, and academic domains.

- In confronting new challenges, systematically review alternative strategies (cognitive-academic, social, and/or behavioral) and select "best bet" and back-up strategies.

- Use hypothetical case studies to practice problem solving.

- Apply problem-solving techniques post hoc when reviewing a student's previous misconduct or poor performance on a test or assignment (i.e., "Let's go back and review how you could have done better if you had stopped and thought carefully about the problem").

- Ask the child to submit work plans and/or "social survival plans" describing how he or she will go about tackling a serious problem or challenge. The Problem-Solving Planner (pp. 255–57) may be used for this.

- Help the child diagram possible pathways of facilitation and inhibition (flow charts) for specific academic assignments and behavioral dilemmas.

- Stimulant medication may help "decelerate" a child and allow for more reflective thinking and behavior; it may simultaneously help with pacing (see next list).

Improper pacing

- Institute time management (scheduling) procedures at home and in school (see p. 136).

- Have the student serve as a time manager in school (e.g., work out schedules for putting on a play, doing a class project, or going on a field trip).

- At home and in school, stress time estimation ("How long should this take me?").

- Avoid providing incentives for frenetic pacing, so that there are no advantages to finishing first or "getting it over with."

- Use time landmarks for writing, reading, and projects (i.e., where you should be when).

- Help the student learn to write in stages (see pp. 377–79).

- Hold regular discussions regarding time and time management.

- Model stepwise approaches to tasks for the student whenever possible.

Deficient self-monitoring and self-righting

- Remind the student to engage in midtask and terminal self-assessment ("How am I doing?" or "How do I think I did?").

- Have the child self-grade and comment (on the quality of the work) *before* submitting tests and assignments, with extra credit given for accurate self-appraisal.

- Use proofreading exercises, and give credit for finding and correcting mistakes (of self and others).

- Require the child to proofread her own work at least forty-eight hours after completion. (N.B.: It is very hard and probably unwise to proofread something you have just created.)

- Use hypothetical case studies to demonstrate the impacts of poor self-monitoring of behavior and interpersonal relating.

- Use the crucial role of self-monitoring in driving a car as an example and metaphor to make the student more aware of the process.

- Remind the student that, in devising work plans (for a project or a report), he should always include "quality control" measures.

- Ask the student to examine her work and try to explain *why* she thinks she made a particular error or where she thinks she went astray.

Low reinforceability

- Stress very consistent consequences for improper actions.

- If necessary, keep modifying incentives or rewards to sustain a child's motivation.

- Use personal diaries on paper or audiocassette to help the student review events of past days and talk about how they might affect her future actions.

- Ask the student to maintain lists of "What I've Done Right Today" and "Where I Went Astray Today" with a stress on lessons learned for the future—the development of a cognitive and behavioral repertoire.

- The child might benefit from having an individual mentor in school to whom he can relate and from whom he can receive official recognition for improvement.

Other Forms of Management

Other modalities of management often warrant consideration when working with children with attention deficits. The following are some of the more important options:

- *Counseling.* Children with attention deficits who also have significant problems relating to their families may benefit from a course of counseling from a mental health professional. The whole family may need to participate. The counseling can help elaborate on and extend the demystification process. It can also deal with issues of day-to-day behavioral management and the resolution of family conflicts. In some cases, the sibling(s) of a child with attention deficits need individualized help in understanding and dealing with that brother or sister. The siblings of highly insatiable children are often very resentful and angry; counseling can be especially necessary in such instances.

- *Help with associated neurodevelopmental dysfunctions and academic subskill deficiencies.* Since it is rare to encounter a child with attention deficits who has no other dysfunctions or subskill weaknesses, educational help is often required. The nature of such support depends on the profile of the child.

- *Social Skills Training.* When a child with attention deficits is experiencing substantial interpersonal difficulty, help with social cognition can be beneficial. Such training is often provided in small groups, using standard curriculum materials (see p. 294).

- *Parent Groups.* Parents of children with attention deficits may derive support from opportunities to meet with other parents who are facing similar challenges. These groups are often led by an experienced parent and/or professional.

- *Medication.* The psychopharmacology of attention deficits has been the subject of considerable scientific and clinical scrutiny (Green 1995). Drugs, especially the psychostimulants, unquestionably have a role to play in the management of children with attention deficits. A clinician prescribing such medications should try to abide by the guidelines set forth in chapter 15.

Possible Indications for the Use of Stimulant Medication

Persistent mental fatigue in school

Hyperactivity and frenetic pacing

Extreme and frequent impulsivity (cognitive and/or behavioral)

Trouble focusing that cannot be accounted for by other dysfunctions or anxiety

Inexplicable serious inconsistencies in school function

- *Long-term follow-up and advocacy.* Children with attention deficits are likely to endure rather turbulent school years. The issues and the decision-making dilemmas undergo constant change. Professionals, such as pediatricians, educational therapists, and mental health specialists, need to offer ongoing support while representing the rights of these children. Ideally, they should see children at least three times a year for follow-up and timely advice.

This chapter has noted that attention deficits are unlikely to occur in isolation. Clearly, it is unwise to manage an attention deficit without also taking into consideration other aspects of a child's neurodevelopmental profile. Memory represents a common area of associated dysfunction, one that will be explored in the next chapter.

Chapter 3

Memory

During six years of Russian communal school, he did not distinguish himself, though he advanced regularly. Only geometry delighted him, he says in My Life, *"In that I was unbeatable. Lines, angles, triangles, squares carried me off toward enchanting horizons."*

—Sidney Alexander, *Marc Chagall: A Biography*

Learning without some form of memory is inconceivable. While memory alone is not sufficient for true learning, it is a major contributor to the learning process. It operates in close collaboration with all other neurodevelopmental functions in the quest to master skills, acquire knowledge, and create products. Therefore, any model of the normal learning processes and learning disorders must factor in the functions and dysfunctions of memory (Swanson and Cooney 1996, Ceci 1984). Memory capacities grow steadily as children develop (Kail 1984). However, the demands on memory intensify progressively. During the school years the stress on memory reaches its apex, as children constantly confront novel topics, subject areas, and demands for skill attainment, all of which heavily usurp memory capacity. Adult careers are characterized by day-to-day redundancy of skill and knowledge requirements, necessitating far less memory.

Memory is by no means a unitary process. Its multiplicity of components, processes, and steps have been well documented (Baddeley 1995). In fact, there are multiple forms of memory and therefore a multitude of potential breakdown sites that might impede learning during childhood. This chapter will review the various forms of memory and make use of a clinical-educational model of memory function to shed light on the memory dysfunctions of children.

The overall memory model underlying this chapter is one which broadly divides this neurodevelopmental construct into three systems, each of which assumes a number of different forms during the educational process. The three systems are: *short-term memory, active working memory,* and *long-term memory.* These three memory systems are highly interactive and are constantly "communicating" with each other. Thus, for short-term memory to work optimally, newly arriving information must be interpreted quickly using skill and knowledge that is stored in long-term memory. Stimuli first enter consciousness and are captured or stabilized for a very brief time (seconds) in short-term memory while undergoing cognitive inspection and preliminary interpretation. While stimuli are being held in short-term memory, a nearly instantaneous decision is made regarding their fate or utilization. The incoming data may be allowed to decay (usually within two seconds) or they may be further stabilized and transferred to active working memory where they are temporarily held in place for utilization in a task, for more in-depth blending with prior knowledge, or while awaiting further definition or elaboration from continuing incoming information. If the information is thought to have the potential for future utility, it can be transferred to long-term or permanent memory. The process tends to be cyclical since, as we have noted, initial interpretations in short-term memory as well as elaborations and clarifications taking place in active working memory constantly require that one draw on prior knowledge and experience that is stored in long-term memory. These processes are depicted further in figure 3-1.

Each of the memory systems serves different functions and has distinct capabilities. Their most basic features are compared in table 3-1.

The next section of this chapter will present each of the memory systems separately and describe first their normal operation and then the dysfunctions that can perturb them.

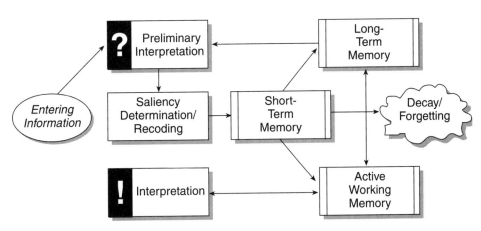

Figure 3-1.   Some interactions between the memory systems

This diagram depicts the close interactions between the three principal memory systems. It can be seen that determinations of saliency and recoding (abbreviating) information for short-term storage depends on making some sense of the incoming data. Such preliminary interpretation demands rapid activation of prior knowledge and experience from long-term storage. Active working memory is a common meeting place for short- and long-term memory, as information is sent from short-term memory to active working memory for further scrutiny and combining with prior knowledge (interpretation). Finally, information in short-term memory can be consolidated directly in long-term memory, sent to active working memory, or forgotten immediately. A similar pattern occurs with information in active working memory, which may either be forgotten or transferred to long-term storage.

Table 3-1. The memory systems: some basic differences

SYSTEM	PRINCIPAL ROLES	RATE OF DATA ENTRY	DATA CAPACITY	DURATION OF ACTIVITY
Short-term memory	Data *stabilization* and disposition: immediate application transfer to other systems	Very rapid	Very small (e.g., 7 numbers)	Very brief (seconds)
Active working memory	Temporary *suspension* within tasks or during ideational development	Moderate	Moderate	Limited (seconds, minutes, hours)
Long-term memory	Permanent *storage* of skills and facts	Slow	Large (seemingly unlimited)	Extended (hours, days, years)

SHORT-TERM MEMORY

Short-term memory captures and holds incoming information just long enough to make a quick decision about what to do with it. The data held in short-term memory can be used immediately for some purpose, they can be transferred rapidly to one of the other memory systems, or they can be deemed useless and be forgotten (allowed to decay) promptly. Information in short-term memory must be utilized, forgotten, or transferred with great speed, since there is always a need to make room for the steady tide of newly arriving data.

There is evidence that a number of processes take place nearly simultaneously within short term-memory. First, incoming information must undergo some rapid preliminary interpretation. Such interpretation may not ultimately coincide with our final understanding of the input, but it represents an approximation, a first attempt at sense making. Second, the incoming stimuli must be sifted through for saliency determination, to both filter out distractions and determine what is important within a message. Third, the salient content goes through a process called *recoding* or *abbreviation*. That is, it must be condensed in order to "fit into" short-term memory, which is a very small-capacity system, one that can barely hold onto a telephone number. Finally, the somewhat understood, salient, recoded information must then be registered in short-term memory with adequate depth of processing. If the processing is too shallow, then the information is likely to decay within two seconds, aborting its further understanding or application. Processing depth is often achieved through what has been called the *articulatory loop*, an actual vocalization, subvocalization, or internal statement of the information. Alternatively, it is possible to make use of the "visual scratch pad," in which case the information is transformed into imagery. These and other techniques, all of which are often called *rehearsal strategies*, are also applied, usually subconsciously, in order to register salient information deeply enough. It should be noted that saliency determination and processing depth are aspects of attention as well as of short-term memory, and therefore represent important junctions between functions. The short-term memory processes are summarized in figure 3-2.

The adequacy of short-term memory function depends intimately on a number of capacities, most of which grow as children develop. These developmental gains occur as a result of normal maturation as well as practice and experience. Short-term memory growth is necessary for learning, and learning is necessary for short-term memory growth.

The following capacities influence short-term memory function:

- The rate of processing incoming information (including rapid access to prior knowledge)

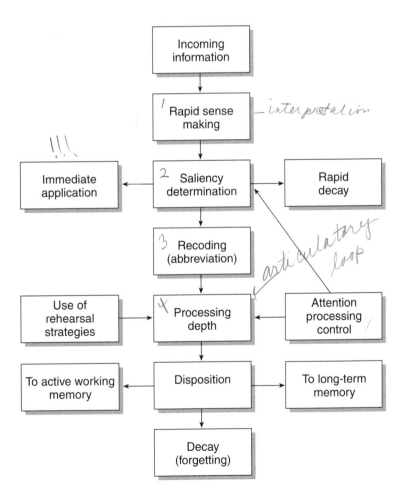

Figure 3-2.   Registration in short-term memory

- The ability to accommodate sufficiently large amounts of data (i.e., the "chunk size" capacity) as well as information density

- The adequacy of processing in specific formats, such as the interpretation of verbal and visual inputs

- The strength of attention processing controls (see chapter 2)

- The use and effectiveness of rehearsal

- Freedom from anxiety

So it is that short-term memory function is intimately bound to a network of other neurodevelopmental capacities and also to the active working and long-term memory systems. Furthermore, it is very likely that little or no information or skill can be stored in long-term memory without first passing through short-term memory. This has major implications for learning and teaching.

As we shall see, the dysfunctions of short-term memory often stem from inadequate capacity in one or more of the above parameters (Siegel and Ryan 1989).

Dysfunctions of Short-Term Memory

There exist many potential breakdown points in short-term memory. This section classifies and describes these conditions and the impaired school performance they create.

Dysfunctions within the Attention-Retention Dimension. There are numerous points at which memory and attention overlap in their functions (Rumbaugh and Washburn 1996). These dysfunctions commonly occur in students with attention deficits. Such students are apt to have their greatest difficulties with saliency determination and processing depth. Their weak saliency determination is frequently manifest in a phenomenon known as *incidental learning* (as opposed to central learning). A student confronting an array of stimuli may have a tendency to register nonessential, incidental data while neglecting more relevant or central material. In preparing for an examination, a student may remember the page number where some technical vocabulary words were introduced and defined, but then might not remember any of the words. Such a person can emerge as a trivia expert but have trouble studying selectively for tests in school.

Shallow processing likewise constrains short-term memory. As described in chapter 2, the result is often trouble following directions, a need for constant repetition, a tendency for information to "go in one ear and out the other." Since short-term memory briefly stabilizes data, these students may be very unreliable when it comes to holding information in place long enough to act on it or respond to it. Shallow processing is exacerbated when a student fails to make use of rehearsal strategies (such as the articulatory loop).

Because performance inconsistency is so much a part of the clinical picture in children with attention deficits, it is not unusual for these students to show inconsistent short-term memory function. At some times or on some days, short-term memory appears highly effective, while at other times it may seem inadequate.

Chunk-Size Dysfunctions. There are some students who exhibit short-term memory gaps that are problematic only when the amount and density of information reaches a certain point, a point that is unfortunately not commensurate with the limits of their classmates. They have difficulty with long sentences, complex diagrams or other visual displays, and, in secondary school, with densely packed information such as that found in many textbooks. In other words, they are unable to generate the rapid processing, saliency determination, and recoding needed to register such material in short-term memory.

A common variant on chunk size dysfunction is found in some students who have specific difficulty with the registration of data that enter the mind configured in "linear chunks." They may have no difficulty assimilating large amounts of information contained in a configuration or gestalt but serious trouble dealing with information arranged in a linear fashion. For example, an eleven-year-old girl did very well when she was tested on reproducing a very complex design from memory, yet she was unable to remember a five-number digit span or imitate some tapping patterns and visual sequences. This girl showed characteristic spelling errors, in that she had difficulty with long words, frequently omitting their medial segments. She left out words in sentences she wrote and neglected parts of long numbers in mathematics. Her problems with short-term memory for linear chunks were associated with diminished accuracy of long-term memory for linear chunks. This pattern of difficulty is not unusual among children with learning disorders.

Rate-Related Dysfunctions. There are some students who are unable to process incoming data fast enough to register them in short-term memory. As already noted, the short-term memory system operates with remarkable speed. Children who process information slowly have difficulty with short-term memory. They may find it hard to keep pace with the flow of instructions, explanations, and other rapid inputs. Some of them are more competent when presented with visual demonstration models and other forms of input that allow for slower processing. Often children with slow processing speed also have attention deficits. It is tempting to speculate that their attentional problems may be secondary to slow processing; distractibility and mental fatigue, for example, may be consequences of their inability to keep pace with the flow of incoming stimuli.

Attribute-Specific Dysfunctions. A child may have difficult entering certain forms of data in short-term memory at the same time that he registers other kinds of data adequately. In such cases one may discover that certain attributes of stimuli elude a particular student. The three major educationally relevant attributes of stimuli are: visual-spatial, verbal (inluding phonological), and sequential/linear. Others, such as kinesthetic, haptic, and olfactory, play minor roles. A child may have trouble registering material that has a strong visual-spatial component (such as a facial appearance or a geometric form) but have no problems at all with verbal inputs or data arranged in linear chunks. Some children have great difficulty registering language sounds (phonemes) in short-term memory. Weaknesses of phonological short-term memory have been studied extensively (Vallar and Papagno 1995). This often highly specific dysfunction can thwart the development of reading and spelling abilities. Virtually any pattern of weakness can be found with respect to these three input attributes. A child may have problems with one or two out of the three (trouble with all three suggesting a more generalized short-term memory deficit). Furthermore, these three attributes depend highly on the rate of input and the chunk size (fig. 3-3), so that a student may have problems registering in short-term memory highly language-laden information but only if it is presented at a fast rate (fig. 3-3). Alternatively, a child may have problems with linear chunks but only when they are densely packed with information (fig. 3-3). Often, incoming messages present themselves in more than one of the three attributes (e.g., they may be both linguistic and visual-spatial, such as written language). It is also possible for a child to exhibit a strength in one attribute that can compensate for relative weaknesses in another. Thus, a student who is excellent at registering linguistic information may be able to retain new spellings easily despite the fact that they are visually presented; the child somehow relies on his well-developed language abilities to capture the input.

Parameters

	Rate	Volume ("chunk size")	Complexity
Spatial attributes			
Sequential/ linear attributes			
Verbal/ phonological attributes			

Attributes

Figure 3-3. The three common sets of attributes of incoming information that is to be recoded and registered in short-term memory

Also shown are the three parameters that further characterize such inputs. Information may have more than one of the attributes (e.g., it may be sequential and spatial). A child with short-term memory problems may have difficulty in any one of the boxes on this diagram (e.g., problems registering rapidly entering phonemes—bottom left box) or may have vertical difficulties (e.g., trouble with rapidly entering data with all three attributes) or there may be horizontal gaps (e.g., difficulty with spatial inputs "across the board").

Rehearsal Failure Dysfunctions. It has been argued that children do not develop more short-term memory capacity as they age; instead, they improve steadily in the ways in which they make use of short-term memory. Specifically, they become increasingly fast and competent at deploying rehearsal strategies that increase the depth and rate of their processing. Some students do not spontaneously acquire such tactics (Miller 1994); they fail to demonstrate rehearsal while using short-term memory (Bauer 1977). They do not make use of subvocalization, imaging, self-testing, or other tactics to fortify short-term memory. These individuals often lack facilitating strategies in many aspects of the learning process; they are "nonmethodologists," performing many tasks the hard way. Some of them may also be passive learners, as described on page 29.

ACTIVE WORKING MEMORY

Active working memory has been called "the workspace of thinking." We have termed it "the cognitive counter space." Active working memory allows one to hold several facts or ideas in mind temporarily while working with them to create a product or while seeking to understand them more fully. While short-term memory briefly preserves information, active working memory extends, modifies, or combines inputs with other incoming or previously stored data. Ample experimental evidence has demonstrated the existence of active working memory as an entitity separate from short-term memory (Halford et al. 1994). Here is a summary of the several different forms of active working memory:

- *Proximal and distal planning.* Many activities require an individual to retain a long-range plan while tending to more immediate (i.e., proximal) needs. For example, while writing a composition a student must retain in active working memory the distal plan or what she intends to write while pausing to deal with a more immediate need, such as how to spell a particular word. If, in the process of trying to spell the word, she loses track of her ideas, her essay will be compromised.

- *Task component suspension.* Most complex academic tasks have multiple subtasks embedded within them, and all need to be preserved while the task is being executed. For example, a student must actively juggle the steps in a math procedure while solving a problem. In the process of carrying a number it is essential to bear in mind what one intended to do after carrying that number. In the process of repairing a bicycle, the repair person needs to remember where she put the wrench she was using earlier in the activity.

- *Progressive ideational development.* It takes time to develop, understand, elaborate on, or complete ideas. While listening to a story or watching a TV show, one needs to remember the earlier parts while listening to and/or watching the concluding sections. Active working memory thus enables us to splice or blend together the parts of a story or explanation or even the ingredients that coalesce to form our own ideas. When comparing and contrasting two entities, active working memory stores one while the other is being described, thereby providing a kind of screen or monitor on which to make the relevant comparisons. Much problem solving and logic demands this form of cognitive working counter space, i.e., room to think.

- *Bridging of short-term and long-term memory.* Often it is crucial to hold a short-term input in suspension while digging into long-term memory for the prior knowledge needed to deal with it. In so doing, the short-term input is transferred to active working memory while long-term memory is being searched. The transfer occurs effortlessly through a kind of automatic transmission that obviates the need to shift gears consciously, to pause and say, "I'd better transfer this to active working memory while I give it some more thought." When asked a question, the respondent must retain the question while sifting through prior knowledge for the precise facts, the right words, and any previously formed opinions needed to generate an acceptable answer.

Facilitators of Active Working Memory

The following conditions greatly enhance the work of active working memory:

- *Attentional strength is great.* Mental fatigue, distractibility, and poor set maintenance are serious deterrents to active working memory performance.

- *The student comprehends well the subject matter or task at hand.* A good grasp of content increases the capacity of active working memory. In particular, active working memory functions best when the elements within an area of knowledge cohere well and interrelate richly.

- *Some aspects of the task or effort are automatic.* If certain components of a task or elements of understanding are so well learned that they require little if any expenditure of mental energy and use of cognitive counter space, active working memory can take on increasingly formidable intellectual challenges.

- *The student has good resistance to retroactive inhibition.* The latter is the tendency of intervening actions or thoughts to erase other recent inputs that are still needed. When writing a report, can one still remember the ideas, even though there was a phone call in the middle. When asked two questions orally, can the student remember the second question after he finishes answering the first? Or, does the act of answering the first question cause him to need repetition of the first question (which, of course, is not such a terrible need)?

- *The student is sufficiently free from anxiety.* Just as anxiety interferes with the function of short-term memory, it reduces the capacity of active working memory by taking up much needed room on cognitive working counter space.

Now that we have considered the roles and the facilitators of active working memory, we can describe the manifestations of active working memory dysfunctions that can seriously thwart learning and work output in students.

Dysfunctions of Active Working Memory

As schoolwork becomes increasingly complex and the demands for extensive output grow steadily, there is increasing demand for active working memory space. In some cases, the demand greatly exceeds the supply. At this time there is not enough research data to substantiate the classification of different subtypes of active working memory dysfunction. Therefore, rather than attempting any such taxonomy, this section will delineate some of the common symptoms of active working memory dysfunction. These findings include:

- A tendency to lose one's way in the middle of a mathematics problem. In the process of performing one part of an arithmetic computation, a student forgets what she was going to execute next. In a sense, she keeps forgetting what she was doing.

- Trouble remembering information from the top of a page or beginning of a chapter while reading the final paragraph.

- A frequent propensity to forget what one was going to say.

- Difficulty thinking through problems or engaging in extensive reasoning in one's head, including problems doing mental arithmetic that can be performed easily on paper.

- Confusion and comprehension problems during extended explanations or instructions. This includes difficulties with comparing and contrasting.

- Problems invoking simultaneously all the different subskills needed for written output. An affected student may have trouble with the simultaneous application of spelling, punctuation, ideation, graphomotor function, etc.

- A tendency for attention to immediate needs to undermine more global or longer range intentions (i.e., proximal planning thwarting distal plans). While sharpening his pencil, a student forgets which sentence he was supposed to copy from the board.

When a student is experiencing the kinds of difficulties described above, attentional dysfunction, poor understanding, or anxiety may be subverting active working memory, or there may exist a primary limitation in active working memory capacity. As with all forms of neurodevelopmental dysfunction, impairment may be due to a primary weakness in a particular function or to the failure of other functions to collaborate effectively with that function—a dysfunction at the junction between two functions. This need to differentiate between mechanisms poses a formidable challenge to the process of assessment, which will be described later in this chapter.

Now that we have examined the phenomenology of the short-term and active working memory systems, we can study the intricacies and mysteries of long-term memory functions.

LONG-TERM MEMORY

Long-term memory is the system that allows for the permanent storage of knowledge, skills, and experiences. Its capacity is seemingly limitless. In fact, long-term memory contains so much data that it confronts us all with a monumental organizational challenge. How can this vast storehouse be arranged to allow for rapid and accurate access to its heaps of content? In fact, any discussion of long-term memory function and dysfunction must focus heavily on issues of information organization—human long-term memory as a filing system. That is precisely what this section will emphasize.

I will divide the discussion of long-term memory into two sections: storage and access. *Storage* subsumes a series of processes involved in the initial consolidation of information, skill, and direct experience in long-term memory. *Access* includes the subsequent attempts to recover that which has been stored. These two functions are obviously closely related; the more systematically material has been stored, the more accessible it is likely to become. Furthermore, the more frequently and accurately one has accessed information from long-term memory, the more firmly and accessibly it becomes stored, which is why "practice makes perfect."

Storage in Long-Term Memory

Consolidation in long-term memory is a slow process, requiring from hours to days for completion. A wide range of factors can either support or deter the process. When it is working well, long-term memory consolidation increases the likelihood of academic mastery, and when it malfunctions it becomes a reason for failure. There are many different filing systems that comprise long-term memory; special storage capacities exist for procedures, for facts (declarative memory), and for autobiographical information.

Long-term memory consolidates information in highly specific formats, each designated to store certain types of acquisitions. However, it is common and desirable for newly acquired information or skill to be filed in more than one format. Five ways of formatting knowledge are especially germane to academic proficiency: paired association, procedural knowledge, rules and regularity, categories, and experience and episodes.

Paired Association

A great deal of knowledge is formatted in pairs. We file names with faces, number symbols with quantities, phonemes (language sounds) with graphemes (letter combinations), cars with logos, and melodies with titles. The academic curriculum makes heavy demands on the process of consolidating paired associations in long-term memory. Linking words with their definitions or synonyms, storing mathematical facts, and learning national capitals are examples of forms of knowledge that need to be stored at least partially in a paired associative format. Tight and unambiguous linkages need to be forged, so that when one half of a pair is encountered, it will reliably elicit its learned counterpart.

Sometimes paired associations are mastered by rote, necessitating a great deal of repetition and drill. At times, they demand the combining of modalities, such as when associating a visual image with a verbal label. Paired association learning, in fact, can be enhanced by recruiting additional sensory pathways whenever possible. Such multisensory approaches to vocabulary building might include looking at a word, pronouncing it, tracing it, using it in a sentence, and then picturing it or drawing it in use.

Teachers should be aware of the specific kinds of paired association that their classes require. Such awareness can enable them to identify the students who are struggling to form certain of these pairings.

Dysfunctions of Paired Association. Paired association breakdowns tend to be highly content specific or processing specific. One is very unlikely to encounter a student with pervasive paired association problems. Rather they present with highly circumscribed difficulty with certain paired associations. The most common forms of dysfunction include trouble with phoneme-grapheme correspondences, problems acquiring new vocabulary (in their native and/or a second language), slow consolidation of math facts, problems with factual knowledge in geography or history, or poor performance in densely factual science classes. It should be stressed, however, that a student may experience frustration forming associations in one of these subject areas but have no problems with one or more of the others.

Paired association breakdowns commonly occur when one half of the pair is incompletely processed. For example, it may be hard to associate a phoneme with a grapheme when a child's weak phonological awareness interferes with the accurate processing of individual language sounds. Similarly, if the appreciation of melodic line is inadequate, it is likely to be harder to associate a song title with its principal melodic themes.

Content-specific paired associative dysfunctions can be more elusive. They may relate to motivation as well as to the level of meaningfulness of specific subject matter. A high school student may form excellent associations in chemistry class but not in history. Another may be able to associate different cars with characteristics of their engines but not be able to associate different countries with their geographic locations. It is no doubt the case that each and every one of us has certain kinds of subject matter that pair easily for us in long-term memory and other forms of knowledge that are highly resistant to the pairing process.

Procedural Knowledge

Clinicians and investigators have continuously upheld the distinction between declarative (i.e., factual) and procedural knowledge. The study of stroke victims has demonstrated consistently that it is possible to suffer an impairment of one without experiencing reduced function in the other, thereby providing evidence for these dual roles. *Declarative knowledge* is stored in all of the other long-term memory formats described here, while *procedural knowledge* is largely confined to its own system of formatting.

Procedural memory can be either motoric or nonmotoric. *Motor procedures* are those demanding significant use of muscle groups. Their memory component is sometimes called a *motor engram* or *kinetic melody,* which is a learned plan that is stored and generally arranged in a sequence of discrete motor actions that create a certain kind of performance. There are *gross motor procedures* (such as kicking a football), *fine motor procedures* (such as knitting), and *graphomotor procedures* (for letter formations) which are limited to the act of writing. Such procedures occur in a relatively fixed sequence, the plans for which are stored in long-term memory. This aspect of function is often referred to as *motor memory.* In the early stages of skill acquisition, verbalization often strengthens consolidation. A learner actually talks through a procedure, thereby facilitating the consolidation process. An example would be the following subvocalized self-coaching strategy used by a novice baseball player: "Let's see, I need to keep the bat off my shoulder, then I have to remember to step in toward the pitcher with my right foot, then swing level and follow through all the way around to my other shoulder and I'd better not ever take my eye off the ball." As such a rising athlete gains proficiency through practice, there is a steadily diminishing need for verbal conditioning.

The mastery of the motor aspects of writing constitutes some of the most demanding challenges for motor procedural memory. Rapid and precise letter formation requires the consolidation of a series of highly complex motor procedures. This is especially true with respect to the storage of cursive writing forms (see chapter 10).

Motor procedures come in two other forms: stereotyped and reactive. *Stereotyped motor procedural storage* involves filing a motor procedure that is always to be used in the same exact way. Letter formation and the motor sequences needed for foul shooting in basketball are examples of procedures that are performed in a fixed manner. Swinging at a baseball, using a scissors, or buttoning a shirt are examples of *reactive motor procedures* that require adaptation or modification to adjust to specific circumstances (such as the speed of the ball, the material to be cut, and the size and shape of the buttons). Driving a car is a prime example of a set of procedures that needs to be learned and then modified or regulated from moment to moment as conditions change. All such activities require the recall of motor procedures at the same time that new information is being processed and applied to adjust those procedures.

Nonmotor procedures also abound in school and are especially common in mathematics, which has procedures for accomplishing long division, for balancing equations, and for reducing fractions. All contain sequences of steps that need to be stored for use when encountering specific demands. Nonmotor procedures are found in other subject areas as well, although they are less pervasive. A student may need to learn how to parse sentences, use a dictionary, or locate a city on a map. Computers provide a very special challenge as they demand the storage of motor (i.e., keyboarding) procedures and nonmotor (i.e., use of software) procedures.

Dysfunctions of Procedural Consolidation.   Children with procedural storage problems are prone to delays in certain academic subskills. They tend to experience some of their greatest impairments in writing and in mathematics. Their writing difficulty is due to incomplete or poor consolidation of the motor sequences for letter formation. These children may write slowly and with great effort. The amount of mental energy expended to recall the letter forms often undermines the application of other subskills, such as spelling, grammatical construction, and the use of language. Mathematical difficulties may be a result of suboptimal consolidation of the nonmotor procedures that are so much a part of arithmetic computation. Weaknesses of procedural consolidation may also impede athletic performance, conformity with daily routines in school, and other aspects of the school day that call for the application of learned sequential steps.

Rules and Regularity

Some of the vital information stored in long-term memory is linked to rules and predictable patterns. The rules themselves may be learned formally or they may be personal observations of regularly recurring patterns. Information consolidated in long-term memory may be either a rule itself or information that pertains to the rule (either obeying it or showing irregularity). The rules help us respond with proper solutions or actions and they help us make good predictions. They are not always correct, but they allow us to set default expectations. In any case, the overall configuration of rules and regularities is "if . . . then," for example, "If this is a proper noun, then it has to start with a capital letter."

Schemata are variants of such self-taught rules. Over time children develop schemata for various settings and circumstances. For example, one may acquire a schema for school cafeterias, so that upon matriculating at a new school, one has expectations regarding the structure and organization of the dining hall. Children can develop schemata for the tests a certain teacher gives, for the way notebooks need to look, and for experiments in a science class. These schemata help prepare students for upcoming challenges and prevent them from having to start from scratch every time they enter a new learning context.

The storage of spelling words presents a typical challenge to rules and regularities. Some words can be filed successfully because they conform to their language's rules and spelling regularities. But other words have as a salient feature the fact that they are irregular and violate the default expectations. The same may be said for the storage of word pronunciations, which also may confirm or deny the expectations set by rules and regularity.

Dysfunctions of Rules and Regularity. Some students have great difficulty engaging in rule-based learning. They are susceptible to problems in all academic areas that stress the mastery of rules (including awareness of rule exceptionality). Grammatical rules, spelling rules, foreign language rules, and mathematical rules may elude such learners. In general, it is difficult for them to memorize and apply rules, and to store information according to its obedience or disobedience of established rules. A student's report card is likely to show evidence that she is experiencing difficulty in all of the courses that require a great deal of rule-based learning. Interviewing such a student can often uncover her problems with rules.

Categories

A substantial part of our knowledge is consolidated in categories of information. Much of declarative memory (memory for factual material) is stored in this way, which enables a progressive growth in knowledge as a child grows older (McKee and Squire 1993). There are subcategories within these categories and more subcategories within the subcategories. If someone tells you that a particular tree is an aspen, then you might categorize the fact under living things and then further subcategorize it under the plant kingdom, subcategorizing it further under trees, and then under trees you have seen in the mountains. Such categorization and subcategorization of data allows us to impart order to the millions of facts we need to remember. Thus, we remember animals, countries, vegetables, and famous people by consolidating them in specific categorical structures within memory. Material consolidated in this way can take the form of mental imagery (e.g., picturing various animals) or it can be largely semantic (e.g., verbally labeling countries in Eastern Europe). Consolidation probably works best when information is categorized with both mental imagery and naming.

Students who are especially competent have the habit of constantly consolidating new facts in multiple categories rather than just one. This practice is part of being an active rather than passive processor (see p. 29). For example, suppose that a teacher states that the Vietnam War was fought during the 1960s and 1970s. The active processor stores this incoming information under: 1) different wars I know about; 2) things we've learned about the Far East; 3) what we studied last year in American history; 4) other stuff I know about the 1960s and 1970s; and 5) experiences my father had when he was in the army. When information is stored in multiple categories rather than a single one, it ultimately becomes more accessible and broadly applicable. Students who are passive processors often fail to make use of cross-categorization. They overrely on simple paired association and rote memory, perhaps repeating to themselves, "Vietnam War 1960s and 1970s, Vietnam War 1960s and 1970s, Vietnam War 1960s and 1970s." This is called *maintenance rehearsal* as opposed to *elaborative rehearsal* (i.e., cross-categorizing).

Dysfunctions of Category Consolidation. During the early years of elementary school, one can begin to identify students who have difficulty with classification and categorization. When asked to name some fruits, they include a sampling of green vegetables. They experience difficulty distinguishing between cities, countries, and continents. Such students are very much at risk for problems with factual storage and access. They are apt to consolidate information without any hierarchical organization. They file the facts to be learned in a disorderly fashion, ultimately limiting the rate and accuracy of access.

The passive consolidation patterns just described represent another common form of dysfunction. Affected children may appreciate how facts fit within categories, but their nonelaborative, passive way of learning prevents them from making good use of cross-categorization tactics during learning.

Experiences and Episodes

Direct experience needs to be consolidated in long-term memory. Direct experiential memory content may be the only form of input that need not always pass through short-term memory to gain a place in long-term memory. Because it circumvents short-term memory, a great deal of nonessential data (i.e., material that has not had to undergo saliency determination) may be stored in this format. Episodes and experiences in life may therefore be consolidated somewhat randomly. Their consolidation in long-term memory can also be subject to the influence of a wide range of emotional factors.

Episodic memory is a conspicuous donor to long-term storage. This form of consolidation entails the storage of details that are closely associated with specific past events. Such memory is usually involuntary or unconscious. Using episodic memory, you store the color of the dress your mother wore at her last birthday party, the dessert you ordered when you ate at that Italian restaurant two years ago, and the baldness of the person working at the toy store. Episodic memory is highly developed in certain children, who frequently astound their parents and teachers with what they remember related to events in their lives. They often reveal a marked discrepancy between their weak semantic memory (the overall set of memory functions required for formal learning) and their incredible episodic memory. A mother may lament: "He can tell you what color shirt Uncle Jim wore when he took us fishing last year, but then he can't remember any of the vocabulary words he studied last weekend. When we go some place where we haven't been for several years, he is the only one who remembers exactly how to get there—and where the men's room is located!" Incidentally, such expanded episodic storage space is commonly found in children with attention deficits, many of whom seem to recall much better when they can bypass the constraints of short-term memory. Such students are often said to be experiential learners; they learn best through direct (i.e., hands-on) experience rather than formal methods. No one retains more from a class field trip than such a student.

Dysfunctions of Episodic and Experiential Memory.   It is unlikely that children experience educationally relevant weaknesses in this form of memory. One might speculate, however, that in adult life, this memory format assumes much greater importance as we benefit from on-the-job training, a form of experiential learning. If dysfunctions exist, they might then exert their greatest impact on careers, where there is less formal learning and more need to consolidate learning experiences.

The five consolidation formats gain in effectiveness as children proceed through their education. This is fortunate, as the demands for long-term storage space grow exponentially through childhood. We have seen that there is marked variation between individuals in the effectiveness of different formats of consolidation. It is unclear, however, whether these differences are entirely inborn, whether they are largely influenced by experience and the quality of teaching a child has received, or whether they depend, in part, on how consciously and systematically a student has been making use of the formats over the years. It is most likely that all three of these explanations pertain to varying degrees from student to student.

Students who are especially strong in consolidating information in long-term memory have facilitating insights and cognitive behaviors. The following are some of the principal ways in which they enhance consolidation:

- *They consolidate information in more than one format.* A student may file a piece of newly acquired knowledge (such as an important date in his country's history) in one or more categories, and he may also consolidate that date as a paired association with an event.

- *They elaborate on new knowledge.* Elaboration strengthens consolidation. All students can benefit from opportunities to expand on new information. Quite frequently this is accomplished through verbal elaboration, which means that students with language production dysfunctions (see chapter 5) may be at a significant disadvantage when it comes to consolidating certain forms of verbally encoded knowledge. There is also reason to believe that the present structure of most schools—rapid shifting from one subject to another—may not allow enough time for students to elaborate on what they have learned and thereby increase the likelihood of strong consolidation. In other words, there is a very good chance that Spanish class has a tendency to erase much of what occurred during the immediately preceding social studies session.

- *They go to sleep immediately after studying.* There is strong evidence that information consolidates especially well during sleep, perhaps because it encounters little interference. Students often discover that they need to memorize and then go right to sleep without interposing a shower, phone call, or any other activity.

- *They have well-developed metamemory. Metamemory* is a form of metacognition that consists of an awareness of memory and how it works, as well as a willingness to apply that knowledge while memorizing. While studying, students with good metamemory ask themselves the simple but crucial question, "How am I going to remember this stuff?" Students with little or no ability to reflect on memory are at a serious disadvantage in school.

- *They plan and make conscious use of memory strategies.* These students are apt to work out novel ways of depicting and extending the information they are seeking to learn. They make provision for systematic review and self-testing.

Access to Long-Term Memory

The recovery of stored knowledge and skill is a never ending challenge for students. On tests, on homework, during class discussions, and in their everyday lives outside of school, there is a relentless need to remember and to apply what they remember. To do so a child must have a clear idea of what she is trying to remember and how to go about finding it. To meet most expectations and to synchronize the flow from memory stores with the rapid engagement of other neurodevelopmental functions (such as language), access to long-term memory must be very fast and often highly precise. In this section we will describe three major, academically relevant access routes: association, recognition, and recall.

Access Through Association. Access through association involves an encounter with one half of a paired association and the often rapid, sometimes automatic, remembering of the other half. One sees a face and instantly associates it with a name. Often arithmetic facts are elicited in this manner. A student hears the question: "How much is five times six?" The oral/phonological utterance "five times six" is quickly and ultimately automatically associated with the number thirty.

Impairments in paired association access were described in the section on consolidation. Suffice to say here that these generally content-specific dysfunctions are common, and that it is not really possible to distinguish between difficulties resulting from incomplete consolidation and those that are manifestations of poor access. Such a distinction is not important in managing these difficulties.

Access Through Pattern Recognition. *Recognition memory* plays an essential role in every subject area. It consists of the ability to encounter a meaningful, cohesive set of stimuli, know that one has seen them before, and respond to them in a way that is based on past experience.

Pattern recognition can be very user friendly and gratifying. If you take a trip to a town you have not seen in four years, on arrival you begin to recognize various features of that metropolis that you never thought you'd remember. You are uplifted by your own exemplary memory performance. For example, you remember instantly the location of the store where you bought a newspaper four years ago. The day before arrival that would have been nearly impossible, but once there, the patterns become apparent, and it is not hard to fill in the supplementary detail.

In school, recognition can be elusive because recurring patterns most often are partially obscured by superficial differences that are potentially misleading. A competent student has the ability to penetrate these superficial differences to recognize the underlying recurring pattern. In a geometry class, for example, a parallelogram first may be studied in isolation but then may return as part of a geometric proof embedded in a circle which is within a trapezoid. It can challenge the student to recognize that the parallelogram pattern is preserved within the other shapes. Word problems likewise call for astute recognition, as students must be sensitive to verbal patterns that connote a mathematical process. These linguistic structures do not reappear on a quiz in identical form but instead as variations with consistent underlying patterns of meaning. Other academic pattern recognition challenges include recurring ideas within a story or a poem, variations on themes in music, functional patterns in biology or chemistry, letter patterns that facilitate sight word recognition, and morphological patterns (see p. 307) that help one to figure out the likely meaning of a new word. Thus the capacity to recognize an underlying pattern in the presence of superficial differences is a requisite for academic success in a multitude of areas.

Pattern recognition assumes its full importance when it results in intelligent responses. It is simply not enough merely to recognize a pattern; one must then accomplish a goal or gain a useful insight. This often requires linking recognition to other access routes. For example, it is common to link pattern recognition with paired association: we might gaze at a withered flower and realize that it is a rose (although it doesn't look much like one at present). However, there is enough rose-ness about the pattern to enable us to associate it with the name *rose*.

To meet a wide range of challenging academic demands, one needs what is called *pattern recognition with procedural transference,* an amalgam of recognition with procedural recall. An example is that of a child who confronts the graphic pattern $34 - 21 = $. He recognizes this as a subtraction pattern and promptly transfers from nonmotor procedural memory the methods needed to compute the answer. Such a dual process is central to all mathematical learning. It likewise plays a substantial part in learning to read music and play an instrument, in becoming proficient at sports, in multiple-choice test taking, and in problem solving in general (see p. 223 for a discussion of pattern recognition in problem solving).

Dysfunctions of pattern recognition. Ineffective pattern recognition can have widespread effects on learning. Pattern recognition deficiencies may be confined to one skill or content area or they may be more generalized. It is also possible to have a recognition dysfunction relating to a particular mode of processing. A student may show evidence of weak visual-spatial pattern recognition or diminished linguistic pattern recognition. Thus, one must always look for recurrent patterns in the expression of a child's pattern recognition problems.

In order to access patterns, one must properly perceive them in the first place. This demands that children gain proficiency with whole-part relationships. When confronting a set of stimuli (visual, verbal, or factual), the student must appreciate what goes with what, where one meaningful set of data ends and another commences. This may be an especially formidable challenge for children in early elementary school, and it constitutes a source of dysfunction in certain students. Their problems with early pattern establishment may ultimately thwart pattern recognition.

Affected children may have trouble acquiring subskills that call for pattern recognition. Among the findings may be difficulty solving word problems, poor understanding and remembering of lengthy text (where repeated patterns should actually facilitate processing), a failure to discern recurring themes in science, social studies, and history classes, and trouble appreciating grammatical construction and parts of speech. Very often students with diminished pattern recognition complain that school is very boring. This is because they are deprived of the intellectual thrill a student experiences when he discovers or uncovers a recurring pattern. Such moments of enlightenment add excitement and feelings of mastery to the learning process. When there is insufficient pattern recognition, the subject matter of education may become fragmented, incoherent, and difficult to assimilate. There are too few analogies and leitmotifs to impart cohesion to learning. A student who fails to find patterns may need to overrely on rote memory and expend excessive mental effort to succeed in school. She may deal with too many problems as if they are entirely novel experiences.

Access Through Recall. *Recall* differs from paired association and pattern recognition in that it involves minimal or no cuing. One simply has a need for some information or a procedure, and one needs to find it. There are no pattern or paired association clues. As children proceed into secondary school and beyond, there is an ever growing stress on recall. Moreover, their recall of frequently used skills and knowledge must become increasingly automatized, accessible instantly with minimal expenditure of mental effort. Such automaticity represents a critical component of normal memory function (Hasher and Zacks 1979).

Recall must respond to the stringent demands imposed by school. These demands are summarized in table 3-2. Over time these demands intensify. Children are expected to recall with growing speed, precision, and simultaneity. They must demonstrate good cumulative memory, especially for course work in which later learning depends entirely on the facilitated recall of earlier consolidated knowledge and skill (such as in foreign languages and mathematics). Also, more and more of what was learned in the past must be accessible automatically, that is, with virtually no expenditure of mental effort and minimal response time. Automatization frees up cognitive counter space for such higher attainments as sophisticated language use, complex problem solving, and creativity.

Dysfunctions of recall. Recall dysfunctions should be suspected in children who do poorly on tests even though they study. These dysfunctions are especially

Table 3.2. Recall demands in school

DEMAND	EXPLANATION	EXAMPLES
Rapid recall	Quick access to stored facts/skills	Answering teacher's query within three seconds; recalling a math fact while multiplying
Convergent recall	Access to one highly specific data bit, when there is only one correct answer	Recalling the spelling of a word, the capital of a country, the name of a general
Divergent or free recall	Access in which a wide range of responses are acceptable	Recalling your favorite television shows or holiday experiences
Simultaneous recall	Access to multiple facts/procedures all at once	Recalling spelling, punctuation, capitalization, and facts while writing a report
Cumulative recall	Access to what you learned early in the year as a basis for what you are now learning	Recalling foreign language vocabulary and grammar
Automatized recall	Instantaneous and effortless access to facts and/or procedures	Recalling specific letter formations or keyboarding while writing a story

prevalent among students with disappointing writing and math performance despite good reading skills.

The following findings are typical of students with dysfunctions of recall:

- Trouble with spelling and with learning math facts and/or procedures

- A history of word-finding problems during the preschool and early elementary grades

- Difficulties with writing (especially in the middle grades), in particular, a tendency to state ideas much better in a discussion than on paper, along with deficiencies in legibility, writing rate, and the application of mechanics during writing

- Excessive time needed to complete homework and tests

- Delayed automatization of needed subskills and/or factual knowledge

- Trouble answering questions that elicit a highly specific answer; better at free or divergent recall

- A tendency to forget in the spring what was learned in the fall, thereby impairing performance in subjects that are highly cumulative in structure (foreign language, chemistry, and algebra, as opposed to English and social studies, which are less cumulative)

- Poor performance on tests, even when the material seemed to have been mastered earlier (e.g., the night before the examination)

A child with recall dysfunctions may not manifest all of the above features, but it is very likely that she will reveal most of them. It is not at all unusual for students to harbor pervasive recall problems that affect all or nearly all academic pursuits. Others, however, exhibit more content-specific recall weaknesses. Examples include circumscribed gaps in the recall of vocabulary, the revisualization of specific geometric forms, or the retrieval of letter formations during writing.

When a student is experiencing problems with recall, it is important to consider the possibility that the difficulty is actually a manifestation of other forms of memory dysfunction. Short-term memory deficits may generate problems with long-term recall; if, in the first place, a child did not process information in appropriate depth or with keen enough saliency determination, the material may not be defined and stable enough to be transmitted accurately to long-term memory. It is also the case that some access problems result from incomplete consolidation; when data are not filed systematically, access to them is likely to be slow and inaccurate. This is analogous to problems that may stem from having a very disorganized dresser in which to store articles of clothing. If underwear and socks are scattered through every drawer, it can be a tedious and time-consuming job to locate a particular pair of brown socks—in fact, you may never manage to find them.

At this point we have presented a conceptual model of memory and the many forms of dysfunction that commonly interfere with school performance. These dysfunctions are further summarized in table 3-3. The assessment of memory function, however, needs to cover more than areas of dysfunction; it can be particularly germane to identify a child's actual or latent memory assets. The next section covers the process of assessment.

BRAIN LOCATIONS OF MEMORY FUNCTIONS

Through the study of brain injuries, strokes, tumors, and other forms of damage, a great deal has been learned about the specific locations of different forms of memory in the human brain. There is clearly no single memory center within the brain; different aspects of mnemonic performance are scattered throughout. Much research remains to be done; we are nowhere near ready to localize the multitude of memory functions delineated in this chapter. However, some generalizations are possible.

Most verbal memory, both short- and long-term, is mediated through structures in the left hemisphere (in about 90 percent of individuals), while most visual and other nonverbal (e.g., *haptic*) memory functions are handled by parts of the right hemispheres. Such modality-specific memory abilities are situated adjacent to the parts of the brain needed for processing in that modality. These neighbors of processing are called *early sensory cortices* or *primary association areas.* Modality-specificity of memory is only a beginning, as there are multiple other memory distinctions that can discerned and localized.

Tranel and Damasio (1995) have provided an excellent summary of what is currently known regarding the neuroanatomy of many aspects of memory. Their rendering is summarized in table 3-4.

Table 3-3. Common forms of memory dysfunction

DYSFUNCTION	EXPLANATION
Short-Term Memory	
Dysfunctions within the attention-retention dimension	Registration problems associated with shallow and nonsalient registration
Chunk size dysfunctions	Registration limitations related to *amount* of incoming data; may be confined to "linear chunks"
Rate-related dysfunctions	Registration limitations related to the *rate* of processing of incoming information
Visual-spatial memory dysfunctions	Weaknesses in the registration of data with visual-spatial attributes
Sequential memory dysfunctions	Weaknesses in the registration of data requiring preservation of serial order
Linguistic memory dysfunctions*	Weaknesses in the registration of data encoded in language
Rehearsal failure dysfunctions	Registration problems stemming from a lack of strategic use of memory
Paraphrasing (recoding) dysfunctions	Problems with the reduction of data inputs for registration

*Includes difficulties with short-term phonological memory

Active Working Memory	
Proximal and distal planning dysfunctions	Difficulty preserving long-term intention while implementing intermediate need(s)
Task component suspension dysfunctions	Trouble simultaneously keeping in mind the subcomponents of a task while implementing that task
Ideational development dysfunctions	Difficulty retaining/manipulating ideas as they are developing
Phonological active working memory deficiencies	Trouble retaining and manipulating language sounds (e.g., for segmenting and reblending during word decoding)
Short-term and long-term memory bridging problems	Difficulty retaining short-term memory input or inputs while accessing long-term memory

Table 3-3. *(Continued)*

DYSFUNCTION	EXPLANATION
Long-Term Memory Consolidation	
Paired association dysfunctions	Problems with the linkage in memory of specific items that co-occur
Procedural knowledge dysfunctions	Trouble with the storage of specific motor and/or nonmotor processes
Rules and regularity dysfunctions	Problems storing rules and data that relate to rule conformity or irregularity
Category use dysfunctions	Difficulty filing information in categories or across categories; often content specific
Experiential and episodic dysfunctions	Poor storage of direct experiences and life episodes; excellence in this function is often seen with other forms of dysfunction
Long-Term Memory Access	
Associative dysfunctions	Same as the paired association dysfunctions described under "Consolidation"
Pattern recognition dysfunctions	Lack of awareness of recurring patterns and/or difficulty integrating patterns with other forms of memory
Recall rate dysfunctions	Problems retrieving information or procedures rapidly enough
Convergent retrieval dysfunctions	Difficulty with the recall of highly specific data (i.e., only one right answer); often with preference for divergent recall
Simultaneous recall dysfunctions	Problems retrieving several forms of information and/or procedures at once
Cumulative recall dysfunctions	Trouble remembering content or skill that forms the foundation for present learning
Automatization dysfunctions	Failure to access sufficient knowledge or skill immediately and effortlessly

ASSESSMENT OF MEMORY

Assessment of the three memory systems and their multiple subcomponents must be an essential part of the evaluation of any student with academic problems. The process can be difficult, however, since many direct tests of memory fail to capture the intricacies and the high specificity of these functions. The most reliable evaluation therefore must include careful history taking, examination of work samples, direct observation in the classroom, and direct testing of those memory functions that can be tapped reliably on examinations.

Table 3-4. Anatomical locations of a sampling of memory functions

MEMORY FUNCTION	LOCATION(S)
Consolidation of new facts (declarative memory) and binding together of memory traces	Hippocampal complex (left side for verbal knowledge, right for nonverbal) located in the medial temporal lobes
Binding together of information (in conjunction with consolidation)	Basal forebrain (just below frontal lobes); delivers neurotransmitters to hippocampal complex and other regions
Retrieval of prior knowledge	"Lower-level" (e.g., sensory) information from association areas, higher-level in other cortical areas in the nonmedial temporal lobes
Storage and retrieval of knowledge in categories, i.e., "non-unique" knowledge	Posterior medial temporal region
Storage and retrieval of discrete "unique" bits of knowledge	Anterior medial temporal region
Pattern recognition (including facial recognition)	Anterior medial temporal region
Emotionally charged memory (e.g., fears, surprises) or "somatic markers"	Ventromedial frontal lobes
Prospective retrieval (remembering to do something later)	Ventromedial frontal lobes
Active working memory	Dorsolateral frontal lobes (the anterior convexity of the cerebral hemispheres)
Procedural memory	Basal ganglia and cerebellum
Habits and automatized nondeclarative memory	Striatal component of the basal ganglia (caudate nucleus and putamen)
Temporal sequencing in memory	Anterior thalamus (along with other possible areas, especially in the left hemisphere)

This discussion of assessment will examine the various parts that must comprise an acceptably complete picture of a child's memory status.

History

Historical information can be gathered through questionnaires from parents and teachers (such as *The ANSER System* Forms 2 and 3) or by directly interviewing these adults as well as the child. Figure 3-4 shows some of the memory items contained in *The ANSER System.*

			TYPICAL PERFORMANCE				VARIABILITY OF PERFORMANCE		
			STRONG FOR AGE	APPROPRIATE FOR AGE	DELAYED LESS THAN 1 YEAR	DELAYED MORE THAN 1 YEAR	CONSISTENT PERFORMANCE	SOMEWHAT VARIABLE	HIGHLY UNPREDICTABLE
		ACADEMIC SUBSKILL OR FUNCTION							
AS52	**Memory**	Remembering over a brief period (i.e., 10–30 secs)							
AS53		Remembering directions							
AS54		Remembering to take things home							
AS55		Remembering on tests							
AS56		Remembering academic rules							
AS57		Remembering how to do things in the right order							
AS58		Recognizing visual patterns							
AS59		Following multistep instructions							
AS60		Remembering skills over time							
AS61		Remembering specific relevant facts							
AS62		Remembering what he/she is doing							

Figure 3-4.   *The ANSER System*'s memory questionnaire

The following algorithmic approach can be used in trying to identify a possible memory dysfunction:

- *Are there general indications that this child is having problems with memory function?* Clues might include tendencies to: 1) have difficulty studying for and taking tests; 2) have problems remembering information that the child appears to understand sufficiently; 3) have great difficulty retaining skills despite considerable practice; 4) have trouble keeping track of what he is doing or listening to; 5) perform most poorly in academic areas that demand memorization; 6) have trouble completing schoolwork when there is a great need for efficient memory function; and/or 7) show particular difficulties with writing and arithmetic.

- *Are there specific signs of short-term memory dysfunction?* The child with short-term memory problems may: 1) often need repetition of instructions/explanations; 2) show evidence of attentional dysfunction (see chapter 2); 3) reveal a lack of rehearsal strategies while listening or while studying; 4) have particular problems retaining information with certain attributes—visual-spatial, linguistic, and/or sequential; 5) have trouble with the rate or chunk size of incoming information; and/or 6) seem not to know things immediately after exposure to them.

- *Are there signs of active working memory dysfunction?* A child so affected may reveal: 1) a tendency to lose track of steps (to "forget what she's doing") amid a task; 2) trouble summarizing narrative or text material; 3) a history of problems decoding multisyllabic words; and/or 4) problems with complex tasks requiring the integration of multiple neurodevelopmental functions.

- *Are there indications of long-term memory dysfunctions?* A student contending with long-term memory dysfunctions is prone to exhibit: 1) trouble remembering facts and/or procedures in mathematics; 2) difficulty answering factual questions quickly; 3) frustration while trying to convey ideas on paper; 4) difficulties with courses requiring cumulative memory; 5) slow pace on tests and some homework; 6) difficulty remembering material that was mastered earlier (i.e., adequate short-term memory but problems with subsequent consolidation and/or access); 7) delayed automatization of basic facts and subskills; 8) difficulty with certain specific forms of paired association; 9) a preference for episodic and divergent recall over convergent and semantic memory; and/or 10) problems knowing what to do when (due to weak pattern recognition and procedural transfer—most observable in mathematics).

Table 3-5 contains a series of quotations typically heard or overheard regarding a student who has memory problems.

Direct Inspections of Work Samples and Direct Observations in the Classroom

Depending on the age and grade level of the student, many different kinds of work samples can be inspected to seek evidence of memory dysfunction. Following are some examples of the kinds of observations that can be made:

- A student writes fairly neatly when copying from the board, less legibly when writing from dictation and considerably less legibly (perhaps even illegibly) when writing a paragraph on his own. This pattern suggests that as the memory load increases, recall of letter formation deteriorates. This might be seen in a student who has problems with simultaneous recall. That student might also show a good appreciation of punctuation but have difficulty punctuating his own written work because of interference form the other memory demands during writing.

- A student may display hesitation while doing a math problem. If you ask her why she is hesitating, you may discover that she is having trouble recalling either math facts or procedures.

Table 3-5. A sampling of typical quotations suggestive of specific memory dysfunctions

QUOTATION	LIKELY INTERPRETATION
"I go over and over his work with him, and he seems to be retaining none of it, but once he knows something, he knows it forever!"	A child with far better consolidation and access than initial registration in short-term memory
"I go over her work with her and I test her; she seems to know it well, but then she misses the exact same items on the test the next day."	A child with far better short-term memory registration than consolidation and access from long-term memory
"He has to keep looking up every couple of seconds when copying from the board."	A child with trouble registering large chunks of visual material in short-term memory
"I keep forgetting what I'm reading about while I'm reading—I get to the end of a chapter and have no idea what I just read."	A child with active working memory problems affecting ideational development
"She seems to forget what she's doing right in the middle of a math problem."	A child with an active working memory problem impairing task integration
"He can remember little details about things that happened a long time ago but he can't remember vocabulary or spelling words he studied for a test."	A child with expanded episodic memory but deficiencies of convergent retrieval
"Everything seems to require too much time and effort when she reads, writes, or does math homework; nothing comes easy."	A child with delayed automaticity of memory function

- A child is noted to be working much more slowly than other students. She seems to have to stop and think too much at points that ought to be straightforward. She may be revealing delayed automaticity in the recall of certain material from long-term memory.

- A student frequently has problems coming up with the right answer when called on in class, even though he seems to know the material. That student may be having difficulty with rapid and/or convergent recall.

- A child is observed trying to study. She never whispers under her breath, writes things down, or tests herself. When asked how she is studying, she simply comments, "I just go over the stuff." This may be a child who experiences difficulty with short-term memory and is devoid of strategies to improve registration.

The close examination of samples of a child's writing, spelling, and arithmetic may reveal error patterns that are strongly suggestive of one or another form of memory dysfunction.

Direct Testing of Memory

There are some direct tests of memory function that can help pinpoint a child's learning difficulty. Such tests, however, are highly susceptible to overinterpretation. Most test items that tap memory are also evaluating other parameters, including attention, freedom from anxiety, rate of processing, and, in some instances, comprehension. But when interpreted along with evidence from the history and direct observations, these items and tests can be helpful. Memory assessment techniques have been reviewed systematically by Mayers (1995). Table 3-6 summarizes the forms of assessment of memory function in school-age children.

Following are some additional guidelines for assessing memory in children:

- In uncovering a particular form of memory dysfunction, it is important to determine whether or not that dysfunction is associated with specific information-processing problems. For example, if a child has trouble registering verbal information in short-term memory, it is reasonable to ask if that child also has problems with understanding (i.e., as well as remembering) linguistic inputs.

- It is very common for students with memory dysfunction to harbor more than one form of memory dysfunction. It is therefore appropriate to seek not just one such problem, but instead, when a memory dysfunction is suspected, to ask the question: Where are the memory breakdowns occurring in this student?

Table 3-6. A summary of assessment methods for memory function

Memory Dysfunctions: General Indicators

Following are some common historical indicators of possible memory dysfunction in students:

- Seeming to know more than is revealed on tests
- Problems in math and writing with fewer problems in reading
- Trouble learning math facts and/or procedures despite drill
- Difficulty expressing ideas on paper despite good oral expression and adequate graphomotor function
- Poor spelling, with errors that are not specifically visual or phonological
- Problems following direction; need for repetition
- Slow rate of work output and delayed automatization or facts and/or subskills
- Organization problems
- Hard time studying for tests

Table 3-6. *(Continued)*

N.B.: Children revealing weaknesses of memory frequently manifest more than one form of memory dysfunction.

General Sources of Evidence for Memory Dysfunctions:

History (possibly from school questionnaire and student report)

Direct observations of the student in the classroom

Samples of work (writing and math)

Short-Term Memory Dysfunctions

The following are some historical indicators of possible short-term memory dysfunction:

- Signs of attentional weakness (especially weak saliency determination, superficial processing, inconsistent focus)
- Trouble following directions
- Significant "chunk size" processing limitations
- Lack of strategic approaches to task completion
- History of frequent repetition of inputs without sufficient registration
- Problems copying from board and/or taking notes

Sources of Evidence and Clarification of Short-Term Memory Dysfunction:

Historical reports from teachers, parents, and students themselves

Classroom observations of the student at work

DIRECT TESTING OF SHORT-TERM MEMORY FUNCTION

Using neurodevelopmental examinations (PEEX 2 and PEERAMID 2):

Tasks involving short-term memory function include Digit Span, Verbal Instructions, Word and Pattern Learning *(PEEX 2),* Paragraph Comprehension, Motor Sequential Imitation, Object Span, Drawing from Memory.

Using psychological tests:

From *The Wide Range Assessment of Memory and Learning (WRAML)* tasks for short-term (Picture Memory, Design Memory, Finger Windows) and verbal memory (Story Memory, Sentence Memory, Number/Letter Memory). Comparable tasks are found on the *Wechsler Memory Scale-Revised (WMS-R)* and the *Woodcock-Johnson Tests of Cognitive Ability (WJ-R).* The *Kaufman Assessment Battery for Children* includes visual and verbal short-term memory tasks for younger children. The *California Verbal Learning Test* requires students to memorize a list of words, offering good opportunities to observe various aspects of registration in short-term memory. Visual memory for detail is tapped on the *Ray-Osterreiff Complex Figure Test,* which requires a child to reproduce a complex design from memory.

In all of these tests, the examiner should note the contributions of attention control and the child's use of rehearsal strategies. It is also possible to modify the rate of administration to uncover possible rate-related registration difficulties. It is important to document any patterns in the child's memory mistakes (e.g., problems maintaining the internal detail of long linear chunks or trouble with the registration of sequences but not configurations.

Table 3-6. *(Continued)*

Active Working Memory Dysfunctions

The following are some historical indicators of possible active working memory dysfunction:

- A tendency to lose place in the middle of a math problem
- Trouble retaining reading material despite adequate one-on-one comprehension
- Writing difficulties; problems with proximal and distal planning, as revealed in difficulty organizing and maintaining thought progression while writing
- Tenuous formation of concepts, and problems with comparing and contrasting ideas
- Foreign language disabilities
- General tendency to forget what one is doing, absentmindedness
- Difficulty decoding multisyllabic words in the presence of adequate phonological awareness

Sources of Evidence and Clarification of Active Working Memory Dysfunctions:
Direct history from parents, teachers, students

DIRECT TESTING OF ACTIVE WORKING MEMORY FUNCTION

Using neurodevelopmental examinations:

Active working memory function is specifically assessed on Alphabet Rearrangement *(PEERAMID 2),* Verbal Instructions, and Passage Comprehension tasks.

Using psychological tests:

Reverse Digit Span compared to forward Digit Span to compare short-term to active working memory (The *WJ-R* and the *WISC-III*). The *WJ-R* and the *WRAML* have Story/Passage Comprehension subtests that can provide some indication of active working memory function. (There is a clear need for tests of active working memory.)

Active working memory functions can be reliably observed during a range of academic tasks involving mental arithmetic, writing, and retention during reading.

Long-Term Memory Dysfunctions

The following are some historical indicators of possible long-term memory dysfunction:

- Incomplete mastery and/or automatization of facts and procedures
- Slow work pace on tasks demanding memory in the presence of adequate pacing of non-mnemonic activities
- Trouble remembering in the spring what was learned in the fall
- Difficulty participating in class discussions that are highly factual
- Writing problems
- Rejection of cursive writing
- Declining legibility with increasing memory load (differences between copying, writing from dictation, and paragraph production)
- Disparity between divergent and convergent recall demands
- Inability to recognize patterns recurring in mathematics (and perhaps elsewhere)

Table 3-6.   *(Continued)*

- Early history of word retrieval problems
- Lack of categorization and classification skills and habits
- Failure to elaborate ideas or new knowledge

Sources of Evidence and Clarification for Long-Term Memory Dysfunctions:

Parent, student, and teacher reports

Work samples (especially writing, spelling, and mathematics)

Overall grades indicative of greatest difficulty in subjects with greatest memory demands

---

DIRECT TESTING OF LONG-TERM MEMORY FUNCTION

Using neurodevelopmental examinations:

Long-term memory is evaluated on tests of rapid naming (e.g., picture naming and category naming), recall of practical sequences, alphabet writing activities, days of the week.

Using psychological tests:

On the *WISC-III* the Picture Completion and Information subtests tap long-term memory function. The *WJ-R* has a long-term retrieval cluster (including Memory for Names, Visual-Auditory Learning, and two Delayed Recall Tasks, the latter possibly entailing active working memory). Delayed recall tests are also found on the *WMS-R,* the *WRAML,* and the *Ray-Ostereiff Complex Figure Test.*

Observation and direct interviewing of the student while working and while "caught in the act" of using memory reveal much about long-term memory. Observations of the recall of spelling, factual content, and mathematics procedures and facts can be most revealing.

MANAGEMENT OF MEMORY DYSFUNCTIONS

As with other areas of dysfunction, the management of memory problems calls for a blending of demystification, bypass strategies, and interventions at the breakdown points. Since no one has a completely good or a totally poor memory, management must be based on a clear understanding of where an individual's mnemonic strengths and weaknesses lie.

Here is a sampling of management recommendations.

General Guidelines

- Students with memory problems have a critical need for demystification, which reassures them that: 1) they are not stupid (i.e., they just have trouble storing certain things in their minds); 2) when they grow up, the memory strain will not be so bad; and 3) they can work on improving their memory capacity for schoolwork and learning. Children can benefit from having a very specific sense of where their memory breakdowns exist and what they are called (e.g., "I've got problems getting linear chunks into my memory—especially when they are real long").

- As part of demystification, teach students about the important differences and interactions between memory and understanding.

- Children with memory dysfunctions need to deploy memory processes and strategies in a conscious (as opposed to a passive or casual) manner. Help them develop *metamemory,* an ability to think about memory before and while using it for a specific purpose.

- New knowledge and skills are best registered and consolidated if: 1) they are deliberately connected to prior acquisitions (i.e., "What does this remind me of that I already know or use?"); 2) they are elaborated on; 3) they are modified in some way (e.g., a format shift); or 4) they get cross-indexed (i.e., filed in more than one way).

- Help secondary school and college students select courses that together do not create a memory overload that exceeds their current capacities.

- Encourage students with memory-based differences in learning to develop written "memory plans" before studying for tests or undertaking extended tasks or projects.

- Instruct affected students in the use of specific mnemonic devices to register, consolidate, and retrieve important information. Devices include forming mental images, using the first letters in a list of terms to form a word or sentence (i.e., acronyms), and remembering key words.

- Ensure that memory-targeted interventions consist of a mix of bypass strategies as well as interventions at the breakdown points (see next two lists).

Short-Term Memory Dysfunctions

Bypass Strategies

- Teach students to circumvent weakly registered attributes (e.g., convert verbal inputs to graphic representations of information).

- Accommodate students' specific parameter weaknesses (e.g., reduce the "chunk size" of linear input or slow the rate of presentation).

- Present new material in more than one format (e.g., visual plus verbal).

- Institute preferential seating, encourage strong eye contact, and repeat inputs.

- Suggest that students use a classmate's notes or teacher handout as backup for note taking and copying.

Interventions at the Breakdown Points

- Have students practice paraphrasing and summarizing inputs.

- Help students develop activities to enhance saliency determination (e.g., underlining).

- Teach students techniques to improve the depth of processing (e.g., subvocalizing, use of the mental imagery "scratch pad").

- Have students engage in intermittent self-testing techniques while studying.

- Emphasize active recoding while studying (e.g., making charts, tables, diagrams).

- Consider using stimulant medication in view of its potential positive effects on processing depth, registration inconsistency, and central (as opposed to incidental) learning.

Active Working Memory Dysfunctions

Bypass Strategies

- Stress doing one thing at a time.

- Help children develop stepwise approaches to academic tasks and use checklists to indicate stages of completion.

- Encourage students to liberally use underlining and subsequent rereading of underlined material in texts and other extended discourse.

- Have students use advanced organizers to help with reading.

- Emphasize self-monitoring following task completion (i.e., "What have I left out?").

- Encourage students to acquire the habit of maintaining "to do" lists and assignment books, and check off completed items.

Interventions at the Breakdown Points

- Have students practice extended mental arithmetic problems to help expand active working memory and help students understand its function more vividly (e.g., multiplying 22×23 in one's head).

- Help children learn to register firmly short-term memory inputs before "consulting" long-term memory (e.g., repeat the question to themselves several times before trying to answer it).

- Help students automatize critical task components to "free up room" in active working memory.

- When practical, have students summarize after reading, listening, observing, or participating in extended activities (e.g., "Can you summarize what happened during today's ball game?").

Long-Term Memory Dysfunctions (of Consolidation and/or Access)

Bypass Strategies

- Place less stress on simultaneous recall, and emphasize staging of tasks and projects (e.g., learning to write in stages).

- Try adding an additional sensory pathway to paired associations that are weak (e.g., presenting or having children create pictures of semantic associations, such as words and definitions).

- Give students more time for recall if needed (e.g., on tests or when calling on an individual for a response).

- Substitute recognition memory for recall to help a student answer questions in class (e.g., "Isn't it true that raccoons are mainly nocturnal animals?" instead of "When are racoons likely to be encountered?").

- Ask questions that have more than one correct answer (e.g., "What are some characteristics of racoons?").

- If necessary, allow children with long-term memory dysfunctions to take open-book tests, and evaluate them on the basis of portfolios and other alternative means of assessing knowledge and skill.

- Allow children to use a calculator in mathematics.

- Have students use a word processor to help with writing (including, of course, spelling).

- Teach students to employ computers to create graphic representations (tables, graphs, diagrams) of material to be consolidated.

- Ensure that grading reflects prioritization (e.g., "Don't worry about spelling this week; it's not a priority").

- Use tutorial support to stress content learned earlier in the year as a means of fortifying cumulative recall.

Interventions at the Breakdown Points

- Induct automatization through rewarded drill (mainly undertaken at home)—especially important for critical paired associations.

- Use tasks that end at the memory breakdown points (e.g., activities that stress search for underlying familiar patterns).

- Train students in systematic study and self-testing techniques to enhance consolidation processes.

- Teach modification, cross-indexing, and elaboration techniques to enhance strength of consolidation (as noted in General Guidelines above).

- Provide opportunities to create tests involving memory of recently learned material.

- Place more stress on experiential learning.

- Give students practice in categorizing and classifying factual content.

- Assign exercises that stress rapid convergent and free recall.

- Establish proper working conditions and timing arrangements for optimal consolidation (e.g., regulation of background noises, studying right before sleeping, morning self-testing).

Chapter 4

Spatial and Temporal-Sequential Ordering

I went to several preparatory schools, beginning at the age of six. The very first was a dame's school at Wimbledon, but my father, as an educational expert, would not let me stay there long. He found me crying one day at the difficulty of the twenty-three-times table. . . . Also, they made me do mental arithmetic to a metronome! I once wetted myself with nervousness under this torture.

—Robert Graves, *Good-bye to All That*

The human brain consciously and unconsciously strives to discover or create order. It does so in part through its attention controls and also through language. Two additional ordering systems deal with alternative formats in which data or information may be arranged, namely, *spatial ordering* and *temporal-sequential ordering*. These systems facilitate the processing of incoming information, the long- and short-term storage of needed facts and procedures, and the output of various "products" or intellectual activities. They do so by allowing us to perceive, remember, and put forth material with particular meaningful whole-part relationships, distinctive borders, and relevant interrelationships between components of an array of data. Spatial ordering arranges these data in a gestalt or configuration, while temporal-sequential ordering arranges data in a sequence or "linear chunk." Working together, these two systems greatly facilitate the learning, academic productivity, and students' overall efficiency. When one or both of these systems is impaired, significant obstacles to learning and working may result. The spatial and temporal-sequential ordering systems operate at five distinct levels: processing (perception), memory, production, organization, and higher-order cognition (see fig. 4-1).

This chapter will examine each of these ordering systems in terms of their operation at the five levels. It will explore their normal functions with respect to school performance and examine their respective neurodevelopmental dysfunctions.

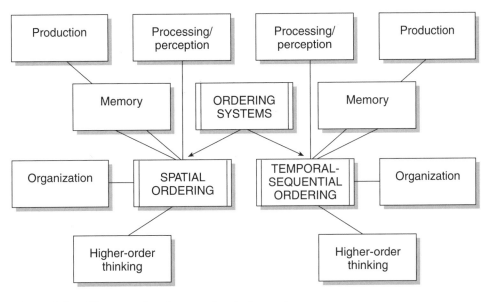

Figure 4-1. The neurodevelopmental ordering systems

SPATIAL ORDERING

As an example of spatial ordering, consider observing and later trying to recall the face of a colleague. First we must define the borders of that face, thereby differentiating it from the neck and shoulders. By also taking into account the relationship between the face and the rest of the body, we further highlight the face as a set of stimuli bound together to form a gestalt or configuration. We also inspect the facial features: sizes of parts, their contours, their locations with respect to the others, as well as other relationships between elements. Our observations are informed as we elicit memories and associations with other faces, attach verbal labels to the face or its parts, and store a mental representation of that face, so that we can recognize it or recall it subsequently. For now, we regard the face, its intrinsic properties and its external relationships.

An example of sequential processing is the conductor on a train. As the train approaches each station, he announces the station's name. As the train departs from the station, he is apt to proclaim, "Next stop. . . ." In other words, he is organizing the trip around a predictable (and observable) sequence. In a sense, his set of stimuli is the entire trip, differentiated from other routes because of its unique sequential pattern of stops.

Much of our experience with processing has spatial overtones. We interpret much of this spatial information visually; however, spatial data need not always pass through visual pathways. *Stereognosis* is an example of spatial processing without visual input. Putting my hand in my pocket, I feel the various spatial attributes of an object that turns out to be the key to my automobile. Believing that the order in which I touched the various parts of the key led to recognition would be as misleading as believing that the order in which I see the parts of someone's face is germane to recognition. Nevertheless, because the *visual* integration and organization of spatial sets of stimuli have been carefully studied over the years and are likely to be the most relevant to the greatest number of childhood pursuits, this chapter concentrates primarily on spatial processing and production.

Spatial Processing Functions and Dysfunctions

Visual perception was one of the first developmental functions to be studied in relation to learning disorders in schoolchildren (Bender 1956, Hermann 1959). In the 1950s and 1960s such dysfunctions were thought to be the nearly exclusive deterrents to acquisition of academic skill. Reading disability was generally believed to be the quintessential learning disorder. Since reading is accomplished with the eyes, it was thought to be logical that problems in reading were secondary to functional disorders along visual pathways. As we shall see, subsequent research has contradicted much of this thinking (Vellutino 1978). But before seeking the true consequences of impaired spatial processing, we will examine normal function in more detail.

Thurstone, a pioneer in characterizing various aspects of "intelligence," listed a series of "primary mental abilities," among which were perceptual speed (ability to grasp visual detail quickly) and space (ability to visualize space or recognize figures in various orientations; Pyle 1979). He subdivided the concept of spatial ability into three distinct elements: the capacity to recognize a particular object when it is seen from varying angles, the capacity to picture movement or internal displacement among parts of a visual pattern, and the capacity to view these relationships from the perspective of the observer's own body. Regardless of the conceptual model used, numerous factor analyses of intelligence tests repeatedly confirmed the existence of a cluster of abilities relating to spatial perception.

In the field of learning disorders, the work of Frostig (1973) was particularly influential. She stressed the importance of visual perceptual abilities as a requisite to effective learning. While she did not consider spatial astuteness to be the sole contributing factor, she is perhaps best known for her work in this area. A diagnostic instrument, the *Marianne Frostig Developmental Test of Visual Perception* (Frostig 1964), divides spatial abilities into the following components:

- *Visual-motor coordination:* the ability to coördinate vision with movements of the body or parts of the body

- *Figure-ground perception:* the ability to attend to one aspect of a visual field while perceiving it in relation to the rest of the field

- *Perception of constancy:* the ability to recognize that an object has invariant properties such as shape, position, and size, in spite of the variability of the impression on the sensory apparatus

- *Perception of position in space:* the awareness of an object's position in relation to the observer (or the perception of the direction in which it is turned)

- *Perception of spatial relationships:* the ability to perceive the position of two or more objects in relation to each other

Frostig's test gained wide use. Curriculum materials were derived from it to remediate students with apparent visual perceptual disabilities. The efficacy of such intervention has remained controversial, as has the relevance of these disabilities to impaired learning. Nevertheless, breaking down the components can be a useful way of conceptualizing this area of development.

Gardner (1983) characterizes "spatial intelligence" as having the following characteristics:

> Spatial intelligence entails a number of loosely related capacities: the ability to recognize instances of the same element; the ability to transform or to recognize a transformation of one element into another; the capacity to conjure up mental imagery and then to transform that imagery; the capacity to produce a graphic likeness of spatial information; and the like. Conceivably, these operations are independent of one another and could develop or break down separately; and yet, just as rhythm and pitch work together in the area of music, so too, the aforementioned capacities typically occur together in the spatial realm. Indeed, they operate as a family, and the use of each operation may well reinforce use of the others. These spatial capacities can be drawn on in a number of different arenas. They are important for orienting oneself in various locales, ranging from rooms to oceans. They are invoked for the recognition of objects in scenes, both when these are encountered in their original surroundings and when some circumstance of the original presentation has been altered. And they are also utilized when one works with graphic depictions—two dimensional or three dimensional versions of real world scenes—as well as other symbols, such as maps, diagrams, or geometrical forms (p. 176).

Thus, spatial abilities, the spatial appreciation of attributes frequently processed through visual pathways, are a source of childhood variability. As children go into, through, and beyond school years, they are likely to vary considerably in the rate at which they acquire spatial abilities, in their effective use of these capacities, and in the versatility and comfort with which they apply these functions. Some schoolchildren may be confused about spatial attributes. Among the most revealing and common of these distorted perceptions are the inordinate difficulties some children experience in dealing with the midsagittal plane (Corballis and *asymmetry* Beale 1976). Not only is spatial awareness simplified when confronting asymmetry, but our own bodies also foster this preference. Using them as a reference, we are unlikely to confuse the tops and bottoms of things or the fronts and backs of things since our own bodies show such dramatic differences between tops and bottoms and backs and fronts. However, employing our bodies for such orientation is not helpful when it comes to the midsagittal plane. If we draw a vertical line through the center of our bodies, dividing both the nose and the umbilicus, the two sides are remarkably similar.

Thus, it should not be surprising that youngsters who are predisposed to difficulties in the spatial domain will have particular problems with left-right discrimination as well as other kinds of mirror-image judgments, including, in particular, the notorious differentiation between *b* and *d*. Such letter reversals may indicate some spatial confusion. However, there are other (and probably more common) causes of reversals (see p. 554). Children with spatial confusion often have difficulty recognizing symbols and, therefore, may be slow to master the alphabet and numbers (see table 4-1). Their relatively weak grasp of the constancy of forms may make visual discrimination an inefficient process. Some children, therefore, may have real trouble readily discerning the differences between visually similar symbols. Confusions over *p* and *g* and *a* and *o*, as well as letter reversals, may ensue. However, the ultimate impact of such early confusion is difficult to gauge. If a child has good selective attention, adequate memory, appropriate language skills, and strong higher-order cognition, it is likely that initial difficulty in distinguishing symbols will be a transient phenomenon, a minor obstacle to learning. Ultimately, with time and effort, the child will master the symbol system. In fact, some highly capable students reverse letters in first grade and even beyond, but ultimately become proficient readers and writers. Spatial confusion may interfere initially with the acquisition of a sight vocabulary (the repertoire of words that can be recognized almost instantly). This, too, in a child with good linguistic and memory abilities, is likely to cause only a temporary setback, if any. More advanced grades increasingly emphasize language abilities and memory functions. Children whose function in these areas is effective compensate readily for spatial deficiencies, relying less and less on visual cues to identify words and numbers.

Fortunately, symbols acquire a host of multimodal associations (their semantic significance, their phonetic uniqueness, and their place in a context), which provide rich cues about pronunciation and meaning.

What, then, are the important impacts of impaired spatial processing of spatial data? Children with a weak foundation in this functional area may later have dif-

Table 4-1. Spatial processing dysfunction: possible effects on learning

AREA	POSSIBLE IMPACT(S)
Reading	Probably only transient effects in early grades; possible delay in sight vocabulary acquisition
Spelling	Possible difficulties with visualization; phonetically correct spelling errors (with intact language skills)
Mathematics	Some difficulty with geometric concepts and appreciation of spatial attributes
Content areas	Problems interpreting maps, diagrams, graphs, and complex charts
Other	Possible left-right confusion; weak facial recognition; deficiency in certain types of nonverbal reasoning; trouble forming mental imagery

ficulty with spelling (Boder 1973). Their inability to *visualize* words may result from indistinct or distorted initial visual registration. Such children who have a strong sense of sound-symbol association may make what Boder calls *dyseidetic* errors—spelling words phonetically (e.g., *l-i-t-e* for *light*), yet incorrectly. Weak visualization may also create problems with writing in general (see chapter 10). An inability to visualize holistically may adversely affect the learning of certain spatial concepts in mathematics. Geometric relationships and the use of graphs and dimensions such as volume or area may be confused. However, children with strong language skills can often bypass this weakness through verbal labeling (see chapter 11) and reasoning.

Other abilities that may be impaired by poor spatial orientation include map reading, a "sense of direction," and interpretation of instructional graphics (charts, graphs, and diagrams). Children who become confused over spatial data and their interrelationships may also be prone to difficulty with geography—relative positions of countries or cities being a source of frequent confusion. On a nonacademic level, such students may become disoriented in a new school, being slow to learn where different rooms are located. They may also have difficulty finding their way in large department stores or shopping malls.

A child's appreciation of spatial attributes (i.e., those components elucidated by Frostig) is quite different from his or her capacity to assimilate visual *detail.* Some children are diagnosed as having visual perceptual problems although their real difficulty is that they can attend to or extract only a limited amount of spatial data. During school years, children are expected to be able to process increasingly complex configurations. The complexity consists not nearly so much of spatial interrelationships as of a steadily expanding *quantity* of elements spatially depicted and required to be spatially integrated. Words become longer while their perceptual complexity remains about the same. Graphic representations, columns of numbers, and geometric arrays confront the student with an increasing need to *integrate, extract* the most salient elements from, *condense,* and *organize* the growing number of stimuli presented at once. As elementary school students move into secondary school, it is increasingly common to find some of them having difficulty not so much with the perceptual content as with the amount of information contained in a spatial pattern.

Spatial processing weaknesses may sometimes be confused with attention deficits. Some children who have difficulty dealing with detail are also found to have attention deficits and are as stressed by detail in the auditory channel as in the visual channel. Some have as much trouble fielding detail in the sequential mode as in the spatial mode. Still others have difficulty exclusively with large amounts of spatial visual detail. They may lose focus in the face of highly intensive, spatial input. Therefore, in evaluating a child's spatial processing, we must distinguish between two related aspects—the appreciation of sophisticated spatial configurations and the integration of many visual details presented as a gestalt. This has significant implications for both assessment and management.

Any discussion of the phenomenology of dysfunction of spatial processing must include comments about children who exhibit strengths in this domain. They are frequently referred to as *visual learners.* That is, whenever possible they prefer to acquire new information and to retain data primarily through visual-spatial (as opposed to sequential) pathways. Many of their learning strategies may be visually based. For example, in mathematics, a child may prefer a visual model of a correctly solved problem to a sequential, verbal explanation of how to do it. In memorizing various facts, such a child may prefer to conjure up visual imagery to reinforce what is being learned.

Furthermore, it is essential to recognize that data presented spatially are often available for a longer period of time than is information coded in a sequence or emanating from spoken language. Thus, children whose processing speed is generally slow may show a distinct preference for and greater proficiency in spatial processing.

Spatial Memory: Functions and Dysfunctions

Individuals need to preserve visual information in memory. Such storage takes the form of *image representations,* which are stored depictions of previously encountered spatial patterns (such as the appearance of a particular spelling word). In a process called *image generation,* these representations can be recognized or recalled on demand. Thus, in forming letters during writing, a child is able to recall the image representation and then generate the image of each letter as she or he begins to transcribe it on paper.

Some children exhibit weaknesses of "visual memory," as a result of which they are susceptible to problems with spelling and writing, and with certain kinds of visual recall that are needed in mathematics (e.g., memory for geometric shapes). A child may have pervasive problems with accurate memory for configurations or, alternatively, he or she may remember images but do so too slowly and with excessive effort. Such labored recall can be especially disabling during writing when the rapid recall of letter forms and spelling needs to keep pace with the flow of ideas and language.

Spatial Production: Functions and Dysfunctions

The spatial manipulation of objects or visual symbols is a challenging component of diverse academic and avocational activities. Consequently, *visual perceptual-motor function* merits consideration. Over the years, the integration of spatial processing with motor production has received a considerable degree of attention. Kephart (1971) stressed what he called the "perceptual-motor match," advancing the hypothesis that a continuing interaction takes place between motor performance and visual perception. This hypothesis has had therapeutic implications, as some professionals have believed that one can enhance spatial processing by using various reinforcing gross and fine motor activities.

This idea was vehemently challenged (Vellutino 1978), and the specific efficacy of this approach has not yet been demonstrated. Nevertheless, it is true that the sensory-motor linkage is a part of many pursuits during childhood (and adulthood; table 4-2). In copying from a chalkboard, drawing, or creating a model airplane, the performer bases much of his or her production on spatial input. A keen awareness of spatial interacting detail, a sensitivity to subtle internal relationships, and a notion of where an array begins and ends all may contribute to production. Many athletic events depend on a good appreciation of spatial data; a variety of outputs are based on the awareness of relative position. Hitting or catching a baseball, timing one's leap in a high jump, or returning a tennis ball all involve a series of motor outputs based on accurate estimations of relative position, distance, trajectory, and location with respect to one's own body.

The appreciation of spatial data is essential for designing academic and nonacademic products. Thus, the arrangement of data on a page may be enhanced by predicting how the components will appear in relation to each other. When interior decorators plan the furnishings of a room or architects the design of a building, they have a clear sense of how elements will relate harmoniously and/or meaningfully as a spatial display. When a child arranges numbers in a column for addition, spatial planning is a pragmatic necessity. During the early years of acquiring writing skills, children are often particularly concerned about spatial planning and the visual arrangement of their sentences, which may be as important to them as the content (Graves 1983). Subsequently, such spatial planning for writing becomes increasingly automatic or unconscious.

Keen appreciation of interrelationships among spatial data can facilitate the acts of fixing and constructing. A person with a vivid picture of spatial interactions is better able to predict the effects of manipulations in the spatial domain. Confronting a piece of machinery that malfunctions, such an individual can survey the spatial interrelationships of its parts and foresee the kinds of manipulation required to repair the damage. The ease and efficiency with which one constructively alters a spatial array depends on a sharp awareness of connections between its elemental parts. Thus, it is not surprising that many children who exhibit strength in the spatial domain have special talents for building and fixing things. Their strong spatial appreciation may extend to the development of extremely sophisticated nonverbal or spatial cognition. Such assets may also contribute to artistic ability.

Table 4-2. Spatial production dysfunction: possible academic and nonacademic effects

Difficulties with certain visual perceptual-motor tasks

Difficulty copying from a chalkboard

Spelling difficulties

Writing difficulties

Difficulty with spatial planning

Possible athletic deficiencies (especially catching, hitting, or kicking a ball)

Spatial Organization: Functions and Dysfunctions

The ability to organize materials is at the core of spatial organization. A child needs to coordinate possessions and implements throughout his or her academic career and beyond. Children with effective spatial organizational abilities are able to impart order to the various objects they need for learning and productivity as well as play. Following are some examples of spatial ordering in the everyday life of a student:

- Arranging written ouput attractively on a page, using paragraphs, margins, and appropriate spacing

- Organizing a desktop

- Arranging and maintaining consistent storage habits in drawers (e.g., having a consistent place in which to keep writing implements or white socks)

- Keeping a notebook in an orderly fashion

- Remembering where you left things

- Remembering what you need to take to school and what you need to bring home with you

For some youngsters spatial organization is an elusive skill. They are often described as highly disorganized. They frequently misplace or lose possessions. It may be exceedingly hard for them to organize a notebook or report so that their work appears reasonably attractive. Some may appear unhygienic and unkempt, as they have trouble arranging their clothing and engaging in daily routines to keep clean. Typically, such a student may work hard to prepare an assignment for school and then leave it on the bus or at the bus stop. Quite commonly these children form virtually no visual associative linkage between an object and the site at which it was last seen.

It is essential to recognize the close interaction between weak production controls (see chapter 2) and spatial disorganization. Some children may appear to have spatial disorganization simply because they undertake so many tasks or activities with little or no planning or self-monitoring and with a frenetic tempo. Of course, there are students who exhibit both attentional problems and spatial ordering weaknesses. Not surprisingly, these are some of the most disorganized children one is likely to encounter.

Spatial Ordering and Higher-Order Cognition: Functions and Dysfunctions

Spatial ordering interacts with a multitude of higher-order cognitive activities. These interactions will be discussed more thoroughly in chapter 7. Well-developed spatial ordering substantially facilitates the formation of nonverbal concepts (such as place value, perimeter, and refraction). In particular, a student's ability to visualize what such concepts are describing solidifies understanding. Such visualization, as we have seen, is a central aspect of spatial ordering.

Spatial ordering also contributes meaningfully to various problem-solving skills. Examples are the ability to find the cause of a malfunctioning computer or the best way to assemble a model car, both of which require analyses of spatial relationships as well as previewing ability. These children are often very good at understanding how things work, which, of course, greatly facilitates the process of figuring out why something is not working properly.

Children with strengths in visual ordering may also be good at discerning and creating rules relating to nonverbal phenomena. They may observe consistent visual relationships between objects or events that can be used to predict occurences (such as the weather). They may also be highly competent at understanding mathematical rules, especially as they pertain to geometric constancies.

Finally, spatial ordering can relate to creativity and brainstorming. Artistic talent and the capacity to generate unique spatial patterns or perspectives on paper (or canvas) are potential byproducts of strengths in this domain. Talent in various areas of design may be an indication of exceptional ability in spatial ordering.

Children with deficiencies of spatial ordering may reveal the following gaps in higher-order cognition:

- Problems mastering certain concepts in mathematics and science

- Weak mechanical aptititude, i.e., trouble understanding how things work and difficulty solving problems in nonverbal domains

- A tendency to perform many mechanical tasks the hard way

- Difficulty in art and craft classes

- Trouble assimilating and applying rules in science and mathematics

Now that we have examined both normal and dysfunctional spatial ordering, we can proceed to describe how to reliably evaluate this area of neurodevelopmental function.

Assessment of Spatial Ordering

The evaluation of spatial processing and production has been a traditional part of psychological assessments for many years.

Direct Observations. Most commonly, the copying of geometric forms is the basis for much testing. The *Bender Visual-Motor Gestalt Test,* the Beery *Developmental Test of Visual-Motor Integration,* and the *Benton Visual Reten-*

tion Test all present designs for a youngster to copy. In the *Benton Visual Retention Test,* the copying is done from memory, thereby tapping visual recall. The underlying assumption is that graphic reproduction is a direct reflection of spatial appreciation. While this is correct, the evaluator of a child must recognize the various contaminating influences that affect the copying of geometric forms. They are:

• *Inattention and impulsiveness.* Children prone to attention deficits (either global or primarily visual) may produce geometric forms that reflect their inattention to detail, impulsiveness, and failure to monitor their work, rather than any spatial dysfunction (see fig. 4-2).

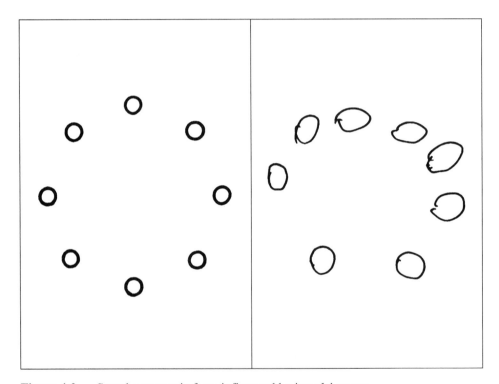

Figure 4-2.   Sample geometric form influenced by impulsiveness

The child whose rendering is displayed above copied this geometric form with incredible speed. She failed to count the number of circles in the configuration and thus was quite superficial in approaching the task. In fact, by the time she had completed half of the design, she had already used up most of her allocation of small circles. Furthermore, she never looked back, seeming unaware of what she was doing. Interestingly, when she was asked to perform the task more slowly, her drawing was nearly perfect. This underscores the importance of closely observing the child's tempo while executing the drawing during the evaluation of form copying.

- *Fine motor dysfunctions.* Clearly, in any form-copying exercise, children must have fairly good pencil control and fine motor praxis (see pp. 194 and 204–5). Children may have difficulty reproducing a geometric form not because they fail to perceive its internal relationships, but because they cannot implement the appropriate motor response. Some children, excessively consumed by the motor demands, lose track of the spatial information—data that they would have grasped had there been no requirement for a complex motor output.

- *Inability to process detail.* Any spatial array encompasses levels of both *quantity* and *sophistication* of interrelationships. Some children may be able to deal with the latter but not with the former. As geometric forms become more complex, the amount of detail rather than the perceptual interrelationships may confuse a child. This is particularly true for those with attention deficits.

- *Inexperience.* Children vary in their previous practice and comfort with writing implements. Ability to copy a geometric design may thus be influenced by the level of prior exposure to such activities, including the frequency with which a child engages in pencil-and-paper tasks at home and in school.

- *Emotional interference.* The *Bender-Gestalt Test is* often used, at least in part, to detect certain "emotional indicators." Heavily preoccupied children, those with high levels of anxiety and specific emotional disturbances, appear to create distorted forms during the copying of geometric forms.

The overall evaluation of a child needs to be taken into consideration in interpreting the copying of geometric forms. Thus, if a child has other indications of significant emotional disturbance, one should consider seriously the extent to which such factors have altered his or her performance. Similarly, a child with a history that suggests attention deficits should cause us to suspect that such dysfunctions may have compromised production.

Some other tests of spatial orientation minimize the effects of some of the contaminants discussed above. In particular, a variety of motor-free assessments require children to match designs. After looking at a visual stimulus and then a variety of others similar to the target design, the child must find one that is identical to the stimulus. Figure 4-3 illustrates such an item from the *Pediatric Early Elementary Examination (PEEX 2;* Levine and Sandler 1996), a neurodevelopmental assessment used for seven- to nine-year-old children.

A more sophisticated challenge is composed of embedded figures. The child, shown or told about a particular configuration, must find it embedded in a context of "visual noise." The background makes it hard to discern or locate the desired pattern or object. Finally, some tests employ a matching task in which the figure sought has been altered in some way, usually by forming its mirror image or rotating it along one of its axes. The ability to match these figures requires a fair degree of sophistication about the kinds of transformations objects can undergo while remaining constant in their identity.

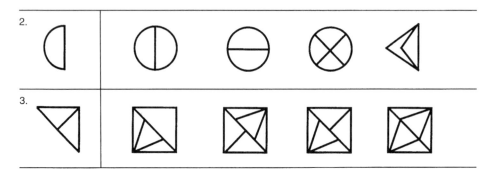

Figure 4-3. Whole-part relationships

These two items are taken from *PEEX 2*. They are used to assess a child's visual discrimination skills as well as her sense of whole-part interactions in the spatial domain. The child is asked to match the part of the design on the left with one of the forms to the right. Children with poor visual attention, trouble with whole-part relationships, or weaknesses of spatial processing may experience difficulty

The *WISC-III,* at this time the most commonly used intelligence test for children, has several tasks that are likely to be particularly difficult for youngsters with spatial deficiencies. A number of the performance subtests are especially sensitive. The Object Assembly and Block Design subtests may document some difficulties with production associated with relatively weak spatial or visual-spatial processing. An optional subtest, Mazes, may be particularly sensitive to problems with spatial planning or formation of strategies.

As with other evaluations of developmental variation, the assessment of spatial ordering and production requires the integration of multiple perspectives and sources of evidence. The following are key components that can facilitate the process:

- A history revealing levels of interest and skill in activities that involve spatial processing and production. Such activities might include ball sports, art and craft activities, mechanical pursuits (repairing and/or constructing objects), and design. Many children with spatial ordering problems reveal difficulties using scissors, tracing, coloring, building models, and other such pursuits. They may avoid such tasks and/or keep asking for help with them.

- A history that elicits information regarding spatial organization. This might include the ability to keep track of possessions, organize a notebook, maintain a functionally neat desk, and have available the materials needed to complete academic tasks (e.g., possessing a pencil when you need one).

- Direct testing of visual attention. There are many tasks that can be used to evaluate visual attention to detail. These are often called *vigilance* or *continuous performance tests.* An example can be found on page 51.

- Direct testing of motor-free visual discrimination. These are assessments that tap visual processing without requiring a significant motor response. Figure 4-2 provides an example. Tests of left-right discrimination can also gauge spatial ordering.

- Direct testing of visual perceptual motor function. This function is generally measured by having a child copy developmentally appropriate geometric designs.

- Direct testing of visual memory for configurations. Often this parameter is assessed by having a child reproduce designs from memory after a predetermined period studying them. Such tasks measure short-term visual memory. Long-term visual memory is evaluated on the Picture Completion subtest of *WISC-III.*

- Direct testing of visual memory.

- Direct testing of nonverbal reasoning and problem solving. This is accomplished by tests of mental rotation of imagery and other assessments involving the mental manipulation of patterns. *Ravens Progressive Matrices* is one such assessment technique.

- Evaluation of academic work. This might include such variables as a child's performance in art classes; facility with maps, charts, and diagrams; patterns of spelling and reading errors (which may be indicative of deficient visualization); and performance in various aspects of mathematical and scientific thinking that require the formation of mental imagery, nonverbal conceptualization, and problem solving.

In all of the above tasks, age norms must be obtained since children's abilities vary through the school years.

The *Kaufman ABC* is an intelligence test, based largely on the distinction between sequential and spatial processing. In fact, the examination contains distinct scales for each. The Spatial Processing subtests provide a great deal of information about this developmental function. They include an assessment of facial recognition, requiring a child to select from a group photograph the one or two faces that were exposed briefly on a preceding page. Another subtest, Gestalt Closure, involves naming an object or scene as depicted in a partially completed inkblot drawing. The Triangles subtest requires assembling several identical triangles into abstract patterns to match a particular model, and the Matrix Analogies subtest requires selecting a meaningful picture or abstract design that completes a visual analogy. This clearly entails some nonverbal reasoning skills. There are also tests of spatial memory as well as a Photo Series subtest, in which photographs must be placed in the correct order to tell a story. Used collectively, these various tasks can help uncover deficiencies or strengths in spatial processing.

It may not be necessary to make *all* of the evaluations listed above. For example, if a child has a history of significant strengths in various aspects of spatial processing, one probably needs to proceed no further. If, on the other hand, she or he has a history that suggests weaknesses, the type of evaluation described above can help pinpoint them more effectively.

Patterns of Academic Dysfunction. Close observation of error patterns in reading, spelling, and writing can reveal difficulties with spatial processing and production. Many children with this dysfunction exhibit spelling inaccuracies that reflect good phonetic approximations that are inaccurate visually. Others have difficulty forming letters because they are unable to visualize them clearly and easily. Their writing, therefore, may be extremely hesitant or dysfluent. They may reverse letters frequently during writing, especially in the earliest grades. They may have difficulty arranging numbers properly in columns for mathematics. Their helter-skelter use of space may result in frequent careless errors. Of course, a similar pattern can be seen, although less consistently, in a highly disorganized, impulsive student.

Problems with spatial processing might be suspected in a child who appears to be better at understanding what she or he is reading than at actually decoding the words. Such a student probably has strong language abilities but some trouble processing whole words, due perhaps to weaknesses of memory or to poor spatial processing with associated weak appreciation of the visual attributes and details within a word. Thus, watching a child read may reveal spatial processing deficiencies. However, a great deal of evidence from direct testing as well as historical data patterns of academic dysfunction are needed to show that a relevant spatial processing dysfunction is interfering with acquisition of academic skills.

TEMPORAL-SEQUENTIAL ORDERING

Temporal-sequential ordering demands the discernment or imposition of serial order. The sequential organization and integration of information is inherent in a wide range of cognitive enterprises (Bryden 1972). Sequential organization plays a role in such diverse activities as programming synchronized motor movements in sports, interpreting complex syntax, and memorizing multiplication tables. Just as we could not avoid alluding repeatedly to *spatial* appreciation in discussing spatial processing, we cannot avoid *time* as a major medium for sequential organization. Learning through sequential analysis requires that we preserve serial order. Spatial stimuli need not be thought of as specific to any one sensory modality. Although most of our discussion focused on visual processing, it was mentioned that simultaneous data also pass through auditory channels and involve stereognosis. Analogously, sequential detail may be processed visually, auditorily, or kinesthetically. Sequential awareness is critical for production since any complex motor activity entails a highly specific sequential ordering of movements (Luria 1980). Not unexpectedly, a process as fundamental as temporal-sequential ordering is likely to have a significant impact on development and learning in schoolchildren. Like other developmental functions, when it is operating well, it serves as a facilitator of learning and performance; when it is deficient, it becomes a source of agonizing frustration.

Temporal-Sequential Processing and Memory: Functions and Dysfunctions

In discussing temporal-sequential ordering it can be nearly impossible to separate perception from memory. This is because the appreciation of serial order most often demands that such order be *preserved in memory*—either short-term memory, active working memory, or long-term memory (see chapter 3). As children progress through their school years, they encounter a steady flow of inputs that are arranged in sequences, the order of whose elements are intimately relevant to meaning and applicability. Over time students are expected to interpret and retain increasingly lengthy chains of sequentially arranged data or steps. Often these sequences become infused with language (as in the serial commands of verbal instruction). Following are some of the developmental progressions that occur as children gain competency in temporal-sequential processing and memory:

- A growing appreciation of units of time (minutes, hours, days of the week) and their relative durations, as well as the ability to tell time

- The capacity to follow increasingly extended multistep directions and explanations

- A progressively improving ability to understand and retain multistep procedures

- A slowly increasing ability to hold long sequences of data in short-term memory

- The evolving capacity to manipulate sequences in active working memory (such as occurs when segmenting and reblending words in reading decoding)

- The capacity to consolidate and retrieve an ever growing repertoire of practical sequences in long-term memory (such as the alphabet, the days of the week, the months of the year, etc.)

These sequential processing and memory capacities are decidedly weak in some children. Recalling that sequential processing "involves the integration of separate elements into groups whose essential nature is temporal" (Kirby and Das 1978), we are not surprised that many children experience academic frustration associated with difficulties dealing with temporal order (table 4-3). Affected students may show varying combinations of difficulties with time and the appreciation, storage, and manipulation of serial order. In the "classic" case, a child may offer early, prophetic hints of dysfunction (Levine 1982a). These

Table 4-3. Signs of sequential processing and memory dysfunctions

- Confusion over time concepts and temporal prepositions *(before, after, until)*
- Delayed mastery of experiential sequences: days of week, months of year
- Slow learning to tell time
- Trouble interpreting multistep directions
- Deficient mastery of multiplication tables
- Difficulty with multistep explanations
- Possible problems understanding certain complex syntax
- Early problems with word segmentation and reblending later (unless compensated for by strong linguistic abilities)

frequently take the form of confusion over time concepts and vocabulary—a preschooler who appears to be acquiring language skills effectively meets up with inordinate delay in mastering time-laden vocabulary. Temporal prepositions (such as *before* and *after*), notions of earlier and later, even rather fundamental distinctions, such as that between *yesterday* and *tomorrow,* are peculiarly troublesome. A child may produce illogical statements such as "I hope my daddy gets home after supper so we can all eat together." An unsuspecting nursery school teacher may be nonplussed when the child inquires, "Are we going to have juice before or did we have it later?" Such comments bespeak bona fide temporal confusion. As our "classic case" enters school, she or he may function fairly well in kindergarten and first grade. Assuming that spatial processing and language functions are intact, letter recognition, the beginnings of a sight vocabulary for reading, and various one-step mathematical operations are generally mastered effectively. Thus, it is not unusual to encounter a six or seven year old with significant problems of sequential organization who seems to have acquired early academic skills.

In school, the first signs of difficulty are often problems processing directions. The following scenario is fairly typical.

The teacher says: "All right, class, settle down. I want you all to take out your workbooks. Turn to page fourteen. All of you should answer the questions at the top of the page. When you are finished, turn to the next page and fill in the blanks next to those new words. When you are finished, close your books, put down your pencils, and sit up straight so I'll know your work is completed."

Jenny, a child with problems in sequential ordering, hears something about "pencils." Because she does not process multistep (i.e., sequential) inputs, she is confused and disoriented. She becomes disheartened as she looks around and observes that all of her peers seem to be oriented; they seem to know what to do.

This creates a high level of anxiety since Jenny, like others her age, wants so much to be like everyone else, to fit in, and, most of all, to avoid humiliation. As the day proceeds and Jenny is constantly bombarded with sequences of input that she cannot integrate, she becomes increasingly anxious. She may need to develop a good strategy to deal with this. She may become aggressive and a behavior problem, a condition she regards as preferable to being considered a "retard" or "dummy" by peers and teachers.

It is also possible that Jenny could develop secondary attention problems. In other words, because sustaining attention to sequences of information fails to yield well-integrated, usable, and storable data, her attention is not reinforced. Jenny begins to tune out, become distracted, yield to appetites and the free flight of ideas, become fidgety, and/or fatigue easily.

Incidentally, Jenny's problems processing these multistep inputs are not limited to school. At home her mother says, "Jenny, why don't you put out the trash and then change into your pajamas and pour yourself a glass of milk and then come back in and watch television with us." Jenny heads for the kitchen. About thirty minutes later, everyone is asking, "Where's Jenny?" In fact, Jenny was able to carry out only the first command. As she headed for the trash can, she became disoriented and was unable to recall the sequence of commands. She then wandered about aimlessly. Because she was not guided by the instructions, she became vulnerable to distraction and was playing with a rubber ball that she and her dog found near the trash barrel.

As a child with problems of temporal-sequential ordering progresses through elementary school, certain academic challenges obstruct progress. In mathematics, the multiplication tables may prove difficult. Additionally, the child may prefer to analyze a particular problem all at once rather than to have it explained in a series of sequential steps. In some instances, spelling can be affected, as can the decoding of long, multisyllabic words.

Very often, the child with sequencing problems is delayed in mastering experiential sequences (Levine 1982a). Initially these include the days of the week (in the correct order), the months of the year, and the ability to tell time. Such children have no difficulty using a digital clock but tend to be confused by the standard clock face, interpretation of which during initial acquisition of skill depends on orienting the hands according to what comes before and what comes after. In the earliest grades these children may find the sequence of letters in the alphabet elusive. When asked what letter comes just before *t,* an affected child may need to sing the entire alphabet song to arrive at the correct answer.

As the school years pass, we can anticipate that children with these impediments will improve in their mastery of experiential sequences. Ultimately, most of them appreciate and recall the days of the week and months of the year (perhaps with some hesitancy) and are able to tell time. In some instances, even some older adolescents have remnants of time confusion. They may have trouble mastering the order of their classes or the opening of a combination lock at the beginning of each academic year. In addition, certain academic skill areas may be troublesome. For example, secondary school students with sequencing difficulties may experience frustration in geometry. Although they are likely to perceive effectively the various geometrical constructs under study, they become confused in understanding and creating proofs. They may have great trouble starting with a premise and proceeding through five or six steps in the correct order to arrive at a conclusion.

Difficulties with sequential analytic processing may have a deleterious effect on a child's receptive language abilities; however, this is variable. Children with intrinsically strong language processing may comprehend adequately despite difficulties with sequential appreciation. In some cases, only time-related vocabulary and syntax are deficient. In other cases, children combine sequencing weaknesses with generalized difficulties in language processing. A subtest on the *PEEX 2* (Levine and Sandler 1996) consists of a series of complex sentences that are read to children. After each, a comprehension question is asked. Seven of these items specifically elicit difficulties with interpretation of time, for example, "The baby crawled to the couch after his mother called him," followed by the question, "When did the baby crawl?" Children who have difficulty discerning temporal order commonly answer this question using one of three styles: "when his mother called him" (a vague response), "before his mother called him" (incorrect interpretation or recall of the preposition), or "because his mother called him" (substitution of a causal relationship for a temporal relationship). It is not unusual to encounter children who perform poorly only on the time-related sentences, and have no difficulty with other syntax. Nevertheless, some children's combined language and sequencing problems are so severe that any subtle variations or manipulations of word order create interpretive havoc.

Children with weaknesses in sequential processing who possess strengths in spatial processing may reveal some characteristic stylistic preferences. Denckla (1978) describes this propensity as a form of "strong right brain." She characterizes such children as follows: "They respond in a holistic big configuration, spatial-sensitive manner of the 'strong right brain'. . . . They have difficulty balancing this style with the detail-attentive, sequential, analytical, linguistic style of the left brain that is so important academically." Denckla uses quotation marks around "strong right brain" to stress that the cerebral localization is not a hard-and-fast or indisputably established phenomenon in such youngsters.

Temporal-Sequential Production: Functions and Dysfunctions

Temporal-sequential ordering contributes significantly to the efficiency and effectiveness of student output in school. In part this is because both motor and nonmotor procedures depend on sequential organization (Luria 1980). In the *fine motor domain,* precise, sequential patterns of muscle contraction and relaxation form the bases for all actions. For example, the order of motor movements required to form letters while writing (i.e., graphomotor output) makes up a distinct *motor sequence.* Other routine procedures, such as tying shoelaces, brushing teeth, and buttoning a shirt, are "programmed" as predictable, sequential patterns of motor sequences. In the *gross motor domain* an analogous phenomenon pertains. Most sports, for example, involve complex, serial motor movements, processes in which the specific order of the elemental actions is crucial to successful outcome. In the huddle, quarterbacks instruct their teammates through sets of serial commands. Each player responds by enacting motoric sequences in a predetermined order. A gymnast working on parallel bars plans and implements, at an automatic "microlevel," a precise set of muscle contractions and relaxations to produce desired formations. Finally, there is *oral motor function*. When one speaks, the component phonemes are arranged in a particular order to form words, the words in a particular order to form sentences, and the sentences in a particular order to form narrative. During speech, a sequentially patterned movement of the oral musculature creates meaningful sounds. Again, the sequence of muscle movements is one critical component of effective output. Commenting on the multiple subcortical, motor sequential programs within the human body completes our discussion of sequential production. Peristaltic movement of intestinal musculature represents an exquisite motor sequence. The various circadian rhythms of bodily function are clearly sequentially organized, as are patterns of sleep and wakefulness. This does not suggest that the motor components of these latter sequences are programmed by the same mechanisms as more voluntary outputs, but only points to the ubiquity of sequential organization as a fundamental function.

Nonmotor sequential procedures are also highly relevant and include many activities common to mathematics. Examples include the ordered steps for balancing an equation, for performing long division, for reducing a fraction, and for balancing an equation.

The generation of logical sequences is an essential feature of many diverse forms of expression. In certain forms of expository essay or narrative account, the sequential order—the logical flow of ideas or events—is mandatory for effective writing. The reporting of scientific experiments, the creation of musical compositions, the description of historical events, and the compilation of geometry proofs all have in common their organization of information: the serial order is germane to meaning. Sequential production provides an important means of organization, without which many academic and nonacademic products would be woefully incoherent.

Sequence can be essential for processes of prediction and planning. When one undertakes a long-range project, a strong sense of sequence aids preparation. As one develops a series of deadlines or breaks down tasks into appropriate stages to be completed at particular times, one is employing sequential organization as a production strategy. A contractor involved in the construction of a new building must base its construction on a series of anticipated sequential steps that might include first clearing the land, then excavating, then assembling the framework, then applying the brick. At exactly the proper point in the sequence, wiring and pipes must be installed. Clearly, the serial ordering of such steps demands strategic planning and the capacity to foresee a stepwise progression. Unquestionably, for the sequential planning of any project, an anticipatory sense of serial order is essential. Sequential organization, therefore, is crucial for allocating time and staging the component steps required to complete a project. Academically, such anticipatory sequencing can have a major impact on study habits, completion of assignments, and overall efficiency.

Developmental Variation and Dysfunction. Some children with dysfunctions involving sequential production manifest a wide range of difficulties, including poorly integrated motor output and difficulty with the mastery and application of multistep procedures (see table 4-4).

A child may be slow to acquire gross motor skills as a result of an inability to appreciate, integrate, recall, and implement the active sequences in the correct order. The same may be seen in the fine motor and graphomotor domains. Letter formation may be slow and awkward as a result of sequential motor disorganization. In some instances, a child may acquire and ultimately master motor skills, but the process may require inordinate *overlearning*. Before this occurs, children may be excessively mechanical, awkward, or slow in their sequential motor output. In other words, they are delayed in achieving *automatization* of motor tasks (see chapter 6). Some children with sequential disorganization fail to display any motor incoordination. Other aspects of their motor function may be so highly proficient that they override their developmental vulnerability.

Some children with sequencing difficulties experience speech production problems. They tend to be among the most severely impaired children. They may have trouble recalling or arranging the order of motor movements to create intelligible, meaningful words. They may be hesitant about combining words into meaningful sentences. They may have difficulty with both sound sequences and syntax. Interestingly, such children may display normal or even superior vocabularies, which are independent of sequential production. As might be expected, children who have trouble with the sequential organization of oral language are likely to have equal or even greater problems with written language. Children who give the punch line first when they tell a joke, whose accounts of what happened at school today are so disorganized that their parents are totally baffled, may experience formidable problems describing and writing about their vacations last summer.

A poorly understood but intriguing question concerns the musical ability of children with sequential difficulties. It is common to encounter children with problems of sequential organization who play a musical instrument adeptly. When we consider the impressive amount of sequential organization required to draw a bow or press keys in the appropriate order, we might think that any musical pro-

Table 4-4. Sequential production dysfunction: possible academic and nonacademic effects

---

- Difficulties with complex sequential motor tasks (as in certain sports and/or crafts)
- Speech problems in sound sequencing
- Difficulty with narrative organization; trouble summarizing; poor sequencing of events or ideas in writing and/or oral retelling
- Poor use of time, lateness, difficulty scheduling stages for completing tasks (especially for projects or long-term assignments)

---

duction is prone to impairment in the presence of poor sequencing. On the other hand, music can be helpful to children with problems of sequential organization because musical sequences are richly reinforced with immediate feedback, with tonal or rhythmic clues, and harmonic meaning. Such pursuits might actually help certain children overcome their sequential disorganization—at least while they are engaging in musical activities. The same might be true for dancing.

Finally, the impact of sequential disorganization on production is variable. Some children excel at sports despite their sequencing deficiencies, which have somehow spared the gross motor area. Advantages such as well-developed body position sense and keen spatial awareness may help certain children circumvent or override sequencing weaknesses so that they perform effectively in the gross motor realm. Similarly, some students with strong expressive language abilities have no difficulty with narrative organization even though they exhibit other sequencing production weaknesses. Their strong innate sense of linguistics provides the necessary "overdrive" to minimize the impact of their sequential confusion. As always, it is necessary to scan a child's entire functional profile to develop insight into the ways in which specific compensatory strengths can alter the clinical phenomenology of a particular dysfunction.

Temporal-Sequential Organization: Function and Dysfunction

Temporal-sequential ordering forms the basis for much of a student's organizational skill. In particular, this form of ordering is necessary for effective time management and for the development of task approaches that entail doing things in logical, manageable steps (rather than attempting to achieve closure all at once). A child's sense of time and sequence is critical for completing assignments on time, for budgeting time during an examination, and for setting aside appropriate amounts of time to get work done. Following are some of the abilities that reflect temporal-sequential organization:

- An ability to meet deadlines and arrive at places on time
- An awareness of time passage (e.g., knowing that you have been out playing for too long and that it's time to come in)
- A sense of how long something will take to complete
- A capacity to allocate time appropriately
- A knowledge of the best order in which to undertake the steps in a complicated task (i.e., what to do when)
- The ability to organize material in a logical sequence (as in a notebook or filing system)
- A proclivity to develop and adhere to schedules

Children with temporal-sequential disorganization often manifest difficulty with most or all of the challenges listed above. As might be expected, using sequence as an organizational scheme may be out of the question for some of these youngsters. Organizing a notebook by using page dividers may be a chronically exasperating challenge. Using time effectively and planning and implementing strategies can also be difficult for these children (Levine 1982a). They may have real problems following a schedule, remembering what to do and when to do it, arriving when they are expected, and figuring out the order in which they should tackle components of a writing task. Often children with deficient sequential organization have trouble completing homework. They typically complain (and their parents echo the lament) that "it's so hard getting started." Because they don't plan a sequence of actions, it is difficult for them to determine how to begin. In some cases, parents need to be urged to help them write the first sentence or, more generally, to develop a sequential plan.

Important interactions occur between the production controls of attention and the phenomena associated with temporal-sequential organization. Most obviously, weaknesses of tempo control (see pp. 37–38) in a child with attention deficits may mimic the effects of temporal-sequential organization. In both instances, the student shows confusion about time relationships and serious problems organizing his or her time. Of course, a child with weak tempo control is likely to exhibit other signs of attentional dysfunction, whereas a youngster with temporal-sequential disorganization should manifest other signs of problematic temporal-sequential ordering. There are some individuals who have problems both with attention and with temporal-sequential organization; they are apt to be especially disorganized and disoriented when it comes to the management of time.

Higher-Order Thinking and Temporal-Sequential Ordering: Functions and Dysfunctions

The precise role of temporal-sequential ordering in higher-order thinking is somewhat speculative. Many sophisticated cognitive activities are organized sequentially. For example, the discernment and analysis of causal relationships depends, in part, on the serial placement of an antecedent cause before its effect. Both inductive and deductive logical thinking require systematic sequential thinking. Psychologists have often employed tests of seriation to evaluate higher-order reasoning. Such assessments present a series of sequential patterns to a child, who has to discern the serial pattern and predict correctly the next item in the series.

Process concepts (see p. 219) require students to comprehend a series of linked steps that comprise a mechanism or way in which something occurs. These concepts include such phenomena as nuclear energy, photosynthesis, and osmosis; their understanding depends on an ability to comprehend the serially linked steps that make the process occur.

Problem solving (see pp. 222–25) is another higher-order thinking function that demands sequencing. A good problem solver is able to think through a challenge, making use of a stepwise approach rather than "jumping to conclusions" or reacting impulsively.

Thus, students with evidence of temporal-sequential ordering problems may be susceptible to problems with those aspects of reasoning, problem solving, and concept formation that utilize a scaffolding based on serial order. Of course, a student with notable strengths in these higher-order thinking processess may be able to override any potentially negative impacts of deficient temporal-sequential ordering.

Assessment of Sequential Ordering and Production

The assessment of sequential processing requires the commingling of historical data with direct observations, because so many of the clinical manifestations of sequential disorganization can be mistaken for other developmental dysfunctions (and vice versa). Virtually all tasks commonly used to assess sequencing also tap other functional areas such as attention, memory, and language. Therefore, an accurate assessment of sequencing abilities requires 1) a history of difficulties acquiring skills that necessitate sequential processing or production; 2) substantial evidence of dysfunction based on direct observation of a variety of sequencing tasks (verbal, nonverbal, visual, and motor); and 3) a pattern of academic dysfunction consistent with reduced sequential function as a contributing factor. As with most other assessments, one probably will never discover a child who meets *all* of the possible criteria for sequential disorganization. One makes a diagnostic case by demonstrating that a child has many of the stigmata which best explain the child's academic and/or behavioral-social plight. The following are key components of an assessment of sequential ordering and production abilities:

- Historical evidence of the ease of mastery of temporal prepositions and other time-laden terminology (e.g., *yesterday, tomorrow, every other week*). Other acquisitions that may have been difficult or readily learned are: days of the week and months of the year, the multiplication tables, and telling time. All of these accomplishments can be delayed or notably elusive in children with dysfunctions of temporal-sequential ordering.

- Historical information regarding multistep processing and production. This should include background regarding a child's ability to process and carry out serial directions or learn various multistep processes (such as long division). Many affected students have problems dealing with complex instructions and procedures. There also may be a history of difficulty narrating events in a story or repeating the parts of a joke in the correct order.

- Historical background with regard to time management. Information should be sought with respect to a child's overall sense of time, ability to allocate time, reason with time, estimate time, meet deadlines, and deal with schedules. These demands are often problematic for children with temporal-sequential ordering weaknesses.

- Direct testing of short-term sequential memory. This should include tasks involving the repetition of auditory sequences (i.e., a digit or word span), visually presented sequences (i.e., imitative tapping in a particular order), and motor sequencing (fine and gross motor rhythm reproduction).

- Academic evidence. Samples of writing may reveal that the child prefers printing to cursive writing (commonly encountered in students with dysfunctions of motor sequential memory). Frequent errors of letter sequence may also be noted in spelling, with a particular propensity to misspell long words, such that the initial and final letters are correct, while the medial letters are incorrect. Written and expository narrative may be highly disorganized. In mathematics the child may become confused and inaccurate when faced with multistep mathematical operations. Problems performing geometric proofs are common among adolescents with temporal-sequential ordering gaps.

Historical Data.   A clinician evaluating a child for possible sequencing dysfunction should probe the child's early history for possible antecedents of temporal-sequential disorganization. Questionnaires can be helpful in this process. Regardless of how information is obtained, it is important to try to uncover early difficulties with time orientation, the mastery of temporal prepositions, and the learning of days of the week, months of the year, the alphabet, and other sequential material. In older youngsters, tracing the acquisition of mathematics skills and, particularly, difficulty with multistep problems and the multiplication tables may reveal the presence of sequential disorganization.

Direct Observations.   An assessment battery to evaluate sequential processing should include items that cover a fairly wide range of possible manifestations. The following types of items should be included in such assessments:

Experiential sequencing. The child's mastery of experiential sequences should be assessed. The precise task depends greatly on the age of the child. During the preschool period, temporal vocabulary (e.g., *before* and *after*) should be included. During early elementary school, the days of the week, telling time, the order of letters in the alphabet, and a further assessment of time-laden vocabulary can be useful. In the upper grades, the days of the week backwards, the months of the year, and some more sophisticated conceptual tasks using time are appropriate.

Auditory sequencing. All of the many traditional tests of auditory-sequential memory do, indeed, involve memory. Most common and perhaps the best standardized task of all is the *digit span,* requiring a child to repeat a list of numbers in the correct order. Children are expected to recall increasingly long sequences of numbers as they grow older. Digit spans are administered in a number of well standardized tests (e.g., the *WISC-R* and the *Detroit Tests of Learning Aptitude).* Reverse digit spans are also often used, but we must remember that they test more than sequencing. They require, in addition to sequential processing, the use of active working memory (i.e., the intake, storage, and reorganization of numbers). Because of its complexity, the reverse digit span is not particularly useful as a pure test of sequencing abilities.

Other stimuli should be included in an assessment of auditory sequential memory. Younger children listen to nonmeaningful sounds (such as *puh-ku-tuh*) and are expected to grasp, store, and restate them in the correct order. Such sequences may be contaminated somewhat by a child's articulation or sound production problems. Word spans can also be effective. The child repeats a series of words in the correct order. For some youngsters, the words provide accessory cues, eliciting a great deal of visual imagery or semantic associations that help reinforce the sequences. In general, both a numerical and verbal sequence should be in one's diagnostic repertoire.

Visual and motor sequencing. Various forms of imitative finger tapping are commonly used to assess visual and motor sequential memory. Typically, a subject may have four or five objects or blocks in front of him or her. The examiner touches them in a particular order; the subject imitates. In some cases, objects are used (object span), while in other instances squares or nonmeaningful shapes are employed as stimuli. The *Illinois Test of Psycholinguistic Abilities (ITPA)* includes a visual and motor sequential memory task that involves rearranging a series of blocks in the correct order to imitate a set of stimuli. Some subjects are confused by a visual sequencing task if they have significant problems with direction. The movement of the examiner's finger from left to right or right to left may create problems that can be mistaken for sequencing difficulties. Some highly distractible subjects may have trouble pointing in the correct order to specific objects. They are, in fact, distracted by the objects themselves, failing therefore to focus on their sequential order.

Motor sequencing. Among the various tasks of fine and gross motor sequencing is showing a subject a particular sequence of finger movements and asking her or him to repeat them in the correct order. This includes both the processing of sequences and their subsequent production. Multistep serial commands tap auditory–gross-motor sequencing. A subject is given a series of directions to perform in a particular order. This primitive form of sensory motor sequencing entails the appreciation of an auditory sequential input and the production of a gross motor sequential response. Some subjects who are particularly adept in gross motor abilities and in spatial appreciation do surprisingly well on complex, multistep serial commands, despite weak sequencing on all other items and a history of such difficulties. This may account for some individuals with major deficiencies of sequential memory who are in serious jeopardy academically in college but perform magnificently on the football field each Saturday afternoon. Although they have serious problems with all of the sequential instructions doled out by professors during the week, they do surprisingly well with the complex motor sequences provided by the quarterback. Their strong body awareness, sensitivity to sensory motor cues, and (no doubt) an extremely high level of motivation all serve to override an underlying vulnerability in sequential memory and production.

The *Kaufman ABC,* an intelligence test partially described earlier in this chapter, contains a Sequential Processing Scale. Three subtests detect problems of sequential processing and production. The Hand Movements task requires a subject to perform a series of manual movements in the same sequence demonstrated by the examiner. The Number Recall subtest is a digit span. The Word Order subtest requires the subject to touch a series of silhouettes of everyday objects in the same sequence as the examiner names each of them. Poor performance on these three tests may indicate sequential processing and production dysfunctions.

Possible contaminations. Testing for sequential disorganization is important but susceptible to misinterpretation. The following factors may distort an evaluation:

- *Confusion with attention deficits.* Virtually all tasks that test a child's assimilation and appreciation of sequences require sustained attention to detail. Thus, a child who concentrates poorly may falter on a sequencing task because of weak attention rather than any true dysfunction of temporal-sequential processing. Often a tip-off to this phenomenon is a child's extreme inconsistency. For example, a child with an attention deficit may be a "streak hitter" on digit spans, succeeding on three spans in a row and then missing the next three of equal length (presumably during a phase of inattention). Furthermore, such a child may succeed on a difficult sequence and subsequently fail or previously have failed on an easier one. One way of detecting this is to avoid administering sequencing items in order of difficulty. By mixing hard and easy items we can discern inconsistent attention and distinguish that from true sequential disorganization. The nature of the errors made yields another important clue. Children with attention deficits may be more apt to insert or omit specific stimuli, while those with sequential disorganization may recall all the bits of data but get them in the wrong order. This latter phenomenon is by no means invariant, since some children with sequencing problems may also omit and insert data in their sequencing.

- *Differentiating between generalized memory phenomena and sequential memory.* Children with pervasive difficulties of short-term memory may do poorly on all sequencing tasks. Most items that tap sequential organization also tap short-term memory. Therefore, any assessment of sequencing should also include other forms of short-term memory assessment to rule out the possibility of more generalized problems with the registration, storage, or recall of data (see chapter 3).

- *Confusion with information-processing weaknesses.* Some children may fare poorly on items testing sequencing not because of true sequential disorganization but because of a weak modality. For example, they may have trouble with an auditory sequencing task (such as a digit span or word span) because of a central auditory processing deficiency (see chapter 5).

- *Dependence on the rate of administration.* Some children are able to process sequences of information, but they cannot do so quickly enough. Generalized slowness of intake and registration may be at the core of their learning problems. Such children may be able to appreciate sequences but not at the usual one-per-second rate at which they are administered on psychological tests. Either a faster or slower speed might eliminate the ostensible sequential dysfunction.

- *Effects of meaningful versus nonmeaningful data.* Some children perform poorly on digit spans but do well on repeating a list of words. Children for whom numbers are relatively meaningless or, in fact, problematic, may have trouble appreciating or integrating a list of numbers but feel much more comfortable repeating sentences or words. For this reason, it is helpful to administer both kinds of items.

- *Ambiguity of production tasks.* Activities that measure motor sequential organization may be contaminated by other aspects of motor coordination. Thus, a child with a motor dyspraxia (see chapter 6), a motor memory deficiency, or weaknesses of eye-hand coordination may have trouble performing sequential motor activities—not because of true motor sequencing deficiencies, but because of those other impairments. This possibility can be inferred if the sequential motor task is part of a more generalized assessment of motor ability.

- *Use of strategies.* Some children may have difficulty with sequencing tasks because they do not employ effective rehearsal strategies (see chapter 3). Thus, children adept at employing memory strategies may perform surprisingly well on sequencing tasks because they apply various techniques to simplify the challenge. Subvocalizing during a digit span is one example of this. Other children are good at imaging, or picturing, the stimuli to reinforce their storage and retrieval. In other instances, children convert the task to their strongest modality. For example, a child who is asked to tap a series of squares in a particular order might number each square and perform the task as if it were a digit span. This can be seen in children who feel more comfortable with auditory than with visual recall. Consequently, assessing sequential organization requires evaluating the presence or absence of memory strategies. This phenomenon is covered in more detail in chapter 3.

- *Other factors.* A number of additional influences can affect direct observations of sequential organization. In general these are the same confounding variables that frequently intrude on assessment. Issues such as motivation or intrinsic interest, anxiety, test-taking ability, and the skills of the test giver seem to be particularly potent factors in assessing temporal-sequential organization.

Patterns of Academic Dysfunction.   In making a case for either strengths or weaknesses in sequential processing and production, it is appropriate to see if diagnostic findings clarify or explain academic performance. This chapter previously described various historical clues and clinical symptoms of sequencing problems. Difficulties following directions, performing multistep mathematics problems, or organizing work effectively might be anticipated. When evaluating a child, it is appropriate to match diagnostic findings to academic outcomes to determine whether what one would anticipate in terms of difficulties is actually the case. The process is not an easy one, however, since sequential processing weaknesses often do not exist in isolation. That is, the academic picture of a child with sequencing problems can be altered significantly depending on what other kinds of difficulties and/or compensatory strengths exist.

BRAIN LOCATIONS OF SPATIAL AND TEMPORAL-SEQUENTIAL ORDERING

Much is known about the localization of spatial functions. In most individuals the right hemisphere is specialized to deal with visually presented (i.e., spatial) data. Association areas near the occipital lobes are involved in perception, in visual attention, and in memory for visual attributes. The thalamus plays an important role in relaying visual messages to higher cortical centers, and that part of the brain can take part in interpreting visual experience.

There is considerably less knowledge of the anatomy of temporal-sequential organization. In all likelihood, the functions subsumed in this construct are far more diffuse in their localization. The anterior thalamus participates actively in temporal sequencing, maintaining the order of inputs for preservation in memory. Arrangements in time and order are also part of the purview of the frontal lobes. In most individuals, the left hemisphere is specialized for sequences (and for language), while the right hemisphere prefers to deal with gestalts and holistic presentations, conglomerations of data that tend to enter the nervous system nearly simultaneously rather than in a preset meaningful sequence.

MANAGEMENT

The relevance of a child's information-processing abilities to educational planning and classroom management has been a subject of conflict among professionals over the last two decades. For our purposes, this conflict converges on the question of whether or not knowledge of a child's strengths or weaknesses in spatial and/or sequential processing and production can be used in the design of a remedial program. Early in the history of the field of learning disabilities many professionals became staunch advocates of treatment based on developmental deficits. For the most part, their therapies were modality oriented. They customarily concentrated on discrete channels of data input, which consisted primarily of auditory, visual, kinesthetic, and tactile pathways. They sought and managed blockages in any or all of these channels as well as in their integration to complete tasks. Programs could be designed either to improve processing through a partic-ular channel or to bypass that modality as much as possible. Over time, many prominent educators reacted strongly against this therapeutic approach. After a period of considerable enthusiasm for visual motor training and the fashioning of curricula to integrate, highlight, or eliminate specific sensory input pathways, there was fairly widespread disillusionment among teachers and clinicians.

Can and should we "fix" deficient processing through a specific modality or in the spatial and sequential systems? Regrettably, this too is a question that remains to be answered scientifically. Present clinical experience suggests a conservative approach, stopping short of total therapeutic nihilism. Remedial techniques, teach-ing methods, and curriculum choices should take into consideration deficits and strengths in these areas without presuming to provide the entire answer or a panacea for a student's learning difficulties. The following management sugges-tions can be incorporated into planning for children who have demonstrated dif-ficulties in spatial or sequential processing—whether these difficulties are generalized or limited only to visual or auditory pathways.

Management of Spatial Processing and Production Dysfunctions

Although spatial processing can occur through visual, auditory, kinesthetic, or tactile pathways, from an academic standpoint we assume that visual spatial arrays are the most common and perhaps relevant of the spatial stimuli. Therapeutics therefore might be aimed at helping a child sustain and analyze visual, spatial information. This might be accomplished by enhancing the ability to discern rela-tionships within a spatial pattern. The more clearly these interactions are processed, the more meaningful and durable the sets of stimuli are likely to be.

Visual training, advocated by many researchers, must be approached cau-tiously. The techniques have often been integrated with motoric, structured activ-ities. The balance beam was one such intervention; various kinds of puzzles and other visual-motor pursuits were another. Frostig (Frostig and Maslow 1973) advocated a wide range of specific curriculum materials to enhance visual per-ceptual functions. They included picture recognition activities, sorting shapes by size and shape, position-in-space activities, left-right discrimination exercises, tracing games, working with blocks, and copying designs or patterns. Through ongoing practice and feedback, it was assumed that children could gain in their visual perceptual abilities. Presumably, various clues about spatial interaction, once fully assimilated, would enhance overall spatial analytic abilities.

Frostig and Maslow (1973) note that "if visual-perceptual training is to help the child most effectively, the teacher must teach for transfer. That means that she must (1) point out to the child the similarities between the games and tasks he uses dur-ing perceptual training and those he undertakes during academic work and (2) develop exercises that help to make the transfer easier" (p. 199). Whether such transfer actually occurs is a matter of fervent controversy. For this reason, such interventions should not form the cornerstone of a program of treatment. While they may offer utilitarian "splinter effects" (such as the enhancement of self-esteem, the development of better organizational skills, and the improvement of subskills such as left-right discrimination), these kinds of activities may or may not influence educational competence. Some of the more extreme examples of visual and/or motor training may actually be misleading and even harmful (see chapter 15).

Overall management must take into account a youngster's visual, perceptual, or spatial processing weaknesses. First, strategies that bypass the weaknesses can alleviate the strain on spatial processing. The manner in which this is done depends largely on other aspects of the child's functional profile. If the child is particularly verbal and linguistically proficient (see chapter 5), verbal mediation should be stressed. That is, the child should "talk through"—verbally label or subvocalize—while studying a spatial configuration such as a long printed word. Because the child may have difficulty with the (spatial) recognition of this word, careful phonetic analysis should be encouraged. She or he should break down the word into its component syllables and blend it. Children with spatial processing problems may be a bit slow to acquire a large sight vocabulary (see chapter 9). On the other hand, they can be taught to be excellent word analysts, especially if sequential organization and language skills are strengths. Wherever possible, convert tasks that involve processing spatial stimuli into tasks that emphasize language and sequential stimuli for these students.

Spatial awareness and processing at the rudimentary level of intake and sorting out of information may not be nearly as important as was once thought (Vellutino 1978, Levine 1984b). Therefore, intensive programs designed to enhance spatial awareness may not be justifiable. It has not been shown conclusively that the improvement of abilities in this area of developmental function is associated with significant transfer to academic areas. Hypothetically, a curriculum might be designed in which children are shown a wide range of different geometric designs and helped to sort out their various attributes. It could train them to discriminate between similar but different designs and identify identical ones. It could help them observe how various objects in space can be rotated or manipulated without losing their essential shape. Such lessons in discrimination and constancy, in fact, were among the first used in remedial programs for children with learning problems. Their lack of generally accepted efficacy has led to considerable skepticism, which raises the question, Why study spatial processing in the absence of useful therapeutic implications? However, an awareness of spatial processing and production weaknesses is useful for curriculum planning and for devising methods of helping students circumvent their deficiencies. Children who have problems with spatial utilization during the early stages of writing can be helped by employing graph paper or some other form of grid to aid in organizing the writing surface. They may need to apply their good verbal skills by describing a plan for effective use of the page. Children who have trouble distinguishing between similar visual symbols may benefit from a multisensory approach, one that stresses tracing letters, hearing and then saying them, or even feeling them (through the use of wooden cutouts). Such an approach supplies additional routes of processing to help fortify or supplement weak spatial appreciation. Awareness that a child has trouble with spatial processing can guide the selection of methods for teaching certain skills. For example, a phonetic approach to reading may be indicated. In this way, a child constantly segments and blends words rather than having to perceive them as gestalts. Children may need to break down words into their component syllables if they have difficulty assimilating an entire configuration spatially.

During the school years, children with spatial processing and production problems may require special help in reading maps, interpreting charts and diagrams, and appreciating geometric forms. In some cases, strong verbal reinforcement can help them overcome their spatial processing dysfunctions. They need to learn to describe what they see in order to retain information most effectively. Children with poor spatial awareness commonly have some difficulties visualizing words for spelling. They may require an emphasis on spelling rules, and less stress on the visual recall of spatial data. Thus, the major therapeutic implications of spatial processing problems rest in the application of various bypass strategies, the selection of curriculum materials, and the design of individualized teaching methods. In addition, the child's own awareness of spatial processing weaknesses can be helpful, as she or he can continue to seek ways to deal with this form of dysfunction if it is creating any academic disability.

Management of Sequential Processing and Production Dysfunctions

Efforts to train a child in sequential processing are likely to be of questionable efficacy. Sequencing training has not attracted the outspoken devotees that visual training has. Nevertheless, the question needs to be raised: Can and should we attempt to strengthen sequential processing when there is evidence of weakness? Although good clinical data regarding the efficacy of training in this area are lacking, my clinical experience (with its inherent limitations) suggests that one can justify a modest effort both to deal with and to work around such documented deficiencies. The following therapeutic recommendations may be helpful:

- The parents, the child, and the teacher need to be keenly aware of the child's difficulties with sequential processing. The child must realize when she is getting lost in sequences. For example, if she feels overwhelmed in class when multistep instructions are given, rather than feeling "dumb," she should say to herself, "Oh, there goes my sequencing problem again. I keep getting mixed up when they give me too many things in a row."

- Help affected students by giving them preferential seating. A teacher should be aware of when a child stops concentrating because of an inability to process and retain sequential data.

- Children with sequencing deficits require repetition, redundancy in instructions, and slow delivery of multistep directions or explanations.

- Many of these children can learn better from worksheets or visual demonstration models than from multistep verbal explanations. For example, in mathematics, a child with sequencing deficiencies may more easily learn a new algorithm (see chapter 11) by studying a correctly solved problem on paper (a spatial presentation) than by listening to the teacher's verbal explanation (a sequential account). Ideally and practically, an integration of both is desirable.

- Beginning in early elementary school, urge these students to subvocalize or use verbal mediation. That is, when they encounter a sequence, they need to talk it through or whisper it back to themselves in order to understand it and register it more firmly in memory (see chapter 3). In other words, children with sequencing deficiencies need to become master strategists when it comes to memorizing.

- Give these children specific help in mastering time concepts and experiential sequences (Lucas 1980), which include the days of the week, the months of the year, the seasons, and the use of various temporal prepositions (e.g., *before* and *after*).

- Beginning in late elementary school, help children with sequencing weaknesses by using various aids to organization. For example, give them long-term assignments and help them organize the assignments into temporal stages of accomplishment. At home, they should always have a calendar pad on their desk. Parents can help them allocate and organize time effectively. The children should determine in advance what time or by what date each stage of an assignment will be completed and then check off these deadlines as they are met. Teachers and parents should continue to reinforce systematic use of time, especially allocation and advance planning.

- Exercises to enhance sequential memory are of dubious value. However, they may increase children's *awareness* of the problem and help them acquire compensatory strategies. Therefore, it is worth at least a modest (if somewhat skeptical) effort. These children may be helped by repeating lists of words in the correct order, practicing digit spans, or retrieving visual sequences (as in the electronic game Simon). If these kinds of activities are undertaken, the children should have some mechanism for measuring their progress. At the very least it can be uplifting for a child to be able to state, "I used to only remember three things in a row. Now I remember five."

- Teachers should anticipate possible difficulties in certain areas. Children with sequential production weaknesses may have trouble organizing their writing, mastering the multiplication tables, constructing geometry proofs, and organizing in a general way throughout secondary school. Foreseeing these roadblocks can be important. It is imperative to help affected students at the earliest stages of these challenges rather than after they have failed inordinately and become disillusioned and/or unmotivated.

- Use knowledge of students' sequencing difficulties to choose curriculum methods. Unless they have particularly strong language skills, such students may be vulnerable to difficulties with word analysis skills or the ability to segment long words into phonemes (individual sound units) and then blend them. The problem comes with their incapacity to segment and recall the sequence. Such students sometimes do better with a whole-word approach to reading (sight reading). In other words, they are apt to be better able to process and retain a gestalt than a series of individual segments that must be assembled in the correct order.

- Some students with sequential production problems may require help with various fine or gross motor pursuits. The services of an occupational or physical therapist may be useful. In some cases, these children benefit from verbalizing their motor output (i.e., talking their way through the steps of motor sequential procedures).

- Musical instruments may enhance appreciation of sequential data and provide an opportunity to improve motor sequential output, although it is not known if beneficial effects will spread to academic areas.

- Students with sequential organizational problems require a heavy emphasis on study skills such as note taking, outlining, underlining, and summarizing or retelling. Approaches to these skills are discussed in chapter 15.

Helping Students Develop Strategies and Organizational Skills

Many children with dysfunctions of spatial and/or temporal-sequential ordering experience difficulty with their organizational skills. While these basic difficulties with ordering are not the only sources of disorganization, they are common culprits. The work of school is just too much work for students so affected. Children who lack organizational skills often feel utterly overwhelmed in the face of academic demands. They tend to do too many things the hard way and use few, if any, strategies to simplify and organize their work output or the learning process. Investigations have shown that children can be taught to acquire and apply strategies (Meltzer 1996). There exist a number of very useful texts to help teachers, parents, and students become aware of the repertoire of strategic approaches that are available (Hoover and Patton 1995; Lenz, Ellis, and Scanlon 1996; Sedita 1989). Adolescents, in particular, can benefit from specific training in reading strategies, techniques to improve writing, and tactics they can use to become more systematic in mathematics (Deshler et al. 1996). Following are some of the methods that can be employed to help children to acquire more organized approaches to schoolwork:

- Teach students to underline key ideas while they read. They might then reread or skim what they have underlined. A cycle of "read, underline, and summarize" must become an established practice that is integrated with writing. It can also be helpful to study with a portable dictating machine; students can record on a cassette what they have underlined (to be played back, for example, at bedtime). Students should purchase their textbooks if possible so that they can mark them up liberally. It is better for them to use a pencil than a highlighter. A pencil allows them to vary their highlighting (underline, circle, asterisk, etc.) and to write brief comments in the margins.

- Help students develop outlining ability and make it nearly automatic. They should use it for oral reporting and ultimately for writing.

- Teach rapid and selective note taking in class. Give students exercises that evaluate their note-taking ability.

- The skills involved in maintaining a neat and accessible notebook may be especially elusive to children with spatial organizational problems. They can benefit considerably from help with this.

- Give specific instructions about maintaining an assignment pad. Coordinate this instruction between home and school. Parents and teachers should review the assignment pad periodically.

- Dividing tasks into stages and allocating sufficient time are critical techniques. Students should always have a calendar pad on their desks at home. Parents should teach them how to allocate specific amounts of time to specific tasks. They should even learn to schedule appropriate breaks and leisure activities. They should have the satisfaction of checking off before bedtime what they have accomplished during a particular day or evening. They should develop a good sense of their own best time patterns for work. For example, many children with memory difficulties come to recognize that they can study best for an examination right before falling asleep (interposing no activity between their memorization and sleep).

- Teach methods of self-assessment. Teach students to reread what they have written—as if grading it from the perspective of the teacher, preparing a critique of what they have produced. Also teach them to self-test to determine if they have understood and retained what they have read.

- Teach summarizing skills. During reading, students should learn to identify main ideas as well as relevant supporting details in paragraphs. Also teach them scanning skills. For example, when using an encyclopedia to complete a report, teach students to read quickly to seek the relevant data they will require.

- Teach students to proofread their work. They should practice detecting their own errors as well as mistakes in other texts. The use of colored pencils for this can sometimes increase motivation.

- Inculcate test-taking skills. Teach students how to allocate time, how to answer easy questions first, and how to relax while taking a test.

- To enhance working capacity, give students a significant amount of homework to complete. Schools that demand little deprive their students of one of the most important contributions of education, namely, the development of working capacity. Students should be discouraged from completing all of their work in study halls, which often encourage them to work too quickly and thus to learn very little, in order to avoid taking home books. In fact, I favor abolition of study halls and much more stress on "getting one's act together" independently at home.

- Set up the "home office" effectively. This is especially critical for students with spatial ordering difficulties. If at all possible, children should *not* work in their bedrooms, which are distracting and very much associated with sleep rather than sustained attention to detail. Establish a predictable site for work at home and a quiet hour each evening for cognitive pursuits. Eliminate distraction by television, loud discussion, or other competing stimuli (with the possible exception of music as white noise). If a student has no particular homework assignments, still set aside a time each evening for productive efforts in cognitive areas. In other words, there should be no incentive to finish work early. Parents can have workbooks, crossword puzzles, or other writing activities available on nights when there is no specific assignment. Make such "evening office hours" part of the normal family routine four or five nights each week.

- Excellent coordination between home and school is essential if organizational tactics are to be effective. That is, techniques being taught at school should be reinforced at home. Methods devised by parents should fit with expectations from the school.

- Develop a scoring or rating system to give a student feedback regarding the status of improving organizational skills.

- Often children who have organizational problems have one or two parents with similar forms of disarray. It can be good for family members to work together to become more organized in time or in space.

- Avoid being overly moralistic about organizational skills (or the lack thereof); do not accuse students of being disorganized. Instead, view the issue as a mild but problematic dysfunction that needs to be worked on.

- Do not expect too much too soon. Organizational problems are often deeply entrenched, and progress may be slow.

- A little disorganization is not so bad; some of the most creative and productive people are somewhat disorganized (e.g., absentminded professors).

- In addition to learning specific strategies, teach children about their own patterns of learning and how they are affecting their work. Such self-awareness has been shown to facilitate the learning and application of good strategies (Meltzer 1996).

SPATIAL AND SEQUENTIAL ORDERING: NORMAL DEVELOPMENTAL VARIATION

Children with problems of spatial and sequential ordering, like those with other forms of dysfunction, provide some interesting clues about normal development in schoolchildren.

During the course of elementary school, children become adept at attending to, integrating, storing, and retrieving increasingly large chunks of data. Sets of stimuli and combinations of sets of stimuli confront them daily. Whether the array is spatial or sequential, normal development permits children to analyze and synthesize material containing more internal detail at a faster rate. Words become longer, and they must initially be processed deliberatively. Using word analysis techniques, the child breaks each word into its component syllables, pronounces the individual syllables, and then reads the word. Once this is accomplished (perhaps several times) the child can deal with that word as a gestalt, a part of the growing collection of sight vocabulary, although even some good readers may continue to process words as sequences of letters (Bayliss and Livesey 1985). During elementary school, children learn to absorb increasingly lengthy sequences of verbal instructions, steps and processes, and words and sentences. At the same time they become more adept at producing their own lengthy sequences— of words, of complex motor rhythms, of daily routines.

During late elementary school and secondary school, children can master not only increasingly large sequential and spatial sets of stimuli, but also increasing internal complexity. In part this is related to attention and the growing capacity to focus on multiple details (see chapter 2). However, a strong sense of internal order facilitates the process. A keen understanding of the interrelationships of the parts of a configuration enables children to focus on it more effectively. A well-developed ability to perceive what comes right before and what comes right after a particular stimulus makes it easier to interpret, store, retrieve, and apply. Throughout elementary school, students grow in the ability to handle more and more internal detail and to understand, recall, and recreate such configurations. Thus, an older child can copy a much more complex design or recall or produce patterns containing much greater spatial or sequential detail.

Finally, as children develop during the school years, they are eager to use spatial and sequential data more effectively to develop strategies, to organize, to conceptualize, and to be creative. It is in these areas, in particular, that we see the emergence in late elementary school (and sometimes earlier) of distinct *cognitive styles,* or preferences. Some children may tend to rely primarily on sequential organization to help solve problems, while others may be predisposed to use a spatial approach.

Bayliss and Livesey (1985) studied both normal and disabled readers and discovered that within both groups there were children who processed visual stimuli preferentially using a spatial (gestalt) approach and a group that leaned toward a sequential (analytic) approach. Their research involved showing children a series of pictures and determining whether they were more likely to recognize them later in the temporal order in which they had been seen or in the spatial (left to right) arrangement. These investigators concluded that a preference for either a sequential or spatial approach to processing constitutes a distinct cognitive style, a variation rather than a dysfunction. They speculated that such preferences, which emerge spontaneously in normal development, can have significant implications for teaching and learning. Students taught to read using methods incompatible with their preferences may be especially at risk. The authors note that "reading disabled children could have experienced difficulties in the early stages of reading when task demands were not congruent with a preferred cognitive style. . . ."

Thus, emergent specialization, either in sequential or spatial function, may be an important normal developmental phenomenon. Teachers and parents need to be vigilant for the possible emergence of such distinct stylistic preferences, which may have therapeutic implications if a child starts to lag in acquiring academic skills.

The development of spatial and sequential processing and production is intimately related to many other capacities in childhood. Various sections of this chapter have commented on close associations and potential confusions among sequential and spatial processing and issues of attention, language, memory, motor output, and cognition. Over time these developmental functions become increasingly integrated so that each serves to enrich processing and production in a harmonious fashion. When one developmental function is relatively weak, others are often able to compensate. A particularly close interaction occurs between spatial and sequential processing and production and language, the construct discussed in the next chapter.

Chapter 5

Language

Most of the lectures of the schoolmaster, an expounder of Quaker doctrine as well as an expounder of the three R's, went over her head; but their severity was lessened by the familiar sound of words and phrases often heard at home on her father's and mother's lips.

—Katharine Anthony, *Dolly Madison, Her Life and Times*

At the Port School, the Reverend Holmes's boy was known to the masters as a boy who (1) read stories behind his mathematics texts and (2) whispered illegally in a steady stream.

—Edward P. Holt, *The Improper Bostonian Dr. Oliver Wendell Holmes*

The vast realm of words, sentences, passages, and books is at once a barrier and a requisite for the processing and production of information. Language plays a pivotal role in academic and social settings. During childhood, linguistic sophistication emerges as a crucial developmental acquisition. Those who assimilate and accommodate new discoveries in language are far more likely to find academic satisfaction and success than are those whose language development involves tedious struggles and delayed or compromised proficiency. Interestingly, the adult world is less likely to make heavy linguistic demands of its citizens. Many worthy and remunerative occupations for adults require little, if any, sophisticated verbal competency. On the other hand, schoolchildren find it nearly impossible to evade the onslaught of complex language input and the pervasive expectation for linguistic facility.

Before describing the various features and developmental phenomenology of language, this chapter will review its protean applications. We can summarize them as follows:

- Language is a critical medium for receiving information.

- Language is a major vehicle for transmitting to others ideas, feelings, or information.

- Language is an essential element for social interaction and influence.

- Language is a prime catalyst for memory.

- Language is a valuable code for reasoning, problem solving, and creativity.

- Language facilitates thinking about thinking.

- Language serves as a means of introspection.

- Language is a tool for learning new motor skills.

This book's discussions of language will be limited to verbal modalities. Clearly there are varieties of unspoken communication, such as facial expression and body language. However, the focus here will be on the language that is most germane to school, namely, spoken and written communication, beginning with a description of some terminology and concepts that enlighten our understanding of language development and variation in schoolchildren. A review of normal and dysfunctional developmental patterns during school years follows, and the chapter concludes with a consideration of assessment and management.

THE LANGUAGE OF LANGUAGE

Professionals interested in psycholinguistics and/or speech and language pathology have developed a specialized vocabulary, which is necessary for tracking linguistic development in schoolchildren. Commonly, language processing and production are divided into components that are the dimensions along which developmental variation may occur (see also table 5-1).

Phonology refers to the sounds and sound sequences that we process and/or produce. Effective phonology (often called *phonological awareness*) consists of a keen appreciation of the distinct nature of individual sounds. *Auditory discrimination* includes the ability to discern differences between sounds or combinations of sounds. *Phonics* refers to association of sounds with specific *graphemes* (visual representations of words; see chapter 9). In common parlance, *phonetics* refers to the analysis of the common sound elements in a language. Children must have a solid appreciation for differences between language sounds as a basis for processing and producing meaningful language. Problems with auditory acuity, such as middle ear pathology, may interfere with such sensitivity. When this occurs during certain critical periods of language acquisition, long-lasting difficulties with language processing may ensue (see chapter 13).

Morphology describes the system of rules for combining *morphemes* (the smallest units of meaning) to form words or phrases. For example, the phrase *untidy bedroom* includes four morphemes: *un* (meaning "not"), *tidy* (referring to the degree of orderliness), *bed* (specifying the type of room), and *room* (identifying the type of site). They are combined according to basic (morphological) rules in our native language. Thus, the system that links these basic units is referred to as morphology, which also includes the use of various modifying prefixes and suffixes and the rules that govern their application in a particular language.

Table 5-1. Key components in the development of language

COMPONENT	DESCRIPTION
Phonology	Appreciation of individual sound units (acoustic signals) and sound sequences comprising language, as well as capacity to discriminate between sounds
Morphology	System of rules for combining units of meaning (morphemes) to convey specific ideas (including uses of prefixes and suffixes and various word roots)
Semantics	Knowledge of specific words and their meanings
Syntax	Methodology of joining words to form meaningful sentences, incorporating rules of grammar
Discourse	Language that goes beyond the boundaries of sentences (i.e., passages and paragraphs)
Pragmatics	Use of language in varied social contexts
Metalinguistic awareness	Ability to make conscious judgments about language and to use language to think about language

Semantics is the dimension in which language and meaning become tightly interwoven. It involves our knowledge of specific word meanings and shades of meanings (i.e., vocabulary) and the understanding of relationships between words (e.g., synonyms or antonyms).

Syntax refers to a system of rules for joining words to make sentences. As we shall see, for the school-age child syntactical development is extremely important. Awareness of syntax includes understanding the alterations in meaning that occur with changes of word order and with other grammatical transformations of sentence structure.

Discourse includes the capacity to organize large volumes of language that go beyond the boundaries of sentences for extended descriptive purposes, either for narrative appreciation (comprehension) or exposition (expression).

Pragmatics is the study of language use in varying contexts. It includes knowledge of the ways in which changes in social milieus alter the linguistic forms we encounter or use. Knowledge of a speaker's true intention depends on a good understanding of pragmatics, because true desires or meanings may not be revealed solely through syntax and semantics. For example, at the dinner table someone may ask, "Can you please pass the salt?" From a semantic and syntactic standpoint, the correct answer is yes. However, by understanding (through pragmatics) the true desires of the tablemate, we know that he or she is not questioning our ability to pass salt but is instead making a request for the salt. Pragmatics is aided by understanding the context in which language is used, by interpreting gestures, and by having previous experience using language in a wide range of social and academic environments.

Metalinguistic awareness is the capacity to make conscious judgments about language. Metalinguistic ability refers to the use of language to describe and think about language (Van Kleeck 1994). Through metalinguistic skill we can form judgments about the adequacy of grammar, about ambiguity in words or sentences, about metaphor, figurative language, humor, paradox, and irony. Much of metalinguistic awareness requires explicit knowledge of language—a sense of the proper structure and use of language. A child who is asked to syllabify a word mobilizes his or her conscious knowledge of word structure and applies it to the task, thus demonstrating metalinguistic awareness.

These components of language ability are graphically illustrated in figure 5-1, which displays their relevance to both expressive and receptive language functions.

Although language has been divided here into seven components for analytic purposes, everyday use of linguistics entails integrated processing and production. These components interact, fortify each other, and take precedence during particular tasks and/or stages of acquisition.

To facilitate a clearer understanding of these processes, this chapter briefly tracks their development and developmental variation during the school years. A far more thorough examination of normal language development can be found in Nelson (1996).

The next section discusses linguistic processing (i.e., comprehension), and the subsequent one considers issues of production (i.e., expression). Relationships between processing and production are unclear. It is unknown whether the ability to understand language develops simultaneously with the capacity to produce it.

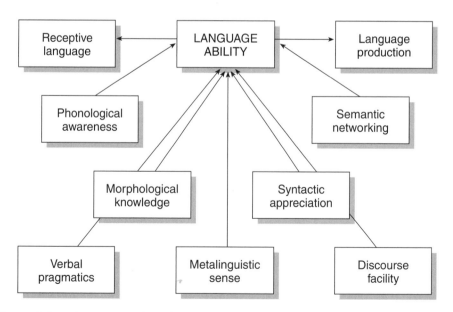

Figure 5-1.   A representation of language ability and its key components

It is likely, however, that a somewhat reciprocal relationship exists between the two; namely, expressing oneself helps the development of understanding, while experience processing language facilitates expressive abilities.

LANGUAGE PROCESSING: DEVELOPMENTAL PHENOMENOLOGY

This consideration of the language development of schoolchildren begins by delineating the evolution of expectations during school years. Young students must undergo a period of language calibration when they leave home and enter school. During the transition from elementary school to secondary school, linguistic expectations increase in both volume and complexity.

Evolving Expectations for Comprehension

At home and even in formal preschool settings, children are exposed to language that is distinct and easily differentiated from the verbal milieu of late elementary school. Parents unconsciously modify their speaking styles significantly when talking to young children. They use considerable redundancy, conscious repetition, simplification, and nonverbal gesturing along with relatively short sentences. Not only that, much of the communication system at home is tightly context bound. Language refers to daily routines; it is readily predictable; it describes mainly current situations and tends to be focused on practical needs, immediate plans, and specific visual reinforcers. Verbal communication with a child at home is often one-to-one. All of this is in direct contrast to language use in school. Teachers must talk to groups of children rather than individualizing their communication. School stresses what has been called "situated meaning" (Cook-Gumperz 1977). That is, children find that an increasing amount of meaning is coded in purely linguistic terms, and much less meaning is available in the nonverbal surrounding context. It is difficult to use context clues from immediate experience to learn about World War I or to discover how to solve quadratic equations. For these reasons, school demands from children the ability to process increasingly sophisticated, context-devoid language easily.

As concepts become complex, the structure of language must become increasingly complex. Embedded clauses, complicated phrases, and longer sentences containing more detail become the rule. Studies of teaching styles have revealed that teachers talk faster, use longer sentences, and employ more complex syntax in late elementary school than in early elementary school. In addition, children are expected to make good pragmatic judgments about their teachers' intentions.

O'Connor and Eldredge (quoted in Nelson 1984) observe that the stringent language demands that confront adolescents require "the understanding to follow the teacher's directions, to focus and derive the main ideas from the teacher's lecture, to organize and store these ideas or facts for retrieval on exams" (p. 158). Finally, there is a growing demand for ever greater metalinguistic awareness, for mastery of rules and regularities of grammar, for understanding of figurative language, and for the discernment of irony, humor, and literary tone. At the same time, much of this comprehension must be transferable from what is heard to what is read. Thus, reading comprehension becomes a major language-processing challenge, relying heavily on verbal proficiency in general.

In late elementary and secondary school, other language demands surface, including the ability to deduce from language, as exemplified by word problems in mathematics. A student's capacity to translate vocabulary and syntax into numerical processes presupposes effective comprehension skills. The ability to comprehend a foreign language is based on good linguistic skills in one's native tongue. Another dimension of change concerns the very quantity of language; the potential exists for an increasing overload of verbal information. Sustained auditory attention and concentration on language in the presence of fatigue and distraction are demanded. Furthermore, the rate of students' language processing is expected to increase to keep up with the accelerating verbal communication emanating from their teachers. Increasingly, they must listen, understand, and perform some other act (such as writing) all at the same time. Writing from dictation and taking notes are examples of the simultaneous integration of listening, comprehension, and other actions. Finally, the need to comprehend under adverse conditions includes the ability to process language within the constraints of time and sometimes heavy emotional stress. This is typified by the demands made during quizzes or examinations.

These rapidly evolving expectations are, in most cases, commensurate with the normal development of verbal processing facility in schoolchildren. However, children who are slow in meeting these expectations can experience agony, misunderstanding, and wasteful underachievement. The developmental progression of language comprehension in schoolchildren has recently been of growing interest to psycholinguists (Wiig and Semel 1984, Wallach and Butler 1984). An understanding of this progression assists us in recognizing and assessing developmental variation.

Phonological Growth.   Over time children develop an increasingly keen appreciation of the individual language sounds that comprise words. These sounds, of course, are relatively arbitrary and, unlike other aspects of language, impart no specific meanings. Thus, the processing of language sounds is a perceptual activity. Children in preschool gradually become aware that words can be divided into syllables, and later are able to recognize that syllables and words can be segmented into individual language sounds. The latter is complicated by the fact that the individual sounds within words tend to be co-articulated: they are pronounced so rapidly that they tend to flow into each other, making them exceedingly hard to distinguish (Liberman and Shankweiler 1985). For example, in the stop consonant *da,* less than 40 milliseconds pass during the transition from the *d* to the *a.* As a result, astute awareness of language sounds demands very rapid processing of acoustic signals. Such an appreciation is vital for the acquisition of skills in reading decoding and in spelling (see pp. 305–7). As they proceed through elementary school, children must not only perceive language sounds clearly, they must also be capable of manipulating these phonemes in their minds, moving them around in words, associating the sounds with graphemes (groups of written letters), and accessing them rapidly from long-term memory.

Semantic Growth. A child's vocabulary grows and diversifies during the school years. Entering kindergartners understand a surprisingly large store of words. What changes markedly is their appreciation and flexible understanding of discrete words in various contexts. Chomsky's (1969) pioneering work on the language development of this age group has demonstrated that certain words pose particular problems for kindergartners and first graders. Children as old as eight interpret verbs that indicate direction of motion (i.e., from a source to a goal) incorrectly. Thus, words such as *come, go, bring*, and *take* may be confusing. Early elementary school students are also weak at distinguishing certain "factive verbs" such as *know, think,* or *believe.* Children from six to ten years old struggle with conjunctions, including *because, if, although,* and *unless.* Older elementary schoolchildren understand with increasing effectiveness these and other words, including *less* and *more, before* and *after, ahead* and *behind,* and *brain* and *mind.* All of these have been the subjects of studies of normal language development reviewed by Palermo (1984). Children who are good linguists tend to develop a very richly woven semantic network. That is, the words that they learn are intimately connected to each other their mind's lexicon. As they learn new vocabulary, they are constantly comparing and contrasting it to words they already know. Thus the words in their vocabulary form a dense connected meshwork, which enhances the depth of their understanding as well as their facility in using words with precision. Finally, an important aspect of semantic growth occurs progressively, as students are expected to master technical vocabulary, an ever expanding collection of words that are encountered exclusively (or nearly so) in educational settings and are generally divorced from familiar contexts. These include terms such as *subtrahend, factoring, despotism,* and *iambic.*

Syntactic Growth. Perhaps the most discernible evolution in language development occurs at the level of syntax (Menyuk 1977) and the production and interpretation of increasingly complex sentences (Scott 1988). This has been studied extensively in school-age children, and Wallach (1984) has characterized it well. She reviewed research on the strategies that children must learn and unlearn as they become increasingly sophisticated in their comprehension of sentences. Two major changes occur in 1) the ability to understand sentences that "violate canonical order"; and 2) in the ability to understand clausal relationships within sentences. Wallach's observations about these two phenomena are described below.

The canonical order strategy. Preschool children are inclined to assume that in sentences with a noun-verb-noun sequence, the first noun is the actor and the second noun is the recipient of the action. *The dog ran after the cat* illustrates canonical order, while *The black dog was chased by the red fox* reverses canonical order. During the toddler years (usually between ages two and three), children can compensate for this preference by "second guessing"; their knowledge of semantics and their sense of probable events help them. For example, although the sentence *The dog was walked by my brother* violates canonical order, it may be interpreted correctly because four year olds are aware that dogs do not walk brothers and so are able to overrule their faith that word order follows the actor-action-recipient regularity. For some kinds of sentences, however, such "second guessing" simply does not work. For example, *The boy was hit by his sister* does not allow for a probable events strategy, since it is equally likely that the sister would strike the boy or that the boy would strike his sister.

Children pass through stages during which they tend to overuse certain linguistic strategies. Thus, during the late preschool years, overuse of canonical order strategies can lead to misinterpretation. As students come to appreciate the subtleties of syntax, they overcome the simplistic canonical order rule and deal with passive forms. This is symptomatic of their growing realization of the relevance of syntax during early elementary school. Another significant element of this development is the use of various clausal strategies.

Clausal strategies. Children first begin to learn that sentences have clauses between the ages of about four and five. Initially, they employ what is called the "order-of-mention" strategy. Under this perceived regulation, they assume that the order in which they hear things in a sentence represents the actual order of events. The sentence *Get a glass of milk before you feed the cat* fulfills this prediction. However, sentences using the word *after* contradict this (as in *Feed the dog after you have a glass of milk*). Four-year-old children tend to follow word order, oblivious to linguistic variations or use of clauses.

Five year olds have a tendency to act out the main clause only. In other words, in the second sentence they may never get to have any milk. Again, sentences in which context is helpful or those that are quite familiar are easier and are acquired sooner. Thus, a sentence such as *The boy eats supper after he washes his hands* is more likely to be mastered. Logical or contextual cues can facilitate surmounting the limitations of primitive sentence processing. Even six year olds who understand the individual vocabulary words *before* and *after* are known to have difficulty processing them when they appear in sentences with subordinate clauses.

During elementary school, strategies and demands are modified. Children are expected to become increasingly proficient with various types of clausal sentences. They become adept at interpreting relative clauses in sentences. Initially, children employ what is called a "parallel function" strategy, which refers to the role of a modified noun within a complex sentence. In a single complex sentence, the noun may be the actor in both clauses. Thus, in the sentence *The girl who borrowed the book walked home from school, girl* has a parallel function. It names the actor both in the independent clause (the one who walks home) and also in the relative clause (the one who borrowed the book). Similarly, the same noun can be the object in both parts of the sentence, as in *The teacher saw the girl who was chased by the dog*. In this example, *girl* is the object of two processes in the same sentence. She was seen by the teacher and chased by the dog—she is the recipient of two actions.

Processing embedded clauses is another key developmental acquisition. In the sentence *The girl who borrowed the book walked home from school,* the clause *who borrowed the book* is embedded. That is, the relative clause interrupts the action of the main clause.

Studies have shown that the processing of parallel functions improves steadily. This is particularly true for "subject relatives," those sentences in which the embedded or nonembedded clause refers to the subject rather than the object (e.g., *The girl who was with the man rode a bicycle*). As we shall see, youngsters with language-related learning problems may be particularly delayed in processing such sentences (see pp. 155–56).

In clausal sentences, such as the examples cited above, it is obviously essential to focus attention on the main clause and then to differentiate it from its subordinate clause. This requires, at least initially, keen attention to detail as well as linguistic skill.

Pronominal Growth. The use of pronouns is another important acquisition during school years. As children gain language experience, they become increasingly adept at identifying precisely who or what a pronoun is substituting for. Chomsky (1969) found that five year olds almost invariably assume that a noun and a pronoun always refer to the same individual regardless of where the pronoun appears in the sentence. For example, in the sentence *Stephen knew he would climb the tree,* a kindergartner lacks awareness of the ambiguity of *he* and is likely to believe that it can only mean that Stephen will be climbing the tree. During early elementary school, children become better at drawing inferences and are less likely to engage in "literal translation" of sentences. Such inferences also allow them to employ pronouns with greater versatility.

Minimal Distance Principle. Chomsky points out that children in preschool and early elementary grades tend to believe in the "minimal distance principle"— that the noun closest to an infinitive must be the subject of that infinitive. Thus, in the sentence *John told Bill to leave,* it is clear that Bill is the one who must do the leaving. The word *promise,* however, causes confusion. In the sentence *Mary promised Jane to buy the candy,* it is Mary who will do the buying. The same kinds of complications occur in sentences with verbs such as *ask* and *tell.* Five-year-old listeners misunderstand these sentences because of their rigid adherence to the minimal distance principle, whereas six to nine year olds gradually learn to violate their faith in it.

The kinds of language processing acquisitions described above emphasize the importance of growing flexibility of semantics and syntactical processing as major landmarks in the development of receptive language ability in school-age children. Certain other elements are also important in the growth of language development.

Drawing Inferences.   During elementary and secondary school, children improve markedly in their ability to draw inferences from language. They become more effective at using context and prior experience to interpret sentences and passages. This facility undergoes striking improvement by age ten or eleven. In one experiment (Paris and Lindauer 1976), children were read series of sentences, some containing explicit language and others omitting important data. Later they were asked to recall the sentences and were given a cue for each. In some instances, the cue contained a word that was in the sentence; while in others, it referred tangentially to something used in the sentence but not mentioned. For example, to help recall the sentence *Her friend swept the kitchen floor,* children were given the clue *broom.* Older elementary school students were able to recall sentences with such implicit clues. Younger children had difficulty with implied content and required actual words from the sentence to trigger recall. As they enter adolescence, students need to engage in higher-order processing of sentences. Challenges include the ability to supply missing information in sentences (inference drawing), the capacity to deal with abstraction, symbolization, and metaphors within sentences, and the ability to resolve ambiguity within sentences.

Pragmatic Growth.   During the elementary school years, children become increasingly adept at understanding language in its social context. Pragmatic language develops steadily, and children become more aware of the importance of social contexts in altering the meaning of sentences. They tune in to variations that convey a speaker's point of view, age, or perspective. This plays a central role in the social development of schoolchildren (see chapter 8).

Metalinguistic Growth.   Schoolchildren become increasingly capable of thinking about language as their metalinguistic skills expand (Van Kleeck 1984). Such growth influences all other aspects of linguistic development (i.e., phonology, semantics, syntactics, and pragmatics). By reflecting on any of these aspects, children can add another dimension to language ability. At an early phonological level, schoolchildren become increasingly adept at taking apart and putting together phonemes, which constitute the smallest units of meaning. Sound blending subtests included in several assessment instruments (see appendix) exemplify this skill. On this task, words are presented, broken into their component parts, and children reassemble them. This entails keen awareness of the elemental sound units.

On a semantic level, children become able to think about words and their meanings. They can increasingly distinguish between easy words, tricky words, and difficult words. As children move toward secondary school, their ability to appreciate ambiguity in words grows considerably, enabling them to understand riddles and language-oriented jokes. They become increasingly aware of synonyms and antonyms.

The use of figurative language—metaphor, simile, analogy, proverbs, and personification—is especially important in the development of metalinguistic skills. Flexible understanding of figurative language does not usually come into full display until adolescence. At this time, students become able to appreciate metaphors, proverbs, and other such constructions. This brings with it new forms of humor. Furthermore, it aids the understanding of irony and the appreciation of symbolism, particularly important literary devices used in prose and poetry.

Another aspect of metalinguistic awareness concerns children's growing abilities to detect errors in their own speech or that of others. Good metalinguistic awareness allows children to determine whether something "sounds right." There is considerable variation in this particular propensity.

The major acquisitions of language processing during the school years are:

- Moderate growth in vocabulary

- Greater understanding of words in varied contexts

- Better interpretation of morphology (e.g., word endings)

- Increased capacity to understand complex syntax (e.g., alterations of word order or embedded clauses) and literate language

- Emergence and enhancement of the ability to think about language (e.g., metalinguistic awareness)

- Better and more sustained capacity for listening (improved rate of language processing)

- Enhanced reading comprehension

- Greater understanding of figurative and abstract language

- Increased ability to discern meaning and saliency in spoken discourse and written text

LANGUAGE PROCESSING: DEVELOPMENTAL VARIATION AND DYSFUNCTION

Language disabilities in children are some of the most common impediments to learning and fulfillment during school years (Johnson and Myklebust 1967, Wiig and Semel 1984). The linguistically deficient child is at a disadvantage in the classroom as well as on the playground. Because of the fundamental and cumulative relevance of language, delays become increasingly pronounced as children age. Defective or lagging language processing can produce secondary effects that compromise attention, memory, socialization, self-esteem, affect, and behavior. It is not unusual for some of these phenomena to be mistaken for the primary cause of a child's dysfunction when, in reality, deficiencies of language are at the core of a frustrated learner's plight.

Recent research has enabled diagnosticians to become more specific about the nature of a child's language-processing deficiencies. Vague terms such as *central auditory processing problem* sound sophisticated but tend to be unhelpful. An empirical approach demands direct observation and description of the kinds of difficulties an individual has in interpreting linguistic inputs or production.

COMPONENTS OF LANGUAGE DYSFUNCTION

This section describes various dysfunctions of receptive language, which are summarized in table 5-2. Children who are having difficulty processing linguistic information are likely to have combinations of the dysfunctions outlined below.

Weak Verbal Attention

The capacity to listen selectively is essential for language processing. Some children have considerable difficulty focusing on verbal detail. In some instances,

Table 5-2. Language processing: common neurodevelopmental dysfunctions

DYSFUNCTION	DESCRIPTION
Weak verbal attention	Poor listening skills; fatigue and distractibility in highly verbal settings
Weak verbal memory	Possible weaknesses of word memory (vocabulary/retrieval), sentence and passage recall, semantic coding in memory, verbal sequential recall, and memory for language rules
Phonological gaps	Problems with discrimination, phonological awareness and manipulation, sound-symbol association (for reading and spelling), and foreign languages
Morphological and semantic dysfunctions	Reduced vocabulary, impoverished word meanings, sparse semantic network, poor reading comprehension, and trouble with word problems in mathematics
Syntactic weaknesses	Poor sentence comprehension; difficulty interpreting word order and grammar
Pragmatic problems	Trouble discerning speakers' true meanings or intentions in social contexts, possible social failure, overly literal interpretation
Poor metalinguistics	Varies with age: early trouble with sound segmentation awareness and blending; later difficulties with figurative language, ambiguity, irony, and paradox
Weaknesses of verbal reasoning	Difficulty reasoning with language; deficient verbal problem-solving skills

their attention controls are weakest in the auditory language domain. In other cases, a child's attention deficit encompasses all channels of processing.

Verbal attention may be the most motorically passive of all attention processes. Requirements for sustained listening are far more stringent and frequent (especially in school) than requirements for sustained (nonlinguistic) watching. Some youngsters have agonizing difficulties with such extended passive listening. In some instances, they are better at listening if they can also be doing something else simultaneously. We might argue, in fact, that the prolonged listening demanded in many school-related settings is unique, thereby placing excessive strain on verbal attention. As with other forms of attention deficit, it is always important to determine whether weaknesses of verbal attention are limited to the language sphere, are part of a broader picture of attention dysfunction, or are secondary to weak processing of language (Berlin, Blank, and Rose 1980).

Weak Verbal Memory

Although children are sometimes said to have deficiencies of "auditory memory," such a description is too vague to be useful. Instead we must ask if weaknesses of verbal memory exist as independent "disabilities," or if they are linked to problems with attention or to gaps in language processing. The following descriptions of some types of verbal memory weakness can help develop an overall picture of a child with language deficiencies.

Poor Memory for Words. This might include difficulties recalling not only specific vocabulary that has already been learned but also synonyms, antonyms, and definitions, as well as related problems of forming rich associations between words. In other words, there may be some weaknesses of associative memory for pairs of words.

Sentence and Passage Memory. Some children may have difficulty recalling whole sentences, making it virtually impossible to infer sufficient meaning from sentence structure. Because of difficulty repeating sentences in their entirety, they may have trouble taking sentence repetition tests or writing from dictation. In most cases, a child who has difficulty recalling sentences may also have some problems interpreting them. Further, confusion over grammar and syntax can make it difficult to store and retrieve complete sentences. Recall of passages may be impaired by poor comprehension, short-term memory weaknesses, generalized language delay, or organizational problems (Brown 1976).

Poor Semantic Encoding. Semantic memory is a process that codes knowledge in an abstract form, independent of the format of input (Wickelgren 1979). Virtually all manner of information—verbal, visual, spatial, and other data formats—may (or perhaps must) be coded semantically. Some children, though, have special problems with coding linguistic information (Miller 1984). They may be very good at recalling visual imagery but have significant weaknesses with the semantic encoding of language, a problem sometimes associated with general memory difficulties.

Verbal Sequential Memory Deficiency. Some students have difficulty processing and recalling multistep verbal information. In particular, they have trouble preserving its serial order (see chapter 4), and their mistakes involve transpositions of sequence. Language coded in a distinct temporal order is hard for them to store and retrieve. A poor score on the Digit Span of the *WISC-III* is not sufficient evidence that a child has problems with verbal sequential memory. Poor performance on a digit span can be a manifestation of other kinds of difficulties, including attention deficits, anxiety, and more deficiencies of short-term memory. It is important to determine whether a child's apparent difficulties with verbal sequential memory are part of a broader picture of language disability or of trouble with temporal-sequential ordering (see chapter 4) or part of a more generalized weakness of short-term memory or attention control.

Weak Recall of Rules. Some children may have particular problems recalling or recognizing rules of grammar. Processing a sentence ordinarily requires comparing it to previously stored correct structures. An inability to do so may be a form of verbal memory weakness; however, it may also reflect relative deficiencies of metalinguistic awareness (see p. 157).

The forms of verbal memory difficulty described above are unlikely to exist in isolation. A suspected verbal memory weakness in a child should be investigated thoroughly since this kind of deficiency does not usually exist in isolation. It is much more likely to be part of a broader language disability, deficit of sequential organization, or problem along the dimension of attention and retention.

Inadequate Phonological Awareness

At the phonological level, language is the transformation of heard sounds into the phonetic constituents of a particular language. In other words, we know that certain sounds, either singly or in combination with others, constitute familiar components of the English language. We are able to distinguish them from sounds whose phonetic features are not part of the native tongue, including utterances that might be familiar in another language as well as those sounds (such as a door slamming) that are nonlinguistic in any language. A phonological dysfunction is a disruption in this process. Children who have this kind of deficit endure considerable stress in attempting to extract from a stream of speech those features that are true phonemic entities. They may be able to discern some features of a word but not all of them. For example, they may mistake the word *sisters* for *scissors* because they process only the first and last phonemes.

In addition, some children have problems distinguishing between similar-sounding phonemes. Thus, they are apt to mistake *bald* for *bold*. This is often referred to as a "breakdown in auditory discrimination." Young children with this problem are simply not able to make clear distinctions between similar-sounding utterances. Still other children have trouble with the sequential organization of phonemes, making it hard for them to discern sequences of sounds within words. Affected students may have particular problems when they are required to decode multisyllabic words, and their reading styles may reflect these weaknesses. The result is deficient word analysis skills (see chapter 9). Some auditory discrimination deficiencies are tied to overall lags in metalinguistic awareness (Van Kleeck 1984). They may also reflect generally poor appreciation of the phonology of language (Liberman 1985).

There are also indications that many children with language impairments have reduced capacity to contain language sounds in active working memory (Montgomery 1995). As a result, it may be hard for them to sustain individual phonemes in active working memory long enough to perceive a whole word and consult long-term memory to derive its meaning. Such an impediment can disrupt the critical linkage of language sound processing to semantics.

Recently, there has been considerable research into the mechanisms underlying reduced phonological awareness in young children. The work of Paula Tallal has received considerable attention. Dr. Tallal and her colleagues have conducted a series of investigations demonstrating that many children with language-based learning difficulties exhibit a *rapid auditory processing deficit;* that is, they have trouble processing fast enough the acoustic signals within a language sound (Tallal et al. 1985) Their problems are accentuated when they are confronted with those language sounds in which the transitions between the signals occur most rapidly. Most notably, the consonant-vowel pairs (*ba/da/la/pa*) often elude them, as the transition times are extremely brief (about 40 milliseconds to go from the *p* to the *a* in *pa*). These children are prone to language comprehension problems, for which they may be able to compensate, especially if other aspects of language (e.g., semantics and syntactical processing) are relatively strong. Such students may show other signs of slow processing of successive signals, even in nonauditory pathways. The academic significance of such nonauditory slow processing is not clear at this point.

Because children who have problems with the phonological aspects of receptive language may be slow to acquire a sense of sound-symbol association, phonetic analysis may be hard for them. Because they have a tenuous grasp of language sounds, it is difficult for them to form rich associations between units of sound and their graphemes, resulting in possible delays in reading. Their spelling may also reflect poorly assimilated phonological knowledge. Words may approximate good spelling in terms of visual configurations but be phonetically impossible in English (see chapter 10). Such children may spell the word *light l-e-g-h-t* or *elephant e-l-g-h-a-r-l*.

Children with poor phonological sense may be predisposed to difficulties learning foreign languages (see chapter 12). Those children with relatively mild weaknesses do not exhibit much difficulty with English (since they are so overexposed to their native tongue), but their mastery of a new language may be seriously impaired by significant difficulties appreciating distinctions between similar sounds or extracting the salient features of long words.

Segmentation Deficits

Often children with reading and spelling impairments appear to lack a very basic awareness that the syllables within words can be segmented into individual, somewhat overlapping sounds (i.e., phonemes). This sense of word segmentation simply eludes many students with deficient phonological awareness. They fail to discern and make use of the stable whole:part interactions that prevail within syllables and words. As a result, the decoding of words becomes an arduous task. In some cases, the problems are associated with poor processing of the individual language sounds, while in others there exists a basic deficiency of segmentation and whole:part relationships that may pervade other areas of learning (such as mathematics).

Semantic and Morphological Dysfunctions

Semantic dysfunctions consist primarily of deficiencies of vocabulary. Johnson and Myklebust (1967) suggested that youngsters with "learning disabilities" knew fewer words, retained restricted meanings of these words, and were too concrete and literal in their symbolization and conceptualization skills. Such deficits of word knowledge may persist into adolescence, when they continue to impair verbal as well as reading comprehension. Students may have increasing difficulty dealing with words that have multiple meanings and with content areas that demand a rapid growth in vocabulary. Certain science courses, foreign languages, and technical subjects may create problems for such students, who may also encounter difficulties with mathematics. Typically, their greatest deficiencies are likely to be with word problems. Because they are limited in their ability to use words flexibly, it may be hard for them to convert a specific word or sentence into a series of mathematical symbols and/or operations. Their capacity to solve word problems and their ability to engage in more direct computational processes may vary widely.

Morphological problems are also common (Wiig, Semel, and Crouse 1973). Affected youngsters may have trouble understanding tenses, plurals, and possessive forms, especially during early elementary school.

Syntactic Weaknesses

The discussion of the normal development of receptive language earlier in this chapter pointed out that some of the major gains for the school-age child occur in the acquisition of syntactical sophistication. Not surprisingly, some of the most troublesome difficulties experienced by children with language-related learning dysfunctions occur in the processing of complex syntax (Wiig and Semel 1984; Liles, Schulman, and Bartlett 1977). Many recent studies have confirmed this phenomenon. Children with such learning problems are apt to experience substantial delays in the acquisition of syntactical abilities. Thus, they have trouble understanding that word order affects the meaning of a sentence. They can have significant difficulties recognizing how a subordinate clause in a sentence relates to and modifies the main one. In general, children with language-related learning problems seem to encounter difficulty with linguistic complexity. They have trouble using the grammatical features of a sentence to extract meaning. Instead, they are likely to rely too heavily on the context in which the sentence is heard, on key words (i.e., semantics rather than syntax), and on their own predictions or expectations from prior experience. This is akin to the processing of preschool children (see p. 144). Interestingly, such a method of interpreting sentences is likely to be quite effective at home, where there is considerable redundancy, predictability, and a tendency for words and sentences to be embedded in the contexts of immediate experience (such as occurs at meals when we are asked to pass the salt and pepper).

As part of their difficulty dealing with linguistic complexity, children with language-related learning problems characteristically become confused over specific types of sentences. One example may be sufficient to demonstrate this. In a study by Wallach (described in Wallach and Butler 1984), children between about eight and fourteen years were assessed on their comprehension of complex sentences. The sample included subjects with appropriate learning and those with learning dysfunctions. Normal subjects had very little difficulty understanding these sentences although they did better when clauses were not embedded. However, subjects with learning dysfunctions had significant problems, especially when nouns did not observe parallel function (e.g., in the sentence *Jim finished his science, which is his favorite subject,* the word *science* is the object of the first clause and the subject of the second one). These children's overreliance on semantic and contextual cues resulted in considerable inaccuracy. They were also especially confused by embedded clauses. When parallel function was observed (especially with subject relatives) and they could use a parallel function strategy (see pp. 147–48), they were most effective.

Problems with Pragmatics

The difficulty detecting pragmatic cues that children with language-related learning problems experience may result in a kind of rigidity of language processing. Affected children may be overly literal in interpretations (Wiig and Semel 1984) because of trouble comprehending speakers' intentions. This results in difficulties understanding in the classroom, at home, and, perhaps most important, in social situations. Problems with pragmatics become an important concomitant of social failure (see chapter 8) and may impair reading comprehension as well, especially during middle and high school.

Reduced Metalinguistic Awareness

Many children with language difficulties have poor metalinguistic awareness, a significant component of development. They remain superficial and reactive in their language processing and have trouble penetrating beneath the verbal surface or perceiving linguistic regularities and irregularities. These difficulties can occur on the level of phonology, syntax, semantics, or even pragmatics. Wiig and Semel's (1984) text on language disabilities notes that affected children have trouble interpreting ambiguous sentences, idioms, puns, metaphors, and words with multiple meanings. They fare poorly with synonyms, verbal opposites, and verbal analogies. Their comprehension may be impaired insofar as they do not perceive any consistent systems in sentence construction or in language in general.

Children lacking metalinguistic awareness may also have trouble assessing what sounds right in their native tongue (Liles, Schulman, and Bartlett 1977). It may be hard for them to detect errors in the speech of others or to decide what is good English and what is not. Poor metalinguistic awareness may even relate to difficulty monitoring their own speech or writing (see pp. 167–68 and 362).

Weaknesses of Verbal Reasoning

Many children with receptive language difficulties have weak verbal reasoning ability. It is hard for them to apply logic or problem-solving strategies that are predominantly verbal. They may be skilled at nonverbal reasoning, but have trouble conceptualizing verbal systems of classification or categorization. They may be better at solving problems without the interposition of linguistic strategies. The next chapter describes such phenomena in some detail.

Systematic Interrelationships

The eight components of language dysfunction elucidated here and summarized in table 5-2 do not ordinarily present themselves as distinct gaps. Children exhibiting a breakdown in receptive language processing are apt to endure difficulties in several or all of these areas. Nevertheless, in assessing and planning therapeutic programs, it is useful to test and inquire about these specific functions.

LANGUAGE PRODUCTION: DEVELOPMENTAL PHENOMENOLOGY

Verbal expression is a valuable facilitator—for social interaction, for affective expression or release, for informing others, and for problem solving (i.e., thinking out loud). Schoolchildren display remarkable growth in language production. Their knowledge of linguistics becomes as important for production as it is for processing. They are able to apply what they have learned about phonology, semantics, syntactics, pragmatics, and metalinguistics to enhance their own communication skills. Although the two systems clearly are intimately related, the rate or quality of development between processing and production is not necessarily parallel. This discussion traces three themes in normal language development during school years: word usage, sentence formulation, and narrative skill (see table 5-3).

Word Usage

Children's skills in morphology (see p. 141) grow considerably during school years. R. Brown (1973) listened to spontaneous speech samples of children and observed that their acquisition of specific morphemes progressed fairly regularly through preschool and early elementary years. Production applications such as present progressives (e.g., *going*), prepositions (e.g., *in* and *on*), regular plurals, irregular past tenses, possessives, and articles fall into place in a predictable chronological sequence. Knowledge of general and specific morphological rules becomes well differentiated over the years. Through elementary school and into adolescence, a child becomes increasingly adept at manipulating highly specific word endings, prefixes, and suffixes to meet more stringent demands for acceptable, meaningful communication.

The ability to find words quickly and easily on demand is another theme in language development. "Language formulation and production must often occur under imposed semantic, linguistic, or social restrictions. Only one word may satisfy the semantic restrictions imposed by a given context" (Wiig and Semel 1984). Such word finding is often described as a requirement for *convergent production ability,* or the capacity to be specific about word choice in a particular context. This capacity is essential for the kinds of responsiveness demanded on classroom quizzes and during formal discussions. When a child is asked to name a particular picture or find the opposite of a specific word, convergent language produc-

Table 5-3. Language production: Acquisitions in three major areas during the school years

AREA	COMPONENTS
Word usage	Increasingly versatile and flexible use of words; enhanced word retrieval; larger active vocabulary; use of abstract and technical (decontextualized) words
Sentence formulation	Deployment of sophisticated syntax; increased overall sentence fluency; greater use of figurative language
Narrative and expository skill	Greater ability to report events in an orderly fashion; better organized discourse; more effective verbal elaboration and creativity

tion is called into play. There is often only one correct answer. This necessitates effective (and often fast) retrieval from long-term memory. Such convergent semantic production ability continues to develop well into adolescence (Guillford 1967) and is tapped by many tests of intelligence and psycholinguistic ability.

Another important event in normal development of school-age children is their acquisition of an active vocabulary. Although a child in the early elementary grades may understand many words, the capacity to use such words effectively, flexibly, and fluently on demand grows significantly well into adolescence. This growth in active vocabulary is quite conspicuous, providing considerably more flexibility for communication.

Formulation of Sentences

Virtually all of the characteristics of acquisition related to the normal development of appreciation of syntax described earlier in this chapter (see pp. 146–48) likewise pertain to the formulation of one's own sentences. As children develop their understanding of rules and regularities of syntax, they are better able to use them for their own production. Effective use of conjunctions, subordinate clauses, and pronouns, leading to the synthesis of increasingly complex sentences, typifies development during school years, enabling children to express sophisticated concepts.

Narrative and Expository Skill

Narrative skills are those abilities that allow for the understanding and exchange of event-structured material (Feagans 1983). One of the major developments in expressive language is the improvement in narrative abilities for storytelling and summarization. In this progression, narrative structures become more tightly controlled, evolving from a collection of events related to each other only by their proximity in time or space; to stories that have a physical or psychological center (that is, a central character or theme); to stories that have a chain of events in temporal or cause-effect sequences; to highly structured narratives in which the events are linked structurally both to a common center or theme and to other events which immediately precede and follow in cause-effect and true temporal relationships (Westby 1984, p. 115).

In other words, children's narrative development progresses from narratives in which children talk about whatever happens to be on their mind with no particular structure or sequence, to increasingly cohesive narratives in which there are elements such as central themes and causal events. As narrative increases in complexity, it includes sections that represent a state of equilibrium or resolution, sections that constitute transitional modes, and others that constitute states of disequilibrium (or presentations of conflict). A child's narrative ability is influenced by memory, cognition, culture, and overall linguistic skill. Narrative ability also forms the basis for increasingly structured written output.

Narrative skill may reflect children's *divergent* (as opposed to convergent) language abilities or "the fluency, flexibility, originality, and elaborations with which language is produced" (Wiig and Semel 1984). Elaborative language is also associated with the growth of verbal creativity as well as overall conceptual ability and the capacity to retrieve rich associative data from memory.

Children develop expository structure parallel with narrative ones. They are able to form detailed explanations and opinions through language with increasing effectiveness. Expository skill is more demanding than narrative skill and develops somewhat later. Furthermore, although the basic rules of language governing semantics and syntax apply to both, there are significant differences which place imposing demands on children's metalinguistic knowledge, language facility and precision, planning skills, content knowledge, higher-order cognition, and convergent retrieval memory. Differences between narrative and expository expression include content abstraction, text structure, grammatic constructions, and semantic precision.

Narratives most generally relate events and emotions that are personally familiar. Thus they demand less convergent retrieval of highly specific, abstract information. In contrast, expository prose, oral and written, is more commonly used to convey specific information and ideational relationships which are often abstract and about which the audience may have little prior knowledge. This requires the child to have sound understanding of the information he wishes to convey, a well-developed semantic network and knowledge of relevant vocabulary, and rapid and precise word retrieval. Vagary and egocentric use of word meanings and implicitness of expression, which lend creativity and color to narratives, have little place in exposition.

Expository discourse also depends on the construction and expression of meaning without the support of familiar story grammar and plot structure. Instead, different text structures are required to express varying expository intents (relay of information, explanation, argument and persuasion, and evaluation) and to express differing ideational relationships (definition-examples, compare-contrast, temporal sequence, procedural sequence, order of priority, and cause-effect). The child must first form a clear purpose for what she wishes to express and then select the text structure that will most effectively present her ideas and meet her intent. This requires previewing and preplanning skills and the ability to foresee the whole before beginning.

Expository text structures frequently are less explicit than plot structure, and children require specific instruction in their recognition and utilization. Furthermore, each text structure involves characteristic semantic and syntactic patterns which govern word selection, usage, morphology, and grammatic constructions. Examples include transition words, pronoun reference, verb tense, and conjunctions. Appropriate use requires a sound understanding of grammar and the effects of word order.

Thus, skill in expository expression does not necessarily follow from narrative ability and necessitates specific evaluation and management.

The various aspects of language production just outlined become important linguistic acquisitions during school years. Breakdowns in these processes can be costly from the standpoint of academic accomplishment, self-esteem, and social effectiveness.

BRAIN LOCATIONS FOR LANGUAGE

The neuroanatomy of language has been studied extensively for many years. Researchers have observed many patients with various forms of aphasia, often following a stroke. Such clinical studies, along with more sophisticated neuro-imaging and neuropsychological investigations, have shed light on the neuroanatomy of language.

The most fundamental notion is that about 95 percent of individuals reveal left hemispheres that are dominant for language. In fact, a great deal of research has focused on the possibility that left hemisphere lesions or underdevelopment account for most language disorders in childhood. Some have speculated that certain individuals may have left hemispheres that are doing too much spatial processing or right hemispheres that are taking on too much of the language burden (so-called incomplete dominance). According to Pirozzolo et al. (1983) affected individuals "suffer from pathologically slow transmission of linguistic information within the left hemisphere."

There has been a sustained interest in the parts of the left hemisphere that are especially germane to the acquisition of reading skills. Several investigators have implicated a part of the left temporal region known as the *temporal planum*. In normal readers, this area has been found to be larger in the left than in the right hemisphere. In several studies, such inequality has not been discerned among children with reading difficulties (Tallal et al. 1991).

Much of the future work on the neuroanatomy of language needs to pass beyond the localization of specific functions and examine carefully language's anatomical connections to other systems, including attention, memory, motor function, and higher-order cognition.

LANGUAGE PRODUCTION: DEVELOPMENTAL VARIATION AND DYSFUNCTION

Although there are many ways to classify the various dysfunctions of language production in schoolchildren, we will limit our discussion to seven categories of dysfunction, which are summarized in table 5-4. Like dysfunctions of receptive

Table 5-4. Language production: Common developmental dysfunctions

DYSFUNCTION	DESCRIPTION
Oral motor problems	Poor articulation, sound sequencing, or other difficulties with the motor aspects of vocalization
Dysfunctions of word retrieval (dysphasia or dysnomia)	Slow, vague, or inaccurate word finding
Morphological problems	Weak sense of the meaningful structure of words, possibly interfering with vocabulary acquisition
Syntactical deficiencies	Inconsistent or inadequate application of rules of grammar, tense, and word order
Deficiencies of verbal pragmatics	Trouble using language appropriate to the social context: inability to take the perspective of the listener
Discourse weaknesses	Difficulty producing extended language orally and/or in writing: problems starting, ordering, emphasizing, and developing concluding thoughts
Poor metalinguistic awareness	Lack of awareness of how one sounds: inability to detect and correct one's language

language, these should not be viewed as discrete; in fact, the dysfunction of affected children is likely to fall into more than one of these categories. The categories, therefore, provide a means of description and a basis for assessment and treatment.

Oral Motor Problems

Dysfunctions in motor production of articulated sound may or may not be associated with other language deficiencies, which include resonance deficits, specific voice dysfunctions, fluency problems, and articulation difficulties (Levine, Brooks, and Shonkoff 1980).

Deficits of resonance—abnormal oral-nasal sound balances—most commonly manifest themselves as hypernasality or hyponasality which can have a disconcerting impact on communication. Voice dysfunctions—deviations in the quality, pitch, or loudness of vocalizations—may have either a psychological or physiological basis. Difficulties with fluency—disruptions in the natural flow of connected speech—are most commonly encountered as stuttering, which can have multiple causes and manifestations. It may consist of pauses, repetitions of sounds, constant revisions of sentences, lapses in responding, and prolongations of sounds. Most stuttering children are identified between the third and fourth years of life. Sometimes, however, the condition may make its initial appearance later—with the first school experience or as a student approaches adolescence.

Articulation problems are the most common speech dysfunctions in childhood. Affected children have trouble with the *praxis,* or motor implementation, of certain speech sounds. They commit a wide range of errors that can be classified into three basic subtypes: *substitutions,* replacements of one sound with another (*wight* for *light*); *omissions,* failure to produce certain speech sounds at all (*boo* for *book*); and *distortions,* inappropriate sounds that replace the correct ones (*chlain* for *train*). The number of consonants and vowels that are misarticulated vary widely. A child's errors can range from only a few, minor misarticulated sounds to speech that is barely intelligible. Poor articulation may be caused by anatomical abnormalities within the oral cavity, including dental irregularities or abnormal shape or structure of the hard palate. Paralysis or weakness of the tongue can also affect this aspect of speech production. Occasionally, poor articulation is a manifestation of hearing loss. Environmental factors and psychological stresses can also predispose children to poor speech production.

A variant of articulation difficulty consists of problems with sound sequencing. Some children have problems constructing the proper order of phonemes to form an articulated multisyllabic word. This may be part of a broader difficulty with motor sequencing and sequential ordering in general (see chapter 4) or it may be an isolated finding.

Dysfunctions of Word Retrieval

Children with various learning dysfunctions commonly exhibit deficient vocabulary throughout their school years. Wiig and Semel (1975) compared teenage subjects with learning problems to their achieving peers. Both groups were asked to name verbal opposites, name pictures or objects, name members of certain semantic categories (i.e., as many foods, animals, or toys as possible), and define specific words. They found that one group of adolescents with learning problems was significantly slower and less accurate in recalling verbal opposites. In addition, it was hard for them to define words and name items within a particular semantic category. When they tried to recall words within a category, they seemed to lack systematic, consistent, or effective retrieval strategies (see pp. 158–59).

Denckla and Rudel (1976) compared good and poor readers between the ages of seven and twelve on a rapid automatic naming test. The groups differed in both accuracy and speed. The poor readers made many more errors and took much longer to name common objects, letters, colors, and numbers as they were presented visually, suggesting the presence of significant problems with retrieval of words. The naming of visual images is closely related to oral reading, an act in which visual symbols are in fact named.

Therefore, it is not surprising that there are high correlations between problems with naming and with retrieving associations between visual symbols and the sounds they represent.

The group of children who have difficulty with naming and word finding are not likely to be homogeneous. Rubin and Liberman (1983) characterized the types of errors in picture naming of a sample of children with learning problems. The following kinds of errors were documented:

- *Phonetic errors without any semantic connection* (4 percent of cases). The subject substitutes a word that sounds similar but has no meaningful connection with the correct answer (for example, *nozzle* for *nostril*).

- *Nonword (i.e., meaningless) phonetic errors* (6 percent of cases). The subject substitutes for a real word a nonexistent word that has some phonetic resemblance to the real word (for example, *helidakter* for *helicopter*).

- *Semantically and phonetically related substitutions* (11 percent of cases). The subject substitutes a word that is fairly close in meaning and also similar in sound to the target word (for example, *popcorn* for *acorn* and *elevator* for *escalator*).

- *Semantically, then phonetically related errors* (6 percent of cases). The subject substitutes a word that is semantically close and somewhat phonetically related (for example, *bed* for *toboggan*, when by *bed* the child means to say *sled*).

- *Semantic errors* (59 percent of cases). The subject substitutes a word that is similar in meaning or related in some way to the picture (for example, *tennis* for *racket*).

- *Circumlocution* (13 percent of cases). The subject substitutes a definition or description of the picture for the precise word (for example, *lamp cover* for *lamp shade*).

A range of terms has been used to describe various word-finding weaknesses. These include *dysnomia, word retrieval weakness,* and *dysphasia.* Johnson and Myklebust (1967) referred to problems with *reauditorization* (in a sense, the language version of visualization). They used this term to describe children who had problems with verbal naming and the retrieval of words (for conversation or other usage) that persisted despite their good verbal comprehension, adequate oral-motor skills, and appropriate verbal imitation of spoken words.

As noted, children with naming problems appear to be at high risk for the development of reading difficulties. Unfortunately, their plight is not limited to frustration with that academic pursuit. Excessive hesitancy and lack of good, readily accessible vocabulary may impose limitations on conversation for social interaction. Children may feel that their relationships are "out of control" because they are unable to integrate interactions effectively with language. Communication skills are an important source of control, an indispensable means of regulating relationships with peers and adults. When this capacity is limited, too strenuous, or frustrating and slow, children may feel socially overwhelmed and become excessively passive, withdrawn, or sometimes overtly aggressive. Children may feel that they must resort to physical means of control (sometimes aggression or violence) because of verbal impotency. Moreover, affected children may feel at a disadvantage during class discussions, living in constant fear of being called on. One patient's frustration and feelings of apprehension are evident in this confession to his pediatrician: "I'm always afraid the teacher will ask me a question. I have a lot of good ideas. I usually know the answers, but by the time I figure out how to say my ideas it's always too late. Either that or what I say sounds dumb. My thinking is much better than my talking." Such a predicament generates considerable anxiety in a classroom.

Paradoxically, some children who seem fluent in conversation have problems with word retrieval. Such children may speak effectively when they are at liberty to select vocabulary and may be quite loquacious, albeit with a restricted vocabulary. However, when called upon to retrieve a specific word at a given moment, problems may surface. Thus, a child's propensity for talking a great deal does not rule out problems with word retrieval. Finally, the recall of precise vocabulary is an essential component of written language; children with these difficulties may encounter significant writing problems (see chapter 10).

Morphological and Syntactic Problems

The plight of children with the language production difficulties described in the previous section may be exacerbated by a relative inability to employ good techniques to govern morphology and syntax. That is, in addition to or instead of problems retrieving specific words, some children may have difficulty manipulating words flexibly to conform to rules of grammar and tense.

Wiig, Semel, and Crouse (1973) found that children at high risk for learning problems had much more trouble than their achieving peers in a number of morphological areas. For example, those with learning dysfunctions were less likely to understand how to form plural possessives such as *the teachers' cars*. The investigators noted that "on the basis of the present data, learning disabled children are concluded to exhibit quantitative morphological deficits when compared to academically achieving controls." Their subjects with learning problems were less able to use rules of word endings (e.g., plurals and past tense) in a flexible manner, suggesting incomplete mastery as well as a lack of what might be called *phonological conditioning* (probably a part of metalinguistic awareness). That is, those with learning problems had more difficulty knowing what sounded right in a sentence they formed.

Difficulties formulating sentences and producing syntax may also complicate the picture. The rules and regularities delineated earlier in this chapter apply to expressive language as much as to comprehension. Children who have difficulty understanding subordinate clauses are prone to experience trouble using them effectively. However, some children's comprehension of syntax may be far superior to their use of it. Children whose abilities to formulate sentences are weak may overindulge in brief declarative sentences. Their spontaneous speech reveals a brief mean length of utterance. Their speech may be characterized by excessive repetition, poor use of pronouns, and the absence of clauses.

Discourse Weaknesses

Many children with expressive language dysfunctions are unable to organize discourse effectively while speaking (or writing) and thus have trouble describing experiences, telling stories, and producing expository reports. In describing these students, Westby (1984) observed that "the individual sentences they produce may be quite adequate, but they are not organized in a systematic, coherent manner so that the listener can understand the story, and their stories lack a theme or plot" (p. 122). To some extent, this reflects poor planning and self-monitoring as well as associated problems in knowing how to go about organizing a narrative when asked to relate a personal experience. These students find it hard to know how to start, to link specific events (sequentially or causally), and to conclude a narrative.

Children with language production problems may be overwhelmed by the need to produce narrative or provide explanations. Since the ultimate product represents a culmination—the combining of effective word finding, morphology, syntax, pragmatics, plus organization—relative weaknesses in one or more of these areas undermine the entire process. Specific indications of their difficulty are summarized on pages 178–80.

The difference between everyday oral language skill and what is called "literate language" is important. The oral language system, the one commonly practiced at home and on the playground, is usually based on events and circumstances that are immediate. Literate language, on the other hand, tends to be more symbolic and oriented toward more remote subject matters. Westby (1984) notes that "narrative and literate language require increasing levels of symbolic representational abilities" (p. 123). Interestingly, such capacities may have their origins in pretend play, which "requires distancing from reality, increasing degrees of symbolic representation, role taking, sequencing, and planning of events, all the skills that are required for narration and written language. Studies show that children who engage in pretend play exhibit longer and more complex utterances, more explicit use of language, and are more sensitive in responding to the cues of others" (Westby 1984, p. 124). This observation suggests that children who participate exclusively in highly structured, nonimaginative activities such as sports may be deprived of the prerequisite practice to develop good literate language and narrative skills. This may be a particular problem in children who are predisposed to weaknesses of expressive language.

Deficiencies of Verbal Pragmatics

The previous discussion of pragmatics as it relates to language processing noted that some children with learning problems have difficulty ferreting out the true intentions of a speaker or a writer. In like manner, these children often fail to consider the needs of the listener when they communicate. Miller (1984) points out that they 1) use personal and indefinite pronouns when specific nomination is called for; 2) use definite articles when an indefinite one is appropriate, which indicates that they have assumed their listeners already know what the antecedent referent is, even if it has not been made explicit; 3) make unjustified assumptions about how much their listeners know about the topic at hand, and talk about it as if the listener had intimate knowledge; and 4) frequently follow the tacit conversational rules of communication without exception, while the exceptions are understood by the majority of speakers as appropriate vehicles for communicating intent. This latter example is evident in the ability of some children to understand that production deficiencies in pragmatics may take many forms in school and at home. Children may have difficulty adjusting language and tone of voice to a specific social situation. They may fail to integrate either accurate or adaptive feelings or emotions with expressive language. Their intonation and word choice, for example, might suggest anger and hostility when this is not actually the case, leading to misunderstanding and sometimes rejection by peers (see chapter 8). In other instances, poor verbal pragmatic strategies may result in a breakdown in communication. Typically, children might leave out key information when relating an experience. They may use people's first names, assuming incorrectly that the listener knows whether people are their sisters, friends, or cousins. Overall, they have an inability to consider the requirements and perspectives of the specific audience in question. In addition to being widely misunderstood or misinterpreted, such children unintentionally commit many faux pas. Their verbal pragmatic problems can cause these children to be rejected by peers or to become exceedingly passive in their relationships. Chapter 8 discusses the signs of verbal pragmatic deficiencies affecting social cognition.

Poor Metalinguistic Awareness

A strong, conscious sense of language not only enables one to improve comprehension but also facilitates production. A child who has a good sense of language knows when something sounds right or wrong. However, many children with expressive language difficulties fail to detect their own linguistic errors. Their self-monitoring is deficient because they lack the capacity to scrutinize language objectively and effectively.

Children with deficient metalinguistic awareness may be delayed in their ability to use figurative language and analogies. They may not have the monitoring capacity to determine whether what they have just said conforms to their intended meaning. Gallagher and Darnton (1978) found that language-dysfunctional children were far less flexible in making verbal adjustments than normal children of their same language level. That is, they were not able to adjust or improve their spoken language. Studies have demonstrated this by having children explain something and interrupting them to ask for clarification. Many children with language-based learning difficulties have great trouble revising or refining what they have said.

Clinically, one commonly encounters children whose use of grammar is significantly different from that of their parents, siblings, and peers. Although they have had substantial opportunity to imitate the speech of others, these children have such diminished metalinguistic awareness that they cannot tell when something sounds right in their native tongue. This exemplifies their lack of metalinguistic self-monitoring.

The Special Challenge of Bilingualism

An especially daunting challenge faces children whose native language differs from that of the country in which their school is located. Such students must struggle on a number of levels if they are to succeed academically. Many of them manage to succeed. However, large numbers of bilingual children struggle and falter academically. The following points can guide our thinking about these children:

- The sound system and the syntactical rules of the second language are likely to differ significantly from those of the native language. Students who have demonstrated some problems with phonological awareness in their native language are apt to have tremendous difficulty superimposing the phonology of a second language.

- Children may face the difficult challenge of not only mastering a second language but also using that new language to acquire academic skills; complex concepts; and new, often technical knowledge.

- There may exist a substantial cultural gap between the content to which these children are exposed in school and the prior knowledge and experience they bring to school, so that much of what they are expected to learn may lack relevance for them.

- If a child is having difficulty learning in a second language, it can be exceedingly difficult to sort out the extent to which the difficulty is a reflection of cultural, environmental, or bilingual factors versus a manifestation of an underlying learning disorder.

- In some settings, these children's problems are exacerbated by the fact that they have minority status within a school dominated by a very different cultural group (Cummins 1989), from which they may feel alienated.

- School problems can be accentuated when children come from families where the parents have had only minimal schooling (Gersten and Woodward 1994).

- Teachers may lack the proper training and cultural backgrounds to understand the plight and the needs of these children, becoming confused and feeling helpless when such children do not make sufficient academic progress.

Many controversial issues surround the education of these students. It is generally agreed that at least some of their learning of knowledge and skill should take place in their native language (Gersten and Woodward 1994). This should include the use of reading materials in that language. However, there is disagreement with respect to the right mix of the two languages. There is also no unanimity regarding the grade levels or ages at which the second language should predominate. Research findings are sparse and inconclusive regarding such decisions. However, at all points in a bilingual child's education, he should be provided with access to learning materials in his native language, at least as a resource. Even in high school or college, complex or abstract material may be more effectively consolidated when there are backup resources in a first language.

Many investigators point out the crucial need for curriculum that is relevant to the cultural backgrounds of bilingual and other minority students. There is evidence, for example, that many of these students acquire greater competency in reading and writing if they pursue topics that they can relate directly to their own experiences in life. For such children, the whole-language approach may attain better results than the more traditional "skill drilling" with worksheets, etc. (Lopez-Reyna 1996).

Bilingual children who are experiencing learning difficulties in school can benefit from an assessment that includes consideration of their language ability and academic subskill status in their native language. It is often possible to detect breakdowns in learning that are interfering with skill acquisition in both languages. These should be managed in the same way that they are managed in students who are not bilingual. Remediation may need to occur in *both* language contexts.

Finally, when a failing child is bilingual and bicultural, it is probably inappropriate to argue over whether or not that student has a learning disorder. As with all of the forms of difficulty described in this book, the problems that these children face are the end result of multiple factors relating to physiological-genetic effects, environmental forces, cultural influences, early health, and life circumstances. If we can identify one or more neurodevelopmental dysfunctions and deal appropriately with additional factors, we can hope to redeem these children.

ASSESSMENT

Assessing language is an essential component of the evaluation of any schoolchild with learning and/or behavioral difficulty. A well-integrated set of observations is necessary to account for the broad range of linguistic functions. An assessment should include not merely a search for deficits but also consideration of underlying or unrecognized linguistic talents that can be mobilized to overcome or bypass developmental dysfunctions in other areas.

Historical Data

The developmental history ought to include questions specifically geared to language acquisition. A diagnostician should document milestones of early language acquisition. The timing and adequacy of language development prior to school entry should be established. Some parents, however, may have trouble recalling their child's language milestones. Some symptoms and signs of language dysfunction are:

- Trouble following directions
- Need for repetition of verbal instructions
- Problems understanding questions
- Difficulty concentrating in verbal settings (such as classrooms) but not in other settings
- Excessive use of simple, declarative, incomplete sentences
- Articulation difficulties
- Verbal hesitancy
- Poor use of connectives in speech (lack of cohesion)
- Expressive repetition or redundancy
- Trouble organizing discourse
- Lack of verbal participation
- Late acquisition of decoding skills for reading
- Poor reading comprehension beyond fourth grade despite good sight vocabulary
- Obscure use of pronouns and names during speech
- Poor written expression
- Difficulty solving word problems in mathematics
- Statements suggesting poor verbal social skill (pragmatic deficiencies)
- Trouble learning a foreign language
- Excessive difficulty mastering grammar
- Diminished vocabulary/trouble acquiring new vocabulary

Considerable research supports the notion that early delays in language acquisition can predict later language-based learning problems. However, some children with language-learning problems during school years experienced no delays earlier in life. Only when the complexity of language demands reached a certain level did these children reveal clinical evidence of disability.

Each of these symptoms and signs may also be found in other types of developmental dysfunction. A large number of symptoms suggests a higher likelihood of language dysfunction.

A careful review of the child's early health and family history can uncover predisposing factors. Some studies have linked recurrent *otitis media* (ear infections) to the later development of language learning problems (Zincus and Gottlieb 1980). Other early health difficulties such as meningitis might also be considered risk factors. A strong family history of problems with language acquisition, comprehension, or speech production can also be an indicator of a language-related learning problem.

The child's current history is most relevant. How a youngster's language comprehension and production compare to those of siblings and peers is of great interest. Are there problems with articulation? Is the child particularly shy or passive in relationships? How effectively does she or he participate in discussions in the classroom? Does the child have problems following verbal directions? Does he or she have trouble telling a story or relating an experience? Are there delays in reading comprehension? Are there indications of difficulty solving word problems in mathematics? Are there specific weaknesses of auditory attention (i.e., listening ability) that may indicate either primary attention deficits or weakness of attention secondary to poor language processing? Further questioning about overall attention patterns (see chapter 2) can help resolve this issue.

It is useful to use multiple sources in obtaining historical data. *The ANSER System* questionnaires probe the language area from the point of view of the parents, school personnel, and the child (if over age nine). Figure 5-2 provides some examples of items from *The ANSER System* that relate specifically to a child's current language status. None of these items is entirely pure; any individual symptom suggests many possible causes. For instance, trouble following instructions is not necessarily due to a language disability. It may relate to problems with sequential organization, more generalized memory difficulty, attention deficits, cultural factors, or difficulties with conceptualization. Only by accruing a significant cluster of items suggesting linguistic dysfunction can one begin to discern a consistent diagnostic pattern. Again, these observations should be derived from multiple observers.

Direct Sampling of Language

The screening and assessment of language is a common practice in clinics and schools. Many diagnostic tools have been developed for this purpose. They deal with the specific areas of function discussed in this chapter and, as such, may have direct therapeutic implications for regular classroom management, communication at home, and specific language intervention.

		ACADEMIC SUBSKILL OR FUNCTION	TYPICAL PERFORMANCE				VARIABILITY OF PERFORMANCE		
			STRONG FOR AGE	APPROPRIATE FOR AGE	DELAYED LESS THAN 1 YEAR	DELAYED MORE THAN 1 YEAR	CONSISTENT PERFORMANCE	SOMEWHAT VARIABLE	HIGHLY UNPREDICTABLE
AS40	Language	Acquiring new vocabulary							
AS41		Understanding verbal directions							
AS42		Understanding stories read to him/her							
AS43		Pronouncing new words							
AS44		Speaking fluently							
AS45		Speaking intelligibly							
AS46		Constructing good spoken sentences							
AS47		Explaining complicated ideas							
AS48		Relating personal experiences							
AS49		Summarizing							
AS50		Elaborating on thoughts verbally							
AS51		Participating in class discussions							

Figure 5-2. Excerpts from *The ANSER System* showing screening items for language processing and production problems

Some hazards that can adversely affect the results and interpretations of language assessments are summarized below.

Cultural Contamination. Separating language and culture is virtually impossible. Of all the aspects of developmental screening and assessment, language is most affected by variability of cultural background. Children who come from well-educated families in which there is a heavy premium on language may appear to be highly proficient in comprehension and production. Conversely, children from backgrounds that are culturally distinct from educational settings may seem to have significant language difficulties, while in fact they communicate and understand perfectly well within the social context in which they are growing up. Any difficulties with language testing may reflect cultural variation rather than a neurologically based deficit. Virtually all aspects of language,

including phonology, semantics, syntax, pragmatics, and metalinguistic awareness, are influenced by one's cultural background. However, all children may
need to survive in a traditional, middle-class-oriented educational setting. Thus,
whether the origins of a language delay are cultural or constitutional, it can be
argued that a deficit is a deficit. If a child is at a disadvantage in language processing and production (for whatever reason), a problem exists, at least during
school.

The youngster with a bilingual background presents a special challenge. Sometimes it is difficult to determine whether a language delay in English is merely a
product of bilingualism or whether it represents a neurologically based language
disability. Testing in both the native tongue and English can help resolve this. It has
been found that many such children have as much difficulty with their own language as they do with English. Here again, it is important to distinguish between
variables in the cultural background and linguistic ones. A child who is bilingual
and comes from a relatively impoverished background culturally and economically may have two reasons for language delay. If the child has a constitutional predisposition to language disability as well, she or he is triply vulnerable.

Specificity of Findings.   Determining whether a child's apparent language
difficulties are limited to the language area is important. For example, children
who have trouble following verbal instructions may be confused by the sequential presentation of those verbal inputs. They may have pervasive problems with
sequential processing rather than a specific language disability. Visual inputs in a
sequence may cause the same difficulty. Confusion between weaknesses of language intake and generalized attention deficits is also a possibility. Children who
are said to have poor narrative organization as revealed by speech and language
assessments may have difficulties with many different aspects of organization.
They may have problems organizing a notebook, finding things at home, or
arranging clothing properly to get dressed in the morning. Again, the issue is
whether a particular finding is unique to the language domain or part of a more
generalized breakdown of systems.

Emotional Factors.   As is true of any assessment procedure, emotional preoccupations may interfere with assessment of language. Children who are particularly inhibited or anxious may reveal erratic and inadequate language processing
and production. Children who are feeling inhibited by the test situation, for example, may be extremely parsimonious when asked to generate narrative. The mean
length of utterances may be reduced, not because of production difficulties, but as
a result of anxiety.

Motivational Factors.   A child's level of cooperation and interest in the testing procedure can affect the assessment of his or her speech patterns. If a child is
not particularly interested in the examination, a language delay may be more
apparent than real.

Artifacts of Testing.   Any testing scenario is intrinsically artificial. Language assessment frequently removes language from its appropriate context. Some children may perform much better under normal circumstances than in the highly contrived testing situation. In some instances, a child's language may appear better on language testing than it is on a day-to-day basis. As with any testing situation, children may rise to the occasion.

The astute clinician who considers various sources of information can likely circumvent these contaminants. By using several kinds of tests and integrating them with historical observations and the results of educational testing, she or he should be able to recognize, correct for, and eliminate these contaminants. Here are some of the forms of assessment clinicians can employ:

Informal Language Assessment.   An evaluation should always include informal measures of language. Conversation with a child during the course of an interview, a testing session, or some other interaction can provide useful clues. Anyone experienced in dealing with children has probably developed internal norms for rating facility of communication. In talking with a child, observations such as the following can yield useful information. Is she or he slow to pick up instructions? Does the speaker need to engage in repetition, simplification, or some other device to facilitate verbal interaction? Does the child use incomplete sentences? How sophisticated is the syntax? How long are the sentences? Is there considerable hesitation? Are there indications of weaknesses of word finding or verbal fluency? Is there difficulty with articulation, stuttering, or unusual voice resonance?

During a physical examination, for example, a physician may wish to look for possible difficulties with language processing or production. Informal conversation can be used to assess how easily and accurately the child follows directions. The physician might say, "I am going to listen to your chest now. Every time I put the stethoscope on your chest, I would like you to take a really deep breath." Then he or she observes how effectively this instruction is carried out. Does the child neglect to take a deep breath? Is repetition necessary?

Asking highly specific questions is another way to perform informal assessments. The examiner can gauge length of response time, accuracy of answers, and comprehension of the questions themselves.

Formal Language Testing.   It is beyond the scope of this section to present a critical review of available language tests. However, a number of them are summarized in the appendix. This book's purpose is not to propose any uniform assessment battery for any aspect of development. Instead, diagnosticians should assemble their own systems of assessments—observations and instruments that they believe help answer specific diagnostic questions. The next section, therefore, deals with the subject of formal assessment according to specific areas of language development, although some examples from standardized tests will be provided.

Formal assessment of language processing. A battery of tests to evaluate language processing should account for specific components. These include discrimination and phonology, vocabulary and semantics, morphology and syntax, metalinguistics, following verbal instructions, and educational testing.

DISCRIMINATION AND PHONOLOGY. Assessing a child's understanding of phonology seems to be most helpful at the preschool or early elementary school level. Ability to break down words into their component phonemes (i.e., segmentation of words) and then reassemble them has been shown to predict success in reading fairly accurately (Liberman et al. 1974). Rosner's *Thirteen Item Auditory Analysis Test* (1971) is one such measure. Subjects listen to a particular word and are then asked to delete one syllable of it. For example, "Say *hospital.* Now say it again, but don't say the *hosp.*" It is quite likely, in fact, that skill in phoneme segmentation is an important prerequisite for dividing familiar words into their component parts. Sound blending subtests, included in several educational instruments, also assesses the ability to recognize the phonemic components of words and reassemble them. A child listens to the several syllables of a word separately and then blends them into the word.

Tests of auditory discrimination tap a child's ability to distinguish between similar-sounding words or phonemes. The *Wepman Auditory Discrimination Test* has become a prototype for many tests assessing auditory discrimination. Children are given pairs of words and asked whether the two words are the same or different. Such discrimination tests, however, are subject to dialectical influences which reduce their validity. In general, these kinds of assessments (segmentation and discrimination) become less valuable as children reach middle elementary school. Therefore, they need not be part of the evaluation of older children and adolescents.

VOCABULARY AND SEMANTICS. Evaluation of language processing should include tests of vocabulary. The most commonly employed test is the *Peabody Picture Vocabulary Test-Revised (PPVT-R*; Dunn and Dunn 1981), which is sometimes used as a measure of verbal intelligence; however, it is more judicious to interpret it as an indicator of receptive vocabulary. Like other vocabulary tests, it has been criticized for its cultural biases. On the *PPVT,* subjects scan a set of pictures and point to the one that corresponds to a specific word spoken by the examiner, thus matching the right picture with the word. No word retrieval is required. Another type of vocabulary test, for example, the Vocabulary subtest of the *WISC-III,* requires the subject to define specific words. Other tests ask children to make up sentences that use a specified word. To varying degrees, vocabulary tests tend to take words out of their usual contexts. Thus, they may not represent a totally reliable indication of a child's day-to-day vocabulary. Nevertheless, with this limitation in mind, it is useful to include some measures of vocabulary at all age levels.

MORPHOLOGY AND SYNTAX. Assessing a child's awareness of the effects on meaning of morphology and syntax should be an important part of evaluation. This chapter noted earlier that sophistication in using morphology as well as syntactical structure marks the most conspicuous dimension of growth in language processing during school years. We can assume, therefore, that youngsters with language-processing deficiencies will be moderately or significantly delayed in this aspect of linguistics.

A number of assessments can be used for this area. Among them are sentence repetition tests. The subject listens to a complex sentence and is asked simply to repeat it. Children with a limited grasp of syntax will have trouble with grammatically correct repetition; they may distort the structure of the sentence because it is not meaningful to them. Sentence comprehension tests can also be useful. They play an important role in the pediatric neurodevelopmental examinations *PEER*, *PEEX 2*, and *PEERAMID 2*. Some sample items are illustrated in figure 5-3. Other language and educational tests include items that require children to detect errors in use of syntax, tenses, comparatives and superlatives, pronouns, word order, and other aspects of language.

METALINGUISTICS. Because children's metalinguistic awareness reportedly increases dramatically from late elementary to secondary school, assessments of older children need to consider this area. Such evaluations often include a child's ability to understand ambiguity, figurative language, paradoxes, and various proverbs. Several subtests in Semel and Wiig's (1994) *CELF-3* instrument and in the *Test of Language Competence* (Secord and Wiig 1988) tap these dimensions.

FOLLOWING VERBAL INSTRUCTIONS. An assessment of a child's capacity to follow verbal instructions represents a combination of linguistic areas, requiring auditory attention to detail, comprehension, active working memory, and some

---

Yes, No, Maybe Text (0 = incorrect; 1 = correct)

Example: Joe might come home early today. Will Joe come home early today?   (M)

1. John said, "Shouldn't you make the knot loose?" Did John think the knot should be loose?   (Y)

2. Ricky won't go to the party unless Ann goes. Will Ricky stay home?   (M)

3. Bob promised Tom, who was hungry, to buy the candy. Did Tom say he would buy the candy?   (N)

4. It's usually safe to climb that mountain although it's very dangerous in the fog. Will it be safe to climb the mountain tomorrow?   (M)

5. Maybe the band would have played last night if the drummer hadn't quit. Did the band play last night?   (N)

Figure 5-3.   Sample sentence comprehension items

The sentences above are excerpts from the *PEERAMID 2* Record Form. After the examiner reads each sentence, the child is asked a question that may be answered by "yes," "no," or "maybe." Children with poor appreciation of syntax may have particular problems with this text, and those with weak auditory attention may also be able to preserve morphological and syntactic structures of increasing complexity.

capacity to integrate language interpretation with (usually) motor responses. The *Token Test* (DeRenzi and Vignolo 1962), used extensively in both children and adults with a diagnosis of aphasia, assesses the comprehension of linguistic materials with only a minimum of redundancy. The fine motor aspects are kept simple to tap language processing as purely as possible. The Concepts and Directions subtest of the *CELF-3* also assesses the ability to follow directions. Verbal Instructions sections of the *PEEX 2* and the *PEERAMID 2* fulfill a similar function. Any assessment of the comprehension of verbal instructions should include observation of the rate of language processing. Hesitancy and/or prolonged response times may suggest that a child is having difficulty keeping pace with language demands.

EDUCATIONAL TESTING. Carefully administered tests of educational skill can provide evidence of language-processing difficulties. The nature of a child's reading comprehension problems may suggest dysfunctional language learning. Certain kinds of spelling errors are frequently associated with poor appreciation of (or memory for) phonology (see chapter 10). A child who appears to have a good sight vocabulary but relative weaknesses in analyzing newly encountered words may have underlying problems with the phonological aspects of language. An older child who is concrete and literal in interpreting written narrative may be manifesting deficiencies of metalinguistic awareness. Carefully interpreted data from educational assessments can support (or negate) findings in the language domain.

Formal assessment of language production. Tests of language production may be particularly susceptible to the diagnostic contaminants cited earlier in this chapter. Nevertheless, such assessments are especially important and potentially helpful to children since specific findings can be used to determine the need for formal speech and language therapy.

TESTS OF ARTICULATION. Much can be learned about a child's articulatory skills through a careful history as well as informal listening to his or her speech. When there are signs of articulation problems, a trained speech and language therapist should formally test articulation. In fact, any child with significant oral-motor problems can benefit from a careful professional assessment.

WORD RETRIEVAL. It may be difficult to separate a child's expressive vocabulary (words available for use) from word retrieval ability. Nonetheless, certain assessment techniques can help make such differentiations possible. Various picture- or object-naming tasks are commonly used. These play an important role in the *PEER*, the *PEEX 2,* and the *PEERAMID 2.* As subjects name pictures, the examiner can assess the accuracy of their naming, the amount of time required to name a particular object, and any tendency to engage in circumlocution. To determine whether a child who hesitates is having problems finding a word or whether that word simply is not in her or his vocabulary, the examiner offers either a phonetic or a semantic clue. If the child then finds the right word, the difficulty was clearly with retrieval. The *Boston Naming Test* (Kaplan and Goodglass 1975) is another tool that requires the verbal identification of pictures.

Several educational and language tests include subtests that require specific recall of synonyms and antonyms. This is one of a number of word association tests. Another type requires the naming of specific items in a category. For example, the *PEERAMID 2* gives the child thirty seconds to name as many different animals as possible, affording the examiner an opportunity to probe word retrieval strategies. All such assessments of word association and retrieval must include careful observation not only of accuracy but also of the amount of effort required, the length of time involved in retrieval, and the various techniques used by the subject. All of these can ultimately be very important in determining the child's efficiency of language production, which is crucial for test taking and participation in class and social discussions.

SENTENCE FORMULATION. Tests of language production should assess a child's ability to use morphology and syntax effectively in sentences. The quality of sentence structure can be judged by having the subject describe a picture stimulus. This is the format of the *Picture Story Language Test (PSLT)* of Myklebust (1965). Several tests use sentence combining and manipulation of word order to change meaning to evaluate syntactic skills in language production. Various sentence repetition tests mentioned in connection with receptive language can also reflect expressive abilities.

The Sentence Formulation test on the *PEERAMID 2* provides the subject with several words to be used in a sentence. Each set of words contains at least one conjunction, thereby necessitating the formulation of a complex sentence. Subjects are scored on correctness of grammar, use of vocabulary, and ease of production.

DISCOURSE SKILL. Formal assessments of discourse ability are difficult to administer and score. Consequently, a diagnostician may need to rely heavily on historical data as well as informal assessment. For research purposes, specific techniques have been used. Depending on the age of a child, we expect increasing ability to organize narrative or expository prose and to integrate the various subcomponents of vocabulary, grammar, and narrative flow.

Research on narrative ability has made use of children's summarization skills. Students are asked to listen to or read a story or expository passage and then retell it. It has been found (Hansen 1978) that children with learning problems have difficulty distinguishing between main ideas and less relevant details when retelling a story. They recall as many details but proportionately fewer main ideas in their narratives. Feagans (1983) notes that "LD students may not have a clear idea about the structure of a story or narrative passage and thus may have less of a concept of a hierarchical structure which makes the narrative a cohesive whole. This implies that learning disabled children may not understand the relationship which exists between sentences and ideas in a passage. This goes beyond, of course, the

meaning of the individual words and the particular syntactic structures which
ds" (p. 102).

roduction can be used as an important indicator
f language as well as a measure of their capaci-
ic linguistic format. By asking children to retell
into both the understanding and production of
ate on and defend their stand on a particular
animals) a good expository sample can be
inventories such as the *Qualitative Reading*
95) include a measure of students' ability to
passages.

ng is undertaken, the following are some key
ing difficulty with language production at the

- Indications that language expression demands excessive effort

- Hesitancy, dysfluency, slow speech

- Excessive use of pause words, such as *like, ummm, you know what I mean,* etc.

- Word retrieval problems and frequent circumlocution (e.g., using a hand gesture or substituting a definition for the actual word)

- Overuse of short, declarative sentences with minimal sophisticated syntax

- Difficulty arranging events or ideas in the best order

- Lack of cohesive ties (words like *but, because, so,* and *then*) that connect sentences effectively

- Tendency to misjudge prior knowledge of the listener (e.g., mentioning "Debbie" without identifying her as "my sister" or "my friend") or providing too much information the listener already knows or can infer

- Redundancy of vocabulary and/or ideas

- Avoidance of pronouns, with frequent repetition of proper nouns

- Brevity, failure to elaborate

- Low ideational density (i.e., relatively few ideas for the amount of verbal output)

- Overuse of high-frequency vocabulary (i.e., one seldom hears an abstract, technical, or somewhat esoteric word)

- Trouble forming, expressing, and justifying an opinion

- Excessive syntactic and morphological errors

- Weak revision skills (difficulty improving upon or clarifying a statement)

In assessing the significance of such findings, it is, of course, essential to take into consideration the child's age and cultural background.

Reconciling Discrepancies. The evaluation of a child for language disability may produce conflicting data. Children may perform differently in different settings. Parents may perceive their youngster as highly verbal while the school perceives language as a problem area. A physician may be struck by how articulate and talkative a particular child seems in the office; in school, however, that child struggles to express himself or herself. The diagnostician must be keenly aware of expectations—of the limits imposed by different scenarios in the life of a child. Social conversation is vastly different from the literate language described earlier in this chapter and demanded in the classroom.

A discrepancy may exist between receptive and expressive language ability. A child may be quite adept at processing language but have great difficulty producing language. Such a child may perform well in reading comprehension and have no difficulty understanding what the teacher says during a lecture. On the other hand, she or he may hesitate when finding words, formulating sentences, and/or organizing narrative. An even more confusing situation occurs when a child is an extremely avid participant in class discussions with strengths in producing discourse yet is an extremely poor performer in language arts subjects. Such a student may be far better at formulating language than at accommodating the linguistic structures of others. The child who, although a good writer, has problems with reading comprehension, is apt to be a better teacher than a student. Depicting or reconstructing knowledge in his or her own linguistic framework is easier than extracting information from other people's speech. The implication is clear: just because a child is verbally fluent and effective does not rule out the possibility of a receptive language dysfunction.

Another common discrepancy is that between divergent and convergent language demands. A child may be proficient (by history and direct observation) at elaborating on ideas, using his or her own linguistic repertoire, but have trouble finding precise words on demand or answering questions with correct verbal responses. Such a student, it seems, must be in complete control of the verbal dialogue to succeed. Other children may be just the opposite—quite skilled at giving precise responses but unskilled at using language in an abstract, elaborative, or imaginary mode.

Other discrepancies involve contrasts between linguistic proficiency in social and in academic settings: children who are slow to "warm up" become increasingly verbal over time; some have language skills especially dependent on the extent to which they are directed to areas of strong interest and expertise.

In view of these disparities, it may be inappropriate simply to describe a child as either language disabled or language competent. The domain of linguistics is so broad and relevant to so many other areas that only a highly specific description of a child's language in various contexts is likely to be helpful and truly representative.

MANAGEMENT

Efforts to manage language difficulties must be based on an understanding of a student's language impairment as well as his or her significant strengths in other areas. As with other disabilities, we do not treat only the language disability; we need to deal with the broad functional profile as well as the dense fabric of temperamental, behavioral, and strategic variation. Nevertheless, some generalizations about therapies are possible. While some of these suggestions may not be appropriate for all affected children, they should provide a general schema for assisting them.

Demystification

It can be exceedingly difficult to explain language and language difficulty to a child who has a language problem. They can have trouble understanding what actually is meant by language. Is it foreign language? Is it language arts? Is it bad language? The demystifier must use concrete analogies and talk about a person's ability to get information out of words and sentences instead of just pictures or visual images. In fact, it is often helpful to discuss the differences between visual learning and language learning. The student needs to acquire a clear notion of which aspects of language are problematic for her. It is therefore important to be specific about whether the problems are mainly expressive or receptive (or both) and whether they affect interpreting language sounds, understanding the meanings of words, or working with sentences.

Bypass Strategies

Regardless of available resources for special education and speech and language, a great deal can be done to circumvent language-related dysfunctions in school. To do so, diagnosticians, school administrators, and regular classroom teachers must communicate effectively. Parents must be keenly aware of a child's language-processing or production deficiencies. The approach to management needs to be consistent and concerted. Teachers, parents, and others should devise a wide range of accommodations such as those listed below, limited only by their own interest, motivation, and creativity.

- Give children with language dysfunctions preferential seating in a classroom— as close to the teacher as possible.

- Repeat instructions and use verbal highlighting ("What I'm about to say is especially important"), along with as much verbal redundancy as possible during the regular class day.

processing weaknesses.

appears to be confused, recognize these cues in
tion or some other form of reinforcement of the

processing weaknesses often benefit from visual rely solved mathematics problem, a worksheet, a diagram,
visual metaphor, or some other nonverbal input is often

reading curriculum to minimize the impact of a language disability. strong visual approach can be helpful if the child has strengths in the visual processing domain. Alternatively, one or more of the various multisensory reading methods (such as Orton-Gillingham) can be used. Such techniques for teaching reading may require the services of a reading specialist.

- Students with language disabilities are prone to foreign language disabilities (see chapter 12). In some cases, they require exemptions from foreign language study altogether, while in others they should delay foreign language training (perhaps until eleventh grade).

- Avoid embarrassing students with expressive language weaknesses in the classroom. A student who has problems with word retrieval or the verbal formulation of a response may be quite tense during class discussions. Phrasing questions so that the student may respond "yes" or "no" can alleviate some of the anxiety.

- Since written language is one of the most difficult forms of verbal expression for a student with weaknesses in language production, special accommodations may be necessary for reports, essays, and narratives of various types. Shorten such assignments or make some allowances for difficulties with grammatical construction, rate of production, and discrepancies between a student's ideation and communication.

- Many students with language dysfunctions suffer lags in acquisition of skills. They are apt to require individualized help or tutorial assistance in a number of basic skills. The special educator needs to be aware of the child's specific language gaps at the same time that she or he fashions interventions based on the child's strengths. Language-impaired children are most likely to require tutorial help in word analysis skills, reading comprehension, spelling, written language, and the comprehension of word problems in mathematics. In secondary school, they may need tutorial help in specific content areas. Social studies and science textbooks, with their ideationally dense prose, may be problematic. Tutoring in foreign languages is also frequently required.

Direct Intervention

Direct intervention to enhance a child's language abilities is apt to vary in effectiveness from student to student. The severity and precise nature of a child's language-processing or production weaknesses will be one determinant of treatment success. The skill of those administering the treatment; the intensity of intervention; and the child's own receptiveness, understanding of the dysfunction, and motivation will also strongly influence the outcome. Following are some examples of interventions to strengthen language ability:

Therapy. Often children with language impairments benefit from direct speech and language therapy from a trained speech and language pathologist. The availability of such services is likely to vary from community to community. In some school systems, speech and language professionals play a major role in providing special education services. At the other extreme are schools in which such programs are unavailable. Because of the frequency of language disabilities and their major impacts on academic and social performance, all school systems should make such services readily available. A trained speech and language pathologist can both diagnose and treat (often simultaneously). During regularly scheduled sessions, a student can receive help with such linguistic parameters as phonological awareness, auditory attention, verbal comprehension, vocabulary, word finding, sentence formulation, the organization of discourse, and, of course, articulation. The speech and language pathologist can also be a valuable asset in informing regular classroom teachers about a child's difficulties and the implications for day-to-day management. The precise content of speech and language therapy is beyond the scope of this book. However, the reader may wish to pursue the subject further in various speech and language texts such as Wiig and Semel (1984) and Gerber (1993).

Phonological Deficits. Children with gaps in phonological awareness may require direct help with auditory discrimination. In many cases, however, they can benefit from activities that simultaneously improve their reading decoding abilities. Thus, drill on sound-symbol associations, possibly employing multisensory methods, may actually result in improved phonological awareness. For those children whose phonological problems are related to slow processing, some recent studies have suggested that technology can actually be used to slow down language sounds as an individual listens to them and to gradually increase the rate of presentation of these sounds (Merzenich et al. 1996). Further validation of such procedures is necessary.

Semantic Weaknesses. Help children with deficient appreciation of word meanings develop a more effectively interconnected semantic network. Emphasize getting them to list or discuss words in categories (e.g., words that describe sadness), compare and contrast pairs of words, and engage in crossword puzzles.

Use various semantic mapping strategies wherein a child creates visual represen-tations of the interactions between words. Such a map is illustrated in figure 5-4.

Sometimes it is appropriate to substitute visual images for the words in the boxes. Students should be taught to create semantic maps of their own for words they find difficult to understand and/or remember.

Sentence Level. Children with syntactical difficulties may benefit from var-ious *cloze* exercises, which are activities in which a child is given a sentence with a word missing and asked to insert one that will be grammatically correct. Sen-tence formulation exercises may also help. A child is given one or two key words and asked to create oral or written sentences that contain these words. The words

Figure 5-4. A semantic map for the word *geese*

This semantic map is typical of those that can be used to help students to develop a stronger sense of word meanings.

should force the student to construct complex sentences (conjunctions such as *unless, until,* and *although* create such conditions).

Discourse Level. Many students simply need intense practice at producing and interpreting discourse. Summarization activities strengthen the ability to process and retain information contained in passages and paragraphs. Children often need as much practice as possible creating their own discourse. There should be a stress on oral presentations, especially within a child's domain of personal interests or affinities. In many subjects students should be required to elaborate, defend their opinions and interpretations verbally, and explain how they did things (as in describing how one solved a mathematics problem). It is helpful to develop elaborative skills in a child's domain of strong interest or affinity. Having substantial accessible prior knowledge about a topic greatly facilitates practice in verbal elaboration.

Verbal Pragmatics. Some children with language difficulties have social problems—perhaps related to their impaired verbal pragmatic strategies (see p. 156). They may need specific counseling in social skills (see chapter 8) to help them acquire a better understanding of how their verbal utterances and interpretations affect their interactions with others.

Reading. Many children with language difficulties are caught in a perpetual vicious cycle: because they have such impairments, they have difficulty reading; because reading is hard for them, they avoid reading. Yet reading is an excellent way to improve language abilities. Over time, affected students read much less than their peers, and the language gap consequently widens. To enhance language skills, affected students should be provided with high-interest reading material that they are highly motivated to read. They should read as much as possible to bolster vocabulary, verbal comprehension, and appreciation of syntax. In some cases, books on tape may be a valuable adjunct.

Word Games. At home and in school highly motivating word games can be helpful. Parents of children in the younger age group should engage regularly in pastimes that involve language. Word games can also be used in school as part of a special educational program for a student. Various games that emphasize word finding, verbal opposites, and naming of items in a category, for example, may help. Crossword puzzles, board games that require spelling, and related activities should be tried.

Rights of the Nonverbal Student

Students with language dysfunctions frequently excel in other forms of information processing and productivity. Yet, they often suffer humiliation in the highly verbal ambience of school. They must have opportunities to practice their specialties, to shine in the areas in which they are more richly endowed. Their artistic abilities, mechanical skills, mathematical talents, and athletic strengths need to be exploited and put on display. A vast number of adult occupations and avocations at all levels of the socioeconomic scale are available to citizens with language impairments. Therefore, it is incumbent on everyone who interacts with such students to make sure that their self-esteem, motivation, and ambition is not thwarted at an early age because of the inordinate but transient stress on language proficiency that occurs during the formative years of schooling.

Up to this point we have explored many direct connections between various forms of information processing and production, on the one hand, and academic proficiency, on the other. The next chapter will examine another important facilitator of school success and of self-concept: neuromotor function.

Chapter 6

Motor
Implementation

He was no student, and he had the added handicap of being left-handed in a right-handed world. His first-grade teacher made him write with his right hand. He never became proficient at it and he put much of the onus for his lackadaisical work in school on his inability to write swiftly and smoothly. "Anything you can't do well and don't enjoy, you generally fall behind in," he observed.
                              —Robert W. Creamer, *Stengel: His Life and Times*

In school, a substantial proportion of a child's daily performance is encoded through various motor pathways. Intentional, skilled motor movements are critical links in the transformation of ideas or plans into products. The principal motor pathways are *gross motor function* (involving large muscles and/or whole body movement), *fine motor function* (usually limited to actions of the hands and fingers), *graphomotor functions* (the motor aspects of writing), and *oral motor function* (speech movements). Gross motor proficiency comes to the fore in sports and in many acts of physical labor. Fine motor skill is evident in knitting and sewing, and in much artwork. Oral motor coordination is revealed in speech. Gratification in one or more of these motor output channels helps schoolchildren feel effective.

Our consideration of motor implementation begins with a discussion of some basic mechanisms. It then surveys gross motor function and dysfunction. It describes the phenomenon of developmental output failure—the common condition in which older school-age children falter and fail in their academic productivity. Within this context, it considers certain issues of graphomotor proficiency. Finally, this chapter explores some alternative channels of output potentially accessible to schoolchildren. Oral motor dysfunction, described in chapter 5, will not be dealt with here.

MOTOR ACTIONS

It is helpful to distinguish between *movement* and *action:* the former is simply an alteration of position in space; the latter is *organized movement.* Action is controlled; it most commonly has a goal and can be modified in the face of unforeseen problems to achieve that goal.

187

A series of *prefunctional programs* is a primitive part of motor control (Wolff 1982). They underlie the simple and more complex reflexes required for postural adjustment and fixed movement sequences, which are not under conscious control most of the time. They enable us to bend down, sit up, and turn over in bed without an extravagant expenditure of mental effort or conscious thought.

On a more sophisticated level are movements under the control of *motor ideas.* A motor idea is a specific plan of action for a series of movements that will achieve a specific goal. Motor ideas, which form the basis for the acquisition of all complex motor skills throughout childhood, may be acquired by direct imitation. In infancy and early childhood, the evolving human commonly makes observations, develops *perceptual images* of observed motor movements, and then imitates them immediately or subsequently. In addition to such apparently visually encoded movements, motor ideas can be verbally encoded. Through a series of experiments, Luria (1980) found that children between eighteen months and five years old frequently guided their motor actions with verbal utterances or subvocalizations. In other words, they kept telling themselves what to do, quite possibly a common manner of mastering a new skill. However, as motor proficiency reaches its peak, verbal motor ideas may be insufficient. Talented musicians or athletes may be at a loss to describe in words how they accomplish their impressive motor feats.

Motor proficiency and experience use sensory data to ensure that an activity will be goal directed. Most motor actions are guided in part by some form of data analysis. When we catch a ball, the data are largely visual and spatial. The catcher makes judgments about the spatial trajectory of the ball, its speed, projected landing site, and arrival time. All such spatial data are used to program an appropriate motor response (running and readying the hands for the catch). For other motor functions, the data may be predominantly kinesthetic, or related to body position.

Repeated motor experience also contributes to information processing. Experience in the visual-spatial world, for example, is commonly gathered through visual-motor activity. Thus, motor participation enhances our knowledge of spatial relationships. We keep learning by performing. Assembling a jigsaw puzzle can help a child understand the relationships of parts to wholes. By speaking French, students are likely to understand the language better than if they only read it. Everyone learns to varying degrees through active engagement or experience. Youngsters who have a great deal of difficulty with the passive receipt and assimilation of knowledge may need to perform in order to learn. Other students can learn as effectively (or more effectively) by listening as by acting. Thus, the extent to which one learns through planned action may be one more element of developmental variation and individual style.

Feedback is another indispensable component of goal-directed movement. Wolff (1982) observes that the actor must have a continuous flow of *reafferent* information about the force, speed, and direction of movement contributed by sensations from the moving limb, and *exafferent* visual information contributed by observing the limb in motion. Furthermore, the actor must be able to organize and compare such information against an internal reference criterion that tells him how closely the actual movements match the movements specified by the goal (p. 205).

In other words, while engaged in a motor action, we frequently watch what we are doing, which enables us to perpetuate, modify, or terminate the action. Such feedback also enhances the progressive development of proficiency. Bernstein (1967) has noted that the process of practice is always a matter of finding new solutions to a motor problem rather than the representation of just one stereotyped method. When young athletes practice a particular basketball shot, they constantly engage in the midtask evaluation of performance, using various revisions and modifications as part of the active practice.

Greenwald (1970) has described the "closed-loop" mechanisms of feedback long studied by psychologists and neurologists. He has observed that a recently accelerating trend in the analysis of skill performance is to regard the performer as an information processor who compares incoming sensory feedback from responses (reafference) with a stored representation of what feedback from correct performance should be (imaged reafference). Performance control is achieved when the information processors detect discrepancies between image and actual reafference, then generate responses that serve to reduce or eliminate these disparities.

Such a closed-loop model is a true *servomechanism*, a part of many engineering concepts. In essence, when performing a motor activity, we have a general idea of that action in mind. We then compare what we are doing to our idea. Proprioceptive and kinesthetic feedback from limbs (or digits or mouth muscles) enter the *motor analyzer* system of the brain to enable us to make the comparisons and effect the needed adjustments.

Memory is another guiding force behind sophisticated motor movement. Most actions involve a specific sequence of basic muscular contractions as well as coordinated rhythms of facilitation and inhibition of motor groups. Luria has described the *kinetic melodies* or *motor engrams,* stored patterns of familiar motor actions. These are not dissimilar to the rolls in an old-fashioned player piano. One simply plugs in the roll (i.e., the kinetic melody), and a particular sequence of motor actions transpires. Luria (1980) points out that "one begins with ideas regarding the purpose of an action and the possible ways of performing that action. These ideas are then translated into specific visual and kinesthetic programs which ultimately generate the required movement. The ideas are stored in the form of 'motor engrams,' 'memory images,' or what are sometimes called 'kinetic melodies.' " When these engrams become "firmly established by previous experience, the movement will be highly automatized in character, the corresponding 'ideas' will be stripped of their complex psychological signs and the act becomes a simplified physiological process."

A process called *serial chaining* governs such continuity of performance. Greenwald (1970) describes this process as the "selection of responses within a routinized action sequence by stimuli produced as feedback from responses earlier in this sequence." Serial chaining is involved in performances of invariant sequential routines. In other words, when we perform an action, the sequence of each unit of motor movement is cued in by what immediately preceded it.

This is typified by the process of learning to perform any routinized series of responses, such as a musical melody. Correct performance may be described as a series of specific responses corresponding to the series of notes comprising the melody. As performance becomes reliable, playing a given note is consistently preceded not only by reception of the situational stimulus to which performance is already conditioned, but also by reception of stimuli produced by performance of the preceding series of notes. The latter stimuli may be auditory, visual, proprioceptive, kinesthetic, and/or tactile. Regardless of modality, these stimuli are directly contingent on the performer's own behavior—that is, they constitute intrinsic sensory feedback from performance (Greenwald 1970).

A strong motor engram of a routine procedure enables the performer to use each step in the process to suggest what comes next. This is true for forming letters with a pencil, assembling the necessary components for a complex gross motor action (such as swimming), or knitting a scarf.

In performing an action, we trigger individual muscle groups in an appropriate order while inhibiting movements that are irrelevant and wasteful. Such *motor inhibition* conserves energy and also smooths out our motor actions. This energy-saving process is exemplified in children's progressive inhibition of associated extraneous movements during the elementary school years (Cohen et al. 1967). When very young children perform a particular motor act, they may show irrelevant associated movements of the mouth or of the opposite limb. Motor inhibition is critical to performance when we try to balance on one foot, defy gravity on a tightrope, or coast on a bicycle. In these instances, muscles may tend to contract spontaneously on one side of the body, causing us to lean in that direction. The balancer must have a good sense of body position, knowing that the swaying is occurring (through reafferent feedback), interpreting that knowledge rapidly, and correcting the position through appropriate motor inhibition. At the same time, motor facilitation on the contralateral side of the body is necessary.

An element of conscious, or at least partially conscious, planning is often inserted within these steps of the motor action process. We may initiate a motor action with a symbolic or concrete image of a specific goal. Then, in the process of *motor planning,* we search for a method of accomplishing that goal and promptly initiate the appropriate technique. Motor planning involves blueprinting the action. To use an analogy, an architect's blueprints must contain not only a representation of the ultimate product (the building) but also an implicit plan for achieving the goal. Implementation of the specific pattern of motor actions constitutes what is commonly referred to as *praxis.*

The motor actions essential for everyday life can be classified according to the degree of conscious effort they exact from the actor. They exist on a continuum, ranging from unconscious postural corrections to the highly deliberative, individual motor components needed to repair an engine, embroider, or build a model airplane.

As we acquire a motor skill, the allocation of conscious effort changes. For example, in the early stages of learning to play the piano, a child must struggle to locate individual keys. Although the ultimate goal is a melody or scale, the child still views production as locating and depressing specific keys on the keyboard. This is a highly deliberative, planned action which relies heavily on visual input and both visual and auditory feedback. The resultant performance is generally slow and marked by frequent self-correction and hesitation. As the child proceeds, he or she relies increasingly on *serial chaining.* That is, one note logically leads to another in producing a melody. Some *simultaneous chaining* also occurs—certain fingers produce analogous movements all at once to create chords. Such serial and simultaneous chaining provide a format for the complex motor action of piano playing. The child continues to rely on proprioceptive, kinesthetic, visual, and auditory feedback for self-correction. However, memory becomes a growing source of programming and self-monitoring. In the final stages, the process of piano playing is likely to become increasingly *automatized.* To perform a sonata, the pianist engages in a well-integrated, unified motor activity and finds it increasingly difficult to articulate how this is being done. Moreover, the process of progressive automatization enables the pianist to play and simultaneously to add interpretation, personal flair, or sophisticated style to the performance.

Figure 6-1 synthesizes the various concepts we have presented into a conceptual model of the implementation of a motor action. The unified model begins with a perceived need for an action and is followed by the selection of the particular action likely to meet that need. This requires intentional behavior and sometimes the use of problem-solving strategies. Then a perceptual image or verbal description predicts what the desired action will look like or how it might be described verbally. This leads to a motor idea, which is a preliminary notion of how one's motor system might respond to implement the action. The motor idea is refined into a highly specific *ideomotor plan* (a blueprint for motor coordination) with the help of verbal instructions, spatial cues from the environment, and/or information from memory about how the action was implemented on previous occasions (motor engrams). This leads to *praxis,* the systematic motor movements that occur (frequently through serial chaining) to create the action itself. Once the action is in progress it is subject to quality control through exafferent (visual) and/or reafferent (kinesthetic) feedback. This proceeds through the motor analyzer in the brain so that adjustments can be made in the ideomotor plan to refine movements in mid-action. Ultimately, the actor determines that the action has either accomplished or failed to accomplish its aim and can be terminated. At this point, if the action is relatively trivial and unusual, it may be allowed to decay. On the other hand, the action may be stored in motor memory as a precedent for future such actions. Under conditions in which there has been a great deal of practice, the steps between the choice of an action and the ideomotor plan can be bypassed or curtailed significantly.

The example of a football player who is alert for the possibility of catching a ball illustrates this conceptual model. First he perceives the need to prepare an action. He chooses to run at the same time that he focuses his vision and prepares his arms and hands for the possible catch. He has a perceptual image of what it will be like to judge the trajectory of the ball and ultimately grab it. This leads to

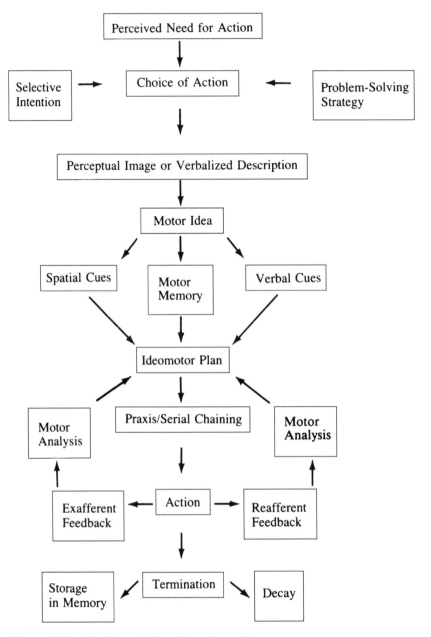

Figure 6-1. Implementation of a motor action

the motor idea of a need to move certain muscle groups in an appropriate manner to catch the ball. As the ball approaches, he makes use of visual spatial cues to the trajectory itself and of memory of previous efforts at ball catching. He may also verbalize the instructions to himself as he chases the ball. The motor idea, combined with the various cues that inform it, creates a highly specific ideomotor plan or sequence of muscular activities that will lead to the action. The plan is then implemented. The player actively pursues the ball. While he is doing so, he is constantly analyzing the relative position of his body, his arms, his eyes, and the ball. Such exafferent and reafferent feedback enables him to alter his running speed and his dynamic body position. This is an ongoing process allowing for self-regulation until he catches the ball. He might then use this isolated experience as a means of enhancing the future pursuit of footballs.

MOTOR DEVELOPMENT

Children's gross and fine motor skills develop steadily during school years. Many frequently used motor actions become more automatic. Tying shoelaces, getting dressed, writing the alphabet, and catching and throwing a ball are procedures likely to become increasingly automatized. When children acquire a new skill, they often trade off speed for accuracy (Wolff 1982). Some youngsters, however, concentrate more on accuracy than speed. Nevertheless, increasing motor speed is an important aspect of developmental progression. Denckla (1973), using a series of finger-tapping exercises, developed norms suggesting that during elementary school, children grow markedly in their rates of motor sequencing. Denckla speculated that this may coincide with increasing velocity of nerve conduction.

Increasing strength and stamina are other developmental accomplishments. Studies of the development of static strength in preschool and elementary school-children usually employ grip strength as recorded by a hand dynamometer. Boys double their grip strength between the ages of six and eleven and show an increase of 359 percent between six and eighteen (Espenschade and Eckert 1980). Girls reveal an increase of only 260 percent during this time. It is difficult to determine to what extent this is cultural, based on the activities of boys and girls, or biological. Development of muscle strength is symmetrical on both sides of the body, although absolute strength is slightly greater on the dominant side. *Dynamic strength,* or *propulsion,* also increases during school years. It is reflected in constantly improved performance in long jump and shot put, two common track and field events. Acceleration also shows pronounced gains during school years.

Increases in strength, propulsion, and acceleration result in highly specific changes in motor performance. Running has been studied extensively in school-children. The speed with which a child can run depends on the length of the stride as well as its tempo. Running speed, which improves steadily during early elementary years, correlates with consistent growth in body size and concomitant gains in lever length and strength, resulting in increased size and tempo of the running stride. A child can endure ever longer distances with increasing age. The development of running speed in boys seems to continue through the age of seventeen or eighteen. Girls, on the other hand, tend to taper off in running speed at about age thirteen or fourteen. Again, this may reflect cultural phenomena (less participation by girls in sports when these studies were performed). Current trends may reverse this tendency.

Jumping (both long jump and high jump) also improves. Greater body size is both advantageous and detrimental; the increased body weight and muscle mass must be overcome by gains in propulsion and strength. Certain children's growth in body weight may outstrip their muscular development. Hurdle jumping also improves continuously and relatively gradually during elementary and secondary school years. As in running speed, the degree of improvement seems to be greater for boys than girls in most studies. However, there appears to be enormous variability in performance. In one study it was found that the average jumper at seven years jumped approximately as far as the poorer 10 percent of eleven year olds, suggesting considerable overlap between ages.

Throwing ability also progresses rapidly. Boys' larger forearm lengths and girths and greater strength give them an advantage over girls in propulsion of an object for distance. Throws for accuracy, on the other hand, do not produce great differences by sex.

Balance is another important developmental acquisition. Static balance (on a beam) increases constantly between the ages of five and eleven with no significant gender differences. Again, a wide range of proficiency is encountered at each age.

Coordination is frequently mentioned as a parameter of gross motor ability. Children are said to be well coordinated when they move easily and when the sequence and timing of their actions are well controlled. Measuring the progression of coordination is difficult since so many subcomponents are involved (see previous section). Most often, coordination is assessed by combining various "stunts." Measures of control, balance, agility, and flexibility are usually combined in characterizing gross motor coordination. Children should be able to change their total-body direction quickly, rapidly flex and extend their arms and hands, and engage in fast serial motor actions. All of these develop dramatically during elementary and high school.

A number of gender differences have already been pointed out. However, they are not consistent and there is considerable overlap. Espenschade and Eckert (1980) remark that "in general, boys have been found to excel in those activities requiring strength and in grosser movements, whereas girls tend to excel in the finer coordination activities such as exactness in walking, speed in grasping, [and] exactness of grasping."

Children's proficiency in fine motor abilities increases, much like proficiency in gross motor abilities. Depending in part on practice and exposure, children become increasingly adept in various tasks of eye-hand coordination. They are better able to integrate sensory inputs (especially visual and kinesthetic) with specific motor plans. Routine functions become automatic, and motor speed improves progressively (Denckla 1973). Increased use of the most distal portions of the fingers allows for finer dexterity in a variety of artistic and mechanical activities. Children also show a marked progression in bimanual coordination, the ability to perform tasks involving either simultaneous or alternating actions of the hands. *Graphomotor facility,* ease with the mechanical aspects of writing, is, of course, the most conspicuous fine motor achievement of the schoolchild. It will be described later under "Developmental Output Failure."

One trend that transcends both fine and gross motor function is the progressive development of motor inhibition—one of the most widely studied developmental phenomena in schoolchildren. *Associated movements* (see p. 553), also called *overflow movements,* are common before the age of seven. As children grow older, these associated movements become increasingly rare (Cohen et al. 1967). In other words, children become more and more able to execute a highly specific motor act on one side of the body without extraneous movement on the contralateral side. During preschool and early elementary school, children commonly move their mouths while they write. Tapping a foot may elicit simultaneous movement of fingers or lips, or performing a task with one hand may cause identical movements with the other hand. Perhaps as a result of progressive myelination of nerve fibers, schoolchildren are increasingly specific in their motor productions. That is, irrelevant motor activities are inhibited. This is part of a general process of judicious selective facilitation and inhibition of muscle groups, a phenomenon that becomes progressively evident during school years and continues through and beyond puberty. The assessment of motor inhibition is a standard part of many evaluations of development in schoolchildren, not only because it indicates motor development but also because it may mark associated attention deficits and possible lags in central nervous system maturation (Denckla and Rudel 1978).

As already noted, children display considerable developmental variation in motor proficiency on both new and practiced actions. It is appropriate now to examine some of these variations and dysfunctions and to consider their impacts on schoolchildren. We begin by surveying common variations and dysfunctions of gross motor function.

GROSS MOTOR ABILITY: DEVELOPMENTAL VARIATION AND DYSFUNCTION

Gross motor proficiency can contribute significantly to self-image and self-competence. Children who are clumsy or awkward commonly feel ineffective and inferior to their peers. Those who are last to be chosen for teams, those who are ridiculed during physical education classes, and those who habitually spoil things for teammates are prone to become disenchanted and to fear taking risks with performance. This may lead to growing social isolation, depression, and more pervasive deprivation of success. In view of these potentially injurious impacts, some form of motor success is likely an indispensable ingredient of healthy child development. Children who are excessively clumsy are vulnerable, particularly if they are unsuccessful in nonmotor areas as well.

Shaw, Levine, and Belfer (1982) observed a phenomenon they called "developmental double jeopardy" in a clinic for learning problems. Children were grouped according to those whose learning problems were complicated by gross motor delays and those whose learning problems were accompanied by adequate or superior gross motor abilities. The two groups were evaluated by a psychologist, who was not aware whether youngsters were well coordinated or not. The testing included various measures of self-concept and emotional health. Children who had both learning problems and gross motor dysfunctions had far more difficulty with self-image and significantly more emotional indicators than those who had only learning problems. Thus, any complete description of a developing child must include consideration of motor mastery and the potential impacts thereof.

Children with gross motor delays form a heterogeneous group. Some appear to have problems in virtually every kind of gross motor performance, while others have discrete deficits affecting only certain forms of pursuit. Denckla (1984) described the following "anomalies of motor development" that are frequently associated with clumsiness: mixed dominance (nonhandedness) or excessive right- (or left-) handedness, skill-preference paradox (the dominant hand does worse than the nondominant one), hand preference manifested too early or too late, persistent overflow movements (i.e., poor motor inhibition), poor reciprocal alternation (such as rapid pronation and supination), difficulty with imitation of a new sequence, and slow or inconsistent motor reaction times. Breakdowns in gross motor output may arise from difficulties in one or more steps in the action processes described earlier in this chapter.

Children may encounter great difficulty with interpretation of sensory data. Denckla has distinguished motor activities that are programmed through "outer spatial" input, and motor activities that are programmed through "inner spatial" input and feedback. The former are likely to be visual or spatial, while the latter are proprioceptive or kinesthetic. A breakdown in programming through outer spatial data could make it hard to judge trajectories for catching a baseball. Proprioceptive and kinesthetic feedback (inner spatial data) help with balance, body position sense, and internal feedback about movement—all of which are important for running, swimming, skiing, and gymnastics. Thus, a breakdown of either of these input modalities may result in clumsiness for those activities that require them.

The term *dyspraxia* is used differently in various contexts and by different clinicians. Here it refers specifically to the integrated activity of particular muscle groups to accomplish a motor action. Some children appear to have a significant gross motor dyspraxia. Some lack ideomotor plans. They may lack a visual or verbal idea of a motor action. Others have a plan and are able to appreciate sensory input and feedback, but they simply cannot perform the act effectively. They are unable to invoke specific coordinated motor group actions to complete the task. One child stated in a frustrated tone, "The other day in gym class the teacher showed us how to slide into second base. I understood exactly, but when I tried, it didn't work. I just couldn't get my own muscles to do what I told them to do. I think I could teach the *other* kids how to do it; I just can't get *my* body to do it." A child may have either a pervasive dyspraxia, affecting all or most complex gross motor actions, or a dyspraxia relevant only to certain gross motor pursuits. Other children may have difficulty with some steps in the motor implementation process but not with others. For example, children with a dyspraxia may perform well on some motor activities if someone helps them get started.

Another form of gross motor delay involves the various deficiencies of motor memory. Some children simply cannot recall the appropriate steps. They may not be able to retrieve the correct serial chain for a continuous motor action. They may have particular problems with rhythmic activities, such as those requiring rapid alternating movements. Gross motor memory is perhaps best illustrated in the mastery of various dance steps. Some individuals can learn a particular motor pattern for dancing with great ease. They have no trouble recalling its specific motor elements in the correct sequence; they make good use of overall motor memory including the cues of serial chaining. Other children have enormous difficulty retrieving such motor sequences for particular kinds of dances. Even the auxiliary cue of the beat of the music is not enough to aid them in their recall of the appropriate kinetic program. They seem to have to relearn the steps each time they reach the dance floor. Gymnastics is another pursuit in which good motor memory is critical. The precise coordination of muscle groups in a sequence of facilitations and inhibitions is essential for proficiency.

Most gross motor dysfunction is extracurricular; there is little, if any, correlation between gross motor proficiency and academic performance. In fact, it may be that certain individuals become scholars partly because of their clumsiness. As a result of their ineptitude, they are not at all distracted by the lure of athletics, and follow instead more contemplative routes toward success.

A lack of success in gross motor pursuits commonly engenders *performance inhibitions.* Victors (1961, quoted in Espenschade and Eckert 1980) notes that "there is a propensity to avoid repetition of combinations of movements that have produced unsuccessful results." If children find a task too difficult or if they face recurrent negative reinforcement or humiliation from its performance, they are apt to avoid engaging in the action. This subsequently superimposes a relative lack of practice over a preexisting insufficiency. Consequently, the gap between a child and his or her peers can widen over the years simply because the latter are more practiced. Such a secondary effect of early demonstrations of inadequacy needs to be considered as part of the clinical picture of gross motor incoordination. Level of interest is another important determinant. Cultural factors, family interest in sports, and role modeling are likely to affect the extent to which children gain practice in motor activities.

A final consideration in the gross motor domain has to do with the structure and conceptual content of sports. Some children may refrain from engaging in athletic activities because they cannot meet the demands on organization or attention. A typical example is the child with attention deficits who joins the Little League and displays superb gross motor skills, exhibiting some dazzling fielding ability and attaining a high batting average. Despite this, the child suddenly quits the sport, refuses to show up for practices, and is dropped from the team. Everyone is bewildered. The truth is that such a child may have had problems delaying gratification (waiting to come up to bat), conceptualizing the rules of the game, fulfilling the intense social demands, remembering when to do things, or sustaining attention to the detail of the game. Some children with language problems shun complex team sports because of the verbal requirements for communication and the processing of instructions. While these factors are not basic components of gross motor ability, they are likely to have an impact on proficiency by secondarily affecting the frequency and intensity of participation in various athletic events. By understanding the exact reasons for a child's reluctance to participate, we can often select an appropriate sport, one that circumvents weaknesses while mobilizing strengths (see chapter 15). Much of this depends on an accurate assessment of any apparent gross motor dysfunction.

Assessment of Gross Motor Function

As with other areas of development, one can evaluate gross motor ability both through careful history taking and some direct observations of performance. In this developmental area, probably more than any other, evaluators need to engage in fastidious task analysis. By finding out which athletic pursuits are easy for a child and which are not, evaluators may succeed in localizing a specific deficit in gross motor production. For example, a youngster who is particularly good at swimming and skiing but who has trouble playing baseball may be experiencing problems primarily with the programming of a gross motor response based on outer spatial (visual) input (perceptual motor ideas) and feedback. In other instances evaluators might suspect dysfunctions involving balance and body position sense (proprioceptive and kinesthetic feedback). Sports that require complex sequential output may be problematic for children with dysfunctions in that area. Evidence can be gathered from reports of proficiency as well as a child's interest in a particular gross motor activity. As noted above, children have a tendency to avoid those pursuits in which they are likely to be humiliated. Thus, relative levels of interest may provide hints about ability.

The ANSER System questionnaires contain a number of items related to gross motor function. They are often used as evidence in compiling a functional profile of a schoolchild's development. Certain children may seek refuge in sports in which there is a great deal of privacy. In some communities, soccer becomes a frequent medium for this form of athletic retreat. In soccer, wherever the ball may be, there tends to be a crowd. This, of course, diminishes individual accountability. Thus, a child may run up and down the soccer field for an entire season, feeling very much a part of the mainstream of athletic action, without ever experiencing any contact between foot and ball. In areas where soccer has become increasingly competitive, individual players may be more visible.

The complete developmental evaluation of a schoolchild should include some direct assessment of gross motor proficiency. As mentioned, an assessment of associated movements (motor inhibition) has become a routine part of such evaluations. Chapter 14 covers this kind of assessment in more detail.

A number of standardized tests of gross motor ability are available, including the Bruininks-Oseretsky (Bruininks 1978) *Test of Motor Proficiency* and the

McCarron (1976) *Assessment of Neuromuscular Development.* The pediatric neurodevelopmental examinations *PEER, PEEX 2,* and *PEERAMID 2* include screening observations of gross motor ability as well as tests of motor inhibition. Assessments of gross motor proficiency should include items relating to eye–upper limb coordination (such as catching a ball), direct assessment of static balance and body position sense (standing on one foot with eyes closed), rapid alternating movement, and the formation and sustenance of various gross motor rhythmic activities.

By combining the direct screening observations of motor function with the reports of parents, teachers, and the child, one can analyze fairly accurately this important area of child development. Accurate analysis can then lead to the prescription of a pursuit that will provide gratification through mastery of at least some gross motor skills.

Causes of Clumsiness.   When performing any gross motor evaluation, a clinician must be aware that clumsiness may be a manifestation of a neurological disorder. While such conditions are relatively rare, detecting them can be important. Careful history taking and a complete neurological examination should make diagnosis of such problems possible. Table 6-1 summarizes these various muscular and neuromuscular disorders.

Sometimes the distinction between mild cerebral palsy and a gross motor delay or clumsiness as a developmental dysfunction is particularly difficult to discern. Although more severe forms of cerebral palsy may be manifest through athetoid movements, extreme hypertonicity, or hypotonicity, the more subtle manifestations of cerebral palsy are often indistinguishable from the low-severity develop-

Table 6-1.   Additional medical and psychological causes of clumsiness

---

Joint inflammation

Hyperthyroidism

Muscular dystrophy

Congenital muscle disorders (myopathies)

Nerve inflammations (neuritis)

Hydrocephalus

Cerebral palsy

Brain tumor (especially in the cerebellum)

Spinal cord disorders

Vision problems

Vestibular problems

Side effects of certain medications (e.g., phenobarbital, lithium, imipramine, theophylline, phenothiazines)

Psychological disorders (e.g., hysteria, malingering, or anxiety)

Substance abuse (alcohol or drugs)

---

mental delays referred to in this chapter. In such cases, it is probably best not to use the term *cerebral palsy* since this may have a potentially negative impact and is unlikely to be helpful to these children.

Gross Motor Dysfunction: Management Issues

As we have noted, athletic pursuits can be an important avenue of productivity, while a lack of gross motor mastery can erode self-esteem and body image during school years. For these reasons, it is essential to offer help to children who are clumsy and unable to achieve in the motor sphere. This is especially important for those students who receive little or no gratification in academic pursuits.

School physical education departments are increasingly recognizing their special responsibilities to children deprived of motor mastery. Remedial physical education programs, which afford opportunities for more structured practice in various motor domains, are increasingly available. Occupational and physical therapists are also available to help children with body awareness, overall coordination, and specific motor skills. These professionals are especially important in the management of children with severe motor impairments.

It is essential to identify areas of motor achievement in which children are likely to succeed, thereby enhancing self-esteem in otherwise deprived students. The entire range of possible motor experiences should be considered, including track and field events, jogging, gymnastics, karate, dancing, hiking and mountain climbing, skiing, wrestling, swimming, golf, and tennis. Some children are not particularly suited for the structured demands and social pressures of team sports but perform better in individual pursuits. Some experience difficulty with athletic activities that are based on the interpretation of outer spatial data for catching and throwing a ball (see pp. 192–93) but can succeed when gross motor outputs are based on inner spatial data, such as that needed for track and field events, swimming, dance, and gymnastics. Any motor rehabilitation program should work on weaknesses but stress potential strengths or areas of demonstrated proficiency. In many cases, it is wise for children with motor problems to specialize in just one gross motor activity rather than strive to star in a different sport each season.

Many students with relative weaknesses in the gross motor domain may acquire adequate skills; however, they require much more time, motivation, and effort to reach particular levels of ability. A major question for these children is how they can obtain the extra practice and have sufficient privacy to avoid derision from peers while they awkwardly perfect their skills. This can be a challenge for physical education teachers and for parents; however, it is more than worth the effort. A student who finds motor gratification for the first time can experience a remarkable elevation in self-esteem and motivation. At the same time, we must recognize the inappropriateness and inhumanity of forcing students to participate in embarrassing gross motor enterprises. Serious thought needs to be given to the rescue of students who endure extreme humiliation in a gym class or after-school sports program. Humanitarian excuses from such endeavors are more than justifiable. Certainly no adults would ever be willing to display the inadequacy of their bodies in front of colleagues or neighbors. Children *and* adults have a right to pride and a right to cover up bodily inadequacies.

Gross Motor Talent: Management Issues

Students who show outstanding athletic abilities may pose some management issues that are just as compelling as those presented by youngsters who are clumsy. In particular, children who experience an enormous amount of gratification in sports may be susceptible to some unfortunate side effects. The athletic pursuits may assume such great importance that virtually no other undertaking can compete effectively for the children's attention and effort. Sometimes academic proficiency can suffer because sports are such an overwhelming distraction. If children have excellent gross motor abilities but disabling developmental dysfunctions in other areas, the athletic field can become a strategic retreat and, in the worst case, a means of avoiding the need to grapple with learning difficulties. In some instances, parents and coaches may unwittingly conspire to overemphasize the importance of sports. Overzealous fathers or mothers may experience such intense vicarious and direct pleasure from their children's athletic triumphs that the youngsters come to see sports as an exclusive source of approval and means of demonstrating talent. In sports, they may actually enjoy too much success too early in life. The inflated gratification may be a "hard act to follow," setting them up for disappointment and despair later in life when their gross motor talents are unlikely to have as great a payoff. The implications for management are clear: parents and coaches as well as the affected children all need to be helped to be more moderate, to avoid making well-coordinated children into celebrities, thereby fostering all kinds of fantasies about professional stardom and crowding out other important and potentially more durable priorities.

Children who are failing academically but succeeding on the playing fields are another common challenge. Some schools have a policy that prohibits students from participating in athletic events if their grades are below a certain level. This practice can certainly be justified in some respects. However, we must be cautious not to remove the sole means of gratification or accomplishment in life. That is, for students whose only triumphs are occurring in sports with significant failures in the academic realm, prohibiting participation in athletics may deliver the final blow to self-esteem. Furthermore, it is unlikely that those students will go home and study poetry instead of attending football practice. It is more probable, in fact, that they will loiter, socialize, or withdraw and become depressed as a result of the action. In the face of academic failure, it might be more beneficial and sensible to *reduce* the amount of time permitted for practice and to substitute supervised study time or tutorial help for that practice time, rather than totally depriving these students of the only activity that generates pride.

The management of gross motor issues—both dysfunction and talent—clearly requires considerable sensitivity and an understanding of the impacts of gross motor performance and expectations on a particular child. As with other developmental functions, the optimal management of problems necessitates close cooperation between parents, school personnel, and (when necessary) professionals outside of the school. There is a need for flexibility, especially in developing policies on such issues as participation in physical education and interscholastic sports. Those formulating rigid policies need to be aware of the potentially damaging effects on individual students as they contend with unique developmental variations.

DEVELOPMENTAL OUTPUT FAILURE: MOTOR UNDERPINNINGS

Gross motor function is a major pathway through which children can exhibit their strengths or reveal their weaknesses. Academic productivity is an even more conspicuous form of display. Large numbers of children are referred for evaluation because of reduced academic productivity. Although many of them have no trouble *learning,* all such children have difficulty *producing.* As we shall see, there are often strong neurodevelopmental deterrents to productivity. These students commonly are accused of laziness, poor motivation, hedonism, and indifference. In other instances, their parents or teachers may be held liable. Affected students usually have difficulty completing assignments, getting ideas on paper quickly and effectively, and taking quizzes or tests. *Developmental output failure* is a term used to describe these children (Levine, Oberklaid, and Meltzer 1981). It is applied, in particular, to children in middle childhood, students between the ages of nine and fifteen whose academic production cannot keep pace with adult expectations and local standards. Our discussion of this phenomenon is included in this chapter on motor implementation because ultimately all such students have difficulty transmitting ideas on paper. The motor implementation of written work is deficient because of a basic fine motor dysfunction and/or difficulties with the input or memory programs needed to guide the writing implement.

Developmental output failure should not be considered a distinct syndrome. The manifestations and developmental characteristics differ somewhat from child to child. Included are children whose output failure represents a late complication of long-standing academic difficulties. Some of them had trouble learning to read and mastering the alphabet in early grades. They may have improved substantially in decoding and comprehension skills but find themselves having significant output problems by fifth or sixth grade. In other cases, children perform well during the primary grades, displaying no difficulty with information processing. They process and master new ideas or concepts with apparent ease. It is not until late elementary school that they deteriorate. The demands for high output and for increasingly sophisticated graphomotor implementation exceed their capacities. There may then occur a relentless decline in grades, in motivation, and in school-related self-esteem (Levine 1984c). This, in turn, can lead to devastating complications, such as antisocial behavior, depression, and alienation.

Evolving Expectations

To appreciate the phenomenology of developmental output failure, it is necessary to review the ways in which academic expectations evolve from early to late elementary school, for it is there that the precipitates of output failure arise. The following list summarizes the evolution of expectations:

- Progression from an emphasis on decoding symbols to an emphasis on motor encoding or creating one's own communication through such symbols, as in writing.

- Movement from simple analysis and synthesis of data to integration of information from multiple sources, including one's own long-term memory and several different current perspectives (the teacher, the reading passage, the class discussion).

- Growing demand for increasingly sustained attention to detail (even amid conditions of fatigue and distraction).

- Increasing reliance on retrieval rather than on recognition memory.

- Heightened demand for *rapid* automatic retrieval memory.

- Progressive need for more *simultaneous* rapid retrieval memory, the capacity to recall almost instantaneously many bits of information in a synchronized manner (such as the need to remember at once punctuation, spelling, capitalization, and grammar during the act of writing).

- Increasing requirements for large chunks of output (especially written) necessitating more delay of gratification and greater endurance.

- Growing need for verbal fluency, quicker and more accurate word finding, and facilitated sentence formulation for participation in class discussion and for effective writing.

- Steadily intensifying demand for speed, appropriate strategies, and organizational skill.

- Increasing call for rapid automatic graphomotor production (i.e., the fine motor efficiency needed for fluent writing).

These expanded requirements commonly converge on motor implementation. Writing becomes the sine qua non of academic productivity. Effectively producing a large amount of writing necessitates more efficient encoding of ideas; effective, fast, and effortless memory; appropriate levels of ability in expressive language, in synthesis, and in organization; sustained attention to detail; and, of course, graphomotor proficiency.

Children with developmental output failure have varying combinations of dysfunctions (see table 6-2) that make it nearly impossible for them to keep pace with

Table 6-2. Possible dysfunctions in developmental output failure (varying combinations of which impede productivity)

DYSFUNCTION	COMMON SUBCOMPONENTS
Graphomotor disability	Motor planning problems Impaired nonvisual feedback Motor memory fluctuation Dyspraxia
Memory deficiency	Generalized slowness of recall, lack of automatization Poor visualization Weak recall of rules Delayed automatization
Attention deficit	Impersistence and fatigue Impulsiveness and poor task planning Dys-synchrony of functions (poor simultaneous recall) Lack of self-monitoring
Expressive language problems	Word retrieval weaknesses Trouble with formulation of sentences Poor narrative and/or expository skills
Organizational problems	Disarray of materials Disorientation in time Poor synthesis and integration

evolving expectations. Some of these dysfunctions have been discussed in earlier chapters and will be reviewed only briefly here. Five general categories of dysfunction—graphomotor output, memory, attention, language, and organization—are variably encountered in these children. They tend to occur in clusters and have a direct impact on the motor implementation of written work.

Graphomotor Function and Motor Implementation

To understand graphomotor function (and therefore dysfunction) in writing, it is helpful to explore some motor components of writing. Typically, a writing implement is held in what is called a *dynamic tripod grasp* (see fig. 10-12). The pen or pencil is grasped between the radial distal surface of the middle finger and the pulp surfaces of the thumb and index finger. The index finger is somewhat less flexed than the other digits, which tend to be in a neutral position. The thumb is relatively fully opposed. Simultaneous flexion or extension of the radial digits (i.e., thumb, index finger, and middle finger), especially at the interphalangeal joints, causes movement in a proximal-distal axis with only a minimum of lateral deviation of the fingers. The principal movement is a simple flexor or extensor synergy. That is, all of the muscles of the fingers act simultaneously and in a coordinated manner to produce the bending or extension movements. During writing, this flexion and extension create the vertical and rotatory dimension of letters. The letter sequences, and to some extent the horizontal component of letter formation, result more from actions of the arm. Thus, the act of writing combines intrinsic and extrinsic movements.

When writing with a dynamic tripod grasp, the writer needs to equilibrate several motoric priorities. First, the writer must stabilize the pen or pencil; a firm grip must prevent it from slipping out of control. Second, the writing implement must be maximally maneuverable; it needs to be easily manipulated, especially in the vertical and rotatory axes. Finally, the implement must move in such a way that it transmits kinesthetic feedback, so that the writer (via the brain's motor analyzer) can maintain awareness of its location within letters and words. This is essential for programming the serial chain of motor movements. These three priorities may be traded off to varying degrees. That is, increased stability may limit mobility. Increased mobility may impair some of the fine-tuned feedback. Certain kinds of developmental dysfunction may promote imbalances in these priorities.

Four basic kinds of motor dysfunction appear clinically to hamper written fluency and accuracy and thereby constitute major contributing factors to developmental output failure.

Impaired Kinesthetic Feedback.   Luria (1980) observed that there must be a constant flow of afferent impulses, not only from external objects that are to be taken into account when the movement is constructed, but also, and primarily, from the subject's own locomotor apparatus, whose every change in position alters the conditions of the movement. That is why the decisive factors in the construction of movement are not so much the effector impulses (which are of a purely executive character), as the complex system of afferent impulses that give precision to the composition of the motor act and that ensure that the movements are subjected to a wide system of correction (see p. 189).

Thus, the complex motor action of writing depends overwhelmingly on accurate, ongoing kinesthetic (reafferent) feedback. Before undertaking the written transcription of a word or sentence, the writer has a kinesthetic plan in mind. She or he then compares ongoing kinesthetic feedback to the original plan in order to correct, persist in, or terminate the graphomotor pattern. A breakdown in the kinesthetic feedback process is a common and insidious deterrent to writing. Impairments of kinesthetic feedback may be associated with a more generalized picture of *finger agnosia,* in which youngsters may have problems localizing their fingers in space. This problem sometimes is said to be part of a condition called the *Developmental Gerstmann Syndrome* (comprised of poor finger localization, sequencing difficulties, and problems in mathematics and spelling). Kinsbourne and Warrington (1964) developed a series of tests of finger localization to determine whether children can appreciate with their eyes closed the simultaneous touching of two of their fingers. Tasks of finger localization (see fig. 6-2) have also been used to detect finger agnosia.

Children with impaired kinesthetic feedback present a fairly typical history. Often they show no impairment whatsoever of other aspects of fine motor function.

In other words, they may have difficulty with writing and pencil control but be very good at sewing and adept at putting together bicycles, small engines, or model airplanes. This discrepancy can occur because the nonwriting tasks consist of predominantly visual input and visual kinesthetic feedback. Often when such children attempt to write, they employ mainly visual monitoring. Consequently, they may write with their eyes too close to the page. Unfortunately, visual feedback during writing is far too slow and mechanical. It is not easy for them to monitor visually the serial chain of motor movements. Thus, writing becomes too slow and much too awkward; as a result, automatization of motor movement is delayed or absent.

The handwriting of a child with impaired kinesthetic feedback may be sufficiently legible. The problem is that production is far too slow, too mechanical, and too demanding on attention. A child with this problem may have trouble writing and remembering, writing and thinking, or writing and applying rules simultaneously. She expends so much effort on the motor act of writing that little remains for other required embellishments.

Very often children with impaired kinesthetic feedback appear to compensate for their problems by developing an awkward, counterproductive pencil grasp. They forgo or never acquire the dynamic tripod described above. Instead, they adopt a wide range of contorted grasps, some of which are illustrated in figure 6-3. They include an extreme hook, a thumb overlap pattern, a perpendicular pencil position, and/or an unusually distal or proximal position of the fingers on the

Figure 6-2. Finger localization

This child is being tested on an imitative finger movement task from the *PEERAMID 2*. The examiner opposes her fingers and the child imitates by moving the same fingers in the same manner. The child can look at the examiner's fingers but not at his own. Children with finger agnosia are hesitant and/or inaccurate on this task, as they have difficulty localizing their own fingers in the absence of visual cues.

shaft of the pen or pencil. In some cases, children use a variable pencil grip; they must keep changing or readjusting, with a distinct sacrifice of stability and consistency of motor movement. Some have a more normal grip while drawing but revert to the awkward version for writing.

Some children with impaired kinesthetic feedback often exert excessive pressure on the pencil. By bearing down hard, they may derive a greater sense of kinesthetic position. Such children may keep breaking their pencil points, necessitating frequent trips to the sharpener or requiring constant reloading of their

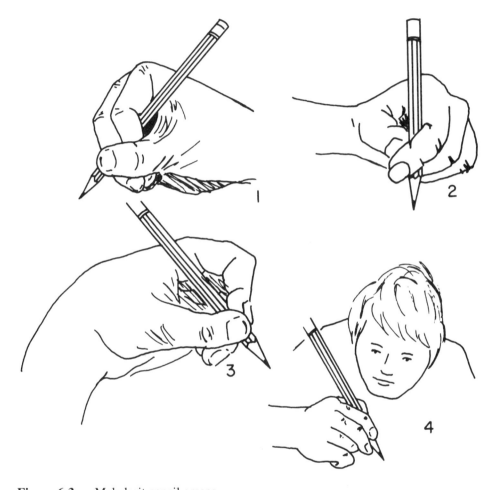

Figure 6-3.   Maladroit pencil grasps

In drawing 1, the child is immobilizing the second and third fingers by placing the thumb across the joints and using mainly wrist movement for implementation and feedback. This grip is commonly associated with finger agnosia. In 2, the pencil is held perpendicular to the page. The second finger, which ordinarily stabilizes the pencil, is not doing so. Thus, an excessive number of joints are mobile during writing. This grasp is found in some children with fine motor dyspraxia. Drawing 3 shows a left-handed hook with the pencil held too tightly (note the hyperextended distal joint of the second finger). In 4, the grip is distal and the child is overrelying on close visual monitoring of the pencil movement. This child may have difficulty appreciating nonvisual feedback during writing.

mechanical pencils. Many children with impaired kinesthetic feedback have great difficulty using ballpoint pens, which tend to be rather slippery; their relative lack of traction is a further deterrent to the appreciation of feedback.

In some cases, the awkward grip represents an attempt to immobilize the most distal digital joints during writing. This forces more liberal use of forearm and shoulder movement, allowing for greater ranges of excursion and less subtle feedback.

The faulty pencil grasp of a child with impaired kinesthetic feedback may work fairly well as a compensatory mechanism in the early grades, when writing consists of producing single words or circling an apple that is a different color from the other apples—when the amount of writing is negligible. However, as the demand for writing increases through elementary school, the maladroit pencil grip can become an increasing liability. Affected children may experience writer's cramp; they may not be able to keep up with the rate requirements for fluent writing. The grip itself may become the problem. In some cases, finger localization abilities improve, but the child is left with the ingrained habit of an awkward, suboptimal pencil grip. Some children produce a significantly diminished quantity of writing. A child with this problem may break all records for brevity of book reports in seventh grade.

Eye-Hand Coordination Problems. Although nonvisual feedback is crucial for writing, some visual feedback is also important. It prevents such faults as writing on the desk, crossing over lines, and creating too steep a downward or upward slant. In other words, visual feedback provides gross monitoring rather than the fine-tuned, kinesthetically transmitted feedback that occurs within letters and words. The history of children with weak eye-hand coordination is likely to be very different from that of children with impaired kinesthetic feedback. Those with poor eye-hand coordination are unlikely to be talented in various mechanical skills. Being a good artist, fixing things, and engaging in various crafts activities depend much more on visual feedback than does writing. When we thread a needle for sewing, for example, there is an initial visual input (the relative spatial positions of the eye of the needle and the end of the thread). We then lead the thread to the eye of the needle by interpreting ongoing, dynamic visual feedback (such as that used by a catcher in estimating the trajectory of a ball) and we base our fine motor responses on such visual exafferent feedback.

Some youngsters may have difficulty arranging numbers in columns and in monitoring the visual aspects of their writing. This may be part of an overall picture of dysfunction in the fine motor area, a history of generalized poor manual dexterity. Thus, the child with impaired kinesthetic feedback may perform many nonwriting tasks quite well, while the child with eye-hand coordination problems may have less difficulty with writing but much more trouble with the slow, deliberative, and generally less rhythmic or automatized motor actions needed for mechanical repairs. Children with eye-hand coordination difficulties may have some problems using the distal portions of their fingers. They may feel more comfortable with proximal muscle movements. Their rate of output on various fine motor tasks is often somewhat diminished. For example, results of the Coding subtest of the *WISC-III* may be low compared to their other demonstrated capacities.

Fine Motor Production.   Dyspraxia has traditionally been described as occurring with specific brain lesions (Luria 1980). It is classically known as *ideational apraxia.* Luria describes two forms of this problem. In one case, a child has difficulty creating an image of the required movement (i.e., formulating an ideomotor plan). In the other form, the central nervous system mechanisms responsible for putting the plan into operation are interrupted. With writing, this applies to children who do not form a good mental image of what it is they are trying to write. Some produce a mental image but fail to see its implications for specific sequences of motor movements. In other words, they have a blueprint for the action but experience difficulty implementing it motorically. Consequently, their writing is slow and awkward. They have serious difficulty with performance. On a writing sample this may reveal itself in significant problems with motor planning and organization. Affected children may use a hieroglyphic type of writing with as much space between letters as there is between words. Such a youngster often writes with considerable hesitation.

Many children with a graphomotor production problem also have some difficulties with oral motor function. As a result, a number of students with a dyspraxia for writing also have had or presently have problems with speech articulation. Less common is an association between a fine motor dyspraxia and a gross motor dyspraxia. In other words, it is quite possible for a child to be a successful athlete and still have difficulties with graphomotor execution. Some children's dyspraxias may be localized very specifically to writing.

Motor Memory Deficits.   The previous section reviewed the way the formation of an ideomotor plan may or may not lead to effective motor implementation. In some instances, difficulty may occur because a child is weak at recalling or maintaining the motor plan. To write well, a student must be able to retrieve the motor patterns of movement effectively and quickly.

In clinics and schools children frequently struggle with motor memory. For them, the retrieval of motor engrams is a slow, strenuous, and sometimes futile exercise. Writing can be thought of as a rotating drum connected to memory; it is a tracing, an indelible record of what is recalled and then transmitted through the writing implement. Children with motor memory deficits have a characteristic handwriting, marred by frequent hesitation, retracing, and illegibility. Memory disorders of this type, in fact, may be the most common cause of poor handwrit-

PENCIL SPEED

START

Figure 6-4.   Eye-hand coordination task

This maze is used on the *PEERAMID* as one indication of a child's graphomotor speed and accuracy. The child is given fifteen seconds to draw a line through the maze without touching its sides.

ing. Typically, children with this form of dysfunction make the same letter several different ways in the same sentence. In other words, they can retrieve no highly specific, consistent ideomotor plan.

Clinical evaluation of children with apparent motor memory dysfunctions most frequently reveals *fluctuating* motor memories. Rather than total motor amnesia, we observe the flickering of a motor memory that waxes and wanes. In the middle of forming a letter, the child seems to forget how. We witness hesitation or retracing, frequent crossing out, and stray lines that suggest not poor pencil control, but erratic motor plans. In general, the writer's fine motor rhythms are likely to be poorly sustained.

Very often children with motor memory disorders compensate for their deficiencies by insisting on using manuscript writing instead of cursive. Printing letters individually produces less strain on the recall of lengthy, complex motor plans and on motor rhythms. A cursive word is likely to be filed in motor memory storage systems as one very long, rhythmic, serial chain or motor engram. Students having difficulty retrieving such traces are more likely to have trouble with sustained, connected motor movements of the type demanded for cursive writing. They are apt to prefer to break down the size of the chunk by using individual symbols (as in manuscript writing) rather than protracted motor sequences (as in cursive writing). In most cases, especially in older children who have really given cursive writing a fair trial, it is probably appropriate to allow them to print for the remainder of their lives.

The close associations between retrieval of ideomotor plans and writing efficacy cannot be overemphasized. On the Self-Administered Student Profile of *The ANSER System,* children frequently check off as "very true for me" an item that states "When I write, my memory gets bad." But, as we are about to see, motor memory is only one component of the drain on storage capacity, although it is very much a part of writing.

Retrieval Memory and Motor Implementation

The requirement for speedy and well-synchronized retrieval memory increases rapidly during elementary school. This is necessary for mathematics, for participation in class discussions, and for success in science, foreign languages, and other content areas. However, nowhere is it of more significance than in the act of writing itself. While writing a report, a child must at once retrieve the motor engrams for letter and word formations (as described above), the correct spellings, the mechanics of grammar, punctuation, and capitalization, the sequential flow or organizational scheme of ideas, and the specific vocabulary needed for expression. For a student to be a successful writer, a growing proportion of these memory demands must become increasingly automatic, requiring minimal expenditure of conscious effort and/or selective attention. This leaves room for higher-order cognitive involvement in what is being produced. In other words, we wish to devote as much of our effort or capacity as possible to the development of ideas, the use of problem-solving strategies, and the employment of analytic or creative functions. Such superimposed sophistication cannot occur while a writer is struggling to recall how to form a letter or produce a word in cursive script.

Not only must retrieval memory be working effectively, but it must also be exquisitely synchronized. It is certainly a major problem if the punctuation of a sentence arrives at the pencil point long after the proper spelling or grammar makes its appearance. The simultaneous recall of all components is imperative. Thus, if one or more retrieval memories is relatively sluggish, vague, or strained, the whole system can give way, as occurs frequently in developmental output failure. Affected students are often limited in their capacity to synchronize retrieval memories. It may be nearly impossible for them to spell, punctuate, capitalize, generate good ideas, and write legibly all at the same time. They may be able to satisfy any one of these requirements when presented with it in isolation. The implications for remediation are clear. At least for a time, these students should be allowed to make retrieval memory functions a priority, for example, be permitted to submit a book report with poor spelling as long as other aspects of retrieval are well and accurately represented. Ultimately, they can strive for the effective blending of all components of memory. Some youngsters simply are not ripe for this challenge soon enough. This delay is a common source of agony, false accusation, and loss of motivation in junior high school.

Any evaluation of a child with output problems must stress the adequacy of rapid retrieval memory, various forms of which need to be assessed. Recall from long-term memory as well as short-term memory should be included. Assessments of visualization (visual retrieval memory) are most important. A child's ability to visualize words is essential for accurate spelling (see chapter 10). This is commonly assessed by having children copy geometric forms from memory. The form should not be terribly complex in spatial relationships, but it should contain a substantial amount of detail.

The Attention Controls and Motor Implementation

Children with attention deficits are apt to encounter serious problems with academic demands for productivity. They may be able to be productive and efficient only when they are pursuing tasks that they really enjoy—highly motivating challenges that stimulate effort. More mundane, moderately (or minimally) motivating activities (such as book reports) may induce fatigue and distraction. The need to sustain mental effort grows with the demands for increased output. The constant threat of fatigue must be thwarted. Youngsters in late elementary school and junior high school often experience fatigued attention at the same time that they have to struggle to remain aroused in the face of increasing detail and the necessity for delay of gratification. Children who are predisposed to attention deficits, some of whom may have displayed relatively mild or no manifestations in the early grades, can have particular troubles in late elementary and junior high school. They may become fatigued, distractible, impulsive, and bored too easily during writing activities. They may have trouble monitoring or proofreading their work since this involves a level of attention to detail that exceeds their capacities. Children with attention deficits may also have problems planning writing, which may be disorganized because of their weak previewing and poor synchronization. Reduced self-monitoring may also result in writing that fails to meet the demands of the assignment. Frequently, students with attention problems do not understand what is expected of them because they really have not listened carefully in the first place.

Language and Motor Implementation

Writing is said to be the highest form of language; individuals who cannot speak lucidly are unlikely to write very lucidly. Children who have mild or moderate dysfunctions of expressive language may encounter serious difficulties when they have to engage in creative or expository writing. Slowness at finding words may decelerate the process. Verbal memory may require too much effort, thereby sabotaging the whole process of writing. Some children with *dysphasia* have trouble not only with their writing but also with participation in class discussions (see chapter 10).

Difficulties with the language components of writing (discussed in more detail in chapter 10) may include a variety of underlying dysfunctions. In addition to the aforementioned word-finding weaknesses, some children have difficulty formulating syntax effectively, grammatical construction being a process that eludes them. In other cases, they have problems with narrative organization, which may be limited to the writing sphere or be part of a broader organizational dysfunction (see next section). Metalinguistic awareness also plays a role in the effectiveness of writing. Good students of language develop a strong sense of what looks and sounds appropriate in an essay. They are able to effect a good match between higher-order cognition and linguistic expression. Students with language problems may find themselves writing things they didn't mean to write, just as they often say things that don't portray their thoughts effectively.

Organization and Motor Implementation

Organization is another dimension of evolving expectations. The accumulation of knowledge and skill can indeed create academic overload unless the student effectively organizes such material. Homework, written assignments, and conformity to daily routines all require an ability to organize. This section considers some forms of disorganization commonly encountered in developmental output failure. It is not at all unusual for floundering or failing junior high school students to be described by their teachers as having "just an organizational problem." As we shall see, such difficulties are common, highly elusive, and often agonizingly resistant to treatment.

Disorganization of Materials. A common form of disorganization involves the mismanagement of the various physical and/or spatial components of schoolwork. This phenomenon is often seen in association with other spatial ordering problems. Common manifestations include an inability to remember which books to take home, difficulty arranging a notebook, trouble finding things (e.g., paper, a pencil, a worksheet), serious problems using the space on a page effectively, and a tendency to leave behind a trail of forgotten belongings.

Students with such spatial organizational difficulties may have real trouble completing homework assignments. It may be hard for them to find a desk, pencil, and paper; to mobilize essential resources (such as the book for the book report); and to arrange material appropriately on the page. In some cases, students may manage to accomplish all of these steps (with some effort) but then forget to take the assignment to school the next morning. A variation on this theme is the student who remembers to take the report from home but leaves it on the bus. Clearly, some children are plagued with this form of material and/or spatial disorganization. They endure formidable problems with the props needed for tasks. Disorganization of materials may be associated with generalized difficulty with spatial ordering (see chapter 4).

Temporal-Sequential Disorganization.   Many children with mild or moderately severe temporal-sequential dysfunction experience significant organizational problems (see chapter 4). These children have a great deal of difficulty allocating time to tasks. They are frequently late for classes. They may experience trouble with the sequential organization of narrative writing. When they write reports, they may be unable to determine what should be the lead sentence, what should follow logically in the middle, and how the essay should end. The sequential flow of thought and language may be problematic for them. They may also have organizational problems when it comes to setting up a geometric proof in high school. Once again, it is hard for them to organize steps in the proper sequence. Their temporal disorganization may result in problems learning the order of their classes at the beginning of the year. Moreover, when they are given long-term assignments to complete, these students may have to struggle to figure out what to do when— how to stage their work in phases. They may require considerable assistance from parents and teachers to accomplish this.

Difficulties with Synthesis.   The capacity to integrate and restate data from various sources is an important skill, a major challenge to organization. Some students find it incredibly difficult to weave together semantic or episodic data from long-term memory, relevant new information, their own thoughts or opinions, and those of others. They then must synthesize these elements for expository writing and for classroom discussion.

An interesting and relevant variation on this theme can compromise reading comprehension. Some youngsters, said by the school to be reading above grade level on the basis of results of group achievement tests such as the *Iowa Test of Basic Skills* or the *California Achievement Test,* deny being able to read. Their parents claim that they never see their child read anything. Thus, we detect a discrepancy between reported reading skill and the child's self-confessed inadequacy. When such children are given a paragraph to read and asked a series of questions about it, they answer the questions accurately. However, when they are given another paragraph to read and are requested to summarize it, they shrug their shoulders and say, "I don't know." In other words, they can answer structured questions about a passage; the questions, in fact, organize it for them. But when they are asked to retell what they have read, they must decide what is salient and what is irrelevant, they must retrieve the important details, and they must restate them effectively in the proper sequence in their own words. They must *formulate* what they have read. Students must not only understand what is in the paragraph but also put it all back together, summarize it, and recreate its essence. This ability is not measured by asking structured questions. Thus, when the format is a multiple-choice test, children with such organizational difficulties are able to cope. They can use recognition memory rather than retrieval memory, and they need to engage in little or no synthesis. Thus, they might perform very well on achievement tests of reading (assuming other information-processing functions are intact). However, participating in class discussions, writing book reports, and effectively using what they have read (i.e., the major application of reading) put them at a distinct disadvantage. Thus, it is possible for a school to overestimate a child's reading ability by not considering his or her capacity to synthesize or organize the content of a passage. Chapter 9 will reconsider this in the context of the discussion of reading.

Difficulties with synthesis may affect listening as well as reading. The capacity to summarize what one has heard is equally germane in school (A.L. Brown 1976). Weaknesses in this area are a common concomitant of learning disorders (Klein-Konigsberg 1984).

The word *integration* is often used in connection with productivity in children. In an earlier era, there was considerable interest in intersensory integration—the capacity to organize responses that brought together two or more sensory and motor channels. This form of integration may be of particular importance for certain kinds of performance. Following directions may require smooth integration of linguistic input with a fine motor response. Copying from the chalkboard may require the integration of visual stimuli with a graphomotor output. The extent to which the integrative step itself is of importance remains difficult to estimate. Nevertheless, in the evaluation and management of children with impaired productivity, it is worth considering whether their problems seem to be localized specifically in areas that require a particular integrative linkage (such as an auditory input with a motor output). The discovery of such an isolated gap in integration can have important implications, especially for the bypassing of that vulnerable linkage.

Functional Profiles and Productivity

The last several sections have outlined a series of developmental dysfunctions that commonly reduce productivity, especially in late elementary and secondary school. In studying this phenomenon in various populations of schoolchildren, some important observations have been made. First, the prevalence of any one of the conditions enumerated (such as fine motor dyspraxia, weakness of attention, and word-finding problems) is high even in randomly selected populations of students. In fact, such dysfunctions occur sporadically in children who are on the honor roll. It is not unusual, for instance, to encounter a successful student with an awkward pencil grasp. It is possible for a child who does extremely well in school to be rather quiet and have some difficulties with word finding. There are even children with attention deficits who may be a bit "spacey" at times but who succeed admirably in most or all subjects. What, then, differentiates children with impaired productivity from their flawed but high-achieving peers? Investigations in schools as well as in clinics have demonstrated fairly clearly that children with developmental output failure have *clusters* of dysfunctions—at least several of the deficiencies enumerated in this chapter. Children who have impaired kinesthetic feedback during writing but who have strong language and organizational skills, good attention and mnemonic strength, and well-developed eye-hand coordination are likely to compensate for poor finger localization and perform effectively despite it. On the other hand, children who have impaired kinesthetic feedback in the presence of relatively weak attention, some difficulties with organization, and language impairment may find the hurdles insurmountable. The natural resiliency of those children is compromised. Consequently, they are unable to meet expectations for productivity.

This finding implies that it is inappropriate to look for single deficits in asking whether or not a child has a disability or some other circumscribed defect. Instead, we need to account for the whole child, compiling a functional profile of strengths and weaknesses (see chapter 14). Certain clusters of dysfunctions reduce productivity. In some instances, individual dysfunctions may be relatively mild. It is their additive effect, their combined influence, that engenders trouble.

Furthermore, some children display these dysfunctions in the absence of any strong compensatory mechanisms that could foster resiliency or help them circumvent their dysfunctions. Empirical research on groups of children has not discerned highly specific clusters or syndromes that impair productivity. In fact, a vast array of combinations of the dysfunctions enumerated in this chapter is possible, requiring that each child be evaluated individually.

At this point, we depart from the precedent set in earlier chapters. To avoid redundancy we will postpone our discussion of management until chapter 10, "Writing and Spelling," since output failure manifests itself so blatantly in those domains.

Repercussions of Developmental Output Failure

Children with developmental output failure are vulnerable to unhappiness throughout adolescence, to serious social maladjustment, and to lifelong underachievement. While delays in learning to read in first grade may be reversed by second, third, or fourth grade, impaired productivity sometimes represents a point of no return. It occurs at a critical age, a time when youngsters are highly sensitive about their own adequacy (or inadequacy). It can become a particularly frustrating problem for those who are bright, who perceive the enormous disparity between their own cognitive capacities and everyday productivity. Students may have a very difficult time dealing with this gap. They may be aware that the quality of their thought processes and overall verbal and ideational fluency are excellent but that what comes out on paper is a poor representation, a humiliating reduction. When these youngsters are accused of not doing their best, of not really trying, the proverbial salt is rubbed into the festering wounds. When a lack of academic productivity is accompanied by a failure to produce results in other channels (such as sports, music, or mechanical skills), they may experience a generalized and profound feeling of inadequacy. This in turn may contribute to a chain of mental health complications, including depression, various adjustment reactions, and conduct disorders.

Chronic deprivation of success may be a developmental time bomb, whose deto-nation can have devastating self-destructive consequences. To prevent catastrophe, there is a clear need for parents, teachers, and clinicians to be aware of the phe-nomenology of developmental output failure, to work toward its prevention, and to treat the child humanely when it is present. Many of the overall guidelines con-tained in chapter 15 are particularly relevant to the management of impaired pro-ductivity. It is hoped that the reader will consider the many therapeutic options available to minimize the potential impact of impaired productivity.

Alternative Production Channels

The concepts presented in this chapter are not intended to imply that athletic proficiency and academic excellence are the only legitimate childhood products. On the contrary, many other channels of production are feasible. The list could be endless, but some of the more common are:

- Artistic endeavors
- Mechanical skills (constructing, repairing, and inventing)
- Proficiency at nonathletic games (e.g., chess or computer games)
- Proficiency at craft work (e.g., sewing, knitting, or pottery)
- Musical talent
- Impressive collections (e.g., stamps, coins, dolls, or comic books)
- Wage earning (holding a job consistently and obtaining positive feedback from work)
- Pets and animals (caring for, riding, showing, or breeding)
- Success at cooperative group activities (e.g., scouts, 4-H, or religious groups)
- Assumption of special responsibilities at school (e.g., working in the health office or tutoring younger children)

Truly praiseworthy performance in one or more active pursuits is essential for optimal child development. This requires production over extended periods, in depth, and with demonstrable evidence of accomplishment and proficiency, as opposed to the tendency to keep switching production tracks. Ideally, children should acquire a healthy lust for the pursuit of depth, accomplishment, and exper-tise. Worthy production also requires the long trail of pursuit to result in respect from peers, siblings (even if grudgingly), and adult mentors. In this way, output channels can be used courageously to verify self-worth.

Chapter 7

Higher-Order Cognition

The minister, of course, taught by rote, a method from which Alva was inclined to disassociate himself. He alternated between letting his mind travel to distant places and putting his body in perpetual motion in his seat. The Reverend Engle, finding him inattentive and unruly, swished his cane. Alva, afraid and out of place, held up a few weeks, then ran away from the school.
— Robert Conot, *A Streak of Luck* (a biography of Thomas Alva Edison)

Higher-order cognition is the pathway to complex thinking. It enables students to grapple with intellectually sophisticated challenges, integrate multiple ideas and facts, undertake difficult problems, and find effective and creative solutions to dilemmas whose answers are not immediately obvious. Higher-order cognition also spares other cognitive functions, as its role in clarifying and blending ideas substantially reduces the burden on memory and attention to detail. In many respects, higher-order cognition represents the ultimate level of intellectual activity in the human mind. Therefore, its progressive development during childhood is an essential ingredient in academic success.

Higher-order cognition is composed of a number of interrelated processes. This chapter will focus on seven highly interactive (sometimes overlapping) areas of higher-order cognition:

- Concept formation

- Problem-solving skill

- Rule development and utilization

- Analogical reasoning

- Classification

- Divergent/creative thinking

- Metacognition

We will then explore some issues related to cognitive development and individual variations in various forms of "intelligence." As we shall see, some of these dimensions of a child's highly individualized cognitive preferences often comprise areas of thinking for which a particular student has a special proclivity.

CONCEPT FORMATION

The Concept of a Concept

Concepts are groupings of facts, attributes, steps in a process, or ideas that commonly go together. These "ingredients" of concepts are known as their *critical features*. Such aggregations acquire a name that subsumes the various critical features within the grouping. The name of the concept becomes a form of cognitive shorthand, allowing the thinker to manipulate and apply the concept broadly without always having to stop and enumerate its critical features. For example, if you understand the concept of "endangered species," and you are told that a particular lizard fits this concept, then you can activate from memory the critical features implicit in being an endangered species, and you know immediately that the lizard under discussion will be hard to find, expensive to purchase for a pet, likely to have been victimized by its environment, and nearly extinct.

To understand or master a concept is called *conceptualization*. A good conceptualizer can readily list the critical features of the concept. She or he knows when the concept is relevant for meeting a current challenge.

Concepts set default expectations. That is, when you encounter a familiar concept, your mind mobilizes a set of expectations. If someone tells you about a bird, you assume that it is a flying animal with feathers. However, there are some exceptions: some birds don't fly and a few lack feathers. You do not allow these exceptions to demolish the concept. Instead, you acknowledge that these rarer forms violate some of the default expectations associated with the concept of bird. Fortunately, most examples of a concept contradict few if any of our default expectations. Sometimes our understanding of a complex idea or process is aided by our understanding of the ways in which it satisfies and the ways in which it strays from default expectations.

Types and Examples of Concepts

Concepts come in a variety of forms. *Concrete* concepts, for example, have a direct sensory identity; they can be seen or touched or heard or felt. An example might be the concept of furniture. *Abstract* concepts have no actual sensory characteristics (unless one derives a metaphor or analogy for them). An example might be the concept of due process in government. *Verbal* concepts are most often thought about with language. The concept of democracy is an example. *Nonverbal* concepts, on the other hand, lend themselves to visualization. The concepts of proportion and perimeter can be understood and applied through mental imagery.

Many concepts can be dealt with either visually or verbally—or both. Sometimes the way a concept is portrayed depends upon the conceptual style of the learner or thinker. Some individuals may have a strong preference for either visual or verbal conceptualization.

Another type of concept is a *process* concept. A process concept is one that describes a mechanism or phenomenon. Examples include the concepts of photosynthesis, kinetic energy, or internal combustion. In these cases, the critical features of the concepts are actually steps in a process. The steps delineate how that phenomenon or process occurs. Thus, if you have a clear notion of the steps involved in internal combustion, you are likely to have a good understanding of how your car engine operates. If someone mentions that a tractor operates with an internal combustion engine, you can transfer the concept to cover the operation of the tractor, thereby avoiding the toil involved in determining all the steps involved in the performance of a tractor. Science courses in school are laden with process concepts.

A perfect example of a concept is called a *prototype* of the concept. It is likely to possess all or nearly all of the critical features within that concept. A bed might be considered a true prototype of furniture. A *nonprototype* fits the concept but is far from being an ideal example of it. Thus, a particular country may display a number of critical features of democracy, but lack a few important ones. Its government could be considered democratic, but the country would not qualify as a prototype of democracy. One effective way to learn concepts is through carefully studying how their perfect prototypes and their nonprototypes meet default expectations.

Conceptual Grasping

Children vary in the extent to which they are able to master concepts, to conceptualize. Eight levels of conceptual grasping pertain to the understanding of specific concepts. Some children may have global difficulties with concepts, while others may have problems only with certain kinds of concepts (such as nonverbal concepts), and all of us have trouble with at least some highly specific concepts. The following list represents the different levels of conceptual grasping:

- *None.* A child may have no understanding whatsoever of a particular concept or even of concepts in general. She or he possesses no default expectations and is unable to cite any critical features.

- *Partial.* In this instance a student may reveal a tenuous grasp. He or she can articulate one or two critical features or perhaps mention a prototype of the concept (e.g., "Democracy, that's kinda like America") without having very much understanding of it.

- *Echoic.* Sometimes a child may be able to repeat the concept as it was told to him or her without truly comprehending it. The child mimics the teacher or other adult but has little or no ability to describe the concept's critical features.

- *Imitative.* At this level the student may be capable of using the concept without actually understanding what it is. For example, a child may succeed on complex subtraction problems without understanding the concept of place value. Imitative grasping is quite common in mathematics learning, where it is sometimes referred to as "the extreme algorithmic approach."

- *Resynthetic.* Conceptual grasping starts to become firm when a student is able to describe the concept in her or his own words. This process of resynthesis enables a child to teach the concept to another person.

- *Extendable.* At this level a student can perform a number of important operations on the concept. She or he can form analogies with the concept (e.g., "proportion is like dividing up a pizza fairly with your brother, so he doesn't get more than his share"). A student can also thread concepts horizontally, linking concepts to each other to compare and contrast them. She or he can explore relationships between fractions, decimals, and percentages, or between liberalism, progressivism, socialism, and conservatism.

- *Manipulable.* As students firmly master concepts, they can manipulate the concepts' contents. A teacher might ask: "Could it still fit the concept of a trapezoid if it had a right angle in it?" or "Can it still be photosynthesis if it yields carbon dioxide?" A learner who has truly grasped the concept can perceive the effects of such alterations in its critical features. Questions such as these are a good way of teaching concepts as well as testing students to determine if they have grasped them.

- *Innovative.* At the innovative level, children are able to apply concepts in novel manners, in valid ways they have not actually been taught. They are also capable of invoking a concept in an unfamiliar context or to meet a new challenge. In this way concepts become generalized and broadened in their applicability as well as their relevance to the student. This represents the ultimate level of conceptual grasping.

Dysfunctions of Concept Formation

All students encounter problems with concept formation at some points in their academic lives. Some, however, are seriously hampered by chronically poor grasp. Their difficulties may be limited to a particular area of academic content or be generalized across the curriculum and possibly in spheres of everyday life.

Following are some common phenomena which may be encountered in children with incomplete conceptualization:

- *Chronic tenuosity.* Affected students proceed through their education with only minimal grasping of important conceptual material. They may seldom appreciate enough of the critical features of concepts to understand and apply them adequately.

- *Overreliance on rote memory.* Students with poor conceptualization may seek to compensate for their dysfunctions by deploying memorization and imitation as substitutes for understanding. Some of these students actually display unusually well-developed long-term memory functions.

- *Poor conceptual comprehension monitoring.* Affected students may not only fail to understand the concepts; they may fail to understand that they don't understand them. Thus, they may exhibit difficulty monitoring their own comprehension and be totally unaware of their tenuous or absent grasp.

- *Problems with verbal concepts.* Some students may experience conceptualization problems only for highly verbal concepts. When they are unable to support their understanding thorough visual imagery or analogy, they may not understand. Their dysfunction can be most problematic in content areas that rely heavily on verbal conceptualization, such as literature, history, and political science. Some of these students have other associated language difficulties (see chapter 5).

- *Problems with nonverbal concepts.* Certain children have greatest difficulty when the concepts they confront need to be thought about without much infusion of language. Areas such as astronomy, physics, geography, and some parts of mathematics may therefore elude them. Some of these students may have associated problems with spatial ordering (chapter 4).

- *Trouble with process concepts.* Concepts that convey a mechanism with which something occurs can be troublesome for certain students. They may have problems linking a sequence of steps to a process and an outcome. It may be hard for them to conceptualize the steps that occur during vaporization or in the process of electricity being generated and then flowing through a wire. Some of these students have underlying difficulties with temporal-sequential ordering (chapter 4). Their problems with sequencing may interfere with their ability to understand and preserve causal relationships, in turn thwarting the acquisition of certain process concepts.

- *Content-specific conceptual difficulties and strengths.* A student may have trouble forming concepts only within a circumscribed content area. There are adolescents, for example, who are good conceptualizers in mathematics and science but experience inordinate frustration with concepts in history class. Others may have great insight into the concepts within a particular sport (such as football) but have problems with the concepts presented to them in their science class.

- *Trouble communicating concepts.* Some students understand concepts fairly well but have difficulty resynthesizing them, stating or explaining the concepts *vocabulary studies* in their own words. This can limit the utility of the concepts. Such difficulty may sometimes be found in children whose receptive language abilities are far superior to their language production or fluency.

- *Excessively concrete conceptualization.* There are many children who seem unable to rise above the level of concrete concept formation. Their problems often become conspicuous in late elementary or middle school as they meet an steadily expanding array of abstract concepts in multiple subject areas. Their teachers and parents will often note that such children are overly concrete and literal in their interpretations of ideas.

PROBLEM-SOLVING SKILL

Problems for Problem Solving

Problem solving is a second important component of higher-order cognition. Effective problem solving requires an individual to slow down and think through a challenge in a deliberative and systematic fashion, as opposed to rushing through a challenge or coming to the first conclusion or action that springs to mind. Problem solving, as we shall see, collaborates meaningfully with other developmental functions. In particular, there are strong ties between strong problem-solving skills and the appropriate functioning of attentional production controls (chapter 2).

This chapter will consider virtually all academic challenges to represent problems that demand solving. Writing a book report, studying for a test, doing algebra homework, and completing a science project all call for problem-solving skills. Outside of school, students need to solve problems concerning conflicts with their friends, siblings, or parents, make decisions regarding issues in their social lives, and resolve highly personal conflicts. All of these confrontations represent problem-solving tasks, whether or not they are recognized as such.

The Critical Steps in Problem Solving

Problem solving must proceed systematically rather than in a random fashion. Therefore, the following somewhat idealized steps (with allowable variation in their precise order or fully conscious utilization) can help define an optimal problem-solving process:

- *Knowing a problem when you see a problem.* To be good problem solvers students must recognize that a problem is problematic. Such recognition serves as a stimulus or trigger for problem solving. Students must acknowledge and respond to the diverse problem-solving challenges enumerated above if they are to approach them systematically.

- *Stating the problem in its entirety.* This step involves the ability to state the problem in a way that includes all of its ramifications, potential complications, and unresolved issues. Instead of stating the problem: "I have to write a report in social studies," the student should expand the problem statement: "I need to write this report and I can't decide what to write about. I am trying to think of an interesting topic, one that's also pretty original because this teacher likes originality. Also, I may not have time to go to the library to get all the right books to read for this report, and I am running out of time." Often the clear and thorough statement of a problem is a key step toward its solution.

- *Recognizing patterns.* In examining the problem, the problem solver should look for familiar patterns, such as questions, situations, or issues that have been dealt with in other problem-solving scenarios. Pattern recognition can enable one to transfer methods or apply rules that have worked in the past in similar circumstances.

- *Using prior knowledge.* A problem solver needs to determine what it is that he or she already knows that can help to solve the current problem. There is a very close kinship between knowledge about a domain and the ability to solve problems within that domain. People who are experts in a field are commonly much better problem solvers in that field than are those without such high levels of declarative and/or procedural knowledge.

- *Previewing the outcome.* It is critically important for a problem solver to preview the final product, to state clearly what he or she would like things to be like once the problem is completely solved. One might ask a child to articulate in detail what it will be like when she is with her friend with whom she has not been getting along once their differences are properly settled. The preview is another great facilitator of problem solving.

- *Assessing feasibility.* The problem solver must decide if the problem is solvable, whether the solution will be easy or difficult, whether outside help will be necessary, and how much time will be required to complete the problem-solving operation successfully.

- *Invoking stepwisdom.* No significant problems can be solved in a single step. Good problem solvers must accept that a sequence of steps will be necessary to arrive at a desirable outcome or product.

- *Researching.* This step entails using outside sources (books, articles, or consultations with other people) to deal with the current problem. A problem solver may need to be highly resourceful in identifying sources of relevant usable information.

- *Considering alternative strategies.* A competent problem solver must consider multiple techniques or strategies that might be applied in dealing with the problem at hand.

- *Selecting the best strategy (without forgetting the others).* The problem solver selects and tries the strategy that seems most likely to succeed with the least effort and risk.

- *Regulating the internal voices.* Problem solving is substantially enhanced by positive internal cheerleading. A good problem solver recruits the self-coaching voices in his or her head to cheer for the problem solver rather than for the opposition. A child might say to himself during a test, "Come on, you can do this, you've taken harder tests. Just keep cool. Don't give up." A self-defeating problem solver might instead say to herself, "No way. This is too hard and I'm such a dummy. I just can't do this. I just can't do this. The internal voices can also communicate advice on such issues as strategy choice and pacing. A problem solver may actually whisper or talk to herself while working on a problem.

- *Pacing.* There is always a need to regulate the pace of problem solving so that the process does not occur too rapidly or drag on wastefully.

- *Monitoring progress.* Throughout the problem-solving process the student must constantly review its progress. Such self-monitoring allows for the detection of erroneous steps, misinformation, or deviations from plans.

- *Dealing with impasses.* The problem solver must be prepared to cope with setbacks or impasses. This may require careful backtracking to determine the point or points at which the problem-solving process went astray or failed to work as expected. At this point, if need be, he or she might try one of the alternative strategies considered earlier.

- *Knowing when the problem is solved.* A good problem solver knows when she has arrived at the best answer or product. In this way, she avoids perseverative tendencies or wasted energy.

- *Projecting future applications.* Once a problem is solved, it is helpful to review the entire process to determine how it might be gainfully deployed in the solution of future problems.

Problem-Solving Breakdowns

Children who have trouble solving problems may reveal distinct breakdowns at one or more of the sites listed in the previous section. Often dysfunctions in other neurodevelopmental constructs (such as attention and memory) can compromise the individual steps required for problem solving. The following list characterizes the common problem-solving difficulties:

- *Weak attention controls.* Children with attention deficits frequently manifest widespread problems with problem solving. There can be multiple reasons for their deficiencies, such as:

  - They may lack the mental energy demanded in systematic problem solving.
  - They may have problems previewing outcomes.
  - They may find it hard to pace themselves.
  - They may fail to monitor their progress.
  - They may not focus on relevant details in stating the problem.
  - They may have trouble estimating time and difficulty.
  - They may not inhibit first responses and consider alternative strategies.

In many respects the word *impulsivity,* which is commonly applied to children with attention deficits, is an antonym for problem solving.

- *Trouble with memory demands.* Problem solving demands substantial memory capacity. A child deficient in recognition memory (pp. 83 – 85) may have trouble perceiving familiar patterns when confronting a seemingly novel challenge. Some children with other weaknesses of long-term memory access may not be able to activate readily the prior knowledge needed for problem solving. Problem solving can be impeded when certain needed procedures or facts cannot be activated with sufficient automaticity (pp. 83–87). In such cases the excessive effort required for recall can usurp mental effort needed for other parts of the problem-solving activity. Finally, problem solving takes up considerable space in active working memory. A child with active working memory limitations (p. 75) may forget one portion of a problem-solving task while engaging in some other aspect of the effort.

- *Lack of prior knowledge.* Some children may lack the factual and procedural knowledge base required for a particular problem-solving scenario. Superficial or absent knowledge in an area dramatically constrains problem-solving ability within that domain.

- *Temporal-sequential disorganization.* Children with sequencing difficulties (chapter 4) often have problems invoking the "stepwisdom" that is required in systematic problem solving. Their shortcomings may result in impulsive or disorganized approaches. Frequently, they complain of feeling overwhelmed when facing a problem-solving task. This is because they are unable to break it down into manageable incremental steps. These same students are sometimes confused about time which, in turn, may cause problems with the establishment of a problem-solving tempo or time management for their problem solving.

- *Cognitive rigidity.* Some children have great difficulty considering and maintaining alternative approaches to tasks. Once they are committed to a method they can see no other way(s) of approaching the problem at hand. They may have problems thinking in terms of alternative strategies and dealing with impasses in a sufficiently flexible manner.

- *Language difficulties.* Good language skills greatly facilitate problem solving. Children with language dysfunctions may encounter trouble when trying to state the problem in a sufficiently elaborated way. They may also be hampered in their use of verbal self-coaching.

- *Modality or domain-specific problems.* It is important to stress that any child may be an excellent problem solver in one or more domains but quite a poor problem solver in other areas. He may have no difficulty understanding what's wrong with his malfunctioning bicycle but be unable to figure out the hidden meaning in a poem. Sometimes such disparities are content specific (dependent on subject areas or topics) while, in other instances, they are modality specific (a child may be more effective in linguistic problem solving than in visual-spatial problem solving).

- *A lack of explicit awareness of the problem-solving process.* There are many children who need to be taught about problem solving in an explicit manner. They seem to lack any intuitive awareness of the steps involved in problem solving. They simply need to be taught what problem solving is and how it works, and need considerable practice applying problem-solving techniques in a conscious way. Such students may not even know a problem-solving challenge when they meet one.

RULE DEVELOPMENT AND UTILIZATION

Use of Rules

The discovery of rules that predict and account for phenomena is a vital developmental acquisition during school years (Siegler 1981). For example, rules of mathematics dictate a systematic and consistent approach to problem solving in that domain. Rules are both taught and discovered; they are probably best acknowledged and used when they conform to previous experience. In many instances, it is better for children to discover a rule after struggling with some direct experience than to be taught that rule and exposed to its application subsequently. This is illustrated in the acquisition of rules of grammar, which simplify the task of making sentences. It would be unbelievably tedious to have to memorize by rote a particular verb tense for every verb, meaning that every time we encountered a new verb, we would be unable to predict how it might be conjugated. Instead, rules of morphology and syntax greatly ease the burden on memory.

Kuczaj (1978) portrayed the development of children in acquiring rules of grammar. Very young children handle the demand for grammar in a haphazard manner; they obey no rules. They consolidate in memory a few past tense verbs (such as *went* and *came*). They discern a vague suggestion of regularity that governs past tenses (such as adding *ed* to the present tense). Thus, they are able to produce some correct regular forms (such as *I walk, I walked*), but then they overgeneralize (such as *I goed, I coined*). Eventually these language abuses are replaced by an incorrect but rule-regulated construction (such as *I spreaded out the sheets*). The latter is typical of an eight-year-old child. At this age rules are being discovered rapidly and, in many cases, too widely applied.

Obviously, experience during childhood requires the understanding of rules in many different domains. Children may discover various rules—of grammar, of mathematics, of science, of games—at different ages. In most cases, however, acquisition of rules follows a fairly predictable pattern. Initial empiricism consists of guesswork and trial and error. The gradual recognition of regularity is often followed by formal teaching of rules. (The formal teaching should conform to previous experience to make sense.) Next follows a period of overapplication of the rules during which a child is not aware of exceptions or degrees of flexibility. Finally, the somewhat flexible, but nevertheless consistent, application of rules emerges. In some educational instances the student learns a rule before he has any experience in a particular field of endeavor, for example, learning the rules of grammar of a foreign language before actually constructing sentences. The initial state of empirical meandering is thereby eliminated, but this may take its toll by making the rules seem less relevant to the learner.

Students become increasingly fascinated with rules in late elementary school. They enjoy fabricating their own rules for games. Discovering the principle of a rule excites them. They enjoy constructing both transformational and non-transformational rules. Adolescents are required to apply rules in many academic subjects. They rely increasingly on rules that govern mathematics (algebra and geometry). As noted, rules play an important role in learning foreign languages as well as in science. As the demands for writing increase, students need to become increasingly automatic in the retrieval and application of rules (of grammar, punctuation, capitalization, and spelling). The more rules make sense (the less they emerge from rote recall), the more they are a comfortable part of the higher-order cognitive repertoire of a child and the more readily and effectively they will be applied to tasks.

Trouble with Rules

Children vary considerably in their capacities to understand, assimilate, and apply rules and regularities. Facility with rules becomes important in a wide range of subject areas (science, grammar, mathematics, and foreign language). The capacity to confront new material and see in it some regularity that suggests a previously encountered and assimilated rule is at the heart of this process, but is also a source of considerable variation. Some children may be able to learn rules by rote memory while exhibiting difficulty understanding how widely and when to apply them. Somehow they are not able to achieve a readily retrievable fit between a frequently recurring event or series of events and the rule(s) that make(s) them predictable.

Nontransformational rules are very much a part of cognitive development and everyday information processing (Ault 1983). The ability to determine whether a rule is being obeyed or violated helps children detect errors and determine what makes sense. Transformational rules, by contrast, govern production. Children have to know when to apply a particular rule for solving a mathematics problem or constructing grammatical English in an essay. Slowness, vagueness, or oblivi-ousness in appreciating and applying rules can seriously handicap children in upper elementary and secondary school. Much of their new knowledge and skill is superimposed on a matrix of preexisting, and presumably fully assimilated, systems of rules.

Some students experience great difficulty acquiring and applying rules. They are apt to experience their most serious academic lags in those subject areas that most depend on systems of rules. As a result they are prone to difficulties in one or more of the following:

- Learning grammar in their native language and subsequently assimilating the grammatical rules of a second language

- Spelling accurately

- Succeeding in mathematics

- Fully understanding and complying with rules of discipline

- Making good use of personal and academic experience to develop personal rules that can simplify work and lessen the burden on memory

- Developing efficient problem-solving skills

As with other forms of higher cognitive dysfunction, a child may exhibit global difficulties with rule development and utilization or, alternatively, the gaps may be highly content specific. Thus, a student may have tremendous difficulty appreciating and applying rules for English spelling but have no problems making good use of rules in a geometry class.

ANALOGICAL REASONING

The ability to form and understand analogies has been used as a marker of higher cognitive development. Tasks of analogical reasoning are frequently part of intelligence tests. Analogies such as the following are typical: *Hammer is to nail as screwdriver is to?* This is a second-order, or standard, analogy. Children in elementary school become increasingly skilled at solving these. To complete the analogy, children first need to encode the various terms in the analogy to hold them in memory. They must then infer the relationships between the terms, deciding that a hammer relates to a nail by acting on the nail during the process of hammering. They must then map the second-order relationship between the halves of the analogy; they must determine what is similar about a hammer and a screwdriver. Then they must apply the relationship to complete the analogy. Finally, they must justify the completion by deciding to what extent it departs from an ideal correspondence. The Similarities subtest of the *WISC-III* taps this kind of process and clearly documents growth in the ability to deal with increasingly subtle analogous relationships.

As children approach adolescence, they are capable of dealing with analogies of the third order (higher-order analogies). They can begin to form analogies between analogies; they can rate how analogous different analogies are. This rather mind-boggling phenomenon is an important step in adolescent reasoning. Sternberg and Downing (1982) describe experiments that reveal that adolescents improve progressively in the ability to use such sophisticated analogous reasoning. They presented subjects with pairs of analogies, such as *sun:day::moon:night* and *sunny:summer::snowy:winter*. The subjects were asked to rate on a one-to-nine scale the degree of relatedness between pairs of words within each of the two analogies. They were then asked to compare the analogies, determining how related individual components of the paired analogies were to each other. Eighth graders, eleventh graders, and college students were studied. Major differences among these age groups were discovered, as older students clearly excelled in discerning relationships in far more difficult third-order analogies.

The capacity to reason using analogies relates to the ability to draw inferences from what is read or discussed in class. As older elementary and secondary school students must draw increasingly sophisticated inferences and extrapolate information, the ability to discern and form analogies is crucial. Children in school are constantly constructing such pictures of reality. They do so by extending what they already know to new territories of inquiry or production. This process of extension can occur by fitting new data into a classification system or category, by perceiving relationships that are analogous to others that were previously assimilated, and by recognizing or even formulating various systems or rules to which new information conforms.

Analogy formation can greatly facilitate comprehension. Our discussion of concept formation noted that analogical thinking facilitates the grasping of concepts. Teachers can enhance comprehension by asking students to build analogies for difficult concepts (e.g., "Can you think of activities in your everyday life that are like balancing an equation?").

Weaknesses of Analogy Formation

Trouble dealing with or developing analogies may seriously limit comprehension. This is especially the case when children are trying to master difficult material. Affected students may find that what they have learned is fragmented and unconnected, as they have trouble discerning (and enjoying) the recurring (i.e., analogous) themes or ideas in their educational experience. Children with weaknesses of analogy formation may have problems with certain aspects of mathematical reasoning. For example, fractions may be hard to ponder without internalizing analogical thinking (e.g., *3 is to 6 as 4 is to 8*). They may also have trouble forming concepts, since conceptual understanding is often enhanced through the use of analogy or metaphor. Problems with analogy formation may be format specific. A student might have much more difficulty analogizing with words than perceiving interesting visual analogies (or vice versa). Such a student may also harbor other forms of language dysfunction (chapter 5).

CLASSIFICATION SKILLS

Elementary schoolchildren often are fascinated with classification. They may become great collectors, accumulating hoards of stamps, coins, tools, dolls, or cards. Frequently the ardent collector arranges and rearranges these prized possessions, incessantly experimenting with categories—with the subdividing of items into classes. Thus, a collection of baseball cards may be subgrouped into leagues, positions, teams, or batting averages. Comic books may be organized according to dates, titles, or subject matter. Dolls may be arranged by size, gender, or age. Numerous studies have indicated that children's abilities to classify objects and words improve with age (Denney and Moulton 1976). A four year old is likely to arrange objects in a manner that is entirely haphazard. In contrast, a twelve year old will be determined to do so systematically, according to an identifiable system of rules.

Various object-sorting exercises can be used to document this developmental progression. When asked to form subgroups of physical objects, two- to four-year-old children tend to group items randomly without any substantial justification for the clusters they developed (e.g., "I like 'em like that"). Children between the ages of four and six for the first time have a basis for grouping objects. Preschoolers might put several toys together because they are all white or all made of wood; however, they seem to have great difficulty being consistent within groups. Typically, five-year-old children will change in the middle of a grouping. They will put together a block and a pencil because they are both made of wood but then add a pen because "You can use that to write, too." Kindergarteners and first graders are apt to discern categories that are a bit far-fetched. They put together an egg and a cup, justifying the link because "When you drop them, they both break." They may form such an association in preference to the more obvious grouping of a cup with a plate and a spoon, and an egg with other foods.

During elementary school, children become far more consistent; they use particular criteria for grouping and maintain them consistently. Throughout a series of trials, they persist in invoking fixed criteria for classification. They begin to favor hierarchical groupings, taking an overall class such as fruits, and including apples, oranges, bananas, and grapes. They can also think about a class such as vegetables and include carrots, peas, beans, and lettuce. They can then combine the fruits and vegetables as all belonging to a superordinate class, foods from plants. This progressive acquisition of class inclusion (the ability to recognize that the same object is simultaneously a member of increasingly broad categories) represents a significant gain in development, often occurring in middle to late elementary school.

Cognition and language converge when words, rather than objects, are sorted. Young children are usually able to group objects that belong to the same class, but tend to group words that might occur together in sentences or that might join to form plausible stories. With both objects and words, younger children tend to make their groupings highly personal, to stress conceptual or functional relationships, and to be inconsistent.

A number of investigators, including Anglin (1970), have presented children with groups of words, asking them to group those that are "most alike." At about age eight or nine, students most frequently classified the words according to common themes because they tended to occur in the same situations or because of their proximity in everyday speech. Thus, they associated black and car because cars are sometimes black. They linked happy and sad because they were opposites. As children entered adolescence, a striking change occurred. They categorized words in like classes not so much thematically, but by parts of speech and similar meanings.

Practical and visible or visualizable features give way to hierarchical organization as children age. Gardner (1978) summarizes adolescent attainment in this domain as follows:

For example, if the task is to group examples of "red reading material," they will pick out not only certain reds or only certain reading materials. Rather, they devise tightly consistent definitions of red and of reading materials, so that their selection includes every example of red but no example of nonred, every reading material but nothing that cannot qualify as readable. Adolescents, but not eight-year-olds, would include in their category of "red reading materials" the crimson inspection seal on a piece of meat, while rejecting a pink magazine or a red picture book. And because they can think logically, their word meanings are now precise, unambiguous, and consistent (p. 417).

In other words, developmental progression in class inclusion is navigating toward a point where consistent and truly sophisticated conceptual groupings can occur.

Chapter 3 discussed retrieval strategies for locating information in memory. We noted how the extraction of information by category is an important mnemonic strategy. Conceptual sorting is thus highly relevant to remembering in school. The ways in which data are stored and retrieved depend on their consolidation in orderly categories or classifications, a cognitively based filing system. This process influences school performance and, in turn, is influenced by school performance. That is, the elementary school student receives a great deal of practice in categorizing and classifying. Cross-cultural studies reveal that this particular function is apt to be absent or significantly delayed in cultures in which children do not attend school.

Deficiencies or Developmental Delays in Classification Skills

Some students exhibit deficiencies in classifying and categorizing. They are susceptible to problems forming concepts (e.g, creating conceptual groupings within a category, such as *reptiles*). Aspects of the curriculum that demand sophisticated classifications may elude these children. A child with a weak sense of classification may have problems learning the parts of speech (and citing examples of each). There may be confusion over various superordinate categories, so that an affected student may not be able to appreciate the difference between a city, a country, a state, and a continent. When asked to name as many countries as he can in thirty seconds, he may respond: "England, New York, Canada, South America, Paris . . ."

Children who have trouble classifying information have some of their greatest difficulties with the use of long-term memory in school. When facts or ideas are not consolidated in specific categories, they are likely to be inaccessible or only slowly accessible on demand. Such students in fact may perform poorly or very slowly on examinations.

DIVERGENT/CREATIVE THINKING

Children are apt to vary considerably in their development of divergent thinking and creative tendencies. The capacity to elaborate, to discover unusual similarities or analogies, to link ideas or objects that are not ordinarily associated with each other and, in so doing, to fuse new meaningful relationships, all constitute part of what is often referred to as *creativity,* another key source of developmental variation. Creativity eludes precise measurement. It is hard to separate from overall intelligence and from the effects of specialization. According to Gardner (1993), "The creative individual is a person who regularly solves problems, fashions products, or defines new questions in a domain in a way that is initially considered novel."

Creativity is often an important component of giftedness (see p. 241). Some investigators who have studied *associative fluency,* the ability to form rich associations easily, think that it is linked to creativity. It is probably a part of creativity, but only a part. An individual's intimate familiarity with a particular medium (such as music, words, paints, or mathematics) is critically important. Building on competency within an area, true creators are able to devise new linkages, rearrangements, or syntheses, resulting in a string quartet, a poem, a remarkable piece of sculpture, or a new way to fix an engine. Creativity does not seem to appear by any particular age during childhood. Its developmental progression is likely to vary considerably. Nevertheless, when it emerges in a child, it is helpful to note the particular time and, of course, to nurture and encourage such divergent thought processes.

It probably does not make sense to postulate the existence of a clinical/educational disorder called "creativity dysfunction." Clearly, some students are more original, divergent, and inventive than others. One can argue that schools and parents need to strive to provide opportunities for all children to seek and try out possible media for personal creativity.

METACOGNITION

It is not at all unusual for children with various delays in the acquisition of academic skills to manifest weaknesses in metacognition. Such children have been termed *inactive learners* (Torgesen 1982). They have difficulty becoming active strategists in learning situations. They lack knowledge about the ways in which they think and therefore are unable to use strategies and study skills effectively. They also have trouble regulating their learning, rarely monitoring themselves systematically because they are unable to step back and conceptualize the learning processes needed to meet task demands. Their lack of metacognitive awareness makes it hard for them to know when they are going astray. In describing this phenomenon, Mann and Sabatino (1985) point out that such students appear to be unsuccessful in school because "they are not knowledgeable about the ways they think, what they know and do not know, or how to apply strategies. Such pupils may well benefit from increased cognitive self-awareness. . . . It has also been found that while many poor readers lack effective cognitive strategies, others may be fully capable of exercising strategies but do not know when or how to best use them. These readers are metacognitively deficient. They don't understand that different strategies are needed to achieve different goals" (pp. 222–23).

Metacognitive Deficiencies

Students with metacognitive deficiencies tend to exhibit a great deal of inflexibility in their academic work while lacking the knowledge needed for effective self-monitoring. In undertaking an academic challenge, they may have great difficulty analyzing what is expected of them. It may be hard for them to evolve strategies based on their understanding of what is entailed. Thus, when studying for an examination, a student with poor metacognition may be unable to reflect on the appropriate ways to combine understanding of the subject matter with techniques for remembering the material. It has been shown that students with written output difficulties have little or no awareness of the interactions between the subskills that comprise writing. To put it another way, effective writers can think about and describe vividly what is involved in writing.

A new assessment tool for use with adolescents is *The Survey of Teenage Readiness and Neurodevelopmental Status (STRANDS;* Levine et al. in preparation). This standardized questionnaire and interview includes sections that elicit a student's metacognitive awareness in various educational domains (see figure 7-1). Of interest is the fact that there is enormous variation among adolescents with respect to their ability to think about thinking. Some students display little or no insight into the processes involved in thinking and learning. Others are capa-

---

HIGHER-ORDER COGNITION—METACOGNITION

1. What's a concept?

2. Can you give some examples of concepts you've learned this year in school?

3. A good problem solver is a person who can figure things out the best way. What do you think are some things a good problem solver does when he/she solves a problem?

4. What are some subjects in school where you think you are good at problem solving?

5. How about outside of school?

6. If you applied for a prize or a scholarship and they asked you to write an essay on anything you wanted, what would you write about?

7. Would you rather they assign you a topic?   Yes ____   No ____

THANK YOU!

Figure 7-1.   Excerpt from the *STRANDS* assessment tool

ble of reaching impressive metacognitive heights. They tend to be more strategic in their approaches to learning and academic productivity; they are likely to be far more successful in school.

SOME ADDED DIMENSIONS OF INDIVIDUAL VARIATION IN HIGHER-ORDER COGNITION

The previous section considered seven areas of higher-order cognition. The following section will review a series of functions that influence and are influenced by higher-order cognitive functions.

Concrete and Formal Operations

Much of our knowledge of children's emergent competencies at classification, analogical reasoning, development of rules, and other forms of higher-order cognition has been stimulated by the influential work of Piaget. Detailed expositions of his theories and their relevance are readily available (Elkind 1976, Ginsburg and Opper 1981). This section outlines briefly Piagetian developmental stages as they relate to acquisitions during school years.

According to Piaget, children between the ages of about eight and twelve are in a developmental period in which they are able to master "concrete operations" (Piaget and Inhelder 1968). This phenomenon is illustrated most strikingly in what is probably the best known experiment in developmental psychology. Piaget and Inhelder, his collaborator, presented children with two identical beakers, each of which contained the same quantity of liquid, and asked whether both containers possessed the same amount of liquid. Necessary adjustments were made until children agreed that they did. Subsequently, with the child watching, the investigator poured the liquid from one beaker into a beaker taller and thinner than either of the other two. The children were then asked, "Does this (i.e., the tall, thin) beaker contain as much water as the other (i.e., the initial) beaker, does it contain more water, or does it contain less?" The researchers were interested in finding out whether children would understand that the amount of liquid is "conserved" regardless of its apparent change of height in the taller and thinner beaker. They wanted to determine whether children could "conserve continuous quantities," providing some evidence that they were able to transcend their own direct sensory observations and appeal to a higher order of logic or reasoning.

In this experiment, four-year-old children commonly believed that the total amount of water had changed. They attended to only one component of what they saw, justifying their responses by saying such things as, "I know there is more; it is higher" or "The glass is bigger, so there is more." Such responses were not altered, even when the experimenter pointed out that no liquid had been added or taken away. Children at age five or six tended to give intermediate responses. Often they were not very sure. Some were able to understand that the liquid was conserved when a difference in appearance was only slight, but had more trouble when it was great. Sometimes they could foresee what would happen (i.e., "When you pour the water, it will stay the same"), but they actually answered incorrectly when confronted with the dramatic visual difference. In other words, they were not yet prepared to overrule sensory data with logical thinking.

Beginning at about age seven or eight, an understanding of genuine conservation was detectable. Subjects were certain that the amount of liquid did not change. Three basic concepts, characterized as "compensation," "identity," and "reversibility" were used to justify their answers. Children invoking compensation noted that although the liquid was higher, the container was thinner and one made up for the other. Those citing identity pointed out that there could be no difference since nothing was added or taken away. Those invoking reversal asserted that if you poured the liquid back into the original container, you could prove that the same amount was there all along. As children gain in their sophistication, they become less exclusively reliant on concrete or sensory data. A child may state, "You know, I really didn't need to look when you were pouring, since I knew you were just pouring. I knew that just by pouring you can't change the amount of water."

It was Piaget's conviction that subjects in the middle childhood years made extensive use of compensation, reversibility, and identity to clarify a multitude of phenomena that went beyond continuous quantities (such as the liquid in the experiment). He included discontinuous quantities such as the conservation of length, of area, of solid substance, and of numbers. For example, conservation of length can be demonstrated by placing on a table a line of five marbles, each approximately one-half inch from the next. Another line of five marbles separated from each other by one inch is displayed and the child is asked which line contains more marbles. A child who is steadfastly loyal to direct sensory information tends to believe that the row that takes up more room contains more marbles.

Piaget called this stage of development *concrete operations. Operations* refers to those mental activities through which a youngster derives a more lucid understanding of time, space, numbers, amount, and related conceptual areas. The operations are *concrete* because they are applied to the physical entities of everyday life, substances such as candy, blocks, and money.

Adolescents reach a higher plane of conceptualization. Piaget and Inhelder (1968) refer to this as *formal operations,* presumably the highest level of thought obtained. The sine qua non of formal operations is the capacity to operate on symbolic statements or propositions. The thinker can grapple with two or more ideas and explore systematically the relationships between them, noting correspondences, contradictions, and implications. In this manner, an adolescent might predict a variety of possible outcomes without having to try out each one.

Examples of the formal operational thinking of adolescents abound. For the first time, they may construct contrary-to-fact hypotheses ("If apples were blue") and reason about them. They can take premises (whether or not they are correct) and extrapolate from them in a logical manner. Thus, they can separate the process of reasoning from specific real-world content, enabling them to solve a wider range of problems.

Followers of Piaget ascribed to formal operational thinking three distinguishing characteristics: generating multiple hypotheses, systematically checking all possible solutions, and operating on operations.

Generally speaking, elementary school students tend to generate one solution to a problem. If the solution is not workable, they are apt to stop, guess, or perhaps concede defeat. Adolescents, however, become increasingly adept at generating a number of alternative solutions even before they begin to solve a problem. They can offer several propositions to explain the same phenomenon and then proceed to evaluate each of them; that is, they engage in the systematic checking of possible alternative solutions to a problem. They usually have a plan prior to the actual testing of a hypothesis. Finally, adolescents who have reached the formal operations stage recognize that hypothetical problems can be solved by using the same rules that exist for concrete problems. The same methods of isolating and testing individual factors can be used in a wide range of circumstances. This organizing of single operations into higher-order ones is referred to as *operating on operations.* An example of this is the mathematics problem, "What number plus 20 equals twice itself?" (Ault 1983). Children working on the level of concrete operations use addition and multiplication on various numbers, employing a trial-and-error technique until they reach the right answer. They might, for example, think of the number 5, insert it in the equation $5 + 20 = 25$ and $2 \times 5 = 10$, and then decide that 5 is incorrect. They continue to try other numbers in this manner until they find the correct one. Adolescents, on the other hand, develop an abstract rule, $x + 20 = 2x$, and solve the formula algebraically, $20 = 2x - x$. The separate operations of addition and multiplication are combined into the higher-order algebraic equation. This is what is meant by operating on operations.

Formal operational processes enable the adolescent to deal with different aspects of a problem simultaneously. This is efficient, allowing for the solution of increasingly complex problems in a shorter time and with less strain on active working memory and attention.

Piaget's developmental model has not gone unchallenged. For one thing, it may be that schooling has a major impact on these acquisitions. In addition, it is known that many adults never attain the stage of formal operations. Nevertheless, it is useful to bear in mind that as school years pass, children become less and less reliant on raw sensory data, better able to generalize, and increasingly skilled at reasoning using principles and rules. As they no longer limit themselves to straightforward empirical observations, children become more and more comfortable with symbols, abstractions, and systems of abstractions. In doing so they become increasingly fascinated with their own higher-order cognition.

Cognitive Preferences

Sometimes expositions of higher cognitive development in childhood assume that all children should acquire these processes in the same order and at the same times, but this is not realistic (Flavell 1982). Clinicians may focus too heavily on deviation, pathological delays, or detours in development. In fact, normal developmental variation occurs in higher-order cognition. During elementary school, children are likely to show preferences for certain higher cognitive pursuits. That is, they may display uneven development. With this uneven development may emerge some unique manifestations of intelligence or talent (Gardner 1983).

A fundamental difference exists between verbal and nonverbal cognition. Some children are capable of reasoning with words but experience frustration with logical processes in nonlinguistic realms. The mastery of rules, the understanding of classifications, the appreciation and use of analogies, and the employment of various problem-solving strategies might all be highly developed in language but primitive in nonverbal thinking. Thus, children who have no difficulty at all interpreting multiple levels of meaning in a poem or a short story may be inept at discerning the rules and processes that enable pieces of wood to be joined together in a systematic fashion to form a desk. These children may have trouble with other problem-solving challenges in the nonlinguistic experiential realm. Confronted with a bicycle that needs repair, they may be unable to diagnose what is wrong, think up hypotheses to account for the malfunction, or know how to test them systematically. The reverse also occurs: some children may be quite talented at nonverbal reasoning but have trouble with verbal cognition. In our society, the educational system favors children with strong, or at least adequate, verbal higher-order cognition. The adult world, of course, needs both types.

Many people whose nonlinguistic reasoning is stronger than their facility with language are able to make important contributions to society. When such uneven development exists, it may be inappropriate to worry about what is normal and what is deviant. Instead, it is essential to identify, acknowledge, and even preserve such stylistic differences, recognizing that certain styles may cause a child to struggle excessively during school years.

Another variable arises in specific content areas. Some children exhibit extraordinary higher-order cognition for certain problem-solving tasks or content areas, while they are not nearly so cognitively talented at other pursuits. One child may be excellent at devising strategies to win a football game but fail dismally at working through hypotheses to solve a mathematics problem. Another might be especially skilled at troubleshooting when a computer is not performing up to expectations but have insurmountable trouble figuring out the meaning of a poem. Variations by subject area have a variety of causes. Certainly motivation plays a role. Children who are particularly excited by an area of inquiry or recreational pursuit are likely to concentrate more intensely and to mobilize all possible latent resources. Practice may also have an effect: children spend more time pursuing what excites them. The more they pursue a content area, the better their problem-solving strategies will be. Other factors, such as the availability of role models and opportunities, may affect cognitive performance in a specific content area. Moreover, it can be difficult to determine whether children are drawn to a type of pursuit because of "natural talent" or innate higher-order cognitive proficiency in that area, whether they develop a preference because they become expert at it, or whether they become expert at it because they like it.

Because children's higher-order cognitive abilities may vary from one content area to another, it is hard to defend a unified definition of "intelligence." Gardner

(1983) proposes what he calls "the theory of multiple intelligences," six different kinds of intelligence: linguistic, musical, logical-mathematical, spatial, bodily-kinesthetic, and a series of what he calls personal intelligences. Each individual displays distinctive profiles of these intelligences. A musical genius may have great difficulty with problem solving and abstract reasoning in linguistics. Another person may have superior visual-spatial intelligence but only average abilities in other areas. At present, there is increasing support for this broad view of intelligence, for a more accommodating and flexible notion of higher cognitive competency.

Sternberg (1985) has assembled further evidence that there exist multiple forms of intelligence. By studying how individuals solve problems, pursue their career goals, and fail or succeed with specific life challenges, he and his colleagues have derived what they term a "triarchic theory of human intelligence." They describe three aspects of intelligence, which are apt to vary considerably from person to person. Some individuals may be especially talented in one of the three and considerably less so in the other two.

The first aspect, *componential intelligence,* requires the capacity to think analytically and critically and to apply effective metacognition when approaching a task. Individuals who are talented in this aspect are likely to be good critical thinkers who are adept at allocating time to tasks. They are clever planners and generally very good at taking tests. For example, a student who has strengths in the componential aspect of intelligence will likely perform especially well in analyzing and responding to questions on standardized multiple-choice tests such as those required for college admission.

The second aspect, *experiential intelligence,* involves the capacity to be highly synthetic in one's thinking. This ability is associated with a high level of creativity. In particular, individuals strong in this area are highly insightful. They are able to engage particularly well in three processes: selective encoding, selective combination, and selective comparison. *Selective encoding* includes the ability to extract significant information when confronting a reading passage, a problem, or a puzzle. *Selective combination* is the ability to assemble multiple facts or bits of data into some interesting product or conceptual model. *Selective comparison* involves the capacity to view old ideas in a new way or new ideas in an old way, allowing one to discern interesting relationships between objects, ideas, or events that others may not detect. Thus, experiential talent can lead to exciting and creative discoveries.

The final aspect, *contextual intelligence,* relates to an individual's ability to adapt to a particular environment. In a sense, this is analogous to being "streetwise." Such ability can have implications for children's academic careers. Adaptability enables students to modify their performances to satisfy the demands of specific courses or teachers. It entails a keen ability to "read" expectations and to work comfortably and fit into an environment—either by being flexible or striving to change the environment.

These three aspects of intelligence are not mutually exclusive. An individual can have strengths in one, two, or all three. It is common to encounter children or adults whose profiles show considerable unevenness in these aspects. Students who have excellent componential abilities may perform extremely well on multiple-choice tests and be very good critics and analysts during class discussions. However, when asked to come up with some original ideas, these students may falter. Other students who are highly creative (strong in the experiential aspect) may perform exceptionally well in subjects that allow considerable latitude and encourage creative and original thinking. These students may have much more trouble in content areas that demand a great deal of critical and/or analytical reasoning. In addition, although they may receive low scores on college entrance examinations, their day-to-day performance as undergraduates may be outstanding. In spite of relatively weak performance on the multiple-choice tests, creative abilities can enable a student to write outstanding term papers and highly original essay examinations. Finally, students who are especially strong in the contextual aspect could be student leaders or thriving entrepreneurs in school (and beyond). In other words, they are remarkably agile at adjusting to varying social and academic contexts. Many successful business executives probably possess this kind of skill.

It is important to emphasize that the types of intelligence described by Gardner and by Sternberg can be diagnostically elusive. Students who are particularly strong in one or more of these areas may not reveal themselves on traditional intelligence tests. Their abilities are likely to emerge as part of their higher cognitive developmental progression. This broader concept of emerging intelligence, which is rapidly gaining acceptance, broadens our notions of higher-order cognition and its relationship to other developmental functions. The broader view requires us to progress beyond simplistic numerical representations of a child's overall mental ability.

During elementary and secondary school, children are likely to issue signals that hint at their higher-order cognitive propensities. The adult world's recognition of a child's progressive individuation represents a vital issue in higher cognitive development; it may also be one of the most neglected. Parents, teachers, and even children themselves often ignore styles that emerge spontaneously. It may be that unheeded styles (those that become underutilized for one reason or another) result in chronic underfulfillment and underachievement.

Awareness of the Hidden Curriculum

It seems appropriate to explore one further acquisition related to higher-order cognition, namely, ability to figure out expectations. A capacity to know what is required, to discern the proper approach to satisfying requirements, and to read between the lines regarding what it takes to please a teacher, a coach, or an institution are all part of what has been called "the hidden curriculum." Snyder (1971) studied the impact of the hidden curriculum at the Massachusetts Institute of Technology. He found that students differed considerably in their understanding of the hidden curriculum. Consequently, they developed different strategies for success. Snyder noted that

> most students discover within the first month of college that they cannot possibly complete all of the assigned work. To finish all the tasks of the formal curriculum would require far more time than is available. In a typical coping pattern, the student finds he must neglect, selectively, certain aspects of the formal curriculum. He

must learn what he can avoid doing, knowing where the risks are minimal and the cost is modest. He is forced to make judgments about what is relevant; he develops a method of study and fixes a way of budgeting his time. But this strategy also fosters a sense of gamesmanship and makes the encounter between the student and the professor a competitive rather than a cooperative one. Some students, for example, schedule their time to the minute; others work hard only under pressure and seem to exist from one academic crisis to another. A third group plays the academic game by ear; another turns it off altogether (p. 12).

Students must become increasingly good diagnosticians of their teachers. At the same time that a teacher is evaluating a student's learning, the student should be implicitly assessing the teacher's teaching, not so much to grade the teacher as to figure out the most direct way of pleasing him or her. This "academic game" constitutes part of the hidden curriculum. Although Snyder studied the phenomenon among college freshmen, we can extrapolate and recognize that it is important even in elementary school. Some children are particularly clever at determining which teachers like highly factual responses on examinations and which prefer more elaborative (divergent) answers. Students are likely to grow in their abilities to predict what will be on a quiz or examination. Some develop an uncanny sense of the structure of a multiple-choice test. Some are better than others at knowing what they know or at knowing when to stop studying because they have sufficient knowledge to satisfy the predictable expectations of a particular teacher. Others may have no idea of this whatsoever. They may think they know more or less than they actually know or need to know.

All of these perceptions form a critical cognitive substrate for a massive problem-solving strategy, namely, figuring out schools and teachers, knowing how to please different adults, and performing in such a way as to meet expectations without much waste or overexpenditure of effort. It appears to be a truism that good students use problem-solving strategies that tend to reduce and simplify the workload. On the other hand, those who are struggling often have no such facilitative methods. The successful become more successful; the unsuccessful more unsuccessful. It is, of course, a remarkable irony that the children who need to have their work simplified seldom simplify their work, while those who can handle more complexity are often doing so by employing strategies that prevent "circuit overload." Any thorough discussion of a child's academic adjustment should include more than casual scrutiny of the extent to which she or he is evolving an understanding of the hidden curriculum, is able to adapt to changes therein, and uses effective techniques to trim the fat from effort and meet expectations efficiently. As yet, there are no developmental norms relating to the mastery of the hidden curriculum. This might well be a promising pathway for future research.

GIFTEDNESS AND GIFTED UNDERACHIEVEMENT

No discussion of variations in higher-order cognition would be complete without including the subject of gifted children. These youngsters are generally talented in one or more areas of performance or capacity. Among the virtues often ascribed to gifted children are a high level of intellectual aptitude (generally revealed on intelligence tests), one or more well-focused zones of extraordinary academic ability, a high level of creativity, leadership skill, and talent in the visual or performing arts. These ingredients are included in the definition of giftedness propounded by Maryland (1972), who also states that "gifted and talented children are those identified by professionally qualified persons who by virtue of outstanding abilities are capable of high performance. These are children who require differentiated educational programs and services beyond those normally provided by the regular school program in order to realize their contribution to self and society." Gallagher (1985), in discussing this definition, notes that giftedness involves something more, namely "the ability to master and use those symbol systems that lie at the heart of the operation of our modern society" (p. 6). Invoking the model espoused in this book, we might state further that a gifted child is one who displays outstanding talents in one or more of the developmental functions we have discussed, and that such a child actually or potentially is able to mobilize these strengths in concert with other developmental functions to acquire skills or attain levels of productivity that are well beyond expectations. For example, a child who is an outstanding linguist may be able to use that verbal aptitude in such a way that—in combination with focused attention, adequate simultaneous and/or sequential processing, and good verbal memory and reasoning—highly precocious or original insights emerge. Gallagher's *Teaching the Gifted Child* (1985) outlines some of the traits that are commonly sought in identifying gifted children. The first, and most prominent, is a high score on an intelligence test. For example, a child with a performance, verbal, or full-scale IQ of 150 would be in the ninety-ninth percentile and, as such, would be considered to have unusually well-developed intellectual ability (or potential). Gallagher's second element is creativity. Gifted children are thought of as highly creative. Torrance (1974) defined the elements of creativity: affluency, flexibility, originality, and elaboration. Children, moreover, may be specialized in their creativity. A gifted child should perform on a high, yet exclusive, level of creative talent in at least one major area of endeavor. Torrance developed a series of tests of creative thinking that present questions with several possibly correct answers limited only by the flexibility, fluency, and originality of the test taker. Both verbal and visual creative opportunities are presented. A high correlation exists between intelligence test scores and the results of assessments of creativity; however, this is not an invariant relationship. Some children with highly convergent thinking (i.e., minds that prefer to seek single, discrete, accurate answers) may attain considerable success on intelligence tests but have little evidence of creativity or divergent thought (i.e., a tendency to elaborate and ponder various possibilities).

Cronbach (1970) distinguishes between *crystallized abilities,* which are highly focused and intimately related to accomplishment (such as musical skill, writing ability, and proficiency at fixing things), and *fluid abilities,* which are the equivalent of the various developmental functions presented in this book (such as language skills, memory, and higher cognition). Gallagher (1985) points out that "a child who shows a great talent for chess playing is showing crystallized abilities in the sense that the original reasoning and problem solving capacities would become focused, or crystallized, around a particular interest or content area" (p. 16). Thus, the degree of crystallization, the extent to which innate strengths in the developmental areas have evolved into performance abilities, is another indicator of giftedness. The development of crystallized abilities is an important goal for all children and an essential aim of education. Identifying specialized areas of higher cognitive ability can help enormously as a child strives toward crystallization.

Many of the capacities described in this chapter are particularly relevant to gifted children, and they can help us distinguish between generalized and specialized talent. Talent can be defined in terms of extraordinary higher cognitive function in one's chosen subject area—such as music, art, or mathematics. It is common (but often inappropriate) to expect that the truly gifted child will display crystallized strengths in several areas.

Of the number of studies of the natural history of giftedness, the most frequently quoted are the longitudinal studies of Terman and his group (1954). Their continuing research began in the 1920s when they first studied a sample of California schoolchildren who met criteria for giftedness. They discovered that children in their population had some describable attributes in common. They were more likely to be superior in their reading and language abilities as well as in their arithmetical reasoning, scientific aptitude, literary skills, and artistic inclinations.

Interestingly, spelling, factual information, history, and arithmetical computation were areas in which gifted children were not found to be as obviously superior. Furthermore, the gifted group had many different hobbies and a tendency to amass collections of objects. They also acquired more knowledge of various games than did their less talented peers. Over time, the gifted children in this sample continued to function quite well as a group. In particular, they displayed persistence and a high level of motivation and had well-defined goals. These children also succeeded socially and tended, as a group, to be quite popular and less susceptible to emotional or psychological problems than other children.

However, not all gifted children achieve academically. The "gifted underachiever" deserves exploration as an important developmental variation.

Gifted Underachievers

In a clinic or school, it is not uncommon to find children who, on the surface, give evidence of being gifted yet whose academic performance is disappointing and not commensurate with fluid abilities. Such gifted underachievers are a common source of consternation to their teachers, parents, and themselves. Many qualify as "gifted" because of high intelligence quotients. Some possess extraordinary creative abilities, highly specialized talents, and unusually well-developed academic skills in circumscribed areas. The disparity between ability and day-to-day performance can lead to chronic difficulties. Gallagher (1985) states that "unless some major attempt is made to counteract these trends at an early age, these underachievers will turn out as relatively nonproductive members of our society, to the detriment of both society and themselves" (p. 416).

What might be some of the causes of underachievement in gifted children? The following should be considered as possible factors, one or more of which may precipitate this condition.

Attention Deficits. One of the most perplexing challenges that a clinician, educator, or parent faces is gifted children with attention deficits. Despite impressively high scores on an intelligence test, these students may have inordinate difficulty completing assignments, tuning in to salient information, and performing consistently on examinations and written reports. The discrepancy between verbal and ideational fluency, on the one hand, and ability to get ideas down on paper, on the other, may be significant. Often these children prefer concepts and theories to details. Like many others with attention deficits, they tend to be impulsive, confusingly inconsistent, distractible, and poor at monitoring themselves. Unlike others with attention deficits, gifted children (in my experience) are likely to be manipulative and more willing and able to rationalize school underachievement. Such children may be either defiant or indifferent, insisting that school is dull, irrelevant, and not really important anyway. Some of these children have very strong competing interests that make schoolwork pedestrian. Others, however, show a remarkable dearth of profound interests. They tend to dabble, almost always on a superficial level, in a wide range of activities. They show few, if any, crystallized abilities despite their obviously fine fluid abilities. In some instances, these are children who are struggling with sleep-arousal imbalance. They require substantial activity or highly motivating, intense experience to remain sufficiently alert and satisfied. Often the classroom fails to fulfill these requirements. It is common to attribute their difficulties to boredom in a mundane school setting. However, many of their fellow gifted students who do not have attention deficits are able to cope with school and to find intrinsic interest in a wide range of subjects, even within a regular classroom program.

An important and common variation on this theme is the child with rich and rapid ideational fluency who underachieves and is poor at concentrating because of an apparent inability to harness or channel thought processes in a productive manner. Such a child may have particular problems slowing down ideation, controlling the free flight of ideas, and focusing on precise detail. He or she may succeed early in an academic year when the subject matter is new and exciting but bog down as the year goes on, when the amount of detail grows and the demand for repetition and disciplined thinking increases.

Gifted underachievers with attention deficits need to be treated in much the same manner as other children with attention difficulties. However, it is particularly essential that these gifted children understand their attention deficits, be helped to crystallize their abilities, and be trained to function under moderately motivating conditions. Their manipulative avoidance tactics need to be dealt with directly through confrontation, counseling, and behavior modification.

Uneven Development. Gifted underachievers often display uneven development. Such children, for example, may show genuine talents in verbal skills, memory, and simultaneous processing and production. However, they may have discrete gaps in one or more areas of development that often elude measurement by intelligence tests. For example, a child may have an active working memory problem but real strengths in other areas, talents that are sufficiently well developed to qualify her or him as "gifted." However, the active working memory difficulties create serious problems with test taking (see p. 75). Another child may have superior information-processing functions (and be labeled "gifted" on the basis of intelligence tests) but have substantial difficulties with production. Discrepancies in fine motor function, organization (of output), or rapid retrieval memory may lead an otherwise highly competent child to underachieve. As in the case of gifted children with attention deficits, the overall picture is likely to suggest a diagnosis of laziness.

Gifted children are sometimes delayed in social development. Despite keen intellectual abilities, they may underachieve in interactions with their peers. They may lack the requisite social skills (see chapter 8) to adjust adequately to the interactional demands of the school years. Disheartening problems can result when the child is placed in accelerated classes with more socially sophisticated classmates and the social delays become even more conspicuous and irksome.

Environmental and Cultural Factors. Some gifted children underachieve because of suboptimal home environments, including culturally deprived backgrounds. A talented child may be unable to perform optimally in school owing to the absence of academic role models at home, failure of the educational system to provide culturally consonant experiences, and lack of recognition by teachers. Poverty, domestic turmoil, and highly stressful life events can preoccupy a child (possibly draining attention) and result in a wide gap between gifted capacity and everyday performance. Gallagher (1985) cites a number of studies showing the frequency of major home-based difficulties and strained family relationships among gifted underachievers. In particular, it has been suggested that there may be characteristic breakdowns in the father-son relationship, the father of the gifted underachiever being less accepting and displaying more hostility toward the child than exists in the families of achieving children (Gallagher 1985, p. 416). Dowdall and Colangelo (1982) pinpointed family instability and social immaturity as key factors of underachievement.

It is also vitally important to acknowledge that not all cultures measure success according to the same standards. A child may be highly successful from the vantage point of his cultural milieu without meeting the expectations of a school curriculum. The concept of underachievement is as highly value laden and potentially culturally biased as is the concept of achievement. There is no universal agreement regarding whom to call a successful child.

Psychological Disturbances. Some studies have suggested that gifted underachievers commonly have low self-esteem and are highly negativistic (Gallagher

1985). They may also harbor aggressive feelings or be depressed. However, it can be difficult to determine whether the depression is secondary to underachievement or a component of predisposition to failure. Whichever it is, feelings of ineffectiveness need to be dealt with directly through counseling and programming activities at which such children can succeed.

Peer Pressure. Some gifted underachievers are likely to fail because they are fearful of success. In particular, some of these children may be overly responsive to peer pressure. They live in an environment in which it is not fashionable to work hard, to please adults, and to achieve academic respectability. They may be embarrassed about taking books home on the bus or ashamed of praise from teachers. Instead, they may prefer to act "cool" to gain a high level of social respectability among their peers.

Educational Understimulation. It is commonly believed that some gifted underachievers are just plain bored in school, with too much repetition and not enough high-level intellectual stimulation to inspire their fertile minds. Because this is sometimes at least partially true, gifted underachievers should have part of each day devoted to some highly stimulating and challenging educational experiences. However, this may not be effective, particularly for those who have attention deficits or signs of uneven development.

Temperamental Factors. Certain gifted underachievers exhibit temperamental features that are incompatible with high levels of productivity. Often these youngsters are slow to warm up and are overly cautious, preferring not to take risks for fear of failing, thereby becoming ultraconservative in their performance patterns. They resign themselves to mediocre levels of achievement despite their apparent intellectual potential. Many lack self-confidence. Some are especially passive in their relationships with adults. It can be difficult to determine whether the temperamental features are learned behaviors or whether they are inborn tendencies that deter achievement. In some instances, these children may appear to be amotivational, exhibiting many of the characteristics of "learned helplessness" (see chapter 13) or inexplicable feelings that success will set them up for future failure.

Pseudointellectualism and Pseudounderachievement. A superior reader is often assumed to be "brilliant." Such a child may be able to read highly sophisticated books at the age of four or five without really understanding or assimilating their content. Another variation is the highly verbal child, one who is especially articulate and widely divergent in social conversation, which may be impressive but, nonetheless, superficial and artificial. A teacher, clinician, or parent may mistake the combination of verbal fluency and the ability to be ingratiating to adults for intellectual giftedness. Such children may seem to underachieve but, in truth, the disparity may be overestimated.

ASSESSMENT OF HIGHER-ORDER COGNITION

As with other constructs, the evaluation of higher-order cognition consists of the search for recurring themes, bits of evidence that reveal strengths and weaknesses in relevant processes. Some evidence may accrue during intelligence testing or other modes of formal assessment. However, an assessor must derive the bulk of evidence for the status of a student's higher-order cognition from everyday observations in natural settings. Teachers are in a particularly advantageous position to make and synthesize such observations. Parents can be helpful as well. Clinicians taking a history can ask questions about specific aspects of higher cognitive function.

Clinicians can pose the following historical questions. Teachers can also use them to guide their observations of higher-order cognitive processes.

Concept Formation:

- Does this child grasp new concepts as readily as other students? Does he or she seem to know what a concept is?

- Does she or he overrely on memorization to compensate for tenuous concept formation?

- Does this student show uneven concept formation, doing better with certain forms of content than with others (e.g., grasping concepts more firmly in science than in social studies)?

- Does this student show a preference for verbal over nonverbal concepts (or vice versa)?

- If you show this child a concept in a textbook chapter she has recently read, can she explain the concept satisfactorily? Can she provide some good examples (i.e., prototypes) of the concept? (A clinician might ask a child to bring her textbooks to a testing session and ask her to elaborate on one or more concepts to which she has recently been exposed in her books.)

- Is there a substantial discrepancy between the child's grasp of concrete versus abstract concepts? Are there problems understanding mechanisms (i.e., process concepts in science and mathematics)?

- Can the child diagram or create a map of a key concept?

- Does this child demonstrate notable strengths in conceptualization? If so, are these generalized or are they conspicuous only in certain domains?

Problem-Solving Skill:

- Does this student tend to perform complex tasks in an impulsive manner?

- Does this student lack strategies when he undertakes a cognitive challenge?

- Does this child or adolescent seem to lack "stepwisdom," the tendency or ability to do things in sequential steps instead of all at once?

- Does this child show flexibility during problem solving or is she excessively rigid and unable to change strategies or methods when she reaches an impasse?

- Is this child uneven, showing good problem solving in certain subjects and ineffective problem solving in others?

- Does this student reveal notable strengths or talent or one or more problem-solving areas?

Rule Development and Utilization:

- Does this child have difficulty mastering rule systems in school (e.g., grammatical rules, spelling rules, foreign language rules)?

- Does this student have his greatest difficulty in those school subjects that contain important rules?

- Does this child comply with and/or memorize academic rules without really understanding them (i.e., make use of a strongly algorithmic approach to learning)?

- Can this child explain rules adequately?

- Does this child generalize well from one lesson to the next? Or, when she learns a rule in one specific context, does she have trouble applying it under slightly different circumstances?

- Are there any indications that this is a student who is good at formulating personal rules, rules that she develops herself to facilitate learning and problem solving?

Analogical Reasoning:

- Does this child seem to grasp metaphors, figurative language, and analogies?

- Is she or he effective at talking about what something (including a concept) is like?

- Can this child comprehend well when the teacher is using an analogy to explain a phenomenon, process, or concept?

Classification:

- Is this student effective at learning information that is arranged in categories (parts of speech, capitals of countries, etc.)?

- Can he organize a notebook, filing system, or a collection into appropriate categories?

Divergent/Creative Thinking:

- Does this student come up with original ideas and/or insights?

- How competent is this child at thinking up topics (for reports, stories, projects, etc.)?

- Are there indications of specific domains of creative talent (e.g., music, art, writing, humor)?

- Is this child willing and able to take risks with thinking, to come up with unusual thoughts or products? Or is she or he a very conservative thinker?

- If this child does exhibit one or more forms of creativity, are these being adequately developed in school and at home?

Metacognition:

- Is this child able to think and talk about how she learns best?

- Does this child appear to understand when taught about study skills, memorization, grammatical construction, and other processes that entail thinking about various aspects of cognition?

Standardized Testing

Standardized testing can shed further light on various higher cognitive functions. The following are some tests and tests items that have been employed for this purpose:

Assessments of Verbal Cognition.   The Similarities subtest of the *WISC-III* is frequently used to assess verbal conceptual ability as well as analogical thinking. Children must apply their understanding of verbal concepts to complete various verbal analogies. On the Likenesses and Differences subtest of the *Detroit Tests of Learning Aptitude,* subjects tell how the pairs of words in a series are similar and how they differ. While this is a vocabulary test, it also assesses how precisely children have mastered certain verbal concepts and categories. For example, when subjects are asked to describe how a spoon and fork are alike, they must recognize the superordinate category of "eating utensils." Thus, this particular subtest simultaneously assesses vocabulary, formation of concepts, and hierarchical categorization or classification.

The *Boehm Test of Basic Concepts* is used with children between the ages of five and eight. The examiner reads aloud statements describing fifty pictures arranged in order of increasing difficulty, and the subject identifies the picture that best illustrates the concept being tested from an array of three or four items. The concepts include quantity, number, time, and space (location, direction, and dimension). *The Woodcock-Johnson Test of Cognitive Ability* includes a subtest that examines concept formation in a way that is uncontaminated by memory function. Also included in this battery is a nonverbal problem-solving task (Spatial Relations), and a test of "reasoning" (Analysis-Synthesis) which at least indirectly assesses a child's ability to generate logical rules.

Assessments of Nonverbal Cognition. The Block Design subtest of the *WISC-III* assesses a subject's ability to form concepts and solve problems in the nonverbal domain. Raven's (1960) *Progressive Matrices* is another assessment of nonverbal reasoning and problem solving. It requires the manipulation of increasingly complex designs. In tests of nonverbal analogies, children are shown a series of pictures of objects or actions. They are asked to look at the relationship between the first two pictures (such as a hammer and a nail) and then to look at a third picture (a screwdriver) and choose from among several options (pliers, a screw, a saw, and a plank of wood) one object that bears the same relationship to the screwdriver that the nail bears to the hammer.

Various tests of *seriation* also assess nonverbal cognition. From a series of numbers or designs the subject must *infer* which of several options most logically comes next. This process can reveal an individual's ability to generate rules. By studying the presented series and determining how each stimulus modifies in some systematic manner the ones preceding it, the subject can predict what comes next by discovering a rule that governs the sequence. Seriation tasks are found on a number of aptitude tests, for example, the *Cognitive Abilities Test* (Thorndike and Hagen 1978).

Assessments of Problem-Solving Strategies. A relatively neglected area in the past, the assessment of problem-solving strategies has become a worthwhile concern of contemporary diagnosticians. Meltzer (1984) has developed a problem-solving battery to assess specifically such strategies in children by observing the entire problem-solving process. Both verbal and nonverbal items are used in an attempt to determine and document how effectively students plan and organize their responses and how flexible they are in employing alternative strategies when required to do so. Sample items are presented in figure 7-2. Various object- and word-sorting tasks have been used to determine how children go about classifying items into categories. Such tasks form a part of a number of intelligence tests (such as the *McCarthy Scales of Children's Abilities* and the *Cognitive Abilities Test;* see appendix). Observing the methods or thought processes used during the act of categorizing can be especially enlightening. The *Wisconsin Card Sorting Test* has been used widely to evaluate children's flexibility and judgment during problem solving. This test is also thought to tap many of the production controls of attention (see chapter 2).

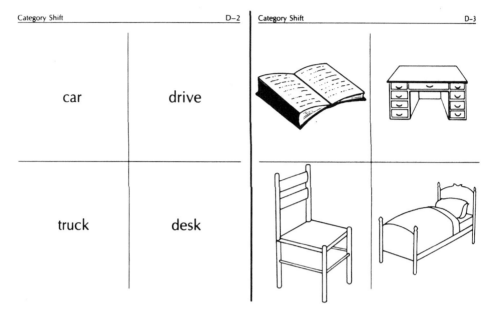

Figure 7-2. Sample *Survey of Problem-Solving Skills* items

The Category Shift task of the *Survey of Problem-Solving Skills* (Meltzer 1986) asks the student to identify which three of the four words or pictures go together and to state how they do so. Then the student is asked to find a different combination of three items that go together. Tasks such as these provide insights into problem-solving abilities, classification skills, verbal and nonverbal reasoning discrepancies, and the flexibility of children's thinking (i.e., how readily they are able to shift from one cognitive strategy to another).

There exist a number of tests of creative thinking. The most frequently cited is the *Torrance Test of Creative Thinking,* which measures flexible and divergent thinking patterns. In general, however, the search for a child's creative propensities should focus on direct historical evidence.

Assessment Interactions between Higher-Order Cognition and Other Neurodevelopmental Constructs

The assessment of higher-order cognition should always be performed in tandem with the evaluation of strengths and weaknesses in the other neurodevelopmental constructs. It is often the case that a higher-order cognitive dysfunction is found in association with a dysfunction in a "lower" area of cognition. Some examples are shown in table 7-1.

It is equally important to acknowledge that strengths in a particular neurodevelopmental construct may facilitate higher-order cognition. Thus, a child with excellent language skills may reveal great linguistic creativity and an excellent grasp of complex verbal concepts. A child with extraordinary spatial ordering could like-

Table 7-1. Common linkages between higher-order cognitive dysfunctions and other forms of neurodevelopmental dysfunction

ASSOCIATED AREA OF DYSFUNCTION	IMPACTS ON HIGHER-ORDER COGNITION
Attentional dysfunction	May impede problem solving, causing a child to use a frenetic, impulsive approach with little or no consideration of strategic alternatives or self-monitoring
Spatial ordering problems	Problems with nonverbal concept formation due to impaired use of mental imagery to reinforce concepts or develop analogies
Temporal-sequential ordering problems	A weak sense of stepwisdom for problem solving; also problems dealing with process concepts
Language dysfunctions	Trouble with highly verbal problem-solving challenges (e.g., interpreting or writing a poem) as well as difficulty forming verbal concepts
Memory dysfunctions	Active working memory problems can impede concept formation; problem solving can be compromised by problems with pattern recognition and/or active working memory

wise exhibit very strong nonverbal problem-solving skills as well as creativity and adept problem solving in the nonverbal domains (e.g., mechanical talent).

It is often the case that higher-order cognitive abilities can only improve significantly if the associated neurodevelopmental dysfunctions are managed well, and if a child's higher cognitive strengths are used to by bypass and strengthen his higher cognitive shortcomings.

MANAGING HIGHER-ORDER COGNITION

All students need help with higher-order cognition. They need to become progressively more effective at dealing with the various components of this construct in a wide range of applications throughout their educational careers and beyond. Every subject is at least implicitly a course in higher-order cognition. In fact, teachers need to think seriously about the ways in which the content they teach actually serves to build higher cognitive capabilities. Much management of higher-order cognition is likely to occur within the context of specific subject areas in school. Becoming proficient in mathematics may enhance problem solving, for example, while dealing with issues in a social studies or science class can also develop this ability. Nevertheless, there are certain general principles that pertain across content areas.

Therapeutic approaches to higher cognitive deficiencies are an important challenge in education. Considerable work has been directed toward enhancing reasoning skills among retarded children and adults. Until recently, relatively little attention was directed toward efforts to improve higher cognition among students with developmental dysfunctions or low-severity disabilities. The development of metacognition, greater conscious use of problem-solving strategies, and the effective use of higher processes such as inferring, analogizing, and categorizing have been the major objectives of such interventions.

As with other areas of development, serious issues are involved in differentiating between styles of learning and true disabilities, or even dysfunctions. Therefore, an important part of management is acknowledging specific learning styles. A child whose nonverbal conceptualization far outstrips verbal concept formation should be encouraged to pursue and strengthen his or her strong (nonverbal) cognitive pathway. A child whose verbal problem solving is intact should be encouraged to "talk through" or verbally mediate tasks whenever possible. In this way, clearly established preferences are further enhanced. More difficult, however, is the generation of an appropriate response to children who are overly concrete, those who have difficulty with abstract thinking in general. Students who fail to apply effective problem-solving strategies, who overrely on rote memory, who do not show sufficient flexibility and efficiency in their various higher cognitive processes are also worthy of attention. Such children may benefit from direct intervention that helps improve these areas through the conscious building of *metacognition,* strategies and methods of conceptualization.

Although there have been many different attempts to train students in higher-order cognition, the work of the Israeli psychologist Reuven Feuerstein has become influential and can serve as a model for our discussion. Espousing what he calls "the theory of cognitive modifiability," Feuerstein has developed a higher cognitive curriculum known as *instrumental enrichment.* The curriculum is based on the premise that much cognitive behavior represents a malleable system amenable to meaningful structural change (Feuerstein and Jensen 1980). Feuerstein et al. (1980) provide a series of learning experiences for their students, some of whom are retarded and some of whom are less impaired. Through intensive training and repetition, the students solve problems and become acutely conscious of the methods they apply. They learn to take in stimuli and to elaborate on them, and thereby, in a conscious manner, to practice good problem solving. Through sharing a whole series of such experiences, students are said to develop insights, to acquire progressive ease and automaticity of reasoning, and to sustain a high level of motivation to continue. An avowed goal of the program consists "in changing drastically the student's perception of himself or herself from a passive recipient of information to an active producer, creator, and generator of new information" (Feuerstein and Jensen 1980, p. 420). Both visual and verbal activities are included in the curriculum. In one task, Organization of Dots, the student is required to recognize standard figures within patterns of dots. It is anticipated that with help the student's perception evolves from an indistinct and very general view to a heightened level of concentration and more precise perception that reveal that the pattern made by a particular number of dots matches a stimulus. Other exercises emphasize categorization, comparisons, and syllogistic thinking. Ultimately, Feuerstein believes that the various tasks (which he calls "instruments") will be generalizable, that children will be more adept at detecting and applying rules, at developing what he calls a linguistic and conceptual repertoire that will be relevant in a wide range of problem-solving situations. Feuerstein and Jensen (1980) note that "tasks involving the same deficient functions are repeated across different instruments, thereby presenting the learner with opportunities to consolidate the different schemata and become efficient in using them" (p. 418). This model emphasizes formation of good learning habits.

The Feuerstein curriculum has been applied in settings throughout the world. Training programs for teachers enable them to administer it. Feuerstein's groups believe that they have demonstrated significant improvement in academic skills as well as cognitive abilities of their students. In one study (Feuerstein and Jensen 1980) subjects were randomly assigned to receive either 300 hours of instrumental enrichment (i.e., structured cognitive exercises) or 300 hours of tutorial help in basic school skills. The authors found that the intensive cognitive training enabled students to do as well or better in various academic areas than those who received only teaching in basic skills. While the Feuerstein approach may not be feasible and available in all settings, the principles involved remain salient. Schools need to make higher cognitive processes more explicit in order to help students develop metacognition. They need to assign exercises that give children and adolescents direct explicit experience engaging in and enhancing critical higher cognitive processes.

Cognitive behavior modification represents a similar approach to intervention for children with apparent higher cognitive deficiencies. Such training involves the direct enhancement of metacognition and has been described by Meichenbaum (1977). His approach is summarized by Mann and Sabatino (1985) as follows:

- *Cognitive modeling.* The child observes an adult performing a particular task while describing aloud what the person is doing.

- *External guidance.* The child performs the same type of task according to the model's instructions.

- *Faded overt self-guidance.* The child whispers the instructions to himself while performing the task.

- *Covert self-instruction.* The child performs the task using inaudible or silent speech to give himself instruction.

It can be seen that Meichenbaum's program entails a great deal of verbal mediation during which children engage in substantial self-instruction. They may instruct themselves to remember to go slowly, to review what they just did, and even to praise themselves when they think they are succeeding. Underlying such techniques is the belief that the children's own verbal coaching will help establish conscious use of metacognitive strategies, which ultimately can lead to less conscious (i.e., covert) forms of monitoring.

The durability and generalizability of such cognitive training models remain to be fully established. Eventually, special education programs may emphasize some form of higher cognitive training. In the meantime, it is justifiable to advocate some direct teaching of metacognition and problem solving. We might argue that these kinds of insights should be instilled in all students as part of any regular curriculum. While this is no doubt true, children with demonstrable deficiencies of higher-order cognition are likely to benefit most from an emphasis on the conscious awareness of learning processes and the active pursuit of problem-solving strategies.

General Management Principles

Formal cognitive training is not the only option for children with deficiencies of higher-order cognition. In addition to or instead of such programs, the following general principles of management merit consideration:

- Encourage students to engage in more elaboration and explanation of facts and ideas rather than rote repetition. At home and in school, have children add personal interpretation, relate new information to prior experience, make use of analogies ("What is this like?") and talk about various future applications of what they are learning.

- Help children become better problem-solving strategists. Stress the right method of accomplishing a task rather than the right answer. Children may also need to recognize alternative methods that they can use if a particular approach proves unrewarding.

- A Problem-Solving Planner (fig. 7-3) can help students develop a more systematic approach to problem solving. Guide children through a wide range of personal and academic problem-solving challenges, and have them document the steps taken in the Problem-Solving Planner. Children can use their areas of higher cognitive ability to develop concepts, rules, and even academic skills. For example, a student who is talented at fixing things can read repair manuals to develop reading skills. While a child figures out how to engage in a new activity on a computer, help her think about problem-solving strategies and rules.

- It can help children to move from the concrete to the abstract and back to the concrete. Children who have trouble dealing with abstract concepts may benefit from the use of concrete materials to reinforce learning. In mathematics, for example, have them study fractions by actively manipulating objects divided into fractional segments. State abstract concepts repeatedly in terms of everyday practical applications.

The Problem-Solving Planner

Name _____ Date _____

Collaborators _____

1. Is there a problem I need to solve?

   Yes_____ No_____ Possibly_____

2. What exactly is the problem?

   Statement of the problem _____

   _____

   _____

   _____

   _____

3. What information do I need to solve this problem? Where do I find this information?

Information Needed	Place(s) to Find it
1.	
2.	
3.	
4.	
5.	
6.	

Figure 7-3. Problem-Solving Planner

4. Can I solve this problem?

- Yes, Easily_____ Yes, with a Lot of Work_____ No_____ Maybe_____
- By Myself_____ With Help_____ From Whom?_____

5. How long will it take?_____ How much time do I have?_____

6. What is familiar in this problem (what I've seen, heard, or been through before)?

   Familiar Patterns _____

   _____

   _____

   _____

7. What should be the order of my stepwise approach for solving the problem?

   (1) _____

   (2) _____

   (3) _____

   (4) _____

   (5) _____

   (6) _____

8. What strategies can I use to solve this problem?

   Strategies_____

   _____

   _____

   _____

   _____

Figure 7-3. *(Continued)*

9. Do I have back-up strategies in case the first one doesn't work? If so, what are they?

Back-Up Strategies _____

_____

10. Roughly, how will this be or look when it is finished or the problem is solved?

Preview or Estimate _____

_____

11. [To be answered in the middle of the problem-solving activity] Are things going according to plan? Am I satisfied with how I'm doing?

Yes_____ No_____ Partly_____

Comments _____

_____

12. [To be answered when the problem has been solved] How did this turn out?

- Very Successful_____ Pretty Successful_____ Unsuccessful_____
- Is Really Finished_____ Could Use Some More Work_____
- Was Harder_____ Was Easier_____ Was As Hard As I Expected_____
- Took Longer_____ Took Less Time_____ Took What I Thought_____

13. Can I use the solution and/or these problem-solving strategies in the future? If so, how?

Future Uses _____

_____

_____

_____

Figure 7-3. *(Continued)*

- Students can benefit from ample experience in concept mapping. Courses containing a considerable amount of conceptual material should encourage the use of *concept atlases,* notebooks in which children create and store the maps for important concepts. Their maps should include critical features of the concept, prototypes, and nonopposite concepts. An example of a concept map can be seen in figure 7-4.

- Be certain that a student has mastered basic concepts before proceeding to more sophisticated concepts. Some children fail to assimilate basic concepts; often they memorize rather than understand. Ultimately, this can lead to difficulty in content areas in which concepts are based on previously taught concepts (such as in mathematics and physics). A tenuous grasp of basic concepts can lead to subsequent misunderstanding and an inability to apply knowledge flexibly. Students with such weak formation of concepts require especially intensive teaching and evaluation in the early stages of learning a new subject.

- Children may need to isolate higher cognition from other functions during the performance of complex tasks. Children with higher cognitive impairments may experience inordinate strain when they attempt to reason at the same time that they are performing in other ways. Some students may find it difficult to write and reason simultaneously or to solve a word problem while trying to retrieve the multiplication tables. Reducing demands on memory may facilitate reasoning. For example, a child might record ideas on a tape recorder and then write a paragraph. Or permit a child to use a calculator whenever trying to solve word problems

- Actively teach metacognition to facilitate acquisition of skills and knowledge. All students can benefit from demystification to help them understand various learning and thinking processes. The course called *The Mind That's Mine* (p. 570) represents one attempt to induce metacognition in all students. Children with higher cognitive dysfunctions may be slow to acquire certain academic skills in the absence of metacognitive knowledge. For example, in reading comprehension they may need help in the following areas (Baker 1982): modifying reading strategies for different purposes (e.g., scanning, looking up something, memorizing), considering how new information relates to old, recognizing the logic in a passage, knowing when and how to reread, and identifying important ideas. In mathematics they may need help identifying key information in a word problem, understanding the rule systems of basic processes (such as long division), and knowing when they do or do not understand a concept (such as the meaning of *equation, place value,* or *proportion*).

- Use reading materials to enhance formation of concepts as well as problem solving. In discussing passages from specific texts, stress distinctions between cause and effect and fact and opinion. In addition, use reading comprehension activities to teach analogous reasoning and the drawing of inferences. Examples of such integrated reading and higher cognitive training are found in a series of workbooks entitled *Reasoning and Reading* (Carlisle 1982).

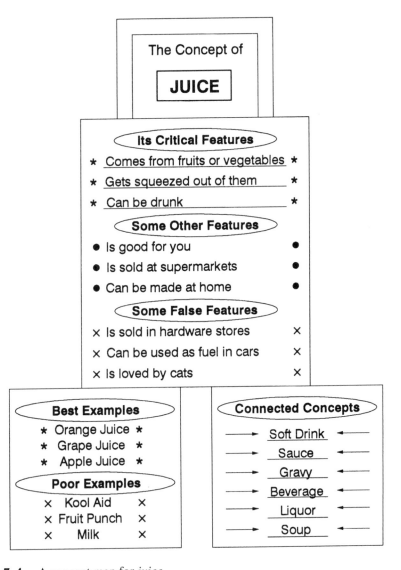

Figure 7-4. A concept map for *juice*

- Encourage and help children to use analogies whenever possible.

- Many students need overt practice at categorizing knowledge. Help a child develop classification skills within her personal areas of expertise. She may practice classifying comic books, trading cards, rocks, pets, etc.

- All children can benefit from ample opportunities to develop their creative tendencies and divergent thinking skills. Encourage them to engage in imaginary play. Discourage them from engaging in too many passive activities, such as television watching, some electronic games, and excessive talking on the telephone. In all subjects, reward children for original, even "far out" thinking.

Assessing and Managing Strengths

Clearly, uncovering deficits is not the sole intent of evaluating higher-order cognition. Specific strengths in higher-order cognitive areas may hold the key to intervention for a child who is struggling. Some children seem to fare particularly well if conceptualization and the use of rules are emphasized—perhaps to overcome difficulties with simultaneous or sequential processing or to lessen demands on memory. Some children with attention deficits can be particularly adept in their higher-order cognitive functions. They may be especially talented at forming concepts, dealing with abstractions, and employing rules. They may discover that such higher-order cognitive manipulations enable them to reduce the total amount of detail in their lives. Since attention to detail can be a formidable challenge for children with attention deficits, these cognitive reduction processes can enable them to succeed. It is not unusual for children with attention deficits and truly excellent higher-order cognitive abilities to bypass (at least somewhat) an attention deficit and mobilize their strong conceptual talents to achieve effectively in a number of areas. This seems to pertain particularly to those endeavors that children find highly motivating.

Children may display extraordinary higher-order conceptual abilities in a discrete subject area or pursuit. Strikingly well-developed problem solving, categorization, and formation of strategies may emerge in music, sports, mathematics, mechanical repairs, or even social interaction (see chapter 8) while children remain conspicuously deficient in other areas. Thus, any good diagnostic account of higher cognitive abilities must include a systematic search for those domains in which higher-order cognition operates most effectively, needs continuous challenges, and has the potential to override weaker functions.

Chapter 8

Social Ability

Kai-Shek showed no signs of special brilliance at school, and was said to have been better at games than at learning. On the whole he seems to have been quiet and rather timid, given to long periods of meditation and solitary walks. . . . By all accounts he was a reserved and lonely youth, who held himself a little apart from the rest.

—Robert Payne, *Chiang Kai-Shek*

In his essay "The Daily Grind," Philip Jackson (1983) comments that "learning to live in a classroom involves, among other things, learning to live in a crowd . . . . Most of the things that are done in school are done with others, or at least in the presence of others, and this fact has profound implications for determining the quality of a student's life" (p. 35). For schoolchildren, this apt observation can be extended to encompass life beyond school as well. Children must make major accommodations as they learn to reckon with the groups in which they are immersed. Satisfying the demands of social life is as critical as fulfilling academic expectations. This chapter focuses on social ability—the aptitudes required to mingle in the crowds of childhood and rehearse for the interactional demands of adult life.

Social success with peers is of paramount importance to most schoolchildren. The avoidance of humiliation at all costs is a relentless campaign, as is the quest for friendship and popularity. During waking hours children are preoccupied with evading embarrassment, face saving, and looking good. During school hours this quest may well take precedence over academic stardom. Social maneuvering drains attention and energy and demands keen skill. The precise nature of that skill, the developmental determinants of social success or failure, have fascinated clinicians and investigators, particularly over the last decade. It is likely that the neurodevelopmental functions delineated in earlier chapters bear (at least indirectly) on social ability. Interaction with peers draws heavily on attention controls, organization, memory, communication, and higher-order cognition. The substantial developmental variation that occurs in acquiring academic skills also applies to building and sustaining human relationships. Like academic success (or failure), social mastery may affect and be affected by self-esteem, self-confidence, and self-image.

Social interaction encompasses relationships with teachers, parents, other adults, siblings, and other children. However, this chapter focuses almost exclusively on the ways in which children relate to each other, the skills they need and develop in doing so, and the phenomenology of variation and dysfunction of social ability. The relative neglect of children's relationships with adults here does not minimize their importance.

Our discussion of social ability begins with a brief description of the social challenge that confronts schoolchildren.

THE SOCIAL SCENE

The French philosopher Jean Paul Sartre once lamented, "Hell is other people," meaning that various people in the outside world inevitably constrain our freedoms. They cramp our styles, condition our behaviors, and alter our goals. Sociologist David Riesman, in his influential book *The Lonely Crowd* (1953), characterized individuals as either *inner-directed* or *other-directed.* The former base their actions and words on predominantly intrinsic values, what Riesman calls an internal "gyroscope," while the latter allow social forces to shape their values and actions. They say and do things that are most likely to be conforming and appealing, especially to their peer group. Much of contemporary society has been characterized as other-directed. Children feel enormous pressure to define themselves by being like others their age. Ironically, much of this pressure is likely to be internally generated. During elementary school, many (perhaps most) children feel legitimated and reinforced only by being comparable to those around them. In late elementary school, this drive toward conformity of behavior, values, and image becomes a nearly tyrannical force in the lives of schoolchildren. The way they talk, dress, move their bodies through space, and act in various settings is supposed to fit the code of their social milieu.

Social conformity necessitates studying and assimilating values or cultural influences that may differ from those of their own homes. Interactions with peers help children increase their self-awareness as they assiduously study the attributes and behaviors of those with whom they are intimate. Peers become allies in the exploration of autonomy and its limits. They collaborate in the satisfaction of appetites and drives.

Social ability undergoes a constant series of tests through childhood. During both elementary and high school, certain settings are particularly provocative. These include the bus stop, the bus, the corridors and lockers, the cafeteria, the gymnasium, the school rest rooms, and the playground. Emotionally laden, fierce social transactions occur on these stages. Interestingly, the classroom may be one of the most protected arenas for peer relationships. The bus stop allows for considerable social dialogue, labeling of peers, and establishment of cliques (with inevitable inclusion and exclusion processes). The bus and the cafeteria provide settings for the sometimes tense drama of who sits with whom and who is actively deprived of such physical intimacy. The corridors, the cafeteria line, and play-ground accommodate the highly charged pushing or shoving of vulnerable indi-viduals; having his books knocked down in the locker area may be an intolerable insult to a seventh-grade student. The gymnasium and the playground afford the potential for invited or denied participation in games.

Being labeled or called names by peers is an ever present threat. Relative immunity from unkind appellations is a sign of social success. Contemporary derogatory terminology includes such words as *wimp, weirdo, nerd, twerp,* and *mental case.* On the other hand, to be called *awesome, cool, neat,* and the like is most gratifying. Children's own names may be unkindly distorted, or nicknames may be a source of prestige, an emblem of coolness.

As youngsters mature, acceptance by the opposite sex becomes increasingly important. Invitations to parties, dating, and perceived attractiveness become cru-cial elements of status.

In middle school or junior high, social pressure appears to reach its utmost intensity. This is an age of conformity, a time when most children feel exquisitely vulnerable. Many are self-conscious, keenly aware of stereotyped gender roles, and heavily preoccupied with the need not to deviate from narrowly set behavioral norms. Children in this age group may be particularly embarrassed by their par-ents. They are often tangled in a major conflict—striving to appear autonomous and adultlike, while highly dependent on their parents and other grown-ups. This period also encompasses the widest variation in cognitive, physical, and psycho-sexual development. It is, of course, ironic that these children show such devel-opmental heterogeneity at a time when they are so intently seeking similarity.

High school students tolerate nonconformity a bit more. There is a growing recognition, even admiration, for individuality. Many students rediscover their inner-directedness at this stage—at least to some extent. High school is also a period of more conscious image building. Students are increasingly aware of their uniqueness and of the need to promote and market the product they think they rep-resent. Increasingly, they become known for their strengths. Particular students are thought of as *jocks* or *brains.* Devotees of cars or motorcycles may become associated with a specialized subgroup. Those who adopt certain styles of cloth-ing and social mores may be considered, for example, *preppies.* High school does not provide generalized acceptance of true individuality as much as tolerance of definable subgroups in which members can gain acceptance. Membership is a key attribute, an identifying feature of the older teenager. This desire to belong con-tinues into the college years—perhaps accounting in part for fraternities, sorori-ties, campus organizations, and other such obligatory subgroupings.

What becomes of the nonconformist? Not all children are willing or able to adhere to the code of social norms. Some prefer a more inner-directed social path through childhood. We might regard such children as modern-day juvenile heroes, especially if they have the capacity to succeed according to local social norms but prefer to be different. The ability of some of these relatively autonomous children to maintain their individuality without experiencing retribution from their peers must be one of the more laudable early-life accomplishments.

SOCIAL DEVELOPMENT

Social ability, like other competencies, accrues during the school years. This section traces several of the major themes of social development that have been studied in recent years. The following principal areas will be explored: the formation of friendships, the understanding of others, and moral development.

Formation of Friendships

The ability to find and keep friends is subject to considerable developmental progression and variation. Children derive an enormous amount of education from their interactions with other children. Stone and Church (1968) state that "the school age child spends as much of his time as possible in the company of his peers, from whom he learns first-hand about social structures, about in-groups and out-groups, about leadership and followership, about justice and injustice, about loyalties, and heroes and ideals" (p. 364).

There have been a number of studies on the development of friendship during school years. Some relevant findings are distilled in the following pages.

The key themes in school-age children's development of friendships are:

- Evolution of friendship from a convenience for play to relationships that embody mutual respect, affection, and the sharing of feelings

- Growing understanding of how personal actions can affect a friend's state of mind and feelings

- Steady acquisition of accurate perspective taking, i.e., the ability to discern and assume the point of view of a friend, to pass beyond egocentricity

- Increasing capacity to distinguish between friends and acquaintances

- Progressive independence from adult participation in friendships

- Enhanced propensity to form "chumships," close relationships with a few friends

- Stronger tendency to display altruism toward friends

Youniss and Volpe (1978) asked children of different ages what they need to do to demonstrate or maintain good social relationships, that is, to provide examples of things they might do to show that they like or are friends with someone. These investigators, like others, discovered that younger children associated friendship with sharing material goods or enjoyable activities. Older children reported that sharing private thoughts and feelings out of a sense of mutual respect and affection is necessary for friendship. The concept of *mutuality* evolves as children's friendships become more sophisticated and their understanding of the relationships between interpersonal acts and personal psychological states becomes more mature. One example cited by Youniss and Volpe is older children's discovering that a gesture of friendship can change a person's state from depression to happiness. Older children recognize increasingly the interdependence between peers—that they need each other and that they can rely on each other. They are less likely to be friends with someone because she or he lives near them or has some toys or facilities that they value. Such convenient relationships are displaced as children seek friends who will "stick by" them, those who will be loyal.

An important contribution to the development of friendships is social perspective taking, a process through which children are able to assume another's point of view and relate it to their own. It represents a dramatic departure from the egocentricity of preschool. Selman (1981), in a review entitled "The Child as a Friendship Philosopher," outlines specific stages and levels of development based largely on the gradual acquisition of social perspective taking. Selman began with a conceptual model based on clinical experience and previous research and then conducted various empirical studies to validate the model. As part of his schema, he defined five levels and five stages. The levels refer to children's growing capacities to coordinate their own and others' social perspectives. The stages refer to their overall understanding of close friendships. These levels and stages are not discrete; there is considerable overlap from age to age. However, they do reveal a predictable progression.

Level 0: Egocentric or undifferentiated perspectives (approximately ages three to seven). At this level, children are unable to distinguish their own perspectives from those of others. They fail to realize that another person may interpret similar social experiences quite differently from the way they do, and they may have trouble determining what is done intentionally or unintentionally. In their understanding of friendships, children conceive of relationships based on physical proximity and on the availability of toys and places in which they can interact. Friendship at this point is described as "playmateship."

Level 1: Subjective or differentiated perspectives (approximately ages four to nine). In this period, children understand that the perspectives of another person may be the same as or different from theirs. They come to recognize the uniqueness of the feelings, values, and attitudes of individuals. During this stage of conceptualizing friendship, children view relationships as important because others can tackle specific activities that they themselves want to see accomplished. In addition, a close friend becomes someone who is *known better* than other persons rather than someone who is in close physical proximity. This knowledge includes an idea of that friend's unique likes and dislikes.

Level 2: Self-reflective or reciprocal perspectives (approximately ages six to twelve). On this level, children are able to think about their own thoughts and feelings from the perspective of someone else. In other words, they can put themselves in someone else's mind and see how they might look to others. This leads to new forms of reciprocity. They become increasingly aware of how their actions and thoughts affect their evaluations of other people. In terms of friendships, Selman has described this as a time of "fair-weather cooperation." He says that "the two-way nature of friendships is exemplified by concern for coordinating and approximating, through adjustment by both self and other, the specific likes and dislikes of self and others, rather than matching one person's actions to the other's fixed standard of expectation." There is reciprocity of thought and feeling but not necessarily reciprocity of action. However, there is clearly more give-and-take, more possible negotiation at this stage.

Level 3: Third person or mutual perspectives (approximately ages nine to fifteen). At this level, children are aware of a so-called third-person perspective. They can distance themselves from both parties in a relationship and study it as a whole. Friendships become a means of developing intimacy and supporting each other. Friends share personal problems. Conflict, when it occurs, does not signal the suspension of the relationship because there is an underlying assumption of continuity between partners. They are no longer fair-weather friends; they can withstand inclement social incidents. The emphasis is still on the two-person clique; there is often intense possessiveness.

Level 4: Societal or in-depth perspectives (approximately ages twelve to adult). At this level, the perspectives become generalized into the concept of society's fabric or a legal or moral point of view. Two persons can share perspectives on a number of levels, including superficial information, common interests, and deeper unverbalized feelings. During this stage of understanding friendship, each person accepts the other's need to establish relations with others and to grow through such experience. Varying degrees of friendship emerge. There is still dependence, reflecting awareness that friends must rely on each other to obtain psychological support, to gain strength, and to develop self-identification.

Thus, as children age, the meaning of friendship becomes increasingly diversified and complicated. To the high school student, friendship represents a commingling of personalities at multiple interfaces; for the preschool and primary schoolchild, it is more simply a facilitator of play.

The capacity to differentiate between friends and acquaintances is another acquired social ability. Newcomb and Brady (1982) studied this phenomenon in second- and sixth-grade boys. As early as second grade, their subjects engaged in a great deal of mutual reinforcement with their close friends. These investigators observed that "the interactions of friends, as compared to nonfriends, were characterized by greater affective expression, and friends were also more likely to match or imitate the affective expression of their partners during their interactions. This tendency to match affective expression was the hallmark of mutuality and harmony. During direct observations, close friends tended to match laughter, match smiling, match looking, and match touching. These matching processes constituted forms of intimacy, signals of mutuality." Newcomb and Brady conclude that "the high social reinforcement value of shared experiences and reciprocated affect experienced by friends may function to provide necessary reaffirmation of existing friendship expectations and, consequently, serve to maintain the existing affective attachment."

In a study of the development of "chumship" during elementary school years, McGuire and Weisz (1982) confirmed Selman's stagelike sequence of interpersonal relationships. In this simple scheme, children were said to move from a stage (two to five years) requiring adult participation in their interactions with peers to a stage (four to eight years) in which children have playmates but interact with them in self-serving ways, and then to a stage (eight to eleven years) described as the period of "chumship." During this third stage, children were said to be able for the first time to form an intense attachment to a same-sex friend, a bond fortified through intimacy and reciprocity. As described earlier in this section, formation of chumships demands intimacy, affective matching, and mutual understanding. It also involves some perspective taking. Chumship moves beyond friendship in general in its acquisition and nurturance of a very few best friends. The most important attributes that reinforce chumships are strong social cognitive skills in general, good perspective taking, and, importantly, altruism. In other words, in the presence of a chum, preadolescent children are less self-centered and engage in more kind acts. This includes such acts as verbal expression of support for a peer whose mother is deriding him, offering to call the parent of a chum who is ill, saving part of one's lunch to share, or assisting physically when a child has had an accident. Interestingly, children who are capable of forming good chumships do not limit their altruism to their chums. They are generally kinder and less self-centered in all their transactions in the social domain.

Gender Differences. In recent years considerable research has been done on the different social pressures and reactive behaviors of the two sexes. Schofield (1981) observes that "a great deal of the interaction within male peer groups seems directed toward proving and displaying athletic skill and physical strength. Informal arm wrestling tournaments are legion, as are a variety of behaviors such as playful shoving, tussling, mock boxing matches, wrestling, and fun fights." This kind of behavior is less apt to be observed among girls and seems to be more than just play. Schofield notes further that "boys often use such interactions to compete with each other for highly valued places at the top of the male dominance hierarchy which they rather systematically set about constructing." This, too, is different from the procedures used by girls, whose social interactions revolve to a great extent around grooming themselves and others. Discussions of hair, clothing, and other elements of physical appearance are very common in late elementary and junior high school. Much of this appears to stem from a desire to be attractive to the opposite sex; in fact, popularity with boys may influence acceptance by other girls.

In elementary school, the major emphasis is on same-sex peer groups. This is often viewed as preparation for future relationships with the opposite sex. Studies of sex differences in the formation of friendships in elementary school show that girls more often confine their friends to a single other person while boys more often have a group of friends (Macoby and Jacklin 1974). Moreover, girls' friendships tend to be more exclusive and more intimate than those of boys. In studies of their ideas about friendships, girls mention intimacy and faithfulness more often than do boys. Girls are more likely to report that they would tell a friend if they did something clumsy or foolish.

Despite these differences, there is similarity in the development of social ability. Both girls and boys face intense pressure to gain acceptance by peers while craving the support and comfort of close friendships.

Developing Understanding of Others

The second area of social development, social behavior, is shaped in part by a child's interpretations of the actions of others. A major confrontation takes place in the primary grades, as children discover that other children differ from them in their values, backgrounds, motives, and interests. L. Ross (1981) observed that "children are egocentric relative to adults—they are less able to anticipate discrepancies between their own view of the world and that of other people . . . they have less capacity than their parents to surround themselves with people who share their values, priorities, impressions, and interests." Ross goes on to speculate that other children "constitute a more random sample of their species than the adult's coworkers and friends." Reckoning with this diversity of values and backgrounds is a noteworthy challenge for primary schoolchildren. They develop skills that enable them to become increasingly astute analyzers and raters of other children. In selecting friends, in communicating with peers, in joining subgroups, and even in adopting personal repertoires of values and social behaviors, children must study the models presented by peers, siblings, and adults. Furthermore, during the elementary school years, they become increasingly aware that they too are being observed and judged—by peers and by adults. They are likely to recognize that the methods or standards they are using to evaluate others may or may not be identical to those applied to them by evaluators.

As children develop their capacities to form judgments about others, an important distinction arises. Children may assume either a *dispositionalist* or *situationalist* viewpoint (L. Ross 1981) about the actions or reactions of their peers. The dispositionalist view holds that people act in a particular way because of their internal, relatively fixed attributes. The situationalist view is that the actions or reactions of people are more likely to be determined by the specific situation in which they find themselves. As children develop during school years, significant changes occur in the extent to which they favor dispositional explanations or situational ones. These changes are best illustrated by an experiment done by L. Ross (1981). It will be discussed at length here because it is so relevant to this critical aspect of social development. The experiment studied subjects at discrete ages (five, eight, eleven, fifteen, and twenty). Each was presented with four versions of three basic stories, one of which is called "boy meets dog," about a little boy's reaction to confronting a dog. The examiner shows the subject a picture of the boy and says:

"This is a picture of Johnny. When Johnny goes to the park with his mother, he doesn't go on the high, slippery slide because he is scared. When he is at school, he doesn't play with kids who are bigger than he is, because sometimes they push him around. Johnny is also scared of the dark."

Then the examiner shows a picture of another little boy, who exhibits considerably more bravery:

"This is a picture of Billy. When Billy goes to the park, he swings really high
on the big swings, and he isn't scared. He plays football with the big kids at school,
and doesn't care if he gets hurt a little. Billy doesn't mind being in dark places."

After the two children with different dispositional types—one a bit timid and the
other admirably courageous—have been introduced, two situations are presented.

"Now here is a picture of a dog. Suppose Johnny was playing by himself in
front of his house one day and this dog in the picture (a large German shepherd)
came running up to him and barked and growled pretty loudly."

"Now here is a picture of a dog (a fluffy white Samoyed). Suppose Billy was
playing by himself in front of the house one day and this particular dog in the picture came running up and wanted to play with him."

The examiner presents four actor-situation pairings of these paragraphs, pairing the timid boy with the fierce dog, the timid boy with the playful dog, the brave
boy with the fierce dog, and the brave boy with the playful dog. The four combinations were presented to youngsters at varying ages to see if their reactions
evolved and how they weighted the potential response of the child based either on
the situation (fierceness or playfulness of the dog) or the disposition (bravery or
fearfulness of the child).

At all ages subjects had no difficulty reckoning with single effects. If one held
constant the type of dog, the predicted reaction of the child (whether or not he
would run away) depended on which dog was used. However, some interesting
developmental trends were discernible when responses to the four possible para-
digms were compared. The five year olds gave the greatest weight to the situation
and the least weight to the disposition. In other words, the major determining factors were not so much how timid or brave the child might be, but rather how
threatening the situation was. Interestingly, the responses of the twenty-year-old
college students were most like those of the five-year-olds. The eight, eleven, and
fifteen year olds, on the other hand, were more inclined than either the five year
olds or the twenty year olds to give great weight to the disposition. Subjects in
middle childhood tended to assume stable personality traits on the part of the
child in the story with relatively little consideration of the specific nature of the
situation. In a second part of this experiment, the subjects were simply asked how
they thought they would react. Almost universally, they stated that they would flee
from the German shepherd but not the Samoyed. The five year olds and the twenty
year olds shared a close match-up between their own situationalist values and
those of the two boys in the stories. On the other hand, subjects in middle childhood tended to view Billy and Johnny as having personality traits that were highly
relevant to their actions.

This experiment can help us understand both the schoolchild's social perspective and the scenario in which she or he is a player. Kindergartners are likely to
find solace in egocentricity, assuming that everybody acts on the same motives
and with the same personality structures that they do. They therefore assume that
in various *situations* others will act as they will act. This allows for a relatively

nonjudgmental and potentially cooperative view of peers. At the same time, they feel assured that other children will identify closely with them and not really question who or what they are since they are fundamentally viewed as dispositionally similar. As children grow older, this view changes dramatically. Belief in disposition increases and belief in situations decreases. That is, children come to feel strongly that individuals have rather fixed attributes or personality traits that are likely to predominate under all circumstances. This proclivity intensifies as they approach the junior high school years. They become increasingly absolute in their attributions of others. People are viewed as unchanging, as highly predictable, as predetermined in their behaviors and reactions. A seventh grader is apt to say, "My English teacher is great. My social studies teacher is weird. Our gym teacher is a phony. Our principal is cool. I can't stand my mother; my father is neat. My little brother is a moron. My best friend is excellent." In other words, everyone is rigidly categorized in some fixed manner, pigeonholed, and labeled. Young adolescents are not able to perceive others as relativistic in their attributes and/or varying in their behaviors depending on the situation. They cannot say, "My science teacher is really nice when you meet him in the corridor or talk to him after school, but he is too strict in class." They don't view other children as fun to be with at a party but not so stimulating in class.

The child in elementary and junior high school often engages in this highly judgmental, diagnostic process. Inclusion or exclusion in a particular social subgroup may depend on the fixed personality traits discerned by peers during this period of life. In late elementary school, children must be especially careful about their own reputations. Since judgments of them are apt to be rigid, and even irreversible, they must live with constant attention to the fixed personality traits that they will project. In other words, image is of paramount relevance. Thus, in approaching and living through junior high school, students need to watch what they say, and act according to social norms so as not to develop a reputation for being dispositionally discordant. It is probably much easier to fall from grace than it is to become acceptable after having been ostracized (although the latter does occur sometimes).

In high school and beyond, the situationalist perspective undergoes a rebirth. High school and college students become increasingly tolerant of a wider variety of personality types. They also come to see that individuals differ under different circumstances. People begin to be perceived as having good points and bad points. Adolescents are increasingly able to recognize and relate to the strengths of others, to find situations that bring out the best in friends and acquaintances. This far more relativistic view of other people also alleviates the pressure on self, allowing for multiple pathways toward a good reputation. While the junior high student may have to fear seeming too competent in the classroom because others may disapprove, believing that any student who is academically proficient is a "wimp," the older student can believe that a classmate can be incredibly bright and even somewhat intellectually arrogant in a classroom and yet be fun at a social gathering. Finally, in high school, students are better able to separate an individual person from a role.

Junior high school students may view the assistant principal as a constant threat, a "bad guy" through and through. High school students can see that person as a "tough cookie" when it comes to law and order in the corridors, but when all is said and done, a "decent" person with "our best interests in mind." Some junior high school students may develop a resentment toward authority as they tend to be extreme in their confusion between roles and attributes. They may fail to recognize that a police officer must be tough as part of the job but that she or he can still be kind and affectionate in other settings.

Clearly there is room for considerable developmental variation in the progression discussed above. Some children adhere to this pattern more than others. Nevertheless, there is predictable evolution from benign egocentrism (with its assumption of uniformity) to increasingly rigid dispositionalism (with the assumption that people tend to have fixed personality traits and are therefore predictable in their actions and qualities) to the growing recognition in high school and college that there is a true integration of dispositions and situations (with the latter often playing a dominant role in determining behavior and personality).

Moral Development

Like the development of friendship and understanding of others, the acquisition of moral values has a significant impact on children's social interactions. A growing awareness of what is ethical, what is fair, or, conversely, what is a moral transgression characterizes the development of schoolchildren. Development of moral values is apt to affect their understanding of others, their personal behavior, and their thinking about appropriate and inappropriate human interactions.

Kohlberg (1963) defined and tested a series of moral stages analogous to the cognitive developmental sequences of Piaget. Kohlberg's scheme proposes the following basic levels: preconventional, conventional, and postconventional (the last also referred to as autonomous or principled). During the preconventional level children are said to be responsive to the cultural rules of good and bad or right and wrong. However, they interpret them with respect to the various consequences of action, such as what will lead to punishment, reward, or exchange of favors. Alternatively, they think of the rules in terms of the physical power or authority behind them. Thus, moral behavior during this early stage is based on obedience and the avoidance of punishment as well as pragmatism (acting in a way that satisfies personal needs and then, if possible, those of others).

At the conventional level, children recognize that maintaining the expectations of a family, a group, or a culture is valuable in its own right, regardless of its consequences. Loyalty to values emerges. At this level, good behavior is defined as that which pleases or helps others and is approved by them. There is conformity to natural behavior, which may be judged by intention (i.e., someone means well). A later acquisition at this level is a law-and-order orientation: good behavior consists of doing your duty, showing respect for others, and maintaining the social order because it is important that it be sustained.

Finally, at the postconventional level, children perceive moral values and principles as valid beyond the authority of people who hold these principles and beyond the individual's own loyalty to the groups to which these values pertain. Correct actions are defined in terms of individual rights and the standards that have been critically examined and agreed on by a whole society. This is not blind loyalty but critical consensus. It represents a reconciliation between personal values and the rules for achieving agreement among people. Ultimately, at this level a person believes that the law can be changed to conform to social utility. Later at this level, children base decisions and actions on carefully chosen ethical principles that are logical, universal, and consistent. The golden rule is one example of this. At this level there exist, in Kohlberg's words, "universal principles of *justice*, of the reciprocity and the quality of the human rights, and of respect for the dignity of human beings as individual persons."

Although Kohlberg's various levels and stages of moral development are not tied specifically to definite age groups, they can be applied in general as we ponder the moral progression of all children. They progress from a self-serving view of morality, in which the fulfillment of personal needs and the avoidance of punishment are the prime considerations, to a desire to maintain law and order and be good in a fairly stereotypical manner. Finally, they become students of morality (i.e., developing a form of moral metacognition), assimilating a sense of the rationale behind laws and of universal ethical principles.

To study these phenomena, Kohlberg used various moral dilemmas, which he posed to children of different ages. A thorough discussion of these can be found in his book on moral reasoning (Kohlberg 1963). For the most part, his findings suggest that most elementary schoolchildren are at the preconventional level. That is, they operate predominantly on the level of punishment avoidance, power acknowledgment, and "if you help me, I'll help you." Beginning at about thirteen years, many children start functioning at the conventional level. Only about 50 percent of adolescents reach the postconventional level.

There has been controversy over the validity of Kohlberg's model, which nevertheless provides a conceptual framework and reminds us of the need to factor in moral reasoning as one component of schoolchild development. Any understanding of the ways in which children act toward each other necessitates consideration of motives, which in turn involves understanding the complex processes of moral reasoning. The ways in which the development of moral reasoning parallel the development of social ability and higher-order cognition are not entirely clear, but are certainly worthy of further clinical and investigative scrutiny.

Popularity and Unpopularity

The preceding description of the social drama of school years and the stages through which children pass as they strive to attain and make use of social ability sets the stage for our discussion of popularity and unpopularity. Not all children are successful or gratified in their interactions, and a minority of them appear to be relatively uninterested in such success. Certain (perhaps inner-directed) children find abundant satisfaction and reinforcement in nonsocial domains and activities. When this constitutes a true affirmation of individuality and independence, it is laudable. When it represents a strategic retreat or concession to social failure, it is regrettable. We would like children to achieve the proverbial happy medium. Ideally a child should become socially adept and acceptable and able to derive pleasure from interaction while not sacrificing too much individuality of behavior, tastes, and values. In other words, we would like to see children interact successfully with their peers without becoming socially intoxicated and incapable of repudiating some of the inevitably imposed behavioral restrictions.

The quest for popularity may be either conscious or unconscious. Some children become popular without really trying, others really try without becoming popular, and still others make a conscious effort and succeed at it. Recently there has been considerable interest in the phenomenology of popularity and unpopularity. A number of social scientists and psychologists have worked to define the social-cognitive requisites of popularity. This section summarizes some of the findings of this research as well as my own clinical experience, and compares the strategies and attributes of popular schoolchildren with those of unpopular schoolchildren. After making these distinctions, we can develop a clearer picture of social competence and lack thereof, while hypothesizing about specific developmental dysfunctions and their relationships to social inability.

For research purposes, investigators have classified children into the following four subgroups that describe their sociometric status among their peers: *popular, controversial, neglected,* and *rejected* (Coie, Dodge, and Coppotelli 1982). *Popular* children are acceptable, sought after, and respected by their peers. *Controversial* children are highly liked by some and highly disliked by others. *Neglected* children are relatively inconspicuous; nobody seems to know them very well. They elicit few if any strong reactions or feelings from peers. We can further subdivide the neglected group into those who have voluntarily made themselves inconspicuous (i.e., not wanting to be a part of the social scene) and those whose personalities or styles are such that they tend not to be noticed. Finally, those in the *rejected* group are actively excluded, sometimes abused, and generally alienated or ostracized. Clearly these are the least successful practitioners of social ability. The differences among these groups have been studied by directly observing schoolchildren in various social settings. In particular, the contrast between popular and rejected children has been scrutinized in an attempt to define behavioral correlates of sociometric status. That is, investigators have sought to uncover the things that rejected children do that differ from the actions of their more popular peers.

In a study reported by Dodge (1983), a group of boys was observed during a series of initial encounters with unfamiliar peers. The boys who ultimately became rejected or neglected tended to engage in more inappropriate play behaviors, such as standing on tables and disrupting the activities of others. They also spent more time in isolated play. However, they did not lack social initiative. In fact, during the early stages, they approached their peers more often than did the boys who eventually became popular. The rejected boys involved themselves in more aggressive, rough-and-tumble play as well as more antisocial acts (insults, threats, contentious statements, and exclusion of peers from their play).

The popular boys, on the other hand, engaged in more cooperative play and social conversation. They did not approach their peers as frequently, but when they did so the interactions were longer and had more positive outcomes. They seemed capable of sustaining their interactions rather than terminating them abruptly. Their peers viewed the popular boys as "good leaders who share things." Even when the popular boys engaged in aggressive play or exclusion of peers, they did so in a way that was less aversive.

Another important attribute of the popular boys was that they tended to be more physically attractive. However, their physical attractiveness alone could not account for their social success. It was found that the attractive children actually had better social skills. The reasons are unclear although we might speculate that attractive children are given more opportunities by their peers to interact and therefore have had more social practice.

The controversial boys engaged in the greatest number of prosocial behaviors. They displayed significant interpersonal skill. However, they had a high level of aggressive play, hostile utterances, exclusion of peers, and, in particular, extraneous verbalizations (noise making). Peers responded to these behaviors negatively. The controversial children obviously got mixed reviews. They were perceived by their peers as being unpredictable. Interestingly, several studies have come up with the same percentage of controversial children (roughly 7 percent) within a group.

In summarizing this and similar research on popularity, Asher (1983) describes three dimensions of social competence: relevance, responsiveness, and "a process view of life." These and a series of factors that stem from my clinical observations (table 8-1) provide the basis for the following discussion of social developmental dysfunction.

Relevance. Asher observes that socially adept children seem to have the ability to read the social situation and adapt their behavior to the ongoing flow of interaction. In other words, socially competent children entering a new social scene are able to perceive and interpret its ambiance, its tone, and drift. They are then able to generate fitting contributions that maintain the existing flow. Suppose a student encounters several others talking in the corridors. One of them suggests that it would be great if the teacher tripped and fell on the way into the classroom this morning. There is considerable joviality connected with this hypothetical event. The popular youngster enters this conversation, discerns its rich blend of absurdity, hostility, and whimsy, and fits in magnificently by suggesting, "Yeah, and what if her glasses broke when she fell, so she couldn't see us messing around in class." This contribution to the dialogue fits perfectly, furthers the mutual cause, and most certainly elicits the respect and affection of the original conversationalists. On the other hand, a rejected child who enters that scene is all too likely to offer a maladaptive, "lead balloon" statement such as, "That's stupid, she won't fall down;

Table 8-1. Social competencies associated with popularity

SKILL/ATTRIBUTE	DESCRIPTION
Relevance	Ability to "read" a social situation and adapt behavior accordingly
Responsiveness	Capacity to be receptive to and reinforce the social initiatives of others
Timing and staging	Capacity to pace relationships; knowing what and when to do or say
Indirect approaches	Awareness that relationships and interactions are often initiated and sustained by indirect means
Feedback cues	Sensitivity to negative and positive social feedback while relating
Resolution of conflict	Aptitude for settling disagreement without resorting to violence (verbal or physical) without aggression
Verbal pragmatics	Understanding and effective use of language in social contexts
Social memory	Recall and use of prior interactional experience
Social prediction	Propensity to foresee the social consequences of one's actions and/or words
Awareness of image	Tendency to present oneself to peers in a socially acceptable way
Affective matching	Ability to discern and reinforce the current feelings of a peer
Recuperative strategies	Ability to compensate for social error

she's not going to fall, and besides, if she does she could get hurt or something." Although the rejected child deserves commendation for her remarkable contact with reality, she is "in hot water" socially, having misread the tone of the dialogue in which she has become involved. When this occurs frequently, a child's reputation is in jeopardy. In social settings, such as the regular classroom, rejected children may have an uncanny ability to say the wrong thing at the wrong time, further undermining their standing with peers. A typical example is the student who raised his hand in class and suggested that everyone try to turn in their book reports three or four days before the due date so that the teacher could grade them before the weekend and thereby be able to enjoy herself on Saturday and Sunday. This goody-goody suggestion did little to engender popularity.

Responsiveness. Asher observes that "children who are especially effective with their peers are those who do not just initiate positively but are positively responsive to the initiation of others." That is, popular children are able to reinforce the actions of their peers in a positive manner. A child seeking out a popular peer for interaction can feel safe in the knowledge that the popular child will take up the call and respond effectively to the overtures so that the effort will be successful. In other words, the popular child is skilled at making others feel wanted, recognized, and accepted when they approach him or her. The popular child is able to seize on their initiatives and reinforce them effectively.

Timing and Staging.   Popular children understand that the formation of relationships requires time and careful staging. This is one part of what is meant by "a process view of life" (Asher 1983). Socially adept children do not take liberties too early in a relationship. This capacity to pace interaction appears to be another contributor to popularity. Rejected children are more likely to rush things, to treat a new relationship as if it were a well-established one. Such children frequently may be found talking to strangers, taking unjustified liberties with other children, and not differentiating at all between ways of acting with those they have known for a long time and those they are just meeting or getting to know. In other words, social actions are not predicated on the degree of familiarity and the historical background of the relationship. Popular children, on the other hand, are able to make such distinctions. They know how to pace themselves, how to take the time to nurture relationships.

Indirect Approaches.   Popular children have an instinctive sense that new relationships are formed by indirect means. This is another component of the "process view of life" described by Asher (1983). They recognize the need to be tangential in establishing meaningful social contacts and are not heavy handed in their approaches. Thus, if we ask a popular child how she would go about becoming the friend of another child in the class, she might say, "I would go up to her during lunch and ask if she'd like to go by bike to the mall with me next Saturday." The same question posed to a rejected child might elicit the following response, "I think I would go up to her and say, 'You know, I really like you. I think you are neat. How about if we become friends from now on. I want you to be my friend, and I will be your friend. Maybe we will be best friends.'" Needless to say, that kind of direct, confessional approach is doomed to failure. Unpopular children do not realize that entry into friendship demands far greater delicateness—a "sideswipe" rather than a head-on collision.

Feedback Cues.   Social interaction, like any other endeavor, is enhanced by appropriate self-monitoring. During the course of a relationship, an individual needs to derive a sense of how things are going. Popular children are much more accurate in their reading of feedback. They are therefore capable of knowing when they have said the wrong thing, undertaken the wrong action, or conveyed the wrong feelings. They are able to read visual feedback on the faces of others. They are able to interpret tones of voice and semantic connotations that suggest either that a relationship is faltering or thriving. This ability affords the opportunity for the maintenance of tone and action, their modification, or their judicious and prompt termination. Rejected children have a great deal of difficulty receiving and/or interpreting such feedback. They are apt to commit one faux pas after another without realizing they are doing so. They may say things that offend others without recognizing the growing consternation etched on the faces or encoded in the words of those with whom they are interacting. Typically, such children keep making social mistakes. Any third-party observer has no trouble detecting such errors, but the children themselves are oblivious to them. These children may feel rejected (which they are), but have no idea why they are so unpopular.

Resolution of Conflict Without Aggression. All continuous interactions between children (to say nothing of adults) run into periodic trouble. Conflict is an integral component of social intercourse. What varies considerably is the capacity to negotiate such conflicts. Popular children seem to be especially skilled at resolving conflicts without resorting to aggression. Suppose two girls are together at one of the youngster's homes. The guest spots a cute windup toy and asks if she can play with it. The host, concerned about breakage, does not want anyone else touching the masterpiece. The popular child in such a position might compromise, allowing the other child to hold it but just for a moment, finding something else for that child to hold, or suggesting a totally different, mutually exciting activity ("How about some ice cream?"). The rejected child, being less socially resourceful, may snatch a toy away, push the other child, or use abusive language. A stalemate is reached or outright verbal or physical combat takes place, and the relationship is placed in serious jeopardy. Often parents report that every time a child comes to visit, fighting or arguing breaks out within a predictably short time. Eventually, other children refuse invitations to play with that child. Studies of rejected children have consistently demonstrated that behavioral and/or verbal aggression is common among them (Coie et al. 1990).

Verbal Pragmatic Strategies. Popular children are often more adept than rejected children at using language effectively in social contexts. Their *verbal pragmatic strategies* (see chapter 5) are clearly superior. Many rejected children are prone to use language injudiciously or imprecisely, at least in social settings. They are more apt to be misunderstood and to misunderstand others. Their selection of words and vocal tone may communicate feelings that they did not really intend. Such children may seem angry or hostile when, in reality, no such feelings are present. The following scenario is typical. A ten-year-old rejected girl comes to school one day carrying a box that looks as if it might contain an interesting toy. A peer approaches and asks what is in the box. The child, who has poor verbal pragmatic skills, answers, "What do you think's in there, dummy?" She in no way means to put down the other child but phrases her answer to the inquiry in such a way that she conveys annoyance, anger, and an air of superiority. The problem is that she did not intend to antagonize the other child. In fact, she would very much like to exploit interest in her toy as a means of enhancing her social reputation. Regrettably, her verbal response will prevent this from occurring, and it is likely she will fail to recognize where her good intentions were derailed.

Children who have difficulty with verbal pragmatic strategies are also apt to misinterpret other people's statements. They may perceive anger when none is present. They may miss salient verbal social cues. They may have difficulty taking the perspective of another child in selecting the right words and syntax. They may be unaware of the need to speak respectfully and supportively to a child whose friendship they wish to cultivate. They may not appreciate the need to adjust language for a listener who is much younger or older. They may not realize that while talking to a teacher in private they should use different kinds of language from what might be employed during a group discussion in front of peers. Children with weak verbal pragmatic skills may also have trouble understanding and using humor. Once again, misunderstandings can occur either in processing other people's wit or in attempts to be jocular. When poor verbal pragmatic skills are combined with a lack of responsiveness to social feedback, a child's reputation is most precarious.

Social Memory.   Children are apt to differ in the extent to which they benefit from social experience. Popular children are more likely to have learned from the trial-and-error processes needed to build good social skills. Some rejected youngsters approach all relationships anew, with little cumulative social wisdom. They have not learned previous lessons. Instead, they commit the same social errors in a variety of settings, as if they are not capable of being reinforced (positively or negatively) by peers.

Social Prediction.   Children differ in their capacities to predict the social consequences of their actions. Some have a strong sense of how others will react to their statements and behaviors. Popular children have a keen awareness of what to do to elicit warm and friendly responses from other children. Rejected children, on the other hand, often have no idea of the social repercussions of intended statements or actions. This compromises their abilities to function as social strategists. When things are not going well with peers, rejected children have great difficulty figuring out what to do or say to minimize the social crisis. Reviewing alternative strategies is not helpful since they have so much trouble predicting which one will succeed. One girl was upset because everyone in school was "picking on her." The next day she took a bag of candy to school and gave it out to all of the other children. Of course her peers accepted these high-calorie bribes, but in doing so they became even more disrespectful of the donor, commenting that she was doing something "really dumb" by handing out sourballs on the playground. One seven-year-old child, wanting to make more friends, went around kissing various boys on the playground. Again, he seemed unable to predict the social consequences of this highly maladaptive strategy. Other such children may make funny noises (imitating birds or monsters) in the back of the classroom, expecting that this will lead to a vaulted reputation. Such poor social predictive ability can be a significant handicap to social initiative taking as well as formation of compensatory strategies.

Awareness of Image. Popular children know how to market themselves. They are aware of dress codes, norms of social behavior, social language, and socially acceptable avocations. Such sensitivities allow them to "package themselves" effectively to be socially acceptable. In a sense they are competent cultural anthropologists of their own culture. They understand the values that their peers appreciate and are able to fashion their images to be the very models of their times and their cultural milieus. Popular students are aware of how to dress, how to talk, how to behave, and how to react to situations in a manner that is in vogue for the time, the place, and the age group. Quite commonly, children who are rejected or controversial present an unacceptable or confusing image to their peers. They dress, talk, or act in a way that does not conform to expectations. Such boys and girls may not realize the extent to which they are out of step. They may select clothing or comb their hair in a way that seems "weird" to other children, but they do not intend to elicit such a negative response. Sometimes parents unknowingly participate in the process by choosing for their children clothing, musical instruments, activities, or lifestyles peers perceive as odd or anachronistic. Of course, it is important to distinguish between children who choose to be different because they *want* to be different or to stand for individualistic values, and those who fall out of step without realizing or wanting to do so.

Affective Matching. Popular children often have keen capacities to read the mood or emotion of another child or group of children and somehow match the affect and intensify it. This is closely related to Asher's concept of "responsiveness." However, it focuses more specifically on emotions than on behaviors. A child, sensing another youngster's sadness, becomes sad, thereby offering commiseration and support. When one child is laughing, another perpetuates (often heightens) the mirth, thereby creating a tight bond and a basis for shared experience. Some unpopular children, on the other hand, too often contradict the prevailing mood. They have difficulty "reading" the emotions of others and therefore either fail at or refrain from affective matching. They constantly undermine the prevailing tone and, in a sense, fail to legitimate or respect the affective communications of their peers.

Recuperative Strategies. Everybody commits social errors; individuals vary in the extent to which they are able to develop strategies to recuperate from misguided actions or statements. Rejected children usually have few such recuperative strategies. When they get into social difficulty, they become anxious and fail to perceive the possibilities for self-righting. Their problem-solving strategies are ineffective and their responses to social stress are often maladaptive, likely resulting in even more difficulty for them. Many children with weak or nonexistent social compensatory strategies keep struggling to overcome their poor reputations. A child may decide to become popular by bribing other children or by boasting or acting in a controlling manner. Such strategies are likely to backfire; the attempted cure further erodes the reputation of the child.

Popularity Versus Chumship

Although some of the same attributes are likely to govern both the formation of intimate friendships and the rise to popularity, there are distinct differences between the two processes. Some children may form several chumships without being truly popular. Other children may be popular without having any very close relationships. The intimacy and altruism described earlier as essential ingredients of chumship are not as central to popularity. Relatively controversial, neglected, or even rejected children may find each other and develop durable bonds that do not require the kinds of insights and production capacities we have enumerated for popularity. Their relationships may be uneven or even tumultuous at times, but nonpopular children nonetheless can form social linkages based on common interests and a mutual need for companionship. Any consideration of the social ability of a child, therefore, needs to encompass both formation of friendships and popularity, two themes that may or may not be covariant.

The shared celebration of tastes emerges as an important source of chumship in late elementary school. Children begin to rally around common interests, recognizing each other for being exquisitely faddish. Their ties to one another may be strengthened by their shared adoration of a pop singer or music group, their joint addiction to a particular dance step, their common interest in clothing, or their enjoyment of cars, sports, or shopping malls.

Young adult or teenage idols become important peer-uniting role models. Chumship cohorts often resort to collaborative adult-imitative experimentation, which in many cases is a socially acceptable replacement for the pretend play of early elementary school. Eleven- and twelve-year-old girls may become obsessed with hairstyles, facial makeup, and the like. Boys may become infatuated with cars as symbols of adult control and autonomy. Young people at this age are apt to initiate smoking as a means of mimicking adult poise while sharing a behavior and taste with their chums.

Chumship may become a convenient escape route for children experiencing heavy stress or deprivation at school and/or at home. Those who sense that they are forever disappointing to adults, as well as those who feel they can never succeed academically, may seek the refuge of a clique or gang. It is not uncommon for groups to be composed entirely of such frustrated, unsuccessful children, who may exploit each other as a surrogate family and an appreciative audience (see pp. 507–8).

DEVELOPMENTAL VARIATION AND DYSFUNCTION

The coexistence of learning problems and social failure has been studied extensively and is well described in the literature. Children with developmental dysfunctions and academic skill delays often have parallel problems in forming and sustaining relationships with peers. However, this is not always the case. Clinicians frequently encounter students who are experiencing tremendous difficulty academically and impressive success socially. Children who are honor students are sometimes socially isolated (neglected or rejected). Some may exhibit deft cognitive strategies for schoolwork but disastrous ones for peer relationships. However, in those frequently encountered children who have both developmental dysfunctions and apparent social inability, it is always tempting to seek correlations to determine whether failure with peers and academic achievement have their origins in analogous constitutional deficits.

Capitulating to this temptation, we can describe certain ways in which the developmental variations elucidated in earlier chapters are apt to play a role in the social failure of certain vulnerable schoolchildren (see table 8-2). Much of what follows in this section is based on clinical impressions, although some studies have documented effectively that relationships between underlying disabilities and social failure have not been fully worked out. Bryan (1974) used a sociometric technique to evaluate the popularity of third-, fourth-, and fifth-grade students, comparing those with identified learning disabilities with others. Children in the underachieving group were considerably less popular with peers than children who were functioning normally in the classroom. A later study (Bryan et al. 1976) suggested that "for a significant number of learning disabled chil-

Table 8-2. Developmental dysfunctions and their potential impacts on social ability

AREA OF DYSFUNCTION	POSSIBLE EFFECTS
Attention and intention	Impulsive, poorly planned (or unplanned) social acts Insensitivity to feedback cues Egocentricity, trouble sharing Lack of attention to social detail Aggression (in some cases) Spatial and temporal-sequential: problems reading nonverbal feedback functions (e.g., facial expression) Sequential: difficulty with social prediction (sequential flow in social contexts)
Memory	Problems with social learning from experience Discrete impediments (e.g., recall of names, faces, appointments)
Language	Poor use of verbal methods of "titrating" relationships Deficient verbal pragmatic strategies
Higher-order cognition	Inadequate social cognition Problems assessing attributions or engaging in moral reasoning
Production capacities	Difficulties with body image Peer ridicule of clumsiness or awkwardness

dren, problems in interpersonal relationships may be critical components of the disability."

One common weakness in studies of the relationship between developmental dysfunctions and social ability has been the failure to be specific about the nature of a child's learning problem. This section will review the different components of development delineated in chapters 2 through 7 and comment on the potential impacts of specific manifestations of these problems.

The Attention Controls

Children with attention deficits may or may not have significant difficulties with the challenge of popularity and chumship. However, it is rare to find a child with significant attention deficits near the top of the popularity poll in school. A variety of reasons can explain the social inability of many children with attention problems.

Affected children who are generally inattentive to detail may have real trouble "reading" the social scene. Their superficiality and impulsiveness may prevent their developing a clear picture of what is going on when they enter a social context, making it quite possible for them to commit errors. Moreover, as discussed in chapter 2, these children are often not at all sensitive to feedback cues. Just as they commit frequent errors when they compute math problems, they may be subject to the same kind of carelessness in interactions with peers. Furthermore, when they make a mistake, they are unaware of it. A faux pas that they do not notice or correct is most certainly observed by others. Thus, failure to appreciate detail, impulsiveness, and impaired sensitivity to feedback may combine to make it hard for children to read a relationship, take the appropriate initiative based on that reading, and monitor the effectiveness of the action.

Children who are highly insatiable (a frequent trait among those with attention deficits) may have serious problems forming and sustaining friendships. They may jump from one contact to another, as described in the section on rejected children. They may be highly egocentric, focusing exclusively on their own appetites or desires. The altruism and mutual understanding required for longer-term interaction may seem unavailable. Such children may have real trouble sharing, compromising, and, in particular, taking the perspective of another child, which can seriously thwart any efforts at sustained interaction.

The timing of relationships as well as the indirect approach may be inordinately hard for highly impulsive children. When they think of something, they do it. Immediate gratification is mandatory. Any activities that require delay create discomfort and restlessness. This can make it difficult to meet the demand for a stepwise relationship, one that intensifies and enriches itself gradually.

Children who are highly impulsive may insist on everything all at once. Moreover, it may be hard for those children to engage in the indirect techniques of building a relationship; bluntness may seem more expedient.

Children who are impulsive may also have trouble predicting social consequences, generating appropriate interactional strategies, and controlling aggressive outbursts. All of these shortcomings are apt to predispose children to rejection. Finally, the inconsistent performance observed in school among children with attention deficits may also pertain to their social lives. The erratic pattern of friendship with such a child can be very difficult for other children to sustain or tolerate.

Many traits associated with attention deficits thus interfere with both popularity and the development of close friendships. In some cases, however, these children have important redeeming features. Physical attractiveness, creativity, good athletic ability, a sense of humor, or expertise in some area (such as computers) may ingratiate them to peers despite maladaptive traits.

Some children with attention deficits are apt to become controversial students. They may appeal to certain subgroups but not to others. For example, a youngster who is predisposed to the free-flight-of-ideas form of distractibility (see pp. 29–30) may be perceived by some children as "spacey" or "weird," while other children may view her or him as a rather interesting character. Even in the high-pressure, homogeneous setting of a junior high school, there may be some toleration for the eccentricity that is found among some children with attention deficits.

A previous section pointed out that rejected children have a tendency to initiate discussions more frequently and for shorter periods of time both with other children and with teachers. This particular pattern may be quite typical of children with attention deficits. They are constantly changing the focus of their communication—frequently starting, terminating, and restarting exchanges of all kinds.

Of all the developmental dysfunctions, attention deficits are the ones most likely to yield high correlations between social and academic effects. Superficial focus and a high level of unintended behaviors are bound to have an impact on reputation.

Spatial and Temporal-Sequential Ordering

The extent to which simultaneous and sequential processing and production affect social interactions is not clear. A considerable amount of research is needed to substantiate any hypotheses. There are indications that some children with learning problems experience inordinate difficulty perceiving nonverbal communication. We might argue that children who have trouble processing arrays of simultaneous visual-spatial information may be prone to difficulty decoding and reacting to nuances of body language and facial expression. This may place them at some disadvantage in planning and implementing their behaviors and verbal communications.

Children with sequencing problems may experience some difficulty with sequential reasoning—the ways in which one step follows from another may elude them. Although there are no data to support this hypothesis, it might be worth studying whether such children have excessive trouble predicting social consequences or sequences of actions. Since the latter occur in a predictable order, these children might be vulnerable.

Memory

The ways in which various aspects of memory relate to social learning are also obscure. Memory for faces and memory for names are considered social frills but may bear some relevance as children grow older. More important is the memory for previous social experience and the capacity to use such experience to condition future actions. Whether children with certain kinds of memory disorders have such problems is not clear, but again the possible correlation merits consideration.

Language

Linguistic proficiency has frequently been shown to relate to socialization. Children's conversational skills play a critical role in the formation and maintenance of relationships (McTear and Conti-Ramsden 1992). Unquestionably, verbally adept children have a distinct advantage in achieving popularity. Both receptive and expressive language skills can contribute generously to formation of friendships and popularity.

Children with intact receptive language ability are better able to detect verbal feedback cues. In one study, Bryan (1978) found that many children with learning disorders had significant problems with the "cognitive-linguistic" analysis of communication (an aspect of verbal pragmatics). This had a demonstrable, negative impact on social achievement with peers. Some children with language-processing problems may have real difficulty drawing appropriate social inferences from what is said. Their tendency to misinterpret their peers, inferring the wrong feelings or intentions, may lead to inappropriate reactive behaviors or statements. As we have noted, this can be perceived by others as inappropriate and perhaps construed as hostile or unfriendly. When inappropriate reactions occur frequently, significant gaps in relationships can occur. Misunderstandings can create chronic feelings of anxiety for all who are involved. Instability and cessation of the relationship may ensue. The same phenomenon may occur with reputation. Repeated misunderstandings with many different peers may ultimately erode a child's overall status.

Expressive language may be especially crucial. Words and sentences are an essential means of gaining control of social situations. If we are to refrain from the use of physical force or violence, expressive language becomes a principal lever of control. It can be used to express admiration, desires, and shared interests. Expressive language is helpful for both altruism and intimacy. It follows that those who have difficulty finding words and formulating sentences are at a disadvantage in forming friendships and (to a lesser extent) in achieving popularity. In fact, students with verbal communication deficiencies have been shown to suffer in their relationships with peers (Donahue and Bryan 1984). Not all nonverbal children are unpopular, however. Many develop compensatory mechanisms or have redeeming features that enable them to bypass this disadvantage.

So-called in-group language is a poorly understood aspect of expressive skill. This slang or jargon is an important part of interaction, especially during middle childhood and adolescence. As students approach secondary school, a social speech style commonly emerges. Allegedly, this facilitates communication with peers. More important, however, in-group language can be used as a means of identification with a group. Donahue and Bryan (1984) note that this closed form of communication "marks the speaker as a member of a particular social group, thereby delineating the insiders from the outsiders." Some students with language disorders are poor at using in-group language. They may have trouble assimilating its vocabulary, slang, and rhythm, making it difficult for them to participate in vitally important banter, friendly teasing, sharing of intimacies, and mutual joking. Students who lack the fluency to keep pace with such activities are likely to be at a disadvantage in the quest for popularity. Not only will they have trouble participating, but they may also misinterpret friendly insults, which are also very much a part of social interchange, especially during adolescence.

In an extensive review of the literature, Donahue, Pearl, and Bryan (1983) conclude that three major aspects of communicative incompetence reduce the social effectiveness of some children with learning disorders. They are poor at imparting intentions to listeners in specific situations; they have difficulty conveying and understanding information; and they have trouble initiating and sustaining conversation.

Another issue in expressive language concerns the speed and efficiency of word finding and sentence formulation. Verbal communication depends, at least in part, on timing. Children need to be quick on the verbal draw. It is especially helpful if children can come up with the right responses without expending a great deal of effort and time. We all know the experience of leaving a social situation and thinking afterwards what it is we should have said. For some children this is a frequent problem. They can never quite get into words the right ideas at the right times to foster relationships or to sound impressive or sufficiently cool at key moments.

Higher-Order Cognition

Children with higher-order cognitive deficiencies may experience difficulties solving social problems, parallel to their troubles solving cognitive problems. Relationships are a constant test of strategic capacities. A child may develop a hypothesis about how to form or sustain a relationship with someone, try it out, and then recognize the need for a new and improved one. The processes of social reasoning may be particularly easy for certain children and unavailable to others. A sense of propriety or an understanding of the rules governing friendships may be less possible for some children than for others. Finally, the introspective capacity to analyze and reflect consciously on personal social ability (social metacognition) may be problematic for certain children who do not seem to be effective observers and analyzers of themselves, the social scene, and its requirements (Flavell 1985).

These youngsters may have trouble meeting the demands of the "hidden curriculum" (see pp. 239–40) as it relates to the social expectations of peer groups. They may also show commensurate delays in their moral development.

Production Capacities

A child's productive abilities may serve as catalysts of popularity and friendship. Being able to pursue an interest in depth or develop a laudable skill can provide a meaningful and long-lasting means of relating. Gross motor proficiency is perhaps the most obvious example. Children who are good athletes may have an inside track on popularity. Their prowess on the playing fields may gain the respect of their peers and even compensate for any social inabilities. For example, if nonverbal children who have tremendous difficulty regulating relationships with words can be heroic on the athletic field, they may emerge as "strong, silent types" and be accepted by their peers without being verbally communicative. Children who are especially adept at working with computers, horseback riding, dance, or other artistic endeavors may gain significant status among peers for being a producer, for demonstrating a high level of accomplishment. While this is not a panacea for social inability, discrete and well-developed production capacity in one or more areas provides a most important redeeming feature. In this regard, children with gross or fine motor dysfunctions may miss out on an opportunity to display socially advantageous products or abilities.

Further Influences

This chapter does not intend to imply that all social ability is based on various endogenous developmental capacities. Unquestionably, social success comes under the influence of many exogenous factors and critical life events. Family and cultural influences are of great importance. Certain family units are so intensely intimate that they consciously or unconsciously discourage vigorous outreach to friends. Some children model themselves after parents who are relatively asocial or even antisocial. Alternatively, those whose families constantly surround themselves with friends, deriving much of their pleasure and measuring their success through interactions with nonfamily members, may become socially precocious. Despite this potent influence, children within the same family can differ quite remarkably in their popularity and sociability. It is not at all unusual (in fact it is almost the rule) to encounter children who differ from their siblings in their social abilities as well as in what might be called their interactional drive, the desire or need for acceptance. Children vary considerably in the extent to which they enjoy being alone and in their compulsion for company. Some children are described by their parents as being happiest when they are pursuing their own projects, working independently, or entertaining themselves to an extent that no peer could compete with. Such laudatory behavior is very much a part of the spectrum of developmental variation in the social domain.

Schools are another influence on social interaction. A "hidden curriculum" exists in the values and pressures exerted by school personnel governing the customs and morality of social life (Purpel and Ryan 1983). Communities and cultures differ in their encouragement and tolerance of varying patterns of social behavior. This has been a long-standing focus of cultural anthropologists.

A rather mixed blessing in school is the contention with body image. Partly due to interest in the opposite sex, preoccupation with appearance increases steadily. Physical attractiveness becomes increasingly important in the higher grades. The social pressures of school create some real tension at the interface of the mind and the body. This is particularly true in late elementary and junior high school, the period for "looking good." At this age, boys and girls typically become exquisitely conscious of their physical attributes. Their sizes and shapes (as compared to peers), their relative psychosexual maturation, and the ways in which they clothe their bodies emerge as momentous issues. They have a nagging belief that how people look is a revelation of their attributes. A truly cool person should look truly cool.

Bodily issues are important in the primary grades too. Children have to deal with potentially embarrassing situations, such as use of the rest room. At the age of six, most children prefer to have others think that they never need to defecate. The use of school rest rooms for this purpose is likely to be out of the question for them. Children in primary school are apt to be particularly modest; in some cases, primary school rest rooms are a source of considerable anxiety, a matter that is seldom, if ever, discussed with any adults. A rather extreme consequence of this hang-up may be seen in some cases of encopresis, a condition in which children become chronically constipated, develop a stretched-out large intestine (a so-called functional megacolon), and ultimately lose control of all bowel function (Levine 1982b). They then proceed to have "accidents" on a regular basis.

Encopresis, or fecal incontinence, can develop as a direct consequence of avoiding rest rooms in school. A primary schoolchild who is accustomed to defecating at home each day late in the morning may find a lack of privacy or some aggression in the school rest room, causing him or her to make the often appropriate decision to withhold a bowel movement until safe at home. However, when the child arrives home later that day, the urge to defecate is gone. As this process repeats itself day after day, stool gradually builds up, constipation develops, and then obstipation. Finally, the colon loses its muscle strength and its sensitivity to feedback from stretch receptors (i.e., the feeling of needing to defecate). The child becomes progressively unable to control bowels, has frequent accidents, and feels terribly shamed and frightened by this primitive loss of control. The situation is apt to be aggravated if the child is made fun of by peers and criticized ruthlessly by parents and siblings. This is a classic example of the inherent tension between children's bodies and the social pressures of the academic setting.

Many other examples of social-somatic conflict could be cited. In early adolescence, many youngsters develop acne. The unsightly pimples of this condition are a source of intolerable embarrassment. A fourteen-year-old girl may observe such a lesion on her nose one morning while washing, and for the remainder of that day perceive herself as a walking pimple. She is convinced that everyone is staring at it, that the teachers in the faculty lounge are discussing her flawed complexion, that no one will want to be friends with her anymore. Throughout her classes she sits with her hand over her nose. She retreats to the back of the school bus and the darkest recesses of corridors to elude discovery. The next day she may attempt to skip school by feigning illness.

Children who are short or who have various forms of delayed puberty, as well as those who are overweight, may fear having to take showers in physical education class. They feel that this violation of their privacy could ruin their social reputations. Still others are concerned about their lack of gross motor coordination. As described in the previous chapter, they are apt to be particularly self-conscious about their bodies during gym classes. Some early adolescent boys develop physiological gynecomastia (temporary enlargement of the breasts). This is a normal event for many boys near the beginning of puberty. It subsides spontaneously, but in the meantime it can create anxiety and the fear of exposure during a time when schoolchildren very much want their fixed attributes (physical as well as dispositional) to resemble those of their peers as much as possible.

Special challenges face certain schoolchildren. The need to wear glasses or orthodontic braces or to sport any other mark of physical deviance may be viewed as a significant social setback by children preoccupied with fostering a robust image.

Obviously, children vary considerably in the extent to which they harbor social-somatic concerns. Those who are particularly affected by them can suffer inordinately and expend considerable energy and attention on designing behavioral and physical camouflages to conceal their bodily flaws.

Self-esteem and self-confidence play a decisive role in social interaction. Children who feel good about themselves in general are apt to confront interactions with conviction and polish. Their peers are usually astute in detecting such personal pride and admire them for it. Children who lack self-confidence, on the other hand, appear to be at a disadvantage among peers. When children feel out of control, believing that the determinants of friendship and popularity are out of their grasp, they are apt to fail and continue failing at social relationships (Diener and Dweck 1978).

Age is also a factor. Children popular in second grade need not remain so in junior high school. Likewise, there is no reason to believe that rejected, neglected, and controversial children are perpetually fixed in their social classifications. On the contrary, it is possible for children to be "discovered" for the first time at preadolescence or in junior high school. Some neglected students emerge with well-differentiated abilities (social and otherwise) for the first time as they approach late middle childhood. A previously unnoticed girl or boy becomes particularly socially adept, physically attractive, academically distinguished, or athletically proficient. These scenarios are common and certainly hold out hope to the socially floundering first or second grader. Students who were repudiated in junior high school because they were a bit different or eccentric may well emerge as very interesting people in high school. Since older adolescents are more tolerant of such differences, they are even likely to admire peers with somewhat obscure orientations or values.

Complications of Social Inability

The exasperated child who is experiencing considerable social failure is apt to react in a number of ways, the most common being low self-esteem, performance anxiety in social situations, and reactive depression. Feelings of worthlessness, loneliness, and alienation commonly ensue. Such children are obviously highly vulnerable to a variety of mental health problems. Children differ considerably in their tolerance of social failure. Some are reconciled to it. They find effective compensatory pursuits—other matters to ponder and pursue. Sometimes, in fact, unpopularity is a blessing in disguise. A child who is not heavily distracted by peers may become a more ardent, dedicated scholar.

Another complication of social alienation occurs when, either intentionally or unintentionally, various adults aggravate the plight of a socially alienated child. For example, a physical education teacher may ask a clumsy child to demonstrate a gymnastic exercise during class, failing to realize that this dyspraxic, marginally socialized child will feel humiliated in front of his or her peers. Being called names by peers can be particularly devastating. Parents and siblings may also inadvertently contribute to feelings of social inadequacy by being overly critical or unsupportive of a child's social struggles. Teasing, even if intended as a friendly gesture, can be humiliating when it comes from parents.

Affected children often develop secondary protective strategies to deal with social failure. Some may withdraw. Others display aggressive, acting-out behaviors. In the lower grades, a child may become a class clown, acting as silly as possible in an effort to project an image that is totally ridiculous since social gratification is unattainable through more natural or spontaneous behavior and speech.

Children who receive a great deal of social abuse at school frequently react very strongly at home. Children who are ridiculed or embarrassed at school may be overtly aggressive and controlling at home that evening. The humiliation delivered by classmates may be transmitted directly to a younger sister or brother. Extremely hostile or violent behavior toward a sibling or even a pet may be the only outlet, the displaced (and of course misplaced) revenge for peer-induced ostracism earlier in the day. When schoolchildren display such behaviors at home, it is important to consider the possibility that they are facing intolerable social failure among peers.

Some children react to their social shortcomings with peers by developing especially strong relationships with nonpeers. A child may become increasingly close to one or both parents, preferring to spend time with them after school. Certain children with social interaction problems are extremely good with younger children. They may be excellent leaders for boys and girls three or four years younger. Some children with social interaction problems are absolutely superb in the company of adults. The latter find such children charming and interesting, while peers think of them as nerds. It should be borne in mind that forming relationships with much younger or much older people (or with animals) may be considerably easier than the formidable challenge of interacting with peers. For adolescents, courtship beyond the confines of the peer group may be an escape—a search for social reinforcement where they can find it.

ASSESSMENT

The evaluation of social skills in children has been a matter of great interest, especially in the psychology literature. However, much of the direct assessment used for research purposes is not practical on a clinical basis. Direct observations of children in various social settings provide important data about normal and troubled peer relationships. Direct tests of social cognition, which present the subject with a story and solicit reactions or solutions, are also primarily an investigative technique.

Another form of direct assessment is use of various inventories in which children can describe their own perceptions of their social lives. The *Piers-Harris Children's Self-Concept Scale* is one that relates mainly to self-concept but also provides insights into interactions. The Self-Administered Student Profile of *The ANSER System* contains a section on social interaction that appears to be quite sensitive, tending to agree with parents' and teachers' observations. It can be used as a rapid screening test, although it depends on the willingness of the child to confess social difficulties. Several other inventories are not in common clinical use. Figure 8-1 is an inventory of social cognitive abilities that I developed. It can be completed by parents or teachers who have some understanding of social skills. This grid can also be used to educate teachers, parents, and clinicians about social skills.

Although straightforward clinical tests are not feasible, no evaluation of the schoolchild is complete without an account of social ability. Three methods should be combined to gather information about this important area. First, observations by parents can be most helpful. Standardized questionnaires (such as *The ANSER System*) that include items pertaining to social interaction can be used (see figure 8-1). Similarly, reports from teachers are helpful; observations made in the classroom, in the corridors, and on the playground over extended periods are reliable indicators of social success or failure. Finally, a sensitive interview with the child is often revealing.

To derive vivid and reliable information from children about their social lives, the interviewer must first establish a trusting alliance. This sense of trust is crucial since, paradoxically, a child's public interactions with peers often are a source of embarrassment, a topic to be avoided, especially if there are serious problems. Children may be reluctant to admit to parents, for example, that there are painful social injuries inflicted in school, out of concern that it may be perceived as a true

Student's Name _____	Grade _____ Date _____
Observer's Name _____	Position _____

A. Nonverbal Functions

SPECIFIC FUNCTION	DESCRIPTION OF FUNCTION	ADEQUACY OF CURRENT PRACTICE		
		− Weak	+/− Adequate	+ Strong
Greeting and entering skills	"Reading" a social scene and acting in a way that fits into it	− Weak	+/− Adequate	+ Strong
Reinforcing behaviors	Making someone else feel good about himself/herself	− Weak	+/− Adequate	+ Strong
Reciprocal behaviors	Showing altruism (e.g., sharing, praising), especially with close friends	− Weak	+/− Adequate	+ Strong
Collaborative behaviors	Being effective at cooperating in play and/or work activities	− Weak	+/− Adequate	+ Strong
Nonverbal cuing	Using appropriate eye contact and body movements in relating to others	− Weak	+/− Adequate	+ Strong
Timing and staging	Pacing relationships; not expecting too much too soon	− Weak	+/− Adequate	+ Strong
Social feedback sensitivity	Knowing how one is faring during or immediately following an interaction	− Weak	+/− Adequate	+ Strong
Behavioral interpretation	Being able to discern reasons for or intent of a peer's actions	− Weak	+/− Adequate	+ Strong
Awareness of impacts	Having awareness of one's overall reputation and general effects on peers	− Weak	+/− Adequate	+ Strong
Conflict resolution	Resolving social conflicts without resorting to aggression	− Weak	+/− Adequate	+ Strong
Social control level	Relating to peers without demanding too much or too little control	− Weak	+/− Adequate	+ Strong
Recuperative strategies	Coping with, recovering from social setbacks	− Weak	+/− Adequate	+ Strong
Self-marketing skill	"Packaging" one's image to be socially acceptable to peers	− Weak	+/− Adequate	+ Strong

Figure 8-1.   A checklist of social cognitive functions

B. Verbal Functions

SPECIFIC FUNCTION	DESCRIPTION OF FUNCTION	ADEQUACY OF CURRENT PRACTICE		
Feelings conveyance	Using language to express feelings accurately, preventing misinterpretation	– Weak	+/– Adequate	+ Strong
Feelings interpretation	"Reading" language cues to infer the feelings of others	– Weak	+/– Adequate	+ Strong
Lingo fluency	Using the language of one's peer group (fluently and credibly)	– Weak	+/– Adequate	+ Strong
Topic selection and maintenance	Knowing what to talk about when, with whom, and for how long	– Weak	+/– Adequate	+ Strong
Humor utilization and calibration	Employing the right kind or level of humor in a current social context	– Weak	+/– Adequate	+ Strong
Code switching	Modifying language expression to fit the expectations of a current audience	– Weak	+/– Adequate	+ Strong
Perspective taking	Knowing what others know and what they need to know from you	– Weak	+/– Adequate	+ Strong
Requesting skills	Asking for something in a nonoffensive manner	– Weak	+/– Adequate	+ Strong
Communication repair	Revising misinterpreted language or fixing miscommunication	– Weak	+/– Adequate	+ Strong
Affective matching	Creating language that complements the prevailing mood(s) of others	– Weak	+/– Adequate	+ Strong

Figure 8-1. *(Continued)*

This inventory can be used to informally survey critical components of a child's social cogntion. By identifying specific areas of weakness, social skills counseling or education can address the subskills that are most lacking in an individual child.

confession of failure in life or an admission that they have disappointed the family in failing a basic test of childhood autonomy. A clinician should initially talk about school and social life without referring to the particular child. They might discuss the universal problems that occur on buses, on playgrounds, or in the cafeteria. The clinician can then ask the child to talk about what goes on in the cafeteria line in his or her school, asking for as vivid a description as possible. The next step is to inquire how that particular child functions in the cafeteria line. "The other children, do they ever push you around? Do you have some trouble finding kids to sit with? Do you ever get made fun of? Other kids get called a lot of names; what names do you get called?" By exploring the critical social hot spots (see pp. 262–63), first generally and then specifically, it is possible to acquire insight into the everyday social scene and to compile both an actual log of events and a portrait of the child's perceptions and feelings.

Using the reports of parents, teachers, and the child, we can compare social patterns to what is known about that youngster's overall development. Parallels between developmental dysfunction and social failure may be postulated, as described earlier in this chapter. Such integrated observations and analyses form the basis for effective counseling and/or direct training in social skills where needed. The clinician may wish to formulate ideas about the extent to which a child's social difficulties are associated with developmental dysfunctions, the degree to which they reflect family or cultural values, and the distinctions between basic manifestations of social ineptitude and secondary effects (such as voluntary withdrawal, overly controlling behaviors at home, aggression, and loss of self-esteem). At the same time, that child's personal priorities and values must be factored in. Not every eleven year old craves or needs popularity. Some may wish to remain rugged individualists. Such a determination must be a part of diagnostic description.

MANAGEMENT

Who is responsible for the social education of children? We might argue effectively that it is a shared responsibility of schools and parents. They must collaborate effectively to rehabilitate children with social skill deficits.

Once a child has been identified as having social difficulties, parents can do much to foster improved socialization. Although it is often traumatic, these children need as much experience and overlearning of social skills as possible. However, they require some guidance to avoid interactional embarrassment. Social activities must be selected carefully and monitored closely. Situations that are most likely to lead to humiliation should be avoided. For example, nonathletically oriented, socially rejected children should not be forced to participate in organized sports at which they are woefully inept. Scouting, musical groups, specialized clubs, religious organizations, and summer camps are possible arenas for social learning (and sometimes failure). Activities in which a child is likely to succeed should be selected. Adult leaders of any such programs should be aware of a child's social difficulties and be available to offer one-to-one attention and ongoing feedback (to the child and the parents).

Counseling

Children with social difficulties need to be well informed about their problems. Many can benefit from individual or group counseling aimed at helping them see what it is they are doing wrong and right. Structured activity groups in certain communities enable several children (all of whom may experience social problems) to participate together in pursuits such as sports, field trips, or crafts. Following their efforts, they meet to talk about socially relevant occurrences that have transpired. Such reviews emphasize how things might have been done differently to preserve friendships, improve communication, or enhance reputations. The general aim is to elevate the social consciousness and sensitivity of unpopular children.

In one-to-one sessions with a child with social problems, a therapist must determine why the child is experiencing difficulties. The various stumbling blocks enumerated in this chapter should be considered. Relevant weaknesses should be dealt with explicitly during counseling sessions. For example, the therapist might help a child who has trouble with verbal pragmatic strategies (e.g., continually saying things in a tone that offends) to see how word choice or tone of voice affects others. She might help a child who has trouble perceiving social feedback to interpret facial expressions and verbal cues. At the very least, the therapist can make children acutely aware of where their faults lie.

Formal Training

Cartledge and Milburn (1980) reviewed a variety of training programs in social skills that can be implemented in schools from preschool through adolescence. Oden and Asher (1977) found that only five sessions of coaching in social skills enhanced acceptance by peers, even at one year following the intervention. Socialization curricula stress instruction and actual practice in affective behaviors relating to interaction with peers, cooperation, application of moral standards, empathy, conceptions of peer status, and play skills. Social ability can be taught to children with problems as well as to those who are functioning normally. However, socially neglected or rejected children need more individualized and substantial intervention in this area. As unpopular children grow older, they are likely to become increasingly motivated to accept advice. Their unhappiness over their social failure often exceeds any anxiety they may feel about doing poorly in school.

The books for children, *All Kinds of Minds* and *Keeping a Head in School* (Levine 1990, 1993), contain extensive sections on social cognition which can be used as part of the counseling and/or education of a child with social difficulties. Case studies are included. Many children with these problems are apt to identify closely with the cases cited in these volumes.

Social "Homework"

Much can be done at home to enhance a child's social skills. First, parents should be aware of difficulties their child is having with peers. To do this, they need to create an atmosphere that is accepting, nonaccusatory, and highly sympathetic. They must be careful not to discount the social problems their child is experiencing. For instance, if a child comes home from school and confesses that he is being called a wimp or a nerd, it is inappropriate for parents to advise him just to ignore his peers. This is tantamount to asking an adult not to worry about losing a job. Fathers and mothers must appreciate the calamitous impact of social rejection. Simply reassuring a child that everything will be all right communicates to that child that we do not understand or perhaps care. This may prevent the child from confiding to us in the future. It is vitally important that the socially rejected child have understanding allies at home. Even if parents cannot offer any good advice about how to cope with a predatory bully in school, they can at least convey to the child that they are willing to suffer with him or her, that they can sympathize, listen, and provide moral support for the struggle. Because children who experience social difficulties may not wish to recount the day's humiliating experiences in front of their siblings, parents may need to spend some private time with them. Any advice offered should be well thought out and realistic. Sometimes parents can offer to help with a situation by talking to a teacher or another parent.

Parents can assist directly with the improvement of social skills through some shared interactions. For example, a father or mother may take a child and two other children to an athletic event or movie, preceded by a visit to a favorite fast-food restaurant. That night, just prior to bedtime, the parent can sit down with the child and review some of the social dynamics that were jointly experienced. The adult might say, "I noticed at lunch that you took one of Gerry's french fries. I also noticed that you kept boasting all the time. Maybe when we go again, you should try to offer Gerry one of your potatoes so she'll like you more. You should also try to say a few nice things about Gerry so she will feel good, and she will want to be your friend even more." Such social coaching and feedback should be proffered in a nonaccusatory manner. It should be accompanied by some positive observations, by pointing out social initiatives or responses that were done well. Parents may wish to set up a formal "talking about friends" hour on a regular basis.

The enhancement of social ability needs further academic study. Its mission is critically important, and has the potential to diminish an enormous amount of unnecessary childhood suffering. As improved techniques become available, social training will be a shared responsibility of professionals and parents. At present, we can concentrate on recognizing deficits in social skills, dealing with them logically, and trying to minimize the psychological wounds they cause and the scars they leave.

Part 2

Academic Skills: The Synchronized Interplay of Developmental Functions

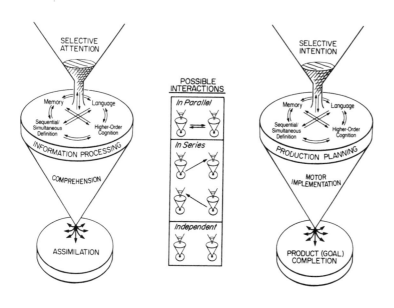

Chapter 9

Reading

My father said that, as I could read, I had better learn to write. This was not nearly so pleasant. Shaky copybooks full of pothooks and hangers still turn up in old drawers. And further exercises or lines of shaky B's and it's, which I seemed to have had great difficulty in distinguishing since I had learned to read by the look of words and not by their letters.

—Agatha Christie, *An Autobiography*

A substantial portion of academic competency throughout school and beyond is reflected in reading ability, a demanding process requiring the integration of multiple intact developmental functions. As a child's central nervous system evolves with time, experience, and education, so reading evolves, perhaps in part as a result of the same influences, creating a succession of new demands and necessitating ever higher levels of efficiency. Within this changing context, the developmental variations described in part 1 serve as powerful determinants of competency in reading.

This chapter first discusses the way most schoolchildren acquire reading skill. It then takes a closer look at components of the reading process, their normal operation, their developmental prerequisites, and variations in performance that are commonly encountered. A discussion of the assessment of reading follows, and the chapter concludes with a consideration of therapeutic options.

THE DEVELOPMENT OF READING ABILITY

Professionals from many disciplines have long been interested in the intricate processes by which children normally acquire reading skills. Over the last 100 years, innumerable articles and books have been devoted to this subject. Specific curricula and teaching methods have been developed based on theories of the normal progression of reading abilities. Furthermore, understanding why certain children fail to read may be predicated on knowledge of how others succeed.

A common approach to the study of reading has been the attempt to discern specific stages in the development of skills.* For example, Gray (1925) described five

---

*The ideas that are the basis for the discussion of reading in this chapter come from Jeanne Chall's book *Stages of Reading Development* (1983).

critical periods: getting ready to read; acquiring initial skills; rapidly perfecting skills; applying reading skills; and refining reading practices, tastes, and attitudes. Gray associated each of the periods with a specific grade level and assigned students definite goals as they arrived at each stage. He also associated distinct expectations for achievement with each stage.

Other educators have refined Gray's stages or offered somewhat different models of developmental reading stages. Chall's (1983) conceptual model is the most relevant to this book. She proposes six reading stages, which describe the ability to read increasingly complex and abstract material (see table 9-1). Chall's stages extend from the prereading of very young children to the highly sophisticated interpretations of educated adults. The progressive acquisition of reading abilities helps us understand reading disabilities as they occur at particular ages and grade levels.

During Chall's prereading stage (stage 0), children acquire a basic sense of language and develop an initial awareness of the printed word. They begin to master the alphabet. In many cases, they are able to identify simple words, usually beginning with their name. This is a time when many preschool children engage in "pseudoreading," pretending to read stories, reading by pictures, and often reading into them what they think the stories ought to be saying rather than what the text contains. This "top-down" approach implies that prereading children superimpose their own ideas on the details of the text. At the same time, children also begin to acquire a sense of narrative structure. Some will insist that a text is not a story unless it begins with "Once upon a time."

During first and second grades (stage 1), children master the true rudiments of reading. They learn about predictable associations between visual symbols and specific sounds in their language. They also begin to build a vocabulary of words recognized by sight. They engage in much trial and error while establishing these associative linkages. Reading aloud is emphasized, but such renditions are typically awkward and dysfluent. In contrast to the prereading stage, those at the initial reading stage become increasingly committed to "bottom-up" reading. That is, they adhere closely to what is on the page, preoccupied with the details of sound-symbol associations and visual configuration, and only secondarily with their own preconceived ideas about meanings.

In second and third grade (stage 2), children acquire a rapidly expanding sight vocabulary, allowing them to read more quickly and efficiently and to begin to infuse their reading with much greater linguistic sophistication. At the same time, they continue to develop word analysis skills, learning more advanced rules of phonics and beginning to recognize the basic structural elements of morphology (suffixes, prefixes, compound words, roots, and syllables). This occurs at a time when language abilities are improving steadily. Children's greater language awareness and sophistication enable them to use context clues as another aid to decoding and comprehension. At this stage, children are reading primarily to confirm what they already know. The language and ideational content of what they are reading is not as sophisticated as that encountered in daily conversation, magazines, newspapers, movies, and television.

Table 9-1. Chall's reading stages

STAGE	APPROXIMATE AGE/GRADE	SOME FEATURES
0. Prereading	Ages 6 months–5 years Preschool	Language appreciation Awareness of printed words Mastery of alphabet and simple words Vocabulary expansion Rhyming awareness Knowledge of language structures "Top-down" approach
1. Initial reading and decoding	Ages 5–7 Kindergarten, first, and second grades	Sound-symbol associations Trial-and-error decoding Growing attachment to the printed word ("the medium") Oral reading Word-by-word (dysfluent) reading "Bottom-up" approach
2. Confirmation, fluency, and ungluing from the print	Ages 7–8 Second and third grades	Reading to confirm existing knowledge Growing sight vocabulary Increasing speed and efficiency Further acquisition of word analysis techniques Linguistic and cognitive content of materials remains beneath student's processing ability
3. Reading for learning the new	Ages 9–14 Fourth grade to junior high school	Reading to acquire new knowledge Expanding grasp of morphology Use of introductory content area texts Growth of silent reading Appearance of new and specialized vocabulary in reading Need for reading recall, summarization skills
4. Multiple viewpoints	Ages 14–17 High school	Reading to discern a perspective Reading to compare ideas Mastery of multiple strata of meaning Greater depth and novelty of subject matter Different literary genres Appreciation of figures of speech, symbolism Awareness of text structures Activation of schemata
5. Construction and reconstruction	Ages 18 + College and beyond	Detailed analysis, synthesis, and judgment of what is read Variable pace: skimming, scanning, studying Creation of one's own views or philosophy based upon reading

In late elementary school and junior high school, reading begins to serve a more specific purpose. Children read to acquire new knowledge (stage 3). The linguistic sophistication of what they are reading catches up to and surpasses the content of everyday speech and much of what they confront in the media. There is more stress on silent reading. Textbooks emerge as an important source of new knowledge. Comprehension skills assume a more decisive role as children are introduced to expository style and as reading content becomes decontextualized, removed from direct experience. There is also, for the first time, a demand for integration of passage reading and memory, as students must store and recall important facts from what they have read. In addition, new and specialized vocabulary is introduced during reading. A student confronts words in a book that are seldom or never encountered in daily conversation. During junior high school, reading rate and efficiency improve considerably. The mechanical act of reading becomes less and less intrusive, allowing students to allocate more attention to meaning and to think and read at the same time.

In high school, reading serves important functions that enhance critical thinking and verbal reasoning abilities. Adolescents read in order to understand particular perspectives or points of view (stage 4). They are able to compare and contrast ideas from a variety of sources. They become adept at discerning varying levels of meaning in a text. The subject matter of what they read becomes increasingly detailed and complex. Reading materials also are characterized by greater language sophistication, and students learn to interpret a variety of literary forms, figures of speech, and verbal ambiguities. In addition to the greater complexity of content and language, students must contend with ever increasing volumes of reading and new information.

By late high school and college, students are becoming increasingly effective literary critics (stage 5). They are able to analyze, synthesize, and form judgments about what they have read. They develop a range of reading styles depending on demands of the subject matter, expectations of the teacher, and the nature of the job at hand. For example, students can vary the pace of their reading. They can skim those materials about which they need only a general idea, scan texts when they are seeking a particular fact, or focus intently when they need to commit material to memory (as in studying for an examination). As part of the construction and reconstruction of what they have read, these older students are able to use reading materials to help them generate a personal perspective or an opinion about a specific issue. Over time, they are able to organize their opinions into an overall philosophy about certain bodies of knowledge (such as religion, politics, or philosophy).

Chall's stage theory introduces some interesting shifts in what she calls the "top-down" and "bottom-up" processes.

> We have classified Stage 0 as top-down [with] only rudimentary word perception skills available for reading. The "pseudo-reading" of the preschooler is based primarily on prediction and memory. The style changes at Stage 1, when it becomes primarily a bottom-up process, focusing on word perception and decoding.

The processing style changes somewhat at Stage 2. It continues in the bottom-up approach of Stage 1, with an increasing backup of a top-down process. From Stages 3 to 5, the emphasis shifts to top-down, with secondary emphasis on bottom-up for materials that become very difficult or unclear (Chall 1983, p. 33).

Similarly, we can note some alternation in the extent to which children give priority to either the message or the medium. Because the medium is still unclear during stage 0, children stress the message; they overuse context, pictures, and prediction to figure out what a story might be about. However, an abrupt shift occurs, and in stage 1 there is a preoccupation with the medium. During stage 2, silent reading is added to oral reading. Increasingly automatic recognition of words and growing fluency in the later stages allow much more emphasis on the message.

In the higher grades (and reading stages), students confront a growing number of words that are unfamiliar to them. At the same time, sentences become longer and the syntax more sophisticated. Passages, which are more tightly written, offer an ever increasing density of facts and concepts. New subjects about which students read become increasingly abstract; they tend to be detached from the occurrences as well as the context of daily life routines. During the earliest years of elementary school, the major challenge for the reader was transforming writing into spoken words. However, the challenge becomes more stringent in stage 3, when the student is expected to comprehend, remember, and draw inferences from text. In stages 4 and 5, students must be keen analysts, able to criticize and elaborate on material, and contribute their own personal creative touches and viewpoints.

During stage 4, the act of reading becomes much more efficient than the process of listening, particularly with complex subject matter, such as that encountered in science or history. It is easier to take it all in while reading than while listening. Reading and the written word allow more time to process meaning than the spoken word, which vanishes as soon as it is uttered.

The expansion of reading vocabulary parallels the stages of reading development. By sixth grade, most children can recognize approximately 6,000 words (Chall 1983, p. 63). This represents dramatic progress, as students' reading vocabularies start to exceed their store of words used in everyday conversation.

Like any conceptual model, Chall's stages of reading development represent approximations that can accommodate variations. Skill acquisition, especially reading decoding in the early stages, is subject to the focus of the teacher and reading curriculum being used. For instance, some place more emphasis on phonics, whereas others stress sight words and a "whole-language" approach. Not all children reach specific stages at the predicted ages. Some encounter more difficulties at one stage than at another; while many individuals reach a stage and never pass beyond it. Many vocations, avocations, and lifestyles do not require highly sophisticated stage 4 or 5 reading. Before pondering developmental variation in more detail, however, it is appropriate to examine the process of reading and its dependency on various developmental functions.

PERFORMANCE VARIATION

Reading ability and disability are controversial subjects. Educators have offered lengthy and varied explanations of how most children learn to read and how others fail to do so. This section presents a tentative, and most certainly condensed, view of the reading process and the developmental vulnerabilities that threaten it. It distinguishes between the processes of decoding and comprehension and between the reading of individual words, the reading of sentences, and the reading of passages.

Reading Words

An adult is rarely called on to figure out a new word in isolation. With the exception of some traffic signs (which tend to be familiar), virtually all of our reading is performed in the meaningful context of sentences and paragraphs. In the beginning stages of reading, however, children must contend with single words, although the *whole-language* approach to teaching reading emphasizes learning to read in context from the very start. *Reading* has been defined as the derivation of meaning from text. Others prefer to define *reading* as the construction of meaning from text, taking into account the background that the reader brings to the text and the interaction that occurs between the reader and the text in the process of arriving at meaning. The process of deriving or constructing meaning entails an appreciation of a range of different characteristics. These have been delineated by Gibson (1971) as a word's *graphic* features (overall visual configuration), *orthographic* features (order of letters), *phonologic* features (the sounds represented), and *semantic* features (meaning). The reader recognizes a written word when the sensory input corresponding to the word makes contact with the representation of the word stored in long-term memory. Words tend to be classified and stored according to their graphic, orthographic, phonologic, and semantic features (Aaron and Baker 1991). During reading, the decoder benefits from these multiple simultaneous cues. Clues relating to the serial order of the symbols (Perfetti 1985) further enhance hints derived from the visual contour of letter combinations. Gestalt and letter order combine to denote a unique sound or combination of sounds. Visual appearance, either with or without the associated sound, directs the reader's search and elicits clear associations with word meanings stored in long-term memory. Ultimately, when the word is embedded in a sentence, further cognitive and semantic hints as well as syntactic (word order and grammatical) clues insinuate themselves.

Decoding individual words requires attention to many details (nearly simultaneous processing of the cues enumerated above). Readers must extract these cues and, through a process often referred to as *lexical access,* search the relevant files stored in their long-term memory. Meaning occurs when accurate correspondence is made. The system by which words are stored has a significant influence on ease of access and recall. Poorly organized mental files have been found to be the source of reading problems, as distinguished from processing dysfunctions (Aaron and Baker 1991). However, the precise manner in which readers construct mental files, extract cues, and activate lexical access is complex and not yet fully understood.

Access to Words. Sight vocabulary and *word analysis skills* are commonly differentiated (Harris and Sipay 1985; Levine, Brooks, and Shonkoff 1980; Roswell and Natchez 1977). *Sight vocabulary* consists of words that the reader instantly recognizes as gestalts or wholes. She needs little time to consciously translate such words into sounds. Although she may perform brief componential analysis (phonologic and/or morphologic), she derives meaning quickly. A reader's sight vocabulary increases with repeated exposure to words. She can decipher sight vocabulary with so little effort that she can allocate considerable cognitive and attention energy to other important aspects of reading, such as comprehension and retention. Although word analysis skills remain relevant throughout life (or as long as we encounter new, lengthy words), we become more and more reliant on sight vocabulary, which allows for greater reading speed, automaticity in accessing words, reading efficiency, comprehension, and enjoyment.

Word analysis is the process of consciously analyzing the components of unfamiliar words and the context in which they occur in order to derive meaning. Word analysis skills fall into three general categories: *phonologic, structural* or *morphologic,* and *contextual.* Decoding unfamiliar words requires attention to many details and nearly simultaneous processing of several cues. A reader must extract the visual configuration, phonemic units, and structural elements that comprise words. Following such detailed analysis, he compares the sound and visual configurations to knowledge of vocabulary stored in long-term memory. Meaning occurs when he finds a correspondence. If this process is insufficient and the word occurs in context, the reader may attempt to search the surrounding content for additional clues.

Phonologic word analysis is the process of segmenting words into their phonemes through associating the written letters with their corresponding sounds and synthesizing the sound units to determine pronunciation and meaning. Phonological decoding consists of a sequence of several steps. A reader must first visualize a word, processing its configuration and letter order. He next engages in phonological coding, translating the visual symbols or segments into meaningful sounds and then synthesizing or blending the sounds to form recognizable words. From this he gains access to his internal semantic dictionary, which enables him to recognize the sound as a word (as opposed to a nonlinguistic sound) and associate it with a specific meaning (Barron 1980, Chomsky 1970).

Segmenting written words calls for a variety of skills. First, children must be able to recognize individual letter symbols. This requires visual attention, visual memory, visual-spatial ability, and visual discrimination. The simultaneous processing of aspects of the individual letters comes into play. It was once widely believed that such visual processing abilities were essential and, therefore, that most children with reading disabilities were likely to have deficiencies of visual perception. Subsequent studies have questioned this (Vellutino et al. 1975, Vellutino 1978); however, the issue is far from settled. The results of more recent studies (Di Lollo et al. 1983, Willows et al. 1988) have shown reading-disabled children to be less accurate and slower in visual recognition of symbols and words. In addition, studies have revealed a developmental factor, with greater differences between normal and disabled readers at younger age levels. Some evidence also suggests that deficits in visual processing speed may diminish with increasing age (Baddock and Lovegrove 1981, Di Lollo et al. 1983, Lovegrove and Brown 1978, Willows et al. 1988). It may be that younger children do not critically analyze letters or words for visual-spatial detail but become more adept with practice. Likewise, older students increase in their visual processing speed through knowledge gained from experience; they know what to look for and can do it quicker. At later ages, also, children are able to apply their greater linguistic knowledge to decoding, whereas beginning readers must rely much more heavily on visual skills. There is no doubt, however, that *combined deficits* such as moderate visual processing problems and difficulties with attention, memory, or language are apt to represent significant impediments. Research thus far has tended to focus on demonstrating the existence of a relationship between specific processing deficits and reading problems. The challenge for the future is not to demonstrate that there is a relationship but to explain how the various basic processing weaknesses interact with each other in causing reading difficulties (Willows 1991).

Once individual letters and letter combinations are discerned, the young reader must associate them with their phonological equivalents. She can articulate the constituent phonemes through subvocalization or actual oral reading. This articulation requires her to register and retrieve a series of fixed visual-phonological associations. Through such paired associative learning, children are increasingly capable of retrieving the sound when perceiving its equivalent visual configuration. At this visual-phonological associative memory level, some children experience difficulty. They have debilitating problems establishing and remembering what unique phoneme a particular letter or letter combination represents.

Presumably, before youngsters can become adept at segmenting written words into phonemes, they must be able to analyze *spoken* words in this manner. A number of studies show a significant correlation between a child's ability to analyze spoken language on various segmentation tasks and the acquisition of beginning reading skills (Blachman 1984, Gerber 1993, Rosner and Simon 1971). This capacity to understand the segmental nature of words is often considered a fundamental element of a child's metalinguistic awareness (see chapter 5).

As a student segments words into their written symbols and associates those symbols with specific sounds, he must hold the sounds in active working memory and then synthesize them, blending them to form a recognizable word. In a sense, a child listens to his own formulation of a word to determine whether the sound matches an existing word in his phonologic lexicon (Aaron and Baker 1991, Liberman et al. 1977). Sequential organization and memory thus are important in the segmentation and synthesis processes.

Finally, to arrive at meaning, a child must compare the composite sound of a word with vocabulary stored in the semantic lexicon of her long-term memory. Children with limited vocabulary may experience difficulty at this stage. There are *hyperlexics,* children who can decode words with correct pronunciation but without understanding. Poorly organized storage of word meanings can also contribute to problems accessing meaning, particularly for words that have multiple meanings which vary according to context and subject area (Aaron and Baker 1991).

Structural or *morphologic word analysis* involves the use of word structure or word parts to determine pronunciation and meaning. As children begin to encounter unfamiliar, multisyllable words in their reading, phonologic analysis and the process of segmenting words by individual phonemes becomes inefficient and severely taxes active working memory, sequencing, and synthesis abilities. By the middle elementary grades, ages 8 to 9, children's linguistic understanding has developed to a sufficient level of sophistication to enable use of structural or morphologic word analysis. Structural word analysis is made up of several components (Miller 1988). *Morphemes* are the smallest meaningful units of language. Words can consist of one or more morphemes. A *free morpheme* is a group of letters that makes up a meaningful word and can stand alone, such as *play, boy, girl.* A *bound morpheme* is a group of letters that can be affixed to a word to change meaning but cannot stand alone. *Suffixes, prefixes, tense markers,* and *inflections* (changes in words made for grammatical purposes, such as adding an *s* to form a plural) are examples of bound morphemes. Other elements of structural analysis include syllables, compound words, and word roots or derivations. In addition to facilitating decoding of long, multisyllable words, structural analysis and morphologic awareness can be a valuable asset in increasing a student's knowledge of word meanings and expanding vocabulary.

Contextual word analysis is the process of determining word meaning and, less often, pronunciation, by examining the context in which a word is found. The context may be the sentence in which the word occurs, adjacent sentences, the paragraph, or an entire passage. There are two broad categories of context clues: *semantic* or *meaning clues* and *syntactic* or *word order clues.* Miller (1988) describes the following five types of context clues:

- *Experience clues:* A reader uses his own experience and prior knowledge to determine meanings of unknown words.

- *Association clues:* A reader associates an unknown word with a related known word in the context (The boy was *ravenous* as a *bear; bear* giving a clue to the meaning of *ravenous*).

- *Synonym clues:* There is a known synonym to the unknown word in the sentence that explains it (The *ancient* dog was so *old* it could barely walk).

- *Summary clues:* Several sentences summarize the meaning of the unknown word.

- *Comparison or contrast clues:* There is a comparison or contrast to the unknown word in the sentence or paragraph that denotes its meaning (After basketball practice, the boy was *ravenous, unlike the rest of his family who had finished eating dinner*).

- *Previous contact clues:* A reader determines the meaning of an unknown word from previous contact with a similar word, often one with a similar root (*hypothetical/hypothesis*).

The whole-language approach to teaching reading is based largely on use of context clues for teaching reading decoding and is introduced at the very beginning stages of reading instruction. However, many young children do not have sufficient linguistic awareness to utilize this method effectively. Furthermore, their vocabulary base and experiential background may be limited, thus further constraining their use of context clues as their primary decoding tool. Older students may rely too heavily on context, especially in content area reading that requires close attention to detail. Context clues also may encourage impulsive guessing, especially dangerous for students who overrely on top-down processing or who are impulsive. Contextual analysis is best used in combination with the other decoding techniques. As a reader gains more sophistication in her linguistic awareness, becomes more proficient in word analysis, and develops automaticity in sight recognition, she uses all decoding methods almost simultaneously.

Developmental Dysfunction: Impacts on Reading Words. The processes summarized in the previous section suggest strongly that the developmental functions discussed in earlier chapters act synergistically to generate skilled reading. It follows, therefore, that specific processing difficulties have the potential to impede the reading of words. The common dysfunctions and their effects are noted in the following paragraphs.

Attention deficits. Attention deficits may or may not affect ability to learn to decode. Children who have strengths (especially linguistic and memory skills) often develop strong visual-verbal associations, which can be retrieved with a minimal expenditure of attention and mental energy. On the other hand, certain children with attention deficits may falter in their efforts to decode words. Superficial attention to detail may obscure for them crucial visual features of letters and words, resulting in inconsistency of visual discrimination. Consequently, unpredictable letter reversals, transpositions of letter sequences, and arbitrary insertions and omissions of symbols may characterize their decoding efforts. If they process only one (possibly irrelevant) visual feature of a letter, it may be associated with an incorrect sound. Weakness in attention may also be at the root of slower processing of information by students with learning problems (Richards et al. 1990). Studies employing a speed sorting task (Copeland and Reiner 1984, Copeland and Wisniewski 1981) showed that subjects with learning disabilities made more errors than controls on stimuli containing more critical features. Cognitive impulsiveness, often seen in children with attention deficits (see chapter 2), may result in their tendency to guess an entire word from some vague configurational attributes, from context (or expectation), or by extrapolating arbitrarily from the first letter or two. Impulsiveness may also result in too rapid phonological or semantic association that fails to take into account the *multiple* features of the word (graphic, orthographic, phonologic, and semantic). A high level of distractibility (such as looking out the window and thinking about next weekend's beach trip) may make it difficult for youngsters to retain the entire decoding process. Finally, poor feedback or self-monitoring can interfere with decoding, as children fail to ask, "Does this sound right?" or "Does this make sense?" As might be expected, children with attention deficits are apt to commit these various errors inconsistently.

Visual processing weaknesses. As mentioned earlier, there is conflicting evidence regarding the degree to which visual perceptual deficiencies are a cause of reading disability in children, although research findings suggest that they may be a contributing factor (Di Lollo et al. 1983, Willows et al. 1988, Vellutino 1979). Studies have more consistently found that the visual processing speed of children with reading problems is slower than that of normal readers, especially for younger children. In the presence of severe dysfunctions, recognition of words is even more likely to be impaired. Confusion over the directionality or other spatial characteristics of a word may result in weak or inaccurate registration in visual memory, possibly creating significant delays in the consolidation of a sight vocabulary. Thus, even words that have been encountered frequently may need to be analyzed anew each time they appear. Delayed acquisition of a sight vocabulary and automatic word recognition have an impact on reading speed and become increasing impediments as the volume of reading accelerates in the middle school years and decoding becomes a tool for learning rather than an end in itself.

Language disabilities. Elements of language processing and production are involved in decoding. Therefore, young children with language disabilities may not be prepared for the challenge (Wiig and Semel 1984, p. 9). Researchers have generally agreed that children with language deficiencies fail to use their own linguistic code to enhance storage and retrieval of information, both visual and verbal. Skilled readers utilize both verbal and visual processing skills for storing and retrieving data, whereas poor readers appear to rely predominantly on the visual route (Spear and Sternberg 1986; Swanson 1983, 1984; Vellutino and Scanlon 1986). Furthermore, children with language deficiencies are likely to bring less linguistic knowledge to the processing of letter configurations that form words and to have greater difficulty integrating the visual print with their verbal correspondences (Gerber 1993, p. 245). Among the language difficulties that may occur (as described in chapter 5) are the following (either isolated or in varying combinations):

- *A poor sense of phonology:* difficulty appreciating the specific phonetic (sound) elements of language

- *Morphological confusion:* a poorly developed grasp of prefixes, roots, suffixes, and other such constituents of single words (Wiig, Semel, and Crouse 1973)

- *Semantic deficiencies:* impoverished vocabulary or trouble associating words or groups of words with their meanings (Lovell, Gray, and Oliver 1964)

- *Syntactic weakness:* poor understanding of the role of word order in affecting the use of words and the meaning of words, phrases, and sentences

- *Problems with metalinguistic awareness:* a weak comprehension of the way we use and understand language (Downing and Oliver 1974, Ryan 1978)

Memory deficiencies. Decoding taps several different aspects of memory. Therefore, weaknesses in one or another mnemonic function undermine the process. In some instances, it is difficult to determine whether the problem is a generalized memory disorder or whether it is limited to the storage and retrieval of specific kinds of verbal information (and perhaps secondary to defective initial processing of such data). Much of our discussion of memory in reading must include exploration at the borderline of memory and phonology. Torgesen (1985) states that "the basic finding that children with specific reading disabilities have particular problems on working memory tasks has led naturally to an examination of their ability to encode verbal stimuli phonologically." The following dysfunctions may be associated with memory problems relevant to decoding:

- *Weaknesses of phonological associative memory:* difficulty establishing easily retrievable (or recognizable) sound-symbol associations and linking the visual form of a word with its phonemic correspondent. Children with these difficulties may (or may not) be skilled at consolidating other kinds of association memory (such as names with faces or places with life episodes).

- *Deficits in sequential memory:* difficulty grasping and retrieving sequences. This may make it hard to blend segmented words during word analysis. Problems with the recall of sequences are often associated with poor reading (Torgesen 1978).

- *Problems with semantic encoding:* difficulty storing and retrieving linguistically encoded data. This can impede the rapid association of written words with their meanings. Individuals with learning disabilities have demonstrated weaknesses in their semantic network, which may impair rapid access (Gerber 1993). Children with such problems may have no difficulty encoding nonverbal material, such as the particulars of various life events.

- *Deficiencies of naming:* problems with the rapid automatic retrieval of the names of things (Denckla and Rudel 1976, Wolf 1984). This differs from phonological associative deficits in that it may be part of a pervasive word retrieval weakness (*dysphasia*). That is, a child may have trouble finding correct words whether the stimulus is graphic (as in written words) or verbal (as in answering a question in class). A number of studies have documented the close relationship between reading and rapid automatized naming.

- *Difficulties with active working memory:* inability to hold one aspect of a word in suspension while processing another component. Weaknesses of such immediate memory have been found in poor readers (Moore et al. 1982). It is closely related to *perceptual span,* the ability to recall the beginning of a word while reading the end of it (Levine 1984b, Rayner 1983). Some children, especially younger ones, with deficient perceptual spans may encounter difficulty holding parts of words together. Affected children may have to take a second look at the beginning of a word after reading the end of it. The compensatory erratic eye movements that result should not be mistaken for the *cause* of the reading problem. In general, problems with perceptual span diminish and disappear spontaneously as children gain proficiency in reading. Active working memory may be dysfunctional in the presence of another primary weakness, when its capability is eclipsed by the combined effects of several mild deficits, or because its current capacity is exceeded. This may occur when one aspect of a task requires so much attention for processing that other components fade, or when the number of elements to be processed and retained is overwhelming. Alternatively, active working memory can be sabotaged by weaknesses of sustained attention and also by excessive anxiety.

Thus, the memory aspects of decoding are intertwined with processing and attention. It may be quite difficult, therefore, to tease out discrete memory gaps as entirely separate problems. A great deal of professional energy can be wasted struggling with the issue of whether visual-verbal associative memory failure is principally a problem of memory, visual processing, or language.

Higher-order cognitive weaknesses. This function gains importance when children are asked to interpret sentences and passages. Nevertheless, during the early stages of reading (such as Chall's stage 1), children's problem-solving strategies and inference drawing in analyzing words require some higher-order cognitive sophistication as they attempt to use pattern recognition, rule application, and context in identifying words.

The potential dysfunctions that may impair decoding can occur in any permutation or combination. Moreover, compensatory strengths in one aspect of decoding may override weaknesses in another, which explains why some children with specific disabilities in one area are nevertheless able to decode words effectively. When the various developmental functions operate synergistically, a child can achieve automaticity of decoding. Once this occurs, it is possible to proceed to Chall's later stages (reading for information and analyzing more sophisticated texts). When one or more dysfunctions are present, decoding may continue to be labored, draining so much attention and cognitive energy that little is left for the more sophisticated processes involved in constructing meaning. Furthermore, as children advance in school, decoding difficulties may have a reciprocal effect on the acquisition of vocabulary and processing of more complex language structures, thus exacerbating decoding difficulties, reducing comprehension and impeding learning. This negative cycle is often referred to as the "Matthew effect" (referring to the gospel according to St. Matthew [Matt. 29:25]: "For unto everyone that hath shall be given, and he shall have abundance; but from him that hath not, shall be taken away even that which he hath." [The rich get richer, and the poor get poorer.])

The various developmental assets and deficiencies that facilitate or impede decoding interact with other compelling forces. Cultural background, socioeconomic status, and emotional health, among other variables, influence ease of decoding. The quality of teaching in the early grades is also highly influential. The mismatching of a child's personal learning style with a teacher's method of teaching reading skills may create problems, especially for certain youngsters whose functional profiles include areas of developmental vulnerability. Prereading experience (Chall's stage 0) can also be crucial. As noted, those who have benefited from strong role models for reading, those who have been read to often, possess a distinct advantage in initial mastery of decoding. Furthermore, current research is providing strong evidence of a linkage between interactive language experience during infancy and early childhood and later cognitive and linguistic development.

Table 9-2 summarizes common decoding errors and potential developmental contributors.

Reading Sentences

Understanding sentences places heavier demands on *syntax* and requires adding context. *Syntax,* discussed in chapter 5, involves word order and grammatical construction. Increasing evidence shows that children who are poor at interpreting the syntax they hear are likely to incompletely understand what they read. The inferences that can be drawn from word order and grammatical construction are necessary for reliable comprehension.

Studies reveal that phonological coding—the translation of written words into their sounds—is as important for processing syntax as it is for deriving meanings from single words. According to Liberman and Shankweiler, "The role of the phonetic representation in speech perception is to hold information about shorter segments (say, words) in short-term memory until the meaning of longer segments (say, sentences) can be extracted" (Liberman and Shankweiler 1979, p. 110). In other words, when reading a sentence, we temporarily store the words as *meaningful sounds* (phonetic units) in verbal memory, while striving to understand the overall meaning of the sentence. Although perceptual span (largely visual and sequential) can maintain a complete word in active working memory, sentences clearly exceed that capacity. Therefore, words may be recoded into language sounds that can be stored just long enough for perusal of the whole sentence. This type of subvocalization is especially likely to occur during the

Table 9-2. Common patterns of reading decoding errors

ERROR PATTERNS	POTENTIAL DEVELOPMENTAL CONTRIBUTORS
Visual approximation to whole word gestalt and some phonemic awareness (e.g., *applesauce* for *applause*)	Weak attention to detail; impulsiveness; poor self-monitoring; weak visual memory
Visually close but little phonemic similarity (e.g., *found* for *friend, make* for *milk*)	Poor understanding of language phonology; weak paired association learning; possible segmentation and sequencing difficulties; inattention to visual detail and impulsiveness
Weak sight recognition and labored sounding out of words	Poor long-term memory skills; weak paired association learning; possible limited vocabulary; lack of reading practice
Mispronunciations and omissions of prefixes and suffixes	Deficiencies in appreciation of language morphology; weakness in vocabulary; poor visual pattern recognition
Phonetically close but misplaced stress or accent	Diminished vocabulary
Poor blending skills; omissions of syllables	Weakness in active working memory; inability to preserve large linear sequences in short-term memory
Accuracy with isolated words but not in oral reading of text	Attention weaknesses, particularly attention to detail and visual distractibility; poor tempo control and self-monitoring; weak semantic and syntactic appreciation; problems with active working memory
Better decoding accuracy in text than of single word	Weak visual retrieval memory with good language appreciation; poor word analysis skills and reliance on context clues
Random, inconsistent errors	Impulsiveness and poor attention control; erratic processing of visual detail; lack of self-monitoring; a good indication that language, word recognition, and word analysis are not primary problems
Mixed pattern of errors	Indicative of weakness in multiple domains, especially at the junctions between attention, memory, and language

early stages of reading sentences and presupposes the ability to decode and attribute meaning to individual words. However, these latter processes themselves may be facilitated during sentence reading (as opposed to identification of individual words) because of the addition of contextual and syntactical clues. Those supplementary clues may be particularly useful to weak decoders who have strong cognitive or conceptual abilities that enable them to make reasoned, educated guesses of what *seems right* (sometimes using top-down strategies). Of course, as such children move into the upper grades, this strategy becomes increasingly unreliable for subjects that are remote from everyday experience (such as mathematics and the sciences).

In some instances, decoding skills deteriorate during sentence reading. Children with significant lapses of active working memory may be struggling so intently to sustain the various elements of the sentence that they have trouble simultaneously segmenting, blending, phonologically coding, and semantically associating a new word. Expending excessive attention on one aspect of the sentence during the reading process can cause failure to attend to other details (such as the difference between *b* and *d*). Thus, a reader who might not ordinarily reverse letters may do so when decoding words is coupled with understanding a sentence.

Developmental Dysfunction: Impacts on Reading Sentences. Reading sentences can be problematic for students with a wide range of developmental dysfunctions. This section begins by assuming that problems that interfere with the decoding of single words quite naturally have an impact on sentence comprehension. However, if a child has adequate decoding skills and significant difficulty with sentence reading, certain discrete developmental dysfunctions should be suspected.

First, some children with attention deficits may have problems with sentences simply because they read in a superficial manner, failing to make good use of context clues, guessing at meaning (overindulging in a top-down approach), and displaying a typically inconsistent focus. The reading of sentences by such students is likely to be unpredictable because of their tendency to tune in and out. Some young readers seem to have difficulty with sentence memory. While they may comprehend sentences, their recall is poor. It can be difficult to determine whether this is because those students are experiencing generalized memory deficiencies or because they have specific language-processing weaknesses. Unless well understood, a sentence is difficult to recall, whether or not a reader has a memory problem.

Some students' difficulties with reading sentences are associated with problems of active working memory. Although this is more likely to affect comprehension of passages (see pp. 320–21), it can also weaken the reading of sentences. Students may have trouble remembering early components of a sentence while reading later parts.

Language disabilities that affect the understanding of syntax could be one of the causes of difficulty with sentence comprehension. Morice and Slaghuis (1985) found significant differences between good and poor readers in the comprehension of syntactically complex sentences. Vogel (1975) also found that children with reading problems commonly had a deficient grasp of word order and grammatical construction. Fry, Johnson, and Muehl (1970) found that children with reading delays had significant difficulty formulating sentences (i.e., using syntax effectively). Not surprisingly, inability to understand and employ syntax has the potential to interfere with sentence comprehension, even if a child is adept at decoding. Furthermore, those children who may have mastered basic syntax sufficient to understand the simple constructions used in beginning readers may have more difficulty with the complex constructions found in more advanced texts, especially when the content is unfamiliar (Roth and Spekman 1989). However, some research data suggest that poor awareness of syntax may not be a specific cause of reading disability, but the association may be part of a broader language disability among children with poor sentence comprehension (Glass and Perna 1986, Kamhi 1988).

As students become more skillful, sentence reading should become increasingly fluent, in part because they are less likely to stumble over vocabulary and are capable of making better use of context clues. Again, children with language dysfunctions are at a distinct disadvantage. Word retrieval problems have been found to be associated with sentence recall and comprehension (Shankweiler and Liberman 1972, Lorsbach and Gray 1986). Lack of rapid access to words and word meanings slows the reading process and places heavier demands on active working memory, often contributing to difficulties with holding on to all the parts of a sentence in order to construct meaning. Circumlocutions associated with word retrieval (e.g., reading *man* for *father*) may result in inaccurate interpretation. Word knowledge has been found to be a powerful determinant of reading comprehension (Fry 1986). Impoverished vocabularies and diminished linguistic awareness may make context clues less accessible. Restricted knowledge of word meanings can be a barrier to comprehension when sentences contain words with multiple meanings. It can make reading comprehension so unrewarding as to deter children from engaging in reading, especially of materials other than those necessary to meet classroom demands. Nevertheless, studies by Nagy and Anderson (1984) found that beginning in about third grade the major determinant of vocabulary growth is the amount of free reading a child does. Once again, the Matthew effect appears to operate: those who read less have poor vocabularies. Those with poor vocabularies remain unskilled readers. Those who have reading problems read less. Their vocabularies remain underdeveloped and they fall further behind (Aaron and Baker 1991).

Reading Passages

The ultimate goal of reading is the extraction of sizable quantities of information, entertainment, or wisdom—more data than can be derived from individual words or single sentences. Chall's later stages of reading skills emphasize reading paragraphs, chapters, and entire texts. As students read for information; to sharpen their critical facilities; to compare ideas, concepts, and writing styles; to distinguish points of view; or even for enjoyment, increasingly sophisticated comprehension of passages becomes paramount.

By the time children are asked to read lengthy passages, it is assumed that decoding is well automatized. A sight vocabulary sufficiently large to permit rapid, effortless reading facilitates the comprehension of words and ideas, allowing the reader to reason, remember, and read all at once. Skillful readers rely less on the translation of visual symbols into phonetic units, although remnants of this process help to register more effectively what is read and are especially useful for mastering complex, factually dense material. Although frequently criticized as a

sign of deficient reading ability, the process of subvocalization strengthens phonological coding, purposely slows the rate, encourages active processing of words
and text, and provides a mnemonic rehearsal strategy for highly deliberate reading (such as studying for an examination). Thus, subvocalization may not only
facilitate comprehension and storage of information but also may increase
metacognitive awareness and self-monitoring of comprehension.

As students read in the academic content areas, they rely heavily on higher-
order cognition to assist with comprehension. The discussion of higher cognitive
function (see chapter 7) described a *schema,* a set of concepts that together form
a framework of knowledge about some specific area (Perfetti 1985, p. 41). A
schema is the background knowledge a reader brings to the text. Schemata provide the mental scaffolding readers use to make sense of what they read. They
provide a guide for determining saliency of information and also trigger cues for
searching memory when information must be recalled (Chapman 1993).

A number of investigators have applied *schema theory* to reading comprehension. McNeil (1984) describes this approach as predicated on four underlying
assumptions. First, what children already know affects what they will learn from
reading. In other words, the schema for a subject influences significantly what is
derived from reading about it.

Second, both *concept-driven* and *data-driven* processes are necessary for comprehending text. The *concept-driven* processes relate closely to the previously
described top-down reading, in which the reader starts with some ideas and pursues the text in such a way that "the reader's goals and expectations determine
what is read." On the other hand, *data-driven* processing takes place when the
reader focuses on the text and then seeks structures (schemata) that fit the incoming information. The reader then pursues data from the bottom up, minimizing initial expectations and allowing new thoughts to be triggered by the text itself.
"Different words and sentences suggest new expectations" (McNeil 1984, p. 4).
Truly sophisticated comprehension of passages requires that a reader be effective
and flexible with both concept-driven (top-down) and data-driven (bottom-up)
processes. McNeil characterizes the problems that occur when one or the other is
used nearly exclusively. "Good readers approach text with a top-down strategy
and then use selected schemata to integrate the text, discarding schemata that are
inappropriate. Less able readers tend to overrely on either a top-down strategy or
a text-driven process, which has a deleterious effect on comprehension. An
overemphasis on top-down processing results in inferences that are not warranted
by the text, while an overemphasis on bottom-up processing—staying close to the
print—results in word calling" (McNeil 1984, p. 4).

The third assumption of schema theory, according to by McNeil, is that the
greater the depth of processing of a text, the more readers will remember and comprehend. Deep processing calls for two techniques: *elaboration* and the use of the
author's *organizational framework. Elaboration* is the ability to extrapolate from
the text, somehow to embellish what is on the page. Students do this by drawing
on prior knowledge, forming inferences, rephrasing the text in their own language,
and continually relating what they are reading to personal experience, ideas, and

values. The use of the author's *organizational framework* requires a keen awareness of the various components of a passage. For example, if readers analyze a narrative into such elements as setting, characterization, theme, key episode, and resolution, they might better understand, analyze, and retrieve it subsequently. For expository selections, "readers achieve deeper processing when they find connections among supporting details, examples, main ideas, and high level abstraction" (McNeil 1984, p. 5).

A final assumption in relating schemata to reading comprehension is that the context in which the reading occurs frequently influences what will be remembered. In one study (Anderson and Pichert 1978), reading passages described children's own homes. The children were told to read the passage from the perspective of a potential buyer and from that of a burglar. The "home buyers" learned and remembered key data relevant to the problems of living in that home. The "burglars" learned and remembered information about security, such as the location of doors, lights, and windows. In other words, the perspective brought to the reading activated particular schemata governing what was to be extracted and registered in memory. Prior knowledge, motives for reading, personal priorities, attitudes, and specific interests are potent determinants of what is gained from the reading process.

Another aspect of schema theory is the organizational patterns in which text is presented. In addition to plot structures that commonly characterize narratives, expository texts also present information within typical structures. Students are better able to understand expository materials when they have been taught to recognize the typical organizational features, such as description, definition-example, cause-effect, compare-contrast, sequence, problem-solution, and thesis-example (May 1990, p. 398). Prior knowledge or early recognition of a text's structure can activate the appropriate schema for comprehension, storage, and retrieval, as well as facilitate selection and use of effective note-taking strategies.

The implications of schema theory are highly relevant to understanding how older children read passages. First, motivation, depth of processing, interpretation, and the ability to assimilate and accommodate new information depend largely on prior knowledge and what the reader brings to the experience. Studies of high school and college students show that inadequate schema or background knowledge is a major source of reading comprehension problems (Chapman 1993). Moreover, children's comprehension is likely to vary depending on the subject matter and the ways in which content matches their own preexistent schemata. Thus, readers with a strong interest and background in computers may exhibit superior reading comprehension of a program manual. However, their reading comprehension may be decidedly inferior when studying irony in a poem by John Donne. Having had experience operating computers, they may have no difficulty elaborating on the program manuals, making good use of the author's organizational framework, and reading for specific information that resonates with personal priorities. Such youngsters gain further gratification from using reading to confirm, embellish, and reinforce established schemata and interests. If they constantly read materials that in no way relate to high-priority schemata, reading text quite possibly will not be a rewarding or happy experience.

The implications of schema theory and research for teaching reading are clear. Students who have an interest in computers have every right to develop their comprehension skills through the reading of materials that relate to their inclinations. At the same time, it is critically important, no matter what the degree of interest a topic holds, that teachers assess students' knowledge base or schema to ensure that it is sufficient, appropriate, and accurate to permit comprehension. Teachers also should not assume that students will automatically activate their prior knowledge or systematically examine their schemata in advance and as they read. These are skills that require direct instruction, demonstration, and guided practice.

As students become increasingly adept at processing passages, they become more versatile and strategic. They perceive the need to modify reading techniques for different purposes. They learn to skim when that is appropriate. They learn to scan passages when they are seeking a specific fact. They learn to differentiate when concept-driven reading and data-driven reading are required. When they have not understood something, they sense the need to reread. They develop techniques for note taking, underlining, and highlighting those components of a passage they must remember or use later on (perhaps in reviewing for a test or writing a report). They become proficient at pinpointing in a text what they do not understand, what does not seem rational, and what is somehow discrepant either within the context of what is read or in reference to personal experience and prior knowledge (their own schema).

As students vary the depth and pace of reading, they alter the extent to which they retain what they have read. Another important reading skill acquisition is *metacognition*, an awareness of how much is being understood and absorbed while reading. The experience of reading an entire chapter and realizing at the end that you have no idea of what you have just read is common. It often connotes a superficial level of processing. A close relative of metacognition is *meta-attention*. Transient lapses of attention during reading are a universal experience. The challenge is to be aware that this has occurred. Some students tune in and out of reading without realizing it. This can result in significant deficiencies of comprehension and recall. It may related to the broader issue of *meta-awareness*, knowing your performance patterns and habits (strengths and weaknesses) and knowing what you know (and don't know), an important aspect of the "hidden curriculum" (see chapter 7).

Distinguishing between comprehending a passage and remembering it may be difficult. Although the two are interrelated, readers may understand content but have real trouble remembering it. Some may read text superficially, thinking they know more than they know. Such children have difficulty answering specific questions about a passage despite having a fairly good grasp of its essence. In order words, they may have overrelied on concept-driven (top-down) reading, tending to ignore detail. Such children may have great difficulty with traditional multiple-choice and short-answer reading achievement tests, which depend on data-driven reading for detail.

In other cases, children who appear able to recall specific detail but falter when it comes to summarizing what they have read may have a form of organizational difficulty. However, other developmental requisites are involved. Children must be able to read and select salient information while rejecting less relevant content. This requires not only good cognitive strategies but also well-honed selective attention. They must sequence the passage's ideas or events in a logical order and differentiate between main ideas and supporting data. Finally, they must synthesize the information, rethinking it and then rephrasing the passage in their own words, within a comfortable frame of reference. These students may do quite well on multiple-choice tests of reading comprehension but have serious problems with retrieving and relating the essence and relevant details of what they have read. Such students may appear to be good readers based on standardized testing but have trouble writing book reports, retaining information on a long-term basis, taking quizzes, and participating in class discussions about what they have read.

Considerable interest has emerged in the ability to summarize as an important dimension in acquisition of reading skill. The capacity to summarize passages, texts, and stories is an essential ingredient for study skills; it is needed for outlining, note taking, report writing, and preparing for examinations. A.L. Brown, Day, and Jones (1983) investigated the growth of summarization skills during elementary school, secondary school, and college, and pointed out that the ability to summarize what one has read is not merely an automatic byproduct of comprehension. It includes the following contributing factors: 1) strategies for concentrating on difficult and important elements; 2) knowing what to include or exclude; 3) determining degrees of relative importance of information within a passage; and 4) using various rules of condensation. "A true summary should be a reduction in length relative to the remembered representation of the text: to summarize implies the ability to condense intelligently what is retained of the gist" (Brown, Day, and Jones 1983, p. 969). In their studies of summarization skills, Brown, Day, and Jones document significant changes over time. Whereas late elementary school students can tease out the single most important idea in a text or story, high school and college students can differentiate varying levels of importance of all the supporting detail. "Older students distribute their attention as a function of the finer degrees of importance that they are able to recognize" (p. 973).

In any text, readers should be able to differentiate details that are central, supportive, or distracting. There is evidence that high school students become particularly adept at distinguishing these levels with great accuracy. Furthermore, when summarizing, high school readers are much more likely to have conscious strategies or plans for summarization.

Brown, Day, and Jones (1983) concluded that

> students as young as fifth grade are able to attempt a written summary of lengthy text, but clear developmental trends are still apparent. College and older high school students outperform younger children in their propensity to plan ahead, in their sensitivity to find gradations of importance in the text, and in their ability to condense more idea units into the same number of words. Under circumstances when a summary is not just a measure of automatic retention, the ability to work recursively on information to render it as succinctly as possible requires judgment and effort, knowledge, and strategies. As such, the ability to provide an adequate written summary of a lengthy text is a late-developing skill that continues to be refined throughout the school years (p. 977).

In Chall's most advanced stages of reading development, students are required to read critically, to select appropriate readings, and to compare and contrast points of view, all of which demand sophisticated schemata, perspective taking, and versatility. Secondary school students should be able to discern recurrent themes, an author's point of view, irony, humor, symbolism, and hidden meaning. They also must become adept at reading a variety of literary genres and analyzing the semantic and syntactic structures pertinent to each.

Developmental Dysfunction: Impacts on Reading Passages. In the upper grades, underlying developmental dysfunctions pose a serious threat to students' abilities to extract knowledge from texts. This inability, in turn, seriously jeopardizes performance in content area subjects (see chapter 12).

An essentially hierarchical model of reading assumes that any developmental dysfunctions that impair decoding and/or sentence comprehension will deter passage reading. A child whose visual and phonological memory capacities are deficient, resulting in a sparse sight vocabulary, will expend too much effort decoding words, so that little attention, active working memory, and higher-order cognition are likely to be available for more sophisticated comprehension. Similarly, a young reader who labors over syntax or is baffled by embedded clauses and the use of conjunctions is less likely to understand a chapter clearly. If a reader has mastered decoding as well as interpretation of sentences, what might interfere with the comprehension of passages? The following paragraphs review some relevant developmental dysfunctions.

Students with attention deficits may have significant difficulties understanding textual materials. Their reading may be highly superficial, passive, and generally unfocused. They may read an entire chapter while thinking about two or three other matters and have no idea of what they have just read. Additionally, they may have trouble with saliency determination (pp. 25–27) and have a weak sense of what is important in a text. Another danger is that careful reading may be replaced by overreliance on probability or context. Students may do too much skimming and not enough careful perusal of the subject matter. Often, students with attention deficits have a tendency to impose their own ideas on the detail in the text (i.e., show excessive "top-down reading"). While this kind of dialogue can be useful and even admirable, overindulgence in the practice distorts meaning. Students with attention deficits may not realize how superficial their reading is. They may equate reading a chapter with finishing it. These students frequently lack meta-awareness of their understanding and absorption and fail to self-monitor their learning as they read.

Difficulties with attention may be mistaken for memory problems. Young readers may have poor recall because they read in a superficial, hurried manner. On the other hand, some students actually have problems with the recall of reading. Although they understand while they are reading, they have significant problems with the consolidation and retrieval of the material. Those with weaknesses of active working memory may forget the beginning of a narrative while reading its middle or final portions. There are also readers with limited memory capacity, so that information contained in longer passages may exceed their factual storage space. These students may recall material from the beginning of texts but not have space left for information that comes at the end.

Some students with deficiencies of sequential organization may have trouble grasping the stepwise organizational scheme of a passage. In particular, when they have to retell or summarize what they have read, they may have difficulty recalling or making use of serial order cues. Procedural concepts in science may be especially difficult for them to master.

Sometimes it is difficult to distinguish between problems remembering what has been read and true gaps in understanding. The latter can stem from several sources. First, children with language dysfunctions, those who have trouble with verbal comprehension in general, are likely to be deficient in understanding passages. Diminished vocabulary, a poor grasp of syntax, trouble drawing inferences in verbal contexts, weak metalinguistic awareness, and poor verbal pragmatics may thwart comprehension. Children with relatively subtle language difficulties may have problems attaining the higher stages of Chall's reading levels. For example, in high school they may be unable to read to discern a point of view, to probe for thematic significance in a novel or short story, or to analyze irregular syntactic structures in poetry.

Bilingualism (see pp. 168–69), although not a true learning disability reflecting a developmental dysfunction, can pose a significant challenge to reading comprehension. Native language interference has been shown to intrude on sound awareness and appreciation of the prosody and rhythm for speaking a second language. Similarly, significant differences in prosody, rhythm, and rate of speaking can compromise understanding of reading, even when a student is proficient in speaking and understanding oral language. Often, without the auditory structure of the sound system of a second language, a reader may revert to the rate, rhythms, and prosody of the native language in reading. This may weaken attention to tense markers, word endings, and punctuation. It also can cause poor sensitivity to phrasing and grammatical structures. The combined effects can cause a major impediment to understanding. Readers may have difficulty comprehending lengthy, complex sentences, interpreting implicit meanings, and appreciating tone and point of view. They may fail to attend to important cohesive ties (connective phrases and transition words) and thus draw inaccurate conclusions. Their comprehension may be extremely fragmentary and disorganized. Having bilingual students with reading comprehension problems read orally can provide valuable clues as to whether or not these factors of native language interference are operating.

Students with discrete or generalized higher-order cognitive deficiencies also are at risk for problems with passage reading. Some may not have the knowledge base needed to understand new materials. Others may read on a level far too concrete to extract meaning from material that is primarily conceptual. Some students may understand concrete examples but have trouble relating these to more abstract concepts. These students are also likely to have difficulty integrating concepts in order to understand broader principles and theories. Students who read at the literal or concrete level often have difficulty interpreting the linguistic ambiguities and symbolic language of literary genres. Still others may show considerable unevenness in their reading comprehension, having discrete higher-order cognitive weakness that affect only certain content areas. Thus, a student who has great trouble understanding science textbooks may be quite skilled at ferreting out the author's perspective in a short story. Developmental variation in higher-order cognition can be an important cause of uneven performance in various subject areas. A particular student may have well-formed schemata for some content areas or topics within a content area but extremely amorphous schemata for others.

Finally, students' organizational skills can affect how well they comprehend texts. Disorganized schemata and systems of filing words and information in their semantic lexicon can impede access and comprehension. The ability to take notes, underline, write in margins, and pace reading are important elements of study skill. Deficiencies in these strategies for selecting and organizing data can significantly reduce comprehension and recall. Competent, organized readers are likely to have effective reading strategies. In addition to systematic note taking, they know when to skim, when to read carefully, and when to scan for specific information. Well-organized students read with a purpose, and they know how and when to reread. Among students with organization problems and attention deficits, failing to remember to take the book home is a common cause of failing to remember the story.

Table 9-3 summarizes common patterns of reading comprehension problems and potential developmental contributors. Additional discussion of reading comprehension skills and dysfunctions pertinent to specific subject areas is included in chapter 12.

Table 9-3. Common patterns of reading comprehension problems

ERROR PATTERN	POTENTIAL DEVELOPMENTAL DYSFUNCTIONS
Slow reading rate with poor recall of information	Weak word identification skills so that the effort of decoding eclipses ability to process meaning; limited vocabulary; insufficient knowledge base; receptive language problems; weaknesses in attention.
Confused understanding at the sentence level	Language dysfunctions: semantic and/or syntactic; problems with active working memory.
Good comprehension at the sentence level, but poor passage recall	Limited memory capacity; weak active working memory. Inadequate sustained attention; lack of metacognition and self-monitoring; poor organization and awareness of content structure.
Better recall of information from the beginning of texts than from the end	Problems preserving large volumes of information in memory. Limited attention maintenance.
Better recall of material from end of texts than from the beginning	Weak active working memory; possibly limited storage; decoding difficulties.

Table 9-3. *(Continued)*

ERROR PATTERN	POTENTIAL DEVELOPMENTAL DYSFUNCTIONS
Good recall of facts but poor grasp of main ideas	Weak saliency determination; poor semantic integration; lack of appreciation of text structure; problems with higher-order cognition; superficial processing; dependence on data-driven processing.
Good grasp of main ideas but weak recall of facts	Problems with convergent retrieval memory; lack of attention to detail; overreliance on top-down or concept-driven processing; superficial reading.
Good explicit understanding but poor inferential comprehension	Weak higher-order cognition and overreliance on literal meaning; organization and integration problems; superficial processing.
Good understanding of narrative, but problems with exposition	Insufficient prior knowledge and deficiency in technical vocabulary; weak appreciation of text structures other than story plot; possible problems with convergent retrieval memory.
Poor understanding of figurative language, point of view, and fact versus opinion	Deficits in higher-order language skills, semantic appreciation, and language pragmatics; weak higher-order cognition and an overly concrete, literal level of interpretation; poor recognition of verbal patterns; possible lack of exposure to more sophisticated literary forms.
Better recall of material read orally than silently	Weak attention controls; passive processing and need for more active engagement; need for auditory reinforcement to process meaning.
Better recall of material read silently than orally	Weak automatic decoding skills so that oral reading usurps attention and eclipses ability to process meaning simultaneously; problems with active working memory; language deficits causing slow processing.
Poor summarization skills	Weak selective attention and inadequate determination of saliency; poor organization skills; problems with retrieval memory; expressive language difficulties.
Good ability to answer questions with text available but poor summarizing and recall	Memory weakness; poor self-monitoring of learning; deficiencies in selective attention and salience determination.
Weak general comprehension despite good decoding	Language dysfunctions, including semantic understanding and knowledge of syntax; passive reading and superficial processing of meaning; lack of self-monitoring; insufficient background knowledge; inappropriate reading tempo; weak cognition.

ASSESSMENT

The business of assessing reading is a well-established, thriving enterprise. Group achievement tests are used nearly universally to assess students' achievement levels, as well as to measure the teaching effectiveness of schools. Individually administered reading instruments, both standardized and informal reading inventories, probe for specific disabilities. This section focuses not on the specific instruments that may be used but rather on the dimensions of assessment and their rationale. Many of the group- and individually administered diagnostic tests are listed in the appendix. The discussion that follows is divided into two major parts: the evaluation of decoding and the evaluation of comprehension.

Assessment of Decoding

Any description of a child's reading ability must include consideration of the efficiency and accuracy of decoding. Sight recognition and word analysis skills, which form the foundation for skilled reading, need to be evaluated during oral reading. The accuracy and sophistication of decoding should be assessed using single words and connected text. In the latter, semantics and various context clues may facilitate word recognition. Higher-order cognition, familiarity with the subject matter (schema), and knowledge of syntax, for example, provide hints as to the identity of a particular word. To assess these abilities, evaluators make observations about the ease and accuracy with which children decipher the phonology and structural elements of an unfamiliar word, their knowledge of vocabulary, and their use of context clues. Some examiners also use nonsense words, a purer test of the knowledge of rules of phonology, the ability to divide words into segments, the appreciation of morphology, and the ability to synthesize or reblend the word parts to form plausible-sounding words.

A number of specific questions should be asked when evaluating a child's word analysis skills:

- Does that youngster focus on the *details* of the word?

- Can the child segment words into their phonemes, and are there certain letters or letter combinations that the child has not yet mastered? Table 9-4 summarizes the various categories of English sound-symbol associations a reader must assimilate to decode effectively.

- Does the reader discern and employ decoding rules (such as the silent-*e* rule)?

- Does the reader recognize common structural/morphological elements (prefixes, suffixes, roots, syllables)? Trying to sound out *-tion* and *-ing* will not be productive.

- Are there problems blending the sounds in the right sequence to form words? Some children are far better at taking words apart than they are at putting them back together. Their deficiencies may be due to active working memory problems, the result either of primary weakness of active working memory or strain imposed by the effort required to process a particular portion of a word.

- Does the reader make use of context clues to assist decoding? This is often reflected by greater accuracy and self-correction in oral reading of text than in reading isolated words.

- What is the rate and efficiency of word analysis? Is it a process that is accurate but so laborious that it is likely to eclipse other functions?

- How do a child's word analysis skills compare to what is expected of children in his or her grade?

During the school years, children are expected to deal effectively with an increasing number of new, lengthy, multisyllabic words. Older schoolchildren are expected to cope with this growing linear sequence of symbols. As we have noted, poor word analysis skills may belie a number of underlying developmental dysfunctions. Common problems include weak visual attention to detail, a poor sense of phonology (making phonetic analysis difficult), weaknesses of associative memory (specifically visual symbol to sound), sequential disorganization (impairing segmentation and blending), poor active working memory, deficient semantic appreciation, problems with spatial processing (appreciation of the configuration of letter combinations), or higher-order cognitive weaknesses interfering with effective problem-solving strategies for word analysis. However, a weakness in *one* of these areas may not necessarily compromise word analysis skills. A child may learn to rely on a developmental strength in order to compensate for relative weaknesses in some other area. For example, children with a strong sense of language may override attention deficits during word analysis.

As has been noted, the higher grades call for students to rely increasingly on instantaneous recognition of words and decreasingly on individual word analysis.

Table 9-4. Categories of sound-symbol associations

TYPE OF SOUND	SAMPLE LETTER OR LETTER COMBINATION	SAMPLE WORD
Short vowels	i	pin
Long vowels	o	hope
Consonants	m	man
Beginning consonant blends	scr	screw
Ending consonant blends	nk	bank
Consonant digraphs	ch	child
Vowel digraphs	ea	seat
Diphthongs	ay	play

A traditional part of reading assessment, therefore, is establishing the adequacy and size of a child's sight vocabulary and speed and efficiency of word recognition. Error patterns that emerge when children have difficulty should also be examined. Several relevant questions should be asked: Does the child substitute visually similar meaningful words? This might suggest impulsiveness, inattention to detail, weak spatial processing, or poor recognition memory. Does the reader seem to have difficulty processing morphology? This might reflect lack of appreciation of prefixes, suffixes, word roots, or other alterations in word form, all of which might suggest either language problems or trouble with the length of visual sequences. Does the child have a tendency to look at the first few letters or some highlights of the word and then guess (often incorrectly)? This may reflect memory difficulties, limited vocabulary, or, once again, impulsiveness. Does the child have trouble pronouncing words, even though she or he seems to recognize them? This suggests weak appreciation of phonology or, perhaps, articulation or oral motor planning problems. Are there prolonged delays in response time? This implies that recognition is not yet automatic, that there may still be an element of word analysis decelerating the process. Consideration should also be given to the presence of word retrieval difficulties. Observation of the fluency of oral expression supplemented by a rapid naming task could provide additional insight. Does the child have trouble recognizing highly irregular words (those that do not conform to rules)? This suggests memory weakness. More generalized weakness in sight recognition could reflect impoverished vocabulary. Furthermore, as children grow older, a simple lack of practice (sometimes a result of fear of failure) may hinder the recognition of irregular words and compromise sight vocabulary in general. Finally, some young children who have been taught to read through a strongly phonetic approach may reveal word analysis skills that are far more effective than their sight vocabulary (usually a temporary discrepancy).

In measuring a child's sight vocabulary, it is important to take into account the speed of word identification. Automatic recognition forms the basis of sophisticated comprehension. Word recognition should not consume more than its share of active working memory. Children whose decoding is weak, especially those with limited sight vocabularies, are apt to engage in word-by-word reading. That is, oral reading is effortful and noticeably dysfluent, marked by hesitation, slowness, and lack of appropriate intonation. Often, comprehension and recall of meaning are compromised. Table 9-5 lists some of the basic parameters of reading decoding.

Silent reading becomes increasingly important as children reach late elementary school. Some children have difficulty reading aloud, remembering what they have read, and understanding the passage all at the same time. Such children may prefer silent reading. Students differ significantly in the extent to which they feel self-conscious reading before their peers. Inhibition and anxiety may thwart fluent decoding. Some children feel more comfortable bypassing phonology and placing greater emphasis on direct extraction of meaning, thereby showing a strong preference for the silent mode. On the other hand, silent reading is a much more passive

Table 9-5. Relevant parameters of reading decoding

COMPONENT	ASSESSMENT PARAMETERS
Sight word recognition	Accuracy Automatic recognition Application of word analysis skills Knowledge of vocabulary Use of context: semantic and syntactic clues Impulsiveness and inattention to detail
Phonologic word analysis	Knowledge of letter-sound associations Rule application Segmentation Synthesis/reblending
Structural/morphologic word analysis	Recognition of prefixes and suffixes as single units Recognition of compound words Appreciation of root words and derivations Syllabication Segmentation by structural elements Synthesis/reblending Knowledge of vocabulary and meanings of prefixes and suffixes
Contextual analysis	Use of word, sentence, and content meaning Use of grammar and syntax Self-monitoring
Oral reading style	Accuracy Omissions and substitutions Place keeping Fluency Phrasing and expression Rate

activity and can result in superficial processing of meaning. The active engagement of reading orally and the auditory feedback may enhance understanding.

Assessment of Comprehension

The evaluation of reading comprehension is a complex undertaking. First of all, as we have seen, comprehension requirements change drastically as children age and reach the more advanced grades, so that increasingly sophisticated measures must be employed. Second, comprehension is confounded by so many variables that it is difficult to measure each in relatively pure form. Attention, memory, language ability, factual knowledge, organizational skill, higher cognition, and adequacy of decoding all influence understanding.

Reading comprehension is usually tested by having children read a paragraph and then answer questions. Both oral and silent reading comprehension are usually assessed in younger students. By the end of elementary school, however, silent reading becomes the primary focus, and oral reading is usually used for clarification if the student's silent reading comprehension is diminished despite adequate decoding of single words. Typically, both narrative and expository content are used in testing. The accuracy of responses to questions is taken as an indication of competency. The questions may relate to specific vocabulary in the passage, its structure, its literal meaning, its main idea and supporting details, the sequence of events, its author's point of view, implicit meanings and plausible inferences, and its stylistic techniques. When a reader does poorly, it may be difficult to distinguish between trouble understanding the question and true difficulty interpreting the passage. The effect of possible memory deficiencies on performance in answering questions also warrants consideration. Sometimes the questions are not consistent with the students' learning style. Some students who are particularly intimidated by multiple-choice questions may receive artificially low scores on group testing but may succeed on reading tests requiring summarization. It is important to compare comprehension of narrative text and expository test. Many students profit from the inherent plot structure of narratives but falter when faced with the less apparent organizational patterns of expository passages. Finally, it is important to assess a student's background knowledge as a factor influencing comprehension. These are some relevant parameters of reading comprehension, oral and silent:

- Decoding single words
- Understanding vocabulary and rapidly incorporating new words and terms
- Interpreting sentences (including appreciation of morphology and syntax)
- Identifying main ideas
- Identifying supporting details
- Rejecting irrelevant or distracting information
- Drawing inferences
- Retelling a passage
- Identifying author's intention and/or point of view*
- Summarizing*
- Understanding figures of speech*
- Prior knowledge

---

*Relatively late acquisitions (i.e., generally late middle school and/or high school).

The following suggestions may help pinpoint specific comprehension deficiencies:

- Have children read a sentence (rather than a passage) and answer a question about it. This reveals whether they have automatized the decoding process, whether they are able to unravel and understand syntax, and whether their vocabulary is adequate. Using a sentence rather than a paragraph has the advantage of requiring relatively little memory and synthesis. If students are able to decode effectively but still have trouble understanding a grade-appropriate sentence, the evaluator should determine whether they also experience problems with oral comprehension by administering an oral sentence comprehension test.

- Have youngsters read a passage silently and ask them specific questions. The questions can stress the parameters delineated in the previous item. Carefully chosen questions can distinguish among problems understanding and remembering, recalling details, determining what is relevant, and appreciating overall themes. It is useful to reveal the topic *before* a student reads the paragraph. Alternatively, one can ask the child to read a passage and seek specific information from key questions provided in advance. At some point during the reading evaluation, it is appropriate to stop a child and probe for comprehension. Having a youngster pause partway through a paragraph or passage and describe the meaning and/or predict what will come next can help differentiate true comprehension difficulties from problems with recall of summarization.

- Have children read passages and ask them questions with the text available for referral; the questions may be presented in written form as well as given orally. Contrasting these results with a child's performance in answering questions without the text can differentiate between problems of memory and comprehension.

- Have children retell or restate a passage in their own words. The various processes required for this have been described on pp. 318–20. Poor performance elicits a rather broad differential diagnosis, which may be the most accurate representation of true reading ability. Some children perform well on multiple-choice tests of reading comprehension but have difficulty on a day-to-day basis—participating in class discussions, taking quizzes, and applying what has been read—because of their poorly developed independent extraction and summarization skills.

- Have older students take notes from or underline a reading text, and later use their notes to answer questions or summarize the passage. Another technique would be to have students complete, fill in, or create a semantic map for a text, the last being the most difficult and perhaps most revealing of their recognition of text organization as well as understanding of content.

- Have students generate test questions for a reading passage. This gives insight into their level of conceptualization and critical reading skills as well as their ability to determine what is most salient.

- Contrast silent and oral reading comprehension skills. Children whose comprehension is significantly stronger for orally read material may benefit from the more active engagement required for oral reading and/or from the auditory feedback to enhance meaning. Silent reading can be more passive and result in superficial processing of meaning and reduced registration and recall. On the other hand, oral reading may usurp attention, require so much effort and/or elicit anxiety so as to inhibit comprehension. In silent reading, also, the reader has more control over the pace and can take more time to process meaning and also to go back and reread when necessary.

Much of the assessment of reading decoding and comprehension just described can be informal. A process-oriented evaluation of reading skills in children who are encountering difficulties may be more valuable than a testing session with the sole objective of generating a series of grade levels and standard scores (in automatic word recognition, word analysis, fluency and rate, and comprehension). Identifying specific flaws or breakdowns in the reading system may be far more germane and has significant implications for educational intervention. For example, the majority of standardized reading tests do little in the way of evaluating the comprehension and recall of longer passages and summarization ability, critical skills as students progress through middle school and beyond. In general, age-normed, standardized testing to document baseline levels and monitor progress should be used in conjunction with ongoing informal assessments that stress processes. Informal reading inventories are available which may be more helpful for examining reading processes. When children are having difficulties, this form of process-oriented evaluation can help determine what factors are causing the breakdown—difficulties with language, recall, organization, or memory.

MANAGEMENT

The remediation of reading difficulties is probably the most well established of skill enhancement programs in schools. Teacher training in special education stresses techniques to improve reading abilities in children with a wide range of dysfunctions. A number of excellent texts offer highly specific suggestions and programs to correct deficiencies. The professional seeking more details about intervention is urged to consult such sources. In addition, the remediation of reading has become a well-established business enterprise. Software programs and materials for parents have become widely available and publicized. The quality of such programs, however, is highly variable. Furthermore, not all programs are equally useful for all children, although advertising publicity and program manuals rarely mention this.

This section offers a sampling of interventions that might be made available to children who are struggling with the reading process. Professionals and parents may build on or extrapolate from these ideas. First, it offers some general suggestions applicable to the diverse population of children with reading problems.

Then, it explores intervention strategies based on awareness of a child's individual dysfunctions, relating them to both decoding and comprehension.

General Recommendations

Following are general suggestions for parents and teachers:

- Research has shown that reading to children from a very young age is an important factor in the development of literacy skills. Parents should read to their preschoolers starting before one year of age on a daily basis. Parents also should model interest in and value for reading by reading regularly in the home.

- Make every to prevent reading phobia or inhibition. Children who have difficulty reading sometimes react by avoiding reading. This results in lack of experience in and exposure to vocabulary, language structures, and information, which compounds their underlying reading difficulties. Encourage children with reading delays to read as much as possible, and read to them regularly.

- As with other skill deficits in childhood, avoid public humiliation. For example, teachers should not ask children with reading deficiencies to read orally in front of classmates. Being laughed at by peers can induce reading phobia as well as a high level of anxiety about school. Practice in oral reading can be done in a very small group (with other children who have similar reading difficulties), with a tutor, or with a parent at home.

- Regular, frequent reading practice helps strengthen reading skills and automatization of sight word recognition. At home, set aside a special reading time on a regular basis and use it for highly motivating responsive reading, ideally with all members of the family reading in order to present a good model and demonstrate that reading is valued. Family members may take turns reading from the same selection or reading something of individual choice. Reading followed by group discussion or description by each member can help develop oral expression, summarization, elaboration, and critical reading skills.

- As early in their education as possible, introduce children predisposed to reading difficulties (as a result of developmental dysfunctions) to the romance of the written word. Subscriptions to interesting magazines can be helpful. Encourage regular trips to the library or bookstore. Discuss newspaper or magazine articles at the dinner table or in the car. Encourage relatives to write letters. Ask children to read traffic signs, labels in the supermarket, and other highly relevant material.

- Limit television viewing. Children with reading problems may discover that it is all too easy to derive entertainment and information effortlessly from a television screen. Strict limits on viewing can help encourage reading. Establish evening hours when there is no television—when the entire family is engaged in cognitive pursuits.

- Teachers can develop children's interest in reading by modeling their own enjoyment and by reading to the class on a regular basis. Classroom discussions about books that have been enjoyed and disliked can stimulate interest.

- At school, children benefit from opportunities to engage in high-motivation reading practice and time set aside for "free reading" on a daily basis. Children might read with partners. Choral reading is another helpful activity for strengthening decoding skills and reading fluency.

- Whenever possible, give children an opportunity to build reading skills using materials that are of particular interest to them. Highly motivating reading can be meaningful at the same time that it responds to a child's personal interests. A child who has a strong interest in automobiles might strengthen decoding and comprehension by reading auto repair manuals or magazines about motor vehicles. Television and movie scripts, song lyrics, and comic books are other sources of high-interest reading.

- Tailor the teaching method to the functional profile of the child with reading problems. Choose reading programs, texts, and approaches carefully. Base methods of teaching reading not only on awareness of the child's developmental dysfunctions but also on recognition of the ways in which that student's strengths can be exploited to enhance reading ability. Table 9-6 lists some of the more common reading approaches with their relevant characteristics.

- At home and in school, use age-appropriate games and scoring systems to help children improve their decoding abilities. Employ computer software, workbooks, flash card games and homemade or improvised activities that make learning fun. Document progress with a vivid graph or score sheet to portray growth. It is particularly meaningful for a child to chart his or her own progress. Self-evaluation can also help develop closer self-monitoring.

- Have the child practice word analysis skills in the context of spelling, writing, and reading, in order to promote consolidation and generalization.

- Make broad-based efforts to improve reading comprehension. Include critical reading, interpretation, thinking, and summarization as well as literal comprehension and factual recall.

- Children almost always need some form of individualized tutorial help. In some cases, parents can work with their own children. However, it is usually more desirable to have a professional nonfamily member provide this service.

- Undertake remedial help, either through the school or an outside tutor, in collaboration with parents, regular classroom teachers, and other therapists that may be involved, especially in speech and language. Collaboration provides reinforcement, promotes consistency in teaching approaches, and ensures mutual understanding of student functioning, performance expectations, and instructional objectives.

- Comprehensive management involves more than remedial reading. Intervention must also address the child's profile of functional development. For example, a child with a language disability probably requires a reading approach that accommodates verbal deficits as well as language therapy. The age of the child is an important factor in considering the intervention program and selecting materials. In addition, specific emotional needs also require attention.

- Do not deprive children with severe reading problems of knowledge, factual acquisition, or exposure to sophisticated language. A child who is delayed in learning to read may need to acquire factual data, concepts, and vocabulary from the content areas through alternative communication channels. Whenever possible, supplement reading with tape-recorded textbooks and leisure reading, movies, filmstrips, picture books, and verbal presentations of material.

Table 9-6. Common reading approaches and relevant characteristics

Basal Reading Series	Used universally. A graded sequential series with controlled vocabulary. Includes reading texts, workbooks, and a detailed teacher's manual. Presents reading skills in word recognition, word attack, and comprehension systematically from year to year. The instructional focus of series varies; some give greater attention to phonics and word analysis while others have a whole-language emphasis.
Distar	A highly structured phonics approach that emphasizes sound-blending skills. Modifies some of the printed letter symbols of the alphabet to provide clues to letter sounds.
Fernald/VAKT	A multisensory approach that includes visual, auditory, kinesthetic, and tactile processing. The child traces the written word on paper with the index finger, saying each part aloud as he traces it, until he can write it without looking at the copy. The child collects words and uses them to write stories. In the final stage, the child generalizes the similarities of learned words to new words.
Gillingham-Stillman (Orton-Gillingham)	A highly structured, sequential, multisensory phonics-based program. Emphasizes learning individual letter-sound associations, then blending the sound to form words, and eventually reading sentences and short passages. Children also practice writing the letters and words as they associate letters with sounds. Reading texts employ highly controlled, phonetically regular words similar to linguistic/word family readers *(The fat cat sat on a rat).* Introduces sight words very gradually.
Language Experience	Uses stories composed and dictated by students and written down by the teacher for instruction in reading skills. In addition to promoting motivation and being personally meaningful, the approach is based on the premises that what a child can talk about, he can write; that the child can read what he says and writes; and that he can read what others write for him to read. Emphasizes sight word learning.

Table 9-6. *(Continued)*

Lindamood	A phonetic approach to reading that emphasizes sound discrimination, segmenting, and blending. Teaches readers to identify sound, number, and order of phonemes heard in a word and to make comparisons between words. Uses real and nonsense words for practice. As auditory discrimination and segmenting skills develop, readers are taught grapho-phoneme relationships and to apply sound segmentation and comparison to the written word in reading and spelling.
Linguistic	Although essentially phonetically based, this method presents sounds not in isolation but as part of a regular pattern. Often referred to as a *word family approach*. Once children have learned the sound for a pattern *(an, ip, op)*, they compare and contrast changes made by altering a single phonemic element and generalize application of the pattern to decode new words. Reading texts contain a highly controlled, phonetically regular vocabulary *(fat, sat, cat; fan, man, van)*.
Neurological Impress	A system of unison reading by student and instructor at a rapid pace. The student sits slightly in front of the instructor so that the instructor's voice is directed into the student's ear. The child points to words as they are read. The method is based on the theory that the auditory feedback from the instructor's and reader's voices will strengthen visual-verbal association and create a new learning process.
Predictable or Pattern Books	Uses stories that contain refrains or phrases that are repeated over and over, enabling readers to predict the next word or line. Examples include *Little Red Hen; The House that Jack Built; Henny Penny; Brown Bear, Brown Bear.*
Rebus	Introduces reading through picture symbols that suggest words. As the reader progresses, pictures are paired with and then replaced by printed words.
Reading Recovery	Developed in New Zealand as an early intervention program for at-risk readers in first grade. It involves one-to-one instruction by a teacher who has undergone a rigorous and lengthy training program. Teaching is formulaic, but individualized for a specific child's learning needs. There are no prescribed materials or word analysis approaches. The essential features are sound segmenting, story segmenting, daily reading practice, and story writing. The program is terminated as soon as the child "catches up."
Whole Language	Teaches reading as an integrated, meaning-related activity. Does not break reading down into separate skills. Emphasizes reading for meaning, and uses regular children's literature. In pure whole-language programs, decoding skills, other than the use of context clues, receive little emphasis. The basic premise of the approach is that children learn naturally from exposure and use rather than from isolated skill lessons and drills. Story writing is an integral part of the approach.

Reading Problems Associated with Attention Deficits

Often, children with attention deficits are adequate readers. On the other hand, when attention deficits are associated with reading weaknesses, the following recommendations merit consideration:

• Give remedial help in short sessions, since children are likely to tire easily and lose their focus during prolonged tutorial sessions. Help improve their concentration by varying the techniques and offering more frequent and shorter sessions. The optimal time and length of tutorial assistance can be determined by trial and error.

• Because of their attention difficulties, affected students should work in very small groups or, ideally, one-to-one. Distractibility, in particular, can make it difficult to remediate reading in a large group or regular classroom.

• These children have difficulty concentrating on minimally or moderately motivating reading materials. Therefore, they have a strong need for attractive content. A *language experience approach* can often help early elementary students. Children select a topic that interests them, and dictate a story on that topic to the teacher or parent, who writes the story, which the child then reads. Older students can be asked to select an exciting topic (e.g., astronauts, cooking, or mythology) and read related books and articles in depth.

• Emphasize reading for detail. Give these children specific questions in advance so that they can read to locate the precise information required. *Cloze exercises*—involving filling in words that are missing from the text—encourage close reading and attention to semantic and syntactic detail. Word searches, proofreading for errors in spelling, and locating word and meaning absurdities are other helpful exercizes.

• To teach decoding, emphasize common letter patterns such as word families and regular structural elements (prefixes, suffixes, root words, and syllables) to help children become less prone to word substitutions due to poor attention to detail.

• Give children questions to answer *during* the reading process (i.e., line-by-line comprehension monitoring). The overall theme should be: "Am I really concentrating while I read?" Label the questions for use at specific points in a text (following a particular page, paragraph, or line). At each of these points, the child answers the question, which should be simple, requiring awareness of a specific detail presented in the last several sentences. Ask questions that stress attention to detail, not comprehension of general themes. If the child cannot answer the question, she or he should reread the section until locating the correct answer. Have the child keep score of the number of rereadings needed.

• Use previewing activities to help students with attention problems identify salient information and reduce distraction by irrelevant detail.

- Have children participate actively while reading. As they grow older, help them acquire the habit of writing while they read: underline, circle key words, place an asterisk or write key words in the margin next to an important section, and inscribe comments when appropriate. Encourage active processing by having students write test questions for reading passages, fill in semantic maps, and write brief summaries. Discourage the use of a highlighter and evaluate underlining skills; children may highlight and underline seemingly important words and sentences without really thinking about the meaning.

- The reader must learn to balance using context clues for reading comprehension with the need to focus on detail. During the earlier grades, when it is easier to guess at meanings, these children should use their often excellent conceptual abilities to aid comprehension. However, such conjecture can be problematic during junior high school, when close attention to what is actually written (as opposed to what is expected) becomes more important.

- Children with attention problems are at risk for difficulty keeping their place as they read. This can interfere with comprehension, so that what they read does not make sense or they miss important segments. Encourage such children to use some type of place marker.

- Ask children whose attention deficits cause them to omit and/or substitute words to make a tape recording of their own reading. Have them play this back and listen to themselves reading while they follow the text closely. They should grade their own reading by marking up the text so that it is a transcript of the tape.

- For some children with attention problems, oral reading may help reduce passive, superficial processing. Hearing what they read may also improve understanding.

- Regular practice in summarizing helps children actively engage in reading and process meaning, select what is most salient, and develop their organization skills. Ask students to tape-record summaries and then check their summaries against the text.

Reading Problems Associated with Memory Deficiencies

Children with primary memory weaknesses can have particular difficulties acquiring reading skills. Memory problems can affect both decoding skills and comprehension. The following general suggestions are likely to benefit those with decoding weaknesses:

- Teaching decoding skills through a multisensory approach has become a mainstay in special education. This method is particularly likely to help children who are experiencing difficulty with associative memory for sounds and visual symbols. Such students presumably benefit from multisensory cues that give the written word an increased number of associations, thereby facilitating consolidation in long-term memory. If a child sees a letter combination, hears it, traces it, and writes it, theoretically the sound-symbol link will be more firmly established. The Orton-Gillingham method, a prototype of this approach, has been widely applied in special education settings as well as in classes for children with significant reading disabilities.

- Tailor other methods of enhancing associative memory to the child's specific strengths. For example, have the struggling reader who has strong visual perceptual and visual analytical skills associate printed words with pictures. Use picture-word books and highly illustrated reading materials (comic books, pictures with captions, and cartoons) to strengthen these associations. Label objects in the home and classroom to reinforce word recognition. Computer software specifically designed to enhance sight vocabulary commonly features strong visual associations.

- Having students create their own letter-sound-picture dictionary and picture-word books promotes interest and active participation, both of which strengthen registration and recall of paired associations.

- Choral reading, echo reading, and repeated reading improve sight word recognition and recall. Flash card drills and games also strengthen word recognition.

- Children with active working memory weakness often experience problems with phonetic blending and synthesis. They benefit from instructional approaches that emphasize common letter patterns and units such as word families, prefixes, suffixes, root words and compound words.

- Use mnemonic tricks to help children who have problems with letter confusions because of difficulties with visual memory for spatial orientation, i.e., *b* and *d*.

- Encourage students with memory problems that impede identification of words by sight to make heavy use of context clues to guess at words.

- Children often benefit from an initial emphasis on recognition rather than on retrieval. For example, have them complete sentences that have single words missing by choosing from a list of visually similar words the one that looks right to them. View such a multiple-choice approach as one step toward identification of complete words.

Memory deficiencies can also result in poor reading comprehension. It is important to rule out the possibility that a child is not understanding because she is having trouble decoding. If possible, establish that her comprehension difficulties are not secondary to primary weaknesses of attention or language. If the child seems to be having trouble understanding because she is not properly sustaining written ideas in memory, interventions such as the following can be particularly helpful:

- Have children practice breaking down paragraphs into specific meaningful components. First, they should read to discern the main idea. Then, on a sheet of paper under the headings *who, what, where, when,* and *why,* they can list specific supporting details in the passage.

- Retelling abilities sometimes must be developed apart from the act of reading. For example, tell a student a story and ask him to summarize it. After a movie, television show, or athletic event, ask him to describe it. Ultimately, retelling should be integrated with reading and remembering.

- To reinforce recall, help children master skills of underlining, circling, writing comments, and other active reading techniques.

- Ask students with strong visual skills to create visual images (pictures) of reading passages to improve their memory.

- *Semantic mapping*—filling in visual diagrams and flow charts—can help children recall reading content, the relationship of ideas, and the sequence of events in reading passages.

- Teach students to recognize the organizational patterns of texts to promote stronger recall as well as facilitate semantic mapping.

- Set a purpose for reading and learning when commencing a reading activity to help strengthen recall. A student is more likely to remember what she needs to find out if there is a plan for what she should gain from the text.

- Help students with memory problems self-monitor their learning. During the process of reading, ask them to stop frequently to summarize the material and ask themselves if they really remember what they have read.

- To help students consolidate information in memory, give them regular practice and instruction in refining their summarizing skills.

- Teach mnemonic strategies to help children recall information from reading. For example, ask them to make up lyrics to a favorite tune or a rap, using information they want to remember.

- When reading to study for an examination, encourage students to develop a deliberate memory plan by considering questions such as the following:
  - What do I need to read for this test?
  - How much time will it take me to read it?
  - How much time should I allow for each chapter or section?
  - Of the material I am reading, what do I have to memorize and what will I be able to figure out if it turns up on the test?
  - What techniques will I use to allow materials to get into my memory several times? Underlining, writing comments, or making charts and diagrams can strengthen reading memory.
  - What other tricks can I use to make sure I learn this material? Should I use a tape recorder? Should I try to picture things in my mind? Should I use a great deal of repetition? Should I concentrate very hard just before I go to sleep?
  - How can I translate this reading material into diagrams or tables?
  - How will I know *when* I know? What self-testing techniques will I use?

Reading Problems Associated with Visual and/or Sequential Ordering Weaknesses

As noted earlier, students with visual processing weakness may experience problems with the spatial orientation of letters and the overall configurations of written words. When there is evidence for an association between poor visual processing and reading delays, try some of the following approaches:

- Encourage children to use a multisensory approach to decoding.

- If the child has relative strengths with language (especially the appreciation and retention of phonology), use a phonics approach to reading. After learning the sounds of vowels, consonants, and blends, children learn to sound out specific words by pronouncing the previously mastered sounds and blending them effectively. They can recognize even unfamiliar words by associating speech sounds with specific letters or combinations thereof. Thus, a phonics approach stresses pronunciation of isolated sounds and their blending into words.

- For children with visual-spatial processing weaknesses (as well as other dysfunctions), emphasize writing at the same time that they are learning reading. The visualization needed for writing and spelling can help reinforce a sight vocabulary for reading.

- Constantly drill with flash cards and/or appropriate computer software to help establish instant recognition of words. Use this approach especially for vocabulary with phonetically irregular spelling.

- Encourage students to make use of context clues for deciphering words not readily recognized. Ask them to guess at words that would make sense in the sentence and context of what they are reading. In the early grades, using context clues to help maintain a reasonable reading rate can help students overcome word-by-word reading, which is so mechanical that it can interfere with comprehension. *Cloze reading exercises,* both oral and silent, which require students to fill in a word missing from the text by using context clues, are especially helpful for this purpose. Create them by deleting every fifth or so word from a reading passage. This technique encourages attention to both semantic and syntactic clues.

- Children with visual processing difficulties may have trouble understanding as they read. Have them preview materials (look over titles, section headings, italics, pictures and diagrams, and chapter questions). Give them a list of new vocabulary words before assigning a reading passage so they can become familiar with them.

Students with sequential processing weaknesses may experience difficulty both with decoding and comprehension. The following suggestions can help remediate their decoding difficulties:

- Give these students exercises that provide practice in segmenting and blending words of increasing length and number of syllables. However, before competent segmentation and blending can occur, these children must have a firm grasp on individual sound-symbol associations.

- Phonetic segmentation and blending can be especially difficult for students with sequential processing weakness. Use decoding approaches that stress chunking strategies, such as use of word families, syllables, and regular structural units. Have students practice these word analysis techniques with words of increasing length.

- When visual-spatial processing is intact, encourage students to use their ability to recognize gestalts. Drill them on increasingly long multisyllabic words with a stress on instant recognition.

- Teach students to use context clues to alleviate decoding difficulties that are due to problems with sequential processing.

- As students are introduced to content area reading, instruct them in structural word analysis skills, using vocabulary from their textbooks.

Children with sequential processing weakness are prone to difficulty with several forms of reading comprehension, including narrative, procedural exposition, and historical sequences. Cause-effect relationships may also be difficult for them to grasp, as they have trouble recalling what came first and what followed. The following techniques may be helpful:

- Ask students to retell what they have read. Have them read passages that contain a logical sequence of ideas or events. Have them practice recalling them in the *correct order,* perhaps creating a numbered list of such ideas or events in the proper sequence.

- Emphasize highly meaningful reading materials with sequentially organized plots (mystery stories are often ideal in this respect). Ask children to retell them in the proper sequence.

- Use activities that stress compliance with multistep directions to enhance sequential memory during reading. Have students read the instructions that accompany a model airplane, or other sets of directions for putting together or building various objects, and then summarize them in a logical sequence.

- Have children order sentences to improve sequential appreciation. Cut up stories and procedural directions, such as recipes or those for constructing models. Alternatively, give children activities that ask them to locate sequential absurdities in stories, and historical events or errors in procedural directions.

- Ask students to fill in outlines, flow charts, and time lines while reading. Depicting ideational and temporal sequences visually may reinforce the sequential flow.

Reading Problems Associated with Language Disabilities

As we have seen, children with language disabilities can be at a disadvantage in reading. They are apt to encounter serious problems with both decoding and comprehension. Decoding problems are likely to be particularly severe for children who have only a tenuous grasp on the basic phonology and morphology of their native language (see chapter 5). The following recommendations can be helpful for decoding:

- Try using a linguistic approach to reading, one that employs a whole-word phonic strategy rather than sounding out and blending phonemes. These methods teach words in word families, with groups of words selected on the basis of similar spelling patterns (e.g., *light, right,* and *tight*). The student masters the relationship between specific speech sounds and letter combinations by discriminating between similar words. Words with irregular spellings are introduced and learned as sight words (i.e., via pure visual or graphemic memory). The presentation of highly consistent phonological and orthographic patterns is the hallmark of this approach.

- Employ multisensory approaches such as the Orton-Gillingham method. Their rationale is that kinesthetic, tactile, visual, and auditory modalities, when presented together, can compensate for relative weaknesses in understanding or retaining distinct language sounds. Generally, such programs stress the mastery of writing and spelling in conjunction with reading.

- Have children work directly on phonological awareness and memory. In the primary grades, ask students to perform exercises to enhance awareness of individual language sounds. For example, beginning readers can participate in rhyming activities. Have them match pictures of objects whose names rhyme. Give them lists of words in a family and ask them to circle the portions of the words that rhyme with each other. Encourage them to compile lists of words that begin with certain letter combinations such as *th* or *tel.* Exercises involving the repetition of phonemes may also be useful.

- Segmenting words into their component sounds and sound manipulation are often stumbling blocks to reading decoding. Have children count the number of syllables or sounds (phonemes) in words to strengthen segmentation awareness. Also ask them to identify initial, final, and medial sounds of words. Sound substitution and pig Latin games may improve skill in phonological manipulation.

- Use *cloze activities,* in which children listen to a word and then fill in the missing parts of its written equivalent, to develop sound segmenting skills.

- Instruction in structural word analysis skills can help students who show strength in visual processing and have problems with segmenting and reblending sounds. Structural analysis facilitates chunking by consistent visual and meaningful units, thus reducing the number of elements that must be maintained in active working memory and then synthesized. Use of chunking strategies becomes increasingly important with the growth in volume of multisyllable words in text in higher grades.

- Sometimes diminished vocabulary compromises decoding. Some children with language difficulties need an emphasis on vocabulary building in general. Stress crossword puzzles, word games, and dictionary work. Drill such children on antonyms and synonyms and directly instruct them in vocabulary and word morphology.

The comprehension problems of children with language disabilities can be particularly troublesome in late elementary and secondary school. When students are having difficulty understanding what they read, it is important to establish first whether their decoding is intact. Sometimes comprehension is impaired because inordinate effort is expended on the act of decoding. Second, it is helpful to determine whether they have difficulties comprehending spoken syntax. Third, it is useful to know whether they have difficulties with comprehension in general (i.e., verbal comprehension) or whether the problems are limited to understanding specific content or concepts. Fourth, it is important to determine whether comprehension problems are due to diminished vocabulary or insufficient background knowledge. Finally, the volume of what is to be processed and understood warrants consideration, especially in older students. An overload of information can overwhelm a student's capacity to comprehend. Use of the following management techniques should be based on answers to these questions.

- Before assigning reading, employ activities that build and activate prior knowledge of content topics. Also introduce new vocabulary.

- Make vocabulary enrichment part of the curriculum for both young and, especially, older students. Instruct them in morphology and word derivations. Give students cards with prefixes, suffixes, and root words and ask them to make up as many words as they can. Have students challenge each other to decipher the possible meaning of words they have constructed.

- Assist students' comprehension by teaching them key words that signal typical organizational structures of reading content.

- Model previewing and predicting skills as aids to comprehension and have students practice them under supervision.

- Older students may have trouble understanding figures of speech. Increase their appreciation by having them create their own.

Reading Problems Associated with Higher-Order Cognitive Weaknesses

Children with difficulties of higher-order cognition may have trouble grasping some concepts while reading. Often their impairments are subject specific. That is, certain kinds of materials will cause more difficulty than others. The following suggestions may be helpful:

- It is especially important to ascertain that an affected reader has the appropriate schema *prior to* reading a passage. For example, to emphasize reading to confirm what is already known (Chall's stage 2), teach a child about a subject and then ask him to read about it as review or confirmation. Some children with higher-order cognitive delays are apt to be late in reaching Chall's stage 3, in which a student reads to acquire new knowledge. Nurture mastery of reading for confirmation before compelling the reader to read for new knowledge.

- Whenever possible, use text that matches the child's cognitive style and interests. Highly motivating materials aimed at the student's conceptual strengths and personal priorities can be beneficial. For example, a learner with well-developed mechanical aptitudes might thrive on books about carpentry, artwork, or electronics.

- Help children with higher-cognitive difficulties assimilate abstract concepts in reading. In the upper grades, assist them in making inferences; comprehending implicit meanings and ambiguities; and interpreting metaphors, similes, and other forms of figurative language. They are apt to feel more comfortable at a concrete level of processing. Assign supplementary reading materials with concrete examples of concepts to increase their grasp.

- The comprehension of different writing styles and literary genres may be particularly troublesome for older students with higher cognitive deficits. Other students may have trouble analyzing the very condensed and terse writing of scientific texts. Teach students *how* to read and interpret different forms of writing.

- The recommendations offered to help with comprehension weaknesses in children with language disabilities (see pp. 341–42) also pertain to those with higher-order cognitive deficiencies.

- Be aware of discrete areas of higher-order cognitive confusion. For example, some children may have difficulty comprehending word problems in mathematics. They may have trouble translating such linguistic presentations into computational processes. Emphasize targeted drill on the transition from words to mathematical algorithms. Others may have trouble interpreting poetry or identifying the author's intention or viewpoint. Employ approaches that strengthen the weak link between reading and ideation. This, too, pertains to both language and higher-order cognitive deficiencies.

Listening As a Corollary of Reading

Listening comprehension is often used as an indicator of reading potential for students with decoding deficits, and it certainly has important implications regarding a student's ability to make use of tape-recorded textbooks. For students who are linguistically adept, removing the barrier of decoding may give them ready access to curriculum reading content. However, there are important differences between reading and listening skills which have particular relevance for very young and older students. In reading, words and text are presented in a visual format and, as such, remain available for reprocessing as many times as necessary for decoding and comprehension. Listening, however, requires very rapid processing of language, close and sustained attention, ready determination of saliency, strong sequencing skills, and excellent memory. Once words are uttered, they are gone and no longer available for referral. Thus, children who are slow to process language are at risk for problems with listening comprehension. Students with attention problems may experience lapses and miss critical pieces of information, thus compromising comprehension. Sequential deficits can interfere with the ability to process and retain multistep directions given orally. Before a child acquires reading skills, she learns mainly by listening. If listening skills are impaired, the child may be at risk for diminished learning of the most basic skills and suffer failure at a very young age. Much of older students' learning also comes via listening in lecture courses and class discussion. Teachers do not restrict classroom instruction to review of reading material but use that as a jumping-off place for delivery of new insights, principles, and generalizations. Furthermore, students not only have to rapidly process oral language, but take notes at the same time. Students who are slow to process language may become lost as they try to listen, understand, and write. Fine-motor difficulties may also interfere with the ability to write and listen simultaneously. In evaluating a child's strengths and weaknesses, it is very important to assess listening skills and taking notes from listening, and not to assume that listening and reading comprehension are equivalent, although they may be compatible.

Assessment of Listening Skills. The following are components of listening ability that should be assessed. They are listed in order of increasing complexity.

1. *Sentence repetition.* Some children do this without processing meaning. One should carefully evaluate errors and whether the child maintains meaning even though he may not directly recall specific words. This can provide insight into a child's approach—whether he uses rote memory or some degree of semantic and syntactic processing.

2. *Sentence comprehension.* Ask the child to answer a question after listening to a sentence. Varying the length of the sentence and the degree of semantic and syntactic complexity can reveal where ability breaks down.

3. *Narrative comprehension.* Ask the child questions after reading her a narrative passage. The questions should include comprehension of main ideas, recall of detail and sequence of events, understanding of vocabulary, and inferential thinking.

4. *Narrative retelling.* Ask the child to retell a narrative after hearing it read. Elements to assess include recall of main ideas, supporting detail, and sequential organization.

5. *Expository comprehension*. This process is similar to narrative comprehension but uses expository passages. Include procedural sequences and recall of multi-step directions.

6. *Expository retelling*. This is similar to narrative recall, with the differences noted under expository comprehension.

7. *Summarizing*. This is different than straight retelling and requires the listener to extract what is most salient.

8. *Taking notes from orally presented material*.

Contrasting a child's skills in retelling and summarizing with her skill in answering questions can help uncover weak organization skills and problems with retrieval memory. Differences between narrative and expository recall may indicate to what degree explicit plot structure is important for comprehension and recall. Differences in sentence comprehension and passage comprehension may indicate problems with processing and storage capacity, active working memory deficits, or weak sustained attention.

Management. Many of the suggestions for language-based reading comprehension problems can help alleviate listening comprehension weaknesses. In particular, children with poor listening abilities require maximum use of visual aids to accompany oral instruction. These may include key words written on the board, a set of written notes or directions, and demonstrations. In addition, the following ideas may be helpful:

• Preview key points before beginning a lesson to alert students what to attend to. Stop to repeat important information to provide reinforcement and give children a second time to hear and write down what is most essential. During the course of a lesson, prime students' listening by warning that something important is about to be imparted.

• Ask students with listening difficulties to subvocalize and repeat to themselves what is being said.

• Allow older students to tape-record lectures and class discussions so that they may give full attention in class and then replay the tape and take notes at their own pace. Tape recorders that have speed adjustment capability are preferable.

• Keep a set of notes or a cassette file of lectures that are available to students. This benefits not only students with listening problems but also those who miss a class due to illness or some other reason.

• Rather than requiring students to take notes entirely on their own, give them outlines to fill in, another means of focusing their listening efforts.

- Allow students who have fine motor problems that impair note taking to use a tape recorder. Or have a set of notes, either written or taped, available for referral.

- Help students develop a type of shorthand to facilitate note-taking speed and efficiency.

- Pair a child with listening problems with another student whom he could ask for clarification or who could act as a note taker.

Reading As Facilitation

The acquisition of reading ability is clearly a major accomplishment in the education of children. Not only do proficient readers gain access to knowledge and to the perspectives of others in an efficient and systematic manner, but reading skill also facilitates the acquisition of other skills. The next chapter explores two of these, writing and spelling skills, that are closely linked to reading and that, like reading, offer insights into the interactions between multiple developmental functions. Subsequent chapters on mathematics and content area subjects also explore the relevance of reading to academic success.

Chapter 10

Writing and Spelling

Clarence had gread difficulty with grammar. No matter how hard he struggled . . . the parts of speech, especially the verb, remained a veiled mystery to him. His teachers and parents kept telling him that he would never be able to write or speak unless he learned grammar. At first, with despair in his heart, he believed them, but gradually a suspicion grew that perhaps they might be wrong. Finally, in the middle of a severe lecture on his grammatical shortcomings, he interrupted the teacher and said through his tears, "When I have something to say, I can always say it!"
—Miriam Gurko, *Clarence Darrow*

The transmission of thoughts onto paper calls for a delicate and highly complex process of neurodevelopmental integration. Writing necessitates synchronizing all of the developmental functions described in part 1. Writing is a final common pathway of these functions, a confluence of processes demanding attention, spatial and sequential production, mnemonic facility, language ability, higher-order cognition, and motor skill.

In the higher grades, children are judged increasingly by what they write. Courses in English, history, science, and mathematics rely heavily on writing as proof of competence. The accuracy, speed, sophistication, and automaticity of writing contribute heavily to scholastic accomplishment. Through a gradual developmental progression, children become able to transcribe their thoughts onto paper, at a rate and quality that match the richness and efficiency of their ideational and verbal fluency, and in a style appropriate to the intended audience. Ultimately, writing may take the leading role in enabling a student to organize thoughts and information, to develop or extract ideas, to solve problems directly on paper, and to communicate with an absentee audience or when face-to-face confrontation is intimidating and inhibiting. We are reminded of the adage, "How can I know what I think until I see what I say?"

WRITING DEVELOPMENT: SIX STAGES

The progressive acquisition of writing skill is a conspicuous indicator of academic attainment. This chapter offers a model of specific writing stages, one that has particular relevance for students with writing problems (see table 10-1). The

347

acquisition of skills in this model is divided into six stages. They acknowledge substantial variation in rates of progress of even normally achieving children. These stages are derived from direct clinical experience and reviews of the literature dealing with the elementary curriculum.

Stage 1: Imitation (preschool to first grade)

During the Imitation stage, children *pretend* to write. They mimic the writing of adults or older siblings, pursuing imaginary writing while making use of authentic implements. Coloring, tracing, and paper-and-pencil games fascinate them. Educational television programs for preschoolers make written symbolism exciting and appealing. Gradually, imitation gives way to greater authenticity as preschoolers and kindergartners master true letter forms. By this age, they usually show preference for a particular hand, although incomplete or mixed dominance is not uncommon. At this time, also, children should begin to master a conventional tripod grip of writing utensils, although fist-like and highly varied grasps are still normal, particularly since the amount of direct teaching in how to hold a pencil is extremely variable.

Imitative writing requires little in the way of organization or sustained attention. It uses relatively primitive motor skills, with no stress on highly distal movements or precise sequential mobilization of movements. Children's writing attempts often show spatial groupings that approximate words, although symbols and symbol sequences may be highly idiosyncratic and creative. During this stage, many normal young children display rhythmic, associated mouth movements while writing. It is not unusual to see a child's tongue undulating sympathetically as the pencil or crayon pursues its course.

Prewriting behavior is important. A young child tantalized by the imaginary appeal of writing is likely to be more responsive to subsequent writing challenges. Familial and cultural influences can be especially potent; a preschooler who never sees anyone in the family writing is likely to be at a disadvantage during the Imitation stage. Early experiences of being read to and looking at books are also important stimulants to interest in writing and words and early writing development. This is a time when early signs of writing inhibition may emerge, particularly in the presence of fine motor weaknesses. Some children become frustrated in their attempts to draw, trace, and color. As early as preschool, observing greater proficiency in their peers can signal the beginnings of self-consciousness and a consequent tendency to abridge writing of any kind. It is of the utmost important to provide young children with encouragement and kind instruction and to avoid criticism at all cost.

During the Imitation stage, writers take pride in their work. They have many grandiose thoughts they would like to document on paper, but, of course, they fall short on technical skills. As they master letter formations, they begin to spell very simple words, but soon discover that they must use invented spellings as well as

Table 10-1. Stages of writing

STAGE	CHARACTERISTICS
1. Imitation (preschool to first grade)	Prewriting and fanciful attraction Attempts to mimic true writing Awareness of spatial arrangement of letter groups (words) and of lines Acquisition of letter and number formations Beginning appreciation of spelling accuracy and use of invented spellings Susceptibility to cultural and familial influences Establishment of hand preference Lack of highly precise graphomotor function and variable utensil grasp
2. Graphic Presentation (first and second grades)	Preoccupation with visual appearances Discovery of conventions of capitalization, punctuation, and sentence structure Growing self-consciousness Increasingly precise and distal fine motor regulation Rapid increase in spelling ability Use of unsophisticated language
3. Progressive Incorporation (late second to fourth grade)	Awareness of writing as a synthetic process Integration of conventions (punctuation, capitalization) with language (morphology, syntax, narrative organization) Written language less sophisticated than speech Little emphasis on well-planned writing Awareness of spatial formats (paragraphs, letters) Beginning of rewriting Start of cursive writing
4. Automatization (fourth to seventh grade)	Writing with less expenditure of conscious effort Growing capacity to write and think or write and remember spatially Attainment of cursive writing fluency Ability to produce larger volumes of writing Written language approximates speech Greater stress on planning and draft writing Early development of report and expository writing and research skills
5. Elaboration (seventh to ninth grade)	Writing used to establish and express a viewpoint Written language exceeds complexity of everyday speech Problem solving and idea development occur through writing Summarization through writing becomes a common task Organization and use of information from multiple sources Extensive use of transitions and cohesive ties (words such as *finally, for example, therefore,* or *but*)
6. Personalization-Diversification (ninth grade and beyond)	Development of individual writing styles Use of different writing styles and formats appropriate to subject matter and purpose (lab reports, research papers, expository essays, poetry) Simplification and greater variation of language use Sophistication of vocabulary and use of figurative language, irony, symbolism Writing as a medium for experimentation Writing as a medium for taking notes Writing as a facilitator for learning and remembering Writing as a method of reasoning, problem solving, and persuasion

other methods of creating an aura of competency as they progress to the next stage, one in which appearance counts the most.

Stage 2: Graphic Presentation (first and second grades)

During the Graphic Presentation stage of writing, children (and teachers) are most preoccupied with the visual appearances of their productions (Graves 1983). They become adept at reproducing the graphic symbols as they master both upper- and lowercase letters and learn the rules for using each appropriately. They acquire facility with the conventions of spacing between words and spatial planning on a page. They discover margins and become acquainted with such conventions as placement of their names and skipping a line at the top of a page. During the early part of this stage, letter reversals are still common. In some cases, they may be due to confusion over directionality and laterality (such as left-right discrimination). More often, such reversals occur due to undeveloped appreciation or memory of these spatial aspects or because the children are concentrating so intently on recalling other attributes of letter configuration that they overlook directionality. During this stage, children equate good writing with visual aesthetic quality. Appearances are everything, often regardless of how the writing utensil is held and manipulated, and teachers and parents regularly reaffirm the value of appearance. Some students whose productions are unattractive become self-conscious and writing inhibited during this stage. They may hide their work and, out of shame and frustration, come to avoid writing.

At this stage, children's capacities for attention usually exceed the demands imposed by early writing. Similarly, there is little stress on sophisticated language and cognition, functions developed well beyond what must be integrated into early writing. Thus, the major emphasis for this age group is on visual processing and production (the recall and reproduction of the gestalts of visual symbols and spatial arrangement of material on the page). Sequential organization, especially the order of letters in the alphabet, the order of letters in one's name, and the visual sequences needed for copying and spelling are emphasized. Writing practice frequently involves a great deal of copying from the board or in workbooks. Copying from the board can present problems for children with attention weaknesses and/or memory difficulties, especially at the beginning of this stage when they often are asked to copy material they are not yet capable of reading. Children may make liberal use of invented spellings, for example, substituting letter names for their sounds (*b-a-b* for *baby*) or relying heavily on phonetic spelling (*muthr* for *mother*). This practice allows graphomotor fluency to proceed unencumbered by the mnemonic strain of true spelling.

Associated mouth movements continue to be present during writing, especially in young boys. However, motor control becomes increasingly distal and selective. Gross motor writing steadily progresses toward more finely regulated use of distal joints. Children start to rely increasingly on proprioceptive and kinesthetic feedback from finger muscles and joints (see chapter 6) during writing. This enables them to write faster. It also allows for more efficient copying, as they can remove their eyes from the page more frequently without disrupting the flow of letter formation. Hand preference becomes fully established, and pencil grip style becomes habitual (for better or for worse). Also during this period, children's letters become smaller to conform to the constraints of ever narrowing lined paper. Throughout this stage, the spatial planning and motor demands in writing are most prominent; struggles with these aspects persist but lessen progressively during the next stage.

Stage 3: Progressive Incorporation (late second to fourth grade)

During the Progressive Incorporation stage, children approach writing as a synthetic process in which multiple systems become amalgamated according to preset rules. Gradually, students incorporate standards of capitalization, punctuation, syntax, and grammar. Concern over spatial planning, motor control, and visual appearances lessens.

During Progressive Incorporation, sophisticated organization of ideas has low priority. A child engaged in expressive writing presents ideas in the order he thinks of them. The language content is likely to be uncomplicated since simple declarative sentences and few subordinate clauses are used. Conversational speech is more sophisticated and syntactically complex than writing, and writing is more often used to state the obvious or relate an experience rather than to solve problems or develop elaborate ideas.

Unlike later writing stages, Progressive Incorporation includes little if any advanced planning of content. Children discover what they will write by writing it. This is not a time for highly deliberative writing, as there are too many mechanical matters and new rules to attend to. It is, however, a period when practices of revision and correction are introduced. The painful process of rewriting makes its educational debut.

A major landmark of this stage is the introduction of cursive writing. Most youngsters have mastered printing, producing manuscript letters with diminishing conscious effort, and they are satisfied with the aesthetic appearance of these symbols. As they become less preoccupied with the spatial attributes of their writing, they are more able to accept the greater efficiency of cursive production. However, cursive writing raises new graphomotor and memory challenges. Fluent motor planning and fluid sequential movement are required in addition to learning a new visual symbol code. Writing fluency may be especially compromised in children who have failed to acquire a regularized tripod utensil grasp.

Thus, during Progressive Incorporation, mastering cursive writing while learning and integrating spatially applied systems of rules challenge the writer, even though highly sophisticated thought and language are not yet demanded.

Stage 4: Automatization (fourth to seventh grade)

During Automatization, teachers expect greater volumes of writing, and demand sustained attention to detail and self-monitoring. Students must increasingly apply rules automatically—quickly syncronizing correct grammar, spelling, punctuation, capitalization, and vocabulary. In addition to these multiple requisites, demands are made on motor memory (see chapter 6) for the rapid, automatic retrieval of motor engrams for writing. Active working memory becomes essential; a student must preserve the meaning of what she is writing while constructing a sentence and at the same time attempt to find the right vocabulary and remember to capitalize, punctuate, and spell correctly. Early in the stage, writers commonly lose track of their train of thought, forgetting what they were going to write or what they have already written. Although awareness of the need to plan what is to be written grows during Automatization, it does not become a major consideration until late in this stage. Teachers give greater emphasis to self-monitoring and proofreading skills. They expect students not only to apply rules of the mechanics of writing with increasing automaticity but to review their work, and recognize and correct errors in sentence structure, grammar, capitalization, punctuation, and spelling.

Language usage becomes increasingly important. As syntax and semantics catch up, written language starts to approximate spoken language. Sentences become longer—often through the use of dependent clauses—and contain more sophisticated vocabulary and conceptual content. For the first time, children use words in writing that they would be unlikely to employ in conversation.

Thus, children are expected not only to amalgamate and synchronize sophisticated language, fluent cursive writing, and systems of rules, but also to consolidate these recent acquisitions into considerably larger amounts of writing, a process demanding sustained selective attention, self-monitoring, and the maintenance of multiple priorities in active working memory.

Late in the stage of Automatization, writing content, rate, and efficiency take on new significance. The systems of rules converge and are assumed to be well integrated and nearly automatic, allowing for greater ideational fluency and sophistication of content. Writing also begins to become an increasingly important indicator of acquisition of subject matter. Children's writing is no longer limited to narrative, and they begin to develop skills in expository writing.

As automatization develops, children can afford and are expected to engage in substantial organization. They start to plan in advance what they are going to write and recognize increasingly that the sequential organization of their thoughts is indispensable to writing. Thus, the development and elaboration of ideas become important. Children learn to make use of punctuation, paragraphing, and cohesive ties or transition words to accomplish this. Students now learn to write in stages. After selecting a topic and collecting ideas, they may create outlines of their thinking, prepare a first draft, revise and edit their work, and finally produce a finished copy. This infusion of organizational skills usually means that ideas are developed before transcription. Furthermore, young writers begin to develop metacognitive awareness and the ability to read and assess the effectiveness of their own writing, an aid to the process of revision. At this stage, writing is not used as an end, a process in itself, or a means of problem solving. Instead, it is strictly for communication, for putting forth ideas for others to read. However, the purposes of communication start to expand to include essays, reports, and display of knowledge on tests. Thus, greater specificity and accuracy in use of vocabulary and language gains importance.

Stage 5: Elaboration (seventh to ninth grade)

During the Elaboration stage, children become increasingly adept at using writing to establish and express a viewpoint. The act of writing is sufficiently automatized and organized that it is now available as a method of developing ideas. Students no longer must devote all their cognitive energy to learning to write, but can begin to write to learn and to influence others. They can begin to use writing for thinking, problem solving, arguing, persuading, and remembering. Writing becomes much more linguistically complex than speaking; students use more extended and sophisticated subordinate clauses. They also make increasing use of cohesive ties (Gregg 1986), words and phrases that clarify and facilitate the flow of ideas. These include appropriately used phrases such as *for example, in fact,* and *of course* and words such as *therefore, finally,* and *however.* The use of relative pronouns grows in sophistication. At the same time, the increasing sophistication of linguistic complexity also calls for greater attention to punctuation and grammatical detail.

As writers begin to plan and organize their ideas, they often find that when they write they have developed better ideas than they had anticipated. Writing at this stage calls for ideational integration. Book reports and essays require children to synthesize ideas from a variety of sources, including books, periodicals, reference volumes, their own personal experiences, and what they have learned recently in class. Writing to summarize and for taking notes become important skills. The capacity to identify main ideas and supporting detail contributes to writing as it does to reading.

The Elaboration stage also sees the reemergence of creative writing. With the mechanics of writing no longer consuming the majority of mental energy, students can once again engage in imaginative thinking, and creative expression becomes more colorful as elaborative skills expand and become more fluent.

However, at the same time that ideational content is expanding and the mechanics of writing are becoming more automatic, the increasing complexity of language use also calls for more sophistication in capitalization, punctuation, word usage, and spelling. Furthermore, students are expected to apply the skills without direction, thus placing substantial demands on attention to detail, self-monitoring, and proofreading ability.

During this stage, many students discover that a word processor facilitates organizing and reorganizing the sequential order of their thoughts in addition to providing checks on spelling and grammar. Processes of rewriting become methods of rethinking, and students use writing as a method of problem solving that helps them explore their own thought processes. They do not yet use writing as a true means of discovery, but as a method of extending or extrapolating ideas. Writers at this stage, as in the Incorporation stage, may not be aware of what they will express until they see it in writing.

Stage 6: Personalization-Diversification (ninth grade and beyond)

The stage of Personalization-Diversification is probably the most variable. This is a time when adolescents develop individualized writing styles and talents. In some cases, this stage may overlap earlier ones. Some writers begin to display distinctive writing styles in the middle of elementary school, while others never really acquire this differentiation.

Students with highly stylized writing use personal expression as a means of discovery or exploration of themselves and their feelings. They may become increasingly creative, in some cases producing poetry, short stories, or plays. Experimentation in a diary may be one means of developing such personalized writing. Diversification should accompany personalization. Students start to vary their writing styles for specific purposes (letter writing, book reports, and love notes, or even to accommodate the perceived tastes of different teachers).

Language use becomes increasingly less stereotyped during the Personalization-Diversification period. During earlier stages, the complexity and length of sentences increased progressively. During this stage, good writers shorten sentence length and vary their use of syntax, ensuring that any particular paragraph contains a mix of simple, compound, and complex sentences. Word selection becomes more deliberate. During the preceding stage, as we have seen, writing surpassed the complexity of everyday speech. During this stage, writers may sometimes revert to more simple, declarative, speechlike writing. They are also likely to experiment with writing. Students begin to play with words and create their own figures of speech. Students become more adept at varying their writing style as appropriate for the purpose of their writing. Those who enjoy writing tend to explore a range of modes of written expression and display considerable creativity, flexibility, and individualization in writing style.

Students who are averse to writing or who find such output unrewarding or too difficult may never reach the stage of Personalization-Diversification. Late in high school, they may still be struggling to achieve proficiency on the Automatization and Elaboration levels. Others continue to develop their personalized and diversified writing throughout their academic careers and beyond. Such styles are heavily influenced by higher education, which may result in some sacrifice of originality and flexibility. Medical and law students, for example, are known to alter (and perhaps damage) their writing styles during training. Constant exposure to legal or scientific writing may result in increasing rigidity and specialization, a regression to the Elaboration stage. Even a personal letter from such an individual may reek of technical jargon. Experimentation and versatility in high school and the first years of college sometimes give way to a rigidity of style characteristic of the later phases of this final stage.

Some Implications of the Writing Stages

In considering stages of writing development, we must confront the dilemmas raised by any model of stages. One issue concerns the stepwise acquisition of skills. This model implies that certain abilities must be acquired and consolidated before a child can progress to more advanced stages of performance. For example, it is difficult to write about personal thoughts while struggling to recall the motor engrams of letter formation. We can think of writing stages partly as a process of progressive stratification. Layers of subskills must be established so that additional abilities can be effectively superimposed. Moreover, children are not readily able to add new layers to writing until they have developed certain functional capacities in nonwriting domains. Obviously children cannot use embedded phrases in writing before they have learned to interpret and use them in speech.

Many requisite acquisitions accrue independently of writing development. Therefore, we can ask whether stages occur only by stratification or also by the introduction of newly acquired abilities in the extra-writing world to the operations of writing. In fact, these two processes most likely combine to generate the writing stages. They interact in a most remarkable manner. While children are progressively automatizing various mechanical components of writing, they are independently growing in cognitive, language, motor, organization, and metacognitive skills, importing these recent acquisitions and superimposing them on appropriately incorporated and automatized writing subskills. Children who are having difficulty with a particular aspect of writing (such as punctuation) will find it harder to introduce recently acquired linguistic abilities and/or stimulating new concepts into their writing. On the other hand, as they effectively consolidate the demands of a particular stage, they become ready, even eager, for the page to become a showcase for their recent acquisitions.

DEVELOPMENTAL DYSFUNCTION

Since writing is a final common pathway of multiple developmental functions, we should be able to account for deficient writing in terms of developmental dysfunctions that impede automatization and reduce the ease and sophistication of writing. Indeed, all of the developmental functions make key contributions to the writing process, although their influence may vary from stage to stage. This section examines developmental functions and the effects of dysfunction on the development of written complexity, effectiveness, and fluency (see table 10-2).

Table 10-2. Developmental dysfunctions and their possible impacts on writing

DYSFUNCTION	POSSIBLE IMPACTS
Attention	Poor planning Uneven tempo Erratic legibility Inconsistent spelling and use of conventions Uneven memory flow Poor self-monitoring, careless errors Impersistence
Spatial production	Poor spatial planning of page Deficient visualization of words and letters Poor margination Organization problems Deficient (dyseidetic) spelling Uneven spacing between letters and words Poor use of lines
Sequential production	Slow learning of serial motor movements for letter forms and connected writing Letter transpositions and omissions in spelling Poor narrative sequencing Organization problems Lack of transitions and cohesive ties
Memory	Weak word retrieval Deficient spelling Fluctuating recall of motor engrams for letters Poor recall of rules (inadequate application of punctuation, capitalization, grammar) Dysfluent writing Poor legibility Preference for printing over cursive writing Loss of train of thought Deterioration of writing skills in continuous writing as compared with words and simple sentences
Language	Impoverished vocabulary Poor written expression Dysphonetic spelling Vague referencing Lack of cohesive ties Awkward phrasing and unconventional grammar Inappropriate use of colloquial language Inadequate narration Simplistic sentence structures and lack of variety
Higher-order cognition	Constricted, simplistic, concrete ideation Lack of development of ideas and descriptive elaboration Poor audience awareness Paucity of written output Weak opinion development
Graphomotor	Diminished amount of writing Slow writing Effortful writing (sometimes "eclipsing" other functions) Poor legibility Awkward pencil grip Lack of fluidity in cursive writing Preference for printing

Attention

Children with attention deficits are prone to writing difficulties. Their hand-writing problems have been thoroughly documented. Early studies of the effec-tiveness of stimulant medication produced dramatic visible improvement in the legibility of treated students' writing (Lerer, Lerer, and Artner 1977), yet the mechanisms through which attention deficits compromise legibility remain obscure. The interactions between attention deficits and disorders of writing have only recently begun to undergo rigorous study, but existing research (Lyon 1994) and clinical experience allow us to propose the following hypotheses:

- The tempo of these writers may lead to a frenetic writing rhythm, their high level of impulsiveness resulting in rapid, unplanned writing, which in this case may represent a faithful rendition of that child's life rhythms. Often, impulsive youngsters attempt to write faster than motor competence permits. In some instances, the rush of their thought processes causes them to accelerate the movement of the writing implement to keep pace. This may not be possible, resulting in poor legibility. When required to write slowly and with care or when given stimulant medication, such children may improve.

- Many children with attention deficits show erratic patterns of retrieval memory. They may be prone to uneven recall of the motor engrams of letters and words. Such uneven recall is reflected on paper. In this case, illegible writing can be thought of as a tracing of erratic memory, much as an EKG is a tracing of erratic heartbeats.

- Chapter 2 described reduced feedback reception in children with attention deficits; these girls and boys seem to have difficulty responding to feedback. Since writing is heavily dependent on ongoing proprioceptive and visual feed-back, children who are relatively impervious to such cues may show poor ongo-ing regulation of their motor movements during writing. Children with intact attention, on the other hand, may notice that letter formation is going astray—that they are crossing over lines or that they are about to write on the desk—and make the necessary corrections. Writers with attention problems are likely to be oblivious to feedback, and when they go astray, they fail to correct the error. In such cases, poor writing is a direct indicator of poor quality control or faulty feedback loops.

- Some students with attention deficits have difficulty dividing their concentration effectively. Writing requires consistent attention to detail. While putting ideas on paper, writers must divide their attention among thought processes, language, recall of rules, and organization. Attention to such well-synchronized details may be too taxing for children with attention deficits, especially if the various targets of attention must withstand competition from irrelevant visual stimuli, background sounds, or daydreams. Because such children may be nearly random in allocating priorities to attention, their writing is unpredictable. Flawless sentences may be interspersed with incomplete, poorly punctuated, or barely legible sentences.

- Many children with attention problems have difficulty with lengthy writing. When they have to write several paragraphs, legibility, application of rules, spelling, and content steadily deteriorate, a manifestation of early burnout. The progressively declining quality indicates impersistence or difficulty sustaining effort and alertness.

- As we know, some students with attention deficits also have other associated dysfunctions, which may make one portion of a task especially difficult for them. For example, youngsters with language weaknesses may need to work so hard to find precise words (see subsequent "Memory" section) that they exhaust their already limited attention. In such instances, low-quality writing indicates reduced capacity for attention that is also being unduly taxed.

- All of the production controls (chapter 2) are involved in written output. Children in whom one or more of these controls are out of control are susceptible to serious writing difficulty.

Children with attention deficits are likely to exhibit any or all of the writing problems just described. As these children reach the upper elementary grades and the stages requiring complex integration of multiple functions in writing, it is not surprising to find that they often receive worsening grades. Some are able to keep up in the primary grades despite problems with concentration. However, the requirements for amalgamating multiple processes during writing, for greater ideational sophistication, planning, and organization, for increased volume requiring sustained effort, and for greater attention to detail and ongoing feedback often lead to difficulties.

Spatial and Sequential Ordering and Production

The appreciation of chunks of data and their order is relevant for the production of information as well as for its processing. Chapter 4 dealt with issues of spatial and sequential ordering. Each makes such a significant contribution to writing that children with difficulty in one of these two areas are apt to falter in writing.

Spatial Production.   An awareness of gestalt and spatial arrangement is helpful, especially during the stage of Graphic Presentation when, as we have noted, children are particularly concerned with the appearance of numbers, letters, and words as displays on a page. This awareness is also crucial during the Progressive Incorporation stage, when substantial attention is directed toward spacing, left-right progression, margination, cursive letter formation, and specialized writing formats (such as those for letters and conventions for name and date placement). Students are challenged by the need to use the writing surface effectively and to practice the skills of paragraphing and planning the use of space on a page, for which they must visualize the arrangement of materials. Spatial organization also is critical as students progress through the stages of Automatization and Elaboration and are introduced to outlining and semantic mapping for purposes of planning and organizing written content. Finally, in the Personalization-Diversification stage, writers have to gain proficiency in new spatial arrangements as dictated by writing conventions for research reports, i.e., footnotes and bibliographies. Writing poetry also requires appreciation of the spatial arrangement of lines and verse formats. Writers using word processing and diagrams are challenged by the need to foresee how various layouts can enhance reporting of information.

Spatial production problems, especially visual-spatial confusions, may give rise to difficulty organizing material on the page, making good use of space, and monitoring letter size. Weaknesses of visual memory and visual feedback may introduce complications, sometimes making it hard for the writer to distinguish between what looks good and what is in disarray. Some students with spatial difficulties have trouble visualizing the configurations of words and letters. This may have an adverse impact on letter formations in the early grades, retard the transition from printing to cursive writing, and compromise spelling. Weak spatial appreciation also has the potential to impede effective proofreading.

Sequential Production. Students with difficulties of sequential organization commonly experience problems with writing. There may be a correlation between poor sequencing and the early motor-sequential organization needed to carry out the serial chains of motor movements to form letters (see chapter 6). Sequencing problems can interfere with spelling, causing poor recall of letter order and syllabication. In addition, children with sequencing problems may display poor sentence construction and awkward phrasing and syntax. Their efforts at story writing may show disorganization in the sequence of events.

Sequential disorganization in later stages (4, 5, and 6) creates problems with the narrative flow of an essay when there is no plot structure to guide the order of ideas. Children with this difficulty may be poor at using cohesive ties that denote temporal order (e.g., *first, second, finally, afterward,* and *subsequently*). A writer may have difficulty knowing where to begin, what the first sentence ought to be, what ideas should be presented in the middle, and what conclusion should be made. This threat worsens in the later stages of writing development. Beginning with the stage of Progressive Incorporation and continuing thereafter, the demand grows for effective sequential synthesis of words and ideas on paper. Students with deficient sequential organization may be challenged by tasks that require several serial steps. They may have difficulty creating outlines, writing drafts, and completing writing projects and reports on time since they lack a sense of the temporal staging of long-term assignments. In some instances, these problems are so severe that a student never really reaches the stages of Elaboration and Personalization-Diversification. Poor sequential organization can interfere with automatization to such an extent that writing may not be available as a medium for logical thinking or extrapolation.

Memory

As discussed in chapters 3 and 6, writing demands smoothly synchronized rapid retrieval memory. Memory difficulties can be an obstacle, especially during the Automatization stage. The child is expected to visualize words for their correct spelling, access the phonological code to associate sounds with written words, recall rules (of punctuation, capitalization, grammar, and spelling), all the while remembering the motor engrams for letter formation. Children who are slow or imprecise with retrieval memory may falter when expected to synchronize these spatial demands. If certain components of memory are relatively weak, a widespread systems breakdown can ensue. One or more of the following retrieval memory processes may impede production:

- *Phonologic memory*—memory for grapheme-phoneme associations

- *Visualization*—memory for the appearance of letters, letter patterns, and words

- *Retrieval of words*—precise naming; mobilization of specific vocabulary

- *Semantic memory*—recall of ideas or facts

- *Passage memory*—serial flow of ideas from what was written earlier in the passage to what will follow

- *Recall of rules*—retrieval and rapid application of the mechanics of writing (e.g., capitalization, punctuation, grammar, and spelling)

- *Motor memory*—recall of motor engrams for letter formation

In addition to these retrieval processes, writing also demands sufficient active working memory. To write effectively, students must remember and think at the same time. They have to ensure that the multiple components of writing cohere. While thinking of the proper punctuation or capitalization for a sentence, students must sustain the narrative flow. Those who experience difficulty with active working memory during writing may keep forgetting what they intended to record. This results in disorganization, in ideational chaos. Some are able to spell single words accurately in a list, but when they compose a paragraph or report, they misspell those very words. Often this occurs because they cannot maintain the multiple memory processes all at once in active working memory. While trying to recall how to punctuate or how to form letters, they lose track of spelling or some other component of the writing process. During earlier stages of writing development they may reverse letters because they cannot recall directionality at the same time that they try to remember spelling or motor engrams for letter forms.

The memory demands of writing must be integrated with other demands, such as motor implementation, language encoding, and reasoning. Figure 10-1 illustrates this process as a working space. Children are expected to retrieve multiple facts, rules, and skills in a synchronized manner during writing. At the same time, they must remember recently presented data (such as the instructions from the teacher

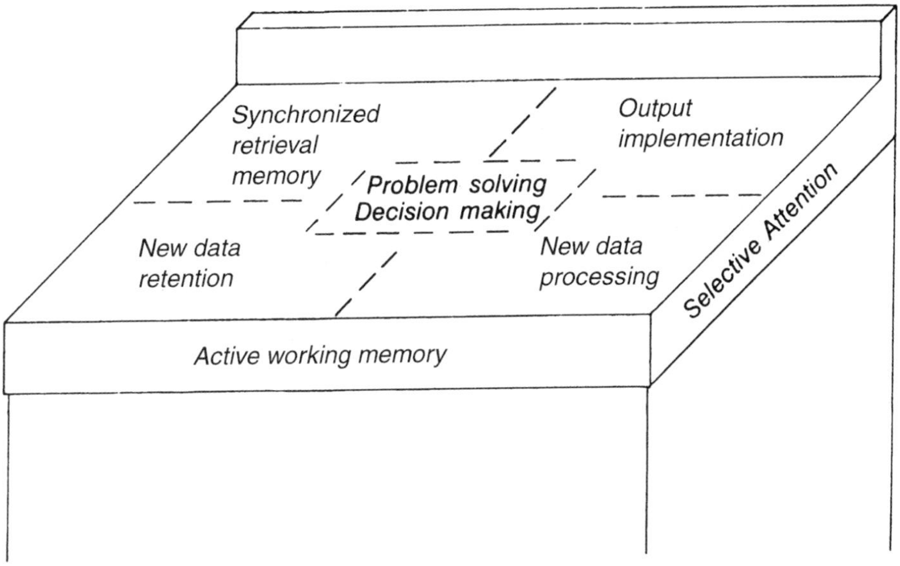

Synchronized
retrieval
memory

Problem solving
Decision making

Output
implementation

New data
retention

New data
processing

Selective Attention

Active working memory

WORKING SPACE EXPANDERS

1. Automatization
2. Strategy employment
3. Checks and balances
4. Staging

WORKING SPACE CONSTRICTORS

1. Anxiety, preoccupation
2. Time and rate factors
3. Dysfunctional component(s)

Figure 10-1. Cognitive working space

This diagram represents the need to maintain multiple developmental functions in spatial operation during academic tasks such as writing. This process is analogous to having limited space upon which to work (such as when cooking). The various operations of memory, processing, problem solving, and motor implementation must all be actively sustained in a coordinated manner. If one of these operations requires too much effort or time, the working space is constricted; a child's working capacity is thereby diminished, and there is a danger that one or more operations will be lost or decline in quality.

regarding what was to be written). Concurrently, they must engage in creative thinking, active reasoning, or problem solving in order to express sufficiently sophisticated and well-developed ideas. Spatially, they must evolve and implement a motor plan. Both attention and active working memory are needed to maintain these multiple contributions to the writing process. Children whose active working memory or attention is weak to begin with may not have adequate working space. Anxiety or preoccupation, a dysfunction in one or more production components (such as graphomotor function), or a particularly slow or rapid rate of ideation can constrict the working space. On the other hand, the employment of effective planning and strategies, the automatization of one or more functions, and a high level of motivation can expand the available space. The conceptual model can be helpful in understanding why some children have difficulties integrating the various components of writing. The model is also applicable to other subject areas, such as mathematics.

Language

Writing is considered the highest form of language. As writing becomes more automatic, written language becomes more complex than everyday speech. Those who suffer from language disabilities are at a disadvantage when striving to express ideas on paper (Israel 1984). Some have word-finding problems (*dysphasias;* Wiig and Semel 1984) that cause trouble locating the vocabulary needed at a particular place in a sentence. This is especially true when precise words are required, when there is little vocabulary leeway.

Students whose understanding and use of syntax are underdeveloped may also experience a significant delay in writing (Gerber 1993, Morris and Crump 1982). They have problems constructing sentences, using clauses effectively, punctuating, and keeping up with the grammatical complications that accompany the demand for the production of increasingly complex syntax. The clarity of their meaning may be clouded by lack of or vagueness in reference between nouns and pronouns. Children whose metalinguistic awareness is underdeveloped have trouble monitoring what they write. They have a weak sense of the efficacy of their own written communication, a serious breakdown in feedback. As they read what they have written, they may not be particularly aware that it is primitive, ungrammatical, or imprecise. They may be unable to alter their writing styles to fit the demands of the occasion or to express a particular viewpoint in writing. Their writing may be concrete, rigid, and frequently inappropriate for the task at hand.

Students who are deficient in language pragmatics may have trouble discerning the needs of the specific audience for whom they are writing. Such awareness increases significantly in importance during the stage of Automatization (grades six and seven) and thereafter. Poor verbal pragmatics may make it hard for a writer to express thoughts effectively to a particular audience, such as a teacher or a parent. Finally, children with language disabilities may have a limited or immature vocabulary as well as a diminished awareness of morphology (word endings and prefixes). Writing samples of older children, especially, may offer strong evidence of underlying linguistic deficiencies (Cicci 1980).

Higher-Order Cognition

Children with difficulties of higher-order cognition may experience problems using writing as an effective medium for developing ideas. Logical writing and the use of discourse to present an argument or point of view elude them. Their writing is likely to be devoid of sophisticated ideas, abstract language, persuasive content, and supportive detail. Yet many students who experience difficulty with the cognitive aspects of writing may be strong in their nonverbal cognition. That is, in pursuing challenges that are less linguistically laden (such as graphic art and mechanical design), these students may be keenly logical and capable of complex abstract thought. In addition, some students may lack the sound cognitive schema needed to elaborate on a particular subject in writing.

The act of writing can be an important means of problem solving and of mastering new concepts. Adept writers can work through various ideas while producing creative or expository discourse. In other words, writing can be used as a medium for reasoning. As students arrange ideas in an appropriate argument or narrative flow, a logical process occurs, and they are likely to gain insights that were not previously available. Myers (1984) observes that "when doing this simple activity (writing), students will be forced to relate information from the lecture to what they already know and to organize and synthesize it so that the concept becomes their own" (p. 23). Many children with higher-order cognitive weaknesses have difficulty reasoning and writing at the same time. Their writing lacks richness and stylistic variation. Efforts at conceptualization are so strenuous that the added burden of writing exceeds their overall capacities. Yet, these students could ultimately benefit from using writing as a facilitator of higher-order cognition. By recording, rereading, revising, and shaping their explanations or arguments, such children could enhance the quality of their reasoning or development of concepts. Nevertheless, students with higher-order cognitive impairments have a tendency to write concretely, without reference to abstract concepts, generalization beyond specifics, or use of symbolism. They often have trouble presenting a coherent argument or a logical flow of ideas in a report. Their writing reads like a list of unintegrated facts or details.

Graphomotor Function

Chapter 6 described various forms of graphomotor dysfunction in terms of their impacts on writing. Difficulties with eye-hand coordination, motor planning *(dyspraxia),* motor memory, and proprioceptive and kinesthetic feedback *(finger agnosia)* have all been shown to compromise the ease of writing production (Levine 1984b).

Assessment

Inadequate writing skills devastate many students with learning disorders (Deno, Marston, and Mirkin 1982). Their brief paragraphs are conspicuous markers of underachievement. Moreover, those able to read well who have problems with writing may be victims of misunderstanding in school, especially at the secondary level. Accusations of laziness, poor motivation, and a reprehensible attitude are often directed toward deficient writers. The result can be a serious loss of incentive—a generalized academic disenchantment and demoralization. Therefore, children with writing problems must receive evaluations at least as meticulous and thoughtful as those of children with reading problems (Poplin 1983).

First (and of paramount importance), *observe* the student during the act of writing. Use age- and grade-appropriate stimuli to elicit writing samples. Include in the assessment alphabet production, copying, spelling, and writing sentences from dictation. For children from third grade onward, evaluate cursive writing skills. In addition, having a student write a paragraph on a subject that affords some thematic latitude can give insight into his ideational fluency, narrative organization, knowledge of rules of mechanics, and capacity for spatial thinking and writing. Elementary schoolchildren might write about a recent movie, a television program, or a trip. At the middle and secondary school levels, ask students to write on a topic that involves some argument, expression of a point of view, or other form of expository composition. In addition, require secondary school students to write a summary of a passage or chapter. Prod the students to write a paragraph of some length and encourage them to use cursive writing—unless cursive script is too taxing and therefore likely to obliterate other functions. Making observations *while* students are writing will likely yield the most useful findings for diagnosis and management. Figures 10-2 through 10-10 show a range of writing samples obtained from children being evaluated for academic difficulties.

The following questions can guide observation of writing:

Affect

Overall affect and facial expression during writing can be revealing. Does the child become notably apprehensive when asked to write? Does he or she comment negatively on the task? Is there any sign of enthusiasm or interest? Is there a change in affect with different types of writing tasks?

Attention and Self-Monitoring

During the act of writing it is interesting to observe attention. Is the student fidgety? Are there signs of distractibility? Does the student self-monitor while working? Do abundant careless errors suggest poor quality control? Is the deterioration in the quality of content, mechanics, and/or legibility suggestive of difficulty sustaining mental energy? Does the child ever review what has been produced? The volume of output is often revealing. Does the child tend to be too brief, clearly striving to write as little as possible? At the completion of a writing assignment, have the student appraise the work. This may be evident in facial expression, but it is also useful to ask the writer whether the paragraph sounds and looks good. Have the student read the paragraph aloud to see if he or she can detect any errors.

Graphomotor Facility

First, evaluate the child's pencil grip. Is she or he using the normal tripod grasp? Or is there a tendency to use one or more of the maladroit pencil grasps (see figure 6-3) suggesting finger agnosia or other forms of tenuous pencil control? How far are the eyes from the page? Is posture awkward? While the older child writes, do associated mouth movements suggest neurological immaturity? Is the child's writing speed fast enough to keep pace with his thinking or with academic demands? Is the motor rhythm smooth or dysfluent? Does the child stabilize the paper with the nonwriting hand?

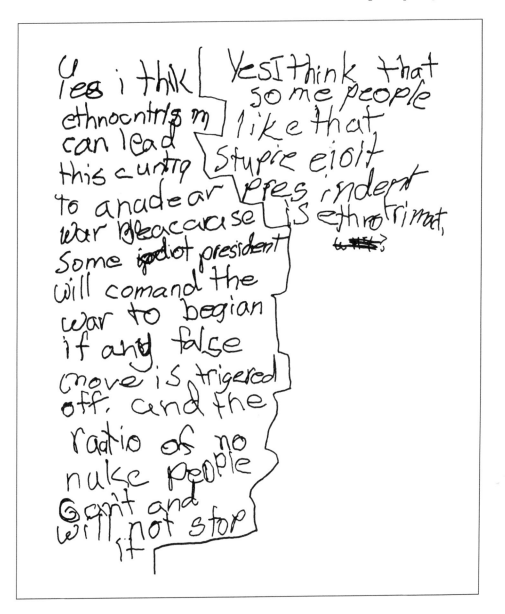

Figure 10-2. Writing sample

The writing sample is that of a thirteen-year-old seventh grade student who, despite being considered highly intelligent and verbal, has performed very poorly in mathematics, English, and social studies. An evaluation found problems with motor memory as well as more generalized difficulties with rapid convergent retrieval. This student also had a strong history of attention difficulties. The paragraph reveals problems with visualization, recall of letter forms, self-monitoring, planning, and the application of mechanics. The author intended to state: "Yes I think ethnocentrism can lead this country to another war because some idiot president will command war to begin if any false move is triggered off. And the nation of no nuke people can't and will not stop it yes I think some people like that stupid idiot president's enthnocentrism."

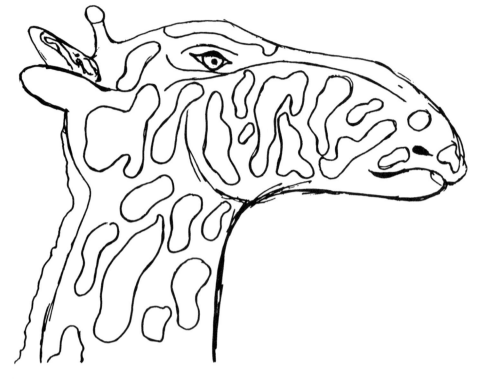

Figure 10-3. Child's drawing

The drawing was created by the same student who wrote the passage in Figure 10-2. Originally thought to have pervasive fine motor weaknesses because of difficulties with writing, this student turned out to be an excellent artist whose works were on display prominently in school. When motor function was liberated from memory, performance was very strong.

When writing is awkward and hesitant, careful observation can identify the impediment(s). Does the child hesitate over letter formation, letter sequences, or at some other characteristic points? Does she or he hesitate within letters (possibly an indication of motor memory deficits)? Finally, assess legibility. Are letter forms consistent in their quality? Are they uniform in size and shape? Are there indications of inconsistent retrieval, such as retracings and crossing out? It is important to go beyond the mere characterization of a student's handwriting as "illegible" and try to describe in more detail what it is that makes it difficult to decipher. A clear description of the illegibility can suggest the source of a child's writing difficulty. Some impulsive students need to be asked specifically to write as slowly as possible as a way of gauging the effects of a frenetic work tempo on graphic appearance.

Planning and Organization

First, evaluate a sentence or paragraph for use of space. Does the writing run uphill or downhill? Are margins and other horizontal constraints maintained? How

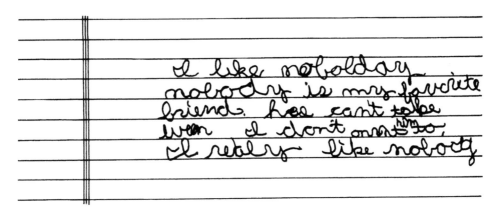

Figure 10-4. Writing sample

The writing sample was created by an eleven-year-old child with attention difficulties who displayed virtually no self-monitoring and created this passage with lightning speed and little attention to detail. The word *nobody* is formed and spelled three different ways in five lines! The sentiment expressed in this passage is consistent with this particular student's problems with socialization.

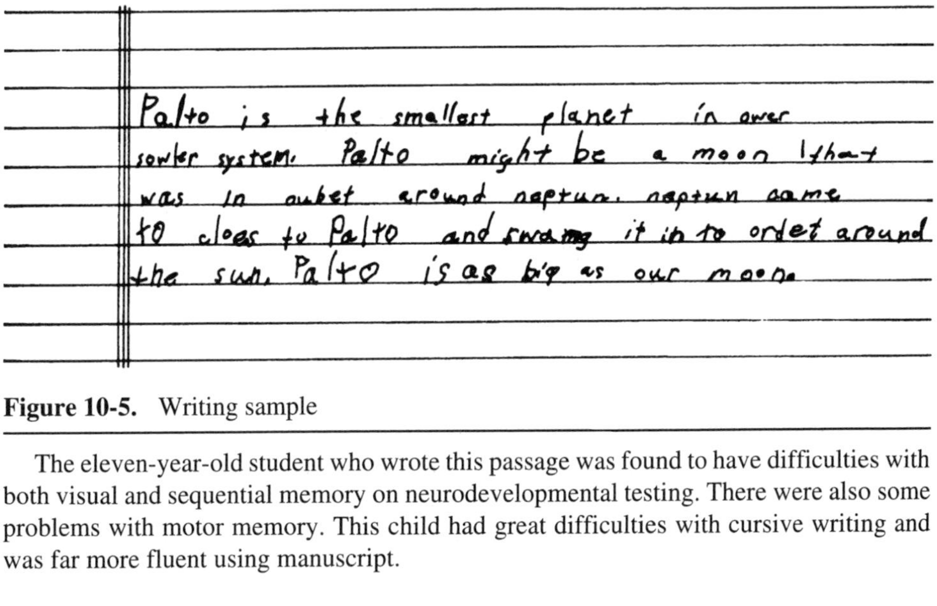

Figure 10-5. Writing sample

The eleven-year-old student who wrote this passage was found to have difficulties with both visual and sequential memory on neurodevelopmental testing. There were also some problems with motor memory. This child had great difficulties with cursive writing and was far more fluent using manuscript.

well does a child use spacing, especially to differentiate letters within a word from spaces between words? Difficulties with spacing suggest poor motor planning, commonly seen in students with dyspraxia. Such children may have real problems with allocation of space—in part because they are so overwhelmed with the demands of motor implementation. Writers with spatial production difficulties may also have trouble predicting appearances and thus organizing space on the

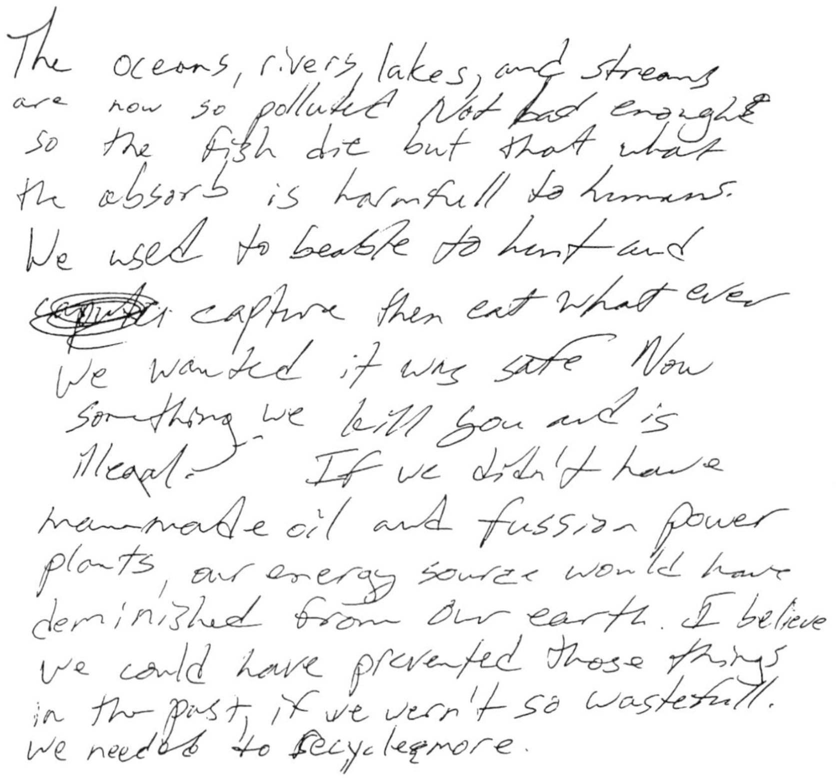

The oceans, rivers, lakes, and streams are now so polluted Not bad enoughe so the fish die but that what the absorb is harmfull to humans. We used to beable to hunt and capture then eat whatever We wanted if was safe Now Something we kill you and is illegal. If we didn't have manmade oil and fussion power plants, our energy source would have deminished from our earth. I believe we could have prevented those things in the past, if we vern't so wastefull. We needed to recycle more.

Figure 10-6a. Writing sample

This sample was obtained from a fifteen-year-old ninth grade student who, at age four-teen, was diagnosed with language difficulties. This paragraph, while revealing multiple errors in sentence structure and syntax, also gives evidence of graphomotor dysfunction.

page. Those with a high level of impulsiveness are apt to be inconsistent; they fail to allot time for planning and organization. Finally, is there an organizational scheme to the flow of ideas? Does the child do any prethinking before commencing to write? Does the child stop to reread while writing? Does the child seem to be able to sequence narrative effectively? Does he or she make effective use of cohesive ties to enhance the flow of ideas?

Memory

Writing strains retrieval memory. Therefore, the observation of writing is an exploration of retrieval memory processes. In particular, prolonged hesitations can be revealing. Does the child seem to be struggling to recall a particular element of the writing task? If so, is she or he hesitating over spelling, correct formation of letters, or mechanical rules? The dictated sentence can be especially useful for this. The child must recall appropriate vocabulary, syntax, and morphology in the sentence while retrieving spelling, punctuation, and letter forms.

THE IRAN-IRAQ WAR

I believe that this has been resolved in one way, and hasn't been resolved in another way. Yes in the way that they will no go to war again about the same issue. Iran and Iraq has to many other issues on there hand to worry about. And no in the sense that their will always be stubborn hatred between each other. It was a war that costed. Many lives died. Some will always have different opinions against this issue. Therefore there will never be a total agreement in which both countries have an "OK". But in regard to all of this, it has led to us still today fighting, on other issues.

Figure 10-6b. Language dysfunctions

This example was produced on a computer by the writer of 10-6a. Although use of the computer circumvented problems with respect to handwriting, it did not resolve the more serious language dysfunctions, especially at the sentence and discourse levels.

This can overload both retrieval and active working memory. A child whose memory is excessively burdened may make errors while writing sentences that do not occur when he is executing specific writing skills in isolation. The clearest example is a writer who has trouble spelling a particular word in a paragraph but who can spell the same word accurately during a conventional spelling test. Children who have difficulties with both spelling and legibility may be struggling with fundamental memory dysfunctions. This is especially the case when their spelling errors are mixed in type. Note the way in which a child copies a sentence. Does she or he recall phrases or groups of words or look back repeatedly at the original stimulus, copying one word or even a few letters at a time? The child's ability to hold entire phrases in memory during copying reflects, in part, reading ability and in part, memory. Examination of the flow of ideas in a paragraph and sentence cohesiveness can provide insights into active working memory. Does the child forget what he means to say as he writes? Are there omissions or contradictions? These often characterize the writing of children with restricted working memory space.

Language

A sentence a child writes from dictation directly reflects the child's awareness of syntax and word order. Retrieving a sentence is much easier when its grammatical construction seems right to the listener. Children with a poor understanding of syntax, particularly those with language disabilities, may have trouble recalling an intact complex sentence. As the child is writing from memory, therefore, look for an appreciable deterioration in syntax. Are there omissions of key conjunctions? Does the student insert superfluous words? Has she

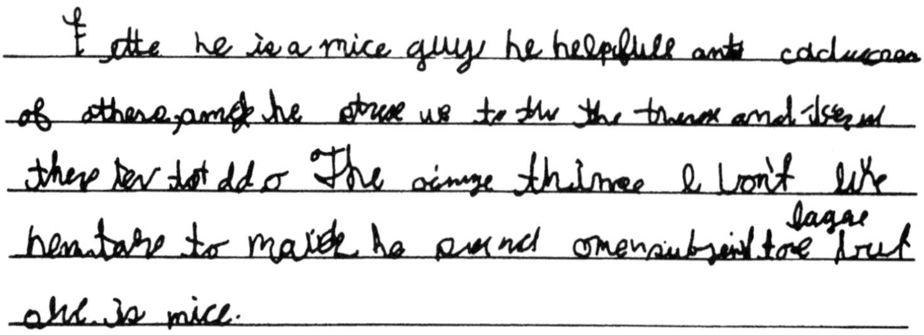

Figure 10-7. Writing sample

This paragraph was created by an eleven-and-a-half-year-old student who was found to have difficulties with the various components of simultaneous retrieval memory needed to create passages. Spelling in isolation was quite good; however, when required to spell, punctuate, use grammar, and come up with appropriate ideas, the multiple demands on memory appeared to exceed his capacity. When asked to read the paragraph, the student gave the following rendition: "Ethan, he is a nice guy. He is helpful and considerate of others, and he stands up to the teachers when they tell him something to do. The only think I don't like that he talks too much and he stays on one subject too long."

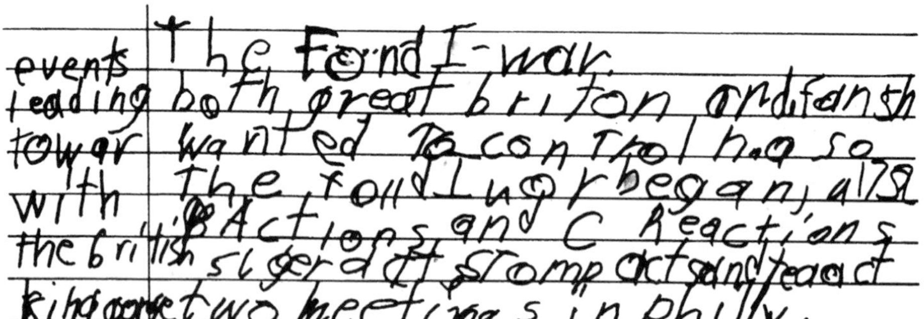

Figure 10-8. Writing sample

This writing sample was submitted by a thirteen-year-old student with evidence of a graphomotor dysfunction. This child also had some articulation problems, reflecting possible oral motor difficulties, a common concomitant of graphomotor weakness. The writing suggests real problems with motor planning as well as with spatial utilization of the page.

altered the meaning of the sentence? Has she produced a simplified version? Does the child preserve elements of morphology such as word endings, prefixes, and tenses? Does she substitute ungrammatical forms? A child who has had difficulty with vocabulary, morphology, or syntax may have inadvertently modified the meaning of the sentence. Any of these findings may suggest language weakness. Comparing a sentence written from dictation with one formulated by the child may help differentiate between memory difficulties and language deficiencies.

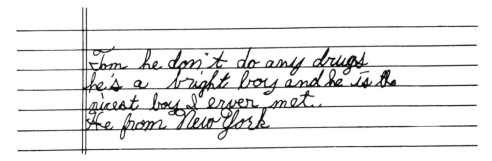

Figure 10-9. Writing sample

This writing sample was taken from a fourteen year old who had been asked to generate a paragraph describing a really good friend. These four lines were produced after
excessive effort and inordinate time. This particular student was struggling academically
because of combined problems with language and higher cognition. The lack of sophistication in this sample reflects such problems.

Figure 10-10. Writing sample

This sample was written by a ten-and-a-half-year-old fourth grader who had been
asked to write about a favorite movie. The paragraph is deciphered as follows: "Capri-
corn #1-they were going to Mars. Then coming home made the life support system for
them was made wrong! A guy pulled them out of the cockpit (T-30). They took them out
in the middle of nowhere!" This student had known language disabilities and particular
problems with phonology. Observe the frequency of preconventional (invented) spellings
in which the names of the letters substitute for their true phonology (as in *m-r-s-s* for
Mars and *t-h-m* for *them*).

Employ the child's paragraph to assess fluent use of language. Do sentences
contain conjunctions and subordinate clauses at a level appropriate to the child's
presumed stage of language and writing, or are they conspicuously choppy, abbreviated, and simple? Is vocabulary sophisticated or simplistic and redundant? To
what extent is there a significant gap between the child's own cognitive ability and
the quality of what appears on paper? Does the child hesitate inordinately over the

right vocabulary to express ideas? Are certain words misused? Are the vocabulary and style of writing sufficiently formal or appropriate for the purpose of writing and intended audience?

Scoring systems have been developed to assess the linguistic sophistication of writing (Morris and Crump 1982). Such parameters as "T-units" (a main clause plus any subordinate clauses attached to it), and counts of the total number of words produced or number of words of seven or more letters have been used as measures of writing. These methods have their limitations because paucity of output does not necessarily suggest a language problem. For example, a writer may write little due to limited knowledge about the topic or because the motor demands, the memory strain, or the stress on sustained attention exceeds his or her capacity. Furthermore, the number of letters in a word does not necessarily indicate level of sophistication; consider the examples *chaos, alien,* and *cohort,* none of which contain seven letters, versus *stopping, animals,* and *helping.* In addition, many of the tools used to evaluate written language skills provide a set stimulus and have time limitations, both of which can constrict writing productivity and ideational fluency. Diagnosing a language-based writing disorder requires some additional documentation of a general antecedent problem with verbal processing, memory, and/or production.

Table 10-3 outlines the basic parameters of written language assessment.

Diagnostic Instruments

Until recently, there have been few standardized measures of writing ability. However, with the growth of concern about deficiencies in students' writing abilities (see Hooper et. al 1994, in Lyon 1994), some measure of written language skills in addition to spelling is now included in many of the most widely used standardized tests of academic achievement, both group and individual. The formats for sampling and the scoring criteria vary, however, and suffer from many of the limitations described in the previous section. Nevertheless, there has been a growing trend toward assessing writing skills within the context of composition rather than in isolation. The *Wechsler Individual Achievement Test* (1992), for example, evaluates ideation, vocabulary, syntax, capitalization/punctuation, spelling, and organization within the framework of a composition written in response to a verbal prompt.

There has also been an increase in the number of tests designed solely for the purpose of evaluating writing skills. The *Picture Story Language Test* (Myklebust 1965), one of the first tests developed exclusively to measure written expression, samples writing by asking the child to compose a story in response to a picture stimulus. The writing sample is scored for syntax, level of abstract thinking, and production fluency (number of words, number of sentences, and sentence length). The *Test of Written Language* (Hammill and Larsen 1996), now in its third revision, contains several subtests that tap separate writing subskills (vocabulary, syntax, grammar, capitalization, punctuation, and spelling)

Table 10-3. Basic parameters of written language assessment

SKILL	COMPONENTS
Handwriting (manuscript/cursive)	Pencil grasp, pressure, and control Automatic recall of letter formations Spatial appreciation Fluid connective strokes Rate Legibility
Sentence copying	Rate Legibility Accuracy Spatial organization Chunking strategies and recall Self-monitoring
Spelling	Visual retrieval of letter sequences Phoneme-grapheme appreciation Rule application Use of word knowledge Consistency Deterioration
Sentence dictation	Handwriting Spelling Application of conventions Semantic appreciation Recall of stimulus Spatial awareness Self-monitoring
Grammar and conventions	Word usage Capitalization Punctuation
Proofreading	Grammar and syntax Capitalization and punctuation Spelling Attention to detail Consistency
Composition: narrative and expository	Planning Ideation Elaboration Organization Cohesive ties Conventions Spelling Ease and fluency Legibility Proofreading
Note taking	Identification of main ideas and salient detail Graphic organization Rate Legibility

and assesses application of these skills in a composition written in response to a picture stimulus. While the format of the last version of the test remains essentially the same as the second, the scoring system has been changed to reflect a more qualitative rather than quantitative analysis. Meltzer (1986) incorporates a systematic observation of writing in the *Survey of Educational Skills*. This screening test of academic skills and subskills includes a series of subtests to evaluate writing fluency, sentence complexity, writing mechanics, accuracy of writing from dictation, and various abilities required for copying. The *Writing Process Test* (Warden and Hutchinson 1992) measures written language skills within the context of composition. The stimulus is a verbal prompt and involves presenting two opposing points of view, thus placing a greater challenge on higher-order cognition and organization. In addition, it includes the option for assessing revision skills and questionnaires to evaluate student knowledge of the writing process and self-evaluation of use of strategies and writing effectiveness.

Comparing results of such standardized batteries with samples of a student's writing from class assignments is especially important. Many children find it difficult to write on immediate command, in the presence of an examiner, or in response to a highly restricted stimulus. Lack of engagement in the subject or anxiety can substantially inhibit written production. Examination of a variety of writing samples from different content areas, including narrative and expository examples, may also reveal differences that are important in diagnosing the nature of writing problems. Several checklists have been developed as systematic guides for informal evaluation of children's writing skills (Hall 1988, Isaacson 1988, Poteet 1980, Weiner 1980). Asking students to evaluate writing samples can provide insight into their appreciation of what constitutes effective writing. In addition, clues from a child's home and school history can reveal useful information regarding the development of written language abilities.

Historical Clues

Probably the most telling bit of historical data is a report that a student hates to write. This loathing is often associated with a generalized distaste for school, especially in late elementary and junior high school grades. There is frequently a concomitant reluctance to complete homework assignments, or even denial that they exist. Using parents' reports, it is useful to compare a child's writing propensities with other manual skills. Does the inhibited writer perform well in artwork, mechanical repair tasks, or craft activities (such as sewing or building models)? A significant discrepancy in overall manual dexterity and the graphomotor elements of writing may suggest problems with finger localization, attention deficits, weaknesses of memory, or deficiencies of language.

The school can report whether a child's writing is highly inconsistent from day to day or week to week. Does writing improve significantly in highly motivating subjects? How do the child's writing rate and sophistication compare to those of classmates? Do timed tests present particular problems? Does the student appear to be overwhelmed by demands for a large amount of writing? Does she or he make more spelling errors in a paragraph than on a spelling test? A particularly interesting finding is a marked discrepancy in the quality of the child's language and cognitive production during class discussions and during writing tasks. A student whose ideational and verbal fluency are well developed but whose grapho-motor output is disappointing is likely to have one or more of the developmental dysfunctions described above. In this instance, the problem is likely to be at the level of motor skill, attention, and/or memory.

Often the student's own reports are helpful. Interviewing the student can provide helpful information about his or her knowledge about the writing process, use of strategies, interest in writing, and difficulties that may be impeding the ability to express ideas on paper effectively. The *Writing Process Test* (Warden and Hutchinson 1992) includes a student self-evaluation questionnaire. *The Writing Interview* (Levine 1994, appendix) is also a revealing tool.

Integrating Findings

Evidence about the nature of a child's writing proficiency or deficiency is abundant; direct observations, reviews of class work, and reports from parents, teachers, and students themselves indicate that certain common dysfunctions account for inadequate output. Bypass strategies and specific remedial techniques can be targeted to deal with them (see the following section on management). The direct evaluation of writing can be enriched by an assessment of neurodevelopmental status. By comparing a child's functional profile to accomplishments (or lack thereof) in writing, an evaluator can compose a valid picture of the relationship between productivity in writing and central nervous system function. The data can then be integrated with a series of other exogenous variables likely to influence writing. These include cultural factors, prior educational experience (both positive and negative), the child's own temperament and coping style, complicating emotional difficulties, and the student's proclivities toward discrete content areas.

MANAGEMENT

Schools have traditionally offered help to students with reading problems and other basic skill deficits. Remediation in writing, until recently, has focused on isolated mechanics, i.e., spelling, grammar, capitalization, punctuation, and use of paragraphs. Only recently has attention been given to alleviation of problems involving the writing process. Programs are increasingly emphasizing ideational content, planning, organization, and revision skills. Students who feel overwhelmed by writing demands may benefit from such interventions, which break down the writing process into a series of manageable steps. Moreover, in the classroom, adjustments are being introduced to reduce the stress imposed by demands for written output.

Bypass Strategies

Writing is frequently measured in terms of ability to transmit skills, knowledge, or ideas effectively on paper. Bypass strategies do not cure writing problems or counteract a diminished working capacity, but they may prevent serious emotional and motivational complications while waiting for the passage of time and more direct remediation to take hold. The following general guidelines can be implemented effectively and without cost in any regular classroom:

Shaping adult attitudes. Parents and teachers working with students who experience writing difficulties need to offer a nonaccusatory, positive approach to remediation. Terms such as *lazy* or *poorly motivated* are not helpful. Criticism in the presence of the peer group is especially lethal and unlikely to cure any student. Instead, a balance between understanding (on the part of the teacher and parents) and accountability (on the part of the student) is the key. A teacher may appropriately disclose to a student in private that "it looks as if your writing problems aren't improving very much. We need to come up with some ideas on how to help you." As is the case with other developmental dysfunctions, always view and discuss the problem as a circumstance that is not the child's fault and let him know that work on improvement will be a collaborative effort. On the other hand, hold the child accountable for *steady improvement*—with the support of the adults in his or her life. Such agreements presuppose that all involved have a good understanding of the underlying cause of the child's problems with writing.

Adjusting amount of writing. Reducing the amount of writing required of students with writing difficulties and then gradually increasing it is a helpful technique. For example, a teacher can arrange for a student's book report to be two well-written pages rather than the five pages required of the rest of the class. Such an arrangement must, of course, be kept private.

Allocating time. Many of those with writing problems require extra time to complete written examinations, reports, and other long-term assignments. Time and quantity are two interacting variables that can be calibrated to accommodate limitations.

Setting priorities. Many students with writing problems feel overwhelmed by the simultaneous demands on memory, motor function, language, and organization. Stressing one or two functions during an assignment but not expecting that all requirements be met can often help. Thus, for a particular written report, a student may be told not to bother very much about spelling or punctuation but to make organization, good ideas, and legibility a priority. A subsequent report can emphasize spelling and other mechanics. Establishing such priorities is especially important during late elementary and junior high school, when students are struggling to automatize writing.

Grading and feedback. Students with writing dysfunctions frequently become hopelessly discouraged, feeling inundated by negative reinforcement. They are often ashamed of their writing and come to dread the inevitability of devastating criticism, which can lead to a refusal to write due to feelings of desperation, futility, and the absence of incentives to be successful. To prevent this phenomenon, teachers need to consider some alternative systems for grading these students. Comments should be positive and based on incremental improvement. Give a student's report separate grades for ideas and for the mechanics of writing, or do grading in stages. Give a grade for content and then have the student rework his writing for mechanics. Allow an overwhelmed student more spelling errors and greater latitude with punctuation in the interest of preserving motivation and getting good ideas on paper. Furthermore, when expression of knowledge is the priority, as on tests, do not take off grades for misspellings or errors in grammar and other mechanics. In other words, it is critically important that these students not be permitted to fail consistently on writing tasks. It is incumbent on adults to break the cycle in which problems with writing lead to poor motivation and poor motivation further compromises writing. This can be done only by providing hope and delivering positive feedback.

Direct Intervention

Written expression is a multifaceted process, composed of several elements that must be integrated into a unified whole. Several models of the production components of written expression have been proposed (Hooper et al. 1994). Cohn and Isaacson (1984) identify the following: content and organization, fluency (the amount of writing), vocabulary, syntactic maturity, conventions, and spelling. To these might be added planning, revision, and proofreading. Handwriting or fine motor ability certainly contributes to the ease and productivity of writing, but management issues will be addressed in a separate section (see pp. 383–85).

Writers engaged in serious composition seldom, if ever, attempt to accomplish all production components simultaneously, but generally go through a series of stages in which they focus on one or two aspects of the writing process at a time and produce multiple drafts before arriving at a final product. It therefore seems obvious that all students would benefit from instruction and practice in the planning and multistage production of long-term writing assignments. Such assistance, however, is critical for students with writing difficulties. Problems with one or more production components may seriously compromise a student's writing efforts or be so overwhelming as to cause a total breakdown in his or her ability to express ideas on paper. Breaking writing assignments, particularly long-term projects, into a series of stages or steps can enable students to focus on one aspect of the writing process at a time.

Staging tasks. The broad stages of the writing process include:

- Selecting a topic, generating ideas, and data collection
- Planning what to say and ordering ideas and information
- Writing a draft
- Elaborating and revising
- Evaluating, revising, and editing
- Writing a final draft
- Rereading and proofreading

For example, to facilitate writing a book report, use the following steps:

1. Divide the book into discrete sections (perhaps chapters).
2. Read each chapter, underline the most important ideas, and write brief comments in the margins.
3. Reread the underlined sections and dictate the most important ones into a tape recorder.
4. Listen to all of the tape-recorded statements and write in your own words the most important ideas.
5. Review these ideas and arrange them in a logical order.
6. Create an outline using this order.
7. Write a first draft of a report in pencil, leaving plenty of space between lines. (This need be legible only to its author.)
8. Review the rough draft and make any corrections.
9. Write a second draft.
10. Revise the second draft using different colored pencils for each type of correction (e.g., red for spelling, blue for punctuation, and green for content).
11. Write a final draft and proofread it.

When giving instruction in the staging process, the teacher should explain and demonstrate each element, assign guided practice, and finally combine and apply the process in its entirety. Effective implementation of staging requires close cooperation between parents and teachers. The steps just listed should be scheduled with care; students should attempt only one or two on a single evening. Many variations are conceivable, but the basic idea is to teach students to reduce formidable tasks to manageable stages by planning, using time efficiently, taking breaks from work, and monitoring their work meticulously.

Using a word processor can facilitate many of the steps, either from the start or beginning at a later stage. Computers are especially helpful to students with memory-based writing problems. Most word-processing programs now have spelling and grammar-checking capability. Software programs that assist students in the planning, organizing, and outlining steps are also useful. There are also computers that can be activated by voice. Much depends on the age of the student and the extent to which the motor aspects and some of the memory strain of writing are to be bypassed permanently.

Content (Ideas and Fluency)

Some students, when presented with a writing assignment, appear to develop thought paralysis. They are totally unable to come up with any ideas at all or, if they do locate a main idea, they are unable to expand on it or provide supportive or descriptive detail. Their writing tends to be abbreviated and terse. For such students, the following suggestions may be helpful.

- Brainstorming activities can help increase ideational fluency. Group brainstorming which involves sharing of ideas is often especially productive.

- Teacher-directed activities to activate background knowledge can enhance thought generation.

- Some students may benefit from structured guidelines for thinking about the various subject matter elements in their writing, i.e., characters (appearance and feelings), setting (time and geography), place (climate, government, economy, culture), and events (what happened, what was the cause, sequence, conclusion, far-reaching results).

- Have students write about topics of particular personal interest to help stimulate more general ideational fluency.

- Group or paired writing projects in which students share thoughts can enhance the flow of ideas and suggest new avenues to pursue.

- Many students do not know where or how to look up information. They may benefit from practice in locating and using resource materials. This may include guidance in using cataloging systems and navigating one's way around a library.

Organization

The effectiveness and clarity of written expression is frequently compromised by poor organization of ideas and/or lack of cohesion. This is especially true for students with poor planning skills, attention problems, and weakness in active working memory. Students may write ideas as they occur without any general plan, or may forget what they have written as they become engrossed in the next thought. Instruction in organization strategies can be helpful.

• Ask students to develop a plan of what they want to say before engaging in writing. This might include forming a general outline of main sections and major elements.

• Preliminary semantic mapping, whereby students categorize ideas and generate a diagram showing how the categories relate, may help in formulating an organization plan (see figure 10-11). A time line is another type of semantic map.

• There are computer software programs designed to assist with outlining and organizing information for writing projects, both narrative and expository.

• Some students, especially those in the elementary grades, benefit from a standardized format for thinking about and organizing writing. An example is: Who/What/When/Where/How/Why. This same format can be used for taking notes and collecting data.

• Once they have made a general plan, ask students to make a more detailed outline of paragraphs to include in each section. This might include a topic sentence and two or three supporting details.

• To improve cohesiveness, give students a list of transition words and practice exercises in using these words to unite sentences and paragraphs. Examples of such words include: *previously, afterward, thenceforth, finally,* and *furthermore.*

Vocabulary

Students with retrieval memory and/or language problems may have difficulty locating words to express their thoughts. The effectiveness of their writing may

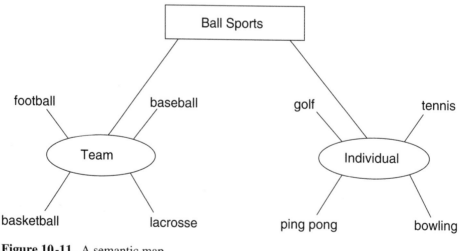

Figure 10-11. A semantic map

suffer from simplistic, repetitive vocabulary; lack of descriptors; and awkward circumlocutions.

- Emphasize instruction in vocabulary enrichment. This might include working with prefixes, suffixes, and root words. Challenge students to create as many words as possible using a selection of morphological elements.

- Ask students to brainstorm about a topic as another useful means of enhancing vocabulary.

- Encourage students to write down words that interest them or that they do not understand from their reading. Use their collections as the basis for group discussion.

- Have students keep a notebook of interesting words to which they can refer while writing, setting aside a section for synonyms and antonyms.

- Research has consistently shown that the amount of reading a child engages in is the most important contributor to vocabulary development. Encourage children to engage in free reading as often as possible, perhaps setting aside a regular time for this each day.

Syntactic Maturity

In the early elementary grades, it is normal for children to write in simple, direct sentence structures. However, as the ideational content of writing becomes more complex, simple sentence structures become increasingly inadequate to express ideas. Syntactic complexity, however, can lead to additional problems of grammatical construction. Vague use of pronouns without referents and errors of tense and agreement are some of the most common problems.

- Assign exercises in sentence combination to help students acquire skills in use of subordinate clauses, compound sentences, and cohesive ties.

- Ask students to diagram sentences to increase their understanding of syntax, use of pronouns, noun/verb/adjective agreement, and grammatical constructions. A good understanding of syntax, grammatical constructions, and agreement also is critical for success in learning a foreign language.

- Have students edit work samples to improve syntactic awareness.

- Assign rewriting exercises to develop more complexity in sentence constructions.

- Too often instruction in syntax involves learning a great deal of technical vocabulary, which has little meaning for most students and frequently results in language arts being the least favorite subject in middle school. The challenge is significantly magnified for students with memory problems. Emphasize the ability to generate and use constructions appropriately and to identify how words and sentence elements are related, rather than the technical vocabulary used to label specific constructions and parts of speech.

Conventions

Conventions usually refer to capitalization, punctuation, specialized formats (e.g., footnotes), and basic rules of grammar such as plurals, tense markers, and word usage (e.g., *who* vs. *whom*). As students become more adept at writing complex sentences, they also must master an increasing volume of rules governing writing conventions. For students with memory difficulties, weak syntactic appreciation, and attention problems, this can pose a monumental hurdle. Furthermore, all too frequently, the rules of conventions are taught singly and as isolated elements rather than as a method of enhancing meaning. For example, the meaning a writer intends to express can alter what punctuation is used.

- Have students read writing aloud to help them identify when punctuation is required. They may find it useful to read their written work onto a tape recorder and then play it back and insert punctuation. This is especially helpful in use of commas, question marks, and exclamations.

- Distribute to all students a checklist with examples which they can use to assist them in applying conventions and in proofreading.

- Assign exercises in correcting work samples (not their own) to increase students' ability to use conventions appropriately. Give them samples and challenge them to find a specified number of errors in punctuation, capitalization, and usage. Grade them according to the number they can locate and correct. This could be done in pairs or teams.

Reviewing and Revising

Reviewing and revising includes proofreading skills, evaluation, cognitive flexibility, language pragmatics, and metalinguistic awareness. These skills require focused attention, knowledge of one's purpose for communication, and appreciation of audience. The writer must have a clear idea of what she meant to say and for whom she wrote it, and then ask if she has expressed the ideas clearly and effectively according to the intent. It is often difficult for a writer to evaluate her own product, but especially problematic for students with writing problems.

- Enhance reviewing and revising skills by having students compare and critique writing samples.

- Students may find it helpful to have someone else read their work and give them feedback. This should be a person whom they feel comfortable having read their work and helping them, and not someone who is likely to be judgmental. The reader should be positive, encouraging, and offer useful advice; he should not simply criticize.

- Compare writing samples in a demonstration to enhance students' appreciation of effective written expression.

- Give students practice in rewriting material for a different audience to increase awareness of audience and expressive flexibility.

Spelling

Spelling, although part of written expression, involves multiple additional factors and will be treated in a separate section (see pp. 385–97).

Graphomotor Function

Students whose writing problems are related to graphomotor difficulties (chapter 6) can benefit from both bypass strategies and direct interventions. These can often be custom fitted to conform to a student's specific fine motor deficits and various compensatory strengths.

Bypass Strategies. Many techniques can be used to minimize the impact of graphomotor problems. Some suggestions are enumerated below:

- Typing can be helpful, especially for young writers with impaired finger localization and/or motor memory problems. The keyboard obviates the demand for total retrieval of letter forms, while it substitutes spatial and sequential automatized motor routines for precise finger localization. Many children with fine motor delays take much longer to learn to type than do their peers without such delays. Nevertheless, the benefits often justify the investment.

- Word processing can be the salvation of some students. While it can benefit those whose motor problems are helped by a keyboard, it can also compensate dramatically for organizational problems, poor use of space, problematic spelling, and a variety of contributing memory deficiencies. Word processing can enable students to produce written work that looks professional and that they can be proud to display. With both typing and word processing, however, some important decisions have to be made about the extent of their use and the timing of their introduction. It is not appropriate for such devices to substitute entirely for writing. Therefore, their exclusive use should probably be postponed until late in middle school. Nevertheless, they should be introduced in elementary school and gradually allowed to take over an increasing number of written assignments. This is especially helpful when problems with writing appear to be relatively resistant to treatment.

• Select appropriate implements for writing. In general, many youngsters with motor problems do quite poorly with ballpoint pens. They need utensils offering more tactile feedback during writing. They should use mechanical pencils with sharp but strong lead (usually about 0.9 millimeters in diameter). These students also seem to enjoy using a variety of writing instruments. They can use pens that provide some friction as well as various types of pencils in varying combinations at different times.

• Vary writing surfaces. Printing on graph paper sometimes helps with organization and spatial planning. Emphasizing the lines on paper, either visually or with tactile cues, can help make students more aware of size and line relationship. Use other kinds of surfaces also, giving students some opportunity to write on a chalkboard with big letters. Tracing letters in sand or with a stylus can strengthen motor engrams.

• At some point, it is necessary to make firm decisions about manuscript writing as opposed to cursive writing. Students with memory deficits often prefer printing to cursive writing. In elementary school, make a concerted effort to teach cursive writing, even if it is painful and arduous. However, allow students who are struggling inordinately and who much prefer to print to do so exclusively. In other words, they should automatize writing in the manuscript rather than the cursive modality. Some of these students may benefit from learning calligraphy or various modified forms of cursive script. This bypass strategy, it should be acknowledged, is not universally accepted.

• For students who have a variable or tenuous grip on the pen or pencil, an auxiliary rubber or plastic grip placed approximately three-quarters of an inch from the point can help strengthen motor control.

A variety of bypass strategies can be employed. As with other such techniques, the range of possibilities is limited only by the creativity of responsible adults.

Direct Intervention. Writing instruction in the early grades is highly variable, and often children are not taught to use a functional pencil grip or the motor sequences for forming letters. Children in the older elementary grades may still benefit from direct instruction in handwriting. A wide variety of specific handwriting programs for children exist. These can help with formation of letters, alignment, spacing, consistency, slant, and writing rate.

Some writers with maladroit pencil grasps benefit from retraining in how to hold a pencil. Any such effort should be made very slowly. Teach the appropriate tripod pencil grip (figure 10-12), requiring students to use this grip for only a few minutes a day initially. Increase the time during which the new grip is employed very slowly over a period of months. Furthermore, writing practice should not involve work which is to be graded for other purposes. Many students, although

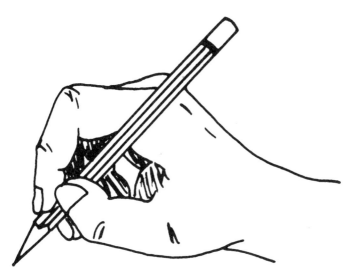

Figure 10-12. Appropriate tripod pencil grip

In a normal tripod grip, the thumb and middle finger effect most of the movement at their middle joints while the forefinger regulates the pressure. The pencil is held at a forty-five-degree angle to the page.

highly resistant at first, ultimately adopt the tripod grasp and are grateful because they can write faster and much more comfortably. Certain students, however, are never able to accommodate a more efficient pencil grip. After several months of effort, giving up is probably justified. However, all children with maladroit pencil grips deserve an opportunity for gradual retraining. The use of an auxiliary rubber grip often facilitates the process.

When fine motor problems are so severe that they cause day-to-day performance to lag significantly below capacity, occupational therapists can be valuable. These professionals intervene directly to try to enhance eye-hand coordination, motor praxis, and speed. Some occupational therapists are particularly adept at dealing with writing problems and can also help in assessment.

Spelling

Research suggests that spelling in English is inherently difficult; studies by Jastak and Wilkinson (1984) revealed that the average adult reaches only an eighth-grade spelling level. Spelling skills are also less responsive to intervention; individuals with decoding and spelling delays showed improved reading skills after appropriate intervention but tended to remain poor spellers (Moats 1994). The ability or inability to spell is not a major lifelong handicap. A person with isolated spelling difficulties is unlikely to experience career failure based solely on this deficiency. On the other hand, when spelling problems are part of a cluster of academic shortcomings, their impact is felt. Spelling is a "multifaceted linguistic skill that integrates and depends on phonological, morphological, semantic, and orthographic knowledge" (Moats 1994, p. 334). Analysis of patterns of spelling errors can indicate fundamental information-processing and memory deficiencies. Studying a child's spelling errors can help elucidate or explain lags in other areas such as reading, mathematics, or writing in general.

Decision Making in Spelling. Accurate spelling is an intriguing model of decision making. The good speller learns to seek clues from several sources to aid in spelling words correctly (Frith 1983). The following pages review the kinds of clues that inform spelling.

A fundamental clue system for spelling is grapheme-phoneme correspondence. Children become increasingly aware of the relationships between visual symbols and sounds. As this capacity develops, they are able to move swiftly in either direction—from sounds to symbols or from symbols to sounds. Auditory analysis enables them to dissect a word they hear into its component phonemes, an operation calling for metalinguistic awareness. Through phonetic analysis, children develop hypotheses about the ways a word *might* be spelled. However, they learn that English is not entirely phonetically reliable; spellings are only sometimes predictable from sounds. Irregular words are common. Therefore, they need other clues to verify or modify hypothesized phonetic spellings.

A solid knowledge of language provides another set of clues to aid in such verification (Chomsky 1970). Beyond the phonological database are other linguistic clues, including vocabulary and morphology. Familiarity with specific words and their uses can help spelling. Various morphological clues, derived from a knowledge of tenses, prefixes, and suffixes, are even more helpful. An understanding of syntax and the ways in which words might be spelled differently in different grammatical settings are closely related.

As children develop their spelling and cognitive abilities, they increasingly rely on an appreciation of what Chomsky (1970) has called the "deep structures" of language. Instead of focusing entirely on superficial characteristics of words (pronunciation and/or visual appearance), students can refer to more profound underlying relationships in language. Chomsky offers the following example of how good spellers use their deeper sense of relationships within language to help them spell accurately:

> When they are not sure how to spell a particular word, the first thing that they do is bring to mind other related words in the hope of finding one that contains the solution. If it is a reduced vowel that is causing the trouble, a differently stressed variant of the word will also provide the answer. For example, there is no way to guess the second vowel of *industry* from the pronunciation of the word, but thinking of *industrial* solves the problem. . . . After all, how *do* we know that the second vowel of *declaration, inspiration,* and *adoration* are written differently, when they are pronounced exactly alike? Obviously because of *declare, inspire,* and *adore.* . . . Once the connection is clear, the correct spelling is automatic. If the child develops the

habit of seeking such connections of thinking of related words that settle his spelling uncertainties for him, he not only spells better, but in the long run he familiarizes himself with the general underlying regularities of the orthography. Instead of memorizing individual words one after the other, he equips himself with the systematic means of dealing with large segments of vocabulary (Chomsky 1970, p. 303).

This process need not be entirely conscious. An internalized sense of how words relate to each other enhances decision making in spelling; a knowledge of common origins or families of words, such as *history, historical,* and *historian,* heightens awareness that in different contexts a root acquires phonetic variations that remain basically loyal to its lexical origins or meanings. Similar associations can be developed for words that retain their phonetic consistency despite the fact that they differ in meaning and display odd grapheme-phoneme correspondences (e.g., *brought, thought,* and *bought).* For adults, these processes are so automatic that they require little or no expenditure of effort. Spelling is substantially strengthened by thorough familiarity with consistencies of the native language.

Through use of these several systems of spelling clues, children can form a hypothesis about the relationship between the visual and phonetic characteristics of a word. They can determine whether this hypothesis fits their knowledge of the language in terms of tense and grammatical construction. They can decide whether this word is a member of a family of words that share deep structures or distinct visual configurations, such as *brought* and *thought* (as opposed to *brawt* and *thawt).*

Children's rote memories for the visual appearance of the desired word provide another clue. The speller has an opportunity to visualize the word. If this system is working optimally, other clues may play only a minimal role in spelling. However, children who have relatively weak visual retrieval memory for word configurations may be tentative, needing to refer more to grapheme-phoneme correspondences and various elements of linguistic awareness to verify a spelling hypothesis.

As with other academic skills, automaticity ultimately arrives. An increasingly large portion of written vocabulary becomes accessible quickly, accurately, and with little if any conscious effort, bypassing the aforementioned systems of clues. In this way, as soon as a word is selected or heard, it is rapidly associated with the proper spelling. This facilitates allocating attention and cognitive energy to other components of the task (such as ideation).

En route to automaticity, individuals may emphasize one form of spelling clue, depending in part on the ways they have been taught to read. Those who have been trained in a phonetic approach to reading may spell by relying on phonetics. Those who have been taught according to a whole-word reading method, one that stresses the processing of gestalts, may be much more inclined toward visualization at an early stage of spelling. Most of their spelling may take place by forming in the memory images of correctly spelled words, what sometimes are called *abstract sequences.* Finally, students who have been taught by linguistic reading methods that stress word families may prefer to spell linguistically. Many of them also make heavy use of spelling rules.

Spelling Development: Six Acquired Insights. It is difficult to document specific stages in the acquisition of spelling skills, since spelling is so dependent on reading ability and on specific instructional methods (Gerber 1993). Nevertheless, we can identify a series of insights that contribute to spelling development and are likely to vary in their importance to a developing speller. Children acquire these insights at different times with some possible variation in chronological order.

- *Preconventional spelling.* This is the spelling that emerges at about the time preschoolers are immersed in imitative writing, the time when the very existence of spelling becomes known. During this period, as we have noted, children are likely to invent spellings that appear bizarre to adults and yet frequently possess a logic of their own. For example, a child may substitute the name of a letter for its sound. The word *began* may be spelled *b-g-a-n*. Or *dresser* may be spelled *d-r-s-r* (Moats 1983). There are many other such primitive types of errors, including various omissions and substitutions that may or may not be phonetically defensible. These are common during the early stages of skill development, when the principal insight is the simple awareness that words are the end product of an encoding process.

- *Growing awareness of grapheme-phoneme relationships.* As children master the alphabet and begin to read, they become more sensitive to a logical system of phonetic equivalency. This can be detected even during preschool (Read 1971). By the end of second grade, most students can spell many words in a phonetically justifiable manner (e.g., *r-i-t-e* for *write*). Most errors they commit are logical when analyzed in terms of grapheme-phoneme correspondences.

- *Integration of language.* As language develops, it allows for greater awareness of morphology and syntax. This awareness can contribute to spelling proficiency. The various linguistic clues described in the previous section integrate and enhance the accuracy of spelling. Knowledge of morphological clues, such as word roots, the effects of syntax, a growing vocabulary, and metalinguistic awareness strengthen spelling abilities (Chomsky 1970).

- *Application of rules.* During elementary school, children deduce the rules that govern spelling. Some of these are self-taught. Others, such as "*i* before *e* except after *c*," may be acquired through formal teaching. The capacity to integrate these rules provides further decision-making guidance and introduces the potential for cross-referencing to establish correct spellings.

- *Enhanced visualization.* Good spellers become increasingly proficient at recalling the visual configurations of words of increasing length and complexity (Farnham-Diggory and Simon 1975). Visual sequential memory and spatial memory become important arbiters of spelling. Good visual recognition memory enables spellers to determine whether a printed word looks right, an important skill for monitoring one's own writing and for taking multiple-choice spelling tests. At a higher level, visual retrieval memory is the capacity to hear or think of a particular word and mobilize an accurate visual image of its spelling. That image contains a correct sequence and a proper overall configuration. An important difference between reading and spelling is that the latter requires full rather than partial visual association. The reader may scan just a few letters, view them in context, and come up with the proper pronunciation and meaning of a word. The speller must recall the entire word with little assistance from context clues, resulting in much more stress on visual memory in *adam's Report* spelling than in reading.

- *Automaticity.* The ultimate objective is to spell accurately while doing something else. Although we periodically encounter words whose spelling requires deliberate decision making and use of the clues discussed in the previous section, a growing storehouse of words is available for automatic retrieval. As noted, this liberates memory, attention, and cognition to engage in more sophisticated intellectual and creative enterprises.

Children vary considerably in the age at which any of the six insights for spelling development first occur and in the extent to which their spelling is influenced by them. For some young spellers, assimilation of language and rules may occur as parallel developments. Thus, the precise interactions of insights depend on a variety of other issues, including variables of curriculum and teaching, a child's own learning style, the presence of talent in spelling, and the existence of any developmental dysfunctions that impede the use and interpretation of the decision-making clues, a phenomenon explored in the next section.

Developmental Dysfunction and Spelling.

Poor spelling is a frequent concomitant of learning difficulty (Critchley 1975). In some cases, *dysorthographia* (spelling disability) exists as an isolated defect; in many instances it is part of a broader picture that includes reading and/or writing problems (Frith 1983).

Recent research has found that children's spelling errors may indicate discrete processing or memory deficiencies. Investigations carried out by Boder (1973) identified three types of disabled spellers. *Dyseidetic spellers* over-relied on a phonological encoding strategy (grapheme-phoneme correspondences) and, because they failed to make use of visualization, had trouble recalling what words looked like. In contrast, *dysphonetic spellers* were poor at coming up with a phonetic equivalent of an unknown word. Both groups often indicated similar propensities in reading. Dyseidetic children had a tendency to overrely on phonetics for either decoding or encoding. They might spell the word *light l-i-t-e*. Dysphonetic children preferred a more visual approach, spelling the word *light l-e-g-h-t*. Although the latter is visually similar to the correct spelling, it bears little phonetic approximation in English. The third group displayed a mixed pattern of spelling errors, both dyseidetic and dysphonetic. These children had the most severe problems and were least responsive to intervention.

Studies of the spelling error patterns of children with reading difficulties have suggested that most of these children commit errors that are predominantly phonetically correct. In fact, Moats (1983) found that the spelling errors of reading-disabled children in late elementary school were nearly identical to those of normal second graders. In other words, there were indications that students with poor reading ability simply had failed to acquire orthographic rules and visualization clues (and perhaps some other insights) to allow them to proceed beyond the level of grapheme-phoneme correspondences. More recently, however, the contribution of problems with phonological segmentation to spelling difficulties has come under investigation. Studies by Lindamood (1992, 1994) have shown that although individuals are usually successful in segmenting syllables of four phonemes, there is a sharp reduction in accuracy when five sounds are involved. This would have particular relevance in the spelling of multisyllable words.

Considerable research is still needed to elucidate the relationships between underlying developmental dysfunctions and patterns of spelling errors. The following section describes some current thinking on these interactions and their impacts.

Attention. As might be anticipated, children with attention deficits are likely to be as inconsistent in spelling as they are in other performance and behavioral areas. Their impulsiveness and lack of self-monitoring, their inattention to fine detail, and their fluctuations in retrieval memory can all combine to yield unpredictable spelling. Within a paragraph they might spell the same word several ways. Because of superficial attention to detail, a student's spelling may capture only the highlights of the visual configuration or some phonetic elements of a word rather than its internal detail. They may frequently omit letters that are unpredictable, or their spelling may tend to deteriorate with time, such as near the end of a written report. They may do well on spelling tests when their attention is focused on words in isolation but show significant deterioration in writing text when their attention is divided between ideas, words, sentence construction, and conventions in addition to spelling. Children who do not monitor their work may not notice when they make impulsive spelling errors. Some highly impulsive spellers who do monitor their work produce writing marred by erasures and crossing out. Monitoring skills may be just good enough for them to notice certain mistakes, but even such quality control is apt to be capricious. Obviously, children with attention deficits who are especially talented in spelling (perhaps due to strong linguistic or visualization abilities) may spell accurately despite these traits. As with so many performance areas, notable strengths in one developmental function (such as visualization) may override a weakness (such as an attention deficit).

Spatial and Sequential Ordering. An appreciation of word configuration is an important outgrowth of visual-spatial processing. Whole-word awareness depends on the spatial coherence of individual elements. Awareness of spatial, directional, and configuration attributes certainly intensifies registration in visual memory, leading to more accurate visualization for spelling. Thus, a student with a visual-spatial processing deficiency may never develop a clear image of a written word and is thus at a disadvantage when it comes to spelling.

The influence of sequencing problems on spelling is questionable. At first glance, we might assume a direct and profound interaction. After all, the letters in a word occur in a predictable and consistent serial order. Therefore, it should follow that children who are confused about sequential organization should have serious problems with spelling. However, this is not inevitably the case. Some students with sequencing problems make liberal use of other clues, so that data about the serial order of letters are less important than visualization of a gestalt, language awareness, and grapheme-phoneme correspondences. Thus, sequential organization may not represent a limiting factor in the retrieval of correct spellings. However, sequential memory and organization can be more germane to the analysis of complex multisyllabic words that have not been encountered or memorized previously. Some children experience problems in dividing and reassembling such words for reading and spelling. They may tease apart a multi-syllabic word but struggle to reassemble the phonemes, some of which they may forget or omit. Furthermore, studies have shown a significant deterioration in sequential sound segmentation as the number of elements increases (Lindamood 1994). Confusions about letter order in spelling may be associated with sequencing problems, but they are as likely to reflect deficiencies of visualization, inconsistent attention to detail, and eclipse phenomena (such as neglecting letter order because of extreme effort required for letter formation, punctuation, or some other component of the task).

Memory. Memory is an essential component of spelling. While it is difficult to separate memory from other contributing functions such as language, attention, and cognition, it is certainly true that many investigations of spelling ability and disability in childhood ultimately stress the importance of access to one or another of several distinct memory banks (Frith 1983). Therefore, children who are struggling with various aspects of retrieval memory might be expected to have spelling difficulties.

In one study of poor spellers, Frith (1983) found that many of those who had both reading disabilities and spelling problems had difficulty with *both* phonological memory and visual (lexical) access, the ability to visualize all the details of real words. The visual memory store accumulates largely from exposure to the printed word. Poor readers may be less attentive to visual orthographic patterns, perhaps because they are giving so much attention to grapheme-phoneme relationships, and thus they form less explicit and accurate visual representations of letter sequences (Moats 1994). Frith and other investigators have found that good readers who are deficient spellers are much more likely to have an adequate or strong phonological memory but significant weaknesses of either visual access or memory for spelling rules. Normal spellers, by contrast, are agile in using both visual and phonological clues as well as spelling rules in such a way that the accurately spelled word is a product of verification and consensus.

Language. Children with language-processing and production problems may be particularly vulnerable to difficulties with phonological memory, as just cited. They may not initially develop a strong sense of grapheme-phoneme equivalency. Sometimes this may be caused by basic problems appreciating the distinctiveness of particular English sounds. Research has shown that students with reading and spelling problems have greater difficulty with particular phonological patterns, such as consonant blends, *r*-controlled vowels, vowel digraphs, and unstressed vowels (Moats 1994). Problems with sound segmentation of multisyllable words also contribute to spelling difficulties (Lindamood 1994). Some children lack the metalinguistic awareness necessary to appreciate the components of words, regularities in the English language, and the many ways context influences spelling. The conventions of the language somehow fail to strike a responsive chord in such students. This may make it difficult for them to gain a true appreciation of orthographic rules. For example, a child struggling to spell a particular word may not realize that it is closely related to a word she or he already knows how to spell, requiring only the addition of a suffix.

Higher-Order Cognition. Strong verbal cognition and cognitive flexibility facilitate spelling. The kinds of manipulations needed to identify the deep structures of words and the internal logic of language relate closely to the search for a word's roots, contexts, and appropriate transformations. That is, children with relative weaknesses of cognitive processing in the verbal domain may have difficulty reasoning out how to spell a word by applying logical principles derived from knowledge of English. They may fail to appreciate and apply their knowledge of common structural/morphological units, such as suffixes, prefixes and root words. They may also have trouble understanding and using spelling rules.

Graphomotor Function. Graphomotor ability appears to be related to spelling. Students who have difficulty with the motor aspects of writing commonly have deficiencies in spelling. In some cases, writing and spelling problems result from combined difficulties with graphomotor function and visual memory. As we have seen, handwriting difficulties may be due to specific motor memory dysfunctions (see chapter 6). Affected children may be poor at recalling both the visual configuration of a word and the ideomotor plan for distinct letter forms. Moreover, at least part of spelling proficiency is derived from the motor act of writing. Transcribing words on paper is a way of registering and consolidating their traces in memory. Those problem writers who are inordinately preoccupied with motor praxis or proprioceptive and kinesthetic feedback for writing may not have sufficient attention to register these lengthy motor engrams as spelling configurations. Furthermore, erratic writing will not provide strong and clear motor reinforcement of the abstract memory images of written words. In addition, poor writing legibility may prevent accurate registration and reinforcement of visual configurations. Thus, there are several reasons why youngsters with graphomotor deficiencies frequently have accompanying delays in spelling skills. Frith (1980) found that students with combined writing and spelling deficiencies produced phonetically correct spellings of nonsense words with almost the same frequency as did normal spellers. Students with significant reading delays, on the other hand, were far less likely to produce such phonetic spellings. This suggests that students with combined writing and spelling difficulties tend to have problems with visualization (and perhaps motor memory) while students with combined reading and spelling difficulties tend to have problems with phonological memory. Table 10-4 describes typical error patterns in spelling and potential developmental contributors.

Assessment of Spelling.   A thorough evaluation of spelling ability requires several different sets of observations. Group tests often include multiple-choice spelling assessments, which can yield some clues about spelling ability. However, some students who are able to *recognize* correct spellings are unable to retrieve entire words. Thus, they may obtain spuriously high scores on multiple-choice spelling tests. Spelling assessments must include graded, dictated spelling lists that require use of all types of clues, and that tap phonological recall, access to visual storage, use of language experience, application of rules, and mobilization of motor engrams for writing words. Spelling should also be examined within the context of written expression.

Standardized spelling lists provide some indication of whether a child is spelling at grade level. Nonetheless, performance is usually measured by the number of words spelled accurately and not the difficulty of the words (length, rule regularity, and exceptions). In view of the complexity of spelling, it is important to do more than assign grade levels; to identify processing strengths and points of breakdown it is necessary to describe accurately the predominant patterns of a child's misspellings. In most cases, students who exhibit deficiencies in spelling commit mixed errors. For example, a study by Finucci et al. (1983) found that children with reading delays and spelling problems were phonologically accurate in 53 to 63 percent of their misspellings. That is, their errors were predominately dyseidetic but not exclusively so. Thus, in inspecting a spelling list, we should not expect to find complete homogeneity of error types but instead should strive to discern misspellings that predominate. The following questions can help characterize such patterns:

• What proportion of misspellings are phonologically accurate (e.g., *l-i-t-e* for *light*)? It has been found that many children and adults who read well but spell poorly have a high proportion of these phonologically accurate misspellings. On the other hand, children with combined reading and spelling delays are more likely to have a predominance of misspellings that reflect inadequate mastery of grapheme-phoneme correspondence.

• To what extent are errors consistent? As we have noted, many children with attention deficits are erratic in their patterns of spelling. This tendency can best be appreciated by studying spelling in the context of a written passage, where the same word may be spelled differently each time it occurs.

Table 10-4. Patterns of spelling errors and potential developmental contributors

ERROR PATTERN	DEVELOPMENTAL CONTRIBUTORS
Close visual approximation but phonetically inaccurate (e.g., *pople* for *people*)	Poor appreciation and/or recall of grapho-phoneme relationships Weak sound segmentation skills Deficient selective attention and self-monitoring
Good phonetic approximation but visually inaccurate (e.g., *bott* for *bought*)	Weak visual retrieval memory Poor attention to visual detail and letter patterns
Letter and/or syllable omissions (e.g., *bogt* for *bought* or *instution* for *institution*)	Difficulty preserving linear sequences Weak sound segmentation skills Diminished active working memory Weak sequential recall
Letter transpositions (e.g., *aminal* for *animal*)	Problems with active working memory Impulsiveness Lack of attention to detail and/or attention eclipsed by other task production components
Trouble with "linear chunks" of data (inaccuracy in middle of long words)	Weak sequential memory Poor retrieval of linear data
Incomplete appreciation of spelling rules and regularities (e.g., *pill* for *pile, rite* for *right*)	Poor understanding and memory of rules Weak pattern recognition Deficient attention Weak higher-order cognition
Poor sense of word structures and derivations	Poor semantic appreciation Language deficiencies Weak higher-order cognition
Inaccurate spelling of homophones (e.g., *there/their/they're*)	Poor semantic awareness and lack of appreciation of context Inattention Overreliance on rote learning
Spellings that violate rules of English regularities (e.g., *rowghte* for *wrote*)	Lack of linguistic appreciation Weak higher-order cognition Poor pattern awareness Inadequate rule understanding and recall
Better recognition of spellings than recall	Weak retrieval memory Superficial learning and registration
Accuracy with isolated words, but not in paragraphs	Weaknesses with simultaneous recall and active working memory Erratic attention Possible fine motor difficulties Multiple function eclipse
Random/inconsistent errors	Attention inconsistency Lack of self-monitoring Multiple function eclipse Deficient motor memory
Mixed spelling errors (dyseidetic and dysphonetic)	Multiplicity of developmental dysfunctions Significant attention deficits

- Are many errors orthographically "illegal"? Such errors consist of words that violate basic rules of spelling, although in many cases they are apt to be phonologically accurate. Examples include ignorance of the vowel-consonant-silent-*e* pattern (e.g., *i-r-r-i-t-a-t* for *irritate*) or ignorance of the *qu* pattern (e.g., *c-w-i-t* for *quit*).

- What proportion of misspellings is phonologically inappropriate but visually close to the correct versions? Some children who overrely on visualization as a strategy may show a preponderance of this form of spelling error.

- Are there frequent errors of letter sequence? This pattern is rare but nevertheless should be looked for, especially in youngsters who have widespread problems with sequential production. Children with poor grapho-phoneme appreciation and/or poor sound segmentation skills may also show this pattern.

- Is there such a distribution of spelling errors that it is impossible to characterize any predominant pattern? It is likely that such students will be especially difficult to remediate. They are apt to have significant gaps in phonological awareness, visualization, and the appreciation and recall of orthographic rules.

It is helpful to observe how a child spells in context. Examining spelling in a paragraph or essay can reveal whether a student is able to integrate syntax effectively with spelling, using words in their proper tense and obeying other rules of morphology. Spelling in context also enables an evaluator to measure the extent to which spelling is automatized as the student simultaneously writes, punctuates, and formulates ideas.

Standardized group and individually administered spelling tests are commonly included as subtests of general achievement tests (see appendix). Although tests can be extremely helpful in characterizing error patterns and grade levels, clearly the day-to-day observations of a perceptive teacher add to the knowledge of a child's spelling level, error patterns, consistency, and automaticity. Nevertheless, children, especially those in the elementary grades, may be thought to have strong spelling abilities because they have strong short-term memory skills and can perform successfully on weekly spelling tests. It is therefore most important that spelling be evaluated in a variety of written contexts.

Combining spelling assessment with neurodevelopmental observations makes it possible to discern links between deficiencies in spelling and underlying, definable dysfunctions of information processing and/or storage.

Management of Spelling Delays.   The remediation of spelling problems may occur in conjunction with remedial reading, particularly if a multisensory approach such as Orton-Gillingham is used (see chapter 9, p. 333). A number of commercial curriculum spelling programs are also available (see Mercer and Mercer 1993, pp. 526–28). As we have noted, isolated spelling deficiencies are not usually major roadblocks to learning. Nevertheless, poor spelling can hinder writing enough to compromise performance in important content areas. Moreover, research has shown that teachers are highly influenced by spelling in their grading of students' work.

Spelling remediation should be based on the error patterns uncovered during an evaluation. A description of these patterns combined with knowledge of neurodevelopmental strengths and dysfunctions can form the basis for remedial teaching strategies. The following examples may be helpful:

- Emphasize visual memory to help students with a preponderance of dysphonetic (i.e., phonologically incorrect) errors and strong visual processing to spell better. Use flash cards and computer software that promotes visual recognition.

- Aim instruction at improving phonological awareness and application. Emphasize exercises to strengthen sound segmentation skills. Ask children to identify the number of syllables and the number of phonemes heard in words (use real and nonsense words). Have them indicate the number by using counters. Once they can identify the number of phonemic units in a stimulus, give them practice in identifying the individual sound units and associating these with the appropriate graphemes.

- Use cloze spelling exercises to improve awareness of letter-sound associations and segmentation. Give children words with certain letters omitted and ask them to fill in the blanks. Use of nonsense words prevents reliance on visual recognition.

- Some children need special emphasis on and review of spelling rules. Employ word search challenges to reinforce rule recognition. Ask children to locate all the words on a page in their reading books that illustrate a given rule. Also have them make up a list of words that follow a specified rule.

- Use flash cards and spelling games such as Scrabble, Hangman, and Spill and Spell to provide motivational practice in spelling skills.

- Confront children who make many orthographically "illegal" errors with several different spellings of the same word. Ask them to select the correct one and to show how the others violate specific rules of English.

- Make children aware of their error patterns. Ask them to keep a notebook of the words they have the most difficulty with. These could be categorized by rules, irregular spellings (the "demons"), letter patterns and word families, and word endings such as *ance/ence*.

- Use any of the number of software programs that provide practice in spelling (Mercer and Mercer 1993, pp. 529–30).

- For students with attention problems and reduced recall of visual detail, use word search puzzles and proofreading challenges. Give them a writing sample and challenge them to find a specified number of spelling errors. Give them one point for each error detected and an additional point for each corrected. Also use this type of exercise with students who display problems with phonological awareness and rule knowledge. The errors could emphasize those patterns in which children show specific weakness.

In general, children should progress from recognizing correct spellings to retrieving and using them in context. Practice in spelling should consist of repeated exposures, followed by a multiple-choice (i.e., recognition) format for locating the correct spellings, attempts to retrieve correctly spelled words, and the use of these same words in writing sentences and paragraphs. Finally, emphasize proofreading to detect one's own spelling errors. This progression of initial exposure and association, recognition, retrieval, spelling in context, and proofreading is likely to benefit all students who are struggling with this academic skill.

Students whose spelling problems coexist with reading delays require an approach to remediation that deals with both areas in a coordinated fashion. A student whose misspellings suggest poor appreciation of grapheme-phoneme correspondence may have reading difficulty caused by the same weakness. A continuing effort to improve phonological awareness through both reading and writing experiences should ultimately have an impact on spelling ability.

While remediating spelling, it is vitally important to allow bypass strategies. Encourage the use of a dictionary. Children may wish to keep a personal log of frequently misspelled words to which they can refer during tests and while completing homework. Require older students who use word processing to make regular use of a spell check, warning them that it is not infallible. To increase their awareness of the weakness of spell check programs, ask them to come up with examples of errors that such a program would not detect. Finally, teachers need to be sympathetic to the plight of children who are feeling overwhelmed by the strain of spelling while writing. Minimize criticism for misspellings. For certain assignments, assure children that their grades will not depend on spelling. At the same time, urge students to proofread carefully and to document that such proofreading has occurred (for example, by correcting any errors with a colored pencil). Tolerate mistakes, as long as there is documentation that the child made every effort to locate and correct them.

For most students, spelling evolves as an increasingly automatic skill, facilitating writing as a means of expression and active problem solving. In a similar manner, children progress in their mathematical proficiency and automaticity. The next chapter will show that students become increasingly adept in basic quantitative skills, an achievement that in turn leads to a growing ability to employ numerical codes and operations as a means of problem solving.

Chapter 11

Mathematics

For the most part Thoreau made little impression on his schoolmates—and they little on him. One thought Thoreau "an odd stick, not very studious or devoted in his lessons, but a thoughtful youth and very fond of reading . . . not given to play or to fellowship with the boys; but shy and silent." On the other hand, it has been reported that the boys used to assemble about Thoreau as he sat on the school fence to hear him talk.

—Walter Harding, *The Days of Henry Thoreau*

Quantitative reasoning and the flexible manipulation of symbols and rules require strenuous intellectual exertion of a child's developing brain. Some students thrive on mathematics while others find the subject a perpetual anathema and a target of phobic avoidances. Some children easily meet the demands for precision, consistency, attention to detail, conceptual agility, problem-solving flexibility, speed of processing and recall, and cumulative learning, but others do not. Moreover, by junior high school, mathematics proficiency becomes a primary gauge by which students measure general intellectual ability. It is not surprising, therefore, that students who are struggling in math often begin to doubt their basic learning capacity, experience profound feelings of intellectual inadequacy, and develop generalized performance anxieties. Such feelings erode academic self-esteem and motivation for learning.

Evolving mathematical challenges interact with all the constructs covered in part 1. Not surprisingly, therefore, close ties exist between developmental variation and patterns of acquiring mathematics skill and daily performance. This chapter portrays these interactions by discussing the following major requisites for mathematical accomplishment during school years, and by describing the ways in which specific developmental dysfunctions can delay or compromise their assimilation:

- Number concepts

- Basic operations

- Graphomotor implementation

- Transfer of knowledge

- Mathematical linguistics

- Visualization

- Problem solving

- Active working memory and mental arithmetic

- Higher-order cognition and abstraction

- Higher-order cognition and proportion

- Higher-order cognition and equation

- Higher-order cognition and proof

- Depth of knowledge and access to knowledge

- Attention to detail and self-monitoring

REQUISITES AND DEVELOPMENTAL FUNCTIONS

This section elaborates on each of the themes and issues just listed that may either facilitate or obstruct the attainment of proficiency in mathematics.

Number Concepts

Preschool children strive to grasp the concept of rational counting and numeration. The representation of quantity by numbers is a significant conceptual acquisition. Through early-life experience, children begin to understand that qualitatively similar objects can differ in size or dimension. Vocabulary such as *more than* and *less than* offers the young mind new insights into numerical representation. Such consciousness is the earliest form of readiness for a true exploration of the meaning of numbers.

In *The Child's Conception of Number* (1965), Piaget describes four underlying concepts necessary to develop a substrate of numerical understanding on which to superimpose higher-order mathematics skills: classification, ordering, one-to-one correspondence, and conservation.

Classification is the capacity to perceive categorical relationships, as discussed in chapter 7. It involves the ability to group objects according to specific properties within consistent categories. A child might sort objects by shape, the material they are made of, or use. This capacity to classify develops rapidly between the ages of five and seven and becomes an important contributor to mathematical reasoning. Some children with higher-order cognitive difficulties may find classification difficult or may be slow to perceive categories, which delays their acquisition of skill in mathematics.

Ordering is the capacity to organize materials in a logical sequence. Arranging items in order of their width, placing things in alphabetical order, or extrapolating from a particular series to what comes next are examples. Seriation tasks necessitate judging which item follows which in a consistent series. Clearly, this ability to order is an important requisite for the assimiliation of numerical concepts and counting. As might be expected, some children with significant sequential disorganization have problems understanding serial order, which can have an impact on their acquisition of mathematics skill.

One-to-one correspondence means that a particular number of objects has a fixed value despite the size or nature of those objects. Children learn to understand that both a pile of five automobile tires and a stack of five pieces of paper contain the same number of objects despite their dramatic differences in visual appearance. During the primary grades, children increasingly come to recognize this truth.

One-to-one correspondence is closely related to the fourth concept, *conservation,* the idea that the volume or quantity of things remains constant regardless of its spatial arrangement and any alteration thereof (see pp. 234–35). This concept is essential for a true understanding of quantities and the use of numbers. In other words, during these early years of education, children come to recognize that numbers have some absolute denotations, that extraneous characteristics do not alter them, and that representing quantities with numbers avoids deceptive and irrelevant sensory data. Children increasingly recognize that numbers are economical—a shorthand for thinking about relative amounts and sizes.

It is unusual for children to show significant delays in the mastery of these basic concepts. Although some students have difficulty fully assimilating them, most feel comfortable with these ideas well before they are nine years old. Ordinarily, children consolidate these concepts through repeated experiential exposures. Verbal explanations, everyday practices, visual demonstrations, and experience in manipulating or counting objects all reinforce classification, seriation, one-to-one correspondence, and conservation. The mastery of these concepts facilitates the use of numbers; the use of numbers further facilitates the mastery of these concepts. Because the opportunities for acquisition are multisensory, children with delayed language skills, poor visual processing, or even sequencing weaknesses may still assimilate the concepts. However, learners probably master them to different degrees; that is, some children grasp them only superficially while others find them strikingly meaningful, widely and automatically applicable. The literature provides some evidence that youngsters who have incompletely mastered these conceptual bases may encounter difficulty later in their educational careers when they need to use this relatively tenuous conceptual substrate for much more sophisticated arithmetical reasoning.

Basic Operations

The basic operations of addition, subtraction, multiplication, and division comprise another early challenge to attaining competency in mathematics. As children master these operations, they prepare for more substantial computational tasks.

Children need to arrive at certain distinct levels of awareness. First, they must acquire a basic understanding of each process, recognizing, for example, that by adding to a quantity, it becomes larger or greater. In most cases, children begin by *visualizing* this effect. Second, they must understand when a particular process is called for—that a plus sign means "to add." Third, children must learn and be able to recall basic number facts, mastering the idea that 2 plus 4 equals 6. Fourth, they must learn the *algorithms,* the series of steps required to solve a particular type of mathematics problem, i.e., a stereotyped problem-solving methodology. Thus, children should recognize that adding 35 to 15 requires a specific procedure. If they compute 35 plus 15 as $3 + 5 + 1 + 5 = 14$, the answer is wrong because an inappropriate algorithm has been employed. This is so despite commendable use of the appropriate operation (addition) and accurate recall of basic facts ($3 + 5 + 1 + 5$ does equal 14).

In the example above, *place value*, an essential part of understanding computation, has been ignored. Place value is the concept that a digit can express a different numerical quantity depending on its position within a multidigit number. (The 4 in 40 represents something considerably different from the 4 in 4000.) Although the concept of place value is introduced early in the elementary grades, it remains an enigma to many students throughout school. An incomplete understanding of place value underlies many errors commonly encountered later on when students must cope with decimals and negative integers. At the early levels of mathematics instruction, teaching and math textbooks frequently emphasize a rote approach to mastering operations, which contributes to conceptual tenuousness and difficulties at more advanced levels.

Identifying the operation, retrieving accurate number facts, following the correct algorithm, and respecting place value are necessary components of addition, subtraction, multiplication, and division. Over time these components become increasingly automatic, allowing competent mathematics students to advance to applying them in word problems, real-life situations, and higher mathematics.

A wide range of developmental dysfunctions can interfere with the comprehension and applications of basic operations (Rourke and Finlayson 1978). Children with attention deficits may be too impulsive and inattentive to detail to attend to correct operational signs. They may add when they should subtract or multiply when they should add. Children who have difficulty with spatial or sequential processing may have trouble reading lengthy numbers or arranging them in columns, which impedes accuracy during computation. Children with language difficulties may have trouble understanding verbal explanations of these operations. They may require visual models or other nonlinguistic reinforcers to understand fully. Students with graphomotor dysfunction may have problems transcribing legible and usable number symbols and arranging them systematically on a page. Weak spatial visualizations may cause confusion with computation of problems that present numbers in irregular columns. Spatial awareness is also important for grasping number-quantity relationships. Dysfunctions of higher-order cognition may limit the degree to which children truly understand arithmetic concepts. Some students memorize and mimic to cover their tenuous understanding of the concepts and algorithms of multiplication and division. The concepts of place value as it applies to regrouping in subtraction, and of part-whole relationships in working with fractions, are especially difficult for students to grasp. Finally, as we shall see, there is a strong relationship between memory and computation. Some children experience difficulty memorizing and recalling basic math facts or even algorithms on demand—especially under timed conditions. Many students with dysfunctions of memory fail to master the multiplication tables (Svien and Sherlock 1979). Students also must learn and remember the meaning of a host of abstract visual symbols used in number notation ($, <, >, =). These symbols are part of the decoding process of math but, unlike in reading, there are no sounds or context clues to assist when memory falters. Problems with active working memory can cause confusion in performing procedures that involve different operations and/or multiple steps, such as long division (see section on "Memory, Computation, and Problem Solving," p. 411, and table 11-1).

Graphomotor Implementation

As noted above, the transcription of numbers on paper can overwhelm certain students (Cohn 1968). Children who have difficulty with motor memory may have problems writing numbers that are sufficiently legible. Orton (1937) used the term *strephosymbolia* to describe this phenomenon. Impulsivity, poor tempo control, and insufficient attention to detail can also contribute to imprecision in forming numbers, resulting in inaccurate computation.

Some students with motor planning problems are poor at spatial utilization (the alignment of numbers in columns, for example). Misaligning numbers alters place value and thereby causes inaccuracy. Vulnerable students often benefit from worksheets with the examples arranged properly. They can then concentrate on thinking through the examples without worrying about writing. Sometimes students are so preoccupied with the motor and spatial aspects of writing numbers that they momentarily forget the algorithm or fail to identify the relevant operation. This "eclipse phenomenon" is common in the early grades. By late elementary school, most children have automatized number formation, but their delay in doing so may have resulted in commensurate delays in acquisition of skills, leaving them struggling to catch up and sometimes having a negative or fatalistic attitude toward mathematics.

Transfer of Knowledge (Equilibration)

A crucial requisite of acquiring arithmetic skill is agility in moving back and forth from formal mathematical learning to everyday applications. This equilibration of knowledge and skill from the abstract to the concrete, from school to home, from home to school, and from formal assignments to everyday problem

Table 11-1. Examples of computation errors frequently characteristic of neurodevelopmental dysfunctions

DYSFUNCTION	EXAMPLES	
Attention	Operational sign	$\begin{array}{r} 201 \\ -185 \\ \hline 386 \end{array}$
	Detail	$\begin{array}{r} 7\overset{1}{5}3 \\ +369 \\ \hline 1112 \end{array}$
	Inconsistency	$\begin{array}{r} \overset{1}{\cancel{5}}43 \\ -276 \\ \hline 273 \end{array} \quad \begin{array}{r} 6\overset{8\,1}{\cancel{9}}2 \\ -495 \\ \hline 297 \end{array}$
Memory	Retrieval of fact	$\begin{array}{r} \overset{1}{7}2 \\ \times 86 \\ \hline 452 \\ 556 \\ \hline 6012 \end{array}$
	Active working memory	$\begin{array}{r} 836 \;^{R6} \\ 8\overline{)670} \\ \underline{64} \\ 30 \\ \underline{24} \\ 54 \\ \underline{48} \\ 6 \end{array}$
		$\begin{array}{r} 4\tfrac{1}{8} = \tfrac{1}{8} \\ -2\tfrac{3}{4} = \tfrac{6}{8} \\ \hline 2 \quad \tfrac{7}{8} \end{array}$
	Procedural memory	$\begin{array}{r} 61 \\ +\ 4 \\ \hline 11 \end{array} \quad \begin{array}{r} 23 \\ \times 42 \\ \hline 86 \end{array}$
		$\begin{array}{r} \tfrac{3}{8} \\ +\ \tfrac{1}{4} \\ \hline \tfrac{4}{12} \end{array}$

Table 11-1. *(Continued)*

Spatial ordering	Alignment	$\begin{array}{r} 604 \\ 7 \\ 5082 \\ 31 \\ \hline 6003 \end{array}$
	Decimal placement	$\begin{array}{r} 61.4 \\ +620 \\ \hline 123.4 \end{array}$
Sequential ordering		$69 \quad \overset{5}{} \quad 8\overline{)970}^{\,R12}$ ...
Conceptual grasp/higher-order cognition		$4\frac{1}{8} = \frac{5}{8} \qquad 2 + \frac{1}{3} = \frac{3}{3} = 1$
		$\frac{3}{8} > \frac{3}{4}$
		$4.0 = 400\%$
Graphomotor	Number formation	
	Size and spacing of symbols	

For the Sequential ordering row:

$$\begin{array}{rr}
 & 111 \;^{R12} \\
69 & 8\,\overline{)970} \\
+46 & 9 \\
\hline
151 & 07 \\
 & 15 \\
 & \overline{12} \\
 & 20 \\
 & \overline{12}
\end{array}$$

$$9 + 7 = 61$$

solving facilitates mathematical fluency (Driscoll 1982, p. 25). Students talented in mathematics relish this ongoing process of extrapolation and elaboration. A child learns about numerical representation and operations in school and then enjoys counting and adding or subtracting money at home. Measurement concepts are applied in purchasing milk, getting fitted for new shoes, telling time, and cooking from a recipe. Children who enjoy sports may derive satisfaction from computing athletic statistics. This capacity to transfer arithmetical knowledge from one context to another allows children to be enchanted by the utility and versatility of numbers.

Exporting mathematics from the classroom creates motivation to learn, and significantly reinforces concepts and operations. Children who perceive formal mathematics education as irrelevant are less likely to attain mastery. Most arithmetic classes encourage equilibration by introducing practical applications along with theoretical and abstract operations. Nevertheless, considerable developmental variation occurs in children's capacities to transfer knowledge and skill from the classroom to the world beyond. Specific cognitive weaknesses, memory deficits, and cultural factors are likely to influence equilibration. Rigid adherence to textbook teaching can also impede development of equilibration.

Mathematical Linguistics

Communication in mathematics may strain both the student and the teacher. For the young child, inconsistency between verbal labels and their number representation may cause confusion, for example, *sixteen* for *16* where the word implies that the six comes first as is the case with numbers 20 and above, i.e., *sixty-one (61)*. Depending on the context and order of words in word problems, *less*, which usually implies subtraction, may actually translate into addition (John has seven pencils. He has three less than Shawn. How many pencils does Shawn have?). Mathematics has a very specialized vocabulary which must be learned. The language used in mathematics textbooks presents an unusually high density of ideas per number of words. Furthermore, in reading and explanations, words are continuously combined with abstract symbols; comprehension depends on the student's ability to memorize the meaning of the symbols and to discern relationships between word and symbols (Curry 1989). Complex verbal explanations, a steadily growing arithmetic vocabulary, and the requirement for precision in mathematical language are utterly essential and, at the same time, a source of potential breakdown (Cohn 1971).

The vocabulary and semantic content of mathematics expands and depends totally on prior entries into semantic memory. That is, content is both new and cumulative. In this respect, mathematics is much like mastering a foreign language. Vocabulary such as *parallelogram, subtrahend,* and *denominator* is far removed from the everyday expression of most students, likely to be heard only within academic confines, not at home or on the playground. Yet, children are expected to become adept in their understanding, use, recall, and application of these terms. As might be expected, students who struggle with semantics in other settings may be confused by mathematics vocabulary, especially when a teacher is not entirely consistent in language use; substituting a synonym for a term, i.e., *minus* for *subtract,* may confuse the youngster who has struggled to learn the literal meaning of the word. Mathematics textbooks may not make clear enough distinctions between words that are truly confusing to young readers. Once again, children with relative weaknesses of language, especially those who are perpetually slow to incorporate new, active vocabulary, will be at a disadvantage.

Rourke and Strang (1983) described children with mathematics disabilities who have apparent dysfunctions of verbal memory. These students had, in addition to their arithmetic deficiencies, delays in reading and spelling.

Kane (1968) and Curry (1989) describe differences between mathematical and nonmathematical English:

- There are differences in letter, word, and syntactical redundancies. That is, single letters such as *x* and *y* occur often in mathematical English, and so do some words such as *infinite* or *greater,* as well as sentences built around conditional phrases such as *if and only if.* Thus, the words, phrases, and symbols that recur frequently in mathematical English are relatively rare terms in everyday English and even the English of language arts courses.

- Words in mathematics generally have only one very specific denotation rather than several. For example, *point, set,* and *prime*, which mean only one thing in mathematics, can carry many possible meanings and be used in a wide range of contexts outside mathematics.

- Students must learn the precise meanings of words, as there are few verbal context clues to help in reading mathematics.

- Mathematical reading is laced with abstract graphic symbols possessing specific meanings that children must memorize.

Various investigators have cited other differences between mathematical and nonmathematical English. Kemme (1981) observed that many mathematical expressions are *hypothetical references,* noting that many students find hypothetical reasoning difficult until they are between fourteen and sixteen years old. Thus, the young adolescent in an elementary algebra course may have trouble understanding the statement "Let the unknown number be *x*." This is particularly true of the student who has not yet reached the stage of formal operations (see chapter 7). Kemme also points out that many verbal expressions in mathematics refer to concepts that are new. In much of their prior experience in school, children have learned vocabulary to account for concepts they have already mastered. In mathematics, they often have to learn words before they have completely worked through the concepts. A British study (Hart 1981) found that a large percentage of fourteen year olds had difficulty with the words *perimeter* and *area* because the students frequently confused the concepts of area and perimeter. A further complication is that mathematics textbooks often define terms using vocabulary that is conceptually obscure. Driscoll (1982) cites the following example: "Polyhedron—a three-dimensional figure all of whose faces are polygonal regions" (p. 32). *Three-dimensional, faces, polygonal,* and *regions* are words that could easily be misunderstood by many students, especially those with semantic dysfunctions.

The language of word problems often presents a formidable challenge in mathematics. Barnett, Sowder, and Vos (1980) delineated differences in ordinary language and word-problem language, noting that word problems tend to be more compact and "conceptually dense" than ordinary prose. A number of key ideas may be compressed into a single sentence, thereby requiring a more intense and thorough reading than ordinarily required outside of mathematics. A single, seemingly unprepossessing word such as *each* may be critical to the correct solution. Students cannot rely on probabilistic language processing (see p. 144) while reading word problems. Moreover, ordinary prose is characterized by a continuity of subject and ideas from sentence to sentence and paragraph to paragraph. Children expect that word problems in a series will be similar to each other. They function well when this occurs but have difficulty when abrupt shifts of operations are required in a series of problems.

Two aspects of word problems that some students find particularly troublesome are the presence of extraneous information, or data not germane to the solution of the problem, and the presentation of numbers in the word problem in an order other than that required for an appropriate computational solution. Children with language disabilities, those who are having difficulty processing essential verbal information as well as some who become confused over word order in general, may fail at solving such word problems.

Word problems may present information in inverted temporal sequence, which can cause confusion. They also require the translation of indirect verbal terms such as *half* and *the same* into numbers. Children with an incomplete understanding of verbal concepts such as *half* may only comprehend it in a single context (*half an apple*) and not know what to do when they are asked to find *half of a number*.

Students with strong language abilities can mobilize these assets to enhance their understanding of mathematics. Their "translation skills" become important for reconstructing arithmetic meaning in language that is most meaningful for them. Other students, however, prefer to resort to nonverbal reasoning; they conceptualize with less use of language. Both learning styles can be successful, since mathematics can be approached through varying combinations of nonverbal logic and language. Terms such as *some, all, neither,* and *nor* often cause confusion and are misused. In one experiment (Driscoll 1982, p. 37), normal high school students were shown a variety of shapes—including circles, squares, and triangles—in two sizes and three colors, each labeled with a letter. The students were asked to "write the letters of all the shapes that are neither small and red nor big and green." Eighty percent of tenth graders and sixty-five percent of eleventh and twelfth graders failed this task. The size of the linguistic "chunk" was too great.

Finally, it should be mentioned that mathematical explanations frequently involve complex sequential processing and memory. Multistep explanations may be particularly elusive for students with language disability as well as for those with dysfunctions of sequential processing and memory. Often these children can benefit from visual representations while struggling to process multistep verbal sequential explanations. Furthermore, these students may be confused both by the complex syntax of explanations and the grammatical complexity of word problems.

Here are examples of some of the linguistic complexities frequently encountered in math word problems:

- *Direct statement.* Sam had four apples. Inez had three apples. How many apples did Sam and Inez have in all?

- *Indirect statement.* Sam had four apples. Inez had *the same number* as Sam. How many apples did Sam and Inez have?

- *Inverted sequence.* After June went to the store, she had three dollars. She spent five dollars on groceries. How much money did June take to the store?

- *Inverted syntax.* Seven puppies *were given to Jack.* Rachel had six puppies. *Together* how many puppies did they have?

- *Too much information.* John and Brittany bought eight cookies. *The cookies cost twenty cents each.* They ate five of the cookies on the way home from the store. How many cookies were left when they got home?

- *Semantic ambuiguity (misleading cue words).* Davon has twelve pens. He has three *more* pens than Sheila. How many pens does Sheila have?

- *Important "little" words.* Connie, Ray, and Ralph bought tacos for supper. They *each* ate three, and there were four left. How many tacos did they buy?

- *Multiple steps.* Patrick sold 410 tickets to the play. He sold twice as many as Ellis. How many tickets did they sell in all?

- *Implicit information.* A plane flies east between two cities at 150 miles per hour. The cities are 300 miles apart. On its return flight the plane flies at 300 miles per hour. What was the plane's average flying speed? *The first trip took twice as long as the second.* (The formula *distance = rate × time* has to be applied to the first and second trips to find the time and then to the combined result in order to determine the average speed.)

Mental Imagery and Spatial Appreciation

Some students often bypass the linguistic stress of mathematics by forming mental imagery. Although the concept of proportion may be difficult to interpret linguistically, it may not be so hard to visualize. The capacity to visualize the quantitative value of numbers, word problems, or other computational exercises is an asset. Children whose nonverbal cognition and visualization are not reliable are at a disadvantage in mathematics. They may have an acute problem dealing with geometric concepts—parameters such as area, volume, and other forms of measurement that are best consolidated with strong visual imagery. Effective visualization often requires appreciation of spatial relationships. The understanding of quantity can be enhanced by visualizing numbers as taking up relative amounts of space. Mental imagery can also be used to create metaphors or analogies for mathematical concepts or processes. A child can visualize the splitting of a pizza while thinking about proportion or fractions.

Problem Solving

Virtually all levels of mathematics depend on problem solving. Many older mathematics students are weak at problem solving despite having well-developed computation skills. A problem can be conceptualized as a "task which the subject is able to understand but for which he does not have an immediate solution" (Bloom and Broder 1950, p. 7). The process of problem solving requires the use of one or more methods to arrive at a solution that satisfies the demands of the problem. In mathematics, students must be methodologists, thinkers who are as concerned with using the right techniques as they are with obtaining the correct answers. An important variation, especially in secondary school students, is the extent to which they are effective methodologists or problem solvers in mathematics (as well as in other subject areas and real-life situations). To be a good problem solver requires a number of capacities and behavioral adjustments that are susceptible to disruption in children with developmental dysfunctions. Bloom and Broder (1950) studied problem solving in college students and pinpointed some distinct differences between good and poor problem solvers that are relevant to younger students.

- Poor problem solvers had trouble getting started. They were often unsure of what was expected. Unlike the good problem solvers, they failed to extract key words or ideas that might suggest the best process to use.

- Poor problem solvers had a tendency to offer correct solutions to a problem, but the problem was not the one they were asked to solve. These students frequently neglected or misinterpreted a term in the directions.

- Good problem solvers were adept at bringing forth relevant knowledge for use in solving a problem. Bloom and Broder (1950) observed that "often the unsuccessful students had within their grasp all the background and technical information necessary for the solution of a problem but were unable to apply the knowledge to the problem" (p. 27). For example, many of the poor problem solvers had trouble relating their readings and lecture notes to a given problem.

- Good problem solvers were substantially more active and systematic. Successful problem solvers reorganized the problem as given to simplify it, pulling out the key terms or ideas, or breaking the problem into simpler subproblems, in order to gain an understanding of the material. If the whole was too complex for easy manipulation, they attempted to deal with each part of the problem separately. Nonsuccessful problem solvers, on the other hand, started the problem with no apparent plan for solution, plunging in, without knowing what was to come next (Bloom and Broder 1950, pp. 29–30).

- The good problem solvers were better able to engage in extended chains of logical reasoning. Their less competent peers kept giving up, forgetting, or otherwise disrupting their trains of thought.

- The poor problem solvers had less self-confidence, tended to be indecisive, and allowed their emotions or opinions about a subject to intrude on objective problem solving. They were also more quickly and easily discouraged.

In addition to the need for attention to detail, appropriate cognitive tempo, and astute monitoring, there are certain kinds of thought processes that also characterize the best mathematical problem solvers. The Russian investigator Krutetskii (quoted in Driscoll 1982) observed gifted mathematics students and characterized them in terms of the attributes of their problem solving as follows:

- Good problem solvers were able to distinguish relevant from irrelevant information in problems.

- Good problem solvers were easily able to discern the mathematical structure of a problem. They possessed the ability to impose a mathematical structure on their perceptions of the world.

- Good problem solvers were able to *generalize* about a wide range of problems. Thus, they might recognize the comparison of similar triangles as a common thread that runs through a variety of problems.

- Good problem solvers were able to remember a problem's mathematical structure for a long time. This enabled those students to reapply the same technique when confronted with a similar problem.

- Good problem solvers were able to be active learners, to think through problems, to be goal oriented and flexible in planning solutions. These qualities demand reflection as well as active participation in the process.

Children lacking in cognitive flexibility, those who fail to recognize recurrent patterns and those who are highly impulsive or inordinately passive learners, are at a disadvantage when it comes to problem solving. Some students simply do not allocate sufficient time to engage in deductive reasoning. The learning style of others makes checking and rechecking and the use of successive approximations and estimations feel alien. Others treat each problem as a novel entity and fail to see commonalities that will lead them quickly to the correct operations. They do everything the hard way. Careful examination of the mathematics sections of the *Scholastic Aptitude Tests* (SATs) has shown that the variety of problems presented is quite limited and that many were a slight alteration of a single pattern.

Estimation

An important part of mathematical competency is the capacity to move from calculation to estimation and then back again to calculation. Mathematically competent students are adept at estimating correct answers. They have a sense of a general solution to a problem and are able to compare their results to what seems credible based on earlier and/or subsequent estimations. Estimating ability has become the subject of recent research into mathematical learning. The capacity to estimate an answer requires considerable flexibility, a strong sense of place value, good spatial visualization skills, and an ability to translate numbers into a more manageable format. We estimate the answer to a complex addition problem, for example, by rounding off the component numbers and adding them in our heads. In doing so, we determine that the correct answer will be within a range of numbers. If the calculation yields an answer outside that range, we recognize that it does not fit prior estimation. Children who for one reason or another lack estimation sense are often inaccurate. Although they have mastered the algorithms, they are susceptible to computational errors, carelessness, and other lapses. Many children with weak previewing control (chapter 2) experience estimation difficulties.

Memory, Computation, and Problem Solving

Several studies suggest that some students with mathematics difficulties have significant problems with short-term memory (Webster 1978, Steeves 1983). More specifically, some students have trouble holding together the elements of a problem while solving it. For example, long division requires remembering what to do next after borrowing a number. In one study of children with mathematics disabilities (Brainerd 1983), "memory probes" were employed while children were calculating. As they worked through various problems, examiners stopped them to see if they remembered what they were doing. Many of those with mathematics disabilities had a tendency to lose track—to forget vital components of the problems they were solving. Word problems also involve an extended process of reasoning that requires holding on to several key elements in order to screen out irrelevant data, selecting the necessary operations and arriving at the correct solution, especially if more than one step and operation are required. Such deficiencies of active working memory generate inaccuracy despite a child's understanding of the conceptual content, knowledge of mathematics facts, and even use of the proper algorithm to solve the problem.

Some children with attention deficits may also have trouble retaining the components of a problem while solving it. Their distractibility and inattention to detail may ultimately impede active working memory. The number of problem components may exceed a child's mental working space so that some get lost. Another phenomenon is when children have difficulty keeping in mind the various components of a mathematical operation because one of them is inordinately taxing. Students struggling with place value, borrowing, or carrying may have a lapse of active working memory and forget that they had intended to add rather than subtract the numbers.

Rapid retrieval memory is critical for the efficient recall of mathematical facts and procedures. Pattern recognition memory (pp. 83–84) also is germane, as students must be alert for recurring patterns as they appear in word problems and in geometrical forms.

Reasoning Processes: Abstraction, Proportion, Equation, and Proof

In mathematics, higher-order cognition is paramount. The reasoning process can be viewed from multiple perspectives. This discussion limits coverage to four aspects of reasoning: abstraction, proportion, equation, and proof.

From the earliest stages of mathematical development, children are expected to operate on a highly abstract symbolic level. Numerals are one step removed from the actual quantities they represent. The algorithms of addition, subtraction, multiplication, and division also involve manipulating symbolic representations of processes. With the introduction of algebra, unknown variables become representational of numbers and must also be manipulated as part of a more generalized system as students encounter abstractions for their abstractions. This necessitates reasoning on an almost totally abstract conceptual level. Some children who are overly concrete are at a disadvantage in higher mathematics. During the Piagetian stage of Formal Operations, most students are able to apply logical principles to totally abstract concepts. In the earlier grades, there is likely to be much more interplay between manipulatives (concrete objects) and abstract representations. Provision is made for students to move in and out of abstraction more frequently than in the later grades.

Proportion offers a vivid example of a concept that begins as a concrete, observable phenomenon and evolves into highly abstract representation. Early in their educational careers, students are taught to recognize simple proportions. The segments of a pie, simple ratios, and the most elementary of fractions may be fairly easy to assimilate. However, as school progresses, children are introduced to complex proportion challenges, which require them to compare two or more ratios. A firm understanding of fractions presupposes the development of formal thinking, which is associated with the gradual development of proportional reasoning. It has been found, for example, that many ninth graders have not yet fully developed formal thinking and appropriate levels of proportional reasoning. This is seen in their frequent inability to understand equivalent fractions (such as 4/6 and 8/12) and in their inappropriate tendency to add when they are asked to adjust one ratio to make it proportional to another. An example of this can be found in the following problem (cited in Driscoll 1982, p. 20): "When Bill made lemonade he used four spoonfuls of sugar and ten spoonfuls of lemon juice. Mary made lemonade with six spoonfuls of sugar. How many spoonfuls of lemon juice must she use so that her lemonade will taste the same as Bill's?" Many children with poor proportional reasoning work this through by subtracting 4 from 6 to get 2 and then adding 2 to 10 to yield the incorrect answer 12. The correct answer is obtained only through proportional thinking (i.e., 4/10 = 6/15). The propensity to use an additive rather than proportional strategy is typical of many students with higher-order cognitive difficulties who have not yet attained true proportional reasoning. Such children have a characteristic tendency to avoid fractions whenever possible. As a result they may encounter difficulty in certain science courses. In particular, chemistry requires a strong aptitude for proportional reasoning, such as that required to convert various solutions while maintaining their relative strengths.

The concept of *equation* is another important but sometimes elusive challenge. A true understanding of the preservation of quantities on two sides of an equal sign is essential for algebra as well as for more advanced forms of mathematical reasoning.

Geometric proofs are one of the more complex higher-order cognitive exercises. Students must ponder several alternative deductive pathways. They must decide on the best one, on the ultimate goal, and on the evidence that must be assembled in the correct order. This requires problem-solving flexibility, strong reasoning ability, active working memory, and well-ingrained sequential organization. *Proof* has been described as the process of reasoning from a set of premises through a series of connected inferences to a conclusion, in such a way that any doubt about the conclusion must be referred back to the premises. This is a frustrating hurdle for some secondary school students. Hoffer (1979) has defined the levels of thinking that are required to understand geometry and execute proofs as follows: *recognition* (of the shape and the vocabulary), *analysis* (of the properties of figures), *categorization* (knowing that all squares are rectangles), *deduction* (recognizing the role of postulates and theorems and their relationships to proofs), and *rigor* (knowing the need for precision). Poor conceptual understanding, inattention to detail, defective sequential organization, and a lack of problem-solving flexibility may imperil performance. In addition, students who have been superficial in their prior mathematical learning may falter when it comes to the complex processes of geometric proof.

Depth of Knowledge and Facility

Like other skills, a portion of mathematical ability must become automatized. Arithmetic is cumulative. As in writing, there must be progressive stratification of underlying skills, allowing the learner to superimpose more sophisticated skills. Basic abilities must become increasingly unconscious and easily mobilized, and must be applied with a minimum expenditure of attention, effort, and cognitive energy. This enables the mathematics student to operate on increasingly abstract and complicated levels.

When mathematical knowledge is first acquired, several degrees of assimilation are possible. In some cases, children seem to have a *poor take*. That is, they are simply unable to make use of explanations—either because of the density and complexity of mathematical language, the elusive nature of the concepts, the burden on memory imposed by a large block of new information, or a failure to have mastered prerequisite skills. Some students maintain a *tenuous grasp*. They understand the new information, but only barely. They cannot fully consolidate or elaborate on it and thus can easily forget what they have learned. Moreover, they have trouble applying new insights and skills in a flexible manner and in varying contexts (such as word problems, real-life situations, and computations). Some students try to learn mathematics through *rote mimicry.* Such children can master and remember formulas, algorithms, and mathematical facts, but they rely too heavily on memory, with commensurate neglect of mathematical reasoning. They may regurgitate what they have learned and perform fairly well in mathematics classes without understanding fully what they are doing. Other mathematics learners engage in *true learning;* they acquire new mathematical skills that they can store, retrieve, apply, and equilibrate. They are prepared to use mathematics in the contexts of science. This is the level at which we find most good mathematics students. Finally, the ultimate learning level is that of exceptional *elaborative capacity.* Children who have mastered new mathematical concepts or facts to this degree are able to extrapolate their new ideas spontaneously, to apply them in a variety of situations, challenges, and problems. They see the relevance of what they have learned to many real-life situations. This is the ideal, the level at which we would aspire to see all students learn mathematics.

Often students struggling with mathematics have either a poor take or a tenuous grasp of recent information; this limits progress. Weak attention, poor language comprehension, and difficulty with the conceptual content can all interfere with true assimilation. Learners who substitute rote mimicry for true learning may experience increasing problems with mathematical processes during late elementary school or secondary school, when there are increasing demands for flexible thinking (processes that are greatly facilitated by elaborative capacity or true learning).

Attention

Focus on detail has already been mentioned as an issue in mathematics. Strength of attention is so important that it is worth further emphasis. The capacity to develop a goal, to reflect on alternative problem-solving strategies, to monitor techniques to determine if they are working, and to be vigilant throughout are essential for success in mathematics, and many children with attention deficits are at a disadvantage. There is close collaboration between the processing and production controls of attention in the pursuit of mathematics. However, there are indeed some youngsters with attention problems who perform well in mathematics. In fact, they may show steady improvement as they progress through school. Such students likely have strong conceptual abilities, a true "mathematical frame of mind," that enables them to reason, estimate, visualize, transfer knowledge, and apply basic operations in a highly flexible manner. Such underlying strengths may go a long way toward countering the effects of weak attention. Furthermore, some students with attention deficits may discover in mathematics a highly motivating experience, thereby overriding their impulsive styles.

Table 11-2 summarizes frequent error patterns in mathematics computation and possible processing and production contributors (see also table 11-1, p. 403).

Table 11-2. Common error patterns in mathematics computation

ERROR PATTERNS	POTENTIAL DEVELOPMENTAL CONTRIBUTORS
Slow or incomplete recall of facts	Weak convergent retrieval memory; poor memorization strategies; lack of pattern recognition; for addition and subtraction, may indicate lack of instructional emphasis.
Poor appreciation of details (e.g., changes in sign, number position in subtraction; carried numbers; number reversals)	Weak attention to visual detail; impulsiveness; lack of self-monitoring; possible weakness in visual processing; weak paired association memory.
Problems with regrouping in subtraction	Tenuous grasp of the concept of place value; weak attention to detail; impulsiveness, poor visual-spatial processing; lack of self-monitoring.
Trouble with algorithms that involve several steps	Poor memory for procedural sequences; weakness in active working memory; lapses in attention; visual-spatial processing difficulties.
Inaccurate calculations, despite knowledge of procedures	Weak convergent retrieval memory for facts; faulty counting strategies; erratic attention; lack of self-monitoring; fine motor deficits impeding finger counting or distinct formation of numbers; deficits in visual-spatial appreciation (e.g., alignment)
Difficulty calculating with fractions and mixed numbers	Poor conceptual understanding of part-whole relationships; poor visual-spatial imaging; weak procedural memory; impulsiveness.
Trouble with problems involving percent and decimals	Weak concept formation and threading; poor understanding of place value; procedural memory difficulties; inattention to visual detail.
Poor conversion skills (e.g., fraction/decimal/percent)	Tenuous conceptual understanding and fragmented or rote learning; weak long-term procedural memory.
Difficulty solving equations	Incomplete understanding of the concept of *equal* as related to equations; weak procedural memory; poor pattern recognition; underdeveloped proportional reasoning abillity.
Problems with geometry	Weak logical, sequential reasoning; poor visual-spatial and part-whole appreciation; sequential memory problems; language dysfunction; weak cumulative memory.
Trouble in advanced algebra and calculus	Poor abstract concept formation; memory deficits; language problems, especially learning and remembering new vocabulary; poor visual and paired association memory for new forms of notation.

Table 11-2. *(Continued)*

ERROR PATTERNS	POTENTIAL DEVELOPMENTAL CONTRIBUTORS
Word problem difficulties	Language (semantic and syntactic) dysfunctions; inadequate conceptual understanding of operations and overreliance on rote learning of computation procedures; poor saliency determination; weak visual-spatial imaging; lack of appreciation of quantity; poor verbal pattern recognition; impulsiveness and weak self-monitoring.
Poor error detection	Attention weaknesses; lack of self-monitoring; poor appreciation of quantity; dependence on rote learning; weak estimation skills.
Random, inconsistent errors	Erratic attention and self-monitoring; possibly a sign of incomplete understanding and reliance on rote learning; tenuous consolidation of procedures in long-term memory.
Mixed pattern of errors	A sign of multiple developmental dysfunction contributors that may occur in varying combinations.

STAGES OF LEARNING

Research has shown that students progress through a series of stages in mathematics learning and that not all students arrive at or pass through the stages at the same rate, age, or grade (Smith and Rivera 1991). The stages include: initial and advanced acquisition, proficiency, maintenance, generalization, and adaptation (Smith 1989, Smith and Robinson 1986). They are described by Smith and Rivera (1991, p. 358) as follows:

Acquisition. Students at this stage learn to perform a skill (initial acquisition) and then, through practice, develop accuracy and consistency (advanced acquisition). The emphasis is on accuracy in skill development.

Proficiency. Students become fluent and develop automaticity in executing skills, while maintaining accuracy. This enables them to progress to more advanced levels and perform more complex mathematical tasks with greater facility. For example, if students have not mastered the multiplication tables, performing advanced multiplication and long division can be a very labored and time-consuming process.

Maintenance. Once students have mastered a skill, they enter the stage of maintenance, which requires regular, periodic practice. Unfortunately, most math curricula move from one skill to another and rarely provide the necessary follow-up review.

Generalization. This is the stage in which students learn to apply a skill in different situations. If students' conceptual grasp of the skill is incomplete or tenuous, they frequently do not achieve flexibility in application of that skill to a variety of contexts. This is characteristic of students who overrely on rote learning.

Adaptation. During the adaptation stage, students learn to apply their understanding of skills and concepts for purposes of problem solving, reasoning, and decision making. Estimation skills are important at this stage.

The stages of learning have important implications for assessment and instruction. Knowing at what stage a student has arrived in skill acquistion, and recognizing the presence or absence of that skill and developmental strengths and weakness, can help direct the focus of instructional intervention.

ASSESSMENT

Mathematics skills, like other academic abilities, must be assessed developmentally. At different ages and grade levels, criteria of proficiency need to be established. Through careful study of a child's approach to mathematical problem solving and through perceptive analyses of error patterns, evaluators can perform assessments that have maximum implications for remediation. Furthermore, systematic observations of mathematical performance can shed light on the status of a variety of developmental functions. This discussion divides mathematics assessment into four academic levels: preschool and kindergarten; early elementary school (grades one to three); late elementary–middle school (grades four to seven); and secondary school (grades eight to twelve).

Preschool and Kindergarten

A number of acquired insights and abilities constitute readiness skills for arithmetic learning in school. During the preschool years, children should develop a sense of the meaning and constancy (i.e., one-to-one correspondence) of numerals. In assessing readiness, therefore, tasks eliciting familiarity with number concepts should be used. Children should show the beginnings of counting skills. They should be able to count aloud by rote, compute the number of objects in a group, and acquire some understanding of one-to-one correspondence. Counting skills are a critical underpinning of understanding quantitative relationships.

Appreciation of relative size and shape provides important foundations for the acquisition of geometric concepts. During preschool, children should demonstrate growing ability to sort objects by size and by shape. They may not be able to produce the language to describe or name such objects, but they should appreciate on a nonverbal level their likenesses and differences. Preschool children should also be developing a mathematical vocabulary. Prepositions indicating spatial directions, words pertaining to size and quantity (*more, less, equal*) and terms relating to fractions and part-whole relationships such as *half* should be mastered. They should be aware of and begin to appreciate left-right discrimination, although accurate labeling is unlikely.

Sequencing abilities are another group of important readiness skills. Preschool children should be able to sequence objects by size and quantity and, by late kindergarten, to sequence numbers between 1 and 10. Beginning appreciation of time concepts and vocabulary as well as familiarity with certain practical time-related materials such as clocks, chronological ages, seasons, and calendars should be appearing. Some elementary money concepts and vocabulary are another aspect of the preacademic mathematics curriculum. Youngsters also should be developing the ability to follow a sequence of two- and three-step commands and to preserve serial order in memory. The latter is especially germane to the mastery of number concepts and arithmetic algorithms in subsequent years.

During preschool and kindergarten, children should begin to learn to recognize number symbols and to associate them with concrete representations of quantity, a process similar to learning to recognize letters and associating them with sounds. Learning to write numbers is closely associated with symbol recognition. Initially, children should have some facility at copying and later, at remembering the motor engrams for number formation. The linguistic inconsistencies of number labels may cause the preschool child confusion in writing numbers. For example, *sixteen* implies that the 6 comes first, as it does in *sixty-one* (61).

By the end of kindergarten, most children have been introduced to the concepts of addition and subtraction and have begun to apply counting skills to perform simple computations with numbers 1 to 10.

Any assessment of general academic readiness should include evaluation of these abilities. Many preschool developmental tests contain items that probe acquisition of these skills and concepts. Informal checklists, skill inventories, and observations can provide additional insights.

Early Elementary School

The evaluation of attainment of mathematics skills in early elementary school needs to be coordinated closely with the pace and content of the curriculum, which can vary in order and rate of skill presentation and emphasis. During the early grades, children should reveal increasing facility with simple addition and subtraction. They should also begin to master basic facts; however, this is often given little emphasis, and students are allowed to proceed using concrete counting strategies. Nevertheless, over time, facts need to become readily accessible and usable with ease so that they can form the bases for the mastery of increasingly complex algorithms. Students must be attentive and respond accurately to mathematical signs. They must become skilled at writing numbers legibly and arranging them in appropriate columns to promote accuracy in completing algorithms.

These necessities require adequate fine motor skills, spatial awareness, and understanding of place value.

Certain major arithmetical concepts emerge and need to be assessed during the early elementary school years. Place value and regrouping are probably the most important of these. Any evaluation of second and third graders should observe and probe the child's understanding of these concepts as well as their application in performing computations. During third grade, students also should show some grasp of the concept of multiplication and emerging mastery of the times tables.

In evaluating the error patterns of children in early elementary school, several key questions should be asked: Has the child applied the wrong operation (e.g., added instead of subtracted), and was this due to inattention, lack of understanding of the operational sign, or incomplete grasp of the procedural steps? Has the child used an incorrect arithmetic fact (e.g., $3 + 2 = 6$), and was this due to inaccurate fact learning and recall or to inadequate counting strategies? Has the child misused an algorithm (e.g., $25 + 14 = 12$; the digits were simply added together)? Does the child overindulge in guessing? Are the guesses simply wild guesses, or do they represent reasonable estimates of the correct answer? During the early elementary school years, effective estimation skills should develop. Often, interviewing the child and asking him to explain the procedures used can provide valuable information about the depth of understanding and where breakdowns may be occurring.

Certain practical applications should also emerge during these years. Children should become increasingly adept at telling time and at making change. Their concepts of money should be developing rapidly. They should also be acquiring notions of measurement (use of a ruler as well as various determinations of volume).

During early elementary school and beyond, it is essential to determine whether students are having trouble in mathematics because of a problem *understanding* the material or whether they understand but are unable to *retrieve* and *apply* effectively what they have learned. Those students who have trouble with the initial understanding of processes or concepts often comment that the teacher does not explain things well enough, that mathematics class is too confusing. Some such students may have difficulties with language processing or with the higher cognitive demands of mathematics. Word problems are introduced during the early elementary grades, and students with language problems experience great difficulty analyzing their syntactic complexities and unusual word order necessary to identify critical information and select the appropriate operations. Those whose mathematics skills are compromised by memory dysfunctions often state (when asked) that they keep forgetting facts or steps, or that they don't remember what to do on a test or homework.

Students who have difficulty with mathematics because of its spatial and nonverbal content overrely on linguistic characterizations of mathematical processes and engage in very little nonverbal cognition. They often have difficulty visualizing quantitative and spatial relationships and display poor estimation abilities.

Problems may occur when these children are required to set up computation algorithms in order to solve word problems. While some students are able to master mathematics using such an exclusively linguistic approach, others (particularly those whose language skills are not outstanding) suffer from striving to transform all mathematical concepts into linguistic rules. Understanding of geometric concepts is especially elusive. Children with attention deficits may be careless and inconsistent in arranging numbers in columns and have trouble with mathematical detail such as changes in operational signs. Some students may make abundant careless errors and/or wild guesses. They are apt to show considerable inconsistency, erring on easy problems while performing better on more complex ones. In fact, greater complexity often is a stimulus for more focused attention. They may also tend to deteriorate over time and neglect to monitor their work.

Late Elementary and Middle School

During this period, students should be demonstrating increasing facility with long multiplication and division problems. They should be steadily automatizing basic mathematics facts, including the multiplication tables. Students should be revealing growing mastery of multistep mathematics problems. During these years, students should become competent with fractions, decimals, and percentages. The relationships between these concepts should become increasingly clear, and students should be able to explain them verbally and graphically. They should understand, for example, the relationship between the segments of a pie and numerical representations of fractions.

By middle school, students should have developed facility with word problems. Any assessment of mathematical ability in this age group needs to take into account the logic of a student's approach and the error patterns in word problems. Is the child able to distinguish relevant from irrelevant information in a word problem? Can the child discern relationships between the content of the word problem and the appropriate mathematical algorithms? Can the child recognize that the order in which information is presented in a word problem is not necessarily the order in which that information must be dealt with to derive a solution? Is the child able to generalize from one problem to another, for example, recognizing that although the wording differs, two problems may call for identical algorithms? Some students, particularly those with language disabilities, are able to perform well in most areas of mathematics but have their greatest frustration coping with word problems. Other students have trouble teasing out relevant mathematical algorithms when they are embedded in the language of a word problem. Sometimes higher cognitive weaknesses thwart their efforts.

It is helpful to watch students perform various mathematical computations, observing whether they plan their work, whether they establish an appropriate work tempo, whether they engage in proofreading or self-monitoring, whether they have automatized basic facts, and whether they are able to work neatly. It is also useful to determine the extent to which students can engage in mental arithmetic. Do they maintain certain steps in memory while undertaking them? Interviewing students and asking them to explain the processes they used in solving problems, both correctly and incorrectly, can provide valuable insights into their conceptual grasp and breakdown points in their knowledge and understanding.

Estimation skills, which should be improving markedly in this age range, are often revealed in a child's capacity to round off numbers. This is also a time for the refinement of geometric concepts and initial calculations of area, perimeter, and volume. During this period, there is a surge in specialized vocabulary which must be mastered.

By the seventh grade, students' automatization of basic arithmetic facts should be at a high level, enabling them to go beyond the calculations of early elementary school and to operate on a more symbolic and abstract level. For example, before students can become adept at the manipulation of unknowns in algebra, they must have automatized algorithms with numbers.

During these years, students should be developing basic computer skills. By seventh grade, they should be comfortable and quick at using a keyboard and aware of computer language and operation. Students should also have had some experience with calculators. Both computer and calculator abilities should be included in assessments in this age range.

Secondary School

During this period, students engage increasingly in formal operations. The demands of algebra, geometry, trigonometry, and calculus necessitate a high level of abstract symbolic thinking. Specialized vocabulary, formulae, and new notation signs place an ever increasing demand on memory. Sequential and cumulative memory are especially taxed in geometry, where the steps in proofs follow a particular order and one proof builds on another. Students also must be able to perceive relationships and make translations between one number form and another, as between decimals, fractions, and percents. Unfortunately, mathematical curricula tend to teach these as separate entities so that students fail to grasp the underlying concepts that enable them to form these relationships and transformations. Assessments at this level should be concerned with students' facility in dealing with equations, formulae, and geometric proofs, and with their ability to translate from one number form to another. The function of graphing takes on new importance at this level. Students must learn to plot equations, which places more demands on accuracy in visual-spatial processes. While evaluating competencies in these areas, it is important to observe the extent to which students engage in planning and self-monitoring; the tempo at which they work; and the level of automatization of earlier acquired facts, algorithms, and more complex processes.

As students proceed to more advanced mathematics courses, it is helpful to determine whether they possess a solid conceptual base for their work. Do they really understand proportion and ratio or are they verbalizing and applying concepts without having fully comprehended them? This is a common phenomenon, one that can ultimately cause difficulties in mathematics and science. Students should be able to explain and illustrate concepts rather than simply applying them. It is often helpful to ask students to describe what an equation is, to use some graphic representations of proportions, or to distinguish between examples and nonexamples of a concept.

Practical application of mathematics also needs to be evaluated during secondary school. Students should exhibit growing ability to deal with problems based on real-life situations. The computation of sales tax and interest, calculations involving automobile mileage (including gasoline consumption and comparisons or relative rates), and skills involving time changes and scheduling are examples. Facility in using calculators and computers for solving problems, and in dealing with statistics and data collection and analysis becomes increasingly important at this level.

Table 11-3 summarizes the basic parameters of mathematics assessment.

Assessment Methods

Many standardized examinations either tap mathematics exclusively or contain relevant subtests and are very useful in measuring skill acquisition. However, they usually report results on the basis of computation accuracy, which may penalize the student with attention problems. Such tests also may be out of synchrony with a school's curriculum. While it is important to make use of such established tools, day-to-day reports from teachers and observation of student performance are essential for documenting a student's level of attainment, characterizing his or her approach to mathematics, and portraying typical error patterns. Often this information can be gained in direct conversations with a mathematics teacher or from a questionnaire. At this stage, interviewing students can be an especially valuable technique in assessing conceptual grasp of, interest in, and affective response to mathematics. Students also can provide helpful insights regarding teaching and study techniques that facilitate and/or inhibit their learning of mathematics.

An indispensable part of assessment is the child's emotional response to learning mathematics. Some students are intensely anxious about this subject. Their anxiety in turn interferes with the acquisition and application of skills. Such "math phobias" often become serious handicaps. Other students, however, despite difficulties, are highly resilient and exuberant about mathematical learning. Any evaluation certainly needs to characterize as closely as possible the affective response and levels of motivation for this subject. In addition, it is helpful to account for the nature of the relationship between a particular student and past and present mathematics teachers. Some students find it especially difficult to communicate their feelings to teachers in this subject. They will often blame the teacher for talking too fast, not explaining things well, being too strict, giving difficult examinations, or embarrassing them in front of their peers. Such concerns, whether real or

Table 11-3. Basic parameters of mathematics assessment

SKILL	COMPONENTS
Basic number knowledge (precomputation)	Rote counting Object counting Symbol recognition Symbol formation (writing) Symbol-quantity association
Math facts	Use of counting strategies Accurate recall Automatic recall
Math notation	Knowledge of operational signs Understanding of quantitative and directional signs, e.g., <, >, ( )
Written computation	Procedure/algorithm knowledge Sequencing of steps Fact recall Alignment Attention to signs Understanding of place value Self-checking
Math vocabulary and verbal concepts	Examples include: *half, dozen, tangent, area, polygon*
Concept formation	Equation Proportional reasoning Propositional reasoning Place value Spatial appreciation Imaging
Problem solving	Identification of relevant information Understanding of syntax and vocabulary Selection of operations Setting up problems Sequence of steps Computation accuracy Self-monitoring Flexibility
Mental calculation and estimation	With number problems With word problelms
Applications	Money, measurement, time
Calculator use	

exaggerated, need to be elicited and dealt with to facilitate progress in the mastery of mathematics at all grade levels.

MANAGEMENT

Ineffective performance in mathematics can be an exasperating and humiliating experience for a student at any age. The precision of computation and problem solving required and the realization that there is only one correct answer induce anxiety, especially in students who lack confidence in their skills. The well-publicized phenomenon of "math phobia," if it exists, is likely to represent a complication of long-standing inability to master and integrate the various processes described in this chapter. It may also stem from traumatic early experience in the subject. The remediation of mathematics disabilities needs to be based on familiarity with students' existing skills and shortcomings in these areas as well as insight into their developmental strengths and deficiencies. At the same time, they must be shielded from personal embarrassment, accusation, and public humiliation.

This section on management is not intended to offer a comprehensive treatment plan. Instead, it is hoped that the suggestions will exemplify the kinds of intervention that can reduce anxiety and promote growth in this important life skill. It begins with a series of general recommendations and then proceeds to some suggestions about children with specific developmental dysfunctions.

General Recommendations

The following measures are likely to be beneficial to a diverse range of children with mathematics difficulties. Additional suggestions for development of specific mathematics skill components and curriculum materials can be found in Mercer and Mercer (1993, pp. 284–338) and Smith and Rivera (1991, pp. 363–69).

- Since mathematics depends on cumulative skills, it is essential that children master prerequisite skills and subskills. Students who have only a superficial or tenuous grasp of previously presented subskills are most vulnerable to failure. They must completely master mathematics facts before they are expected to become proficient in complex processes using these facts. Students who have not fully automatized multiplication tables will obviously feel stressed during long division and fractions. Remedial assistance, therefore, must often include a return to fundamentals.

- Whenever possible, mobilize students' developmental strengths to help them overcome skill delays resulting from developmental dysfunctions. The following pages contain examples of this.

- To prevent phobic reactions or excessive anxiety, mathematics teachers need to be compassionate, nonaccusatory, and supportive. Whenever possible, respect students' privacy. Do not call on deficient students when it is likely that they will err in public. The papers of a child with mathematics difficulties should not be checked by a more competent fellow student, passed back through the class, or left in a general stack. Do not display grades publicly. Avoid devastating written or spoken comments implying that a mathematics deficiency is the result of laziness or some other moral transgression.

- "Modeling" techniques may be useful (Smith 1981). With the student watching, the teacher solves the first example on the page, which consists of examples similar to the first one. This provides a model to which the student can refer. At home, parents can do the same. Integrate such techniques with discussions of the conceptual content or rationale for the processes being demonstrated.

- In evaluating a student's work it may be more helpful to designate or mark those problems done correctly than the errors. This focuses the student's attention on good examples or models. The student might then earn back credit for each error that he identifies and corrects. This encourages and reinforces self-monitoring and performing the correct procedures.

- Exercises that require students to correct work samples can serve a variety of purposes. They can increase attention to detail, strengthen knowledge of algorithms and the sequence of steps, improve self-monitoring, develop accurate and automatic recall of facts, and enhance identification of salient information in word problems.

- Use a student's breakdown point as the end object of assignments. For example, give a student who has trouble identifying the appropriate operations for solving word problems a selection of problems and ask her to write down what operation is needed (e.g., multiplication, subtraction), write down the operational sign, or identify all the problems that call for division. Similarly, ask a student who fails to attend to the need for regrouping and consistently subtracts the lesser from the greater number to go through a worksheet and circle all the instances where regrouping is required. Ask children who have trouble identifying extraneous information in word problems to go through examples and cross out any information that is superfluous.

- Set specific goals for acquiring skills, with a deadline for each stage. Deadlines must be attainable by the struggling student. For example, decide that by the first Wednesday of next month, the multiplication tables will be mastered through the fives. Students should have some clear-cut documentation of their progress, possibly through the use of graphs or other charts.

- Students with mathematics disabilities often have significant test-taking anxiety, which complicates their plight. Try giving these students fewer examples to solve, because time constraints intensify their anxiety. Emphasize test-taking skills in general. Teach estimating correct answers, monitoring, pacing, and such strategies as performing the easiest examples first.

- Use highly motivating games wherever possible. Entertaining computer software can alleviate the tedium of drill for those who are slow to assimilate basic facts. Mathematics teachers are often familiar with mathematically oriented instructional games such as *Math War, Basketball Math, Fraction Blackjack,* and *Arithmetic Squares* (Mercer and Mercer 1981). Dice and playing cards offer a wide range of possibilities. Monopoly can provide practice in strategic planning and money management as well as in calculation. These games can be easily taught to parents and pursued outside of school for practice and reinforcement of skills. There also are a number of computer software programs in game format that can be used for drill and allow students to work independently as well as in adult-directed groups, since they provide direct feedback and thus avoid allowing a student to practice errors.

- Homework is a particularly important part of mathematics learning. Homework should not involve learning something new but provide students opportunities for needed practice and application of skills that have been taught and require strengthening and consolidation. It is also helpful for parents to periodically work with their children to assure that mathematics is done slowly and deliberately. Students should employ a systematic approach that is well paced and fosters reasoning, reflection, and self-monitoring.

- Instruction and practice of skills using materials relating to high-interest subject matter may make learning more meaningful and practice more tolerable. Sports, woodworking, planning trips, and cooking offer a wealth of possibilities.

- Many students who have trouble with arithmetic can benefit from individualized help in a resource room or tutorial setting. The teacher offering this kind of service needs to strive to establish a strong alliance with the student. The setting should be nonthreatening and the ambience cheerful, to help combat the apprehension with which many of these learners approach mathematics.

- It is especially important for teachers to model algorithmic procedures and good work strategies (planning, a slow and deliberate approach, estimation, and monitoring). Make demonstration, accompanied by talking through the sequence or strategy, a part of classroom instruction. Simply having students mimic examples from the board or textbook can result in mislearning, lack of real understanding, and acquisition of poor work habits.

- Mathematical skills are particularly subject to loss over time if not practiced regularly. Require all students to maintain a cumulative notebook or file of math concepts and procedures throughout elementary and junior high school from which they are given regular review tests. Such reviews should be continued in all high school math courses.

Management for Specific Developmental Dysfunctions

Attention Deficits.   Children with mathematics difficulties and attention weaknesses need to stress methods and planning. Their approach to mathematics must become less impulsive; their tempo must be slower and more detail oriented. Teach them to examine all the problems and highlight or cue operational signs and/or those examples that require regrouping, especially in subtraction, before beginning calculations. Require them to check over their work, making corrections with colored pencil. Use of a calculator for the initial checking step might make the process less arduous. Encourage them to devise a plan for solving a problem and to articulate this plan before beginning the actual solution. Estimating answers before beginning calculations can enhance attention and depth of processing. Sometimes, devising a plan or problem estimation might be the end objective of an assignment. Or, withhold the pencil until the child has described a strategy for solving the problem. Encourage children who work too quickly to take more time to solve each of several computations. Tell the student, "Usually you do a problem like that very quickly. I want to see if you can do that problem in two minutes instead of in fifteen seconds."

Children with attention deficits need preferential seating in the classroom. Encourage them to subvocalize while working in mathematics (Smith 1981). Such verbal mediation helps focus attention on work, thereby enhancing accuracy. Teachers, tutors, and parents need to ascertain that youngsters with attention deficits truly understand what they have just learned. Because of their tendency to mimic rather than master and their relatively superficial approach to some learning, these students may not fully assimilate new concepts. Their mathematical careers may thus be vulnerable because of a superficial grasp on earlier learning. Remediation entails ongoing review and assurance that children have a firm understanding and recall of antecedent materials. While this is true for all students, it is especially the case for those with attention deficits.

Spatial Ordering Deficiencies.   Students with visual-spatial processing dysfunctions may be frustrated (especially during preschool and kindergarten) with the recognition and reproduction of numbers, particularly those that are similar in general configuration (6 and 9) or involve the same digits (15 and 51). As they proceed, they may have some difficulties aligning numbers in columns and using space effectively for calculations. They can benefit from using structured work sheets. Sometimes, the use of graph paper can facilitate spatial arrangement of numbers, as individual symbols are placed in separate squares on the grid. Lined paper held horizontally can also assist students with alignment, is less obvious and stigmatizing, and can strengthen the concept of place value. Conceptualization of quantitative relationships and time may prove difficult. Use of concrete and manipulative materials may make them more meaningful. A number line and/or ruler can help students visualize quantitative relationships between numbers and facilitate grasp of the concepts of basic operations and fraction equivalence. These students are also vulnerable to problems with the purely spatial aspects of mathematics. Geometric concepts, in particular, may be elusive. They may benefit from a highly verbal approach to geometric learning. For example, active verbalization of the characteristics of an equilateral triangle can help such students. They may also need to develop and memorize rules governing processes such as the measurement of volume or area. Students with poor visual-spatial processing and relatively intact language skills should thoroughly master mathematical vocabulary and system of rules. Drawing graphic representations of verbalized descriptions and word problems may increase their spatial appreciation.

Sequential Ordering Weaknesses.   Students with these problems are susceptible to difficulties following multistep explanations, poor mastery of the multiplication tables, weaknesses affecting the establishment of time concepts, and trouble implementing multistep computations. These students benefit from extensive drill on the multiplication tables. A strong visual-gestalt approach is recommended. Use flash cards, computer software, and mathematics games to drill facts. Have these children visualize and verbalize simultaneously. Their assimilation of multiplication tables can be based on what "sounds correct." Thus, while using flash cards, encourage them to articulate the entire fact (e.g., "four times six is twenty-four").

For these students, repeat multistep verbal explanations of mathematics processes. Visual demonstration models are especially important. Always have several models of correctly solved examples available for the students' homework assignments. For multistep mathematics processes, give these learners substantial opportunity to articulate the steps required in the correct order. Sometimes this should be done graphically. Students might make a list of the correct steps for solving a particular long-division problem rather than actually computing the correct answer. Practice in explaining/teaching algorithmic procedures can help solidify the sequence of steps. Mnemonic aids that signal the steps can be helpful; an example for division is, "**D**oes **M**cDonalds **S**ell **C**heese **B**urgers"—**D**ivide, **M**ultiply, **S**ubtract, **C**heck subtraction, **B**ring down. Give these students considerable drill on time conceptualization. Work with calendars, clocks, and schedules can be useful. Scheduling time for completion of daily and long-term assignments becomes increasingly important as students progress through middle and high school. Regularly require students to estimate how much time they ought to allow to complete different nightly assignments as well as different stages of long-term projects. Have them write out plans for homework and long-term projects and block out schedules on daily and monthly calendars; a large wall calendar may be helpful.

Memory Dysfunctions.   The formidable mnemonic demands of mathematics overwhelm some students, who thus benefit from a more cognitive, visual, and linguistic approach, with less stress on memorization. They require more time during examinations, an emphasis on rules and concepts, and considerable rote drill. Visualization strategies should receive instructional emphasis. Children with active working memory deficiencies can have particular problems taking mathematics tests. Encourage them to write down as much as possible so as not to rely too heavily on mental arithmetic operations. Counting strategies and mnemonic aids can help students who have difficulty recalling math facts; for example, addition and subtraction facts involving 9 present their own answer: $9 + 7 = 16, 6 + 1 = 7; 9 + 3 = 12, 1 + 2 = 3; 14 − 9 = 5, 1 + 4 = 5$. The *Touch Math* system is based on counting strategies whereby numbers 1–9 are accorded a representative number of dots. Often these are the students who can benefit most from using a calculator for homework and tests. Although this is not recommended as a panacea, it can be the salvation of some students with mathematics deficiencies. Calculators enable students to continue learning mathematics concepts, problem-solving strategies, and practical applications despite their trouble with the automatic recall of basic facts. This bypass strategy can be defensible for a wide range of developmental dysfunctions, but it is particularly germane to those who are debilitated by the memory strain imposed by mathematics. These students also need an active approach to studying for examinations. They need to give themselves practice tests, to come up with specific memory plans that include such self-testing strategies. Such plans should be articulated to parents and/or teachers beginning several days before the examination. Decisions about allocating time, drill techniques, and predictions of what will be on tests should be part of the intense study campaign.

Children with memory problems suffer when they do not practice skills regularly. Since mathematics depends so much on cumulative memory, these students are especially vulnerable. Require them to keep a cumulative notebook of examples of processes, concepts, and formulae and engage in regular practice as part of their homework. Reinforce learning by periodic review tests. Students can carry over such a notebook or file from year to year and keep it on a computer.

Language Disability. Students with language difficulties may have problems with the verbal aspects of mathematics learning. They require careful drill on mathematics vocabulary. They need visual models and considerable repetition of verbal explanations as well as seating as close to the teacher as possible. They can benefit from an emphasis on graphic work sheets. Computer software, with its predominantly visual mode of presentation, can be especially helpful for these students.

Struggling students are apt to need special help with solving word problems. Tutorial assistance should stress a systematic, step-by-step approach to word problems, including identification of relevant and irrelevant data, isolation of key words within a problem, translation of these words into numerical symbols and/or processes, and identification of relevant rules or formulas for arriving at a solution. Although students with language difficulties are not the only ones threatened by word problems, they are especially vulnerable and need help with the translation of these verbal arrays into computational formats.

Have students with language difficulties work on developing estimation skills. These skills can lead them to the correct operations when they are stymied by language complexities. Give students who are struggling with word problems exercises in which they are asked to identify those examples that require a specific operation. Students with language problems may also benefit from practice in writing word problems that require a specified operation or represent a particular formula.

Higher Cognitive Weaknesses.   Some students have great difficulty with the higher cognitive aspects of mathematics. Their problems can be pervasive or limited to either the verbal or nonverbal cognitive realms. A teacher who is aware of cognitive weakness can aim material at the stronger of the student's reasoning channels. For example, one girl with well-developed language abilities had a great deal of difficulty conceptualizing the properties of various geometric forms. She was helped considerably by being allowed to prepare brief lectures on various topics in geometry. She recorded them, played them back, and wrote them out for her teacher. Applying her expressive linguistic talents, in a sense translating nonverbal conceptual material into her own words, greatly facilitated her learning. Students who seem to have much more pervasive difficulties with higher-order cognition can benefit from a less abstract approach to mathematics. Concepts such as fractions, equations, and proofs can be taught with manipulatives. Cuisenaire Rods and the Sterns program with structured boxes and color-coded blocks exemplify materials that can be visualized and handled to vividly illustrate quantitative relationships, place value, and the four basic mathematics operations. A color-coded abacus and fraction pies are other examples. Affected students also benefit from practical mathematics applications. Measuring, making change, dividing materials into equal or unequal proportions, cooking and adapting recipes for varying numbers of servings, and calculating the relative speeds of moving objects or other prototypes of real-life situations are likely to have greater meaning to students frustrated by the abstract elements of mathematics.

Graphomotor Dysfunction.   Some students have difficulty with the graphomotor components of mathematics. Their work may be sloppy. They may make many careless errors because of poor alignment of numbers in a column or illegible number formation. These students can benefit from the use of a good mechanical pencil, the writing of numbers in squares on graph paper, the use of columns on lined paper, a strong emphasis on deliberative slowness, the use of a calculator, and an emphasis on monitoring their work. Some students need to be drilled on number formation, with regular practice forming legible symbols.

MATHEMATICS SURVIVAL

Every effort should be made to teach mathematics so that the subject becomes less intimidating to apprehensive students. Mastering mathematics and any phobic tendencies can be an enormous source of satisfaction. The teaching of mathematics to students with developmental dysfunctions can represent a real challenge to the creativity of the educator. As with other academic subjects, it is possible to make use of a particular student's academic and/or developmental strengths to facilitate learning and make the subject matter more palatable. An example of this is the use of writing to master mathematical concepts. Nahrgang and Petersen (1986) describe the use of journal writing sessions in a mathematics course. Entries in a journal were substituted for mathematics quizzes. As part of their journal writing, students were expected to describe linkages between mathematics processes and other life experiences. In all likelihood, this kind of activity makes the conceptual content much more accessible to students who may be poor at taking mathematics quizzes but relatively strong in expository and creative writing. Some divergent thinkers might find this form of mathematics learning and extrapolation satisfying and helpful. Nahrgang and Petersen cite an example in which students were told to "think of a nonmathematical relationship that is analogous to the process of finding a product and factoring." One student gave the following response:

> One relationship similar to finding a product versus factoring is that of taking a carburetor apart and then putting it back together. When the carburetor is together, it is difficult to clean and repair. Therefore, it is disassembled to make it easier to work with. This is analogous to factoring.
>
> When the parts of the carburetor are in working condition, they must be put back together before they will work as desired. This is analogous to finding a product (p. 465).

Alternatively, one might ask children to write essays about the ways in which balancing an equation is similar to techniques needed to keep friendships or relate to one's parents.

The mastery of mathematics concepts offers students a rigorous set of thought processes and problem-solving strategies. Furthermore, mathematics abilities are essential for meeting daily life challenges at work and on the domestic scene. However, when all else fails and it is likely that a student will ultimately fall far short of adequate mathematics performance, priorities must be considered to assure that mathematics survival skills will be in place (Smith 1981). These include a wide range of practical needs such as finance-based vocabulary, number symbols, the capacity to read common measuring instruments (time schedules, clocks, gauges, and calendars), the use of dry and liquid measures, the ability to read maps, the ability to interpret graphs and statistical data such as those used in sports and financial reporting, and comprehension of financial concepts used in banking and other business transactions.

Mathematics, reading, writing, and spelling are basic skills. These abilities provide gratification in their own right, and also they facilitate the acquisition of highly specific bodies of knowledge. Such learning traditionally occurs within predetermined categorical contexts, such as science, social studies, and literature. The various content areas and elective subjects, which the next chapter explores, present a series of unique challenges and opportunities that often serve to dramatize individual differences and preferences. Performance in these areas depends highly on skills acquired in other contexts and is likely to reveal specific strengths and shortcomings in the developmental functions.

Chapter 12

Academic Content Areas

Until then [age fourteen], de Gaulle appears to have given unexpectedly little atten-
tion to his formal studies. Absorbed by his martial games, by adventure stories, and
by his beloved poets and writers, he spent more time writing verses of his own than
studying. . . . His astonishing memory—which he had already begun to train by
speaking words spelt backwards—usually carried him through.
                                                    —Brian Crozier, *De Gaulle*

The early years of educational experience prepare students to deal with the academic content of various subject areas. As academic skills are progressively acquired and automatized, they increasingly afford access to specific domains of knowledge. Students must make the transition from learning specific skills to applying them to obtain new knowledge and broaden their understanding and reasoning capabilities. Reading, for example, becomes a tool for acquiring facts, skills, and concepts and for learning to make judgments. The content areas predominate in secondary education. History, science, foreign languages, and literature are among specialized subjects that require students to make use of previously acquired skills and knowledge to extract and manipulate ideas and engage in critical thinking. Mathematics also becomes content oriented, and computer literacy emerges as an important addition to content specialties. The steadily expanding emphasis on content areas poses a formidable set of new demands for all students, but some or all of these areas may be highly stressful for those with developmental dysfunctions and incompletely assimilated skills in learning and producing.

In considering content area subjects, it is helpful to bear in mind their potential for fostering either a new level of academic independence or a growing maladaptation. This section summarizes some important determinants of the impacts content area subjects have on students.

Content area teachers may assume that students have well-developed and appropriately automatized basic skills in writing, reading, and mathematics. When underlying skills are inadequate, not yet automatized, or notably inconsistent, students experience difficulty fulfilling content area demands.

Teachers also frequently assume that students possess the specialized reading techniques required by specific subject matter and materials. Reading literature allows for a divergent approach and flexibility in interpretation, whereas science and mathematics require precision in reading and understanding vocabulary and concepts.

Different teachers teach different subjects and also different sections of the same subject. Not only must students accommodate to varying subject matter, but they must also adapt their learning, productivity, and classroom behavior to a wide range of teaching styles, expectations, classroom routines, grading systems, and personality matches between themselves and individual teachers. Students must somehow discern the varying requirements as they proceed from class to class and strive to interpret and satisfy expectations. Such "reading" of what it takes is part of the "hidden curriculum" described in chapter 7.

Content area teachers may sometimes be more interested in their specific subjects than in the problems or styles of individual learners. Moreover, they have more students to deal with than do elementary school teachers. This may result in some sacrifice of individualization. Students with highly specific needs or unusual learning styles may suffer from the relative anonymity of junior high and high school classrooms. This is particularly the case when students have received substantial help or accommodation during earlier grades.

As the content areas increase in difficulty, demand for sophisticated reading and writing intensifies. Students must have strong summarization abilities, good interpretative skills, a capacity to integrate knowledge from numerous sources, keen critical thinking, and the ability to analyze different textual styles and genres.

Sufficient and accurate prior knowledge is essential for understanding and learning in content areas, a fact frequently assumed by both teachers and the writers of textbooks. Incorrect preconceptions must be dispelled and an appropriate knowledge base built for understanding and learning to occur. Furthermore, students must learn how and when to activate their fund of background information and prior learning.

Students must recognize the diverse expectations that emanate from different content areas. Certain subjects, such as literature, allow for risk taking, creativity, divergent memory, and imagination. Others, such as chemistry, demand convergent memory and precision. Content area subjects require that students develop variable reading intensities and apply them in the proper circumstances. Skimming (reading to derive a general impression), scanning (reading to locate specific information), and intensive reading (to find out how to do something) are examples (Deshler, Ellis, and Lenz 1996). Appropriate application requires establishing a purpose for reading, assessing prior knowledge of the topic, and evaluating text difficulty. Students must also gain flexibility and discernment in selecting appropriate study techniques according to the nature of the material, learning purpose, or test.

Mastering unfamiliar vocabulary in reading is another challenge. Students must be adept at discovering word meanings through context clues, linguistic knowledge, and dictionary usage.

The demands for students to process and learn increasing volumes of new material, the need for cumulative learning, and the growing length of individual assignments make it especially important that students engage in metacognitive self-evaluation of their learning, stopping regularly to assess their understanding and memory.

Content area subjects require organization, storage, and efficient access to increasing amounts of information. Maintaining class notebooks, collecting and organizing data for reports, and locating information from prior classes for review and referral (particularly important in courses where learning is cumulative) is an overwhelming task, and most students would benefit from guidance in establishing a consistent, organized system. With the ever increasing availability of computers, required instruction in database management for all students should be seriously considered. Database management software enables rapid access to information, comparison and contrast between files, continuous, cumulative updating of information, and an organized storage system. It can be implemented effectively in all content areas (Lungren 1989).

The content areas have the potential to arouse special interest. A student may be turned on by history, biology, Spanish, or computer science. A sudden surge of enthusiasm for learning, a drive to master a subject (independent of academic requirements), or the mysterious resonance of a topic with a child's processing systems and interests kindles motivation, which sometimes even spreads to other academic content areas. Conversely, the student who finds no content area attractive but works only to avoid ostracism may continue to struggle to sustain effort and endure the tedium of school.

These factors are an important part of our survey of content area subjects. This chapter describes the demands they place on students and examines possible effects of developmental variation and dysfunction. It does not cover every content area; instead it provides an overview of some of the more common subjects.

ENGLISH AND LITERATURE

Courses that stress literary skills of reading and writing are universal in the curricula of secondary schools. Most students perceive them as a direct continuation of earlier tutelage in reading, spelling, and writing. However, unlike the stories contained in elementary basic readers, in which content, context, and language emulate familiar experience, literary content comes in many forms and generally is conceived of as an artistic creation. As such it presents multiple layers and shades of meaning expressed in indirect, ambiguous, and often idiosyncratic language and syntactic patterns, and presented in a variety of literary genres. These pose enormous challenges for language skills. Teachers of English and related literature courses are perhaps less likely than other content area teachers to neglect instruction in the reading skills specific to a work, author, or literary genre. Nevertheless, they are apt to presuppose (or hope for) the existence of adequate reading comprehension and writing ability.

The study of literature necessitates that students become adept at discerning and manipulating reading content in sophisticated ways. They must be able to read a paragraph or passage and identify its main idea as well as supporting details (see pp. 318–19). This is problematic for many students. Donlan (1980) found that many junior high school readers think that whatever is stated in the first sentence is the main idea.

Students must be able to abstract, summarize, and retell what they have read in their own words (see pp. 318–319). This requires comprehension, the ability to distinguish saliency, and the capacity to organize and express ideas effectively. Examinations complicate this process by placing heavy demands on retrieval memory and active working memory.

Literature classes require that students engage in different levels of critical reading and interpretation. Herber (1985) identifies three levels of comprehension: literal, interpretive, and evaluative. The *literal* level requires concrete understanding of the words as written. The *interpretive* level involves discernment of the author's intent and requires comprehension of verbal ambiguities, figures of speech, and idiosyncratic use of vocabulary and syntax. *Evaluative* comprehension includes identification of broader principles that go beyond the specific context of the text. Literature courses further require that students develop special interpretive skills for different genres; students must adjust to varying literary techniques as they read poetry, plays, short stories, novels, and biographies (Fishel 1984). Some students may experience difficulty moving with facility from one genre to another.

As students deal with larger amounts of literary material, the need to relate parts to wholes increases. They must develop an overview and determine how specific elements contribute to a total literary work. In reading a novel or a short story, they must determine the author's intention, ferret out recurring themes or symbols that help fulfill that intention, follow the plot, identify complicating factors, and demonstrate an appreciation of the resolution (McNeil 1984). Such processes entail sustained attention to detail, good organizational skills, appropriate processing of sequence, substantial active working memory, good retrieval, well-developed language abilities, and effective higher-order cognition. Language skills, in particular, are challenged as students must deal with figures of speech, semantic ambiguity, syntactic complexities, and cultural variations in word usage and meaning.

Thus, multiple developmental functions work in concert to foster success in literature courses. Once students have developed skill and confidence in interpretation, they have the opportunity to interject a personal point of view, to achieve the supreme integration of a reader's perspective with that of the writer, so that reading becomes a creative, constructive, interactive process. These capacities suggest Chall's later reading stages (3 to 5; see chapter 9).

In addition to well-developed reading skills, the literature student must also possess adequate writing skills. The abilities described in chapter 10 are called for in book reports, essays, quizzes, and examinations. The tenth-grade literature teacher is likely to assume that students are totally adept at letter formation, are capable of capitalizing and punctuating, know rules of grammar, can spell, and are able to write, think, and remember simultaneously. Clearly, writers whose developmental dysfunctions have thwarted automatization will be at a disadvantage in such courses. Their own literary ideas may be sacrificed during transcription onto paper. This can be a disheartening experience for bright thinkers who find this reduction in quality intolerable.

Creative writing may be either the bane or the salvation of certain students. Many of those with attention deficits, for example, possess rich imaginations and have a strong aptitude for placing the free flight of ideas on paper. This can be a highly motivating experience for such students. In other cases, students may be devoid of literary ideas. They may be paralyzed by the need to choose a topic for a composition or to provide descriptive elaboration. Frequently, it helps to identify an area of unusual talent, interest, or aptitude and encourage students to write about that. For example, youngsters who are very interested in cars or animals may do their best writing about those subjects. The area itself may be so highly motivating that it facilitates development of ideas and other writing skills. Brainstorming activities can also enhance a student's ideational and elaborative fluency.

Class discussions may be problematic for some students with expressive language difficulties, memory weaknesses, or attention deficits. They may have trouble keeping up with the flow of conversation, following the sequence of thought in debating interpretive nuances, quickly retrieving information about their reading, or expressing ideas about what they have read.

Effects of Dysfunctions on English and Literature

Literature courses tap heavily the basic skills of reading and writing. Therefore, the impacts of dysfunction cited in chapters 9 and 10 pertain directly to this content area. Receptive language abilities, including phonology, vocabulary, morphology, syntax, semantic discourse, pragmatics, and metalinguistic awareness, are essential requisites for the interpretation of reading material. Developmental functions facilitating oral expression and writing skills are equally germane. When underlying skills are weak, students may appear to know less than they actually do. This can lead to a significant reduction in incentive and motivation to work. As we shall see, special allowances may have to be made to accommodate such students in their English courses. They need opportunities to savor the ideational content and creative expression of the different literary genres (novels, plays, poetry, and biography) despite delays in decoding ability and inadequate comprehension skills.

The presence or absence of literary talent is likely to be a question of higher-order verbal cognitive facility. A student may have significant difficulties with verbal reasoning and trouble constructing schemata required for literary criticism and creativity. Devices such as irony, metaphor, simile, and symbolism may be too abstract for a student who tends to be linguistically concrete. Teaching such students to deal with analogies may enhance their understanding of abstract devices (Bellows 1980). A student who has problems with literature may nevertheless do well in science and history courses, in which the language is more direct and comprehension is literal and less dependent on creative interpretation. Or he may be admirably clever at mathematics, playing music, or fixing a computer. Thus, cognitive style becomes highly germane to success in a content area. A child who is baffled when constrained to interpret a poem need not be viewed as "disabled" but perhaps as engaging in the wrong specialty. That is not to say we should grant an exemption from poetry, but rather that we should understand that his particular pursuit of this type of reading may exact Herculean effort and could conceivably yield relatively low satisfaction and success for that child. Of course, the great challenge is to entice those who lack a natural affinity for literature and to maximize the rewards of such experiences.

FOREIGN LANGUAGE

The mastery of a second language can be a source of enormous gratification. Such a new skill allows one to savor other cultures, to find new modalities of communication, to gain access to a foreign literature, and to appreciate better the intricacies of one's native language. A multilingual scholar is held in high esteem. Foreign language proficiency is taken as a sign of advanced educational attainment in our society; it also has become a very valuable career asset. Unfortunately, for certain students, learning a foreign language is an anathema. They may work exceedingly hard only to discover that their minds reject a second language as vigorously as their bodies might reject an organ transplant. It is not unusual for an adolescent to become increasingly frustrated with her inability to master a foreign language, and the consequent demoralization can spread to other subject areas. She spends so much time and mental energy struggling with the foreign language (and fretting over it) that there is little left in reserve for other content areas. Unfortunately, identifying the difficulties that make language learning so futile for certain students is not always easy.

Learning a foreign language requires facility with verbal comprehension, reading, speaking, and writing (Cziko 1978). These four abilities are closely related and, in most cases, develop parallel to each other. Foreign language courses also place varying demands on expertise with oral and written modes of communication, both receptive and expressive. Some students may be much better at understanding than speaking. Others may progress rapidly with reading but slowly with writing. A student may be fluent in oral conversation but struggle when attempting to translate thoughts into written form. Another may be able to read and comprehend written text but be at a loss in understanding what is transmitted orally. Foreign language courses tend to increase in complexity, in demands on memory, and in the expectation for growing fluency. Some students keep pace during the early learning stages when they are highly attracted to the subject matter and there is a modicum of strain on cumulative memory, only to plummet into a catastrophic slump by February or March of the first year. At this point, demands for memory, vocabulary, and some automaticity in comprehension and expression increase, and grammar becomes more complex.

Considerable research has explored what constitutes foreign language aptitude. Some of the best studies were done as part of military research on the prediction of success in intensive foreign language training. A wide range of test batteries evaluated which recruits were most likely to succeed in rapidly acquiring language skills applicable to military settings. Some of this research has been reported by Carroll (1962), who identified the following four elements of language aptitude discovered to predict talents:

- *Phonetic coding.* A student's ability to mimic unusual sounds and to code them in such a way that they can be retrieved later is one of the primary foreign language aptitudes. First, the learner must be able to imitate the sounds effectively, even though the particular phonemes to be mastered are not characteristic of the native language. Once the sound has been formed accurately, it must somehow be associated with a grapheme (visual representation) and then filed for subsequent recognition, retrieval, or association. Adept students are good at both imitating and storing such novel sound units.

- *Grammatical sensitivity.* Those who are adept at foreign languages are attuned to nuances of grammatical construction. They are likely to display keen sensitivity to word functions, to the effects of word order, to the construction and interpretation of subordinate clauses, and to other forms of syntactic structure and the ways in which they alter meanings.

- *Rote memory for foreign language materials.* A good language learner is especially skilled with memory for language and is able to form strong associations between foreign words and their meanings. Such a student can retrieve previously acquired vocabulary quickly and with little effort.

- *Inductive language learning ability.* Carroll (1962) describes this as "the ability to infer linguistic forms, rules, and patterns from new linguistic content itself with a minimum of supervision or guidance" (p. 130). He describes a form of foreign metalinguistic awareness. That is, proficient students have an innate sense of the structure of a foreign language; they know what sounds right, what fits. They have assimilated the deep structure of the language and discerned its regularities and irregularities so that they can make accurate independent predictions about vocabulary, morphology, and sentence structure.

Barriers to Foreign Language Acquisition

Although multiple developmental, motivational, and cultural obstacles can stand in the way of foreign language mastery, five common impediments are discussed here.

Pronunciation Problems.   Some students simply have difficulty articulating the sound of a foreign language, that is, imitating its phonemes even after repeated exposures (Mead 1983). They may have trouble employing the foreign sounds in the varying combinations and sequences of sounds in words and contexts. In addition, a number of students are poor at *discriminating* between sounds in a foreign language. Phonemes seem indistinct to them. They are unable to distinguish the end of one word from the beginning of another. These shortcomings of auditory discrimination seriously impede vocabulary acquisition and speaking ability. Students may have particular trouble pronouncing and/or hearing differences between sounds that seem similar. Still others have a seeming oral motor *dyspraxia* (inflexibility), making it difficult for them to derive and implement the motor engrams to imitate the unfamiliar phonemes. Many children with phonologically based foreign language difficulty have had at least mild problems with the sound system in their first language.

Foreign language aptitude requires not just internalizing and mimicking foreign language sounds but also recalling them. Developing an effective memory for foreign phonology can be a significant problem.

Certain languages, such as Spanish and Latin, are phonetically regular and are therefore particularly well suited for those who lack a strong visual memory for letter patterns. Nevertheless, even these require a firm sense of sound-symbol association and rhythm, good auditory discrimination abilities, and strong paired association memory skills. Students lacking in these prerequisite functions may encounter obstacles even with highly phonetic languages.

Although sound discrimination and pronunciation problems may hinder development of oral comprehension and conversation skills, students with otherwise strong language, visual processing, and memory abilities may become competent readers and even writers of a foreign language. This is especially true for languages that are highly regular and rule governed, such as Latin.

Native Language Interference.   A major barrier that affects pronunciation and appreciation of sounds (as well as other aspects of learning a foreign language) is the common phenomenon of *native language interference* (Mead 1983). Some students are slow to part with the system of sounds in their native language. They are so wedded to its prosody and rhythm that they have trouble adjusting to an alternative mode. As children become older, they are more susceptible to native language interference. If students master a foreign language when very young, they have a better chance of speaking it with little or no accent. With increasing age, the likelihood of a strong accent grows. Native language interference may also occur when students have had to struggle to acquire language skills in their own tongue. When articulation and acquisition of vocabulary in the native language have been laborious, time is apt to bring a loss of flexibility, which is likely to depend on automatization of the first language. That is, if the native sounds have not been very easily and deeply integrated, it is difficult to move from them to a whole new system of sound.

Morphology Problems. Some language learners are slow to grasp patterns of roots, suffixes, and prefixes in new languages (Politzer 1965). Latin and German are examples of languages in which these are vitally relevant, in fact, more relevant than in English. Even adjectives in these languages change their endings to acknowledge grammatical constraints. Students must master these regularities of word structure at the same time that they become aware of notable exceptions to the rules. To a large extent, the regularities and irregularities of morphology must be learned through rote memory. However, the process is substantially facilitated for those students who have a strong intuitive language learning ability. Somehow, the morphology makes sense to them. Native language interference can make it difficult to assimilate patterns of morphology at variance with one's native tongue. Again, this is likely to be particularly true for those who had to struggle to master their own language. Residual language disabilities return to haunt such students when they confront a second language.

Vocabulary Problems. The acquisition of a foreign vocabulary is yet another hurdle, one in which memory plays a critical role. In particular, paired associative learning is essential. Students must form a tight link between a word in their native language and its equivalent in the new one. Often this entails rote memorization; sometimes, however, roots are similar in both languages, facilitating mastery. Occasionally, even this can be deceptive. A common fallacy is to equate incorrectly a foreign word with a native one. In French, such words are referred to as *faux amis*—words that look the same in French and English but have different meanings. An example is *crayon,* which means "pencil" in French. Students must learn the different meanings of words that look alike.

In addition to memorizing vocabulary, students must recognize that meanings often change according to contexts. Thus, learning vocabulary is more than just memorizing a list of words and native language equivalents. Also involved are the various usages of those words and their contextual dependency. Mastery of idioms also requires a heavy reliance on context cues as well as sheer memorization. Other words may be highly culture specific. These, too, have to be learned independently.

There is now evidence that vocabulary learning must be carefully paced for all students. For example, one study demonstrated much more effective learning when drill took place on consecutive days for short time periods rather than in extended sessions (Bloom and Shuell 1981).

Over time, foreign language vocabulary must become increasingly automatized. In order to read sophisticated literature in a second language, the meanings of words must be readily accessible (Mackay, Barkman, and Jordan 1979). If too many words have to be looked up in a dictionary, if detection of meaning requires too much time and effort or a prolonged search of memory stores, the reader may exceed the capacity of active working memory, sacrificing overall comprehension, connotation, an author's point of view, and other sophisticated elements of literary interpretation.

When writing or speaking in a foreign language, fluency is essential. Students who are dysfluent, who have serious word-finding problems in the foreign language, may have trouble expressing themselves. They may need to settle for unsophisticated vocabulary that falls short of capturing complex ideas. Again, a prolonged search for words may take its toll on overall expressive sophistication.

Syntactical Problems. Mastering a new grammatical system can challenge the foreign language learner (Politzer 1965). Syntax barriers may be substantial. Many students who appear to demonstrate competence in use of the syntactic structures of their own language are operating on "automatic pilot," relying on "what sounds right." However, their understanding of word functions, anaphora (features that distinguish referents from nonreferents, as in the use of relative pronouns), and clause structure is quite tenuous. Students who have an incomplete understanding of word functions in their native language have even greater difficulty learning new rules of grammatical construction. They are unable to comprehend how systems of word order and syntax work. Native language interference may be the culprit, there being a strong tendency to impose the grammatical system of the native language on that of the new language. This tendency may cause an English-speaking student to use English word order in constructing German sentences. Students with a poor sense of foreign language (or those with poorly automatized English language processing) may have real difficulty determining what sounds right grammatically in a foreign language. Some of them overrely on word order as a mediator of meaning. In certain languages (such as German) word endings are more important than word order.

Effects of Dysfunction on Foreign Language Learning

No single content area threatens children with learning difficulties more than foreign languages. Often, we can predict that students who have floundered in other academic areas will flounder when it comes to absorbing a second language. In some instances, students seem to have overcome dysfunctions that have affected other academic areas but are left with residual dysfunction that is rekindled by foreign language learning. Attention deficits, language disabilities, specific memory dysfunctions, sequential disorganization, and weaknesses of verbal cognition, singly or in clusters, impede foreign language learning. Probably the most relevant dysfunctions are those involving language and/or memory. Some children with relatively mild or subclinical language disabilities may ultimately have learned to comprehend and express themselves in their native language because they have been so overexposed to it. In a sense, they have overlearned their language although they were vulnerable to problems with it. Constant immersion and exposure may allow a child to develop competence in the skills of his or her native language without a real understanding of the underlying rules that govern the systems of how words function. Ultimately, however, she encounters difficulties when she attempts to master a second language. Language weaknesses in the native tongue become conspicuous when tackling a second language without the opportunity to overlearn it. Children with discrete problems in memory, especially those with active working memory weaknesses or problems with paired associative memory (for words) may falter and become extremely frustrated when challenged with both a new vocabulary and a new system of morphology and syntax. Deficiencies of active memory and retrieval may create inordinate barriers for such youngsters. Their foreign language learning may be a source of continual frustration despite their having fairly good language skills in general.

Assessment of Foreign Language Ability

Certain methods to evaluate aptitude for foreign language (Dinklage 1971) have been used in educational settings at the middle school, secondary, and college levels. Among these are the *Modern Language Aptitude Test* (Carroll and Sapon 1959) and the *Pimsleur Language Aptitude Battery* (Pimsleur 1966). The norms are old, and neither their reliability nor their predictive validity has been fully established. These assessments should not be relied on exclusively. Frequently, tests assessing phonological skills in the context of nonsense words are employed as indicators of aptitude for foreign language learning. Studies of Swedish-, French-, and Italian-speaking children revealed phonological abilities to be highly correlated with later reading achievement (Lundberg, Olofsson, and Wall 1980; Alegria, Pignot, and Morais 1982; Cossu et al. 1988). This gives some support to use of assessment of phonological abilities as an indicator of success in foreign language aptitude, but little research has been done to substantiate this. Nevertheless, schools often need to know whether a student is poorly motivated or uninterested in foreign language or is contending with a disability that makes foreign language learning futile, or nearly so. One useful method of reconciling such conflicts is to have the student in question spend time alone with a foreign language teacher. Five or six private lessons might be tried during which a specific body of material is taught. The teacher should be able to develop a sense of how difficult it is for that student to assimilate the language and how effectively what is learned on a one-to-one basis is retained over time. Such trial learning may also provide insight into methods of instruction and practice that are particularly effective for that student. This technique can serve as a reliable indicator of foreign language teachability; however, it is vitally important that such trial lessons include a variety of requisite skills for language learning (vocabulary, sound-symbol learning, pronunciation, and grammar).

To supplement information gained from such assessments, a thorough review of the student's developmental history and early acquisition of language skills may be valuable in revealing the presence of underlying language weaknesses which the student has compensated for in his native language by constant immersion and overexposure. Assessing a student's reading rate and comprehension of grade-level content area material may also provide helpful insights into that student's basic language aptitude and fluency. Evaluation of knowledge of the grammatical structures of English and their application, through structured tasks and examination of writing samples, may provide additional information regarding a student's linguistic knowledge and facility.

Management of Foreign Language Disability

Symptoms of foreign language disability require special services. The precise content of such intervention is likely to differ depending on the specific characteristics and needs of the student. Drill on vocabulary, comprehension, and verbal expression needs to take place in a language laboratory with some privacy or in a one-to-one tutorial setting. The teacher must have an excellent grasp on the student's areas of relative strength and weakness. Some students, for example, have particular difficulties understanding a spoken foreign language but have none or few in comprehending what they read. A learner's apparent strength or facility should be emphasized (at least initially). Thus, if students derive more meaning from reading than from listening, much of the vocabulary and grammar should be taught through the use of texts. In other instances, students learn best through oral expression. They are apt to benefit from an emphasis on encoding their ideas into the foreign language.

Often students need highly specific drill to master the grammatical rules of a language. Many students with learning problems have a tendency to gloss over such regularities; their understanding of parts of speech and word functions is tenuous at best. As the complexity of spoken and written material increases during the year, their lack of a true, basic understanding of language structures catches up with them. For this reason, fundamentals—word order, morphology, and syntax—need to be constantly emphasized. This return to basics has to be the cornerstone of remedial help for floundering language learners. At the same time, attention to vocabulary building should continue. It should be based on an understanding of differences between the new language and English and on an awareness of common roots. The *logic* of the foreign language should be stressed as much as possible.

A variety of methods of drill can be employed with students with foreign language learning problems. Teachers should consider computer software packages, especially those that emphasize vocabulary and sentence structure. Diagramming sentences may improve a student's understanding of syntax and use of rules of grammar. Students need to engage in frequent self-testing, use flash cards, and use tape recordings of their own readings. Cloze procedures, in which students are given sentences or paragraphs with words or phrases missing, can be used. Students fill in the missing words or phrases, using context clues to help them with grammatical construction and vocabulary. Teachers should permit students to make liberal use of a dictionary in working through these exercises. Foreign language tapes can improve listening skills. Students can also record their own productions and compare them with tapes as a means of developing pronunciation and oral expressive skills.

Foreign language learning is generally hindered by traditional teaching methods which limit exposure and practice to a single class period and homework assignment per day. All students, but especially those with language learning difficulties, would benefit from more frequent practice, particularly of oral skills. In addition to language tapes, interactive software has enormous potential for practicing oral skills, listening, and speaking. Having foreign language tables at lunch provides another opportunity for practice. A foreign language pen pal could offer motivational practice in reading and writing. Many students with significant foreign language difficulties have benefited greatly from immersion in the culture of a country where the language is spoken. A summer spent in such a setting can do a great deal to enhance motivation and provide practice. There are also foreign language summer camps that can provide similar experiences.

It is not unusual for students intimidated by a foreign language to develop a phobic reaction. Foreign language learning becomes associated with profound feelings of inadequacy. Sometimes differentiating between impaired learning resulting from anxiety and difficulties stemming from a true foreign language disability can be difficult. Early detection of a foreign language phobia is essential. Affected or vulnerable students need to be handled with care. As with mathematics phobia and other such academic inhibitions, students should not be humiliated in public and should be given prompt assistance when problems surface.

The choice of the most suitable, or perhaps the easiest, foreign languages frequently confronts parents and teachers of children with learning problems. Often, such students are advised to pursue a highly phonetic language, such as Spanish. It is assumed that less phonetically consistent languages are likely to create serious problems for students with developmental dysfunctions. While no scientific evidence for this idea exists, it does make intuitive sense, particularly for students who have demonstrated competence in learning and applying phonetic skills in their native language. However, while a language may be phonetically regular, it may be grammatically complex and challenge the student whose language weaknesses lay in this sphere. Furthermore, if the sound-symbol codes of a foreign language differ significantly, native language interference may impede sound discrimination and acquisition of the new code. Teachers should also consider the student's oral pronunciation abilities. Latin, which is rarely spoken as a conversational language, might be a better choice for a student who has oral expressive and pronunciation problems.

Other factors may be more important in selecting a language for a vulnerable student. Consideration should be given to the language likely to induce the greatest motivation. If other family members speak French, a student may particularly desire to learn French (or to learn an entirely different language). If Spanish is spoken widely in the community, it may be perceived as having relevance. If a child has always had a desire to travel to a particular land, its language may have the greatest allure. Some students may be drawn by more unusual, "exotic" languages such as Chinese or Norwegian. Career interests such as international business and foreign affairs may influence the choice of a foreign language. Certain ethnic groups and religions value the acquisition of a second language, such as Hebrew. For the student with learning problems, the learning of such a language should be considered as fulfilling school requirements.

Another important factor is the quality and nature of the teaching of particular foreign languages in an individual school. A child with learning problems desperately needs the most understanding, patient, and flexible foreign language teacher. If that particular person teaches German, then that might be the most appropriate language. Students should work with a foreign language teacher who has had experience dealing with children with learning problems, one who is comfortable proceeding at a slower pace and offering individual help, one who will grade somewhat liberally and will help a student avoid a phobic response to frustration. Generally, the availability of such a person should take precedence over the specific language to be learned.

Deciding when to introduce foreign language instruction is of paramount importance. For children with learning problems, it is safest to introduce a foreign language either as early as possible or as late as possible. Some students with learning problems can benefit from gradual introduction of a second language in early elementary school (or even preschool). This lessens some of the heavy demand on memory. If such a student starts to have a difficult time with language learning toward middle and late elementary school, the classes should probably be tapered off or even suspended. On the other hand, many children with learning problems actually benefit from such early immersion in foreign language learning. The sole exception is likely to be those who have substantial language dysfunctions in English. They often become confused and have difficulty keeping the two languages separate in their minds. Alternatively, many students with learning problems need to postpone learning a foreign language until late in high school—perhaps eleventh grade. Foreign languages are commonly introduced in junior high school or in ninth grade, a period in which there is an enormous strain on memory and linguistic functions. For many students who are struggling academically, the addition of a foreign language in eighth or ninth grade is the proverbial straw that breaks the camel's back. Unless a student with memory and/or language dysfunctions has a particularly strong aptitude or motivation for foreign languages, postponement beyond ninth grade is strongly recommended. Even then, the student may require tutorial support or a summer school course to keep pace with the linguistic and mnemonic demands of a foreign language.

Exempting a student from foreign language study is always a controversial issue. Many colleges require that applicants demonstrate mastery in this area. Some secondary schools demand two or three years of foreign language study for graduation; the practice is regrettable. Some students indeed seem unable to learn a second language. Often, they spend torturous hours struggling in vain. Ultimately, the wasted time and anxiety begin to erode competence in other subject areas as well. At some point, it seems appropriate to call a halt to such a losing effort. It is certainly not worth sacrificing a child's academic career for the sake

of a foreign language. High schools and colleges must become alert to this phenomenon. Flexibility with regard to course requirements may provide a viable
alternative. Some students may succeed in courses that emphasize reading in a foreign language but in which classroom instruction, tests, and papers are done in
English. Alternatively, others might specialize in conversational courses that place
minimal demands on reading and writing. Certain students, especially those who
have not been able to benefit from an intensive program of remedial help, should
certainly be exempted from the traditional foreign language requirement for graduation and for college admission. These students might be required to take litera-
ture-in-translation courses and develop in-depth expertise about a foreign country
instead of learning its language. Opportunities to pursue advanced studies in other
areas that are culturally broadening (such as history, geography, political science,
or world literature) might be substituted. Some schools offer sign language and
computer language courses as alternatives.

SOCIAL STUDIES AND HISTORY

Beginning in elementary school, the social sciences afford an opportunity for
students to demonstrate well-integrated application of their basic skills in association with critical thinking abilities. Often social studies is the subject that introduces children to the quest for information through reading (Cassidy 1978). By
secondary school, most teachers of social studies and history assume that their
pupils are able to keep pace with the requirement for silent reading comprehension at a rapid rate. Well-developed word analysis skills and an accessible sight
vocabulary are essential requirements. The social studies student must be able
simultaneously to read and interpret, read and associate, read and retain, and read
and think. What she gleans from social studies reading must be available for elaboration and broad application. However, Otero and Moeller (1977) note that
"often teachers assume that students understand a concept if they can simply read
the words in a textbook or use the term in a discussion" (p. 43).

Certain aspects of social studies reading are unique—especially at the time
they are introduced during middle childhood. These have been summarized by
Blake (1975). First, students must become adept in general comprehension. They
must distinguish between main ideas and supporting details and draw conclusions
from such distinctions. They must discern specific causes and effects as they are
described in reading passages. The critical events leading up to a particular war,
the forces behind and impacts of a particular election outcome, or the reasons for
and consequences of a country's prosperity are examples of such patterns that
must be teased out of reading materials.

A second common aspect of social studies reading is comparing and contrasting. The reader must peruse a passage and recognize that the likenesses and
differences of two countries, two presidents, or two governments are being examined. A student needs keen awareness of language, effective active working

memory, adequate prior knowledge, and a good conceptual framework to judge which attributes favor which sides of the comparison.

A third common reading pattern is that of sequential events. In this type of reading, the student must preserve serial order, as it is essential to the discourse and to understanding events leading up to a particular situation or crisis.

A fourth aspect of social studies reading requires distinguishing between fact and opinion. Cassidy (1978) calls this "propaganda recognition." Within a passage (such as a newspaper editorial), students must be able to distinguish fact from opinion and be astute at identifying a point of view and comparing it with their own and that of others. This type of reading also entails the application of critical thinking skills, the development of which must be a major goal of the social studies curriculum (Rubin 1983).

Finally, Blake (1975) identified the "graphic pattern" in reading: students must read and develop a clear picture of what is being described in the paragraph. This requires some visualization of scenes, of maps, or of imaginary diagrams. Consequently, social studies puts active reading comprehension skills to the test. Five major processes—cause and effect, comparison and contrast, sequential events, fact versus opinion, and graphic representation—comprise the major challenges.

In addition to the processes delineated by Blake, students must learn to identify and classify data according to different categories of information (social, economic, geographic, and political) and then perceive interactions between them. How a student structures knowledge influences interpretation and can facilitate or hinder learning and retrieval (Hayes and Peters 1989).

Both for their reading and for classroom survival, students must develop a technical social studies vocabulary, which facilitates the understanding of historical, geographical, and political concepts. Children with a relatively meager general vocabulary may have particular problems acquiring such technical vocabulary.

Prior knowledge assumes importance in social studies. Students who approach the subject with a broad and well-established factual base gained from experience, previous classes, discussion at home, and independent reading are likely to comprehend and integrate knowledge and form broad insights from a variety of perspectives. Those who are capable of elaborating and of perceiving multiple implications in what they learn are apt to thrive in a social studies class. For this to occur, however, it is frequently necessary for the teacher to include activities that help students activate their prior knowledge and provide them with sufficient background if it is lacking.

Textbooks in social studies tend to be geared to students who are at or above grade level in reading skill. The readability of textbooks is apt to vary considerably; some students with poorly automatized reading skills may find it difficult to adjust. Learning how to use a textbook is another potential obstacle. Students vary considerably in the flexibility and skill with which they accomplish this. Understanding how to manage the table of contents, the index, and the glossary as well as the overall structure of the book can be confusing. Students may vary in their capacities to integrate graphic material in a textbook with what they read. They also vary in their capacities to recognize where material is being summarized and where it is being introduced. For some this is a nearly intuitive process. Some students must devote extensive time and effort to analyzing the organizational structure of text material, and there are others who can never grasp it.

Social studies textbooks and reading materials require students to develop a clear-cut purpose for reading. They undertake (often for the first time) the mission of reading to locate specific information. For example, students who are writing reports about a particular country's principal exports must know where to locate such factual material, how to recognize it when they see it, and what is most relevant to extract from the reading. Students must develop a considerable degree of flexibility in reading style and rate. In particular, they must know how and when to read intently, how and when to skim, and how and when to scan.

Courses in social studies require students to extract factual data from multiple sources. Frequently, original and contemporary materials supplement textbook reading. A student's understanding may be impaired by lack of sufficient background knowledge or difficulties interpreting language forms. Students may not know how to extract historical data from writing forms such as biographies, speeches, or narratives. In addition to traditional learning from listening to the teacher, many classes include movies, filmstrips, field trips, and computer software. Equally challenging is the adjustment to a variety of graphic materials such as maps, graphs, charts, and diagrams. Visual attention, nonverbal cognition, simultaneous memory, and cognitive flexibility are needed to derive sufficient meaning from such materials. Students must also have some transformation agility in order to integrate graphic and verbal data, translate graphic data into language, and ultimately enter it into semantic memory.

Social studies reading stresses higher cognitive abilities. Gaskins (1981) has pointed out that text materials contain a very high "concept density." A number of new ideas are often introduced on the same page, such as *balance of power, realpolitik,* or *benevolent despotism.* Such concepts commonly emerge from descriptions of specific situations, governmental structures, or political circumstances. Students who are weak in higher cognitive abilities may have trouble mastering new ideas or generalizations, especially when they occur in great density in texts and/or with terse explanations. Students must also be capable of separating concepts from facts and of engaging in an integrative, constructive thinking process, moving from facts, to concepts, to principles, and finally to theories. Many students with higher cognitive learning dysfunctions get stuck at the concrete factual level and fail to perceive broad implications. Those who have difficulty dealing with abstractions may not be able to negotiate the transitions from factual data to conceptual content. They may be confused by social studies texts and reveal poor overall comprehension of what they have read. They may fail to perceive unifying principles or to generalize from specific instances and make broad applications.

At the secondary level, students are introduced to a plethora of nontextbook reading materials. They are expected to peruse articles from magazines and newspapers. They must locate information in encyclopedias and other reference works and often have to undertake research in a library. Research presents a particular challenge. Its structure and its routine or procedures can baffle students who have difficulty with attention and organization. Navigating library stacks, card catalogs, and computerized databases can be disorienting to students with a poor sense of space and difficulties with sequential ordering. Furthermore, some find libraries incredibly distracting; they seem even to be distracted by the unusual silence in which every little sound or movement is magnified. Certain children have even greater difficulty "filtering out" their peers in the library than they do in the classroom.

Social studies also requires efficient study skills (Rubin 1983), and virtually all of the major organizational abilities. In secondary school, a student's social studies performance will be heavily affected by his organizational capacities and behaviors. Note taking, underlining, outlining, and developing strategies to study for tests become of great importance. Students must be able to use time effectively as they prepare projects or written reports. They must organize information from diverse sources. They need to learn to work in stages and to meet deadlines without last-minute panic. Social studies is an appropriate subject in which to develop such skills and behaviors. It is also a subject in which highly disorganized students can experience considerable underachievement.

Writing abilities are indispensable in social studies. The subject often requires well-organized, lucid expository writing—discourses that juxtapose factual reporting with interpretation. Students must progressively master in writing the same five structures that they have mastered in reading: cause and effect, comparison and contrast, sequential events, fact versus opinion, and graphic representation. In addition, writing a research paper requires students to learn and apply specific procedural rules of format such as those for footnotes and bibliographies.

A further consideration in social studies education is the likelihood that the relevance of the material to a particular student fluctuates markedly from subject to subject and from class session to class session. Some students may become invested and stimulated when social studies class discussions cover subjects seen on the evening news or overheard at the dinner table. On the other hand, they may have difficulty identifying or perceiving the relevance of a discussion of the Franco-Prussian War. Students who have trouble with cognitive flexibility and poor temporal awareness may find it difficult to take a <u>historical perspective</u>, comprehend events that occurred in the distant past, and percive relationships between the past and present. Wide variation in immediacy or familiarity is characteristic of the subject matter of social studies and history, creating a need for flexibility and imagination on the part of the student (and the teacher).

Effects of Dysfunction on Social Studies Mastery

From the preceding description, it can be seen that social studies courses, beginning in elementary school, require <u>well-developed reading and writing skills</u> as well as a variety of underlying developmental competencies. Effective reading for information demands vigilant attention. Good comprehension in class and in reading necessitates well-developed receptive language abilities. Understanding the course of historical events is a major challenge to a student's sequential organization and memory. Associating capital cities with countries, dates with wars, and political leaders with their countries taps the ability to form strong associations for coding in semantic memory. Comprehension and interpretation of historical events require a high degree of cognitive flexibility and imaginative conceptualization. Students must be able to switch cultural and temporal perspectives. Report writing calls for the mobilization of the multiple developmental function and skills described in chapter 10 as well as the assimilation and application of specific rules of format. Map reading, interpretation of graphs, and the use of charts necessitate effective simultaneous processing, higher-order cognition, and organizational skill. Children with difficulties in one or more of these areas are likely to struggle inordinately with the subject matter and requirements of social studies courses.

Social studies is a subject in which certain students who have had learning difficulties rise to the occasion. Some of them are attracted by the lure of history, geography, and politics. Some students with deficient academic skills excel in class discussions. Their strong conceptual and verbal abilities enable them to grasp concepts and elaborate on them whenever this does not require a heavy loading of skills, sustained attention to detail, memory of specific facts, high volumes of output, or organizational demands. Thus, it is not at all unusual for someone who performs poorly in social studies to tantalize, often astound, and certainly confuse a teacher by making an extraordinary contribution to class discussions while failing on examinations and homework. This can lead to some fierce accusations, as the student keeps hearing that "You can do better" or "If you would only apply yourself, you would be an honor student, since we know you have a good grasp of the material."

Management of Social Studies Problems

Students who contend in vain with the social studies curriculum may have diverse reasons for doing so. The following general guidelines should be considered in offering remedial help as well as for regular classroom accommodation:

- Determining whether a student is having difficulty in social studies class because of underlying deficits in basic skills is essential. If such deficits are discovered, provide remedial help. Deficiencies of reading comprehension and writing are most likely to be problematic.

- Developing strong study skills may be necessary, especially for those with attention weaknesses, organization problems, and memory deficiencies. Such social studies students need particular assistance in arranging a regular time to study, allocating time to complete work, maintaining an assignment pad and work schedule, and having a well-organized and definite site for homework (preferably outside the bedroom). Instruct these students in identifying a specific purpose and focus for reading and studying, and in effective outlining and note taking. Introduce and have students practice these kinds of skills over a long time period and with a variety of assignments and subject materials. Establish close coordination between the classroom teacher, tutor, study skills instructor, and parents in order to develop and reinforce consistent work habits.

- Summarization skills are of special importance in social studies, which often requires much reading. Students who have difficulties with language and memory, in particular, may feel overwhelmed by the information overload. They are likely to need a great deal of practice in summarizing material. A first step is to read a chapter and simply circle its most important ideas. The next step is to copy the ideas and rate the importance of each (i.e., 1 = very important, 2 = pretty important, and 3 = possibly important). Ultimately, students need extra practice in writing abstracts. First they should write a one-hundred-word summary and, as a second assignment, condense it to fifty words. Students who are struggling with writing can dictate summaries on tape and then transcribe them.

- Students, especially those with higher cognitive or language delays, may need help with critical thinking skills. Often they need assistance reading or listening to a passage (such as a newspaper editorial) and then identifying the point of view or argument of the author. Following this, they can express their own views on the subject and contrast their views with those of the writer. Reading and writing activities that require students to respond to materials on different levels (literal, interpretive and evaluative) can advance critical reading and thinking abilities.

- Improve students' comprehension and writing skills through instruction in recognizing and using different patterns of text organization (Blake 1975). Often, the use of semantic mapping can enhance a student's ability to perceive relationships and to integrate events and concepts. Students can use different diagrammatic schemata to emphasize different organizational patterns. Some examples are illustrated in figure 12-1.

- Social studies vocabulary is another source of difficulty. In particular, students need to understand various roots and combining forms. In the upper grades, connotative meanings of words become especially important. The way in which the choices of specific words connote points of view requires careful emphasis. Rubin (1983) stresses the need for students to learn consciously how word choice reflects the biases of writers. This is likely to be a particular challenge for students experiencing problems with the pragmatics of language.

- Some students with spatial processing deficiencies may benefit from specialized help in interpreting graphic materials. Map reading, in particular, may be frustrating for them. Give these students considerable guided practice in translating graphs, diagrams, and maps into linguistic contexts. In particular, geography can present significant problems. Some students with relative weaknesses of visual

Cause and Effect

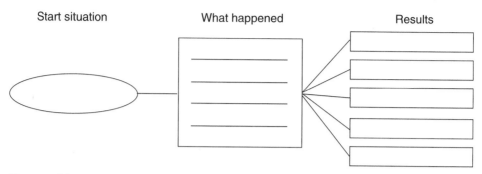

Start situation   What happened   Results

Temporal Sequence (Time Line)

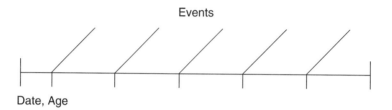

Events

Date, Age

Compare-Contrast

What Is Being Compared

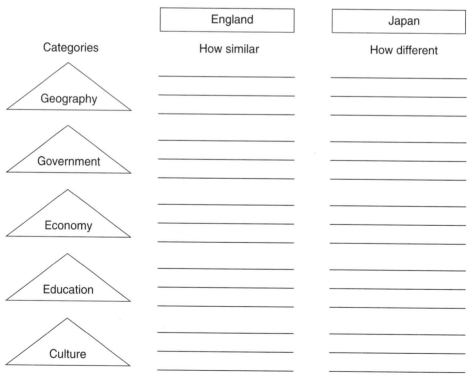

	England	Japan
Categories	How similar	How different
Geography		
Government		
Economy		
Education		
Culture		

Figure 12-1. Diagrammatic schemata or semantic maps for organizing information

memory may have trouble visualizing maps. Teach them to use strong verbal cues, describing relative locations of specific areas.

- Some students have difficulty with rote memory work in social studies. In particular, this may impair the learning of history. Certain elementary and secondary school students simply see no relevance in historical events. For some reason, what is in the past does not resonate with their cognitive and/or motivational states. Such students resort to minimally motivating tasks such as memorization of dates, sequences of events, and laws. Clearly, every effort must be made to get such learners out of the memorization mode, to induce them to see the romance and relevance of the past, perhaps by discerning logic in historical sequences and similarities between the past and the present. Nevertheless, some students persist in finding history dull. Some of them have developmental dysfunctions that create frustration when they try to master the subject matter. Some students with attention deficits have difficulty dealing with the detail of social studies. They may perform much better in discussions of current events (which allow for divergent thinking and are immediate and highly motivating for them) than in taking tests that tap specific facts in history. There may be a notable discrepancy between the quality of participation in class discussion and their scores on quizzes. Some students require specific help in studying for tests. They need to become highly active learners—taking notes, underlining, writing comments while they read, and making lists of key events in the correct order. They need particular help in testing themselves and in determining what is important in a historical context. The use of mnemonic devices such as acronyms, rhymes, and melodies can also assist factual learning.

- Since comprehension in social studies is highly dependent on background knowledge, it is important that teachers not take this for granted and incorporate activities that will build a broad knowledge base, activate prior knowledge, and link new learning to old. Brainstorming can be especially effective for this purpose, as well as for developing a fund of text-relevant vocabulary.

- When original sources supplement textbook reading, teachers should model and provide guided practice in how to read and use the material and extract relevant information.

- Teach research skills, especially to students who have organization problems. They need to learn how to use a book, including the table of contents, the index, the organization of chapters, and the levels of subheadings. They need to familiarize themselves with reference works in libraries. Escort struggling students through the process of researching and writing a report and help them frame specific questions, develop strategies for locating the answers, and use various types of reading materials efficiently.

- Give students an illustrated checklist of format mechanics specific to research and report writing.

- Research report writing is often best completed in a series of steps. Teach a staged approach to data collection and writing to enhance the quality and organization of a student's written output.

- Maintaining a notebook is an overwhelming task for certain students. It becomes particularly problematic in the content areas of social studies and science. Some students are overwhelmed by paperwork. They never have a good idea of where to put a work sheet, a map, or other material that has been handed out. They frequently misplace important documents. The folders or notebooks they try to maintain are simply a mess. By November or December they are totally confused and panicky, perpetually unable to locate what they need, and often embarrassed by the disarray. Students who have a track record of such organizational chaos need help from the very beginning of the year to maintain a neat and tightly organized set of files, folders, or notebooks. Parents can be of assistance. Each evening they should review the notebook, particularly its organization and neatness. It is important not to wait to do this until the middle of the academic year when disorganization is likely to be virtually irreversible, even by parents and teachers. Highly impulsive students need to decelerate enough to make conscious decisions about the disposition of particular materials. A well-organized "office" at home, one that includes a filing cabinet that is jointly run by parents and the student, may be beneficial.

SCIENCE LEARNING

Course material in the biological and physical sciences varies considerably from year to year, from teacher to teacher, and from level to level. The many different modes of imparting scientific knowledge afford abundant opportunity either for matching or mismatching learning and teaching styles. Despite the potential for a widely diverse range of experiences in mastering a science curriculum, this section focuses on certain common features.

Science reading materials are laden with diagrams, tables, charts, graphs, and specialized symbolic notation. Furthermore, many science courses interweave mathematics with linguistic content. The student must learn to integrate written text, graphic representation, quantitative concepts, and numeric functions and to translate from one mode to another. This calls for higher-order cognition and flexibility, substantial memorization, sequential organization, and sustained attention to detail.

Science textbooks as well as class discussions and explanations require sophisticated receptive and expressive language abilities (Weidler 1984). The prose of science textbooks is terse, with little repetition and frequent use of anaphoras (reference to a preceding word by a grammatical substitute). The difficulty is often compounded by causal chaining, that is, a long series of causal linkages used to explain a particular phenomenon. Eisenberg gives an example (quoted by Weidler

1984) in a study of the structure of science language: "The water thundering over the spillway possesses kinetic energy, which is converted to mechanical energy as it turns the blade of the turbine at the foot of the waterfall. The generator converts the mechanical energy to electrical energy, which is used to light a bulb, which in turn gives off light energy. In this process, some of the electrical energy is also converted to heat" (p. 55).

The passage illustrates both prolonged causal chaining and anaphora (the pronoun *which* refers to *kinetic energy, electrical energy,* and *bulb).* The passage is made even more difficult because *which* refers to three different nouns. Weidler (1984) observes that causal chaining "requires the reader to follow and infer such changes and meaning sequentially in the context" (p. 55). The writer assumes that the readers' well-honed reading comprehension skills and strong active working memories will enable them to maintain a grasp on the various nouns in the paragraph in order to relate them to specific conjunctions and pronouns. Furthermore, scientific writing tends to include an unusually large number of passive verbs and complex embedded clauses, further heightening the challenge to reading comprehension, language processing, and memory. At the same time, however, scientific writing also employs a formal structure and precise use of terminology and concepts; sentences and syntax also tend to follow a consistent pattern, and the presentation of information is well organized. Once a student has cracked the linguistic and organizational codes, comprehension of scientific text may be easier than interpreting the linguistic ambiguities and stylistic variations of literature.

Another common hurdle in science courses can be described as the "heaping" of definitions. In most scientific curricula, students are required to master new technical vocabulary (such as *mechanical energy* and *electrical energy* as cited above). Almost as soon as they are assumed to have assimilated these new terms, they encounter newer vocabulary whose definitions make liberal use of the recently acquired (and perhaps not fully consolidated) terms. Constant use of recently acquired terms and concepts is a basis for understanding subsequent ideas and vocabulary and for building a network of concepts in order to form broader, unifying principles. Students who have not fully understood, mastered, or elaborated on a definition are likely to become confused or overwhelmed when a new one is heaped on the partially assimilated one. Clearly, students who are quick at appreciating and readily applying newly acquired language and conceptual material will have an advantage in many science courses. Those who memorize definitions without really understanding them may enjoy a temporary refuge from confusion, but ultimately their tenuous hold is likely to reveal itself as the heaps of definitions based on other definitions become increasingly top-heavy and inadequately supported.

Even more than in social studies and history, some prior knowledge is essential for understanding science texts and class discussion. For example, a student who has never had any exposure to the concepts, vocabulary, and formulaic notations of chemistry would find trying to understand a chemistry textbook as baffling as trying to understand a foreign language without any previous contact. Background knowledge is frequently referred to as *schema.* It provides the mental scaffolding readers use to make sense of incoming information and to guide systematic search of memory when the information must be recalled (Chapman 1993). Furthermore, the background knowledge needs to be accurate and activated. Too often, textbooks and teachers make unrealistic assumptions regarding students' background knowledge. Teachers also fail to assess its appropriateness and accuracy and assume that students will know when and how to call on it. These issues can be especially problematic in the sciences, which depend on cumulative learning.

The mathematical content of science courses can be a source of problems for certain students and of clarification for others. Physics, chemistry, and certain computer science courses may be laden with demands for mathematical reasoning. As with quantitative subjects in general, students need to maintain the delicate balance between memory and cognitive problem solving. Some students in high school physics memorize, regurgitate, and dutifully plug numbers into formulas without ever truly understanding the material. Overreliance on rote registration and recall ultimately may lead to trouble, although it is unlikely that such students actually fail courses. Others act in the opposite manner, believing they can figure everything out without bothering to master critical facts and algorithms. As in courses in mathematics, the best students move with impressive agility from memory to reasoning and back to memory again.

The chapter on mathematics mentioned that the concepts of proportion and equation are significant acquisitions in secondary school. They are especially relevant in chemistry. A common downfall of students who have not totally assimilated these crucial schemata occurs when they study various concentrations of materials in solution and must be skilled at manipulating proportions. To understand the meaning of a *molar solution* (grams per hundred milliliters), proportional reasoning is essential. Chemical equations likewise necessitate a lucid mastery of the symbolic statements that equations make. Understanding how manipulations on each side of an equation must preserve equality is imperative. Although chemistry entails a fair amount of memorization (of symbols, valences, and definitions), as with other sciences, an equilibrium between memory and cognition must be reached.

The performance of experiments in various scientific courses is another potential source of gratification or frustration. Most laboratory demonstrations require that a student be able to follow directions. This requires knowledge of technical vocabulary, and a well-organized, sequential, and reflective approach. Attention to detail and spatial accuracy in measurement is essential. Fine motor skill, eye-hand coordination, and well-developed self-monitoring abilities are also needed. The scientific method can provide a series of organizing principles that help many students (Rubin 1983). The regimen required in writing up laboratory experiments may greatly help some who have difficulty with organization. On the other hand, these reports require meticulous attention to detail, a terse writing style, a high degree of accuracy in reporting, and exactness in use of terminology. Some students fail to meet these standards and fall far behind in submitting laboratory

reports and/or maintaining a science notebook. Conducting and reporting laboratory experiments often requires both the reading and drawing of diagrams, placing additional demands on spatial and visual–fine motor functions.

Effects of Dysfunction in Science

Success in scientific content areas is likely to depend on developmental competencies equilibrated with innate attraction to the subject matter. Students with
dysfunctions that have interfered with the acquisition of basic skills may approach
secondary level science courses at a decided disadvantage. Textbooks and teachers may assume that well-automatized basic skills exist. Significant clusters of
developmental dysfunction, even to a mild degree, can interfere with the acquisition of scientific knowledge and reasoning. Some students with attention deficits
fail to focus selectively and with sufficient depth of processing to absorb the
densely packed details in a science textbook. The processing of such nonrepeti-
tive material requires a high level of alertness and sustained concentration. Students with language disabilities and specific deficits of memory (such as a lack of
effective mnemonic strategies) are also likely to falter in their scientific pursuits.
Difficulties with sequential organization may interfere with the processing of
causal chaining and the reporting of experimental results, which involves presenting data in the proper order. All of the various dysfunctions that can interfere
with mathematical proficiency may similarly thwart scientific learning. In addition, spatial and visual–fine motor skill deficits have the potential to cause problems, more so than in many of the other content areas.

Management of Problems in Science

Individual science courses tap different developmental functions. Nevertheless, here are some general recommendations.

- As with other content area subjects, it is essential that a science teacher uncover
  any underlying basic skill deficiencies. Without specific remedial attention,
  such deficiencies may impede the acquisition of knowledge in science. Problems in reading, writing, and mathematics may be particularly troublesome for
  science students.

- Science subjects require reading in depth. Superficial perusal of a chemistry
  textbook can only lead to trouble. Students with attention weaknesses may try
  to overgeneralize from context. They may be able to use logic and strong conceptual abilities to survive during the early months of a science course, but
  ultimately their lack of attention to detail and their superficial mastery of the
  material may return to haunt them. Beginning early in the academic year,

encourage students to read deliberately, particularly those who have a history of science difficulties. Have them purchase their own textbooks so they can underline key concepts. Ask vulnerable students to copy down the most important points while reading a chapter and to keep testing themselves. Because of the importance of definitions in science, they should maintain a personal dictionary. Every time they encounter a new word in a text, they should copy it on a three-by-five-inch card and keep it in a personal file for periodic review.

- Specifically instruct students with reading comprehension problems in how to read and learn from science texts. Show them how to read slowly and deliberately, to underline, dictate, copy, or otherwise extract the most important facts, concepts, and definitions. Teach them how to activate and use prior knowledge or schemata.

- Teaching students to recognize and interpret common organizational patterns of scientific writing can facilitate comprehension. May (1990) found that students were better able to handle expository text when they could recognize its organizational features: definition, description, sequence, enumeration, cause-effect, compare-contrast, thesis-example, and problem-solution.

- Concept mapping or diagramming can assist students in perceiving relationships as well as in organizing information for written reports. Being able to read and to create flow charts can also assist with following procedures and directions.

- Few students have sufficient background knowledge to pick up a science text and understand it on their own. Give some prereading instruction that introduces new vocabulary and explains new concepts and principles and relates them to what has already been learned. Activities that require students to explain concepts in their own words and collect examples are especially helpful for developing a sound understanding.

- Students with language-related problems and those with apparent higher-order cognitive deficits (generalized or specific to science) should not overrely on memory. Tutorial sessions should focus on the logic of science. Help students to see that there are good reasons for studying science.

- Many students with learning problems confront science in a confused manner because they are unclear about what they should memorize and what they should try to figure out. Tutorial sessions may be needed to sort out various priorities for students.

- Advanced problem-solving strategies may be helpful for chemistry and physics. Students must have the right schemata or conceptual backgrounds to be effective in these subjects. Concepts such as proportion and equation must be fully assimilated before students can perform effectively in chemistry. Some students need specific help in refining such conceptual underpinnings.

- Assist students with learning problems in learning the procedures for conducting experiments, using equipment, applying scientific methodology, and writing laboratory reports. Those with organization problems may have difficulty adhering to the structural constraints of scientific writing. Escort them through the process on a regular basis. In addition to modeling procedures for them, give them written guidelines that delineate the steps involved.

- Some students with fine motor dyspraxia and related dysfunctions may have difficulty performing laboratory experiments. Implementing specific procedures may elude them, leading to some humiliation and general feelings of frustration. Place such students on a team of experimenters with one or more dexterous classmates. Adjust the assignment to minimize the impacts of fine motor dysfunction.

- For students who are impulsive and disorganized, maintaining a science notebook may be particularly troublesome. They are likely to need special assistance.

- Learning how to study for examinations can be especially important in science. Teach vulnerable students to predict what will be on an examination, to develop the best possible techniques for active reading, to use good memorization techniques, and to test themselves.

- Many students profit from learning test-taking skills. Allocating time, doing the easier problems first, checking work, making good use of scrap paper, using estimation skills for quantitative answers, and "keeping cool" can be taught specifically within the context of the science subject.

- Some special materials exist to help students with science difficulties. Videotapes, computer software, and various self-testing packages can help a student improve science reading comprehension, study habits, experimentation, writing skills, and data organization.

- Teachers should be aware that students are apt to vary considerably in the rate at which they can master scientific subject matter. Some learners have a very strong attraction or highly effective schemata on which to superimpose new scientific learning. Others fail to see the relevance of scientific course work, and for a variety of reasons, lack the conceptual scaffolding that can support the subject matter. Science teachers, perhaps more than those in any other content area, face the challenge of individualizing material for specific students. To some extent, offering courses at different levels of sophistication and rates of presentation is helpful. Nevertheless, teachers need to recognize that certain students, through no fault of their own, will find scientific learning laborious, often unrewarding, and sometimes destructive of initiative. Teachers of such students must try to be good salespersons of their curriculum while at the same time protecting these students from inordinate humiliation and the consequent development of phobic reactions to scientific material. Teachers in these areas should consider the reluctant scientist a challenge.

MATHEMATICS LEARNING

At the secondary level, mathematics essentially becomes a content area subject. As in science, course material varies considerable from year to year, and instruction varies from teacher to teacher, thus providing opportunities for alternating success and frustration. For example, the student with strong language and memory skills may do well in geometry but find trigonometry and calculus enigmas. For a full discussion of mathematics, see chapter 11.

COMPUTER SCIENCE

In contemporary society, computer literacy is an essential goal of education. Children are expected to be knowledgeable and skilled in computer theory and applications. Computer courses have become an increasingly important part of the school curriculum, and many school systems now require some degree of computer literacy for high school graduation. Use of computers often is introduced as early as kindergarten and first grade. Abilities in this area enable students to make use of sophisticated word-processing equipment, to benefit from educational software as a means of enhancing skill and knowledge in a range of academic subjects, to organize information in an effective and usable format, and to acquire new approaches to and expansion of problem-solving capability. By high school, database management can facilitate the systematic organization and storage of large volumes of information in all subject areas and allow for continuous updating. A variety of software programs are available to assist with expository and technical writing.

Educational computer programs can be grouped into two broad categories: general application and computer-assisted instruction (Mathison and Lungren 1989). *General application* software includes word processing, database management, spreadsheets, and graphics. These assist students in collecting, organizing, and comparing data in a variety of subjects; enable better planning; enhance writing skills; and facilitate acquisition of more sophisticated approaches to problem solving. By using word-processing and graphics software, students with skill and developmental function weaknesses can produce professional-looking documents which enhance self-esteem and raise motivation for learning.

Computer-assisted instruction focuses on specific skill and content learning. The primary purposes are to remediate skill deficiencies, to provide opportunities for practice, and to supplement class and textbook materials. Mathison and Lungren (1989) have identified five categories of computer-assisted instruction programs:

- *Drill and practice:* programs, frequently in game format, that provide review of information and skill-strengthening exercises.

- *Demonstration:* self-instruction and tutorial programs that teach new information and procedural steps through verbal explanation, graphic illustration, and examples.

- *Simulations:* programs that imitate real and imaginary situations for purposes of skill application, consolidation, and generalization.

- *Instructional games:* programs to develop logical reasoning and problem-solving abilities.

- *Curriculum correlates:* programs, similar to workbooks, that are specifically tailored to a written text or classroom program.

Computer skills call for a number of developmental functions:

Fine motor function. Facility with a keyboard entails considerable motor sequential organization, motor memory, and motor speed. Children must be able to locate the appropriate keys accurately with little effort. Lack of motor memory for key position may result in a labored search which can compromise other aspects of computer operation. For example, children may forget the command they wish to implement or lose their train of thought while looking for a particular key. Their motor dysfluency may prevent their fingers from keeping pace with their flow of ideas. Children with fine motor dysfunctions can ultimately master the keyboard, but some require a great deal of time and practice. In the near future, voice-activated computers will provide an alternative to the finger-activated keyboards.

Spatial and sequential processing and production. Sequential organization and memory are important in computer science. The various commands needed to operate a computer effectively are frequently coded in extended sequences. Some students find this language difficult to master. The precise order of various computer inputs eludes them; they expend substantial time and attention as they constantly refer to manuals or seek out the teacher for guidance. While spatial processing is not an essential part of computer use, it can play a role in the appreciation of graphic displays on a monitor, the creation of charts and diagrams, or the design of spreadsheets to exhibit collections of data. The latter can emerge as an important computer application in high school and beyond. Students with poor spatial appreciation may have difficulty foreseeing or planning such displays. Often the graphic representation used in instructional software programs is cluttered, confusing, and fast moving, requiring very rapid visual-spatial processing and skillful scanning abilities.

Attention controls. Children with attention deficits may encounter distinct problems using a computer. First, they may be too impulsive and inattentive to detail to cope with the precise commands needed to operate most computers. Second, they may find that too much time elapses before information appears on a screen or emerges on a printout. In other words, the computer may not be able to keep pace with their rapid cognitive tempos. It is not unusual to hear of children who are initially excited about computers but who progressively lose interest as the novelty of the device wanes and the requirements for precise attention to detail grow. Parents of children with attention deficits may lament having purchased a computer that the child used only for three weeks or for fast-paced recreational games. Frequently, the feedback for incorrect responses may be amusing and so gratifying that students may lose track of the intention of the program and repeat mistakes purposefully, thus strengthening error patterns.

Memory. We have already noted that sequential memory plays a crucial role in the mastery of computer commands. However, other aspects of retrieval memory also come into play as children study different computer languages. Assimilation of detailed material from a manual requires systematic consolidation and later, rapid retrieval. It is not unusual to encounter some high school students who have difficulties with both computer science and a foreign language. This combination is often found in those who manifest weaknesses of convergent retrieval memory. They have as much trouble recalling foreign language vocabulary as they do recalling computer language. Computer use also requires paired association learning and memory of a graphic symbol code, similar to learning to identify letters, numbers, and math notation signs.

Higher-order cognition. Many computer-oriented tasks require flexible reasoning and application of rules. Students who design their own computer programs must be good cognitive strategists. Nonverbal cognition can be put to use in the design of innovative approaches to problem solving and information storage. Verbal reasoning can enhance effective use of databases as means of organizing information for purposes of comparison and contrast.

An intriguing and controversial developmental implication of computers concerns the extent to which they can enhance and substitute for human developmental functions. Facility with a computer is most likely beneficial to children with developmental dysfunctions. In fact, the same dysfunctions that may make computer learning difficult in the long run may be bypassed or strengthened through sustained practice operating the computer. For example, children with fine motor dyspraxia may have tremendous difficulty learning to master a computer keyboard; however, with persistence they can do it. Once such mastery occurs, continued use of the keyboard can facilitate report writing, thereby bypassing cursive writing (a far more complex motor action). At the same time, it is conceivable that continued frequent use of the keyboard may enhance fine motor abilities in those students. Similarly, children with spatial ordering problems may have initial difficulties planning or thinking about a spreadsheet of data, but ultimately the computer can facilitate the process for them. Thus, children with developmental dysfunctions may need to surmount formidable initial hurdles in order to reach the point where a computer can become both a useful tool and a means of enhancing and bypassing developmental dysfunctions.

Some students, despite the presence of developmental dysfunctions, appear to resonate with computers. Somehow, the logic of these devices makes enormous sense to them. Their higher-order cognition is well matched to the workings of hardware and software. Often such children are also attracted to computers, thereby mobilizing high motivational energy for this pursuit. For many such children, computers are such a high personal priority that computer science becomes more accessible than any other form of academic performance. These children, in particular, can benefit from using computers to learn and enhance skills in other academic areas.

While computers can be a valuable tool, computer programs and software vary enormously in quality and complexity, which can either enhance their use and instructional efficacy or impede their use for purposes of learning. Therefore, it is critical to carefully evaluate programs for clarity of directions, readability, presentation format, speed of processing and response, level of abstraction, assumption of prior knowledge, amount of practice, and feedback. Feedback should not be simply evaluative but should be positive and encouraging, offer correction, and be specific in responding to individual errors.

ADDITIONAL SUBJECT AREAS

Not only the major content areas are worthy of analysis; so too are courses such as music, art, dance, photography, industrial arts, home economics, health, and physical education, each of which poses its unique opportunities and demands. Teaching styles may in part determine the nature of these exigencies. In some cases, requirements for selective attention, tightly organized study skills, or verbal comprehension are important. Each subject area presents its own specialized vocabulary and writing style which may challenge students with language and/or memory weaknesses. Courses vary in the degree to which they encourage creativity and/or demand rigor. Thus, neurodevelopmental vulnerability may be problematic. For example, students with visual-spatial difficulty or memory problems may be slow to learn to read music, learn dance routines, or interpret play diagrams in sports. Those with gross motor dyspraxias may feel humiliated in a dance class. Students slow to automatize and synchronize new motor skills may be devastated (even endangered) in drivers' education courses. Artistic abilities are likely to vary considerably. Some children with poor eye-hand coordination and generally weak visual processing may fare poorly in art classes; while others who have writing difficulties (perhaps due to proprioceptive and kinesthetic feedback deficits or motor memory deficiencies) are talented when it comes to drawing and painting, pursuits that entail very different kinds of visual-motor integration plus creativity and insight. Other students with language and/or visual-spatial problems may struggle in art history courses which require forming associations between written text and graphic representation. Likewise, health textbooks are laden with graphs and diagrams which require special skills to interpret and thus may baffle and confuse students with visual-spatial weaknesses. Learning to interpret road signs in drivers' education requires mastering yet another visual symbol code, which may challenge students who have problems with paired association memory.

Various industrial, home economics, and vocational courses can be a major source of success for certain youngsters. There may also be highly motivating incentives in some cases. On the other hand, there is justification for exercising great caution in the use of potentially dangerous power tools, kitchen implements, or an automobile by students who are impulsive, inattentive to detail, and poor at self-monitoring. This is especially true when these traits are complicated by eye-hand coordination deficiencies.

Courses such as music, art, photography, and industrial arts may also serve to help children overcome specific developmental dysfunctions. This is especially true for those students who find pleasure or satisfaction in one or more of these pursuits. It is likely, for example, that learning to play a musical instrument can enhance appreciation of sequences and sequential memory. The melodic line provides constant feedback about the adequacy of sequential organization. Courses in art can help improve students' spatial planning and fine motor execution. In all of these areas children can learn to acquire skills in a systematic way. These courses can promote planning, self-monitoring, persistence at tasks, and delay of gratification. Students can learn how to blend a disciplined approach to techniques with their own creative interpretations or ideas. They can experience pride in their skill and, at the same time, learn to tolerate and make use of criticism, which is essential in becoming a good artist or craftsperson. So it is that these subjects can become an especially vital part of the educational experience of children who have had to struggle inordinately as a result of developmental dysfunctions.

Elective courses have the potential to provide an avenue for remediating skill deficiencies, build critical reading and writing skills, develop study strategies and expand problem-solving abilities. Students' interest in sports, driving, fitness, photography, or carpentry can be a catalyst to reengage those who have lost their motivation due to chronic academic failure, and to develop skills that will enable them to achieve greater success in regular content area subjects. For example, comparing news articles about the same sports event can improve critical reading skills; carpentry and home economics can provide opportunities for strengthening the understanding of fractions and measurement. Students can develop writing and expressive language skills through reporting on school events in the school newspaper or on a school-run radio show. Special area courses also have the potential for improving developmental dysfunctions. Spatial awareness might be strengthened through courses in photography; drama presents possibilities for enhancing language and social pragmatics and for expanding memory skills; and dance has the potential for improving motor coordination.

Children vary considerably in the extent to which they find specific elective subjects especially appealing and relevant, or notably dull and remote. In a real sense, differences in the allure of subject matter help students individuate. They even enable some children to excel despite serious developmental dysfunctions and skill deficits. At times, elective courses such as art and music have significant vocational and avocational implications, possibly more enduring and relevant than classes in English literature or algebra. For many success-deprived students, learning to play a musical instrument, having artwork on display, acquiring skill in photography, creating a special recipe, or excelling in automobile mechanics may provide the opportunity to experience mastery, a reprieve from pervasive feelings of inadequacy.

Health courses have come to play an important role in the curriculum. These can be especially important for students who experience too much failure. Many of them have somatic concerns. In addition, some may be especially vulnerable to substance abuse and confusion over sexual practices or identification. Education in these areas can be vital in preventing needless mistakes. Health courses frequently rely on a variety of media, so that students with significant reading or language problems may still be able to gain a great deal from exposure to the content.

A final advantage of these elective courses is that students can often exercise some choice over their selection. This allows them to feel more in control of the curriculum through participation in the decision of what to learn. In a sense, motivation and performance in such courses should be seen as yielding evidence of a student's preferred areas of interest and learning.

Part 3

Seeing and Influencing Change

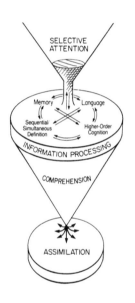
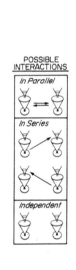
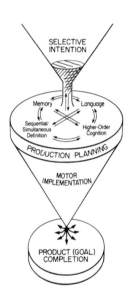

Chapter 13

Predispositions, Complications, and Mechanisms

My eyes were always on the clock waiting for lunch. I loved the taste of the school cabbage and mashed potatoes. I would eat plates and plates of it, going back for more. . . . Whenever I looked at my timetable and saw "gym" I'd feel ill. Mum wrote me notes. "Please excuse George . . . " When she refused I'd write them myself.
—*Take It Like a Man: The Autobiography of Boy George*

This book has stressed the ways in which variations in developmental function become associated with divergent manifestations of performance such as disability and handicap. Academic proficiency, social success, and motor efficacy are three cardinal examples of performance realms that are highly dependent on the fit between a set of expectations and a functional profile of strengths and weaknesses that either facilitates or hampers arrival at a predetermined level of skill. Multiple causes of delay or thwarted attainment are likely. Although a child's endogenous profile of strengths and weaknesses is a major determinant, other environmental, temperamental, and accidental factors are likely to be influential as well. Discussion of the causes of disability, whether for research or clinical purposes, are often laden with conflict and confusion. It may be senseless or frustrating to probe for a discrete etiology for a functional variation in an individual case. To seek an ultimate cause for the fine motor dysfunction that is interfering with a child's writing may be as irrelevant and fruitless as pursuing the reason why someone is a talented musician. Nevertheless, we often feel compelled to identify causative factors as a means of enhancing our understanding of dysfunctions and disabilities, with an eye toward better prevention and management. In seeking such explanations, either in research or during the evaluation of a child, some pitfalls must be avoided.

Confusion between association and causality. The existence of both a particular performance problem and a specific stress in a child's life does not necessarily denote a direct causal link between the two. For example, a child's failing sixth grade when she or he did well the year before is not necessarily related causally to the parents' recent divorce. Researchers might discover that mean scores on a test for anxiety are significantly lower among children who are doing poorly in school as compared to normally achieving classmates. Investigators might be tempted to conclude that excessive anxiety is a common *cause* of school failure. In this case, it can be very difficult to sort out which phenomenon (anxiety or school failure) occurred first, whether both result from a common source, or whether each continuously worsens the impact of the other.

Dangers of oversimplification. There exists an understandable tendency to look for single or simple truths. In reality, human behavior and developmental function are far more complex than many of us care to think. Most disappointing performance in childhood is likely due to multiple, convergent risk factors rather than single causes.

Vague definitions. Individual evaluations or studies of groups of children are often plagued by problems of taxonomy. Many studies of "dyslexia" or "hyperactivity" have been undermined because of loose criteria for diagnosis. Different investigators may find contradictory causes because they are not all clearly studying the same problem. For example, the mere presence of overactivity, impulsiveness, and several other traits reported on a questionnaire need not necessarily define a "pure" clinical sample of primary attention deficits.

Confusion between causes, complications, and secondary effects. It is often difficult to determine whether a particular biological or environmental factor is etiologically related to a child's difficulty, whether it brings out a preexisting tendency or complicates an already difficult clinical situation, or whether, in fact, it is irrelevant. Such a determination can challenge both evaluations of single cases and the design of research studies.

This chapter explores factors likely to shape the lives of children whose developmental variations are dysfunctional. It provides an overview of predispositions, mechanisms (processes that lead to problems), and complications. It consists of descriptions of potential factors to be reckoned with and described in individual cases or research efforts. In clinics or schools, we can identify such factors in particular students. However, the relative weighting of these factors is apt to be difficult and subject to bias. Therefore, a descriptive approach is suggested, one in which the therapeutic implications of important life influences are elucidated, dealt with objectively, and used meticulously.

PREDISPOSITIONS

This section surveys some common risk factors that may predispose children to dysfunction. The overview includes the following eight areas: genetic factors, perinatal health stresses, health and somatic factors, sociodemographic influences, family life effects, critical life events, issues of behavior and personality, and educational impacts. Substantial research literature exists in each of these domains. The following summary comprises only a modest sampling of what is known or suspected. It is hoped that this will sufficiently justify the need for a multifactorial model in which performance during childhood is viewed as a final common pathway made up of multiple predispositions.

Genetic Factors

Reading disabilities and "hyperactivity" have been widely studied in relation to possible hereditary or familial predisposition. In an early investigation, Hallgren (1950) studied large numbers of families in a psychiatric clinic in Sweden. He used the term *dyslexia* for learning disorders in which delayed reading was the major symptom. Investigating detailed family histories, he concluded that a large percentage of his sample experienced direct inheritance of their reading problem through a dominant mode.

He believed that he had evidence that this reading disorder was carried on a particular gene on a chromosome other than a sex chromosome. Most of the further refinements of Hallgren's study cast doubt on his view of a dominant mode of inheritance (Owen 1978). Volger, DeFries, and Decker (1984) studied self-reported accounts of reading ability of parents of 174 children with severe reading difficulties and 182 controls. They found that "the risk for reading disability is increased substantially (by a factor from about 4 to 13) if either parent has had difficulty in learning to read." The authors stress that "the absolute risk appears to be sufficiently high to warrant clinical application of family history information as one component of a multifactorial risk assessment battery" (p. 616). More recently, Pennington (1995) studied four samples of families (n = 718) and found strong evidence supporting the contention that dyslexia is both familial and heritable. Pennington also found indications that the transmission of normal variations in reading skills were familial and heritable. For example, in one of the family samples, primary relatives had a correlation for reading skill of .40. The past decade of genetic research has supported the claim of familial dyslexia (Culbertson and Edmonds 1996), and it has become accepted that dyslexia and other learning disabilities are neurodevelopmental disorders (Pennington 1995).

Owen (1978) studied a large cohort of educationally handicapped children with a range of disabilities and discovered a strikingly high prevalence of positive family history in this group as compared to a normal control sample. Neurological examinations performed on these children and their siblings revealed some remarkably similar patterns of dysfunction, suggesting again some strong familial tendencies. In a study conducted by one of the authors and colleagues (Levine 1984) of children between the ages of nine and fourteen, those whose academic productivity was low were more than twice as likely to have a mother or father who had been retained in school as a child. Grade retention of siblings was also much higher in the reduced productivity cohort than in controls. In this study, 18 percent of mothers and 20 percent of fathers had had reading problems, significantly more than in the control group of normally achieving students.

Although a large research effort has focused on possible genetic transmissions of attention deficits, these studies have been plagued by serious methodological flaws. In particular, a lack of clear-cut diagnostic criteria has undermined many efforts. In one typical study, Morrison and Stewart (1973) reported a significantly higher prevalence of "hyperactivity" in the parents (mainly the fathers) as well as in second-degree relatives (uncles, aunts, grandparents) of "hyperactive" children. Recently, Faraone, Biederman, and Milberger (1994) conducted a study of 140 6- to 17-year-old males identified as having attention deficits with hyperactivity disorder, 454 of their first-degree relatives, and 1201 of their second-degree relatives. They found that the greatest risk for attention deficit with hyperactivity disorder occurred when the father and grandfather had attention deficits with hyperactivity disorder. A problem with this study was that the information about the second-degree relatives was obtained from the parents of the subjects. When interviewing procedures are used, studies such as these have been weakened by the parents themselves being the reporters. For example, fathers of such children may identify closely with their sons and indiscriminately associate their own early life behaviors with those of their offspring.

A number of studies have shown a relationship between attention deficits in children and parents with alcoholism and antisocial behavior. Some of these investigations have been compromised because they took place in psychiatric clinics where the investigators did not fully control for the high prevalence of such family problems in other behavior disorders as well. Nevertheless, a consistent link has been reported between alcoholism in a biological parent and attention deficits in a child. It is certainly tempting to speculate on the intuitively appearing association of insatiability in childhood and substance use in later life. It may be that insatiable, substance-abusing men father children whose attention deficits are characterized in part by the same degree of insatiability. This link merits further study.

Twin and adoption studies have also been used to isolate genetic factors. A twin study of 91 identical and 105 same-sex fraternal twins found heritability of activity level ratings to be .75, and that for attention deficit measures to be .76 (Stevenson 1992). Although twin studies have many advantages, one significant problem has been cultural beliefs about monozygotic and dizygotic twins. Parents and teachers who provide information about the twins may tend to overestimate the similarity of identical twins.

Adoption research has also held some promise in isolating genetic factors. Safe (1973) investigated "minimal cerebral dysfunction" by studying full and half siblings who had been assigned foster homes at an early age, thus making a distinction between genetic preposition and environmental factors. Ten of the nineteen full siblings also had "minimal cerebral dysfunction" as compared with only two of the twenty-two half siblings.

There have been several reports of overrepresentation of adopted children among clinic patients with attention deficits (Weinberg 1982). Environmental or cultural interpretations might account for this, but genetic explanations must also be considered. Recently, Hechtman (1994) reviewed studies of genetic and neurobiological aspects of attention deficit hyperactivity disorder, and reported that recent adoption studies supported a genetic component of hyperactivity, but that there is important interaction between genetic and environmental factors.

A subgroup of children put up for adoption by their biological parents may have been the products of unstable relationships between one or two individuals who had had trouble delaying gratification, who were impulsive, or who were insatiable. In other words, it may be that if a child is born out of wedlock, there is more than a random chance that one or both parents had many of the traits of attention deficits, which were transmitted in some instances to the child put up for adoption. This does not negate a variety of other possibilities, including inferior prenatal care, mismatching between an adoptive child and his or her adoptive parents, and possible deprivation in the earliest (preadoptive) days of life.

Goodman and Stevenson (1989) compared monozygotic and dizygotic twins and found "that genetic effects account for roughly half of the explainable variance in trait measures of hyperactivity and inattentiveness" (p. 707). Ross and Ross (1982), in their monograph on hyperactivity, suggest that there is considerable support for a theory of "polyfactorial transmission," which "implies a genetic predisposition to hyperactivity that puts the individual at risk so that the extent to which he is affected by hyperactivity, if he is affected at all, is determined by various environmental influences that operate on the substrate of the genetic predisposition" (pp. 71–72). This, of course, is entirely consistent with our model of multiple risk factors in the generation of disability.

Another genetic impact on development is when a known genetic disorder influences developmental functions. This is well illustrated in studies of the effects of phenylketonuria (PKU). In this inherited condition, infants are born with an inability to metabolize the amino acid phenylalanine. Their lack of an enzyme needed for its metabolic breakdown results in toxic accumulation that is known to have a deleterious affect on brain development. Consequently, when PKU is detected, children are routinely placed on a low-phenylalanine diet. One study (Holtzman et al. 1986) found that when a low-phenylalanine diet was discontinued early (before the age of six years), children performed much more poorly on tests of IQ and achievement as well as on a behavioral rating checklist than did those who continued on the diet. The findings made it clear that the diet needs to be maintained beyond age six. Additionally, the study provided an example of the way in which a genetic metabolic disorder (i.e., PKU) affects academic disabilities and behavioral change.

It has been found that although dietary supplementation prevents mental retardation in most of the children affected with PKU, these children still have an increased rate of cognitive and behavioral problems (Pennington 1995). A recent review of neuropsychological functioning in treated phenylketonurias supports this finding. Waisbren et al. (1994) found that "studies have established that abstract reasoning, problem solving, reaction time, speed of mental processing and sustained attention appear to be consistently deficient in treated patients with PKU" (p. 102).

Chromosomal Disorders. Abnormalities of chromosomes are associated with developmental delays of various types. Alterations in the number of autosomes (i.e., nonsex chromosomes), including Down syndrome (trisomy 21), commonly predispose children to varying degrees of disability. Sex chromosome anomalies are often associated with specific developmental dysfunctions rather than global retardation. Turner syndrome (45,X), in which the second X chromosome is missing, has been particularly well studied. Affected girls as a group often display significant visual-spatial dysfunction. They tend to have low performance IQs and serious problems with drawing, copying designs, writing the alphabet, and map reading. With their apparently normal or above average verbal abilities, they do not appear to have significant problems with reading or spelling. However, Pennington et al.'s (1982) investigations indicated that these students had difficulties with geometry and other abstract subject matter. More recent investigations have revealed that children with Turner syndrome tend to be at greater risk than their cohorts for underachievement in arithmetic, specifically for numerical ability, mental calculation, geometry, and reasoning, as well as selective impairments in visual-spatial processing and areas of memory (Rovet 1993).

One study (McCauley et al. 1995) used parent and self-report measures to compare social competence, self-esteem, and behavior of 7- to 14-year-old girls with Turner syndrome (n=97) to girls without Turner syndrome (n=93). The girls with Turner syndrome were reported as having weaker social relationships, school performance, and self-esteem.

Other investigations have shown that 47,XXX girls tend to have generalized learning problems, while 47,XXY males have significant language disabilities, including delays in speech and language development as well as depressed verbal subtests on the *WISC-R*.

In a longitudinal study, Pennington et al. (1982) found distinct karyotype specificity in the IQ profiles and learning problems displayed by different forms of sex chromosome abnormality. Furthermore, they uncovered somewhat predictable educational patterns. These authors note that

> about half of the 45,X girls showed an unusual difficulty in the development of printing that seemed to reflect visual-spatial and visual-motor difficulty. These girls appeared to compensate fairly well for this problem by 8 or 9, which may account for why this aspect of Turner Syndrome has not been reported in previous studies which have examined 45,X adults and adolescents. Finally, the 47,XXX boys seem least affected so far in the number and kinds of learning problems but show a greater tendency to have specific delays in reading, and spelling, a finding which is consistent with their depressed verbal subtest scores (pp. 1187–88).

These investigators also comment on youngsters with a 47,XXX karyotype: "This group differs from children with specific developmental dyslexia in showing more difficulty with higher level conceptual skills (which are required on the mathematics and reading comprehension subtests) and with lower levels on phonic and decoding skills (which are tapped by the reading recognition and spelling subtests)" (p. 1188). Of interest was a remarkably low association between sex chromosome abnormalities and problems with attention activity. This is consistent with the findings of Hier, Atkins, and Perlo (1980) who also found a very low incidence of "hyperactivity" during childhood in their retrospective study of sex chromosome abnormalities in adults (many of whom had experienced other learning problems).

Fragile X syndrome is an important model of the diverse effects of a chromosomal aberration (Hagerman and McBogg 1983). In this inherited disorder, there is a fragile site on the X chromosome, resulting in a variety of physical and developmental manifestations. In many cases among males, the abnormality is associated with mental retardation. However, it has been found that a substantial number of affected children exhibit specific developmental dysfunctions, including attention deficits and some overactivity. They experience a variety of forms of academic delay. The majority of affected males exhibit autistic-like features, especially poor eye contact. They may also display what are called "hand stereotypes," such as flapping, hand biting, or other unusual hand movements. Some exhibit perseverative or repetitive speech.

The classic Fragile X syndrome is more common in boys than in girls. Affected children are likely to show certain phenotypic features related to the fact that they appear to have a defect in connective tissue. Consequently, they often exhibit floppy or large ears (greater than seven centimeters in school-age children). Their faces are often long and narrow (especially after puberty), and they may have high-arched palates. They frequently have a large head circumference with a bulbous forehead. The males commonly have enlarged testicles. Other feature include hyperextensible finger joints, loose skin, and pectus excavatum (a sunken chest). Approximately 50 percent have mitral valve prolapse, a heart problem that can cause some difficulties in later life.

It was once thought that Fragile X syndrome affected males exclusively. Now it is recognized that girls who carry the trait may have some of the manifestations. It has been reported that 30 percent of carrier females are retarded and 30 percent manifest low-severity dysfunctions, including attention difficulties and higher cognitive problems dealing with abstraction (Hagerman and McBogg 1983). Females with full mutation are reported as having weaknesses in executive function, attention, and visual-spatial skills (Mazzocco, Pennington, and Hagerman 1993), deficits in interpersonal social skills, and are viewed as more withdrawn and depressed than their peers (Freund, Reiss, and Abrams 1993). They also appear to have a high prevalence of finger agnosia. Most commonly, the sisters of affected boys exhibit some learning problems (especially in mathematics), prominent ears, a normal IQ, and, in a number of cases, hyperextensible joints.

Fragile X syndrome may be the most common inherited cause of mental retardation. It may also turn out to be a common source of developmental dysfunction, especially among female carriers. For this reason, it is important to be aware of this condition and to consider the diagnosis, particularly in children with learning problems and a compelling family history of mental retardation.

Thus, the association of chromosomal abnormalities with developmental dysfunction is well established. The precise mechanisms through which this occurs have not been elucidated. Specific abnormalities correlate highly with certain distinct patterns of dysfunction. However, these associations are by no means invariant. Within a given karyotype there are exceptions. Once again, we must acknowledge interactions between a particular risk factor (such as an abnormal karyotype) and the various other influences with which it must interact to produce a specific pattern of developmental dysfunction and performance delay.

Further research is needed on the possible influence of minor autosomal as well as sex chromosomal anomalies that could predispose a child to developmental dysfunctions. It is now recognized that at least some of them could have significant impacts on cognition, learning, and behavior.

Implications. Most clinicians active in evaluating children with learning problems are quick to tell us how frequently they hear from a parent, "I had exactly the same thing when I was a kid." It is not at all unusual when discussing test findings with a mother or father to encounter a refrain such as "I've always had that kind of trouble; I can never remember things in the correct order." Such anecdotal feedback, although seemingly too common to be a chance occurrence, is subject to considerable bias or contamination. Nevertheless, a substantial body of research suggests that genetic and chromosomal factors play a prominent role in the predisposition to developmental dysfunctions. While attention deficits and reading disabilities have been studied most thoroughly, we might also find hereditary predispositions to problems with socialization, productivity, higher-order conceptualization, and motor dysfunction. For these reasons, epidemiological research as well as good clinical history taking requires investigators to factor in possible inherited predispositions as part of their documentation of risk factors. At the same time, they must cautiously differentiate hereditary patterns from environmental and/or familial influences or from cultural effects that can easily be taken for genetic phenomena.

Perinatal Health Stresses

There has long been considerable interest in the extent to which children's cognitive development and educational attainment are compromised by difficulties in and around birth. Traumatic delivery, prematurity, smallness for gestational age, maternal alcohol ingestion, and neonatal hypoglycemia are among the many conditions that have aroused concern over long-term outcomes. Maternal illnesses such as diabetes, toxemia, and alcoholism have also come under scrutiny.

Much of the research into the effects of perinatal stresses has revealed surprisingly little influence on later learning. A famous and often quoted longitudinal project, the Kauai Study, found that the ultimate effects of perinatal status were mediated by the quality of the child's environment (Werner, Bierman, and French 1971). That is, infants born with significant perinatal stresses were more likely to encounter subsequent developmental and educational problems if they grew up in deprived or low socioeconomic environments. In more affluent settings there were signs of greater central nervous system resiliency. In another large, collaborative study, Willerman, Broman, and Fiedler (1970) found that infants who had endured major perinatal complications displayed low cognitive function in later life if they were reared in poverty-stricken surroundings.

Longitudinal studies of low birth weight children have also revealed a relatively minor influence of perinatal stresses. Few studies of normal children or of children with disabilities have found positive correlations between pre- and perinatal complications and learning disorders or behavior problems (Esser, Laucht, and Schmidt 1996). A study of subjects from the Children of the National Longitudinal Survey of Youth revealed that preterm children exhibited cognitive delays only until age six (Lee and Barratt 1993). Feingold (1994) found that the quality of the home environment correlated significantly with cognitive development, while birth weight and education level of the mother did not.

Very early descriptions of "hyperactivity" (Still 1902) frequently attributed the condition to specific kinds of brain damage resulting from perinatal problems. However, studies have suggested that stresses in and around the time of birth are not a major cause of attention deficits or "hyperactivity" (Werry and Sprague 1970). Although it is true that some children with severe brain damage become overactive and have difficulty concentrating, large numbers of children do not have attention problems because of complications of pregnancy, labor, or delivery.

Another line of research, however, has tended to contradict this finding. Waldrop et al. (1978) conduced a series of investigations of minor congenital anomalies (features of no medical or cosmetic consequence that constitute mild malformations) and documented an association between clusters of these anomalies and difficulties with the control of activity and attention. The anomalies themselves are thought to be a result of either genetically determined alterations in embryo formation or insidious complications during the early stages of pregnancy.

In 1980, Shaywitz, Cohen, and Shaywitz reported on a group of children whose mothers had a history of very heavy drinking during pregnancy. The children were patients attending a clinic for learning problems. They had somewhat small heads and a postnatal growth deficiency. All had various dysmorphic features; most had intelligence in the normal range and significant academic problems frequently associated with attention problems. In a recent prospective longitudinal study, prenatal exposure to alcohol had little effect on size after eight months (Streissguth et al. 1994). The same study notes that from birth to fourteen years, there were "dose-dependent effects on neurobehavioral functions [including] problems with attention, speed of information processing, and learning problems, especially arithmetic" (p. 89).

In a recent review of research on prenatal exposure to alcohol, Jenkins and Culbertson (1996) discuss some of the emerging evidence from longitudinal studies. The spectrum of difficulties found by various researchers include: central nervous system dysfunction, cognitive development, auditory problems, delayed language acquisition, speech impairments, hyperactivity, distractibility, impulsivity, short attention span, poor math skills, and poor interpersonal social skills. Prenatal alcohol exposure demonstrates a continuum of impacts; children born to women in the earliest phases of alcoholism seem to have milder learning difficulties than those whose mothers were chronic alcoholics. Fetal alcohol syndrome appears to engender a spectrum of difficulties.

In the past decade, there has been an increase in the number of infants prenatally exposed to crack cocaine. Maternal cocaine use can affect the fetus's central nervous system development and cause fetal distress and premature delivery. The mother who uses cocaine is likely to lack proper nutrition and appropriate prenatal care (Singer, Farks, and Kliegman 1992). In a review of the effects of maternal cocaine use, Singer et al. (1992) found findings to be inconsistent for investigations of newborn abnormalities. There are many methodological issues in determining the effects of maternal cocaine use, such as socioeconomic conditions, parental caretaking skills, mother-infant interaction, mother's use of other drugs and alcohol, and the amount of cocaine used during different stages of the pregnancy (Singer et al. 1992, Hutchings 1993). Hutchings (1993) notes that "it is tentatively suggested that the teratogenic effects of prenatal cocaine may be produced only in those infants exposed to the highest doses reported in the literature" (p. 281). Long-term effects of maternal cocaine use will not be evident until methodological problems are addressed.

Well-controlled studies are also needed to determine the neuropsychological and developmental effects of perinatally acquired human immunodeficiency virus (HIV) infection and acquired immunodeficiency syndrome (AIDS). Improved treatment has increased the length of survival of these children (Armstrong, Seidel, and Swales 1993). Armstrong et al. (1993) state that research on infants with HIV infection has found neuroradiological and neuropathological findings of "(a) cerebral atrophy (sulcal widening and ventricular dilation); (b) calcification of the basal ganglia; and (c) reduction in white matter" (p. 94). They also noted that studies have found these infants to have cognitive delays resulting in learning disabilities, mental retardation, visual-spatial difficulties, both receptive and expressive language delays, and a decrease in alertness.

Implications.   The variable developmental impacts of specific perinatal health stresses have been described elsewhere (Healy, Hein, and Rubin 1983; Jenkins and Culbertson 1996), but considerably more research is needed. Many of the longitudinal studies examining the effects of such difficulties have not extended into the later school grades. Others have used sophisticated measures of family functioning, prenatal stress, and early development, but have applied relatively crude outcome measures during school years. In the future, it will be essential to determine the extent to which perinatal stresses influence the development functions described in part 1 of this book. It will be important to examine their impacts on the various constituent features of attention and intention, the subtleties of language, memory, productivity, social ability, and higher-order cognition. More precise and clinically relevant outcome measures need to be devised and applied. Present knowledge about perinatal stresses supports the need for a multifactorial model of causation and the continuing assessment of the accumulation and evolution of risk factors.

Health and Somatic Factors

Specific illnesses or medical conditions are not commonly encountered in association with developmental dysfunctions. Although acute or chronic diseases can be important risk factors, studies of groups of children with school problems tend not to uncover large numbers with major illnesses. On the other hand, some studies of specific medical conditions or stresses suggest that they may have short- and long-term impacts on behavior and school performance. This section, therefore, explores some of the more commonly cited health issues.

Nutrition. Past years have seen considerable discussion and relentless controversy over the possible effects of diet on behavior and learning (Golden 1984). The most widely discussed interaction is the possible role of certain food additives in precipitating "hyperactive behavior." The notion was popularized by Dr. Benjamin Feingold, whose book *Why Your Child Is Hyperactive* (1975) reported that nearly half of the "hyperactive" children in his clinical practice became essentially free of all symptoms within four weeks after being placed on a strict diet that excluded all salicylates and artificial food coloring or flavoring. Feingold pointed out that this phenomenon represented a constitutional idiosyncrasy or predisposition rather than an allergy. Since he introduced the concept, there has been a substantial body of research to document the effects of these substances, including double-blind and provocative studies, that does not support Feingold's claim (Barkley 1991). Studies have found that about the same number of students on the diet improved as those on the placebo (Ferguson 1990). However, other studies indicate that at least a few children are indeed affected adversely by salicylates and food colorings (Kinsbourne 1984, Ferguson 1990). The effects appear to be more pronounced in younger children (under four years). Moreover, the impacts of these dietary substances are only a small part of the story, even in those who are affected.

While long-term, multimodal treatment is the most effective way to approach attention deficit disorders, many controversial therapies have emerged over the past decades. While Feingold's diet is the best known, others include avoiding allergens, megavitamin therapy, regulating blood sugar levels, and biofeedback. While these methods have their advocates, they lack rigorous research and have not been found to be significantly effective (Lerner, Lowenthal, and Lerner 1995).

The role of carbohydrates in worsening the behavior and learning of certain children is another focus of interest. Highly reliable parents report that their sons or daughters deteriorate shortly after consuming chocolate bars, ice cream, or the like. In a review of the literature on this subject, Wolraich et al. (1985) note that "changes in behavior and personality following the ingestion of a product containing refined sugar are reported by parents to be both dramatic and relatively rapid" (p. 675). These investigators concluded that "the results obtained to date from a series of challenge studies have been uniform in suggesting that sugar ingestion does not adversely affect the learning or behavior of these children. The responsibility rests with the proponents of the association between inappropriate behavior and sugar ingestion to demonstrate objectively any effects before continuing to recommend restriction of sugar intake for the purposes of modifying children's behavior" (p. 681). Wolraich et al. (1994) recently supported this statement by undertaking a double-blind study of twenty-five preschool and twenty-three school-age children whose parents described them as sensitive to sugar. The results suggested there were no significant differences in cognitive function and behavior due to an increase in the children's sucrose or aspartame intake. The authors noted that "despite the generally negative findings of this study, it is possible that there are some children who respond adversely to sugar and aspartame" (pp. 305–6).

How then can we account for the common parental observation of behavioral deterioration after sugar ingestion? One possibility is that certain children with attention deficits have a great deal of difficulty managing pleasure. Chapter 2 described characteristics of attention deficits, including insatiability, chronic restlessness, and inability to find satisfaction. Many children who are highly insatiable have a great deal of difficulty handling pleasurable experiences. They are apt to deteriorate around the Christmas three, at a birthday party, or anywhere else where the stimulation is intense and the pleasure level high. A candy bar may be one such heightened experience. Moreover, the allegedly deleterious effects of sugar may be mimicked when the child receives a glittering new bicycle or some other longed-for material asset. Indeed, it may not be so coincidental that all of the foods that allegedly engender behavioral aberration happen to be childhood delicacies. Thus, we have yet to encounter children whose behavior or learning is impaired by broccoli or brussels sprouts.

The specter of hypoglycemia also looms. There has been widespread speculation that some children may have learning and behavior difficulties because of low blood sugars (Golden 1984). Sometimes it is reasoned that since very low blood sugar can cause significant brain damage, levels somewhat below average should cause low-severity disabilities or disturbances of behavior. As yet, there is no rigorous evidence to substantiate this seductive notion. There is currently widespread interest in the relationship between food intake and behavior. It is reasonable to suspect that children may be adversely affected by certain substances; carefully controlled research will be needed to confirm this hypothesis.

Allergies.   The idea that a direct connection exists between specific allergies and problems with behavior and learning is not a new one, and has been the subject of considerable investigation and clinical claims over the years. Speer (1958) was one of the first to describe the "allergic-tension-fatigue syndrome," said to be caused by certain specific forms of hypersensitivity. Affected children were said to show "exaggerated neuropsychic activity" in the form of hyperkinesis and generalized heightened sensitivity. This hypothesis, unlike Feingold's, suggested that certain foods impaired behavior through an allergic mechanism, rather than a toxic or idiosyncratic one.

The role of allergy has had a number of strong advocates (Rapp 1979). While it has been shown that some children have allergic reactions to certain foods

(Ferguson 1990), only sporadic reports in the literature have associated specific forms of allergy with various learning and behavior difficulties. Unfortunately, there has been a dearth of carefully controlled and rigorous epidemiological research; much of what exists has to be classified as anecdotal or empirical observation.

Allergies and learning problems are probably two of the most common chronic disorders of childhood. Therefore, it should not be at all surprising that these conditions often coexist in the same children, which should in no way imply any causal relationship. On the other hand, we can certainly argue convincingly that allergies can *aggravate* an underlying developmental dysfunction. A child who is wheezing from bronchial asthma, one whose head is congested due to chronic sinusitis, or one who feels uncomfortable and is constantly scratching eczema is likely to pay a price in behavior and school performance. It is difficult to concentrate on detail and learn effectively amid the dulling effects of fluid-filled sinuses. Furthermore, medication such as antihistamines or theophylline-containing drugs frequently exerts a further negative effect on selective attention and possibly on memory (Rachelefsky et al. 1986).

Food allergies are frequently cited as causes of learning difficulty. By implication, their elimination should improve function. Well-controlled studies to prove this, however, have fallen short of being able to convince even the most open-minded skeptics.

Infections. A variety of significant infectious conditions might predispose children to learning and behavior dysfunctions, most notably the infectious conditions of the central nervous system, such as meningitis and encephalitis. The ultimate developmental impacts of these diseases depends on their severity, initial response to treatment, and the ages at which they occur. Meningitis (usually accompanied by septicemia) in the newborn often has dire consequences. Bell and McCormick (1981) reviewed various studies and reported serious developmental delays as well as other forms of brain damage in 31 to 65 percent of infants who survived neonatal bacterial meningitis. Many of them have severe retardation rather than developmental dysfunction, although attention deficits and other learning problems are also common (Bresnan and Hicks 1983).

Tuberculous meningitis has been found to induce attention deficits as well as other forms of low-severity disability among 20 percent of survivors. Pertussis (whooping cough) encephalitis has also been associated with learning and attention difficulties. Based on existing data, most cases of bacterial and viral meningitis and encephalitis have been shown either to cause severe neurological and cognitive damage or none at all (Bresnan and Hicks 1983). However, considerable research needs to be done to uncover possible subtle or inapparent developmental dysfunctions that may result in these conditions. Grimwood et al. (1995) conducted a longitudinal study of 130 bacterial meningitis survivors' school outcomes. At fourteen years old, these students performed poorly compared to controls on tests of fine motor function; verbal IQ; visual-motor, memory, learning, and executive skills; and reading ability (accuracy and comprehension).

The effects of recurrent ear infections have been widely studied. The results are varied and still somewhat inconclusive (Reichman and Healey 1983). Some evidence suggests that repeated episodes of mild hearing loss during certain critical developmental stages may interfere with the acquisition of language processing mechanisms, which in turn could thwart the development of speech and language skills Gottlieb (1983) reports the following mechanism: "Chronic otitis media → recurrent conductive hearing loss → disturbed central auditory processing skills → speech and language delays → impaired educational progress" (p. 466). He acknowledges, however, that there exist "few controlled studies further establishing this link between transient conductive hearing impairment and subsequent neurodevelopmental disorders" (p. 466). Nevertheless, there is some compelling retrospective evidence. For example, Bennett, Runska, and Sherman (1980) assessed seventy-three suburban students in a full-time learning disability program and compared them with seventy-three matched controls. Those with learning difficulties had significantly more frequent histories of otitis media and were more likely to have abnormal audiograms and tympanograms. There was even a high incidence of active unrecognized middle ear infection or congestion in the learning-disabled group. But in a recent prospective study, Roberts, Burchinal and Clarke-Klen (1995) uncovered no relationship between early childhood otitis media effusion and the results of standardized tests of intelligence and academic performance, behavior, or attention at the age of twelve. These investigators acknowledged the small sample size, that all subjects were from low-income families, and that more sensitive outcome assessments might have detected differences.

As further research documents or disproves a relationship between recurrent otitis media and later learning difficulty, some critical considerations need to be examined: extraneous variables may create the appearance of a causal relationship without the existence of such a relationship. For example, relatively immature swallowing mechanisms during infancy may cause some regurgitation of feedings through the eustachian tubes and into the middle ears. This may lead to the development of otitis media. The child subsequently exhibits learning problems. However, the otitis media and the learning problems may have stemmed from a common cause, namely, neurological immaturity or inefficiency (which caused the initial minor feeding difficulty). Other children may develop recurrent otitis media because they have always had the bottle propped during feedings. This may also result in some involuntary regurgitation. The bottle propping is part of a picture of maternal deprivation, which may also have fostered a learning problem. Finally, we must not assume that recurrent otitis media causes difficulties exclusively with language processing. A general lack of alertness during a critical period may weaken selective attention or even visual processing. Moreover, it is possible also that a chronic infection, like any other health stressor, is likely to exert its greatest impact on developmental functions that were weak or vulnerable to begin with. In the meantime, clinicians are probably justified in considering recurrent otitis media as a risk factor for various forms of developmental dysfunction.

Sensory Organ Deficits. Hearing loss obviously has a significant impact on learning. It is well known that behavior and learning problems are significantly higher among deaf children than among hearing children (Gottlieb 1983). Less is known about mild deficits of hearing or fluctuating hearing loss (perhaps secondary to recurrent otitis media). Some recent studies suggest a relationship between learning problems and unilateral hearing loss. This intriguing association is compelling enough to warrant careful observation of this group of children.

The relationship between visual function and learning has been even more controversial. Optometrists have been strong advocates of a central role of visual function in multiple areas of skill acquisition. These clinicians have associated problems of extraocular movement and accommodation with difficulties learning to read and other kinds of school problems (Getman 1985). Once again, there have been no carefully controlled, unbiased investigations that include control groups who are doing well in school and outcomes measured by objective, experimentally blind observers. There has been no compelling evidence of any relationship between myopia (nearsightedness), astigmatism, or color blindness and learning problems. While such difficulties may be associated with academic underachievement in individual cases, they do not appear to be important causes of developmental dysfunction among large numbers of children. Furthermore, there is no notably high incidence of strabismus among students with school problems. Disorders of visual perception are another area of controversy; their relationship to learning was discussed in chapter 4.

Toxins. Graef (1983) notes that "for children, life in an industrialized society includes exposure to the byproducts of the technological age" (p. 429). He cites the threat to children of a wide range of toxic hazards, including the broad categories of heavy metals, air pollution, cigarette smoke, and low-level ionizing radiation. Added to these are such common exposures as asbestos, polyhalogenated hydrocarbons, and insecticides. As these various toxic threats increasingly permeate our society, it is logical to wonder which of them are apt to have an impact on learning and behavior.

Probably the most convincing investigations of toxic impacts have been conducted by Needleman et al. (1979). They studied tooth lead levels of two thousand schoolchildren from two lower-middle-income communities. They administered a wide range of double-blind neuropsychological tests and obtained ratings from teachers. Reportedly this research revealed a direct relationship between moderately high tooth lead levels and the existence of many difficulties with attention. Students with higher lead levels were likely to be more distractible, less persistent at tasks, disorganized, and unable to process sequences. Interestingly, subsequent studies and analyses have been critical of these findings, citing incomplete control of extraneous variables (Ernhart, Landa, and Wolf 1985).

McMichael et al. (1994) studied lead levels of 262 children who were followed from birth to seven years of age. They measured tooth lead concentration in the children and collected *WISC-R* assessments of the children's development. Results showed that tooth lead was negatively correlated with intellectual development. Baghurst et al. (1995) studied environmental lead exposure in blood lead concentrations and visual-motor skills in a sample of 494 children at seven years old, which included McMichael et al.'s (1994) sample of children. The authors adjusted for potential confounding factors and found that there was a dose-related inverse association with visual-motor integration.

As Bellinger (1995) states, over the past two and a half decades, there has been a drastic reduction in the United States population's blood lead levels. "Exposure to lead tends to account only for small amounts of variance in children's cognitive performance. . . . No single study provides a definitive answer to the question, 'Under what environmental conditions do different patterns of lead exposure produce measurable impairments at which ages in which behavioral end points in which type of population?'" (p. 210). The potential of other toxins such as cadmium, mercury, arsenic, and various hydrocarbons for predisposing children to developmental dysfunction has not been fully investigated.

Anemia. It should not be surprising that children who are anemic are apt to experience a decreased state of alertness and general cognitive fatigue, especially in school. Howell (1971) observed that three- to five-year-old children with iron deficiency anemia revealed low levels of attention. In an investigation of twelve- to fourteen-year-old students from an economically deprived school, Webb and Oski (1973) reported that anemic subjects scored lower than nonanemic peers on standardized achievement tests. Pollit and Leibel (1976) described diverse affects on attention and behavior in children with iron deficiency (even in the absence of anemia). At this point it is difficult to determine whether anemia per se predisposes children to difficulty with attention or whether it is the iron deficiency, with possible impacts on certain brain enzymes, that results in cognitive or behavioral deterioration. Children who display declining attention certainly need to be evaluated for possible iron deficiency. As further investigation proceeds, it may be that iron levels of all children with difficulties with attention will need to be studied.

Malnutrition. A number of studies have suggested that children with poor nutrition are predisposed to developmental problems. Sometimes these problems are self-limited. For example, Lloyd-Still et al. (1974) tested children with a variety of abnormalities associated with malabsorption and consequent malnutrition. Among younger children they found reduced scores on scales of development. However, such findings were not evident in their older patients. Botha-Antou, Babyan, and Harfouce (1968) followed longitudinally a cohort of children, who after an uneventful early infancy, ultimately fell below the third percentile for length and weight and developed signs of malnutrition at age three months. They were compared to a group of matched controls. The malnourished group walked and talked somewhat later than the controls. Most dramatic, however, was that at age four to five there were significant differences on the verbal and performance scores of the *Stanford-Binet Intelligence Scale*. Many other studies confirm the finding that early-life malnutrition is a significant neurobehavioral risk factor (Howard 1983, Cravioto and Arrieta 1983). Problems with attention, language skills, overall intelligence, and behavior have been well documented. The possible effects of mild to moderate degrees of malnutrition are difficult to investigate, and thus remain unclear (Sigman 1995). It is likely that the long-term impact of mild malnutrition is less dramatic and convincing or more apt to be compensated for in later childhood.

Physical Maturation. Any perceptive parent, teacher, or clinician will have difficulty separating physical appearance and growth from overall competence in a child. Many important issues emerge at the interface of growth and development. Are children who are slow to grow also slow to develop? Is there a relationship between physical and neurological maturation? To what extent do children's self-concepts depend on body image, which in turn relates to their perceptions of the adequacy of growth? Gross and Duke (1983) offer a compelling model in their studies comparing early- and late-maturing children during adolescence. In all of the education-related variables that they surveyed, the late-maturing males performed worse than did those who matured earlier. These investigators noted that "they were less likely to want to complete college and less frequently expected to do so. Their parents concurred in their lower expectations and aspirations. The teachers less often characterized late maturing males as above average in intellectual ability and less often in the upper third of their class in terms of academic achievement" (p. 152). The later maturers also had lower scores on the *Weschler Intelligence Scale for Children (WISC)* and the *Wide Range Achievement Test (WRAT)*. In the same national study, females failed to demonstrate such clear associations between early and late maturation and between educational and intellectual achievement.

Certainly it is fair to say that children themselves are concerned about, even preoccupied with, the adequacy of their bodies. Those who believe they are somatically different, those who are dissatisfied with their growth rate or maturational status, are at a disadvantage. They carry with them throughout the day a heavy preoccupation. Students with learning difficulties plus body image concerns are likely to be particularly troubled. Growth and maturation, furthermore, are apt to relate also to athletic ability, social success, and overall physical appearance. Some children with defective body images think they must develop a repertoire of face-saving strategies, which ultimately can interfere both with behavioral adjustment and day-to-day academic performance and socialization. In some cases, their manner of coping is worse than the perceived problem.

Trauma. Central nervous system trauma can have long-standing developmental consequences. Such damage can occur as part of the birth process or as a critical event at any time during childhood. Long-term outcomes, of course, are quite variable. It is not unusual for a clinician to encounter a child with learning problems and a history of serious head trauma earlier in life. Parents often wonder whether there is a connection between the concussion or fracture and the present developmental dysfunction. In one investigation, Heiskanen and Kaste (1974) studied thirty-six children four to ten years after severe head injury (with prolonged unconsciousness). Poor school performance was characteristic of a large proportion of them, although nearly half were performing well. It appears that the length of unconsciousness following head injury is likely to relate to later developmental prognosis. In extreme cases, such as children who remain unconscious for two weeks, adequate school performance occurs only rarely (Abroms 1983). In studying the epidemiology and outcome of head injury, Teasdale et al. (1979a) introduced the idea that prognosis depends on the age of the patient, the presence or absence of any other systemic disease, the psychosocial status of the child, the severity of the brain dysfunction on initial assessment, the presence or absence of early complications, and the rate of recovery following the injury. Snow and Hooper (1994) confirm these and state that "for most pediatric patients, outcome continues to be defined largely by school attendance, school performance, neuropsychological functioning and parent/teacher reports of cognitive and emotional symptoms" (p. 37).

Follow-up studies by Teasdale et al. (1979b) found that those who had suffered intracranial hematoma had the poorest prognosis. Snow and Hooper (1994) in reviewing the literature on pediatric traumatic brain injury, confirm that penetrating head injuries will primarily result in deficits related to that area of the brain that is damaged. Nonpenetrating head injuries can effect neurocognitive outcomes, including intellectual performance, motor and visual-motor functions, attention, language, memory, and specific academic problems in reading, writing, and mathematics.

It is likely that most cases of incidental head trauma (especially those without any measurable period of unconsciousness) have little lasting effect on developmental functions, learning, and behavior. In several retrospective studies of juvenile delinquents, Lewis, Shanok, and Balla (1979) documented significant histories of recurring head trauma. These delinquents were also found to have problems with learning, some minor neurological findings, and, of course, severe social maladjustment (Lewis et al. 1979). In such investigations, however, it is difficult to establish whether the head trauma predisposed a child to delinquency or whether some preexisting conditions (such as impulsiveness or poor self-monitoring) set the stage both for recurrent head trauma and maladaptive behavior. Data from The Middle Childhood Project at The Children's Hospital in Boston (1984) revealed that students between the ages of nine and fourteen who exhibited reduced productivity in school had a much higher prevalence of recurring lacerations requiring sutures than did their normally achieving peers. In this study, there was no difference in the prevalence of frequent head trauma, accidental poisoning, or fractures.

Implications. The identification of health-related risk factors should not be neglected either in research or as part of clinical evaluation. On the other hand, as we have seen, it can be extremely difficult to establish clear causal relationships. Like other risk factors, these health-related risk factors probably interact with preexisting central nervous system strengths and dysfunctions as well as with other environmental conditions and life experiences to shape developmental outcomes in later childhood.

Further complicating matters is the issue of *neuroplasticity*, the notion that damage or insult to a part of the brain early in life may not lead to a permanent or immediate loss of function, since an alternative part of the brain may assume the role of the damaged portion or, in fact, some regeneration of that damaged portion may occur. At some point in development, however, such plasticity may prove inadequate. Bashir et al. (1983) note that "since behaviors mediated by specific brain areas may not emerge normally until a later developmental stage, identification of injuries to these areas may not be discerned until the behavior is expected or required. Alternatively, early in life, the behaviors associated with a given brain area may be successfully mediated by other brain structures capable of similar function. As task complexity increases, the ability of the usurped area to support that level of task complexity decreases" (p. 94). Thus, there can be a significant "sleeper effect," or time gap, between the occurrence of medical trauma or stress and its effect on processing and productivity. As complexity of tasks grows, vulnerable or barely compensated developmental functions may (sometimes suddenly) fail to suffice.

In some instances, a medical condition may arouse high anxiety in a parent. On hearing that there might be a causal relationship between a child's recurrent otitis media, for example, and the later development of learning problems, a mother or father may be seized with guilt. They may feel terrible about not having given the prescribed antibiotic for the full ten days during a recent episode of otitis media or for not having summoned the physician sooner. They may be angry at certain doctors who they believe failed to diagnose the condition properly or accurately. Such parents need reassurance that it is unlikely that anything they might have done could have changed substantially the child's present state. Once again, it is important for all concerned to understand the difference between a true causal relationship and an occurrence that is but one of a multitude of confluent risk factors. Parents also need to be aware that many (probably most) children with recurrent ear infections (as well as other health-related risks) ultimately perform adequately in school, at home, and on the playground.

The preventive implications of health risk factors need to be taken seriously. When there is a suspicion that a particular health-related condition could have long-term developmental consequences, it obviously needs to be diagnosed early and treated thoroughly. Dysfunction-predisposing illnesses require more diligent developmental-behavioral follow-up. As it becomes increasingly clear that a relationship exists between recurrent otitis media, for example, and later learning problems, it becomes ever more obvious that there is a need to monitor recovery, to perform regular hearing tests, and perhaps to extend treatment in predisposed patients.

Public policy implications are also important, especially in the area of environmental toxins. Preventive measures need to be stressed as public awareness grows.

Finally, it is important for all concerned to maintain a somewhat skeptical attitude toward health risk factors. Teachers, parents, and diagnosticians are all hungry for explanations of the seemingly inexplicable gamut of developmental dysfunctions. Discrete medical conditions (especially common ones) can provide enticing, but greatly oversimplified, explanations. They are easy to sell. However, years of research in many fields have demonstrated amply that logical and appealing explanations for phenomena often disintegrate under conditions of rigorous scientific scrutiny. All of those working with children with developmental dysfunctions must be willing to repudiate that which seems to be intuitively satisfying and proper, especially when the simplistic explanation has strong therapeutic implications (such as diets and expensive exercise programs).

Sociodemographic Influences

It would be absurd to think that juvenile central nervous systems evolve and individuate themselves within a developmental vacuum. On the contrary, the evolving functional profile of a child is under the constant influence of environmental forces. This section delineates four forces—economic, cultural, community, and lifestyle—known to affect the academic and social performances of children, both as individuals and in groups.

Economic Forces. It is not surprising that children who grow up in poverty are vulnerable and less likely than advantaged children to be spontaneously resilient in development and ultimate performance in life. Schorr (1983), in a review chapter on the subject, describes the many well-documented examples of this phenomenon. Among the various liabilities of poor children, she lists school absenteeism, a tendency toward lower birth weight, and an association between low birth weight and subsequent poor performance on intelligence tests. The association of elevated blood lead levels and poor behavior and classroom performance is nine times as high for children in families whose income is less than six thousand dollars than for those in families whose income exceeds fifteen thousand dollars. There appears to be a strong correlation between low socioeconomic status and residual hearing impairment from otitis media (which, in turn, may be associated with the aforementioned learning disorders). Schorr goes on to document a higher prevalence of congenital infections with subsequent development complications, more frequent anemia, a higher incidence of teenage pregnancy, and a greater likelihood of child abuse.

The well-known longitudinal study of the children of Kauai (Werner, Bierman, and French 1971) revealed most clearly that outcomes are determined by a complex interplay between the child's constitutional characteristics and various environmental phenomena and critical life events (Werner and Smith 1982).

Strong relationships between specific learning problems and low socioeconomic status have been well documented. Eisenberg (1966) performed some classic studies of "reading retardation" in Baltimore, Maryland. His data revealed a tight link between poverty and delayed acquisition of reading skill. Other investigators have produced similar findings. In a prospective, longitudinal study, Walker et al. (1994) found that socioeconomic status was related to children's receptive language, verbal ability, and reading and spelling achievement. Earlier differences, assessed when the children were between seven and thirty-six months old, predicted the children's language and reading achievement at seven years old. The differences were not attributable to minority or cultural background but to socioeconomic factors (Walker et al. 1994). Thus, low socioeconomic status must be considered a major risk factor. However, the precise mechanisms through which it exerts its negative effects are not entirely clear. One potent variable appears to be maternal educational level, which may be an important marker of socioeconomic status. It is fair to conclude that in the complex of factors that constitute life in poverty there exist variables that, especially in the face of other risk factors, are very likely to impede the development and learning of children.

Thus, a child who was born prematurely in a low socioeconomic environment is more likely to experience handicapping developmental dysfunctions during school years than is an equally premature child reared in less economically deprived circumstances. Several longitudinal, low birth weight studies have shown that once students reach elementary school, developmental differences are attributable to socioeconomic factors, not birth weight. Once again we perceive the recurrent theme of this chapter, namely, that multiple risk factors dampen the natural resiliency or self-righting tendencies of children.

At the other extreme, we can argue that affluence may also take its toll. Schorr (1983) summarizes four major negative influences potentially present in wealthy families: 1) weak family ties due to inconsistent parental presence; 2) overuse of substitute caretakers; 3) unrealistic or destructive parental expectations; and 4) a surfeit of possessions with less need for choice and relatively easy access to cars, drugs, and alcohol. The very special pressures and high expectations implicit in affluence may create a competitive atmosphere, a tension-filled environment in which to grow up. Schools in upper middle-class neighborhoods as well as private day and boarding schools may be especially rigid in their curriculum requirements, concepts of good learning and behavior, and cultural values. This can impose a weighty burden on children who are eccentric, specialized in talents or interests, or, in fact, deficient in some area deemed absolutely essential by local arbiters of childhood standards of excellence.

Cultural Forces. Cultural values can also be potent determinants of performance. The establishment of children's personal identities may depend in part on the cultures from which they emerge. A sense of identity, in turn, is likely to relate to the strivings of a given student, to motivation, and to his attitude toward learning and accomplishment. Among the kinds of values that may influence learning are concepts of gender role, ethnic identifications, and differences in dialect or even language. Children whose cultural backgrounds differ from that of the majority are likely to experience particular stress. Such students may strain to bridge the gap between values at home and those at school. Moreover, children whose cultural backgrounds diverge from those of their peers must also cope with the processes of social stereotyping that may affect the way others view them.

Teachers, fellow students, and adults in the community may tend to overgeneralize about children from a particular ethnic or minority cultural background and somehow alter their expectations of them. Affected children may need to struggle to overcome such constraints.

Children whose language at home differs from that at school may endure special stress. Bilingual students eventually have little or no difficulty with the principal language in school. However, in some cases, their learning disorders may be overlooked and attributed entirely to their bilingual backgrounds. When children are bilingual and living in poverty, some educational backwardness may be all too readily blamed on retardation, which in turn can lead to some unfortunate self-fulfilling prophecies. Students with conspicuous dialects may also experience difficulty in school despite having ostensibly the same native tongue as that of the majority. Students who have such dialects may also be at a disadvantage in understanding the standard English spoken by the classroom teacher. This may differ markedly from the language spoken at home and in the neighborhood.

Finally, different cultural groups may vary in the importance they place on specific areas of educational competence, athletics, popularity, and religious participation. However, it may be that some scholars and policy makers place too much emphasis on these kinds of differences. Gordon (1983) observes that "students of cultural and ethnic groups increasingly assert that differences *within groups* are as important as differences between them" (p. 190). In other words, there may be too great a tendency to identify particular cultural groups with distinctive (and artificial) levels of aspiration, leading to some unfortunate prejudices.

Community Forces.   Children's attitudes toward learning are likely to be conditioned in part by the expectations and propensities of the neighborhoods in which they live. The existence of role models in the community may have either a negative or a positive impact on children's performances. If students identify with a group of older adolescents who have dropped out of school and are primarily concerned with automobiles or the consumption of alcohol, the younger protégés may discern no value in education. There may be a disincentive to work hard or take school seriously. Children who have never seen anyone in their neighborhood carrying a book home may find it hard to muster up the motivation to learn fluent reading. When there is little hope in a community that children can achieve at a certain level or obtain certain forms of employment, again there may be little reason to strive academically.

Peers exert an enormous influence; in particular, during the late elementary and junior high school years, the drive to conform to peers predominates. If local public opinion and practice dictate against taking books home from school, doing homework, getting good grades, and pleasing adults, then students are probably wise either to join forces with peers in a kind of boldly indifferent, anti-intellectual campaign or to become underground achievers. In other settings, peers may act as positive energizing influences. An atmosphere of accomplishment that values learning and intellectual development may be a much better climate for the pursuit of scholastic excellence. In some instances, peers inflict too heavy an influence, eliciting a strong competitive atmosphere in school. This is especially true with certain upper middle-class communities with a prevailing achievement-oriented ethic.

Lifestyle Forces. At any particular time in history, certain predictable trends colonize the time and space of childhood. Much of a child's life may be consumed by the passions of a particular era. Television is a prime example of this. The 1990 *Nielson Report on Television* revealed that 2 to 5 year olds watch an average of 25 hours of television a week, 6 to 11 year olds average 23 hours a week, and adolescents average 22 hours a week. With these rates, "by the time a 2 year old finishes high school, almost 3 years will have been spent watching television (Dietz and Strasburger 1991).

A number of studies have assayed the effects of heavy television viewing on the development and behavior of schoolchildren. Television is said to induce increased passivity and disengagement as well as have negative effects on cognitive learning (Schorr 1983). While few studies have shown that television significantly affects cognitive development, the negative effects of television appear related to the amount and content of the television watched (Dietz and Strasburger 1991). Setting aside considerations about violence and the trivialization of sex (both of which are certainly important), we will consider the ways in which this medium may have a particularly negative or positive impact on children with developmental dysfunctions.

Some students may be especially vulnerable to negative effects of television because of their own functional profiles. Television provides the viewer with very small chunks of information. If children have difficulty attending to detail over time their problems may be reinforced by an overdose of rapid return stimuli on a television screen. The content of many programs is highly redundant, impulsive, predictable, and intellectually unchallenging. Scriptwriters judiciously avoid sophisticated vocabulary and complex syntax. Thus, young viewers who overindulge in television may spend long segments of their waking hours understimulated. Contemporary rock music may have some of the same effects. The mean length of a melodic theme is brief and likely to repeat itself with great frequency. Thus, careful listening is not demanded. Finally, these frequent repetitions call for little in the way of encoding, planning, organization, sustained attention, memory, self-monitoring, or higher cognitive reasoning. For most children, these factors are likely to be trivial in the long run. For children with developmental dysfunctions, the popular media have the potential to accentuate or aggravate their vulnerabilities.

Other lifestyle forces may also be important. In some suburban middle-class communities, children may be too highly programmed. There may be little free time in which to use imagination, plan and organize activities independently, and encode or implement original ideas. Certain schools emphasize after-school athletics or other organized pursuits. Some students may suffer from a lack of opportunity to develop more spontaneous talents. Obviously, a more balanced approach is most desirable. There is a need for highly structured, adult-supervised activities, but, at the same time, it is crucial that children employ such neglected functions as imagination, organization, initiative, and the development of a personal system of rules to govern leisure. Such functional capacities should not be stifled by zealous parents or teachers who overprogram compliant children.

Family Life Effects

No characterization of a struggling child's condition is complete without a careful analysis of family life. Domestic turmoil often preoccupies children. In the presence of developmental dysfunctions, serious concerns about home may exert a particularly strong negative impact. Research has shown that children from unhappy homes are at greater risk for learning and behavior difficulties (Emery and O'Leary 1982). Frequent domestic quarrels can lead to disruptive behaviors on the part of the child. Youngsters who are chronically depressed or anxious about their lives at home may be able to reserve little attention for academic function.

Children who are abused are another group that has been shown to be at risk for negative developmental outcomes. Kurtz, Gaudin, Wodarski, and Howing (1993) found that abused children exhibited pervasive and severe academic and socioemotional difficulties, and neglected children exhibited severe academic delays. Both groups displayed strengths on adaptive behavior measures. Other studies have shown impacts on emotional status, self-esteem, self-worth, and feelings of helplessness among children who were abused or neglected in troubled families (Cerezo and Frias 1994).

Children are understandably concerned about their parents' perceptions of them. Those with developmental dysfunctions who believe that they are disappointing may give up all hope. They may experience enormous despair, a loss of incentive, and feelings that they will never be able to please a father and/or mother whose criteria of success are well beyond them. In some instances, a child may wish to punish or embarrass a parent whose standards are perceived as too high. Academic performance may be used as a weapon by boys or girls who are angry at their parents.

Siblings are a frequently overlooked factor. Intense competition between brothers and sisters is common in families. More insidious, however, is the tendency of siblings to compare themselves with each other. The child with a developmental dysfunction who is chronically struggling in school is of particular concern, especially if she or he has a sibling whose achievement level is high and who attains her accomplishments with seemingly little effort. This can promote hostility, efforts at aggressive revenge, and a generalized disenchantment on the part of the floundering brother or sister. In certain cases, a child may feel that it is much safer not to compete at all than to keep coming up short in the perpetual processes of comparison. Such a child may stop doing homework, seek alternative forms of gratification (sometimes quite maladaptive or antisocial), or become withdrawn.

A number of studies that have examined birth order as a possible determinant of performance have yielded inconclusive results. Some recent research found that birth order affects the total number of years of education, but only for students raised in a middle-class home (Travis and Kohli 1995). Somewhat more compelling have been data about family size, as it has been shown that large family size has a negative effect on intellect (Schubert, Wagner, and Schubert 1983). However, once again, this implies a multifactorial approach since large families with ample economic resources show no such effect. Again, the association of large family size and low socioeconomic level may predispose schoolchildren to functional problems.

Critical Life Events

Adventitious circumstances and crises certainly must be factored into a historical compilation. Losses, separations, and other disruptive life events may interfere with personality development and affect social and academic performance in later years. In one retrospective study, Bowlby (1960) found that delinquent adolescents commonly had a history of prolonged separation from their mothers or families during the first year of life. Studies of the effects of divorce and death, as might be expected, have revealed the potential for impacts on school function and social interaction. With both death and divorce, the ultimate impacts appear to depend on a series of modifying variables, which Wallerstein (1991) has described with reference to the effects of divorce. In reviewing longitudinal and large-scale divorce studies, she notes that the age of the child is a particularly significant factor. After parents remarry, relationships with stepparents are particularly difficult for older children. The social setting and the availability of outside supports may also affect long-range impacts. Children are apt to vary considerably in their capacities to withstand acute stresses. Wallerstein (1991) emphasizes that to a child a divorce is not always a "short-lived crisis" (p. 359).

Critical life events need not always exert negative impacts. Klaus and Kennell (1982) have performed considerable research on the effects of early parent-infant bonding. In their view, the early days of life are a "particularly sensitive period." A high degree of early contact between mothers and babies at this point is said to have a positive long-range effect on subsequent behavior and competency. Thus, such early bonding can be viewed as a highly influential life event. This example, as is the case with other seemingly influential episodes or periods, is a subject of some controversy because of the poorly understood interplay between the impact of some triggered event or condition over a relatively short period and the long-term dilutional effects of time and the continuing infusion of new experience. Moreover, major unknowns are the dimensions of malleability (the extent to which children can be helped to develop optimally) and resiliency (the remarkable, spontaneous recuperative propensity that characterizes children to different degrees; Gallagher and Ramey 1987; Compas, Hinden, and Gerhardt 1995). At its best, such resiliency is seen in children who are said to be invincible or seemingly immune to any lasting impairment (Werner and Smith 1982). They, as well as their more fragile peers, need to be studied further in order to elucidate the elements of resiliency and invincibility.

Glib attributions of causality can easily distort the role of critical life events in leading to academic underachievement or poor social adjustment. It is easy to proclaim unequivocally that family disruption is causing the poor school performance of a child whose parents happen to be in the process of obtaining a divorce. Some clinicians may be too quick to blame the home situation. They may overlook the fact that a particular student's problems were festering before there was family turmoil or that another student has two siblings who are performing well academically despite a divorce. Often family problems or critical life events are invoked as a reason not to provide services to a child in school. It is easy to forget that setbacks and stresses are virtually universal elements of family life. It is tempting to blame them for a child's failure, thereby overlooking the idea that problems at home may have little to do with the struggles in school. Such stresses may indeed aggravate the difficulties, but they are seldom the sole cause thereof. Parents are often reassured when told that their son or daughter would have been having problems (although maybe less severe ones) even in the most blissful of homes.

Issues of Behavior and Personality

The previous section commented on resiliency, the self-righting tendency of most children. It is likely that temperament is a significant factor—that certain innate behavioral styles allow for more recuperative strength in the face of adversity or dysfunction than do others. Thomas and Chess (1980), in their New York Longitudinal Study, tried to identify and rate individual differences in the intrinsic behavioral styles of children. They identified the following nine significant factors, some similar in certain respects to the traits we associate with attention deficits: activity level, rhythmicity (regularity or predictability), approach or withdrawal (response to a new stimulus), adaptability (response to altered situations), threshold of responsiveness (intensity of stimulation needed to evoke a response), intensity of reaction, quality of mood, distractibility, and persistence of attention. From the examination of these components, Thomas and Chess characterized children in four general patterns: "the easy child," "the difficult child," the "slow-to-warm-up child," and a group of children (approximately 35 percent) who fit none of these categories.

In a series of studies, Carey (1982b) employed questionnaires to document these behavioral styles. He found that certain temperamental patterns predispose a child to vulnerability. In particular, the "difficult child"—who early in life is likely to show irregular sleep and feeding schedules; slow acceptance of new foods; prolonged adjustment periods to new routines, people, and situations; and relatively frequent and loud periods of crying—had a high likelihood of developing behavior problems in early and middle childhood. Similarly, in the New York Longitudinal Study, 70 percent of this group went on to display significant behavior disorders before age ten (Thomas and Chess 1980).

Recent data have shown a significant relationship between temperament and academic performance. Carey (1985) notes that "how children perform expected tasks, school work in particular, has been recognized in recent years as being strongly influenced by the child's individual temperament. Several traits, especially adaptability and persistence, affect academic performance both directly and indirectly. In brief, children who can sustain attention and be flexible will probably work more efficiently, and those who are diligent and sociable will reap secondary gains by evoking more positive stimuli from their teachers" (p. 104). The New York Longitudinal Study (Thomas and Chess 1980) linked the traits of approach and adaptability to higher scores on academic achievement tests.

Since many of the traits of poor adaptability and impersistence overlap with descriptions of attention deficits, some differentiations must be made. In a study comparing difficult temperament with minimal cerebral dysfunction, Carey, McDevitt, and Baker (1979) documented this similarity. They concluded that many children diagnosed as having a neurological problem affecting attention and behavior might be diagnosed instead as having certain temperamental traits characteristic of the "difficult child." In a review of risk factors for school failure, Brier (1995) discusses the contributions of temperament, intelligence, school attitude, peer influence, and parenting practices. Brier states that a "difficult" temperament can contribute significantly to antisocial behavior. "Empirically, the association among temperament, school failure, and delinquency is evident in several studies. The risk of delinquency has been shown to be elevated among youngsters who spend relatively less time on task, and are more careless when doing school work, do homework less often, and plan and organize more poorly" (p. 273).

In extrapolating from studies of temperament to the classroom and the playground, a particularly important component is likely to be a child's coping ability. The use of appropriate mechanisms to deal with frustrating social and academic demand or conflicts is one element of coping. Some children exhibit commendable coping styles, being able to appropriate the right response at the right time in an awkward or conflictual situation. Other children display maladaptive coping. Their defenses or strategies to deal with stress serve only to aggravate their circumstances. Related to coping ability are such propensities as persisting or quitting, facing adversity or avoiding it, accepting defeat graciously or denying it, and prolonging the agony or recovering promptly after setbacks. Children vary remarkably in their temperamental repertoires. Parents are often surprised to find wide variation among their children, all of whom have grown up together. The origins of temperament are likely to be constitutional, inborn propensities influenced somewhat by the environment and cumulative life events and experiences.

We can justifiably conclude that any diagnostic description and explanation of a child is incomplete without at least some consideration of his or her unique array of temperamental traits and how they may either ameliorate predisposing developmental dysfunctions or exaggerate their effects.

Educational Impacts

The school experience itself occupies a central role in ultimate academic performance. Extremely negative or notably positive experiences in school can either facilitate or constrain motivation and incentive. Students who must endure recurrent embarrassment before their peers in a classroom are likely to bear the scars of these exposures. An overly critical teacher, a curriculum that completely baffles a student, or an academic setting that is truly incompatible with the child's own learning profile can create significant negative pressure, ultimately resulting in alienation and academic disenchantment. The potential positive benefits of educational experience are inestimable. A highly supportive teacher, a co-conspirator in the campaign to avoid humiliation, can be an extraordinary asset and facilitator of development in a child who is predisposed to failure.

Considerable research has indicated sizable variations in schools and the degrees to which they can tolerate individuality in childhood. In some cases the major variable is the school or headmaster, who may set the tone for an entire faculty. An attitude such as "I don't believe in learning disabilities" may filter down to an entire teaching staff. On the other hand, a school principal who can also serve as an advocate, who recognizes developmental variation or even celebrates it, can do a great deal to foster performance strengths in vulnerable students.

The studies of Rutter et al. (1979) revealed marked individual differences between educational institutions. Their prospective study of 1500 children in secondary schools in London found that these schools differed substantially in rates of attendance and dropout, student success on examinations, and prevalence of delinquency. Financial resources, size or age of the school, and number of students per classroom did not strongly relate to these outcomes. What made a difference was the general atmosphere in the school, the attitudes of the faculty, and the overall scholarly ambiance of the place. Students fared better in schools in which they received more open praise in the classroom. Teachers who provided a sense of respect for their students (such as displaying their work prominently) seemed to foster better performance. Schools in which the teachers themselves were positive models of organization and academic skill were the ones where students performed better. Schools that gave more homework were more likely to produce successful graduates, as were those in which curriculum and discipline were agreed on and supported by the entire staff in a consistent manner.

These data as well as results of other studies and reports strongly suggest that schools, teachers, and administrators need to be keenly aware of the enormous influence they are likely to have on their students. In many instances this impact may be at least as great as the power of parents.

COMPLICATIONS

The scenarios of children with developmental dysfunctions are seldom straightforward. There is a constant interplay between their endogenous endowments and a variety of life circumstances, experiences, confrontations with expectations, and acquired coping mechanisms. The end result is heterogeneity and complexity. This section explores a group of commonly encountered complications, phenomena that both result from and aggravate learning disorders, and that influence the prognosis and educational or clinical course of a child with developmental dys-functions.

At times it can be very difficult to distinguish between a predisposition and com-plication. For example, poverty may be considered a risk factor for school failure. A child born into a poor family may not receive adequate stimulation and education early in life. This deprivation can cause a delay in the acquisition of readiness skills. That child may subsequently develop academic difficulties which, in turn, are *com-plicated* by his or her school's being located in an inner-city area where resources are scarce and special education programs are unable to keep pace with the demand for services. In this example, poverty helps create problems for the child and an impoverished school system complicates matters. Sometimes failure itself creates complications. A child who is slow to grasp mathematical concepts or decoding skills in reading may become increasingly ashamed in the classroom. The shame itself may lead to the appropriation of maladaptive face-saving behaviors (such as clowning). The difficult behavior then becomes a complication, which in itself deters development and learning. Similarly, some children with a long record of repeated failures experience a progressive erosion of motivation.

Loss of Motivation

It is not unusual for children who have experienced an overdose of frustrated achievement to give up. To comprehend often misunderstood mechanisms behind motivation and failure of motivation, it is useful to review some recent concepts. Some of the most important work in this area has been the research and theory of Dweck.

Dweck (1989) states that "the study of motivation deals with the causes of goal-oriented activity" (p. 104). She points out that children may have two types of goals in their academic pursuits: *learning goals,* those that involve an attempt to increase confidence or master some new material, and *performance goals,* those toward which they strive either to gain favorable judgment of their competence or to avoid negative feedback and its consequences. Dweck (1989) contrasts good and poor motivation as follows: "Adaptive motivational patterns are basically those that promote the establishment, maintenance, and attainment of personally challenging and personally valued achievement goals. Maladaptive patterns, then, are associated with a failure to establish reasonable, valued goals, to maintain effective striving toward those goals, or, ultimately to obtain valued goals that are potentially within one's reach" (p. 1040). These adaptive ("mastery-oriented") and maladaptive ("helpless") patterns "can have profound effects on cognitive performance" (p. 1041).

Variations in motivation are likely to be influenced by multiple factors. Some children may be motivated to strive in certain situations but not in others. A stu-dent may be extremely motivated in English class but barely, if at all, motivated in mathematics. Some students display conspicuously high motivation on the playing fields but little, if any, in the classroom. Still others are highly motivated to please their friends and totally unmotivated to please their parents. *Goal value* plays a crucial role, as children find certain kinds of pursuits more attractive, more closely associated with status or prestige, or more alluring for obscure reasons. *Goal expectancy* also produces variation. Children rapidly lose motivation when they perceive the likelihood of success as minimal. Children have little tolerance for failure and are commonly drained of motivation when they are least likely to succeed. They have a common, innate sense that it is better not to try at all than to make an effort and fail. This is true in the classroom, on the playing field, and in social settings. The *means value* is also significant. If a particular goal requires too much effort or too much delay of gratification, or if it greatly exceeds the capacity of a child's attention, it may be abandoned. Thus, the irrelevancy or unattractiveness of an academic goal, a likelihood of not being able to attain it, or the pain of the effort itself singly or in combination may dampen motivation and led to chronic failure to strive in a child with developmental dysfunctions (Levine and Zallen 1984). As might be expected, the loss of motivation, often induced by the failure itself, is likely to perpetuate or aggravate that very failure.

An important clinical question concerns the extent of a child's loss of motivation. Is it limited to areas of perceived irrelevance, improbability of success, and unpleasant means, or does it extend to virtually all potential areas of interest and effort? If it is extensive, a child's condition has been complicated by a pervasive motivational state, often as part of a clinical pattern that may culminate in depression.

A child's personal understanding of why he or she succeeds or fails is relevant. Licht and Dweck (1984) describe two kinds of responses to difficulty or obstacles in achievement situations. They observe that "some children respond in a 'mastery-oriented' fashion. Effort and concentration are intensified, and task performance may be enhanced as a result. Indeed, sometimes these children show *more* mature problem-solving strategies than they have shown before encountering obstacles. Other children, however, respond in a 'helpless' fashion. When difficulties occur, they show decreases in their effort and concentration, which are often accompanied by a deterioration of problem-solving strategies and task performance" (p. 628). There is considerable evidence that children's causal attributions (personal analyses of reasons) for failure are good predictors of their responses to difficulties in achievement situations. Those who believe somehow that uncontrollable forces, such as their innate inability, caused them to fail are likely to respond in a helpless fashion. This is typically accompanied by a loss of motivation, a sense of diminished expectancy from goals. Those who are mastery oriented are more apt to feel that they are in control, that if they work harder they will do better, that intelligence or ability is not a fixed entity but that it can keep expanding with effort and practice.

In a recent study, Cain and Dweck (1995) studied first, third, and fifth graders' beliefs about their ability and achievement, and their motivational responses to challenging puzzles. "A sizable minority of children at all ages showed the maladaptive helpless pattern (nonpersistence, negative expectations, etc.). Among older children, the helpless and mastery orientations were associated with differences in whether intelligence was seen as fixed or malleable. Younger children with the helpless pattern gave outcome-oriented explanations for school grades, whereas those with a mastery orientation gave process-oriented explanations" (p. 25).

Smiley and Dweck (1994) found that even preschoolers are capable of helpless responses. In studying achievement goals in four and five year olds, they found these young children to display individual differences in achievement goals.

Children confront specific tasks, challenges, or courses in school by superimposing their own beliefs, rules, and representations about how competent they are, how difficult tasks are for them, what will determine their success or failure, how much fun or torture will be involved in the effort, and how valued the ultimate goal seems. Some students are consistently upbeat when they confront challenges, while others doom themselves to failure.

It is likely that a common complication of developmental dysfunction is the acquisition of a fatalistic view, or a sense that one simply does not have the ability to succeed and therefore any intensification of effort would be doomed to failure. This particular response pattern is termed *learned helplessness,* the perceived inability to surmount failure (Diener and Dweck 1978). Learned helplessness contrasts with the conviction that failures are related to controllable factors such as effort or good strategies. A mastery-oriented attitude helps children maintain confidence and momentum in the face of obstacles. It also implies to students that harder work will have a payoff. Interestingly, researchers into these phenomena have discovered repeatedly that the pattern of learned helplessness is not necessarily limited to children with low ability; some competent students are fatalistic about their own capacities. On the other hand, some of those with learning problems are incredibly optimistic and able to maintain a strong sense that their personal efforts ultimately will win out. The latter phenomenon is a positive prognostic indicator.

Implications. The word *motivation* may be one of the most misused of all terms. All too often it acquires a distinct moral tinge. Children with development dysfunctions are frequently told that they are doing poorly because of low motivation. However, the accuser has seldom explored the true complexity of the term. It is never enough to say that children are poorly motivated. We must go one step further and determine the reasons. Is the subject matter somehow not meaningful to this child? Is the effort required so great that it exceeds attention and the capacity to persist? Is the likelihood of failure or disappointment so high that effort simply cannot be mobilized? If children are pessimistic about outcome, if they feel that considerable painful effort is most likely to engender mediocre feedback or evaluation (at best), the failure to strive is apt to ensue. Accusations of a "poor attitude," "laziness," or "moral turpitude" are seldom helpful. If anything, accusatory stances by parents and teachers can only reinforce a negative self-image and promote learned helplessness.

Children with low motivation and learned helplessness most likely need a nonaccusatory, positive approach as they search for motivation. A three-pronged attach may be most effective. First, the subject matter must somehow be made more attractive so that learning goals (motivation to increase competence) can become as important as performance goals (those designed to acquire good evaluations). This is very much a challenge to teaching. Second, students with low motivation must acquire a sense that they can indeed attain goals, that there is a possibility for success. Third, efforts must be made to simplify the means when the struggle is too time-consuming, too difficult, or too self-defeating. This requires recognizing a student's strengths and weaknesses and being willing to accommodate them through the use of interventions and bypass strategies. With continuing success and support, a student may quite possibly become more optimistic, more in control, and, of course, more motivated. A major goal for those working with children with developmental dysfunctions must therefore be the prevention of learned helplessness.

Low Self-Esteem

Various studies of children with learning problems have suggested that a loss of self-esteem is a major complication. As self-esteem dwindles, feelings of learned helplessness are frequent concomitants. High levels of performance anxiety and even clinical depression may be further complications. Self-deprecatory comments (such as "I'm a dummy" or "I guess I'm just a retard") are the early warning signs of declining self-esteem. In determining their own worth, schoolchildren are comparing themselves to siblings, to peers, and to adult role models. These quiet comparisons are further reinforced by formal evaluations such as report cards, test results, and overt praise or criticism from other children and grown-ups.

Success is essential for normal development. Children who are achieving mastery in no area, those with no recent triumphs, are very much at risk. The identification of strengths and prescriptions for success become indispensable in preventing or curing low self-esteem.

Maladaptive Face-Saving Strategies

Children who are failing vary markedly in the strategies they use to save face, to regain a sense of pride, and sometimes to try to fool themselves and others. In some instances, the strategies are effective; in other cases they become complications. The following are some examples of maladaptive strategies (Levine, Brooks, and Shonkoff 1980).

Quitting. Children may practice avoidance as a strategy. Sometimes they may denigrate a particular activity, calling it boring or dumb, as a means of escaping any direct confrontation with the subject matter. A pattern of quitting can become self-perpetuating and habit forming. Undoubtedly, some avoidance of highly aversive, potentially humiliating scenarios is desirable. However, when avoidance becomes a lifestyle, it can lead to chronic underachievement and a highly conservative coping pattern with no risk taking. Every effort has to be made to confront children with the maladaptive strategy and help them see how its overuse actually thwarts achievement.

Cheating. Some children using cheating in varying degrees as a way of dealing with the threat of failure. Such strategies may range from copying the answers of others to overrelying on certain kinds of help at home (from parents, siblings, or friends). Sometime an enormous amount of energy goes into the development of cheating techniques. The same output appropriately diverted could obviate the need for cheating. Once again, confrontation and dispassionate discussion are important. At the same time, it is essential to understand why a child feels the need to cheat. This maladaptive strategy often emerges from profound feelings of desperation.

Controlling. Some children who feel inadequate and overwhelmed in school compensate by having to be the boss whenever possible, exhibiting an inordinate need to be the overseer and oppressor in social situations. A child may return from a humiliating day at school and exert tight control over siblings and parents. Bossiness may be an effort to conceal a deep and painful perception of vulnerability and helplessness, extending to domination over peers while playing games in the neighborhood. Some children express their need to control by playing with younger children whom they can lead. Others, who exert control by taking advantage of other students with problems, may overindulge in name calling, scapegoating, and excessive aggression. At home they may exert control by disobeying rules, defying the authority of their parents (e.g., "you can't *make* me do it," or constantly threatening to do things that would embarrass others. Like other maladaptive strategies, controlling can become a habit. It deserves and requires careful analysis and appropriate therapeutic counseling.

Aggression. Some children with developmental dysfunctions compensate by becoming aggressive. In part, this helps them exercise control. In some instances it represents the outward manifestation of deep feelings of anger and/or jealousy. A child feeling vulnerable may strike back to get revenge or save face, somehow sensing that the best defense is a good offense. Sometimes she will employ verbal aggressive tactics. In other cases, children direct their rage at objects, destroying material things, overturning furniture, throwing rocks, or defacing walls. Such aggressive tactics can spiral and intensify, culminating ultimately in extreme antisocial behavior and even delinquency.

Regressing. A tendency to regress may represent a form of escape for certain children who feel caged in or trapped among the stresses of their own age. These children may revert to behaviors and actions of an earlier age. Students confronted with a frustrating mathematics assignment may begin giggling, fall on the floor, or offer an inaccurate response in baby talk. Children who have difficulty mustering up the social skills to relate to peers may indulge in the antics of much younger children.

Withdrawing. Some children seek a strategic retreat. They become isolated and withdrawn. They avoid contact with other children and/or with adults outside the family. In group situations, such as those that occur on the playground, they may go off by themselves, interacting only minimally with anyone else. Unlike their aggressive peers, children who are withdrawn might not be recognized by the school as problems. Extreme passivity may be characteristic of some who prefer not to be noticed, who fear exposure of their inadequacies. Some of these children may become addicted to the safety and security of television watching. Alternatively, they may pursue reclusive hobbies or areas of interest. While the ability to be happy by oneself is a commendable attribute, excessive withdrawal or isolation as a means of avoidance of stress is likely to be maladaptive in the long run.

These behavioral complications of developmental dysfunctions have the reciprocal quality of many of the other complications reviewed in this chapter. That is, they can be engendered by failure, and at the same time they can worsen that failure. In attempting to break the vicious cycle, clinicians, teachers, and parents must have a keen understanding of why children perceive the need to employ a particular strategy. In attempting a "cure," we must not require children to eliminate a strategy without dealing with the reasons for its use in the first place. In general, it is inappropriate to remove a maladaptive strategy without replacing it with a better (i.e., adaptive) one.

Somatic Complications

The maladaptive strategies discussed above are sometimes carefully calculated or premeditated. In other instances they may be unconscious or semiconscious methods of dealing with the threat of failure. Somatic symptoms in association with developmental dysfunctions are common and are rarely conscious or premeditated.

Among the common somatic concomitants of dysfunction are the various aches and pains that may plague certain schoolchildren. Many children with learning problems appear to have lowered pain thresholds. In some instances, this may be a direct manifestation of distractibility. In other cases, somatic complaints stem from anxiety or stress. In other instances, they are a source of secondary gain or a diversionary tactic. Sometimes somatic complaints (such as abdominal pain or headache) are part of a general picture of school phobia. Children wishing to avoid school may feel such pains intensely, especially in the mornings. They are not malingering or pretending to have symptoms. In most cases, they genuinely perceive discomfort. In fact, there are often underlying physical factors promoting the pain (Levine and Rappaport 1984), tendencies brought forth by their lowered pain thresholds and the frustrations they experience. Overt school phobia (with or without pain) is not necessarily limited to children with developmental dysfunctions. In fact, surprisingly few children with school problems refuse to go to school, and it is not unusual for an honor student to develop a school phobia, along with an array of somatic complaints.

Excessive somatization may first be revealed in a high level of absenteeism. Alternatively, there may be frequent trips to the health office. Parents and teachers may report that a particular student appears preoccupied with his or her body and tends to overreact to perceived discomfort. Such a child may have problems with body image or self-concept, feeling vulnerable or fragile. It is not unusual for somatic complaints to accompany low self-esteem in the face of academic disappointment.

Certain specific conditions warrant mention. A common and seldom discussed disorder is encopresis (Levine 1982b), a chronic disorder in which children lose control of large intestinal function. They are apt to soil their underwear, most commonly in the afternoons. Most of these children are often constipated, although their parents may not realize it. In some cases, the constipation and loss of bowel control result from a reaction to school and, more specifically, avoidance of school rest rooms. In other cases, children with attention deficits tend to be impersistent, sometimes even in their bowel habits. When they defecate, they fail to empty themselves completely. Over time, they accumulate stool, ultimately become constipated, and finally incontinent. Many different pathways lead to a loss of bowel control. Once this state is reached, however, the secondary effects are profound. Children with encopresis often become withdrawn and lose confidence in themselves. They live in constant fear of being discovered by their peers (Levine 1982b) and expend enormous energy trying not to be smelled. Their level of shame is understandably high. They feel that they lack one of the most primitive forms of control. Encopresis is a condition that warrants immediate medical, and sometimes psychological, attention.

Enuresis can also complicate or accompany learning problems. Children who wet their beds at night and those who wet during the day also feel that they have lost a basic kind of control. Children who awaken in a puddle of urine have difficulty entirely forgetting this while at school. It can be an added preoccupation for children who are struggling with social and/or academic demands. While there is not a very strong association between learning problems and enuresis, when the two coincide in the same child, low self-esteem and feelings of helplessness may ensue.

Headaches and abdominal pain are especially common in schoolchildren. These conditions can result from multiple causes (Gascon 1984, Leaven and Rapport 1984), but the stresses of school may intensify and be intensified by these conditions. The most common complaints of 186 students who were surveyed when visiting their high school nurse were headaches, infections, stomach aches, dizziness, and tiredness (Schneider, Friedman, and Fisher 1995). The most common reasons students gave for these complaints were stress, depression, not eating well, not sleeping well, family problems, and school problems.

Many other somatic manifestations can complicate learning disorders. Included are the various eating problems such as anorexia nervosa and bulimia, a variety of chronic diseases such as bronchial asthma and inflammatory bowel disease, and virtually any long-standing or recurring illness. While developmental dysfunctions do not cause such conditions, reciprocal complicating effects are commonly evident.

Depression *predispositions complications*

Childhood depression is a common psychiatric complication of developmental dysfunction. Between 10 percent and 20 percent of children with "learning disabilities" have been found to have significant depression (Stevenson and Romney 1984). There are varying results in studies of depression in students displaying "hyperactive" behavior; the percentage of the population with these co-occurring characteristics ranges from 0 to 75 percent (Joseph 1992). From a clinical standpoint, it can be extremely difficult to differentiate the manifestations of depression and the direct symptoms of certain developmental dysfunctions, especially in children with attention deficits. A number of the symptoms of childhood depression overlap those of attention deficits (Levine 1984d). One can argue endlessly whether children are depressed because they have attention deficits and consequent overexposure to failure, or whether children are failing and having trouble concentrating because they are depressed. Ultimately, such exercises are fruitless. It is likely that the children need help with both the depression and the attention difficulties.

Puig-Antich and Rabinovich (1983) characterize major depressive disorders in children as either a persistent depressive mood or pervasive loss of interest of pleasure in all or many usual activities. In trying to uncover depression in a child, these authors suggest that one inquire about eight different labels that children might use: *sad, depressed, low, down, down in the dumps, empty, blue, very unhappy,* or *bad feelings inside.*

Any or all such terms may be used by depressed children in describing their feelings. Puig-Antich and Rabinovich state that to make a diagnosis of depression the dysphoric mood must persist for at least three continuous hours and occur at least three times a week.

The *Diagnostic and Statistical Manual of Mental Disorders-Fourth Edition* (1994) delineates specific symptoms of childhood depression. The cardinal symptoms are dysphoric mood and/or loss of interest or pleasure in almost all usual activities and pastimes. Seven other symptoms are listed in the manual, of which four need to be met for a diagnosis of depression in conjunction with either depressed mood or loss of interest or pleasure: poor appetite or significant weight loss, trouble with sleep, psychomotor agitation or retardation, loss of energy or fatigue, feelings of worthlessness or guilt, difficulty with concentration or decisiveness, and recurrent thoughts of death or suicide. Children with attention deficits, of course, may have difficult with sleep, psychomotor agitation, feelings of worthlessness, and difficulties with concentration. Therefore, they often satisfy at least four of the eight criteria. If a child with attention problems is also sad, it may be particularly hard to differentiate the underlying dysfunction from depression. However, it is perfectly plausible for a child to have two superimposed conditions. An important criterion concerns any recent change in mood. A child who is becoming increasingly dysphoric or is progressively losing interest in usual activities may be more likely to be depressed.

Bipolar (manic-depressive illness is most unusual before puberty. However, during adolescence, we may see the emergence of this condition in certain teenagers who appeared to have "pure" attention deficits during earlier childhood. Their manic episodes are marked by elevated, expansive, or irritated moods, often with accompanying hyperactivity, pressured speech, free flight of ideas, inflated self-esteem, decreased need for sleep, distractibility, or engagement in various hazardous activities. Sometimes the mood may be described as euphoric, or unusually cheerful or happy. In other instances, irritability is the predominant symptom. The depressive episodes are as described above. Often children who develop bipolar illness in adolescence have a family history of this condition (Compas, Hinden, and Gerhardt 1995).

Some of the dilemmas involved in diagnosing depression may ultimately be helped by certain chemical tests. In recent years, considerable research has been done on the neuroendocrine correlates of depression. Much of the research, performed on adults, has focused on the hypersecretion of cortisol and its lack of inhibition during dexamethasone depression testing. There has also been research on the inhibition of the cortisol response to d-amphetamine as well as growth hormone hyperresponsivity to insulin-induced hypoglycemia. Although children have not been the subjects of as much research, there is now some evidence that certain of these physiological correlates of major depressive disorders may be discernible during childhood (Puig-Antich and Rabinovich 1983). Other major psychiatric disorders can be complications of developmental dysfunction, although they are much rarer. Phobias, schizophrenia, extreme separation anxiety, and obsessive-compulsive disorders unquestionably complicate learning problems. They certainly need to be considered in cases where bizarre or extreme behaviors are interfering with the learning process. Prompt psychiatric evaluation and treatment are essential in these cases.

Suicidal Behavior

Suicide is the most dreaded of all complications of developmental dysfunction. It is essential to include this tragic phenomenon, even though it is more an outcome than a complication. From 1980 to 1992, the suicide rate increased 120 percent for young adolescents (Carnegie Council on Adolescent Development 1995), and the rate of suicide for fifteen to nineteen year olds in 1990 was 11.1 per 100,000 (Berman and Jobes 1995). There has been concomitant rise in suicide threats and unsuccessful attempts. In many cases, chronic depression and suicide are closely linked. Suicidal ideation is, of course, a psychiatric emergency. Children who threaten or discuss the possibility of suicide need immediate attention. Studies or risk factors for suicidal behavior have tended to emphasize troubled family relationships (Berman and Jobes 1995), and recognize mood, psychotic, and disruptive disorders, and substance abuse as the main risk factors (Brent 1995). Pfeffer et al. (1982) identified a series of common factors that may contribute to the expression of suicidal behavior, including severe anxiety, aggression, multiple deficits in reality testing and impulse control, learning disabilities, preoccupation with school failure, disturbed peer relationships, fear of parental punishment, parental separation, and abusive home atmosphere. Inspection of this list reveals that at least some of these factors are apt to be present in children with developmental dysfunction. Nevertheless, it must be considered as the ultimate threat and the supreme justification for early identification and intervention.

Severe Aggression and Delinquency

Several studies have documented clearly an association between juvenile delinquency and developmental dysfunctions. In one investigation (Karniski et al. 1982), neurodevelopmental examinations were administered to incarcerated delinquents as well as a series of controls from the same geographical regions. Not surprisingly, the delinquent subjects more commonly displayed significant areas of dysfunction. They tended to have clusters of impairments. A large percentage of them had experienced educational failure beginning at an early age. Their developmental dysfunctions varied considerably but included a substantial number of attention deficits and even more language problems. Levine et al. (1985) showed that delinquents tended to amass multiple risk factors. They were much more likely than controls to have combinations of neurodevelopmental dysfunctions plus behavior disorders plus social and economic disadvantages and family disruption. These delinquents had "risk factor complexes," or combinations of risk factors, that together predisposed them to delinquency and reduced any natural resiliency. Other studies have confirmed the strong association between "learning disability" and delinquency, especially among lower socioeconomic groups. In a review of studies of the antecedents of male delinquency, Loeber and Dishion (1983) note that "the school studies in the present review reinforce the image of delinquency-prone children who are underachievers in an educational sense. At the end of elementary school, low achievement, low vocabulary, and poor verbal reasoning improved the prediction of delinquency by 27%" (p. 82).

Children who display many aggressive behaviors early in life also seem to be at risk for later delinquency (Offord 1984). These "antisocial" children with conduct disorders have consistent tendencies toward disruptive acting-out behaviors. It can sometimes be difficult to differentiate between children with "conduct disorders" and those with attention deficits. There is certainly a subgroup with attention weakness whose impulsiveness and poor self-monitoring of behavior take the form of aggression and disruptive behavior. Considerably more research is needed to understand the various pathways that lead to and from aggressive behavior during childhood. Offord, in his review on antisocial behaviors in childhood (1984), notes that "what needs to be done is to determine the degree of overlap among these diagnoses using clear-cut inclusion and exclusion criteria. We must further learn the extent to which children within a category, such as conduct disorder, differ in important respects if they are subdivided on the basis of the presence or absence of a second diagnosis" (p. 265). Offord identifies a series of factors that seem to predispose children to chronic acting-out tendencies. He includes genetic factors, acquired brain damage, learning problems, difficult temperament, and society's labeling of these children (with subsequent self-fulfilling prophecies). He proposes that it is often the cumulative effects or interactions of these various factors that ultimately produce intransigent tendencies toward aggression and thence delinquency. "Given the interactions and transactions among social, familial, linguistic, and neurobehavioral variables that may culminate in the overlap between underachievement and externalizing behavior, teasing apart the effects of any single background factor is likely to be quite difficult or even misguided" (Hinshaw 1992, p. 151).

Substance abuse is devastating potential complication, and it is estimated that 58 percent of high school seniors have used illicit drugs (Fox and Forbing 1991). Some students with a long record of school failure appear predisposed to abuse drugs (Johnson 1973, Millman and Botvin 1983). There are a number of other potential contributing risk factors including modeling, family environment, stress, inadequate social support, and temperament and personality characteristics (Brown, Mott, and Stewart 1992). In some instances, chemical substances provide the sole pleasure in their lives. In other cases, predisposition to abuse resides in the traits of unfulfilled insatiability that may be part of the clinical picture of long-standing attention deficits. It is not at all difficult to imagine that a highly insatiable child might be prone to substance abuse, especially when deprived of success. Researchers caution against misidentifying a student with a substance abuse problem as having a learning disability, behavioral disorder, or attention deficit (Fox and Forbing 1991). As with other complications, substance abuse can aggravate a preexisting learning problem. Chronic use of marijuana or cocaine may have a deleterious effect on memory and/or attention.

Children who have suffered the effects of developmental dysfunctions may express anger or disenchantment through minor antisocial acts as they approach adolescence. Petty thievery, including stealing at home from parents or siblings, is one such manifestation. The use of excessively unacceptable language is another. These early warning signals frequently betoken underlying frustration and anxiety.

Another common phenomenon is antisocial gangs. In many communities children with developmental dysfunctions tend to congregate, especially during early adolescence. They are apt to form what appears to be a new family, one that is preferable to the one at home. These often success-deprived individuals feel good about themselves only when are with each other. They develop virtually blind loyalties to the group and to one another. They laugh at each other's jokes, savor each other's linguistic forays, and sometimes go so far as to commit petty (or more substantial) crimes to win further adulation. The parents of these gang members may blame the others in the group, believing that they are having a bad influence on their child. Various prohibitions may be issued in an effort to extract a son or daughter from an antisocial group; however, such attempts may lead to anger, rebellion, and intensified family tension. The bonds that form between these peers are extremely durable. The value system that they adopt is difficult to alter; it commonly features such attributes as defiance, bravery, grace under pressure, and the repudiation of adult authority. This frequent complication of learning disorders and deprivation of success further erodes school performance. Often such groups have no tolerance whatsoever for a member who displays motivation in school. The predicament posed by the gang is difficult to resolve. Every effort should be made to prevent its formation in the first place by ensuring that elementary school-children receive sufficient success and praise and feel respected by the adults in their lives. Often intensive counseling, a complete change in environment (such as boarding school when desirable or possible), or the precipitation of a major crisis (such as going to court) is needed to break up the gang and facilitate more positive developmental progression. As with other such phenomena, however, it is totally inappropriate to destroy this refuge without first having a clear idea of what will be substituted for it.

Teenage Pregnancy

Teenage pregnancy is another social problem that may be partly a consequence of inordinate failure to achieve. While school problems are unlikely to be the sole cause of this phenomenon, academic failure is certainly a contributing element. Moreover, adolescents who are highly insatiable, those who tend to form unstable peer relationships, and those who have some difficulty predicting the consequences of their actions may be especially predisposed to having children out of wedlock.

Undeveloped Talent

The final complication mentioned in this section is the phenomenon of central nervous system talent or strength that is not permitted (or encouraged) to develop. putting the lid on a proclivity may seriously deter the developmental health of a child. Parents, teachers, and clinicians need to be vigilant for previously unrecognized talent, particularly in students who are struggling academically and/or socially. When children are strongly oriented toward an area, it is imperative that they be allowed to develop competency in that area. It may, in fact, be more helpful to strengthen strengths than it is to remediate deficiencies. Young children who show mechanical skills, such as facility with engines or cars, must have plenty of opportunity to develop those skills. Children with musical, artistic, mathematical, or athletic strengths must have the chance to exercise them to their full extent. They should never have their area of talent removed as a punishment ("If you don't study harder, you can't play the drums"). Children who for one reason or another are not permitted to practice their specialties, who are required to be full-time practitioners of their weaknesses, endure a significant complication of their dysfunctions. Awareness of this complication is important since it is so easily treated and reversed.

MECHANISMS

Consistent with its empirical and phenomenological outlook, this book has not until now stressed theories of physiological mechanisms underlying dysfunction. Many disciplines have made concerted efforts to describe the disordered neurobiological processes that prevent or decelerate learning. Although explanations may bear only an indirect relationship to intervention, they are important, interesting, and certainly complementary to the more descriptive approach advocated in this book. In the long run, it is likely that the richest picture of childhood dysfunction will emerge from a lively interplay of keen empiricism with neuroscientific data.

This section provides examples of the major thrusts of investigation into relevant brain mechanisms. The brief overview begins by considering anatomical localization of function in the central nervous system and the disorders said to be associated with neuropsychological models.

Neuroanatomical and Neuropsychological Models

Many investigators in the fields of neuropsychology and neurology have focused on the localization of specific functions in the brain. The clinical study of adult stroke victims has produced major gains in the understanding of brain function. The study of post-traumatic brain injuries as well as a variety of experimental procedures have contributed to our knowledge. In recent years, strong interest has developed in brain localization and its evolution during childhood.

With this interest have come efforts to relate inappropriate localization phenomena to the development of various learning disorders. The impetus for such efforts has been the belief that an anatomical model can help explain failure to acquire skills and can allow for the definition of subtypes of learning disorder corresponding to specific central nervous system lesions or patterns of unusual localization (Hooper and Willis 1989). Probably the greatest and most sustained level of scrutiny has centered around investigations of hemispheric specialization and cerebral dominance as they relate to reading disability.

Cerebral Dominance.   Many investigators have attributed reading difficulties to problems with cerebral dominance (Hiscock and Kinsbourne 1982). The two hemispheres of the brain are interconnected by the corpus callosum and relatively specialized in their functions. The dominant hemisphere (the left in most people) is generally recognized to have linguistic superiority. It is also known to predominate in all aspects of sequential output (including complex speech), in finger recognition, and in the verbal mediation of tasks. The nondominant hemisphere (the right in most people) is said to be superior in interpreting visual-spatial stimuli. It functions when visual inputs are integrated with some form of fine motor output. The right hemisphere (when it is nondominant) is also important for visual memory (both recognition and retrieval), color discrimination, and certain aspects of music recognition and appreciation. Typically, the left side is said to play a major role in language. While this is true, the generalization pertains primarily to expressive language. Certain elements of comprehension or receptive processing may well reside in the nondominant hemisphere. "The left hemisphere is not just linguistically based and the right hemisphere visual-spatially based; rather, they complement each other" (Semrud-Clikeman and Hynd 1990, p. 96).

These and other left-right distinctions have captured the fancy of many individuals. Some devotees have extended the model to include a wide range of personality traits characteristic of "left brain" or "right brain" persons. However, little experimental evidence justifies many of these generalizations and overextensions. "Such literature renders a disservice to the discipline of neuropsychology by its oversimplification, and it is especially problematic when applied to treatments for learning disabled children" (Hooper and Willis 1989, p. 33). A steady accumulation of evidence proves that there are significant anatomical differences between the two hemispheres, but that "the two hemispheres work together, possessing a reciprocal and interacting variety of hemispheric specialized functions" (Gaddes and Edgell 1994, p. 211).

Using sophisticated methods of injecting dye into arteries, leMay and Culebras (1972) showed that the sylvan fissure (a region of the brain known to play a major role in language function) is greater in the left hemisphere than in the right in an adult population. Geschwind and Levitsky (1968) reported a difference in the width of the planum temporale, measured on horizontal sections of pathology specimens. This again is said to represent superior language function on a structural basis in the dominant hemisphere.

Numerous techniques have been used in the past to study the degree of lateralization of specific functions. Examples are the surgical removal of a damaged hemisphere or portion thereof, temporary incapacitation of a portion of one hemisphere (frequently with the injection of a barbituate—the Wada technique), electrical stimulation of certain regions, and one-sided electroconvulsive shock. Each of these methods has some methodological limitations, and less invasive procedures have been applied more recently. Electroencephalogram (EEG) technique records the brain's alpha and beta waves by measuring the change in voltage at the subject's scalp. This voltage change reveals intracortical connections both within and between hemispheres, and allows for investigations of the development of the brain, frontal lobe activity, and the function of different of regions in emotional behavior (Torello 1992). While a particular kind of stimulus (e.g., visual, auditory, or written language) is presented to the subject, an EEG tracing is obtained and, with the help of computers, information is derived about the site(s) where the input is processed.

In another procedure, dichotic listening techniques enable a subject to hear two stimuli simultaneously, one directed toward each ear. Whichever side is heard preferentially is assumed to be contralateral to the side of the brain that processes predominantly verbal inputs, because nerve fibers coming from the ears cross before reaching their final destinations in the higher cortical centers of the brain.

Visual half-field investigations are based on some similar assumptions. Subjects are presented briefly with visual stimuli on one or the other visual half-field (areas to the left or right of visualization). There is evidence that stimulation from either side, if brief enough so as to disappear before an eye movement can be made, is conducted more directly to the opposite hemisphere than to the one on the same side. In this way, attempts are made to lateralize visual-spatial processing. As Hiscock and Kinsbourne (1982) point out, however, both dichotic listening asymmetries and visual half-field observations may be biased by specific patterns of attention rather than true localizations of processing. The same is true with certain studies of tactile recognition. In general, most children and adults recognize objects (without looking at them) in their left hands better than in their right hands. This is often taken to mean that such recognition (*stereognosis*) is mediated on the right side.

Probably the oldest and simplest correlate of cerebral lateralization is the association with lateral preferences, most commonly handedness. One of the least controversial findings in the field of neuropsychology is the frequency of left- and right-hemispheric speech in right-handed adults. Many investigations have established that between 95 and 99 percent of right-handed adults have speech control lateralized to the left cerebral hemisphere. Lateralization in left-handed individuals is estimated to be more variable but is said to be between 60 and 70 percent for left-lateralized speech (Gaddes and Edgell 1994). Moreover, left-handed people are far more likely to have bilateral speech representation. Ambidextrous individuals are said to be indistinguishable from left-handers in their prevalence of different patterns of speech lateralization. Another important issue is the degree of handedness and its possible relationship to the degree of lateralization. There is some evidence that auditory asymmetry varies with the strength of handedness—particularly in left-handed males. The data relating cerebral function to eye preference are less compelling. A greater correlation likely exists between handedness and footedness than between handedness and eyedness. About 33 percent of the population is said to be right-eyed, while only 8 to 10 percent is left-handed (Gaddes and Edgell 1994). Therefore, a significant number of normal adults and children clearly have crossed eye-hand dominance; thus, eye preference and hand preference must be quite independent of each other.

Studies have not demonstrated convincingly that left-handed individuals have more learning problems than right-handed individuals. Hiscock and Kinsbourne (1982) state that "the preponderance of negative findings, especially those based upon large and representative samples, suggests that left-handers in the general population are as intelligent as their right-handed counterparts. Consequently, we conclude, that when deviant lateralization of speech is found in the absence of brain pathology, there are no detrimental effects with respect to cognitive ability" (p. 211).

Cerebral dominance and reading disability. Orton (1937) presented a model of what he called *strephosymbolia* to explain reading difficulties. In his model the hemispheres differed in their representation of stimuli: the left hemisphere ordinarily exerted control over its opposite half. When, for some reason, dominance of the left hemisphere failed, the two hemispheres were actually competing. If the right hemisphere took over at a time when the accuracy of a response depended on the perceived orientation of the stimulus, a reversal error might occur. Inconsistent domination of the right hemisphere by the left might then engender erratic performance. Interhemispheric competition would decrease overall reading efficiency.

Another interesting model (Hiscock and Kinsbourne 1982) is characterized as a breakdown of corpus callosal function. Galin et al. (1979) have speculated that callosal processes (i.e., those that allow communication between the two hemispheres) are undeveloped in young children. In other words, it may be that the cerebral hemispheres of very young children function independently. In this model, reading difficulties are blamed on a delay in the maturation of the corpus callosum in two hypothetical ways: one in which the callosum transfers too much information and one in which it transfers too little. Some studies have investigated the callosal size in children with dysphasia, dyslexia, and general learning disabilities (Njiokiktjien, deSonneville, and Vaal 1994); however, there is yet little evidence to support these mechanisms.

Some studies examining postmortem brain specimens taken from patients who had had severe reading disabilities revealed the presence of distinct architectural abnormalities of the left hemisphere (Galaburda 1983). The abnormalities included an increase in certain cells (*polymicrogyria*) in the speech region of the brain. In addition, *cortical dysplasias* (unusual patterns in the cerebral cortex) were observed in a number of key areas. Further, some of the usual temporal lobe asymmetries found in most of the general population were not present among those with reading disabilities. In a review of these findings, Duane (1985) notes that "the extent to which the physical alterations were causal to the educational underachievement cannot be stated. However, the observations clearly raised the possibility of such a causal relationship and suggested continuing studies of a similar nature should be carried out" (p. 19).

Another commonly advanced model presupposes a "translocation" of function, so that in some instances the right hemisphere does what the left should do and vice versa. According to this model, there is either a complete reversal of functions (mirror image) or both sides of the brain attempt to carry out both spatial and verbal processes. Alternatively, it may be that the left hemisphere practices both verbal and spatial processing, while the right limits itself to spatial functions (or vice versa). All of these models have in common a reversal of the normal responsibilities between the two hemispheres. These reversal theories are based on the premise that it is advantageous to have verbal functions on the left and visual-spatial ones on the right. Any reversal of this normal pattern of lateralization might have a damaging impact on verbal functions and/or visual-spatial processing.

One intriguing theory is that of Bakker (1983, 1994), who pointed out that the right hemisphere is likely to be the primary processor of perceptually demanding letters. Certain studies have found that the right hemisphere is more likely to process information set in nonconventional typefaces while the left hemisphere is better at processing information set in conventional typefaces. These discoveries were made using the visual half-field technique. Reading during the early stages of acquiring skills appears to entail right-hemispheric strategies since normal print to the very young is perceptually complex. As readers gain more experience, they concentrate less on processing the perceptual characteristics of symbols and more on syntax, semantics, and other linguistic components of the reading process. Consequently, as children progress in their reading abilities, there is less emphasis on right-hemispheric processing and more emphasis on the left. In accounting for reading disabilities, Bakker (1983) describes two types of children. The first group (which he calls *L-type dyslexics*) shows left-hemispheric mediation of speech, possibly with a weak right-hemispheric specialization for visual perceptual abilities. Although readers must perform perceptual analysis in the early phase of learning to read, they may tend to overlook the perceptual features and have a difficult time. They may read relatively quickly but make many errors. Such readers are similar to those described by Boder (1973) as "dyseidetic," by Kinsbourne and Warrington (1966) as "gestalt-weak," and by Mattis (1978) as poor in visual-spatial function. In other words, these readers may overuse language during a time of acquiring skills when it is preferable to focus on the visual appearances of the symbols of graphemes. Bakker states that "due to a *relative* overdevelopment of left hemispheric function, the scale is turned in favor of linguistic (semantic) approaches in L-type dyslexics" (p. 504). He calls the other type of reading disability *P-type dyslexia*, which is the opposite phenomenon. These readers overrely on perceptual strategies. Bakker explains that "while perceptual feature analysis is required in early reading and subsequent slowness is allowed, the ultimate aim of reading is fluency. Left hemispheric mechanisms are most appropriate to subsume fluent reading. Thus readers should shift from a perceptual to a linguistic (semantic) reading strategy at some point during their development. Some of them may not be in a position to do so; they go on relying on right hemispheric strategies (P-type dyslexics). Their problem may be due to relatively overdeveloped right hemisphere function" (p. 504). Bakker compares this group to the group Boder (1973) called *dysphonetics* and the group other writers called *language-disturbed*.

Bakker (1979) calls the conceptualization of dyslexics as L-types and P-types the "balance model." He cites a considerable body of experimental evidence to support his view (Bakke 1994). Gaddes and Edgell (1994) conclude that "the causes of developmental dyslexia are far from clear and possibly more complex. Most CT and MRI studies of developmental dyslexics have shown no detectable brain injury, and this suggests a possible genetic, developmental, or physiological dysfunction" (p. 383).

From this discussion it can be inferred that much remains to be done before we can subscribe wholeheartedly to the role of aberrant cerebral dominance in reading disability. Nevertheless, the justifiable effort to describe subtypes will continue.

Slow Processing and Production As a Mechanism.   Tallal, Star, and Mellits (1985) studied groups of children with language impairment and discovered that these subjects have particular problems with the *rate* of processing and production. The investigators found that children thought to have complex linguistic difficulties such as those described in chapter 5 were instead having significant problems keeping pace with the rapidly changing flow of stimuli into their central nervous systems. These language-disabled children also have problems processing and producing nonverbal material at a rapid rate. Thus, they appeared to be deficient at perceiving rapidly changing sequential stimuli. It was found, for example, that these children had much more trouble appreciating speech sounds containing rapidly changing acoustical qualities than those sounds that remained more stable (i.e., stimuli that can be dealt with more slowly). This has led to some speculation that many children with language and sequencing problems may, in fact, be encountering difficulty with the *rate* of their processing and production rather than its quality. Since language is a phenomenon requiring rapid processing, it would not be surprising if such individuals have their greatest difficulties in the linguistic domain. Visual-spatial data, on the other hand, tend to remain stable so that there is less demand for extremely rapid processing. The visual perceptual features of an array of stimuli usually do not change quickly, while language comes and goes with great rapidity. This has led to Tallal's proposition (1985) that the left hemisphere may be specialized for rapid processing of information (and therefore language) while the right hemisphere in most individuals processes at a slower rate (and therefore accommodates much of the visual-spatial demand). The extent to which such rate factors constitute common mechanisms for dysfunction has yet to be determined. However, the evidence is attractive and most certainly suggests the need for continuing study. It may be that an important subgroup of children with language and sequencing deficiencies is struggling to keep pace with the demands for quick processing. Because these children cannot operate at an adequate rate, they may miss a great deal of input. It is possible, for example, that the higher linguistic functions such as syntax, semantics, and morphology become reduced secondarily because of a chronic inability to keep up with the language flow and a consequent loss of language experience.

The Search for Neuropsychological Syndromes

The quest to uncover highly specific syndromes into which groups of children with learning problems will fit has been implicit in much of neuropsychological research. There has been considerable speculation about the existence of various predictable clusters of findings or symptoms. The syndrome model is well illustrated by Developmental Gerstmann syndrome, which was first described by Josef Gerstmann (1940). He related focal disease in the dominant parietal occipital region (in the left hemisphere in most subjects) to a constellation of four distinct findings: right-left disorientation, bilateral finger agnosia, writing disability, and problems with mathematics. Over the years, clinicians have continued to search for this symptom complex. Many agree that there is a tendency for the four deficits to coexist in patients with left parietal problems. However, a wide range of variations have been described (Benton 1977), leading many observers to wonder how pure or true the syndrome may actually be. Of the specific syndromes that Semrud-Clikeman and Hynd (1990) reviewed (Asperger's syndrome, Developmental Gerstmann syndrome, left hemisyndrome classification, right hemisphere syndrome, and right parietal lobe syndrome), Developmental Gerstmann syndrome had the least support for right hemispheric learning disabilities. "Whether Developmental Gerstmann Syndrome can be considered to reflect left or right hemispheric dysfunctional or bilateral disturbance in children is unclear, as the pattern of symptoms could implicate many different dysfunctional systems" (Semrud-Clikeman and Hynd 1990, p. 204).

Just as Developmental Gerstmann syndrome describes a cluster of findings associated with parietal lobe lesions, other syndromes describe findings associated with other specific regions of the brain. For example, the frontal lobe syndrome results in a reduced ability to plan and follow through, as well as some deficits in recent memory, weakened ability for mental extraction, personality alterations, diminished concern for the future, impulsiveness, some euphoria, and a seeming lack of initiative or spontaneity (Benton 1968a). This description contains some recognizable features of attention deficit (especially the impulsiveness and lack of planning). Hynd and his colleagues found that the subjects with attention deficit hyperactivity disorder had more symmetric frontal lobes, and therefore smaller right frontal regions, than the control subjects. Regions of the corpus callosum were also smaller in the subjects with attention deficit hyperactivity disorder (Filipek, Kennedy, and Caviness 1992; Gaddes and Edgell 1994). These parts of the brain, along with the basal ganglia, are related to inattentive behavior, and a lack of response inhibition. Brain function studies reveal that synaptic conduction is slower in subjects with and without attention deficit hyperactivity disorder (Gaddes and Edgell 1994).

Other syndromes have associated certain social cognitive abilities with frontal lobe function. Social cognitive abilities and frontal lobe functions are exemplified by Gaddes's (1980) description of an adult patient with a right frontal lobe lesion. Gaddes noted that the patient had real problems "because of a loss of the ability for subtle judgment, and for the understanding of fine nuances of meaning in evaluating and handling social group situations" (p. 86). We might argue from this that some children with attention problems understandably have social cognitive deficiencies.

Asperger's syndrome was first used in 1943 to describe "children with a congenital inability to relate emotionally to others" (Klin et al. 1995). The recent definition in the *Diagnostic and Statistical Manual of Mental Disorders-Fourth Edition* (1994) states that essential features include "severe and sustained impairment in social interaction . . . the development of restricted, repetitive patterns of behavior, interests, and activities . . . the disturbance must cause clinically significant impairment in social, occupation, or other important areas of functioning . . . [and] there are no clinically significant delays in cognitive development or in the development of age-appropriate self-help skills, adaptive behavior (other than in social interaction), and curiosity about the environment in childhood" (p. 75). It has been disputed whether Asperger's is a mild form of autism or a distinct syndrome

(Semrud-Clikeman and Hynd 1990). The *Diagnostic and Statistical Manual of Mental Disorders-Fourth Edition* (1994) defines Asperger's Disorder as differing from Autistic Disorder in that "there are no clinically significant delays in language" (p. 75).

Another proposed neuropsychological syndrome is Rourke's nonverbal learning disabilities syndrome. Since the 1970s Rourke and his colleagues have sought to define nonverbal learning disabilities within cognitive processes and cerebral organization, specifically, "central processing deficiencies" (Gaddes and Edgell 1994). Rourke and his colleagues believe that cerebral hemispheric organization develops from the right to left hemisphere, and that nonverbal learning disabilities result when there is a disturbance of the white matter in the brain. Rourke et al. (1990) state that the nonverbal learning disability syndrome "would be expected to develop under any set of circumstances that interferes significantly with (a) the functioning of the right hemispheral systems (as in the case of any general deterioration of white matter or with substantial destruction of white matter in the right hemisphere) and/or (b) access to (neuronal intercommunication with) these systems (as in the case of colossal agenesis)" (p. 381). This syndrome includes elements of tactile and visual perception, attention and memory, exploratory behavior, concept formation, problem solving, and elements of speech and language (Rourke 1995). It remains controversial.

Tourette disorder is another syndrome that has features of multiple motor tics, and vocal tics that occur a number of times a day for a period of more than one year (*Diagnostic and Statistical Manual of Mental Disorders-Fourth Edition* 1994). This neuropsychological impairment is most commonly accompanied by obsessive-compulsive disorder, and attention deficits with and without hyperactivity (Singer, Schuerholz, and Denckla 1995). Learning disabilities are also common. Burd, Kauffman, and Kerbeshian (1992) reviewed the records of forty-two children with Tourette syndrome and found that 21 percent met the two standard deviations discrepancy criteria in one subject area (reading decoding, reading comprehension, mathematics, or spelling) for learning disabilities, 9.5 percent in two or more areas, and 2.4 percent for three or more areas.

Certain forms of memory disorder appear to be related to function of the hippocampus and other parts of the limbic circuit on the inner surfaces of the temporal lobe near the brain stem. Luria (1980) points out that lesions in these areas lead to severe disturbances of memory. Gaddes and Edgell (1994) note that "short-term memory deficits may result from disturbances in the posterior parietal, temporal, and front cortices. The storage sites for long-term memory also are distributed in cortical networks throughout the cortex. The lateral temporal cortices are important in long-term memory, whereas the mesial temporal areas are important in short-term memory. The mechanism of transfer from short-term memory into long-term memory may be localized in the hippocampus, amygdala, and closely related structures and is vulnerable to insult" (p. 296). Thus, specific patterns of disordered memory may be attributed to this kind of neuropsychological picture.

The search for anatomical accountability for childhood learning disorders remains active. It has yet to be established that the kinds of neuropsychological generalizations made about adults (such as stroke victims) also pertain to children. Convincing statistical evidence for the existence of highly specific syndromes is still in short supply. There is even some evidence to the contrary. The Middle Childhood Project, conducted at The Children's Hospital in Boston (1984), gave a group of children with learning problems complete neurodevelopmental examinations, assessing multiple developmental functions (including attention, motor output, visual processing, sequential organization, language, neuromaturation, and memory). Using these seven developmental functions, an effort was made to see whether children with significant learning problems tended to fall into distinct, predictable subtypes based on clusters of dysfunction. Analysis of the data revealed that 86 of a possible 128 combinations of deficits were encountered in 222 children. None of the functional profiles represented a significantly large portion of the group. In other words, there were more ways to be different than there were to be the same. A high level of diversity was found among children with learning problems. Such a finding argues against emphasizing the search for major syndromes, although the need remains to relate highly specific performance deficits (such as a particularly troublesome propensity in spelling) to a discrete anatomical disorder. Although much research is being conducted along these lines, none of the studies have been exemplary. In the meantime, the therapeutic approach can safely proceed in the absence of clear-cut identifications of syndromes.

Newer Techniques for Elucidating Mechanisms

Some very promising technologies are advancing rapidly and should be able to provide clues about anatomical localization. Brain imaging provides images of the structure and/or functions of the brain, which once seemed inaccessible. "The establishment of human brain-behavior relationships once rested upon post-mortem and 'war wound' behavioral-anatomical correlations. However, the past decade has seen a quantum leap in our ability to extract anatomical and functional brain indices from the intact human head via the now well-known CT, NMR, MRI, PET, and SPECT scans" (Duffy 1994, p. 93). Unfortunately much of this new technology has been invasive, expensive, scarce, or inappropriate for children. The electroencephalogram (EEG) has been the most widely used technique to study the brain's electrical activity, and is a noninvasive procedure that is less expensive than other techniques.

Over the past decade, EEG analysis techniques have been developed, including a "quantified EEG" technique, also called *quantified neurophysiology, neurometrics, brain electrical activity mapping,* or *mapping* (Duffy 1994). Some of the seminal work in this field has been done by Duffy and McAnulty (1985). Their Brain Electrical Activity Mapping (BEAM) is a technique using minicomputers equipped with advanced graphic display devices to represent brain functions in progress. The methodology combined the classical approach to topographically mapping electroencephalograms with the use of evoked potential data. With the aid of a computer, the EEG tracing during certain activities or with distinct inputs is measured with a graphic display of the results. The image on the screen can be represented by a series of numbers that can be employed statistically. The clinician detects unusual patterns by comparing the map of a particular subject to that of a control group. A statistic may reflect "deviation from the normal." In this manner, normal and reading-disabled boys have been compared in terms of possible electrophysiological differences during the act of reading. In some preliminary studies, Duffy et al. (1980) found differences in the frontal and temporal regions, seeming to suggest some physiological correlates in these patients.

The new advances in brain imaging promise more precise definition of subgroups of children with learning problems. Many of the brain-behavior research has focused on dyslexia. MRI (magnetic resonance imaging) studies, such as those by Hynd and his colleagues, have investigated the chemical composition of subjects with dyslexia, and Torello (1992) reviews the conflicting findings of EEG studies and dyslexia. He reports that studies have found increases in theta and alpha activity, abnormal bifrontal and left temporal alpha activity. Others report no abnormal activity at all. Hynd, Semrud-Clikeman, and Lyytinen (1991) reviewed eight CT (computed tomography) and MRI studies of dyslexia. Seven out of the eight studies found no detectable brain injury. Six out of the eight studies found more left-right symmetry. Acknowledging methodological concerns, the use of CT/MRI procedures has provided some "limited evidence that alterations in normal patterns of brain asymmetry in the region of the left planum temporal and parietoccipital cortex may correlate with the behaviorally defined syndrome of developmental dyslexia" (Hynd, Semrud-Clikeman, and Lyytinen 1991, p. 494).

Other helpful techniques study differential blood flow to different parts of the brain. There is some suggestion that for certain kinds of learning and/or attention problems, abnormalities of cerebral blood flow (particularly inconsistent or erratic patterns) may be operating. Some research has found that subjects with attention deficit hyperactivity disorder have decreased blood flow to the frontal lobes. Other studies have found a reduced blood flow to the basal ganglia, the motor cortex, and the primary sensory cortex (Gaddes and Edgell 1994).

At the present time these brain imaging procedures convey little of therapeutic significance and are limited to research. Ultimately, they may find a clinical application.

Symptom Complexes

Further hopes for explanatory mechanisms have sometimes occurred in the attempt to perform epidemiological studies that relate diverse conditions to each other. Geschwind and Behan (1982) described one such promising attempt. They were struck by a group of disorders that appeared to be particularly common in left-handed individuals. These included various autoimmune conditions such as ulcerative colitis, celiac disease, Hashimoto's thyroiditis, and migraine. They also believe that certain "developmental learning disorders" were present in increased frequency among left-handers (although, as we have noted above, not everyone agrees with that). They also linked this symptom complex to some learning disorders. These relationships were found to be true mainly in boys.

Geschwind and Behan proposed the following mechanism for the phenomenon cited above: they noted that left-hemispheric growth *in utero* is slowed down by testosterone, the normal hormone of males. The delayed growth in the left hemisphere accounts for the greater frequency of left-handedness in males. In those cases where the effects of testosterone are more marked, there is greater interference with neuronal migration and there are such distinct abnormalities in the formation of the left hemisphere (again, especially in males) that the left temporal speech area is impaired. At the same time during fetal life, the immune system is maturing. Testosterone has important depressive effects on the thymus (an organ that has a critical role in the development of normal patterns of immunity). During periods of unusually high secretion of testosterone, maturation of the immune system is also likely to be affected adversely. Suppression of thymic growth during fetal life might therefore favor the development of autoimmunity in subsequent life. Extrapolating from this hypothesis, some abnormally high or uneven secretion of the male hormone creates a predisposition both to autoimmune diseases and learning disorders secondary to underdevelopment of the left cerebral cortex. Recently, Bryden, McManus, and Bulman-Fleming (1994, 1995) evaluated the Geschwind-Behan-Galaburda model of cerebral lateralization, and while the model has stimulated interesting research in cerebral lateralization, studies testing the effects of testosterone on the hypothesized traits have provided "little empirical support" (Berenbaum and Denburg 1995).

The hypothesis above requires much more validation—both biological and epidemiological. However, it should serve as a model of the kind of far-reaching thinking that may help elucidate mechanisms for some of the phenomenology described in this book.

Biochemical Correlates

Faced with highly complex behavior and learning difficulties, parents and professionals alike have sought clarification in the intricate series of equilibria that characterize body chemistry. Sometimes parents hope ardently that a difficult child will be found to have a "chemical imbalance." This has led to some heavy consumer demand for diagnoses of hypoglycemia (low blood sugar) and abnormal carbohydrate metabolism. Other chemical quests have included the search for enzymatic defects, subtle vitamin deficiencies, and abnormalities in the metabolism of heavy metals. Each of these hypotheses implies an underlying biochemical "defect." As yet, these have not been substantiated in any scientific manner. The theories are often upheld on the basis of anecdotal evidence of successful treatment.

One promising area of biochemical research has been the study of neurotransmitter substances, the chemical agents that convey electrical activity (and therefore information) from one nerve ending to another within the brain. There has been extensive research into the possibility that some children may actually suffer defects in the production, use, and/or turnover (degradation) of these compounds. The possibility that such defects are at least partly responsible for some attentional difficulties has been of particular interest. Norepinephrine and dopamine are two chemicals that are produced in the peripheral and central nervous system and play an important role as neurotransmitters. Both are synthesized from the amino acid tyrosine, found in dietary proteins. Through a series of chemical reactions tyrosine is converted either into dopamine or norepinephrine, which can be in activated by incorporation into the nerve endings. Chemical degradation is regulated by two specific enzymes. The various metabolites (breakdown products) of these neurotransmitters have been measured in the blood, in urine, and in cerebrospinal fluid.

Several studies have shown that certain metabolites are significantly lower in children clinically diagnosed as having attention deficits. Another relevant finding has been that a major product of dopamine is found in lower concentrations in the spinal fluid of children with attention deficits (plus overactivity) than in normal children (Shaywitz, Cohen, and Bowers 1977). Shaywitz, Yager, and Klopper (1976), using rats, showed that neonatal damage to the systems that produce dopamine ultimately yields rates with behavioral profiles that resemble remarkably those of children with attention deficits and overactivity. These investigators observed that following neonatal dopamine depletion in rats, animals become significantly more active than their littermate controls and exhibit profound learning deficits. There is a growing body of evidence implicating abnormal dopamine and norepinephrine metabolism in the pathogenesis of attention deficits.

Further compelling evidence has arisen from studies of the effects of stimulant medication on neurotransmitter function. Two commonly used drugs, dextroamphetamine (Dexedrine) and methylphenidate (Ritalin), have been investigated. The main mechanism of action of an amphetamine is to block the reuptake inactivation and increase the presynaptic release of neurotransmitters. The end result is that larger quantities of these substances are secreted by nerve endings and smaller amounts are inactivated. Furthermore, amphetamine seems to inhibit the enzyme (monoamine oxidase) that degrades norepinephrine and dopamine. Methylphenidate works somewhat differently. It seems to stimulate release of certain stores of dopamine. The effect is similar—more available neurotransmitter substances at nerve junctions. Seemingly contradictory, however, is the observation confirmed in many studies that levels of catecholamine (neurotransmitter) metabolites decrease rather than increase when affected children are taking stimulant drugs. If more neurotransmitters resulted from these medications, we would expect to encounter higher levels of urinary metabolites. Rapoport (1983) has suggested that the ultimate therapeutic effect of stimulant drugs may be to increase the amount of active norepinephrine. That may not have such a major impact of metabolites in the urine since norepinephrine is so potent. In a review article on the subject, Raskin et al. (1984) conclude that "it is clear that future research is needed in order to understand the neurochemical changes that underlie stimulant-enhanced performance" (p. 394). This kind of research is in its infancy. Undoubtedly, future studies will elucidate further the mechanisms of normal and dysfunctional neurotransmitter metabolism and performance. As for the study of attention deficits, there will first need to be a much clearer taxonomy and a better understanding of the multiple clinical disorders of which this symptom complex may be one component.

Additional Mechanisms

It is important to remain open-minded about biological mechanisms. Compelling hypotheses that merit further investigation include abnormalities or unusual patterns of brain blood flow, disorders of various endocrine systems (such as hypothyroidism), and a variety of forms of embryonic dysgenesis. New hypotheses will need to be scrutinized according to scientific methods, utilizing combinations of clinical studies, epidemiological investigations, and other rigorous techniques. In all such cases, hesitancy must precede widespread public acceptance. There needs to be greater recognition that an explanation may be logical and intuitively appealing but nevertheless untrue. In particular, it is exceedingly important to avoid drawing premature therapeutic implications from mechanisms that have not been scientifically established.

Natural Diversity

In accounting for the mechanisms underlying developmental dysfunctions, we run the risk of dramatizing deviation while neglecting variation. Indeed, it is quite likely that there is no particular explanation for the "abnormalities" of many children with learning problems because it is not clear that they are truly "abnormal." A brain that is highly specialized need not be considered pathological. Therefore, an important mechanism is the natural range of variation in the "wirings" of nervous systems within a population. The chapters of the book have presented one variable after another in a seemingly endless procession of possibilities for childhood function and dysfunction. The infinite variety of combinations of these endogenous, environmental, and stylistic elements must of necessity culminate in the propagation of highly individual and individualistic prototypes. Drawing a line can be most difficult. The distinction between variation and deviation is apt to blur as we attempt to delineate handicapped states. Therefore, we must reserve for at least a portion of children with learning difficulties the possibility that the mechanism for their dysfunction is physiological rather than pathological, part of a normal distribution of assets and deficits, an explanation that demands no invocation of damage or pathology.

Chapter 14

Approaches to Assessment

"I was always a bad learner," he recalled, "and although I loved knowledge from my cradle, I like to acquire it my own way. I think I was born with a detestation of grammar."

—Stanley Weintraub, *Disraeli, A Biography*

Her grades were good enough though she did not seem in any sense precocious. She did not excel at spelling, a humbling deficiency because the spelling bee was one of the social events of the school year.

—Allen Freeman Davis,
American Heroine: The Life and Legend of Jane Addams

Evaluating children with learning problems and associated neurodevelopmental dysfunctions challenges the thoroughness, sensitivity, and open-mindedness of the evaluator. The most effective assessment of children describes them without reducing them to labels. This chapter advocates an approach that stresses observation and description, an empirical accounting of the various functions, subskills, and skills elaborated in earlier chapters. To understand and treat underachievement and/or maladaptation, we need to be the best possible describers of the child in question. Table 14-1 summarizes the objectives of an assessment.

DESCRIBING

Descriptive assessments demand the search for recurrent themes (figure 14-1). No one piece of evidence, regardless of its source, leads to definitive formulation without considerable supporting evidence from other perspectives or sources. In other words, the diagnostician should function like an attorney preparing a brief. Numerous interlocking data are needed to substantiate an argument. A scholar analyzing a novel by Dostoyevsky or Melville must be vigilant for recurring themes or symbols that provide insights into the author's intention or points of view. A similar process should be followed in evaluating a child. The diagnostician systematically searches for evidence based on consistencies in historical data,

Table 14-1. Objectives of an evaluation

1. Accurately formulate the possible reasons for a child's learning problems
2. Compile a description of a child that can form the basis for optimal management
3. Enhance the insight of parents, teachers, and the child
4. Answer the specific questions or concerns of parents, teachers, and the child
5. Provide a baseline for monitoring progress and for judging the effectiveness of services
6. Alleviate anxiety, pessimism, and guilt
7. Determine specific service needs
8. Identify strengths that can be utilized to enhance performance and self-esteem
9. Determine eligibility for school-based and other services
10. Detect and describe complicating factors that require management

test results, and direct observations. Prematurely formed conclusions based on one test or subtest score or a single teacher's observations may be misleading and therefore unfair to the child in question.

The astute evaluator must formulate a description that encompasses all available information to portray the complexity of a disappointing child. In seeking recurrent themes, evaluators must begin with a conceptual framework. In the medical realm this is called a *differential diagnosis,* a series of possible explanations for a clinical phenomenon. For example, diagnosing a child who has difficulty reading begins with a series of possible developmental explanations, including problems within the developmental functions of language, memory, spatial and temporal-sequential ordering, and attention. Once the list of possibilities is established, the ways in which each is to be ruled in or out must be determined. An assessment should be based on specific, predetermined diagnostic possibilities. At the same time, an evaluator must be prepared to encounter phenomena that she or he has never before uncovered. A frequent tendency, especially in schools, has been to start with tests and then proceed to diagnoses, thereby defining learning disorders by test results. This may lead to mistaken notions that children could not possibly have learning disorders if they excel on a *WISC-III* or fail to show discrepancies between intelligence and achievement test scores. This kind of thinking is, of course, far too narrow and is likely to exclude many disabling problems affecting learning and productivity. Attention difficulties, productivity problems, higher-order cognitive weaknesses, poor understanding of syntax, active working memory dysfunctions, and debilitating organizational problems often pass through the sieves of such rigid diagnostic systems. Evaluators of children need to begin by compiling a list of the major functions they wish to investigate. For example, they might use the headings of chapters 2 through 8 of this book to delineate the constructs to be assessed for differential diagnosis. A hierarchical approach, as depicted below, can be used in assessing neurodevelopmental function and academic performance:

The evaluator should make explicit decisions about the best ways to assess relevant neurodevelopmental functions and academic subskills and processes at

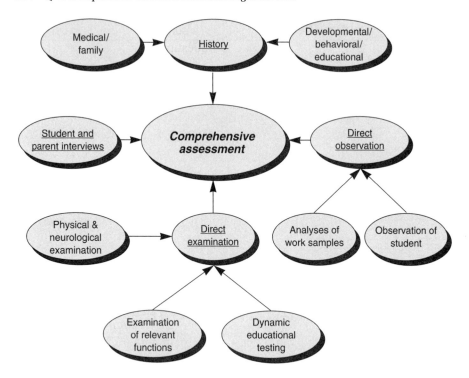

Figure 14-1. Comprehensive assessment and the search for recurring themes

The diagram illustrates the use of multiple sources of information in assessing a child's learning difficulties. From these varied forms of information a clinician can discover the recurring themes that point to a student's strengths and weaknesses.

- Characterization of current academic skills and productivity
- Identification of weak skills and/or areas of reduced productivity
- Determination of weak subskills or processes within area(s) of weak skill or reduced productivity
- Identification of neurodevelopmental dysfunction(s)
- Impeding acquisition of subskill(s) or productivity in school

Following are two examples of this approach:

Example A. A Reading Problem
- Evaluation reveals strengths in mathematics and writing, delay in reading.
- Analysis of reading subskills shows a deficiency in word decoding.
- Neurodevelopmental evaluation uncovers poor phonological awareness.

Example B. An Organizational Problem
- Evaluation reveals that student is highly disorganized.
- Further assessment shows student is especially weak at managing time.
- Neurodevelopmental evaluation shows dysfunction of temporal-sequential ordering.

specific ages or grade levels. How will we (as a school or clinic) detect third graders with attention deficits? Should we use questionnaires, classroom observations, direct assessment, or combinations of these methods? How will we assess spatial and temporal-sequential ordering in our sixth graders? How do we evaluate saliency determination and summarization skills in our sixteen year olds? Can we use questionnaires? Will certain subtests of existing standardized examinations be particularly revealing in these areas? What customized assessment approach will best answer our specific diagnostic questions? Planning of evaluation procedures in schools, clinics, physicians' offices, and private consultation settings should take into account these types of questions. Rather than starting with an instrument, the astute diagnostician should begin with developmentally relevant questions and then determine the most accurate and feasible methods for deriving answers.

Avoiding Labels

It should be clear by now that this book discourages the practice of labeling children. A major decision must be made as to whether a diagnostic label is to be a goal of assessment. The following are some arguments against such an approach:

- Labels such as *dyslexia, learning disability,* and *ADHD* are apt to oversimplify complex phenomena.

- Many labels have a pejorative connotation. Often it is difficult to distinguish between variation and deviation. Applying a label commits the evaluator to a deviant or pathological mode.

- Certain labels erode the self-image of children or their families. The evaluator needs to be concerned with the effects on a child of being labeled "emotionally disturbed" or "brain damaged." Some of these labels can become self-fulfilling prophesies and thus be more harmful than the conditions they describe.

- Labels connote to some professionals that children have only one difficulty. This promotes artificial concepts of mutual exclusivity. That is, an evaluator may come to believe that children who have behavior problems cannot also have learning difficulties. In reality, the two commonly coexist and may or may not be causally linked.

- Many labels are intrinsically pessimistic, creating an aura of permanence rather than potential recovery from a problem. Children who are implacably labeled as having a "conduct disorder" may continue to behave as labeled because of certain persistent mind-sets that condition them to continue in the labeled role.

- If a discrete label is the ultimate aim of an evaluation, evaluators may tend to be superficial in their assessments. For example, once they have established that a child is "severely emotionally disturbed," they may stop there and fail to look for the other relevant attributes that together form a functional profile of a child.

In some settings these antilabeling arguments may represent ideals that cannot be achieved. For instance, communities commonly state that children cannot receive services unless they have been labeled (e.g., "learning disabled" or "brain damaged"). Often this requirement has been put in place by legislators who fear overuse of special education services. Or a clinician may not received third-party reimbursement for services without a label. In such cases, although a label is required, the evaluation should still be broad and thorough. Additionally, evaluators should see to it that the label does not adhere too tightly, that teachers and parents perceive it as a formality rather than the outcome of an assessment.

It is important to avoid the temptation to dwell on imponderable issues such as which problem came first and which is more important when children have more than one manifestation or difficulty. For example, if a student does poorly in several subjects and also exhibits low motivation in those classes, the debate as to whether the student is doing poorly because of poor motivation or whether poor motivation stems from doing poorly can be endless. Similarly, if a child is acting out and failing academically, discussion of whether the learning problem results from the misbehavior or whether the misbehavior is a cover-up for not learning can be interminable. Analogous and equally fruitless are discussions of what the primary problem might be. Enormous energy can be wasted in attempting to decide whether children are "primarily emotionally disturbed" or "primarily neurologically impaired." It is more sensible, less time-consuming, and certainly most helpful to state, for example, that a child has trouble with behavior in the classroom and also trouble remembering instructions. The behavior and the difficulty with instructions both call for therapeutic attention. We need not determine how heavily to weight one or the other. It is unfortunate when children need to be assigned to a particular room that carries only a single label (such as a class for the "emotionally disturbed"). It is hoped that in the future such oversimplified programs will be modified to accommodate a broader, more generic view of childhood function and dysfunction.

Finally, it is vitally important to avoid pseudolabels when describing children. These terms really have no definition. The most blatant example is "immaturity," for which there are virtually no clinical criteria. Many behavior difficulties can be glibly characterized as "immaturity." That many normal two year olds have trouble sitting still and are often disruptive should in no way be interpreted to mean that a seven year old with the same pattern is "immature." Regrettably, the term "immaturity" has weighty therapeutic implications despite the absence of diagnostic standards. For example, children casually termed "immature" might be retained in their current grade and given little or no services because it is assumed that they will outgrow the condition. Since there are no tests for immaturity (except possibly an X ray of the wrist to determine bone age), use of the term masks important problems that could benefit from intervention. Other pseudolabels include "attitude problem," "effort problem," and the common overuse of the word *potential* (as in "not living up to one's potential").

Avoiding Diagnostic Biases

When children undergo evaluation, there is a real possibility that evaluator biases can contaminate results. Most of the time such distortions are unintentional and unrecognized. Probably the most common are disciplinary biases; professionals tend to diagnose conditions or characterize problems in a manner consistent with their training and current interests. A speech and language pathologist may have a strong bias toward language disability as an explanation for most learning problems. A neurologist may have a tendency to perceive more "brain damage" than would other professionals. An education specialist may be more likely to attribute certain learning problems to the nature of children's early education experiences. A psychodynamically oriented psychiatrist or clinical psychologist may stress family factors or affective disorders. A clinician devoted to psychopharmacology may tend to diagnose problems that can be treated with medication. A pediatrician may too often perceive normal variation. Such natural proclivities may distort or oversimplify complex disorders. The best prevention for this is a truly multidisciplinary assessment, one that includes individuals from several professional backgrounds. Although these people should work as a team, they should be more than willing to disagree with one another and to assemble findings in a way that makes it possible to discern and serve all the facets of children's needs.

Another bias is the conflict of interest introduced when confounding factors compromise objective assessment. A school team performing an evaluation when the special education budget is tight may avoid stressing learning problems that require costly services. In such cases, the community is evaluating its fiscal health at the same time that it is assessing the developmental status of particular students. This can certainly alter results of an evaluation. Other, more insidious threats exist. Evaluators may blame "a home situation" too readily when faced with a problem partly caused by a nonunderstanding or unsympathetic teacher or school. If a seventh grader has been struggling for several years, the evaluation team may be reluctant to diagnose a learning problem because the parents might then wonder why it was not detected earlier. There may also be a tendency to avoid disagreeing with certain key people on a diagnostic team. Members of a team may be hesitant about contradicting a classroom teacher who is convinced that a child has "emotional problems," perhaps not wanting to hurt the feelings or damage the morale of a respected colleague. Some diagnosticians on evaluation teams also report that they feel somewhat apprehensive about offending or antagonizing school administrators. Knowing that certain diagnoses and formulations of need are not what the school principal or director of special education has in mind can also taint an assessment.

The window of a large pharmacy one block from Harvard Medical School displayed for many years a large sign stating, "If we don't have it, you don't need it." This philosophy sometimes prevails when it comes to evaluating and serving children. Unavailability of particular services may diminish the possibility of diagnoses in those areas. For example, if a school has no speech and language therapist, an evaluation team may tend (perhaps unconsciously) not to diagnose language disabilities.

Another potential conflict of interest may compromise independent evaluations or assessments (often second opinions) that are performed outside of school. Evaluators who receive large numbers of referrals from a particular school and who depend for their livelihoods on a continuing tide of such referrals may be tempted to avoid making certain diagnoses requiring services that the school does not wish to provide. This, too, can distort the evaluation. Another form of this problem occurs when the person performing the independent evaluation would like to have the child and parents as clients for further services. Such a situation may occur when a clinician who sees a child has an opening for counseling or medication follow-up and is tempted to use the referral from the school to fill up a practice. While this can be acceptable and beneficial, the potential for conflict of interest exists, as evaluations for schools may be used to market therapeutic services. All of these considerations need to be borne in mind, but they are not intended to induce widespread mistrust or diagnostic paranoia. Most schools are highly conscientious and eager to help children overcome dysfunctions. Most independent evaluators are well trained and want to make the correct diagnoses. However, consumers of assessment services must be vigilant and critical to ensure the most objective and accurate portrayal of a disappointing child's problems and needs. Table 14-2 summarizes some questions that can be asked in assessing the quality of a child's assessment.

COMPONENTS OF ASSESSMENT

The content of an evaluation for learning problems is likely to vary from site to site. There is a growing commitment to multidisciplinary processes in schools, clinics, and other settings. The exact composition of an evaluation team may vary, depending on local resources, the availability of expertise, and the degree of interest of various professionals. Nevertheless, we can describe components appropriate for all such diagnostic efforts. History taking and direct observation are the two pillars of assessment. The following sections will consider the methods used for each of these.

History Taking

Traditionally, much of the "narrowing down" stage of medical diagnosis occurs as a result of careful, systematic history taking. A meticulous history and its analysis are at least as important as any set of test scores. Historical data should be sought from multiple perspectives, incorporating the views of parents, teachers, consultants (when relevant), individuals providing special services and, of course, the child. Consistent themes should be pursued, although even contradictory data

Table 14-2.   Evaluating an assessment

The following questions should be considered in evaluating the quality and utility of a general assessment of a child with learning problems:

1. Is the evaluation sufficiently multidisciplinary, reflecting the contributions of individuals from varied relevant professional backgrounds either directly or indirectly (through previous reports)?

2. Does the assessment include evaluation of a broad range of neurodevelopmental functions or is it too narrowly focused?

3. Does the assessment reflect any possible professional disciplinary, political, or economic biases or conflicts of interest?

4. Does the assessment lead to practical suggestions for management at home and in school?

5. Does the assessment provide satisfactory answers to specific questions raised by teachers and parents?

6. Does the assessment consider the child's strengths and affinities as well as specific weaknesses?

7. Does the assessment provide rich descriptions of the child's behavior and approach to tasks rather than simply listing test scores and age levels?

8. Are the diagnostic conclusions based on well-substantiated evidence?

9. Does the formulation of a child's difficulties go beyond the mere spawning of diagnostic labels?

10. Does the assessment take into consideration possible emotional, temperamental, cultural, and environmental factors that may complicate or predispose the child to learning problems?

11. Does the assessment deal effectively with the impacts of the learning problem on the child and the family?

12. Is the assessment process itself therapeutic, fostering optimism and positive feelings on the part of the child, the family, and the teachers?

13. Do the recommendations include provisions for follow-up and long-term monitoring of the child's difficulties?

Some of these questions may not pertain to a highly specialized evaluation performed by a consultant in a particular specialty.

---

have implications for reconciliation through counseling and education. As part of the analyses of historical data, clinicians and educators need to extract those factors most significant and relevant to the child's current underachievement. Ultimately, they should refine the history to a succinct summarization of its key components. This can be part of an overall narrative description. The history taking can be divided into five components:

The basic problem. Make an attempt to state succinctly what in medicine is commonly called "the chief complaint." This statement should characterize in one or two sentences a consensus regarding the child's principal problem(s).

The basic questions. Delineate the major questions (explicit or implicit) that are being asked. Include a direct response to these questions. They may come from parents, teachers, the child's physician, and other professionals. Examples of such questions include: What is the best way to teach reading to this child? How can we control the overactivity in the classroom? Why does this child keep fighting with his or her brothers and sisters? Could she or he be depressed at this time? Why does this adolescent, who seems so smart, have so much trouble completing assignments?

Current academic performance. Document the child's skill levels and the status of relevant subskills and other processes in all grade-relevant areas. In addition, include in the historical compilation information about day-to-day performance in various school settings. Mention any observable phenomena (such as an awkward pencil grip or apparent word retrieval difficulties) that teachers or parents have noted.

Associated traits. Describe various symptoms and attributes that cluster around the child's basic problems. These traits need not be negative. Cite areas of strength as well as weaknesses. Include social behaviors with peers and with adults; somatic complaints such as headaches, abdominal pains, or bed-wetting; affective observations such as mood swings, sadness, or irritability; unusually aggressive behaviors; coping abilities such as responses to stress and the ability to recover after frustration or disappointments; and the use of social and academic strategies.

Background conditions. Examine three aspects of the child's environment: educational setting, the home, and the community. In examining conditions at school, evaluate the classroom, including its size, structure, and organization, the curriculum, the overall level of proficiency of students in that class, and the availability of individualized help. Account for any special services the child is receiving as well as others that are available in the school. Evaluate home environmental conditions, including the present family constellation, current household members, and space allocation, as well as any prominent stresses, signs of turmoil, or notable strengths within the family. Finally, a number of demographic variables are relevant, including the family's socioeconomic status and how it compares to the rest of the community, various cultural factors in and around the family, and the quality of the neighborhood (its intimacy, safety, and supportiveness).

Family History. A carefully elicited history of any problems in the family is increasingly recognized as an essential part of any evaluation. Since genetic and familial tendencies toward dysfunction are common, careful documentation can provide some valuable clues about the nature of a child's learning difficulties. Many parents will describe attention difficulties or other information-processing or production weaknesses in themselves, their parents, their brothers, their sisters, or the siblings of the child in question.

Certain clinical conditions may be characterized by a strong family history. For example, a child with attention problems who has a number of mentally retarded relatives should be evaluated for a possible chromosomal disorder such as Fragile X syndrome. It is now recognized that many children with Tourette syndrome have a family history of the condition. There are families in which one or more individuals suffers from depression or some other type of affective disorder. A child with attention difficulties in such a family may actually be manifesting emergent initial symptoms of depression or bipolar illness.

In addition to these direct etiological clues derived from a complete family history, a range of therapeutically helpful perspectives can emerge. If a parent has had particular difficulties learning to read, he or she may be exquisitely sensitive to the struggles of a child who is enduring the same frustrations. In some instances, a parent who experienced a learning disorder during childhood is now performing well in life. That parent may assume that the child will also "grow out of it." It may be, however, that the affected child has a problem that is more severe or complicated than the one suffered by the parent. The tendency to assume spontaneous resiliency on the part of the child may not be appropriate. This can emerge as an issue for counseling and further discussion. By contrast, a parent may overreact to a child's learning difficulty because that parent or a relative suffered a dire consequence of a similar problem. Again, counseling and discussion can promote a balance between complacency and overreaction in those cases in which the family history is compelling. For these reasons, it is essential to document the existence of learning problems, behavior difficulties, mental retardation, mental illness, alcoholism, substance abuse, delinquency, and other negative outcomes in the families of children with learning disorders.

Antecedents. The child's past history also contributes to diagnosis. The health history should include a careful survey, beginning with the mother's pregnancy. It should include the birth history, any relevant early medical events, and current health status. It is important, in particular, to document stressors such as perinatal complications, central nervous system infections, recurrent otitis media, seizures, and sensory deficits. Health problems such as chronic illness, allergy, anemia, or hospitalization should also be documented.

The child's temperamental history can be highly revealing (see pp. 494–95). A retrospective account of behavioral style in infancy, in the toddler years, and on school entry is useful. Early behavioral patterns can aid in understanding current ways the child deals with transitions, challenges, and stresses.

The developmental history is another component of history taking. Early-life developmental milestones should always be surveyed. Accounts of motor development, language acquisition, and the attainment of various self-help skills, such as tying shoelaces and dressing, are important. However, most children with developmental dysfunctions during school years have normal early-life developmental histories. Thus, a child who is having significant language disabilities in fifth grade may well have, according to his parents, a history of normal language acquisition during preschool.

A direct extension of the developmental history is an account of any experiences in early education. If a preschooler attended day care or a nursery school, it is helpful to obtain a description of both developmental and behavioral function in that setting. Finally, it is essential to document previous evaluations as well as any interventions that have been provided.

History-Taking Methods. Depicting the complexities of the child's current predicament as well as its historical precursors can be exhausting and time-consuming. To facilitate history taking, I use questionnaires that systematically probe relevant issues. These questionnaires have been published and are known collectively as *The ANSER System* (Levine 1996). Separate versions are available for three different age groups: three to five year olds, six to eleven year olds, and adolescents. Each of these chronological levels has a parent and a school questionnaire. In addition, children nine years old and above are given a Self-Administered Student Profile (Form 4 of *The ANSER System*) to complete (Levine, Clarke, and Ferb 1981). The profile consists of statements made by children who have had learning problems. Students are asked to indicate which of these statements might also pertain to them. The quotations are grouped to correspond primarily to specific areas of development (such as attention, language, memory, and motor function). In addition to this inventory of quotations, the Self-Administered Student Profile asks for personal accounts of skills, interests, and ambitions; probes feelings of effectiveness, social interactions, and overall outlook for the future; and includes an open-ended section for general comments. The Parent Questionnaires include systematic inventories that help describe the perinatal period and any stresses occurring therein, the child's early life and current health, developmental milestones, temperament during infancy and the preschool years, family history, current skills and interests, patterns of activity and attention, other aspects of behavior, and perceived strengths. The School Questionnaire for each level includes descriptions of services and curriculum, previous test scores, current levels of educational skill and subskill, specific observations of particular areas of development (such as language, memory, and visual processing), patterns of attention and activity, and a detailed behavior inventory similar to the one completed by parents. A sample portion of *The ANSER System* questionnaires is illustrated in figure 14-2.

The ANSER System provides a standardized, systematic approach to history taking from multiple sources. It offers a rich database that can aid in assessment as well as follow-up. The questionnaires are not psychometric instruments; they are not meant to be scored. They are intended for use with other tools in the search for recurring themes.

Many school systems and clinics have developed their own questionnaires designed for their formats and approaches; such instruments are valuable probes. Of course, questionnaires have both advantages and disadvantages. On the positive side, they facilitate history taking. An enormous amount of information can be collected very economically. A clinician can scan a well-organized questionnaire and tease out critical elements for further elaboration during an interview. The act of completing a detailed questionnaire can help a teacher or a parent, for the activity itself can be revealing and even therapeutic. Some parents have

	EARLY LIFE PROBLEMS	Never	0–3 months	4–6 months	7–12 months	13–18 months	19–24 months	2–3 years	3–4 years	4–5 years	5–7 years	Since 7 years
EL01	Shyness with strangers											
EL02	Bashfulness with other children											
EL03	Refusal to go to school/daycare											
EL04	Difficulty in keeping to a schedule											
EL05	Problems going along with change in daily routine											
EL06	Extreme restlessness											
EL07	Tendency to become overexcited											
EL08	Trouble getting satisfied											
EL09	Desire to be held too often											
EL10	Difficulty getting consoled											
EL11	Over-reaction to sights or noises											
EL12	Extreme reaction to tastes or touching											
EL13	Temper tantrums											
EL14	Irritability											
EL15	Cried often and easily											
EL16	Yelled a lot											
EL17	Was too sad or too happy											
EL18	Head banging											
EL19	Rocking in bed											
EL20	Self-destructive behavior											
EL21	Trouble making eye contact											
EL22	Failure to be affectionate											
EL23	Making of odd sounds, grunts or noises											
EL24	Jerking arms or head often											
EL25	Feeding difficulty											
EL26	Extremes of hunger											
EL27	Eating non-foods											
EL28	Poor appetite											
EL29	Colic											
EL30	Constipation											
EL31	Stomach aches											
EL32	Trouble falling asleep											
EL33	Trouble staying asleep											
EL34	Very heavy sleep											
EL35	Noisy breathing/snoring in sleep											
EL36	Frequent naps during day											
EL37	Unpredictable length of sleep											
EL38	Stiffness or rigidity											
EL39	Looseness or floppiness											

EL40   Was child breast-fed?   ❑ Yes (until age _____ months)   ❑ No

Figure 14-2. A sample from *The ANSER System* parent questionnaire

commented after completing *The ANSER System* questionnaire that it is the longest time they have ever spent discussing their child and that they grew to understand him or her better simply by responding to the questions on the form.

Among the drawbacks of questionnaires are the limitations of some individuals asked to complete them. Poorly educated families and those with language barriers may have trouble interpreting some of the questions. They may need help to complete the forms. Even in the most educated families, a questionnaire can exhaust long-term memory. Parents may not precisely recall developmental milestones or infant temperament patterns, especially for an older child or adolescent. Moreover, when there are three or more children in a family, it may be understandably hard to recall one child's toddler milestones. There is even some evidence that the more troubles a family has had, the less they are likely to remember key events form early years. Moreover, some parents may not feel comfortable reporting critical issues about which they are very sensitive. They may be reluctant to document a drinking problem, marital infidelity, or child abuse. Therefore, it is essential to recognize that not all information can or should be sought on a questionnaire.

In lieu of questionnaires, an evaluator may want to use an in-depth interview. This approach can be time-consuming and therefore expensive, but it can elicit more private information. Since an interview can never provide access to as much data as can be revealed on a questionnaire, the most satisfactory approach is a combination of questionnaire and interview. The following sequence is commonly followed. First, parents (sometimes with help) and teachers fill out questionnaires. The clinician then uses the forms to provide historical background and also to guide an interview that might last an hour. During this session with parents, the clinician can elucidate further items indicated as problems or important issues on the questionnaire, and explore matters not covered on the form.

The Self-Administered Student Profile can be especially useful in guiding an interview. Often school-age children are conspicuously taciturn during a formal interview with a professional. They may over indulge in monosyllabic responses and show little interest. Open-ended questions yield notoriously meager replies. The questionnaire can be used as a basis for discussion. The clinician can say, "I noticed you checked off that when you write, your memory gets bad. A lot of kids check that one off. I was wondering what you meant by that." This level of specificity often helps break the ice and stimulates the student to communicate. Therefore, the combined use of the questionnaire and separate interviews with the parents and the child is likely to yield the richest database.

Direct Observation and Assessments

Recurrent themes in a child's current life struggles emerge from the kind of historical compilation described in the previous section. Further evidence accrues from direct testing. This section describes seven common approaches to the examination of children: educational evaluation, aptitude and admission tests, intelligence testing, neurodevelopmental or neuropsychological assessment, health examination, personality testing, and specialized consultation. The choice of specific assessment techniques depends on the differential diagnoses under consideration. Direct assessments are used to confirm or eliminate specific developmental and personal factors constraining or facilitating current performance. The identification of these elements should have major implications for remediation.

Evaluation of Educational Skill. The assessment of specific educational skills has a long tradition in schools, clinics, and private consultants' offices. Group achievement tests are administered routinely at regular intervals in many public and private schools. Although such machine-scored examinations do not often permit fine-grained analyses of error patterns and methods of approaching tasks, they provide a fair approximation of skill levels. Results are usually expressed in terms of grade equivalents and/or percentile scores. The latter may be broken down into local, national, and (when relevant) independent school norms. The frequent discrepancy in these three separate standards dramatizes demographic variations in performance. These differences are apt to stem from socioeconomic and cultural factors as well as regional influences.

The appendix contains a list of some of the commonly used achievement tests. Instruments such as these are widely used and have an enormous impact on educational planning. In certain communities, a particular score on a group achievement test may help quality or disqualify a child from special services. It has been common to define a "learning disability" by comparing achievement test results to intelligence quotients, using such a process to differentiate true underachievement from general slowness or broadly defined innate inability. Such rigid eligibility criteria are misleading and harmful. Many students with developmental dysfunctions who would benefit from special education help would fail to meet such eligibility criteria.

Although group achievement testing can be a good method of screening for delays and of general assessment of a school's educational program, its limitations must be borne in mind to avoid potential misunderstandings:

- Children differ in their ability to take tests in a group. Some, especially those with attention deficits, may be unduly distracted by their peers and may not exhibit their true abilities.

- Of necessity, group achievement tests fail to replicate the situation in a classroom and do not authentically measure the full scope of academic demands. Such important abilities as organization, writing, summarizing, following verbal instructions, easily mastering new skills, and employing good study habits are among the many facets of educational experience that elude measurement on group tests. Thus, for example, many youngsters with developmental output failure, particularly those who have real trouble getting ideas down on paper, may appear educationally competent on a group achievement test.

- A multiple-choice format may favor some students and discriminate against others. Some children appear to be particularly comfortable with multiple-choice questions, while others find them difficult to interpret and fare much better on essay tests or short-answer questions. Certain test takers may not particularly like any of five possible titles for a paragraph, but would do very well creating one of their own. Some highly creative and adept readers will not exhibit their true merit on this kind of test. Conversely, some who are superb at taking multiple-choice tests have much more difficulty on a day-to-day basis. As noted in chapter 9, students may have no trouble selecting the best answer for a reading comprehension test question but have a great deal of difficulty extracting what is most salient from a paragraph, recalling all the supporting details, and summarizing in class or in a book report. They may perform well on achievement tests but have trouble succeeding in English class.

- Most group achievement tests are timed. Some students who are relatively effective readers and mathematicians have trouble working at a rapid rate.

- Students are apt to vary considerably in their levels of motivation and degrees of anxiety during group testing. These extraneous variables can certainly have an impact on test performance.

- Although a test publisher or author takes a great deal of care in establishing norms, such norms may not be entirely appropriate in a given school at a particular time. Adhering too closely to a set of performance standards may be misleading. Any school employing such tests should have thorough familiarity with the antecedent field testing. Local norms, even norms limited to a particular school or neighborhood in a community, should continue to be established.

- Some group achievement tests have cultural biases in spite of efforts to eliminate them. Those administering these examinations should review the content and identify elements that may discriminate against particular groups of children.

Despite these limitations, group achievement tests can play a significant screening role. However, they should never be the sole criterion for identifying children with problems. Instead, group tests should take their place with several other sources of data in contributing to a holistic view of the student.

Aptitude and Admissions Tests. Closely related to group achievement tests are the various instruments used to measure scholastic aptitude and, frequently, eligibility for admission to a particular educational program (such as a university or independent school). Typically, such tests assess an amalgam of acquired educational skills and innate abilities. In addition to measuring acquisition of specific skills, these instruments commonly tap such areas as vocabulary, quantitative reasoning, and general language abilities. The aptitudes measured, however, can never be cleanly separated from academic accomplishments.

These tests often cause enormous anxiety since students perceive them as critical hurdles to success in life. Unfortunately, such examinations are susceptible to the same limitations described in the previous sections. Some students perform admirably on multiple-choice aptitude tests, but subsequently perform abysmally in secondary school or college. Some, especially those with organizational problems and output limitations, have no difficulty with the format of such tests, since the tests organize materials for the test taker. Others, whose performance on multiple-choice standardized tests is consistently disappointing, may function competently on a day-to-day basis and, in fact, appear to overachieve. Their unique cognitive styles are not suited to the format of an aptitude test. We must hope that admissions committees are able to identify such students and place less emphasis on their scores.

Individual educational testing. Individual educational testing is important when students, on the basis of daily performance as well as group achievement tests, are determined to have significant learning problems. Judiciously selected and administered individual assessments can overcome most, if not all, weaknesses inherent in group testing. During individual evaluation, children can be monitored closely as they apply academic skills. The examiner can observe them reading, writing, computing, and spelling. This allows for multidimensional assessments. An astute evaluator will address the following kinds of questions:

- What is the status of the child's academic skills and subskills? What kinds of errors or error patterns does the student commonly display? In reading, for example, is there a problem with sight vocabulary, word analysis skills, comprehension, oral reading, retention, keeping place, rate, or using appropriate inflection and sustaining fluency? Is the child have particular difficulties with certain kinds of word or letter combinations (such as digraphs or consonant blends)? Such observations can be the basis for targeted intervention. Similar error analyses can localize precise educational difficulties in spelling, mathematics, and writing.

- What patterns of attention, planning, and self-monitoring does the student display as he undertakes specific tasks?

- Does the child or adolescent employ effective problem-solving strategies? Is she reasonably flexible in shifting from one technique to another when necessary?

- Does the student work efficiently and at an appropriate rate? Are previously acquired skills sufficiently automatized?

- How does the child or adolescent respond affectively during particular kinds of educational efforts? Do certain areas of skill incite anxiety?

- How does the student deal with criticism or correction?

- How easy is it to teach him or her a new skill or strategy?

- Is it difficult or easy to form an alliance with the student? Is the child slow to warm up, unduly passive, defiant, hostile, resistant, or easy to interact with?

These kinds of observations are consistent with an approach that is sometimes referred to as *dynamic assessment.* This is an approach that advocates very flexible use of tests. For example, a diagnostician may actually change a task that a child has missed to find out a way for the child to succeed. Also, the clinician can actually stop and ask the student why she had problem with an item or, alternatively, what technique she used to be so successful on that item. Applying dynamic assessment, the diagnostician may take significant liberties with the test manual but learn an enormous amount about a child's ways of learning.

These multidimensional observations can have a major impact on educational planning. In addition to establishing levels of attainment in various skills, such evaluations by a skilled psychoeducational specialist (sometimes referred to as an educational diagnostician) can have major prescriptive value.

The appendix describes tests that are commonly used for individual educational assessments. In this form of testing, the choice of instruments is not nearly as significant as the astuteness and clinical perspective of the clinician-interpreter. Direct assessments vary considerably in the areas they measure; a thorough assessment will include the following (depending in part on the age of the child):

- Word recognition
- Word analysis of new and/or multisyllabic words
- Oral reading fluency
- Reading rate
- Reading comprehension and memory (assessed by structured questions as well as the child's own retelling or summarization) from silent reading of text
- Spelling individual dictated words
- Spelling in context from dictation
- Mathematics facts
- Mathematics computational ability (algorithms)
- Solving mathematical word problems
- Copying written material
- Writing from dictation
- Writing from memory
- Expressive writing on a specific topic
- Organizational and study skills (e.g., outlining, summarizing, note taking)

In addition, other areas relevant to specific grades and ages can be assessed.

Classroom work. Whenever possible, the results of group and individual testing should be compared to samples of daily work in class in order to estimate the reliability of the testing. For independent assessments outside of school, parents can provide typical samples of the child's writing, mathematics calculations, notebooks, and other schoolwork. For evaluations done within a school, it is helpful to have a diagnostician spend time observing the child in the classroom. A systematic inventory or informal observation can document, for example,

Memory

ELEMENTS	INDICATION(S) OF DYSFUNCTION	-	Adeq	+	INDICATION(S) OF STRENGTH
Registration in Memory	Requires repetition, misses key inputs				Seems to remember things right after hearing/seeing them
Strategy Use in Memory	Does not use techniques such as subvocalization, self-testing				Uses memorization techniques, such as subvocalization, self-testing
Active Working Memory	Loses key parts of tasks while working on them				Seems able to retain task components while working or writing during classroom activities
Rapid Recall	Is slow to recall known facts				Is quick to recall facts from long-term memory during a test or class discussion
Simultaneous Recall	Has trouble recalling multiple things at once that are known individually				Is able to recall skills and facts simultaneously with ease and efficiency (as in writing)
Activation of Prior Knowledge	Seems slow or poor at activating prior knowledge				Is quick to associate new information with prior knowledge
Automatization of Basic Skills	Shows slow/laborious recall of basic skills				Can recall basic skills effortlessly

Attention

ELEMENTS	INDICATION(S) OF DYSFUNCTION	-	Adeq	+	INDICATION(S) OF STRENGTH
Selectivity	Stares into space, tunes out, doesn't take in important stimuli; easily distracted				Seldom misses important information conveyed in class; is not distractible
Mental Effort	Yawns, stretches, generally appears tired; burns out quickly				Never appears fatigued; looks alert; can focus on detail effectively
Planning and Tempo Control	Rushes through work quickly; doesn't stop to plan before or while working				Appears to plan and organize before and while working; paces himself/herself effectively
Self-Monitoring	Seldom or never checks over work				Can be seen checking over work
Consistency	Is extremely variable, unpredictable with work				Performs at a steady level; quality of work is predictable from day to day
Activity Level	Is fidgety, has trouble sitting still in seat				Is able to sit still and listen without excessive or unusual movement of feet, hands, or whole body

Figure 14-3. A portion of The Teacher's View, showing observations of memory and attention that can be made within the classroom

patterns of attention and activity, organizational abilities, interactions with peers, mood swings, and use of time.

Teachers can be educated to become astute observes of the neurodevelopmental constructs in action. In the SCHOOLS ATTUNED program (see p. 602), teachers are taught to systematically observe students, making use of The Teacher's View (fig. 14-3). They can then integrate their observations with analyses of work samples, a knowledge of the child's history, and the results of testing. In consultation with a school psychologist or special educator, these observations can contribute to the formulation of an effective management plan for a student.

Student interviews. A direct interview with a student who has learning problems can be most revealing. One of the authors (MDL) has participated in the recent development of a standardized neurodevelopmental interview for adolescents. The *STRANDS (Survey of Teenage Readiness and Neurodevelopmental Status)* takes about forty-five minutes to administer and consists of open- and close-ended questions about key neurodevelopmental functions. Students are asked to reflect and rate whether or not they have difficulty with the specific functions. A sample page is shown in figure 7-1.

More specialized interview formats can be used to assess reading, writing, and mathematical proficiency. It is best to administer such interviews immediately after the student works on a mathematics or writing assignment, so that any impediments are fresh in her mind. Examples of these specialized academic interviews have been published in Levine (1994).

Intelligence Testing. The concept of intelligence is both fascinating and controversial. Measures of intelligence have been said to reflect current ability, potential for future learning accomplishment, speed of development (with respect to current age), and capacity to profit from experience. In general, definers of intelligence grapple with notions of innate cognitive ability (Sattler 1974). Some have simply defined intelligence operationally, as what intelligence tests measure. Over the years, a variety of conceptual models of intelligence have been advanced (Pyle 1979). These have attempted to portray the basic elements that comprise intelligence as well as a fundamental trait, or "g factor," that defines such cognitive competency. Intelligence tests are commonly administered in schools, clinics, and professional offices. Through such assessments, IQ scores are derived; these intelligence quotients represent ratios of mental age and chronological age. The *Stanford Binet*, the *Wechsler Intelligence Scale for Children* (*WISC-III*), and the *Kaufman Assessment Battery for Children* have been widely used to estimate intelligence in children. Each has a series of subtests, which, in the opinion of its advocates, comprise a valid representation of general intelligence. IQ scores are likely to be particularly helpful at the extremes—at low levels of demonstrated mental ability and at the peaks (in the gifted range). In the midrange, however, global scores for children with learning problems (as in other testing procedures) are less valuable than are the profiles of performance subtests.

As with other diagnostic processes, therefore, it is essential to understand the limitation of IQ tests. They may be summarized as follows:

- Intelligence test scores do not represent absolute measurements with a zero point. A score merely states a child's status compared with the status of other children who have taken the test. The underlying assumption in the bell-shaped curve along which intelligence is normally distributed has been criticized.

- Test items are generally selected not to reflect how children learn and develop but to show differences between age groups and correlations with school performance.

- Intelligence tests may be susceptible to significant cultural biases.

- The subtests of an intelligence test require careful task analysis. There may be a number of reasons why a child does poorly (or well) on a particular component of an intelligence test.

- Intelligence tests were not designed to diagnose a broad range of developmental dysfunctions. Using them for this purpose creates the potential for misdiagnosis (Galvin 1981). For example, if the verbal subtests of the *WISC-III* are employed to assess language ability, some important capacities and potential dysfunctions may be overlooked. In fact, the verbal subtests do *not* comprise a form of language evaluation. The capacity to understand and formulate complex sentences is a critical element of language ability, likely to be a major hallmark of language ability in elementary school. The verbal subtests of the *WISC-III* fail to tap sentence production. Language pragmatics, phonological awareness, metalinguistics, the rate of language processing, and the appreciation of morphology represent additional linguistic dimensions that elude the subtests of the *WISC-III*. A child with significant language gaps may not be identified by the IQ test.

- The notion that one can have a significant learning problem only if there is a measurable discrepancy between sections or subtests of an intelligence test is wrong. Children can have perfectly consistent results across subtests and still have endogenous problems with learning. These difficulties may be in areas not measured by the test, or dysfunctions may result in a generalized depression of scores.

- Intelligence tests may not be reliable for certain children. Those who are very anxious in test-taking situations may have artificially low scores. Children with attention deficits are likely to display poor test-retest reliability because their inconsistent performance contaminates testing. Diagnostic referral centers commonly encounter students with attention deficits who have had intelligence testing performed on several occasions. Their overall scores as well as subtest patterns vary widely from test to test, reflecting their erratic patterns of mental energy control (see chapter 2).

- Intelligence tests may not tap some important facilitators or strengths. Creativity, good use of strategies, organizational skill, interest and motivation, and strong attention may be critical ingredients of ability that an IQ score cannot always capture.

- Certain arbitrary components of an IQ test may not be entirely relevant to significant challenges of childhood. For example, a number of *WISC-III* performance (visual and motor-oriented) subtests are timed. It may be that the rate of processing or producing *verbal information* is much more related to accomplishment in our society than is the speed of assembling the parts of a puzzle.

- Intelligence tests may correlate well with school performance when the entire range of scores is considered. However, in the midrange (90–110), the correlations weaken significantly.

- Intelligence tests may be based on the assumption that there is only one kind of intelligence. As we have noted, scholars (Sternberg and Downing 1982, Gardner 1983) have taken the position that there are multiple intelligences, not merely the one variety assessed by IQ testing. The study of individual differences or cognitive preferences among children has further motivated clinicians and educators to examine individual areas of relevant function rather than global IQ scores (Jonassen and Grabowski 1993).

• As with achievement and aptitude testing, students are likely to vary in their intelligence-test-taking ability. Some may rise to the occasion, while others are indifferent or unable to adapt to this particular kind of challenge. Consequently, an intelligence test may not elicit their true abilities (and talents).

• Intelligence tests are subject to considerable overinterpretation and misuse (as are all tests). Rigid adherence to certain cutoff criteria can lead to unfortunate labeling. Some children may be called "dull-normal" when, in reality, they have more ability than is apparent on the test, as the IQ score was depressed because of developmental dysfunctions in discrete areas. Some students may have above average scores on the Similarities subtest of the *WISC-III* but be relatively low in other areas. A high score on the Similarities subtest suggests strong verbal reasoning abilities. However, because other scores are depressed, a highly verbal student may be considered "dull-normal." We can ask whether any individual can pass through school in a dignified manner when viewed by the adult world as "dull-normal."

Intelligence tests are not particularly helpful in creating what Cruickshank (1975) once called "the psychoeducational match," the process by which children's psychological characteristics can influence the ways they are taught. In commenting on the limitations of intelligence testing, Cruickshank states, "This is not to say that the concepts of the intelligence quotient and of mental age are unimportant. They are, however, much less important in the day-to-day educational planning by a teacher for a child than has been generally assumed in the past. Quantitative data generally does not provide the basis for a full realistic educational framework for a child. Another approach appears to be required in order to accomplish that which educators have stated for years to be their obligation; mainly, 'to meet the needs of a child' " (p. 72).

Despite the potential for abuse and the clear limitations of IQ tests, they deserve a place in the assessment of some children with learning difficulties. However, like other components of evaluation, they need to be viewed in a broader context, one that includes observations of day-to-day performance, educational testing, and other forms of assessment. The specific subtests of an intelligence test can contribute to the formulation of a child's profile of strengths and weaknesses. This is likely to be more valuable and less harmful than the overall IQ score.

More detailed discussion of such assessments can be found in several works (Pyle 1979, Sattler 1974). Once again, the choice of an instrument is not nearly as important as its interpretation by the examiner. As with other forms of tests, an intelligence assessment affords an excellent opportunity to make process-oriented observations—informal evaluations of attention, affect, use of strategies, and organizational skills.

Tests of Neurodevelopmental Function. One of the goals of evaluation is the generation of a functional profile, a balance sheet of neurodevelopmental strengths and weakness that can contribute to both diagnosis and treatment. Children's areas of strength can be used effectively in selecting a particular kind of curriculum, in remediating discrete weaknesses, and in providing successful experiences when they are otherwise deprived of mastery. Parent and school questionnaires, intelligence testing, and assessments of educational skill can all furnish presumptive evidence about strengths and weaknesses in the developmental areas covered in chapters 2 through 8. However, direct testing of specific functions can help facilitate and refine diagnostic formulations.

The interpretation of specific findings on tests of neurodevelopmental function can be somewhat hazardous. In particular, the clinician is faced with the perpetual problem of establishing causality. The fact that a child has some difficulties with visual perception and is delayed in reading does not necessarily mean that the child is delayed in reading because of the visual perceptual problems. In fact, some children may acquire a developmental dysfunction as a direct consequence of not having acquired particular academic subskills and skills. Stanovich (1986) describes "reciprocal relationships" (so-called Matthew effects), or instances in which certain cognitive processes may be adversely affected by a lack of reading ability. Illustrating this concept, we might evaluate a fourteen-year-old student with severe reading comprehension problems and discover a delay in language function. It might be tempting to conclude that the reading problem is a direct result of the language problem. On the other hand, because of reciprocal relationships between skills and neurodevelopmental functions, it is possible that the child's language skills have stagnated because of a lack of experience in reading. The well-functioning peers of that student may have acquired vocabulary as well as a growing appreciation of syntax and verbal discourse by having read a great deal. As children grow older, such reciprocal relationships between subskill attainment and neurodevelopmental functions need to be considered in the evaluation process.

In many cases, it is likely that bidirectional phenomena operate; that is, a pre-existing neurodevelopmental dysfunction creates an academic lag, which in turn slows the development of that function. In a descriptive evaluation, however, we need not overemphasize causality as an issue. In the example just cited, the fourteen year old needs help with both language and reading, and to facilitate such service, the evaluator needs to acquire a good understanding of the precise nature of that youngster's language deficits in reading skills.

Tests of various underlying neurodevelopmental strengths and weaknesses exist in a variety of formats. Since it is not possible to describe all of them, a few examples should suffice. The *Wide Range Assessment of Memory and Learning (WRAML)* is an assessment tool that focuses largely on memory functions, allowing a clinician to examine highly specific aspects of short- and long-term memory function. The *CELF (Clinical Evaluation of Language Function)* allows for in-depth assessment of critical parameters of language ability. These and other similar assessments place greater stress on individual test components than on an overall score for the total procedure. However, these evaluations can also yield more global ratings.

Neuropsychological test batteries are used, especially in large diagnostic centers. These are also designed to detect functional strengths and weaknesses. For example, the *Halstead Neuropsychological Test Battery for Children* is designed not only to uncover relative strengths and weaknesses, but to do so in such a way as to suggest specific areas of the brain that may be involved in a child's dysfunction. Such testing can be useful, although the assumptions made about brain localization are subject to the concerns elucidated in chapter 13.

Neurodevelopmental examinations represent a broad form of assessment oriented toward age-related development, rather than issues of brain localization. Over the years, neurodevelopmental examinations have been compiled and refined for different age groups (Blackman, Levine, and Markowitz 1986; Levine and Schneider 1982; Levine and Rappaport 1983; Levine 1985). These instruments include the *PEET,* the *PEER,* the *PEEX 2,* and the *PEERAMID 2* (each for a different age group). They tap such diverse components as the presence or absence of minor neurological indicators (pp. 552–55), gross motor function, fine motor output, visual processing, language, and memory. Unlike intelligence tests, neurodevelopmental examinations yield no overall score. In fact, they do not even generate subtest scores. Instead, normal ranges of performance exist for each task and each overall developmental construct at each age level, enabling the examiner to derive a profile of relative strengths and weaknesses. Each task on a neurodevelopmental examination is acknowledged to measure more than one function or ability (fig. 14-4). Thus, an examiner can make simultaneous observations of attention, strategy use, and memory function while a student performs a particular task. Findings from neurodevelopmental examinations are intended for incorporation into a narrative description, one that blends findings from the examination with other test scores, results of educational assessments, and questionnaire and interview data. Thus, the neurodevelopmental examinations are never used in isolation.

It is often helpful to administer neurodevelopmental examinations with the parents present as observers. Special Observer Guidelines exist for *PEEX 2* and *PEERAMID 2* (fig. 14-5). Parents are helped to understand the specific tasks, and are encouraged to make their own observations of the child's performance. In this way mothers and/or fathers become a part of the assessment team. They are apt to learn from the experience, while participating in the evaluation by commenting on the typicality of the observed performance. Their presence can also enrich the quality of feedback at the end of an evaluation since the examiner and the parents have witnessed the same performance.

In some clinics, practices, and schools, "customized" diagnostic packages are compiled by diagnosticians who use portions of various tests in the evaluation of children with learning problems. Provided that the subtests are appropriately standardized for age, this practice can be justified. However, subtests are standardized within the context of an entire examination, and their use in isolation or with subtests from other examinations may alter their standardization. When dynamic assessment is applied, and examinations are not given with rigidity, this should not be a problem.

A most important consideration is that the decision as to which test or subtest to use should be based on a prior determination of a differential diagnosis. Sometimes the testing should be fitted to the child's problems. For example, children with output problems may need quite a different set of assessments of ability from

MEMORY FUNCTIONS

Drawing from Memory   (7-second exposures)

Deduct 1 point for extraneous detail (maximum deduction 1 point per drawing).

Short-term memory		
Visual registration		
Attention		
Visual processing functions		
Chunk size		
Planning/Organization		

A. X and O present in proper positions	(0,1)	___
B. Number of symbols accurate	(0–3)	___
C. Horizontal and upper vertical line	(0,1)	___
Diagonal line	(0,1)	___
Both vertical lines	(0,1)	___
D. Four symbols	(0,1)	___
Number of symbols accurate	(0–4)	___
Sequence	(0,1)	___
E. Outer rectangle	(0,1)	___
3 sections	(0,1)	___
Left diagonal	(0,1)	___
Center blank	(0,1)	___
Horizontal line	(0,1)	___
Vertical line	(0,1)	___
Small diagonal	(0,1)	___
Total score	(0–20)	___ ___
Correct drawings	(0–5)	___
Strategy use (e.g., rehearsal, imaging, verbal mediation)	(0,1)	___ STRATS

Total Score	
I	II
15–18	17–19

Comments:

Figure 14-4.   A sample page from the Record Form of *PEERAMID 2*. The box in the upper right provides a task analysis, suggesting functions that might be deficient if a child has trouble drawing designs from memory.

those with pure reading problems or signs of poor attention. Schools, clinics, and private offices may use different diagnostic algorithms for different problems. Beginning with knowledge of the possible causes of the problem rather than just a series of tests for "learning disabilities" will likely lead to more accurate and sophisticated diagnoses.

Health Examinations.   Examination of a child's health is an important part of assessment. It is essential not to overlook medical factors that contribute to or aggravate a child's underlying dysfunction. Whenever possible, the examination of a school-age child should take place without the parents in the room so that the child can feel free to voice any potentially embarrassing somatic concerns.

General appearance. A child's appearance is often revealing. Pediatricians have traditionally considered the overall appearance of an acutely ill patient,

LANGUAGE

The language section of the *PEEX 2* measures many different aspects of verbal ability that are critical for success in school. The section begins by assessing ability with language sounds (phonology), then with words, sentences, and discourse (language that goes beyond the boundaries of sentences). Various tasks tap both receptive language (understanding) and expressive language (production of language).

PHONOLOGICAL AWARENESS
(Language Sounds—Receptive and Expressive)

These tasks are meant to detect difficulties with the processing of and/or memory for sounds in the English language. Such difficulties are commonly associated with problems acquiring reading and spelling skills. The rhyming task taps long-term memory for language sounds as well as the precision of a child's awareness of the "families" of sounds that are found in English. The phonemic segmentation task (dividing words into their individual sounds) tests a child's ability to discern the distinct language sounds within a word. Such tasks have been found to correlate highly with decoding skill in reading. The deletion and substitution task also relates to decoding skill. It elicits information about a child's ability to manipulate language sounds in active working memory—a skill essential for decoding multisyllabic words.

PICTURE NAMING
(Words—Expressive)

Ability to name objects rapidly is likely to be one predictor of a child's capacity to develop a good sight vocabulary—a store of words that can be instantly or automatically recognized during reading. This task involves rapid visual processing (quick visual recognition of the objects) and convergent retrieval memory (immediate association with highly specific words). As children proceed through school, they must develop such highly automatic memory in many skill areas such as mastering math facts and spelling and forming letters in writing. This task provides one indication of automaticity.

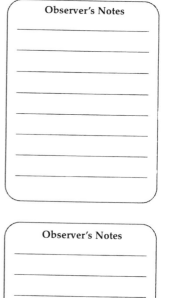

Figure 14-5. A sample page from the *PEEX 2* Observer's Guide. Each item is explained, and parents can record their own observations during the session.

whether a child "looks sick," in deciding on the need for any further tests or treatments. Assessing the general appearance of a child with learning problems, however, is not such a well-established procedure, yet it is likely that professionals react subjectively and unconsciously to a child's overall appearance. It is helpful, therefore, to be systematic. Several specific questions should be raised.

- Does the child project physical features, aspects of posture, dress, or mannerisms that may be inviting verbal abuse by peers? Is the child unusually obese, tall, small, or fragile? Are there any atypical physical features such as lop ears, a large nose, or a conspicuous birthmark? A clinician who notes these findings should consider offering the child an opportunity to discuss their significance and social impact. Confidentiality should be promised since many such intimate body image concerns are deeply sequestered secrets.

- Some research has suggested a relationship between certain developmental problems and the existence of minor physical anomalies (Quinn and Rapoport 1974). These include various mild defects such as a crooked finger, an extra eye fold, or a double whorl in the occipital region of the scalp. There are indications that these may represent genetic or prenatal effects that may also predispose a child to learning or behavior dysfunctions. A number of clinicians now include them as part of their diagnostic evaluation. Their ultimate significance and especially their therapeutic value remain questionable.

- How are the child's personal hygiene, general body care, and self-image related? Some children appear to be chronically unkempt and poorly nourished. Subjective observations of this sort need to be interpreted with some caution; isolated instances may occur by chance, but chronic extremes can be revealing. The immaculately groomed, obsessive-compulsive child may have a significant preoccupation with body image, while a malodorous child who enters the room with nose running, socks of two different colors, and a label prominently displayed on the front of an inside-out shirt may be demonstrating underlying behavioral disorganization, dyspraxia, absent self-monitoring, or chronic neglect. Any interpretation of these features must take into account the constantly evolving, faddish, stylistic variations of youth.

The standard physical examination. The physical assessment of a schoolchild with learning problems includes careful measurements of blood pressure as well as percentile documentation of height, weight, and head circumference. There should be an evaluation of overall physical maturity. For early and late adolescents, assessment of the development of secondary sexual characteristics (by using Tanner ratings which quantify maturity level) is vital. Adolescents with delayed maturation may be carrying an enormous psychological burden; reassuring counseling can be liberating. As noted in chapter 13, there are distinct relationships between the rate of sexual maturation and school performance. *Dentition* (tooth development) is another physical parameter that may be useful in assessing physical maturity. Significantly short stature often suggests the need for an X-ray study of the wrist for bone age. A child with short stature and learning problems may need further evaluation to rule out an endocrinopathy or a chromosomal abnormality (such as Turner or Klinefelter syndrome). Although associations between delayed bone age, dental immaturity, and neuromaturational lag have not yet been clarified, their clinical coincidence may suggest delay. Throughout the examination, the clinician needs to be vigilant for dysmorphic features or other signs that might suggest a genetic or chromosomal disorder.

Structures in and around the head should be carefully examined. Lesions in the hard or soft palate may have led to recurrent ear infections. Serous otitis media or chronic scarring of the tympanic membranes, especially in conjunction with a history of hearing loss, suggests the need for audiometry and/or tympanometry. Anatomical abnormalities of the buccal cavity or palate may be associated with difficulties in sound production and articulation that require further assessment by a speech and language pathologist. Skin lesions on the face (or on the trunk and limbs) may suggest a range of rarely occurring disorders called the phakomatoses (e.g., neurofibromatosis or Sturge-Weber syndrome). Signs of chronic conditions such as allergic rhinitis and sinusitis are more common phenomena that can drain attention, cause fatigue, and result in school absenteeism. Finally, a careful optic fundoscopic examination should be performed as well as an assessment of oculomotor function to rule out strabismus.

Examination of the neck should include palpation of thyroid tissue. Although previously undiagnosed congenital hypothyroidism is unlikely to occur as a subtle learning disorder in the schoolchild, acquired hypothyroidism secondary to subacute thyroid conditions (with high antithyroid antibody levels) may be an unsuspected cause of underachievement. Thyrotoxicosis can be associated with school problems and "hyperactivity," but this too is unusual.

Examination of the chest should include cardiac auscultation and pulmonary evaluation. In this age group, the yield of previously undetected cardiac findings will be very small. Wheezing or diminished respiratory exchange may indicate chronic pulmonary obstruction with resultant increased fatigability. Precocious, delayed, or asymmetric breast development in adolescent girls and gynecomastia in pubescent boys can be sources of anxiety. When these benign conditions are detected, reassurance is helpful.

The examination of the abdomen does not offer abundant educationally relevant data. However, the physician should be alert for evidence of retained feces. Stool retention and encopresis are frequent concomitants of learning disorders. Children with attention deficits appear to have a particular tendency toward bowel dysfunction.

The genitalia should be examined, particularly with regard to maturational status during early adolescence. The inspection of this private area may occasionally elicit concerns that have counseling implications. Older children should be asked directly whether they have any questions about sexual development or anatomic normality. Menarchal girls, for example, may have unsettling fantasies about this natural function. Some obese boys worry about their genitalia, believing they are too small, when actually they are merely embedded in a prepubic fat pad. The clinician should feel comfortable in promising confidentiality and taking the initiative in discussing potentially sensitive issues such as these. The child should always be reassured that confidentiality will be maintained and that other children have similar concerns. In boys it is helpful to screen for the enlarged testicles associated with Fragile X syndrome and gonadal dystrophy, as found in Klinefelter syndrome. Both of these conditions are associated with learning and attentional difficulties.

Examination of the extremities should include observation of any orthopedic deformities that may impair gross or fine motor function. Significant muscle asymmetries should be noted. In addition, any discrepancies or asymmetries of muscle tone merit careful assessment. Specific somatic complaints should be investigated carefully in a child with school problems. Recurrent abdominal pain may be related to severe constipation as well as to other causes (Levine and Rappaport 1984). Sometimes the link between a learning disorder and a medical complaint can be very important. For example, a child with learning problems and recurrent localized headaches may have an arteriovenous malformation, migraine, or tension headaches. Gascon (1984) discusses other significant possibilities.

During a physical examination, the clinician can inquire about additional health-related issues. The child may have questions about his overall physical development as well as other preoccupying somatic concerns. There can also be some discussion about nutritional habits and attitudes toward food intake. It is important to find out about any medications the child is taking since some drugs may alter certain neurodevelopmental functions. It is especially essential to uncover any propensity toward substance abuse, which can have a dramatic impact on both learning and behavior.

Laboratory studies. Parents and teachers sometimes voice considerable interest in having laboratory tests performed on children with learning disorders. Fortunately (or unfortunately), the yield of positive findings tends to be low. There is considerable consumer demand for metabolic causes of learning problems, but tests of blood sugar, calcium, zinc, and various enzymes usually fail to fulfill the hope for easy answers. Tests of nutrition are, of course, very hard to perform. Blood tests are unlikely to reveal subtle forms of poor nutrition. A nutritional history and physical examination are more apt to provide data in this area. Hypoglycemia is a rare cause of learning problems; therefore, there is seldom any need to perform a glucose tolerance test.

Electroencephalograms (EEGs), CT (computerized tomography) scans, skull X rays, and other forms of neuroimaging are sometimes included in a comprehensive developmental evaluation (Satterfield 1973). Again, relevant positive findings are uncommon. Some studies have suggested that there are characteristic EEG findings in children with learning disorders or attention difficulties. Millichap (1977) reported that 7 to 8 percent of these children had seizure discharges, 20 percent had moderate disturbances suggestive of seizures, and a large number had borderline abnormalities. Posterior slow waves have been reported most frequently, although studies in this area remain inconclusive. Very few of the reported positive tracings have direct therapeutic implications. In fact, such findings can be harmful if they create the stigma of "brain damage" in a child. When a seizure disorder is suspected because there are episodic lapses of attention, an EEG (with a sleep tracing and hyperventilation) is useful. Petit mal and temporal lobe epilepsy as well as more generalized seizure problems can be diagnosed in this way. Denckla, LeMay, and Chapman (1985) performed CT brain scans on thirty-two children attending a learning disability clinic. Of these, five showed mild abnormalities. The clinical relevance of such findings was questionable, and meaningful hemispheric asymmetries were not evident. Newer, more specialized studies with auditory or visually evoked potentials offer promise for the future. At this time they, too, have only minimal implications for therapy. At some point some of the new imaging techniques may become a routine part of the evaluation of children with learning difficulties. The BEAM (see pp. 517–18) is a technique that, in conjunction with others forms of assessment, may provide insight into the constitutional nature of a child's learning difficulties. At present, however, its therapeutic relevance is not clear. It remains largely a research tool.

In recent years, there has been a rapid growth in neuroimaging technology. PET (positron emission topography) scans can now be employed to measure cerebral blood flow. MRI (magnetic resonance imaging) provides images of the brain in action during specific tasks. Such views depict the actual functioning of a child's brain. Another technique, called magnetoencephalography (MEG) records magnetic signals during an electroencephalographic examination (George et al. 1995). These signals provide evidence for the site and duration of specific brain activities (such as reading a word). Neuroimaging techniques hold great promise for research on learning disorders. As Lyon and Rumsey (1996) note: "Much remains to be learned about how best to adapt tasks found in the behavioral literature to the neuroimaging situation and about how secondary variables affect patterns of activation demonstrated with functional imaging." At the time of this writing, neuroimaging technology shows great promise for helping elucidate specific forms of neurodevelopmental dysfunction and the brain localizations. However, these techniques are not yet practical and therapeutically relevant for the routine clinical and educational evaluation of students.

A complete blood count can be useful in youngsters who show signs of anemia, which can cause considerable fatigue and weaken attention. Some children may have difficulty concentrating or processing information because of iron deficiency. In these cases a serum ferritin, or iron level, may be useful. It should be stressed that not all children with low serum ferritin show signs of anemia.

In young children (especially those with attention problems), laboratory determinations of lead intoxication are important. When there is a past record of possible lead intoxication, X-ray films of bones (especially of the knees) may reveal lead lines. Assays of tooth lead levels (from deciduous teeth) have been used to demonstrate earlier ingestions possibly associated with attention problems (Needleman et al. 1979). Those with a history of pica must also be investigated.

Physical findings that occasionally suggest the possibility of a chromosomal abnormality (see pp. 473–76) point to the need for chromosomal analysis. This should be accompanied by a carefully elucidated family history. Among the possible chromosomal abnormalities sought are Turner syndrome, Klinefelter syndrome, various autosomal anomalies, and Fragile X syndrome or carrier state.

Children who have shown a recent distinct deterioration in school performance sometimes require special investigations. For example, Wilson's disease has been uncovered in certain patients whose school performance and personality changed for the worse during early adolescence (Adams and Lyon 1982). A number of them show characteristic involuntary movements associated with this condition. They may also have visible Kaiser-Fleischer Rings, typical findings detected on an ocular examination. Confirmatory laboratory studies include a blood copper and ceruloplasmin level.

Sensory assessments. Vision and hearing examinations should be included in the assessment of any child with learning disorders. The visual assessment is usually performed with Snellen Charts or similar materials. Visual defects alone rarely lead to learning problems, but myopia or astigmatism can contribute to visual inattention and weak visual discrimination in the classroom. A student may be unaware of difficulty focusing on the chalkboard or a written paragraph, making direct assessment especially important. In addition to screening for acuity, the clinician should look for evidence of oculomotor difficulty (such as strabismus). Assessment of color vision may be revealing; children with red-green color blindness (protanopia or deuteranopia) need to be made aware of their problems. Studies have not demonstrated a significant association between color blindness and learning disorders. Any child with suspected visual abnormalities should be referred to an ophthalmologist for further evaluation and management.

Audiological assessment is a bit more complex. Many primary care physicians are unable to conduct reliable screening tests using office audiometers. Such procedures tend to have a high rate of false positive and false negative results because of testing rooms that are not truly soundproof and instruments that are unreliably calibrated. If a child is thought to be at high risk for a hearing loss, referral to a hospital or speech and language center can be most useful. School-age children with articulation problems as well as those with apparent language disabilities and auditory attention difficulties should be studied especially carefully to uncover possible mild to moderate hearing losses.

Neurological examinations. There is considerable misunderstanding about the usefulness of neurological examinations in the evaluation of children with learning disorders. Sometimes parents and schools have unrealistic expectations. They may expect the neurological exam to diagnose the child or discover the "cause" of the problems. They may believe that a neurological examination will answer once and for all the question of whether a child's difficulties are organic or emotional. Despite this potential for overinterpretation and inflated expectation, a carefully performed and judiciously interpreted neurological examination can be helpful.

The neurological examination of a child has two distinct components: the standard neurological assessment and the examination for minor neurological indicators, sometimes call *soft neurological signs.* The standard neurological examination can uncover localized central nervous system deficits. In rare instances, actual lesions or pathological processes may be suspected. In the vast majority of cases, however, a precise pathological process is not identified. The absence of such findings does not rule out learning problems on a neurological or endogenous basis.

The neurological examination should include a careful survey of the cranial nerves, some assessment of sensation to touch and pain, evaluation of cerebellar function (including finger-to-nose and heel-knee-shin tests, along with the Romberg sign), an evaluation of visual fields, and an assessment of muscle strength and symmetry. There should be a careful elicitation of deep tendon reflexes, including notations as to their symmetry and strength. Any pathological reflexes should be noted.

The standard neurological examination should attempt to discover any localizing or lateralizing signs of neurological disorder (Paine and Oppe 1966). This quest becomes particularly important in children whose learning problems seem to be worsening or exhibiting recent dramatic deterioration. In these cases, some of the very rare causes of learning difficulty need to be considered, including various degenerative diseases, brain tumors, and arteriovenous malformations.

Observations for minor neurological indicators. Indicators of central nervous system inefficiency and immaturity have been referred to traditionally as *soft neurological signs.* A number of studies have suggested that the existence of these signs and school failure are closely linked. Although they have no direct therapeutic implications, they can be important markers of central nervous system dysfunction.

The systematic search for such indicators has been useful clinically (Peters, Romine, and Dykman 1975). Two types have been described—those whose clinical significance is determined by the child's chronological age, and those that represent mild, borderline versions of neurological signs that are abnormal at any age. The former, which include such phenomena as synkinesias (mirror movements; see p. 553), can generally be determined with fairly good interobserver reliability. The latter, on the other hand, include findings such as equivocal hypertonia (which may elicit less consistent agreement between examiners). Although the neurology literature has not differentiated consistently between those two types of soft signs, the second appears to reflect a localized neurological deficit, whereas the first type suggests the possibility of neuromaturational delay or generalized inefficiency. Such distinctions, however, remain hypotheses, given the present state of knowledge (or ignorance) about brain function.

Age-dependent minor neurological indicators are nearly universal in young children and become progressively rare during the later elementary school years. Whether through myelinization or increasing dendritic connections or by yet undiscovered mechanisms, these findings appear to be linked to central nervous system maturation. Some signs reappear during senescence. The persistence of these neuromaturational indicators beyond the ages at which they generally disappear has been associated with learning disorders, behavior problems, and other manifestations of developmental dysfunction.

Minor neurological indicators are subject to several types of misinterpretation or overinterpretation. First, a single sign in isolation may not be meaningful. Highly successful children may show one or more of these indicators, whereas children with significant developmental dysfunction may have no evidence whatsoever of neuromaturational delay or minor indicators. Clusters of signs appear to be more accurate discriminators than any single, isolated sign. The pediatric neurodevelopmental examinations (*PEEX 2* and *PEERAMID 2*) seek clusters of minor neurological indicators as they are elicited on multiple tasks. Efforts are currently being made to quantify these findings, a process which should make them more useful. Second, it is inappropriate to use neuromaturational indicators as evidence that a child will catch up eventually. The word *maturation* is misused widely in children with learning disorders. A so-called maturational lag in no way implies that there will be a spontaneous developmental growth spurt. Evidence of "immaturity," therefore, should not be used as justification for therapeutic inaction. Instead, such findings can suggest a constitutional component in a child's learning or behavior problems. Finally, evaluators must always relate the presence of minor neurological indicators to a child's age. A six year old with many such indicators, for example, is not nearly as likely to be "dysfunctional" as an eleven or twelve year old with the same cluster.

The most commonly elicited minor neurological indicators include the following:

Synkinetic (mirror) movements. In these motor phenomena, one side of the body mimics an activity carried out on the contralateral side. When a child is asked to oppose the thumb and forefinger repeatedly, for example, the other hand mirrors the action. Synkinesias are common in preschool children but less prevalent and less mirrorlike as children mature during elementary school. In older schoolchildren, synkinetic movements may be elicited by more complex unilateral acts. Persistence of true mirror movements beyond the age of eight years is unusual; it tends to occur commonly in children with learning and behavior disorders (Cohen et al. 1967, Woods and Eby 1982). One revealing study demonstrated that a battery of motor tests, including a range of tasks eliciting synkinesias, was able to predict later academic performance in kindergartners and first graders (Wolff, Gunnoe, and Cohen 1985).

Other associated movements ("overflow"). Other forms of extraneous or inefficient movement may also be interpreted as evidence of a neuromaturational lag in older children (Touwen and Prechtl 1970). For example, some children consistently display rhythmic mouth movements or head bobbing in conjunction with another activity occurring lower in the body. While rapidly apposing the thumb and forefinger, or even while writing, children may exhibit tongue movements. Most associated movements tend to proceed caudocranially in direction. Thus, rapid finger movements may elicit associated mouth movements, but rapid tongue movements are unlikely to elicit associated movements in the fingers. In assessing gross and fine motor function, the physician should be alert for associated movements as an indication of immature and inefficient performance.

Dysdiodochokinesis. The ability to perform a rapid alternating movements can be tested by sequential pronation and supination of the hands, for example, pretending to turn a doorknob back and forth rapidly, while holding the elbows against the sides. Some children seem unable to suppress activity in proximal muscle groups, exhibiting excessive flailing of the arms (Touwen and Prechtl 1970). This phenomenon is normal and common in preschool children but is associated with dysfunction in older children.

Stimulus extinction. Young children have difficulty perceiving simultaneously presented sensory stimuli (Kraft 1968). In some cases, more proximal stimuli are noticed over distal ones, or two-point discrimination in generally may be poor. For example, children with eyes closed may be touched simultaneously on the hand and face but report only the touch on the face (sometimes referred to as *rostral dominance*). This response pattern is common in younger children but is not generally encountered after the age of seven. Its persistence may be associated with dysfunction. One study, however, has suggested that sometimes poor performance is related to expectations, "mind-sets," or conceptual presumptions (involving interpretation of the instructions) rather than neuromaturational delay (Nolan and Kagan 1978).

Motor impersistence. The inability to maintain a fixed motor stance with arms extended, mouth open, and tongue protruding is a sign originally described in association with established "brain damage" (Garfield 1964). It is commonly observed in children with attention deficits.

Choreiform movements. Involuntary rotatory and rhythmic movements, when present, are most commonly seen in the outstretched fingers or protruded tongue when children are asked to close their eyes, extend both arms, spread their fingers, open their mouths, protrude their tongues, and sustain the posture for at least thirty seconds. A number of studies in older children have correlated such involuntary movements with school failure and behavior problems (Wolff and Hurwitz 1966). Prechtl and Stemmer (1962) originally described "the choreiform syndrome" in characterizing children with this finding and a history of hyperactivity, impulsiveness, emotional liability, poor tolerance for frustration, and difficulties with reading and social interaction. Since such symptoms may be found in children with learning disorders of all types, however, the existence of this particular "syndrome" can be questioned.

Lateral preference. A propensity to use one side of the body preferentially may reflect the development of one hemisphere of the brain for a particular set of functions (Hiscock and Kinsbourne 1982). Hand preference is usually well established between four and six years. Eye preference is often established by age two. Ear and foot preference can also be evaluated, but less is known about their clinical significance. Ear preference may be helpful in determining which hemisphere of the brain is predominantly language oriented. Children with delays in establishing lateral preferences may have problems in other developmental areas. However, this has been a controversial subject in the child development, psychological, and neurological literature. Mixed preference (especially a tendency to be left-handed and right-eyed) has been associated with an increased incidence of reading disabilities (Corballis and Beale 1976, Denckla 1985). There have been no consistent documented associations between left-handedness and learning disorders (Hiscock and Kinsbourne 1982).

Left-right discrimination. It is important to distinguish between a sense of laterality and the ability to respond to left and right commands; the latter involves a high degree of attention to detail and language efficiency. As children grow older, they become progressively competent in this area, but in some cases delayed left-right differentiation may be part of a developmental lag (Benton 1968a). By age six, most children can tell left from right on their own bodies. Before their eighth birthdays, they are usually able to cross the midline (e.g., "Touch your right ear with your left hand"). By age nine or ten they usually can identify right and left on the examiner (e.g., "Touch my right knee with your left hand"). By early adolescence, children are competent at rapidly distinguishing left and right, starting from new bases in space (e.g., "right face, left face," as in military commands). Problems with left-right discrimination may result from complex manifestations of maturational, developmental, or basic processing problems. Such deficits may be associated with learning disorders (Croxen and Lytton 1971). Left-right reversals of letters and consequent reading retardation were described in the early and influential studies of Orton (1937). He attributed such confusion to incomplete cerebral lateralization (dominance).

The minor neurological indicators described in this section are often sought in the evaluation of dysfunctioning children. They are part of the neurodevelopmental examinations described earlier in this chapter. Although they do not have direct implications for intervention, they may suggest strong "constitutional loadings" which may have relevance for direct counseling and for feedback to teachers and parents. In some cases, delay in neuromaturation is accompanied by other forms of maturational lag, such as in skeletal age, dentition, emotional or social sophistication, onset of puberty, or physical stature. Studies showing strong correlations between these areas are not yet available. Evidence of neuromaturational delay is of little value out of context. When combined with environmental, developmental, health, emotional, and educational performance issues, however, it contributes to the clinical formulation of a child's problems.

The ultimate significance of these minor neurological indicators is a matter of continuing controversy. While certain studies, such as the report of Gottesman et al. (1984), have shown strong correlations with certain learning problems, some investigators have been skeptical (Shaffer et al. 1983), noting that there are a large number of normal children who show these signs. Others (Shafer, O'Connor, and Stokman 1983) have pointed to a number of biases that enter into the rating and interpretation of these kinds of findings. Many investigators conclude, therefore, that minor neurological indicators need to be described with care and viewed in the context of a whole child. In the presence of indications of developmental dysfunction, they may add to the body of evidence favoring a strong neurological basis for a child's difficulties.

Personality Testing. The use of projective tests has become a standard procedure, especially in the field of child psychology (Brooks 1983). Such testing is intended to uncover underlying preoccupations, feelings that a child may have difficulty expressing directly, and emotional issues that are potentially important for diagnosis and therapy. Brooks (1983) has reviewed the subject of projective testing. He describes the following five types of commonly used tests:

- *Associative tests* require children to respond to stimuli with the first word, image, or idea that comes to mind. The *Rorschach* and *Early Memories* tests are examples of this type.

- *Construction procedures* stimulate children to create something, usually in response to a visual stimulus. Several different tests use thematic cards or pictures on which the child bases a story.

- *Completion tests* have the subjects finish an incomplete sentence or drawing. The *Sentence Completion Test* and Winnicott's "Squiggle Game" are assessments of this type.

- *Choice or ordering responses* are assessments in which children are asked to list some things in order of preference. The *Miniature Situations Test* designed by Santostefano is an example of this.

- *Expressive techniques* are those in which children engage in free play, artwork, or the use of puppets and dolls as well as tests that require them to draw themselves, another person, or their family.

Using such techniques, a diagnostician attempts to identify areas of conflict, unusual patterns of response (perhaps suggesting major psychopathology), and deeply sequestered feelings. Projective techniques need to be administered and interpreted with great care. Gittelman (1980), in a comprehensive review of research on this subject, reminds us that validation studies of various projective tests used in children often have failed to show that they really measure what they claim to measure. Moreover, she states that "the current status of projective tests in children can be summarized succinctly: sometimes they tell us poorly something we already know. On the basis of empirical data, it is clear that the use of projective testing in children does not deserve a high priority." On the other side, there are strong clinical advocates for such techniques (Rabin and Haworth 1960). However, these tests need to be viewed in the same manner as individual items on a neurodevelopmental or neuropsychological battery, as intelligence test scores, as parent observations, or as teacher ratings. That is, they form one fragmentary piece of a total picture of a child. Their interpretation may be highly subjective and thus susceptible to disciplinary biases and other conflicts of interest. When findings on projective testing fit with and account for the phenomenology of a child's failure, when they are rigorously confirmed by data from other sources, they can be useful adjuncts to evaluation. On the other hand, when they are given too much weight, when they are overinterpreted by inexperienced or zealous clinicians, when they are administered by individuals who appear to obsess on their results and overreact to them, they can be dangerous, even to the point of violating the civil rights and privacy of a child. Some children with language difficulties may produce unusual responses as a result of their production dysfunctions. Children with attention deficits may give impulsive answers or overindulge in the free flight of ideas. Such variations lend themselves to being misinterpreted as indications of significant psychopathology.

Direct interviewing. Interviewing children and/or their family members can be especially revealing. A skilled pediatrician, nurse, social worker, psychologist, or child psychiatrist may elicit a rich store of information. Some claim that this kind of direct approach is more valuable than projective testing. When assessing children in a clinic or private office, interviewing is especially important. The orchestration of such interviews is relevant. Beginning by talking to the parents alone enables them to discuss issues they may not feel comfortable mentioning in front of their child. It also allows them to get at any "skeletons in the closet." For example, it is always useful to find out why parents want a child evaluated now. Is it because they have a relative who resembles this child and who now suffers from a drinking problem, has gone to prison, or just entered a mental hospital? Is there something that has changed significantly about this child or the family? What are the parents' worst fears? What do they believe is wrong? Do they have a strong sense of guilt? Do they feel they have caused the problem? Are they in agreement in their perceptions of the child and in their rearing practices? Are they having marital difficulties or other family problems that are creating anxiety in the child that becomes indistinguishable from the child's learning problems? Are they entangled in conflict and political strife with the school? Do they perceive the child's positive attributes? What are their expectations from the evaluation? What specific questions do they have?

Following an interview with the parents, it is useful to see the child alone (either the same day or during a subsequent appointment). *The ANSER System*'s Self-Administered Student Profile (Levine 1980), the questionnaire about perceived strengths and weaknesses, can be used to break the ice and initiate discussion. Whenever possible, open-ended questions such as "How do you like school?" or "Are you popular?" should be avoided. Instead, the child might describe various daily scenarios at the bus stop, in the cafeteria, or in the classroom. After the youngster describes what goes on in these settings, the examiner should ask him to portray his roles and/or problems therein. The examiner should reassure the child that any problems also occur among other children. School-age children are often afraid to reveal their concerns and conflicts out of fear of being too unusual (i.e., "weird"). Therefore, to obtain useful information, the clinician needs to keep reassuring the child that his or her concerns are not unique.

If a physical examination is to be performed by a pediatrician, it can be combined with an interview. As mentioned previously, schoolchildren should usually have a physical examination without parents in the room so that they can comment on any bodily concerns. During the physical assessment as well as the general interview, a clinician needs to reassure the children that any discussion of private matters will be treated confidentially.

At some point, interviewing the child and parents together allows observations of their interactions. It is not a good idea to test and/or interview a child and then immediately see the parents alone. This creates understandable anxiety for the patient, who wonders what bad news the clinician is imparting. "Do they think I'm a mental case?" "Maybe the doctor's telling them I'm a retard." "Do I have a brain tumor or something?" If speaking alone with the parents is essential, it should be done during a subsequent appointment or over the telephone.

Specialized Consultations.   The result of a basic evaluation of a child, one that has included assessment of educational status, health, individual developmental functions, and emotional well-being, may be a need for further evaluation in one or more specific areas. More detailed assessment may be required by professionals from fields such as hearing and speech pathology, occupational therapy, physical therapy, social work, or psychology. More refined educational testing by a reading specialist or someone who can focus primarily upon mathematics disabilities may be necessary. Various medical specialists may also need to be consulted, including neurologists (when a "hard" neurological disorder is suspected), otolaryngologists, ophthalmologists, or child psychiatrists. Some older adolescents may be helped by a vocational-rehabilitation counselor.

Feedback and Formulation

Once an evaluation is completed, its results must be reported in such a manner that those who will use it can understand it and discern its implications for treatment. This is often accomplished through both verbal feedback and a written report. Shortly after an evaluation, it is helpful for a clinician or members of a team to meet with the parents and the child to provide feedback. The technique for providing such feedback is discussed in chapter 15. To prevent anxiety, this should be done as soon as possible after completion of the evaluations.

The written report should include a summary that explains the child's difficulties. This diagnostic formulation should be concise, positive, relatively nontechnical, and upbeat. Figure 14-6 gives two examples of such formulations as they might appear in a report. Immediately following the diagnostic formulation should be a list of specific recommendations (see chapter 15). The formulation should attempt to incorporate the findings of various disciplines. It should be written by one individual who can integrate and state effectively these viewpoints and their implications for the child, the family, and the school.

Assessment and the Provision of Services in Schools

Children have a right to an appropriate education, one that is geared to their individual profiles of strengths and weakness. In recent years in the United States as well as in other countries, this right has been safeguarded and implemented through various forms of special educational legislation. Public Law 94-142 and, more recently, IDEA (the Individuals with Disabilities Education Act) have provided for the educational care of students with a wide range of developmental delays. Clinicians, teachers, and parents need to be familiar with the provisions of current legislation, so that they can advocate effectively for the kinds of children described in this book.

For our purposes it will be useful to examine the content of IDEA with amendments for implementation in 1998 to determine the ways in which this legislation can serve affected children and adolescents. The following are some of the most relevant facets of this important legislation:

- The legislation provides that children with a wide range of developmental delays must be served within their schools. Children under nine *need not* be categorized or labeled to receive services. However, their delays need to be well documented.

- Students are expected to be educated in the least restrictive environment. Inclusionary models are strongly encouraged and facilitated in this legislation, along with a strong emphasis on regular classroom accommodations.

- For each child to be served, an Individualized Educational Program (IEP) is developed by a team of individuals, which usually includes: a special educator, the regular classroom teacher, the parents, possibly the student, and others who have expertise regarding the student.

- The IEP report is required to include the following information: 1) a statement documenting the current level of a child's educational attainment and describing her or his disability and how it is impacting performance; 2) a description of the child's strengths; 3) a delineation of annual educational goals and how their accomplishment will be measured; 4) a detailed description of special education services, other interventions, and classroom accommodations to be provided; 5) provisions for notifying the parents regarding the student's progress;

A. Betsy

Betsy shows strengths in many areas. She has well-developed visual processing abilities. She shows strong sequential organization and generally adequate fine motor skills. She is known to have well-developed artistic and mechanical abilities as well as a rich imagination. On the other hand, there are concerns about Betsy's current function at home, in the classroom, and among her peers, as a result of which Betsy is experiencing profound feelings of inadequacy. There are several reasons for this. First, Betsy does have some underlying developmental dysfunctions that are making academic work and socialization difficult. There are signs of a mild language disability, and the processing and production of verbal material are problematic. There are also suggestions of moderate speech dysfluency. Her linguistic shortcomings exert an impact on her writing and also on the processing of instructions and explanations. On the expressive side, she cannot mobilize language at an appropriate rate, which most certainly impairs her efficiency and reduces her comfort in academic settings. Betsy also has some significant organizational problems. In particular, she is not a reflective student. She does not develop good strategies or simplification techniques prior to undertaking a task. Thus, she is often overwhelmed or confused. Her lack of strategies renders her work overly mechanical, which means that she must put forth inordinate effort to accomplish an end. This inefficiency is particularly evident in her writing, where there are real problems with graphomotor planning. It also has an impact on mathematics, as documented in the psychoeducational testing during the evaluation. In other academic areas, Betsy is functioning fairly well. However, we are beginning to see some vulnerability in her reading comprehension, likely the result of her mild language dysfunctions.

Betsy also has difficulties with her social skills. She does not have optimal instincts about peer interaction. It is likely that she fails to use good strategies in forming and maintaining relationships with other children, a difficulty that parallels her cognitive dysfunction. At home, Betsy obviously has to compete to keep up with her sisters. This is likely to be another source of frustration for her.

At this time, there are blatant signs of low self-esteem and yet Betsy sustains motivation and wants very much to experience mastery. She will need a considerable degree of help if she is to overcome her anxiety, avoid adolescent depression, and begin to feel effective as a student, family member, and child.

B. Mark

Mark exhibits a great many assets. He has a very appealing personality and good social skills, especially when it comes to relating to adults. He obviously also possesses strong visual processing abilities and well-developed visual motor function. Mark is a very imaginative boy with a lively mind capable of highly original insights. He shows relative strengths in his expressive language skills that, combined with his divergent thinking abilities, make him a rich contributor to classroom discussion. When stimulated and attentive, Mark's ideation is both creative and keenly analytical.

It is certainly true that Mark shows a significant gap between his capacities and his day-to-day performance. To a large extent, this is the result of an attention deficit, which tends to plague him especially in school. He has great difficulty sustaining his focus. He becomes particularly "burned out" in highly verbal surroundings. That is, Mark's auditory attention is not nearly as strong as his visual focus. Therefore, in classroom settings, he tends to drift and become distracted. Mark's attention problems are also marked by a considerable degree of impulsiveness and poor planning, some performance inconsistency, restlessness, and deficient self-monitoring. These particular characteristics make it difficult for him to remain oriented in class. His relatively weak auditory attention is associated with significant weaknesses of verbal memory, so that it is hard for Mark to process and retain spoken instructions, especially when they are complex and composed of multiple steps. For this reason, he is likely to be disoriented at least some of the time in the classroom. It is also conceivable that he is missing out on a considerable amount of informational input throughout the school day. Thus, he is perpetually struggling to keep pace despite incomplete information processing and erratic retention. Mark is obviously concerned about his disappointing school performance. He is motivated and would like very much to succeed. However, he is becoming increasingly anxious about himself. At the same time, there are indications that he is experiencing a precipitous decline in his self-image. His obesity is creating significant social problems for him at the same time that it is further eroding his self-esteem. There are now signs that Mark's increasing anxiety is becoming a potent distraction in itself. Over the coming years it will be important for Mark to receive considerable support and empathy so that he can overcome his attention difficulties and achieve at a level commensurate with his strong reasoning and creative abilities. If he can experience sustained success, it is likely that Mark will be able to surmount his current feelings of worthlessness and anxiety and become a more productive and gratified student.

Figure 14-6. Examples of formulations

6) possible modifications in state testing requirements for this individual; and 7) a statement of any transition needs of older students (see figure 14-7).

- The assessment of a child to determine his or her eligibility for services is to be determined using valid measures. No determination is made based on a single instrument or perspective. Instead, multiple sources of information must be sought (including significant input from the parents).

- Students who attend private or parochial schools are eligible to receive assessments and educational services.

- Periodic re-evaluation is required to determine if the student remains eligible for services.

- The law includes various provisions for the management of associated behavior problems and guidelines for the discipline of disabled students with maladaptive behavior. In some cases, there is a need for a child to be evaluated to deter-

---

1. Is the plan based on a sufficiently thorough, multifaceted evaluation of the student?
2. Does the plan reflect an adequate understanding of the full range and degree of a student's problems and service needs?
3. Does it state treatment objectives clearly?
4. Does it establish deadlines for the achievement of specified objectives?
5. If the student is to receive services in a special classroom or learning center, does the plan specify the skills and/or developmental functions to be remedied and the methods of curricula to be used in that setting?
6. Is the plan specific about the amount of time per week or day during which the student will receive services and about the student-teacher ratio for the special services?
7. Is the level of special education sufficient in view of the degree and impact of the academic delays?
8. If specialized services are to be provided (e.g., language therapy or counseling), does the plan delineate specific issues that such services need to address?
9. Does the plan make sufficient use of the student's strengths?
10. Does the plan delineate appropriate accommodations in the regular classroom(s), including measures to minimize humiliation in front of peers?
11. Is there a provision for reevaluation and ongoing monitoring of the student's problems?
12. Are mechanisms in place for communication between special educators (and other specialists) and regular educators working with the student?
13. Are mechanisms in place for communication between school personnel and the parents regarding issues such as homework and study habits?
14. Does the plan provide for ongoing demystification and maintenance of the child's self-esteem?
15. Does the plan contain new interventions for a student who is not making sufficient progress?
16. Does the plan deal adequately with behavioral issues?
17. Does the plan suggest accommodations for the classroom testing of the child?
18. Does the plan reflect input from the parents, the regular classroom teacher, and (in many cases) the student?
19. Is there general agreement among the parents and school personnel about diagnostic conclusions and the services offered, or is there a need for an independent (outside) evaluation?
20. Is the child being educated in the least restrictive environment?

Figure 14-7. Guidelines for evaluating an Individualized Educational Program

mine the extent to which her or his behavior problems are a direct result of the disability. Children or adolescents who display violent or dangerous behaviors cannot have their special services terminated.

- IDEA also protects the rights of students for whom English is a second language and for those with sensory deficits.

- Students with disabilities are included in the data when communities are required to submit their districtwide academic performance assessments.

Clinicians, parents, and others involved in the assessment and management of a child with learning problems need to ensure that their knowledge of the student will contribute meaningfully to a student's IEP. They should also be active in reviewing any plans that are developed and helping monitor the progress of the student. It is also important to educate the child regarding his or her educational program and the reasons for it. This process can be included in the student's demystification (see pp. 568–71).

Legislation such as IDEA undergoes regular modification and re-authorization. Those who work with students who have learning disorders need to remain informed about changes in the laws and about the ways in which their states or provinces are implementing the regulations. It is also important that parents, educators, and clinicians exert their influence publicly, so that future legislation can protect and support affected students.

Monitoring and Follow-Up

Whether or not a student is eligible for services with IDEA, the evaluation process should never cease following an initial assessment. Ongoing monitoring and periodic reevaluations are essential. They should include a review of the child's interim history. *The ANSER System Follow-Up Questionnaires* (Levine 1984a) have been used for this purpose. They include parent, teacher, and self-administered follow-up items. Figure 14-8 shows excerpts from one of these instruments. In addition, follow-up educational testing and an interview with the child and the parents is appropriate.

The child's current management should be reviewed critically, including a determination of need to increase, decrease, or alter the treatment plan as well as the current diagnostic formulation.

Preschool Screening

This book is about school-age children. Notwithstanding, the potential importance of early diagnosis and intervention must be acknowledged. Many communities offer screening of preschool (three- to five-year-old children in an effort to discover potential "learning disabilities" or "behavior problems." Such efforts are to be commended. They, too, should obviously be of very high quality. Preschool screening tests are not new; many procedures are available (Frankenburg 1983). If one attempts to screen children, then covering a broad range of developmental areas is essential. In fact, it is strongly suggested that communities screen for

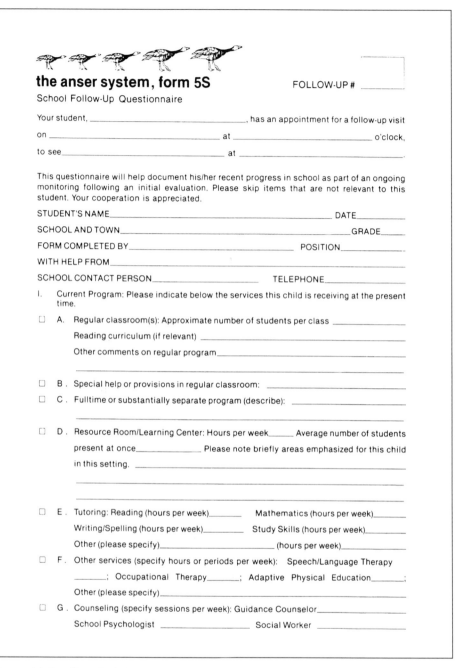

the anser system, form 5S

School Follow-Up Questionnaire

FOLLOW-UP # _____

Your student, _____, has an appointment for a follow-up visit

on _____ at _____ o'clock,

to see_____ at _____.

This questionnaire will help document his/her recent progress in school as part of an ongoing monitoring following an initial evaluation. Please skip items that are not relevant to this student. Your cooperation is appreciated.

STUDENT'S NAME_____ DATE_____

SCHOOL AND TOWN_____GRADE_____

FORM COMPLETED BY_____ POSITION_____.

WITH HELP FROM_____

SCHOOL CONTACT PERSON_____ TELEPHONE_____

I. Current Program: Please indicate below the services this child is receiving at the present time.

☐ A. Regular classroom(s): Approximate number of students per class _____

Reading curriculum (if relevant) _____

Other comments on regular program_____

_____

☐ B. Special help or provisions in regular classroom: _____

☐ C. Fulltime or substantially separate program (describe): _____

_____

☐ D. Resource Room/Learning Center: Hours per week_____ Average number of students

present at once_____ Please note briefly areas emphasized for this child

in this setting. _____

_____

_____

☐ E. Tutoring: Reading (hours per week)_____ Mathematics (hours per week)_____

Writing/Spelling (hours per week)_____ Study Skills (hours per week)_____

Other (please specify)_____ (hours per week)_____

☐ F. Other services (specify hours or periods per week): Speech/Language Therapy

_____; Occupational Therapy_____; Adaptive Physical Education_____;

Other (please specify)_____

☐ G. Counseling (specify sessions per week): Guidance Counselor_____

School Psychologist _____ Social Worker _____

Figure 14-8. Sample follow-up questionnaire

This form is part of the teacher questionnaire from *The ANSER System Follow-up Questionnaires*. Clinicians frequently use it as one method of assessing the academic, developmental, and behavioral progress of a child. A similar form is completed the by parents, and older children fill out a questionnaire entitled "How I Think I'm Doing." Inspecting these three questionnaires can guide the clinician in offering further management advice, determining the need for additional assessment, and regulating other therapies (such as medication).

III. Please indicate any questions or concerns you have, as well as your thoughts about this student's rate of progress and general school performance and adjustment.

_____
_____
_____
_____
_____
_____
_____

IV. Please record or attach information about any recent standardized testing and/or new Individualized Educational Plan.

_____
_____
_____
_____
_____
_____

V. Do you have any suggestions regarding this follow-up visit?   Yes ☐   No ☐

If so, please specify._____

_____
_____

This form was compiled by
Melvin D. Levine, MD, FAAP
The Children's Hospital, Boston, Massachusetts
Copyright 1984 by Melvin D. Levine
All rights reserved

eps

EDUCATORS PUBLISHING SERVICE, INC.
31 Smith Place, Cambridge, MA 02138-1000
ISBN 0-8388–1762-9
February, 1996 Printing

Figure 14-8. *(Continued)*

difficulties in the major developmental areas surveyed in this book. Early indications of attention deficits, problems with simultaneous or sequential processing, language disabilities, memory problems, motor implementation, higher-order cognitive weaknesses, or social skill deficits should be sought.

In addition, the child's overall health and sensory (visual and auditory) functions should be screened. As with evaluation in older children, it is helpful to combine direct observations with systematic collection of historical data. *The ANSER System* preschool questionnaires are useful for this purpose. They facilitate collecting data from parents as well as any preschool or nursery school teach-

II. CURRENT PROGRESS

Please complete the table below by putting an X in the appropriate column based on recent performance.

	Never a problem (to my knowledge)	Was a problem; no longer a problem	Some improvement; still a problem	No improvement; still a problem	Is worse; has a new problem	Cannot say; not relevant	COMMENTS (Please point out areas of great inconsistency)
PERFORMANCE							
Overall academic performance							
Reading – decoding							
Reading comprehension							
Reading rate							
Enjoyment of reading							
Spelling accuracy							
Writing – legibility							
Writing – rate/efficiency							
Written expression (language)							
Mathematics concepts							
Mathematics accuracy							
Foreign language							
Science							
History/Social Studies							
Independent work							
Physical education/ sports							
Other:							
SUBSKILLS							
Ability to express ideas orally							
Verbal comprehension							
Visual/spatial abilities							
Memory for skills							
Memory for facts							
Grasp of new concepts							
Organization							
Study habits							
Report writing							
Test taking							
ATTENTION/ACTIVITY							
Selective attention/concentration							
Control of impulses							
Control of activity level							
Alertness in class							
Consistency of work quality							
Planning and self-monitoring							
Completion of tasks							
SOCIALIZATION/AFFECT							
Confidence/self-esteem							
Peer relationships							
Happiness in school							
Handling of stress							
Cooperativeness							
Level of anxiety							
Relationships with teacher(s)							
OTHERS (please list)							

Figure 14-8. *(Continued)*

ers. In some communities, questionnaires are used to identify high-risk children, who then undergo testing. It is preferable to test children at high risk thoroughly rather than to assess directly every child in the community in a superficial or skimpy manner. One should be wary of quick screening tests that may be calibrated to detect mental retardation but are relatively insensitive to specific neurodevelopmental dysfunctions. If this book has successfully demonstrated the complexity and variety of issues involved in childhood school function, then professionals and parents alike should hesitate to rely on the rapid screening test, a procedure that is likely to have a high false negative rate. Studies of the predictive validity of preschool screening tests have shown mixed results. One can legitimately ask whether it is possible to diagnose neurodevelopmental dysfunctions at an early age. If so, how early? Undoubtedly, the answer depends on the individual disability, its severity, and the availability of well-standardized instruments to measure it. Much remains to be done in this area. Once we have defined the specific dysfunctions of older children, we can address the issue of detecting these dysfunctions as early as possible. For instance, if it is agreed that problems with active working memory cause trouble in older students attempting to succeed in mathematics, can we devise a test for this function for four year olds? Quite possibly active working memory has not been developed adequately in this age group, and therefore either it or its antecedents remain beyond the scope of early diagnosis. Issues such as these require further investigation.

The nature of children's learning problems tends to change as they grow older, because they require different functions to perform effectively at different ages and because evolving subject matter calls for different capacities in different grades. Therefore, a child with developmental dysfunctions may not have been affected by them previously and may not be affected subsequently. Furthermore, a developmental dysfunction diagnosed previously may have improved when the child is assessed several years later. For this reason, early evaluations may not necessarily agree with those performed once a child is in school. And an evaluation done in early elementary school may not agree with one done in high school.

Thus, we can anticipate some instability of findings on that basis alone. In conclusion, community screening, especially of high-risk preschoolers, can be beneficial. However, we need to be aware of its limitations, of the possibility that some children will show remarkable improvement once they are in school while others will develop problems that may not have been apparent earlier.

Preschool assessments should never be used to label a youngster but rather to define a subgroup that may require special services early or careful monitoring and follow-up.

Description and Prescription

Any good evaluation of a child should have direct implications for remediation. The ultimate aim of assessment is to alter the ways in which we view a struggling child. The next chapter considers the ways in which unbiased, accurate description can beget effective prescription.

Chapter 15

Approaches to
Management

*"Instead of applying closely with my studies, I preferred to go with my friends in
search of birds' nests. . . . I usually made for the field, my little basked filled with
eatables for lunch at school, but to burst with nests, eggs, lichens, flowers, and even
pebbles from the shore of some rivulet by the time I came home at evening."*
—John James Audubon, from Alice Ford, *Audubon, By Himself*

Previous chapters have offered suggestions for managing various forms of
developmental dysfunction and academic delay. This chapter presents a broader
consideration of the philosophy, content, potential hazards, and potential benefits
associated with attempts to rehabilitate a disappointing child.

SETTING GOALS

Any management program that deals with developmental dysfunctions and
accompanying learning or behavior difficulties must meet certain objectives.
Seven major goals are summarized here:

Enhancement of subskills and skills. Clearly, a principal objective of any habil-
itative or rehabilitative effort is the enhancement of skills needed to survive and
thrive during childhood and the transition to adulthood. The wide spectrum of
these skills ranges from traditional academic abilities such as the three R's to
social skills, cognitive strategies, and the capacity for avocational pleasure. Not
all children need all skills. Not all children need the same skills. But, in the process
of developing expected skills, all children need to cultivate their unique abilities
and affinities.

Discovery and facilitation of pathways for individual success. Every child has
a right to practice his or her specialty. Each needs to find personal fulfillment
through one or more forms of endeavor. Special attention must be given to children with developmental dysfunctions to ensure that they experience success.
Teachers and parents must mobilize their interests and abilities so that they can

achieve in one or more areas, for they can best learn to seek excellence by experiencing it firsthand.

Prevention of complications. The complications of developmental dysfunction are often devastating. As we have seen, chronic deprivation of success, mental illness, delinquency, maladaptive social bonds, and paralyzing amotivational states are common sequelae. Two forms of complication merit active prevention: first, the tragic consequences of the dysfunctions themselves and the failure, embarrassment, and feelings of anxiety they generate; and second, the iatrogenic effects, the suffering caused by adults who fail to understand, accommodate, and help disappointing children. Included are the deleterious effects of overdoses of criticism, public ridicule, false attributions (such as calling a learning disorder an "attitude problem"), and long-standing failure to receive respect from any adult audience.

Assurance of gratification. Any therapeutic program must balance current service needs with a child's requirements for ongoing gratification. Parents and teachers must collaborate to ensure that a student's life is sufficiently rich, that there are enough varied, stimulating experiences, and that the child is experiencing adequate success and fulfillment. In other words, in our zeal to prepare children for adulthood, we must not ignore the quality of life during childhood. If discipline and education are especially painful to children with developmental dysfunctions, there must be enough plasticity in the system to promote short-term gratification as well as preparation for life.

Facilitation of critical transitions. Any therapeutic program must create readiness for what comes next. Certain of these transitions are especially critical—the junctions between preschool and kindergarten, entry into junior high school, entry into high school, and entry into college or the workplace. To be effective, a management program must analyze what comes next; counseling and planning must facilitate the next step.

Preservation of authenticity. It is always appropriate to wonder how much we have a right to change a child. Clinicians often hear parents simultaneously lamenting and loving the attributes of a struggling offspring. A child who seems hopelessly disorganized may possess a delightfully scintillating imagination. We would like to impart organization and structure but not at the cost of stifling originality and spark. Therefore, every therapeutic program must practice human conversation by preserving, supporting, and even encouraging children as individuals with unique capabilities, insights, and eccentricities. Children have the right to be different, and we have an obligation to uphold their right.

Fostering self-esteem and motivation. Management plans should enable students to feel that they are effective human beings. They should be able to sustain a sufficiently high level of aspiration in life, fortified by feelings of self-efficacy. Further, they need to believe that personal effort will pay off, that their motivation is worth maintaining at a high level.

The pages that follow will first present an overview of a systematic approach to children with learning disorders. The second half of this chapter will examine some additional options and models of service for helping these students.

MANAGEMENT BY PROFILE

A management program for a child with developmental dysfunctions should include some basic ingredients, all of which have been discussed in the management sections of earlier chapters. The following description is intended to be a basic structural framework for intervention. The approach advocated here is called "management by profile." This phrase signifies that a management plan must fit the profile of a child's neurodevelopmental strengths and weaknesses as well as the child's current academic subskills. Instead of managing an attention deficit or a delay in reading ability, one must manage the whole child.

Management by profile consists of six major steps: 1) demystification; 2) bypass strategies; 3) interventions; 4) the enhancement of strengths and content affinities; 5) humiliation protection; and 6) additional services.

Demystification

A good prescription should be based on a good description. Once we have compiled and integrated a vivid description of the elements of development, patterns of behavior, mechanisms of coping, and other key variables affecting performance, it becomes possible to share the formulation with the principal actors. We call this process of explication *demystification,* a process in which a child's plight is described so that it contains as little myth, fantasy, and mystery as possible. Weaknesses and strengths are described in concrete terms with as little use of technical terminology, diagnostic jargon, or facile labeling as possible. Demystification should help alleviate guilt, dispel fantasies, and minimize condemnation and accusation. It should also serve to convince children and parents of their ability to affect future outcomes. Such explanations should be provided by an articulate member of a diagnostic team or by an individual clinician who is coordinating an assessment or undertaking a major role in it. They should communicate the results in nontechnical language. The clinician should always begin by citing the child's strengths and creating a sense of optimism. The clinician should present results in a nonaccusatory, positive, highly supportive manner. He or she should explain the child's dysfunctions as clearly as possible, and whenever feasible, use concrete examples. These might include specific citations from a questionnaire or examples of errors the child made during educational testing or neurodevelopmental (neuropsychological) examination. The clinician should encourage the child and parents to ask questions freely. Such a feedback session can do more than provide information. It can be the first meaningful step in the rehabilitation of a child. The demystification that takes place can in itself repair a considerable amount of injury and misapprehension.

The recipients of the explanation might include the child, the parents, the regular classroom teacher, and other important school personnel. Sometimes demystification needs to be extended to include siblings, grandparents, other relatives, the child's physician, a member of the clergy, and even neighbors. Parents can often provide secondary transmission to some of these individuals. Therefore, it is often a good idea to have parents present during a demystification session with the child.

This book recommends following the sequence shown in table 15-1 when offering demystification to a student.

The following points expand on the contents of table 15-1:

- Children with learning difficulties may feel self-conscious during the demystification session. Destigmatization—reassuring a student that many or all people have some sort of learning problem—can help put a child at ease.

- When telling a child about her strengths, avoid using false praise or praising a child for something that most others of that age can do very easily. Moreover, it is helpful to offer concrete evidence for the praise you are giving. Instead of just saying, "Susan, you are such a good artist . . ." refer to some specific piece of her artwork that you have seen. Also, it is often helpful to include comparisons with other children in the expressed praise (e.g., "I have seen many children draw horses, but yours is among the best").

- When discussing weaknesses, the use of a number (i.e., "There are three things you need to be working on . . .") convinces a child that he is not pervasively defective or mentally retarded. The number used initially and later reviewed with the student puts borders around the child's dysfunctions, enabling him to feel more in control. At the end of the demystification the child should be asked to recall and restate the areas he needs to be working on. It is also helpful for the student to offer examples of times when his dysfunction has caused problems for him.

- An optimistic tone is critical. Many children with learning problems believe their lives are to have unhappy endings, that they were born to lose. Demystification must dispel this illusion. The clinician should help the child see bright possibilities for herself in the future.

Table 15-1. A systematic approach to demystification

COMPONENT	CONTENT
Destigmatization	Assurance that all people have strengths and weaknesses; the sooner they learn about them the better; possibly cite examples of successful people with dysfunctions or mention own deficits
Strength delineation	Description of strengths: concrete, highly specific, using examples or samples, compare to others when possible; legitimization of affinities
Weakness enumeration	Cite *number* of problems (e.g., "there are three areas that need work . . .") before, during, and after discussion; possible use of graphics; child reiterates, gives own examples
Induction of optimism	Projection to future; descriptions of possibilities for career and future education; restoration of self-esteem, internal locus of control
Alliance formation	Communication of desire to be helpful and supportive in the future; including student as active partner in planning for education

- It is especially important for the child to feel that the person providing the demystification has a real commitment and wants to be helpful.

- Demystification should be provided in a tone that is supportive, nonpreachy, and upbeat.

- It can be very helpful to have parents present during a demystification session. Their participation enables them to continue the discussion at home and to be consistent in frames of reference and terminology used to refer to the child's learning difficulties.

- Various visual aids can assist in demystification. For example, "The Concentration Cockpit" (figure 2-4) is a device that a teacher or clinician can use to help a child understand better the problems he is having with attention controls. The Cockpit and manual enable the clinician or teachers to record the child's comments and self-ratings of the various attention controls.

- The clinician can give children materials to read (or audio cassettes to listen to) to supplement and enhance demystification. My books, *All Kinds of Minds* (1993), for elementary schoolchildren, and *Keeping a Head in School* (1990), for older students, are examples. These books contain case material or vignettes that can help students realize that many other children share the problems they face, a vitally important realization.

- Demystification can also be conducted with groups of children. Participating students first fill out a self-rating form ("The Student's View") that covers specific areas of neurodevelopmental function, academic subskills, and behavioral issues. These materials are part of the SCHOOLS ATTUNED project (see p. 602). The students take their Student's View to the group demystification discussions and get to compare self-perceptions and discuss key aspect of learning. This process has evolved into a complete course for students called "The Mind That's Mine." This curriculum includes considerable demystification and is designed to provide an education in neurodevelopmental function and dysfunction for all schoolchildren.

When offering demystification to students, establish a balance between empathy and accountability. Help children understand that adults are sympathetic and compassionate. On the other hand, hold these children accountable for incremental progress.

One cannot command students to improve dramatically in a short time, but one can expect slow and steady progress. The following example illustrates this point:

> I'm sure that when you get older, you'd like to drive a car. On the other hand, you remember we discussed how impulsive you are. This can be a real problem when you're driving. Let's suppose you're driving along and you come to a red light. You impulsively decide to go through the light. But a police officer sees you and stops your car. You roll down the window and say to the police officer that you are impulsive and that you were born that way so it's not your fault that you passed the red light. The police officer will get angry. Even impulsive people have to stop for red lights. Your explanation may sound like a fake excuse. Our society can sympathize with a problem but people still have to do something about their problems. Some-

one who has bad vision has to wear glasses when driving a car. This is not blaming that person for poor eyesight but requiring that something be done about it. The same is true for you with your problem.

This kind of counseling can set the tone for an effective balance between empathy and accountability in school, at home, and on the playground. The goal of insight, optimism, and accountability is illustrated in the letter shown in figure 15-1.

When resources for special education and other services are lacking, when children's social circumstances are seriously problematic, or when they have little will to succeed, the process of demystification is particularly important. Even when children cannot receive adequate services, the processes involved in demystification can justify the evaluation process and at least some of the complications of chronic, unresolved, and misinterpreted failure at a young age.

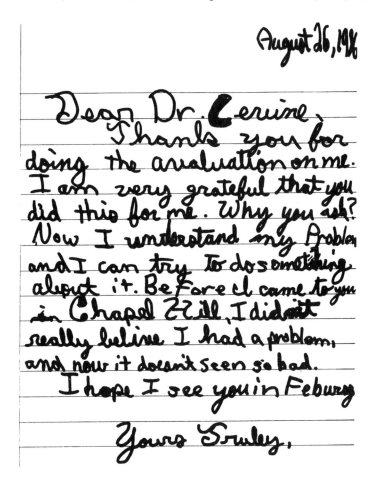

Figure 15-1. Demystification

I received this letter shortly after completing a multidisciplinary assessment of the twelve-year-old boy. The child had been reluctant to undergo evaluation and was practicing a fair amount of denial. The demystification process may have been particularly effective in this case.

Bypass Strategies

Teachers are apt to vary considerably in their abilities to be creative and effective at circumvention. As inclusionary models of education are implemented and increasing numbers of children with learning disorders are served in regular classrooms, bypass strategies become more essential than ever. Some teachers lament that they have too many children in their classroom to worry about the special requirements of a particular one. At the other end of the spectrum are the many talented teachers who find it natural and professionally gratifying to individualize and make provisions for dysfunctioning students despite having thirty-three others to teach and relate to. Some part of educational planning may need to focus on selecting the teacher who can best tolerate individual differences and is willing and able to adjust expectations, curriculum, and daily procedures to meet the needs of a particular struggling child. Earlier chapters of this book have provided specific examples of bypass strategies. Bypass strategies assume many different forms; one can roughly divide them into *presentation strategies* and *production strategies*. *Presentation bypass strategies* are modifications in the ways teachers present information to affected students, while *production bypass strategies* represent alterations in how the child will produce for the teacher. Table 15-2 depicts these options for circumvention.

Table 15-2. The use of bypass strategies

FORM OF BYPASS	PRESENTATION EXAMPLES	PRODUCTION EXAMPLES
Rate modification	Stopping frequently to review and summarize material	Warning day before calling on student; more time on SAT
Volume reduction	Highlighting textbooks, reducing reading load	Allowing shorter written reports
Complexity adjustment	Giving multiple practical examples of abstract concepts	Giving tests that don't mix types of problems
Prioritization	Emphasizing key points to be learned from lesson	Grading only for content and not spelling
Curriculum changes	Not overloading with subjects that stress language processing	Letting a child print instead of using cursive writing
Special devices	Using reminder cards, wall chart of assignment staging	Using a calculator, word processor, spell check
Alteration of routines	Changing subject schedules, allowing collaborative learning	Permitting breaks, allowing doodling, use of hands
Formal shifts	Showing films, allowing experiential learning	Using oral reports, recognition memory, portfolios
Feedback modifications	Providing encouragement while teaching	Requiring self-rating, private conferences, modified grading

Following are additional guidelines for the use of bypass strategies:

- Be sure that the student understands the bypass strategies. The demystification process should help a child understand the rationale for the accommodation.

- Provide bypass strategies in a way that is not embarrassing and does not imply disrespect or "a writing off" of the child.

- One can "charge a price" (e.g., suggesting a student read an extra book instead of writing a report). Sometimes the student might be asked to perform a service for the school (such as drawing a poster for the front hall) in exchange for a bypass strategy. This often makes students feel much better about the accommodation. Affected children are less apt to feel that they are being treated as invalids.

- A teacher and a student can reach a "secret agreement" regarding accommodations, such as prepared questions, private teacher-to-student signals, and options for format choice (e.g., written or oral reports).

- Whenever possible, let the entire class know that bypass options are available to everyone if they can be justified in individual cases.

- Some teachers may need help in understanding that bypass strategies are not unethical, that it is actually fair to treat different students differently. To treat them all the same is ultimately *unequal treatment*, since it will clearly favor some who have particular ways of learning.

Parents may also need to practice techniques to circumvent a child's difficulties. Realizing that a child has receptive language or short-term memory dysfunctions, a parent may need to repeat or simplify verbal directions. Life at home may need to take into account such specific developmental dysfunctions so as not to cause needless frustration or embarrassment. Professionals may also need to accommodate. A professional who is counseling a child or a family, for example, should be aware that a particular client has difficulty with verbal expression or abstract concepts. Such recognition may alter the kinds of therapeutic modalities selected.

Interventions at the Breakdown Points

Bypassing a weak subskill or neurodevelopmental function is by no means the only option. It is frequently possible to work toward the direct improvement of a deficiency. Interventions at the breakdown points are techniques that can be used at home and in school to repair the weak links in the learning process. *Breakdown points* are stages or components of a task or expected skill with which a particular student has difficulty and which therefore thwart successful performance or mastery. They can be identified through careful task analyses and multifaceted assessment of the student. Table 15-3 describes the common forms of intervention at the breakdown points.

Table 15-3. Types of interventions at the breakdown points

INTERVENTION TYPE	DESCRIPTION/EXAMPLES
Automatization of subskills and/or neurodevelopmental function	Reversion and practice at earlier learning stage; e.g., drill on math facts, sound-symbol associations
Scaffolding	Provision of a structure or component of a task; e.g., use of a report developer or problem-solving plan; use of cloze procedures
Design of tasks that end at the breakdown point	Accentuation of weak component by making it an end in itself; e.g., sorting out word problems by the process demanded, underlining, paraphrasing
Separation of breakdown points	Slowing down, verbalizing at breakdown point; e.g., doing punctuation as a separate, verbalized, decelerated step during writing
Staging	The organization of tasks into manageable steps; e.g., separating brainstorming from actual writing, from application of mechanics, from proofreading
Use of multiple formats	Presentation of material in multiple ways/contexts; e.g., concept mapping, demonstration models, verbal summarization, syntheses
Deployment of strengths and affinities	Enabling student to use strong pathways; e.g., learning math via demonstration models, improving comprehension by reading about special interests, verbalizing nonverbal concepts
Modeling	Demonstrating, having student try, and demonstrating again an operation at the breakdown point; e.g., showing how to use a stepwise approach to a math problem
Strategy use	Showing student a technique to strengthen a breakdown point; e.g., imparting rehearsal and self-testing techniques for studying
Directed retraining	Reteaching specific functions or skills; e.g., helping a student develop a better pencil grip

Some interventions at the breakdown points are best implemented at home, when feasible (see section on "Home Management" later in this chapter). For example, the automatization of subskills (such as arithmetic facts or letter formations) can be difficult to achieve exclusively within school. Nightly practice or drill at home substantially facilitates the attainment of automaticity. Often the school can write a "prescription" for remediation which might then be carried out largely at home.

Many interventions at the breakdown points can be implemented within regular classroom settings. Often an intervention designed to help a particular student with a learning problem can actually benefit all of the other children in the classroom as well. This is because the function or subskill that is causing a child great difficulty is likely to constitute a struggle (albeit somewhat less arduous) for all students.

The therapeutics of developmental dysfunction are controversial, especially in the extent to which we can justify direct efforts to fix a dysfunction. Should children with weak simultaneous processing receive services to improve this function? Should those with sequential organization deficiencies be trained to be better sequencers? Many respected clinicians and investigators question the value of such intervention. Two questions permeate discussions in this controversial area: Can we repair a dysfunction? If so, does it make any real difference? Scientific proof of the efficacy and ultimate value of such intervention does not yet exist. On the other hand, the futility of such intervention has not been demonstrated either. In fact, there may be a tendency to be overly nihilistic in this regard, a propensity toward the proverbial throwing out of the baby with the bath water. First, it is likely that certain dysfunctions are more apt to respond to therapeutic intervention than others. For example, a child with language difficulties may improve with direct intervention from a speech and language therapist. Second, the effectiveness of such treatment may depend on many factors, including the child's motivation, the presence or absence of other areas of developmental dysfunction, the availability of compensatory strengths, and the talents and techniques of the individual educator or therapist. Rigorously controlling these variables in any studies of the efficacy of direct intervention would be difficult. Even if it were demonstrated that it is possible to strengthen substantially a child's sequencing, memory, language, or visual processing, there would remain the question of whether this results in improved performance in reading, writing, arithmetic, and social studies. Such a transfer process may or may not take place. If it did occur, it might be hard to separate the effects of intense caring and attention of an adult from the direct and specific impacts of work on a particular developmental dysfunction.

Given the uncertainties that exist, it is probably justifiable to recommend a middle ground. Intervention should never focus exclusively on the remediation of developmental dysfunctions. On the other hand, specific work in that area can serve to enrich the demystification process, help a child devise strategies to deal with an area of dysfunction, and perhaps even result in some strengthening and transfer. Therefore, I suggest that clinicians direct a modest effort toward strengthening developmental functions in all age groups. In the meantime, research must progress beyond generalizations about this kind of intervention. We must carefully scrutinize specific ways of improving individual developmental functions. It may turn out that direct intervention is effective in improving higher-order cognition, language, sequencing, and attention, but less effective in improving visual processing or memory. Further research is critical.

Enhancing Strengths and Affinities

In many respects the potency of an individual's strengths are more important than the severity of her weaknesses. Consequently, any management plan must make provision for the continuing enhancement of a child's neurodevelopmental assets. If a child reveals strong spatial abilities or mechanical aptitude, the parents and the school should provide opportunities for the child to apply these abilities frequently. At the same time, if possible, the student should receive continuing instruction in that strong domain. A child who is able to sense that his strengths are becoming stronger and more "marketable" to peers and to adults is likely to experience a notable upsurge in self-esteem and motivation. Conversely, it is nothing less than tragic when a child has strengths that are wilting or that can find no application whatsoever until she arrives at adulthood. The plight is especially compelling in a child with learning disorders, one who is experiencing excessive failure and not much success during the school years.

Content affinities are as germane as neurodevelopmental strengths. Many children demonstrate specific foci of interest in certain subjects. An affinity might consist of a love for horses, an interest in cars, a strong orientation toward dance, or a fascination with computers. It is critically important that parents and teachers encourage children to develop passionate interests, to focus consistently and over long periods of their lives on the areas of content with which their minds appear to resonate. Adults should help a child develop his interests into domains of expertise. Substantial knowledge in an area greatly facilitates the growth of neurodevelopmental functions, and it can even bolster academic subskills. It has been shown, for example, that the best way to learn how to read well is to read about something one knows a lot about. Furthermore, expertise in an area of affinity can elevate the self-esteem of a success-deprived student.

Parents, clinicians, and teachers do not select a child's neurodevelopmental strengths and content affinities. It is only through sensitive observation that these highly individualized tendencies can be identified.

Humiliation Protection

For all school-age children the avoidance of public humiliation is perhaps the most compelling preoccupation throughout the school day. The constant threat of embarrassment in front of peers nags them. The fear is apt to be especially profound among children with learning disorders. Concerns about being called on in class, self-consciousness about spelling or handwriting, and a fear of being laughed at in physical education classes or while reading aloud are gnawing apprehensions for many children with neurodevelopmental dysfunctions. Adults need to reassure these students that they will make very effort to help them avoid public exposure of their learning and developmental weaknesses. Teachers should take care to preserve the privacy of these children. Parents should take care not to embarrass a child in front of her friends. Thus, humiliation protection should always be considered explicitly when evolving a plan of management for a child with learning difficulties.

Additional Services

There are many individualized services that can be provided to specific children with learning disorders. Some may be available within a school, while other services may be obtained in the community.

Interventions at the breakdown points may be implemented by tutors or educational therapists who work in areas such as remedial reading or mathematics, organizational skills and study habits, and foreign languages. Trained special educators or tutors exist in most communities and are available to offer such expert intervention. In many cases this takes place exclusively within schools. In other instances, parents seek private tutorial help. This remediation should be closely coordinated with the work of the regular classroom teacher as well as any other special service provided by the school. The precise techniques used by such professionals are the subject of many other texts and are beyond the scope of this one. Knowledge of a child's profile of developmental strengths and weaknesses can help a tutor select appropriate techniques for remediation. Tutorial help enables a child to receive intensive teaching in an area of weakness. At the same time, small-group or one-to-one intervention may minimize the effects of attention deficits and anxiety, allowing the educator to adjust to the learning style, affect, and pace of the individual student.

A vast range of other special services exists for children with developmental dysfunctions. Their availability varies from community to community and even from school to school within a town. However, it is important to be aware of the general options that exist. They include speech and language pathology, occupational therapy, social work, psychotherapy (provided by various types of mental health professionals), social skills training, guidance, vocational counseling, and recreational therapy (specializing in many different modalities). Many of these services may be available within a school system; sometimes a child must go outside the academic setting to receive them.

Medical Therapies. Treating medical predisposing factors or complications can facilitate development and learning. Health needs of academically struggling students must be met. Children with allergies may be predisposed to recurrent sinusitis, asthmatic bronchitis, serious otitis, and frequent absences from school. Any or all of these can complicate learning difficulties. Optimal management of the medical problem is therefore essential. Analogously, a seizure disorder, recurrent abdominal pain, headaches, hearing or vision difficulties, and conditions affecting body image (such as short stature, obesity, delayed puberty, or acne) should receive prompt attention.

Using medications to enhance learning and behavior is an option. Stimulant drugs are most commonly used (see chapter 2) to deal with attention deficits. Specific medications to help other kinds of processing deficiencies and memory disorders have not yet been scientifically substantiated. Major tranquilizers or antidepressant medications, which may be indicated for certain youngsters (Gualtieri, Goldin, and Fahs 1983), should be administered and monitored for therapeutic effects and side effects by a psychiatrist or other physician experienced in psychopharmacology. Table 15-4 provides a summary of currently used medications. However, this compilation is likely be outdated almost as soon as it is published. Therefore, those interested in the role of specific drugs should consult current psychopharmacology journals.

The following principles should always be applied when using medication in the management of a child with learning disorders:

- Drugs should never be prescribed until a child has had a thorough evaluation to rule out associated medical problems, emotional difficulties, and learning problems. The latter, in particular, may have a profound effect on attention. Thus, if a child has language-processing weaknesses, that area of dysfunction could be a major source of his attentional difficulty and/or anxiety. If that student is placed on medication with no awareness of the underlying language difficulty, in the long run academic problems and behavioral reactions to them are apt to worsen, even when the medication may seem to help in certain ways.

- Medication is absolutely never the whole answer. It should be used as one part of an overall management plan for a child. That plan should include other forms of intervention, as elaborated on in this chapter.

- Children on medication require close follow-up from a physician. There should be two or more follow-up visits to discuss the effects of the medication and adjust dosages and the choice of medication as needed. The child should have a complete physical examination during these follow-up visits to ensure there are no side effects or complicating health factors that might be relevant to the medication regime.

- A clinician who places a child on medication needs to be readily accessible to the parents and possibly to the child himself by telephone.

- The child may need to be helped to understand what the medication does and also what it does not do (e.g., "It doesn't make you smarter; it just helps you use your abilities better").

- Parents, too, should be educated in the potential benefits as well as any important side effects of the drug.

- There should always be a plan to wean the child from the medication. There should be periodic drug holidays, during which the child tries to function without medication.

- So-called polypharmacy should be avoided if possible. Children should only take one medication at a time.

- Physicians should try to use the smallest possible effective dose. Levels approaching drug toxicity should definitely be avoided.

- Medication should never be used to make a diagnosis. The fact that a child improves on a drug in no way proves that she has the condition the drug is meant to treat. There are many nonspecific and placebo effects of pharmacological intervention. Similarly, if medication does not seem to work, the child may still have the condition it was intended to treat. For example, it is possible for an individual to have problems with the attention controls that are not responsive to stimulant medication.

- The school should be informed that a child is taking medication (even if no dose is given during school hours). Teachers should know what benefits and side effects need to be monitored over time.

Alternative Controversial Therapies. Not surprisingly, the neurodevelopmental dysfunctions described in this book engender widespread speculation about therapeutic possibilities. Unfortunately, there is a strong tendency for hypotheses to be prematurely accepted as facts (Golden 1984). If a "cure" sounds logical, it is easy to sell to desperate parents and teachers. Placebo effects and the benefits of time may permit a particular panacea to appear more effective than it actually is. Therapies then become highly susceptible to the distortions of anecdotal reports of success and highly inflated claims of efficacy. Some options for remediation have value, but only to a limited extent. Their advocates, with unbridled exuberance, may fail to take into account serious limitations. At times, a particular form of treatment stirs such passion that it attracts a kind of therapeutic cult. Sometimes the response is intensified by the excellent marketing strategies of individuals who have a pecuniary interest in the widespread acceptance of the treatment. Examples of some of the more controversial therapeutic approaches and their characteristics follow (Storm 1983, Silver 1984).

Dietary interventions. Various special diets have been tried on children with attention and learning dysfunctions. The most widely known of these is the Feingold Diet, described in the book *Why Your Child Is Hyperactive* (Feingold 1975). It presents the hypothesis that various food additives and dyes appear to be associated with "hyperactivity." The use of his special diet has been studied extensively (Kinsbourne 1984). Although there appear to be some favorable responders, the overall results have been disappointing for most children. An enormous amount of effort is required to implement the Feingold Diet, and the gains do not appear to be all that great. Furthermore, it appears that many of the children who respond to the diet respond even more favorably to stimulant medication. Nevertheless, such dietary intervention is worthy of further investigation.

Table 15-4. Medications prescribed for children and adolescents with problems affecting learning, behavior, and/or mood

CLASS	DRUG	COMMON INDICATIONS	MOST COMMON SIDE EFFECTS	COMMENTS
Psychostimulants	Methylphenidate (Ritalin)	Attention deficits	Rebound problems; insomnia; loss of appetite	Probably contraindicated in children with seizures and in those with Tourette's syndrome
	Pemoline (Cylert)	Attention deficits	Same as above; also elevated liver enzymes	Long-acting, serum half-life of 12 hours, improvement often very gradual
	Dextroamphetamine (Dexedrine, Dextrostat, Adderall)	Attention deficits	Same as for methylphenidate	Less likely than methylphenidate to lower seizure threshold; may have stronger effect on production controls
Tricyclic antidepressants	Imipramine (Tofranil)	Anxiety/attention deficits	Cardiac arrythmias, headaches, dry mouth, abdominal pain, possible effect on blood pressure	Usually not for use under age 12; serum levels, EKGs helpful for monitoring
	Amitriptyline (Elavil, Endep)	Depression	Same as above	Same as above

Drug	Indication	Side effects	Notes
Desipramine (Norpramin, Pertofrane)	Depression	Same as above	Same as above; reports of sudden cardiac death in the literature
Clomipramine (Anafranil)	Depression, obsessive-compulsive disorder	Seizures, insomnia, dizziness, headache, cardiovascular effects	Not approved under age 10; drug of choice for obsessive-compulsive disorder
Selective serotonin reuptake inhibitors — Fluoxetine (Prozac)	Anxiety, depression, obsessive-compulsive disorder	Nausea, insomnia, excessive sweating, impulsivity, suicidal ideation, mania, hyperactivity	Not approved for use in children and younger adolescents; very long half-life—up to one week or more
Sertraline (Zoloft)	Depression	Same as above	Has 24-hr. elimination half-life; full effect may be delayed weeks
Paroxetine (Paxil)	Depression	Same as above, may be more sedating	Same as above

Table 15-4. (*Continued*)

CLASS	DRUG	COMMON INDICATIONS	MOST COMMON SIDE EFFECTS	COMMENTS
Other antidepressants	Bupropion (Wellbutrin)	Severe depression	Seizures, agitation, insomnia, headache, gastrointestinal symptoms	Only approved for over 18; may have positive effect on memory function
	Venlafaxine (Effexor)	Depression; possibly attention deficits	Hypertension, anxiety, mania, anorexia, weight loss, sedation	Generally used for short-term treatment; not fully established for use under 18 years
Lithium	Lithium Carbonate (Eskalith, Lithobid)	Bipolar illness, manic episodes	Tremor, kidney problems, weight gain, headache, G.I. problems, thyroid disease	Not approved for children under 12; requires close monitoring for side effects
Antianxiety drugs	Benzodiazepines (Valium, Librium, Xanax, Klonopin, etc.)	Anxiety, panic disorders	Oversedation, fatigue, ataxia, confusion, behavioral paradoxical effects, hallucinations, nightmares	Mainly used acutely in older children and adolescents for several weeks, then discontinued; Klonopin may be useful in Tourette syndrome

Class	Drug	Use	Side effects	Comments
Antiepileptic drugs	Carbamazepine (Tegretol)	Seizures—psychomotor or or temporal lobe	Dizziness, fatigue, ataxia, G.I. symptoms	No "official" use for behavior or learning problems
	Valproic acid (Depakene, Depakote)	Seizures—absence spells	Liver failure (potentially fatal), sedation, GI symptoms, blood changes	Same as above
β-Adrenergic blockers	Propanolol (Inderal)	Anxiety, phobias	Hypotension, insomnia, lethargy, G.I. symptoms	Thought to be especially effective in reducing physical signs of anxiety
α-Adrenergic agonists	Clonidine (Catapres)	Behavioral impulsivity, aggression, sleep problems	Hypotension, oversedation	Should be discontinued gradually; may worsen attention deficits while reducing hyperactivity; has short behavioral half-life (3–4 hours)
	Guaneficine (Tenex)	Behavioral impulsivity, aggression	Probably same as above, but not completely studied	Has fewer negative effects on attention than does clonidine
Other	Melatonin	Sleep disorders	Excessive daytime sedation; not used with lupus, autoimmune disorders, lymphoma	Over-the-counter not FDA controlled; vast differences in quality of preparations

Megavitamin treatment for children with learning difficulties has been advocated (Cott 1971). Such orthomolecular therapy has not been substantiated by other investigators. At present, there is no reason to recommend it.

Many parents believe that their child's consumption of carbohydrates or, in particular, sweets, aggravates behavior and/or learning difficulty. The anecdotal evidence is often quite compelling. However, little evidence exists for the efficacy of treatments that restrict consumption of these foods. Carefully controlled studies have not shown carbohydrate challenges to elicit deterioration of behavior; nor have sugar-free diets been found effective (Wolraich 1985). So-called hypoglycemic diets have also been studied. They consist of numerous very small meals containing a modicum of carbohydrates. As yet, there has been no evidence that they are effective.

Hypoallergenic diets are based on the assumption that some children's learning difficulties are a result of specific food allergies. There are strong advocates for this position. However, truly independent, carefully controlled research has not yet shown any effects. Further research is clearly called for. Other dietary interventions have included trace elements. Sometimes these diets are prescribed following allegedly meticulous "biochemical evaluations," which have not been scientifically substantiated. Nor is there evidence in any responsible scientific literature that the replacement of trace elements plays a role in the remediation of learning or behavior difficulties.

Neuromotor programs. Several controversial therapies focus on the neuromotor systems. One of the most widely publicized of these is the effort at patterning advocated by Delacato (1959). In this program children are subjected to extensive exercise, the rebreathing of air, and restriction of fluids, as well as certain dietary constraints, in an effort to rehabilitate their brains. The exercises are particularly taxing, often requiring the assistance of neighbors and other volunteers in the community. The evaluations and treatments are expensive, time-consuming, and potentially liable to induce guilt and feelings of frustration in parents. Various professional groups, including the American Academy of Pediatrics and the American Academy of Cerebral Palsy, have condemned this kind of intervention. Most educational and medical professionals strongly advise parents to avoid this form of intervention.

Optometric training is one of the most controversial of all of the controversial treatments. Some optometrists believe that learning problems are commonly caused or complicated by difficulties with visual function. To overcome these problems, they employ a variety of perceptual motor and visual training techniques (Solan 1981). Various eye muscle exercise are included as well as activities to strengthen visual perception. The American Academy of Pediatrics and the American Academy of Ophthalmology and Otolaryngology have issued statements critical of this approach. Some professionals believe, however, that optometric training may have a limited role with a small group of youngsters whose visual function may aggravate, but not cause, a learning disorder.

Ayres (1972) has advocated a system of treatment called sensory integration therapy. An occupational therapist, she has written books and given courses to train individuals in her discipline to employ a series of exercises and various sensory experiences. The goal is to control sensory input and enhance the capacity of the brain to integrate various pathways, allegedly facilitating better connections between the vestibular (inner ear) and tactile senses as well as between the visual and auditory senses. Thus, it is claimed that vestibular stimulation can even help improve language-processing dysfunctions. It is likely that these claims have been inflated (Polatajko 1985, Carte et al. 1984). An occupational therapist can be a valuable contributor to the rehabilitation of a child with learning problems, especially ones that involve fine or gross motor dysfunctions. However, sensory integration therapy has not been scientifically justified through investigations by unbiased professionals. It may be difficult in this case to distinguish the nonspecific beneficial impacts of support and attention paid to a child from the alleged targeted effects of sensory integration treatment.

Levinson (1981) proposed that some types of "dyslexia" are attributable to problems in the vestibular system and cerebellum. He stated that these types of dyslexia could be corrected by using medications such as meclizine (Antivert), drugs that cure motion sickness. He reported in his book *A Solution to the Riddle Dyslexia* (1981) that reading difficulties can be improved dramatically by his treatment. Unfortunately, Levinson's work, largely personal and anecdotal, has not been replicated by impartial investigators. Moreover, the tendency to combine this treatment with educational intervention, advice, and sometimes stimulant medication makes it especially hard to evaluate Levinson's hypothesis and the specific therapy he offers. Once again, extreme caution is advised.

There exist a multitude of other controversial interventions too numerous to mention here. Included are Irlen lenses for reading problems, biofeedback for attention deficits, and various forms of chiropractic treatment. Like other such treatments, these approaches need to be evaluated rigorously by individual parents, parent groups, and, most importantly, unbiased scientists before they are adopted.

These therapies have been described in more detail in a book for parents entitled *The Misunderstood Child* (Silver 1984), a work that can help sort out therapeutic options.

Evaluating alternative and/or controversial treatments. Professionals confronting the steadily increasing possibilities for treatment have a responsibility to serve as scientific consumer advocates for parents and children. All of those involved in advising families need to be critically and ruthlessly honest in appraising therapies. The uncritical acceptance of a poorly substantiated alternative treatment can result in significant delays in implementing educational intervention, false hopes, and a tendency to ignore significant complications (such as mental health problems). For these reasons, it is essential that all alternative therapies meet stringent criteria of efficacy. The following are some guidelines:

- The efficacy of a treatment must be established scientifically through studies undertaken (at least in part) by individuals who have no particular vested interest in their outcomes. Whenever possible, a therapeutic approach should be studied and validated by individuals who are not in the professional discipline gainfully involved in administering it. Findings should be replicated by more than one investigation and investigative group.

- Studies of treatment effectiveness must conform to standards of good science, including careful attention to criteria for sample selection and diagnosis, use of randomized control groups, and sound statistical analyses of outcomes.

- Scientific studies and their results should be published in peer-reviewed journals (periodicals that accept only articles that have been read by other experts and granted approval).

- Professionals and consumers should be highly skeptical about anecdotal reports of success.

- Professionals and consumers should be suspicious of therapies that claim to be the "whole cure" for any child and equally cautious about treatment programs boasting of applicability to all or most children with a learning problem. For example, there is unlikely to be any single intervention that is likely to help *all* children who have attention deficits. Readers of this book should recognize the complexity of children with developmental dysfunctions as well as the diversity of factors that create and perpetuate their difficulties. Furthermore, the extreme heterogeneity of this population and, therefore, the marked variation in its therapeutic needs should be evident.

- It is important that we not be therapeutically nihilistic. A hypothesis can, indeed, prove to be correct. All those working in this field need to be open and receptive to such occurrences. At the same time, they must avoid premature acceptance and uncritical therapeutic bandwagons.

Counseling. Children who are heavily preoccupied with stresses at home may become intensely preoccupied at school. Regular classroom activities as well as special education services may be limited in their effectiveness because of troublesome competing stimuli. Any home management program therefore needs to include specific help with serious domestic problems. Family problems such as marital discord, alcoholism, economic woes, or serious conflict with siblings must be dealt with. At the very least, children must develop a sense of personal security and alleviate active or latent feelings of guilt. Personal difficulties that students are experiencing outside of school and the family also need to be considered. A drug problem, trouble with neighbors, confusion about psychosexual development, and ostracism by peers are examples of conditions that commonly create internal turmoil, which in turn reduces attention available for learning. Professional counseling should be recommended and implemented when such preoccupations prevail. Even among children who do not appear to have major environmental stresses, significant emotional turmoil can interfere with learning. Those who exhibit identifiable psychiatric symptoms, especially students who are clinically depressed, can benefit from psychotherapy. Referral to a qualified child psychiatrist or child psychologist can be critical. It is essential, however, that a therapist understand fully the nature of the learning difficulties and not assume that the emotional problems or family stresses are the exclusive reasons for a child's academic underachievement. Many child therapists have had little or no training in neurodevelopmental functions and dysfunctions. If a psychotherapist believes that all of the problems are due to emotional factors, while the school and other personnel are contending with the effects of developmental dysfunctions, the parents, the child, and other individuals trying to help are likely to be caught in a web of confusion and conflict. Therefore, it is most useful if the psychotherapist can deal with issues surrounding the ways in which emotional difficulties and family problems are interacting with underlying developmental dysfunctions.

Parents certainly need to participate in the management of children whose behaviors are clearly maladaptive. They can benefit from advice that helps them deal consistently with specific problems. Counseling should be aimed at facilitating communication, developing consistent routines at home, setting realistic expectations, and learning what to anticipate and at what rate change should occur. When behavior problems are severe, parents need ongoing professional help. Sometimes an entire family needs to participate in counseling sessions to develop consistent approaches, frames of reference, and attitudes toward a member with difficult patterns of behavior. In addition to counseling and advice giving, some families can benefit from enrollment in a behavior modification program so that systems of reinforcement can be implemented consistently. The administration of such a program requires the services of a trained behavioral therapist (Hirsch and Russo 1983). In instances in which parents themselves are unable to use advice or implement behavioral therapies, more intensive psychotherapy and various analytic techniques can be tried.

ADDITIONAL SERVICE OPTIONS

Educational Options

Educational services need to serve the best interest of the child. Once appropriate recommendations are assembled, suitable help tailored for the child in school and perhaps in the community must be found and implemented. Physicians, psychologists, and other professionals can serve as case managers, identifying available and appropriate resources. Services within the school include a range of prototypes that are delineated below.

Full-Time Private School. The number of full-time, privately funded programs for children with learning problems is increasing. These schools offer small classes, highly individualized prescriptive programs, and personnel that have been trained to work with students who have special needs. Quality, costs, and content are likely to vary considerably. Some such schools avow special philosophies or particular curricula. Certain programs, for example, may be based on Orton-Gillingham principles. In evaluating the appropriateness of such a school, it is essential to understand its philosophy as well as its teaching methods or orientations. Some schools, for example, may zealously embrace dietary, optometric, and/or motor-training programs. Those making referrals should be cautious about schools that have become enthusiastic about unscientific approaches.

The decision to send a child to a private school is based on many factors. High cost and the lack of a mainstream education may be important deterrents. On the other hand, the expertise and intensity of learning as well as some reduction in peer pressure may justify at least one or two years in a special school, especially when a public school system is unable or unwilling to accommodate the child.

Full-Time Special Classes. In this rapidly vanishing prototype, a child is given full-time instruction in a special classroom, usually in a public school. Sometimes the child is grouped with others who have similar difficulties. Alternatively, a more "generic" model brings together a heterogeneous mix of handicapped children. My colleagues and I have delineated criteria for judging such classes in another publication (Levine, Brooks, and Shonkoff 1980). The following questions should be considered: How severely impaired are other children in the classroom and what is the nature of their difficulties? What types of curriculum materials will be used? What is the size of the class? What is the teacher-student ratio? Are the teachers qualified to teach special education? What are the relative proportions of specific educational intervention and support? Will the child be spending any portion of the day in a regular classroom (e.g., for physical education, recess, industrial arts, and music)? To what extent does the child in question reveal behavior patterns similar to those of other children in the class? If a student has not been acting out or displaying antisocial behaviors and is placed in a class composed of children with behavior difficulties, his or her best interests may be unmet. Parents need to be aware that special classes can stigmatize their child. For example, participants in a class for "the emotionally disturbed" (as well as their parents) may be insidiously labeled. Also, there may be too much emphasis on behavior and too little on learning. Ideally, such classes should not be named.

To place an overactive, inattentive child in a room for emotionally disturbed children often communicates that the primary problem is related to psychodynamic issues (usually at home). Such an implication can be harmful to a child and his family, especially if the youngster's problems are largely constitutional. Moreover, a label can define the mission of the classroom in such a way that the emphasis is on behavioral manageability, with little stress on special education needs (Levine, Brooks, and Shonkoff 1980, p. 156).

Resource Room or Learning Center. This facility, reserved for specialized part-time help for children with learning disorders, is the mainstay of low-severity special education programs. Within the resource room, students are provided help in very small groups (usually fewer than eight). Assistance may take the form of enhancing educational skills, specific help with classroom work or homework assignments, or remediating the youngster's specific developmental dysfunctions. Children's participation in a learning center or resource room may range from one hour a week to several hours per day. For the remainder of the school day (or week), students are mainstreamed in regular classes. It is essential for the resource room teacher to communicate freely and frequently with the regular classroom teacher in order to coordinate their approaches to the child. Some students (especially in late elementary and junior high school) feel stigmatized by having to go to such a facility. Understandably, children who are accused by peers of going to the "mental room" or the "retard center" may offer resistance. Counseling is of paramount importance to help these students save face and to recognize the substantial benefits of such individualized attention. Abusive fellow students may also need counseling.

Tutorial Help. Remedial reading or other forms of specific tutoring from a reading specialist or other educational specialist may be offered, in most cases on a one-to-one or small-group basis. Tutorial help tends to be skill or subject oriented, with an emphasis on continuing practice or drill, and may be offered during the school day or after school.

Full Inclusion. In recent years there has been a growing movement toward the full inclusion of children with learning disorders within regular (so-called mainstream) classes. This normalization model allows these students to feel less stigmatized or different from their peers. Some schools advocate inclusionary programs that preclude any pull-out services at all, while others supplement inclusion with a full range of more individualized services (such as language therapy or tutoring). In all cases, however, an emphasis is placed on the regular education of children with a wide range of dysfunctions and disabilities. When students with neurodevelopmental dysfunctions receive all or most of their education in regular classrooms, it is mandatory that teachers receive training to enable them to understand and manage affected children appropriately. Demystification, bypass strategies, and interventions at the breakdown points become critical within inclusionary service models.

Within the educational setting exists a series of additional options that may be beneficial. Some are controversial but all merit consideration.

Curriculum Choice and Design. It is often necessary to fashion a particular curriculum to match a child's functional profile of strengths and weaknesses. In the upper grades, course selection and levels of difficulty need to be factored in with educational planning. The ultimate aim is to stack the deck to make sure that children will experience success. It is dangerous to overchallenge floundering students. It is generally better to aim lower and foster feelings of effectiveness. Students who begin to get good grades (even in low levels or easy subjects) can become addicted to the taste of mastery, striving thence to achieve over increasingly broad domains.

Exemptions from specific courses need to be considered carefully. Although there are many possibilities, some of the most controversial involve excuses from studying a foreign language. Students who struggle inordinately to master a second language may become pervasively disenchanted with school. The amount of time they spend contending with the foreign language detracts from other subjects and also creates a loss of self-esteem and feelings of hopelessness. Modifications in other areas (such as mathematics and science) may be needed for certain students. Such individualization can be extraordinarily helpful in fostering students' educational careers and preserving their motivation.

So-called magnet schools offer excellent options for some students. These are schools that are organized around a particular theme (often a content area) that can appeal to and motivate certain students who may have affinities consistent with the orientation of the school. A good match between a student and such a school often results in an upsurge of motivation and interest.

The choice of curriculum and selection of courses should always consider students' strengths and interests. Every plan should have in it some subject area(s) in which a student with learning problems is apt to excel and to perceive high relevance. For some who are strong in manual skills and mechanical aptitudes, industrial art programs, automobile mechanics, and other such endeavors can be redemptive. Home economics courses, art classes, and music can be therapeutic, enabling struggling students to find creative outlets and to feel competent.

Grade Retention. In many school systems, especially those with limited special education resources, it is common to retain a child who is not keeping pace with demands. This step should not be taken without careful deliberation. Being kept back can be a major traumatic defeat to a school child. It is often interpreted as punitive. A retained child may dread the jibes of the peer group in the fall and is likely to feel that he has failed a major life challenge, that he or she has disappointed parents and teachers. Decades after having been retained in school, adults frequently report having recurring bad dreams about that horrendous setback. Retention is a major life crisis and has the potential for creating a permanent scar on self-esteem, an enduring sense of inadequacy. Therefore, the decision to retain should never be made lightly. Children are likely to pay a substantial price.

In general, children should not be retained. If necessary, exceptions can be made especially for repeating first grade or staying back in twelfth grade. In between, the consequences are not likely to be worth any advantage. It has never really been shown that retention is helpful in the long run. Whenever possible, it is preferable to promote a student and offer increased services rather than retaining and recapitulating that which is ineffective. Retention may be more justifiable if a child is changing schools and peer groups or moving to a new community.

When retention is absolutely mandatory, the student should be adequately prepared for it. Sensitive counseling should be offered; the child should be helped to deal with either real or perceived ridicule by peers.

A related issue has to do with the delayed start of school for preschool children. An extra year in kindergarten may be justified to reinforce readiness skills, especially for children with attention deficits, language disabilities, and simultaneous processing deficiencies. Significant deficits in social skills may also respond to late entry into first grade. In pondering this move, the word *immaturity* is not helpful. From a clinical standpoint, it is virtually impossible to diagnose "immaturity." By calling a child "immature", we are likely to overlook significant problems such as attention deficits, problems with social skills, or other dysfunctions. A second year in kindergarten or preschool should focus not on oversimplified notions of generalized "immaturity" but rather on highly specific areas of demonstrated deficiency. Therefore, most children appearing to require such delayed entry should undergo careful evaluation prior to their second year in kindergarten (or its equivalent).

Vocational and/or Technical Training.   As students approach secondary school, some of them have a vital need to engage in technical training. Much of their educational program needs to be directed towards this. Certain vocationally relevant components can be blended with a regular school curriculum. Vocational or technical schools offer a more substantial introduction to a career. Such options should be available at an earlier age. Many ten, eleven, and twelve year olds desperately need to do what they are good at—for at least part of each school day. More vigorous programs of this type are a critical need in our society.

Transitional Options.   For high school students who are not quite ready for the job market or college, certain transitional options exist. One of these is a year off, during which the student has time to arrange priorities and to decide on future education. Although this can be a disconcerting option for many parents, in some cases it proves to be a most important formative year. The young adult can be expected to hold a job, albeit in an area unrelated to future career. It might also be appropriate to take one academic course, perhaps at night. During the year, with as little interference as possible from parents, the older adolescent should be allowed to reckon with personal values, ambitions, and self-knowledge. Sometimes counseling from a professional is helpful during this interval. Junior colleges and trade schools of various types can also ease the transition from high school to adult life. They deserve careful exploration by parents and students. Some schools provide a transition year following twelfth grade; it can be another facilitator of the transition to young adulthood.

Summer School.   In certain cases, students may benefit from a summer program to enhance educational skills. Sometimes it is part of the regular school system, and sometimes it has to be sought privately. Summer school should never be served up as a punishment. It should be perceived as an opportunity to catch up or move ahead. It should never occupy an entire summer vacation. Ideally, a good summer program should include recreational activity. For some students with a tenuous grasp on skills, tutoring during summers helps them maintain what they have learned, consolidating their skills and inducing greater automatization. Such tutorial programs should extend through approximately 75 percent of the summer.

An initial period might be free of any formal educational content, consisting instead of recreational pursuits.

Home Management.   It is not unusual for parents to ask what they can do to help. Many of them want very much to be a part of the management team. Their desires to help should be acknowledged and exploited. This section offers some general guidelines for home management.

Often parents want to know whether they should tutor their own children. Sometimes tutorial help from parents is practical and effective, and in other instances it creates a great deal of tension and accomplishes little or nothing. Much depends on the nature of the relationship between the parent and the child. In general, it is best for parents to assist with organization rather than with content. They can provide an appropriate place and schedule for working at home. They can facilitate getting started (an impressive hurdle for some students). They can provide sporadic assistance when a student feels stuck or seriously discouraged during an assignment. Parents must not be too heavy handed in their offers of assistance. Too much interference can be perceived as "hassling" or "bugging." In protest and to avoid unpleasantness, a student may start pretending there is no homework or rushing through it in school as a means of averting the bad scenes each evening. Parents may need counseling to temper extreme emotional involvement in homework while still serving as useful resources.

Home Schooling.   Increasing numbers of parents are assuming prime responsibility for the education of their children. This has been especially common when a child is experiencing academic difficulties, and the parents believe that the school is not responding effectively to her or his needs. Although there are definite drawbacks (such as a child's lack of social experience with peers and "overexposure" to a parent), home schooling can be highly effective. The parent administering the program needs to gain access to the proper curriculum materials, and the child must undergo periodic testing to ensure that sufficient academic progress is being made.

Managing Leisure Time.   Parents have a central role in helping orchestrate activities outside of school. They should avoid overly coercive direction but should help generate ideas, provide access, and encourage follow-through. They can facilitate participation in activities in which their child can feel successful and develop good habits and skills. The careful choice of such pursuits can yield therapeutic dividends. Some examples are:

- *Athletic activities.* Sports in which the child shows an interest and is likely to succeed should be encouraged. Forced participation and possible humiliation before peers must be avoided. Some children, especially those with gross motor lags and attention deficits, may have real trouble coping with team sports. Children with weak attention may have difficulty playing in the outfield on a baseball or football team. They may continuously stray and readily lose interest.

Such children may make excellent catchers in baseball because involvement is required at all times. Every effort must be made to avoid the overly zealous coach who overemphasizes winning, often to the detriment of a struggling child. Certain children should abstain from sports in which there is a great deal of catching and throwing since their visual-spatial abilities might preclude competency. These choices are covered in more detail on page 200.

- *Musical instruments.* Select these to conform to needs and abilities. Children who have problems with social skills may benefit from playing instruments that allow participation in a variety of groups, such as a band or an orchestra. Such children should shy away from solo instruments, such as the piano. Children with low self-esteem may benefit from learning a "macho" musical instrument, such as drums or guitar. Musical instruments that depend heavily on rhythms may be helpful to those who have difficulty with sequential organization. Recurring sets of stimuli in a particular order may help to reinforce sequential organization, although this idea is admittedly speculative and intuitive.

- *Recreational activity in groups.* These activities can enhance self-esteem at the same time that they bolster social skills. Scouting, religious groups, 4-H, and other programs of this type should be chosen carefully. In many communities, children with learning problems benefit from specialized recreational interventions, such as dance therapy, art therapy, and music therapy. Specially trained professionals conduct these programs, which can foster feelings of effectiveness as well as strengthen social skills, attention, and other functions (DeAngelis 1983).

- *Free time and imaginative play.* Children with neurodevelopmental dysfunctions (as well as others) need enough unstructured time to pursue imaginative games and individual (perhaps capricious) ventures. There is real danger in having children grow up with too much structuring by adults. Children who have adult-guided activities every afternoon are deprived of the opportunity to invent and engage in imaginary games, to organize and structure time, and to relax. Children can learn important lessons from each of these kinds of pursuits, skills applicable throughout childhood and adulthood. Boys and girls playing house or doing lessons of one sort or another each day are learning mainly to comply with a set of rigid expectations. What is more appropriate is a good balance between structured and unstructured activity. Children can also choose to use free time to enhance areas of strength, to pursue activities that they really enjoy, and to do so independently. Parents can assist only by facilitating the process, providing the necessary materials and appropriate amounts of free time.

Additional Services. Key individuals in school offer services closely coordinated with the work of special educators and regular classroom teachers to help support and remediate children with learning disorders. The availability and case loads of such individuals are apt to vary considerably from school to school. In general, the following school professionals are often present and their potential contributions to a child merit consideration:

School psychologists. The school psychologist commonly plays a pivotal role in the school and in the implementation of Public Law 94-142 as well as the Individuals with Disabilities Act. She or he is an essential part of the diagnostic process. In addition, the school psychologist in some settings is able to offer school-based counseling as well as ongoing consultation to regular classroom teachers. Under inclusion, school psychologists have a vital role to play in advising and supporting a school's faculty. A well-trained school psychologist should be sensitive to both neurodevelopmental and crucial environmental, social, cultural, and academic issues in the life of a child.

School nurses. School nurses can occupy a valuable position in the assessment and management processes by helping coordinate various medical therapies. They can serve as links between the school and the children's primary care or consulting physicians. In some settings, school nurses are becoming more involved in neurodevelopmental assessment. They can be particularly helpful when a child with learning difficulties also has somatic concerns such as headaches, abdominal pain, obesity, or asthma. In some schools, the school nurse works closely with the school physician to provide medical consultation and to conduct screening programs of various types. In many areas, however, budgetary constraints have resulted in significant reductions in such services. In those communities with strong school health programs (either in the schools themselves or as part of the public health department), parents, teachers, and children can find such consultation and liaison useful.

Guidance counselors. Many guidance counselors in school are especially sensitive to issues surrounding a child's everyday life in the class and on the playground. They can offer important advice to students who are having academic, behavior, and/or social troubles. They can also advise on course selection and can inform teachers about the emotional issues that confront disappointing students.

School social workers. Many schools employ social workers to assist in evaluating and managing children who are having learning and behavior problems. The school social worker can be an indispensable link between teachers and a child's family. He or she can visit the home to evaluate the child's environment and to make suggestions for home management. Some school social workers (and guidance counselors) are adept at offering group therapy for children with behavior problems. Some such groups are directed toward training in social skills for youngsters who are experiencing difficulties with peer interactions.

Speech and language therapists. Many schools now employ professionals with expertise in the field of speech and language pathology. They can offer a wide range of therapeutic options, including training for children with articulation difficulties or for those with processing and other production problems. School personnel and parents must be aware that speech therapists are not necessarily trained as language therapists. They may not have very much experience in dealing, for example, with early adolescents who have trouble with the appreciation of syntax and are deficient in their metalinguistic awareness. Therefore, the qualifications, experience, and orientation of a particular speech and language pathologist must be taken into consideration before services are recommended.

Other potentially useful individuals. Within any school there may be certain staff members who are especially sensitive to the life scenarios of disappointing children. A physical education, woodworking, art, music, or drama teacher may play a special, even heroic, role in the life of a child whose only real success exists in the particular specialty of that person. Sometimes these teachers conduct special programs for children who need help or need to experience mastery in their areas. For example, many schools are now offering adaptive physical education for children with gross motor delays (Wiseman 1982). A coach or teacher can become an important confidant and mentor, helping to sustain the child's self-esteem by offering positive reinforcement and opportunities to experience mastery. The principal and/or the assistant principal can represent a substantial force in the life of a child with learning problems. Such an individual is likely to be respected or even revered by the student. He or she can be of great help in forming a close supportive relationship with that child, offering encouragement and sensitivity while vigorously supporting the efforts of special educators and regular classroom teachers. The principal or headmaster can play a major role in shaping an entire faculty's attitudes about children who have learning problems.

Many children with learning disorders benefit enormously from being asked to perform a special service for the school. Such privileged responsibilities merit serious consideration in the planning of a child's educational experience. For example, a high school student with learning difficulties may derive high levels of gratification and status from taking charge of the lighting and/or audio at a school play.

Legal Entitlements

The Individuals with Disabilities Education Act (IDEA) has been enacted and re-authorized several times with various modifications. This act has great implications for children with learning and attentional difficulties. The details of this law have been delineated in chapter 14.

Treatment Recommendations from Independent Evaluations. An outside evaluator, a professional or team that is independent from the public school system, is obligated to make recommendations that cover the multiple needs of a child. In many cases this can best be done by a diagnostic team rather than an individual, who may not have knowledge over a wide range of issues. Independent evaluators need to compile a multifaceted functional profile of a child, accounting for strengths, weaknesses, and other relevant characteristics and life circumstances as outlined in chapter 14. From these formulations, specific recommendations can be derived; however, such recommendations need not carry legal weight. The school is not obligated to implement the suggestions of an independent evaluator. However, in the event of a hearing or mediation, the recommendations themselves constitute specific needs for which one can advocate. Awareness of the law, good diplomacy, and intellectual integrity are the cornerstones of sound independent evaluations.

Samples of the kinds of recommendations that an independent evaluator might make are found in figure 15-2. They cover such management issues as the specific educational prototype, bypass strategies, the need for additional services, and provisions for follow-up and monitoring. No report can contain a comprehensive management program; instead there should be key suggestions as well as a sampling of the kinds of techniques that might be beneficial.

Early Intervention and Prevention

It is unclear whether we can prevent learning disorders. However, there is reason to believe that we can minimize the impacts of a wide range of dysfunctions and other risk factors, as discussed in chapter 13, through early recognition and prompt management.

Any efforts at early education or early intervention raise one central issue: Is change really possible? If a particular child harbors a series of risk factors for learning difficulty, does early exposure to educational input prevent or minimize the ultimate problems? Much of the research in this area has focused on the ability of such programs to alter the intelligence quotients of young children. Ramey, Yeates, and Short (1984) did in fact show that IQ could be raised as a result of early education for economically disadvantaged children. This suggests the existence of some "plasticity" or malleability in the young human nervous system. McCall (1981) argued that mental development is "canalized," that is, during certain periods (especially the first two years of life) strong species-specific tendencies prevail, so that there is a more or less biologically determined course of mental development. Moreover, so-called self-righting tendencies during early infancy allow substantial resistance to stress. During the toddler years, there is greater opportunity to alter developmental functions. Presumably, this is when early intervention is particularly important. The toddler and preschool years may be critical periods in which to take advantage of the plasticity of intellectual development prior to the onset of significant academic problems, loss of motivation, and secondary maladaptation of behavior. In addition to children from economically disadvantaged circumstances, preschoolers with signs of language delays, motor incoordination, and other apparent dysfunctions will likely benefit from early exposure to structured education experience.

Not all preschool children with evident developmental dysfunctions are likely to gain dramatically from a preschool experience. In a recent study, Palfrey et al. (1985) found that young children with early symptoms of attention deficit were the most likely to show little or no improvement in behavioral function as a result of a preschool program. On the other hand, substantial gains were experienced by those with language delays, health problems, and motor deficiencies.

The Brookline Early Education Project was a landmark demonstration model designed to evaluate the efficacy of entering all children in public school six months before birth. "Students" participating in this project received periodic health and extensive developmental assessment. Their parents were taught to enhance relevant emerging developmental functions at specific ages during infancy and the preschool years. Data generated within this project showed that these early life interventions had lasting cognitive benefits for the children involved (Hauser-Cram et al. 1991).

We have every reason to believe that if developmental dysfunctions are identified early, intensive intervention may minimize their damaging effects. The ultimate goal is not necessarily to eliminate dysfunction but rather to soften its impact. Intensive social programs, language enrichment, and other forms of early intervention are especially valuable for children found to be delayed developmentally as well as for those who display temperament and/or behavior difficulties. Currently under investigation is the possibility that ongoing developmental surveillance and service may be helpful to babies and toddlers who have endured high-risk births. Graduates of newborn intensive care units, for example, bear close watching, as do very small premature infants. Earliest intervention can consist of helping parents offer cognitive and language stimulation to their young children. Home visits as well as educational programs promote the process. Specialized day care or nursery school curricula can provide intensified developmental training for toddlers and preschoolers. Future research needs to investigate the efficacy of early detection and intervention as well as to continue to scrutinize its ultimate usefulness. Early results are encouraging.

Learning Disorders in College

Having considered the complexities of early intervention, it is equally appropriate to examine management issues as they relate to university undergraduates. Learning disorders commonly follow students into college, where neurodevelopmental dysfunctions present significant challenges to the young adult as well to the institution of higher learning (Cox and Klas 1996). Many colleges and universities have tried to develop programs to help affected students. Their success has been variable.

The following points are relevant to the management of college students with learning disorders:

- It is common for freshmen with learning difficulties to try to deny their problems, to make believe they have completely overcome their learning difficulties. Frequently, they are able to "pull this off" during the first few months of college. All too commonly, however, they unknowingly fall behind and become overwhelmed later in the year. The first year of college can be a formidable barrier for these students, especially when they conceal their problems and engage in what has been termed the "hide out" stage (Allard et al. 1987), a period during which they try to camouflage their dysfunctions. According to Allard et al., "Using long-established avoidance patterns, these students enter the hide out phase of their college education, generally a short-lived period during which they attend classes, carry books, and exhibit behavior suggesting 'no problem.' "

Betsy

1. Betsy would benefit from tutoring once or twice a week to develop problem-solving and organizational skills and reading comprehension abilities.

2. To improve reading comprehension, she might be preassigned specific questions to read for: these questions should require interpretation of information (drawing conclusions, making inferences) and defining vocabulary phrases.

3. Listening comprehension could be developed in a similar manner by preassigning her specific questions to answer after listening to a passage.

4. Betsy could also be given a series of passages on a similar topic to read and then summarize.

5. To improved unaided recall of material, Betsy might read a passage, retell it onto a tape recorder, and then listen to the tape and check it against the passage. She might chart her progress in the number of facts she can recall in the correct order.

6. Use of a mapping strategy might assist with organizing and summarizing material. After listening to or reading material, Betsy should jot down everything she can remember. She would then categorize the details according to common concepts. The next step would be to order the categories, and finally, to summarize the material. This process can be done effectively as a group activity.

7. To develop problem-solving and analysis strategies in mathematics, Betsy could be asked to act as a teacher and explain how to do problems. She should also be given exercises in estimating answers; this also could be done as a group activity.

8. To expand her expressive language and organizational skills, Betsy might collect clippings, pictures, and materials on an area of particular interest. She could then dictate onto a tape or do an oral or written report on her collection. The mapping strategy might be useful for this.

9. It will very important for Betsy to develop some areas of interest to differentiate her from her siblings. She should participate in sports, musical activities, or hobbies that differ from those of her older sister, in particular. Every effort should be made to allow her to perform in different ways and to make it clear to her that she need not replicate the activities of other family members. The emphasis should be on how important it is for different children in the same family to differ from each other.

10. Betsy could benefit from counseling. This should be very directive, aimed at helping her to develop her social skills at the same time that it assists her in acquiring better insight into her personal strengths and weaknesses. Attempts should be made to bolster her self-esteem. There should be some opportunity for play and role-playing experiences, aimed at teaching her strategies for monitoring her feelings and behavior to avoid unnecessary interpersonal conflict. At the same time, she should practice compiling strategies for resolving conflicts when they do arise. In other words, Betsy needs to be taught coping skills. It is possible that this counseling could be combined with some cognitive therapy and tutoring. This has been discussed with Betsy's parents.

11. At this time, we are unable to document primary attention deficits. It is likely that much of her inattention is secondary to anxiety as well as her language inefficiencies and organizational problems. On the other hand, it would be a good idea to monitor her progress. If, in the future, she is having problems with concentration and attention to detail, some consideration can be given to the use of stimulant medications.

12. It is very important that Betsy's teachers be aware of the difficulties she is experiencing. In her regular classes, she should be given preferential seating. Whenever possible, she should be given the opportunity to exhibit strengths to her classmates. Her artistic capacities should be exploited both at home and school. She could benefit from art lessons and an opportunity to exhibit her talents.

13. We would be very interested in monitoring Betsy's progress. She should be seen for follow-up visits approximately twice each year. At each visit, follow-up psychoeducational testing will be performed. We would be happy to participate in future course selection and education planning for her. As questions arise, Dr. Smith can be reached during his call hour (from 7 to 8 A.M.).

Figure 15-2. Examples of recommendations derived from the independent evaluation*

Mark

1. During the coming academic year, Mark would benefit from several hours per week of tutorial support. This could be provided in his school's resource room or by a tutor in the community. Study skills and organizational strategies within the context of reading and writing in the content areas should be emphasized. Individual tutoring over the summer months might also be helpful.

2. Mark should be taught to monitor his comprehension as he reads. The following procedures might facilitate this. His teacher could provide information at individual points to highlight important ideas (e.g., "page 1, paragraph 2. Pay special attention to this section. Why do you think Will acted in this fashion? We will discuss your ideas later."). He could also be given a partially completed outline to fill out while he is reading. In addition, drawing attention to key words such as *who, what, when, where*, and *why* might be helpful.

3. Mark should also work on summarizing or restating what he has read. This might help develop his reading recall as well as enhance his planning and organizational skills. For example, Mark might be given a passage to read (in a content area) and asked to number and underline major events as they occur. He could then put what he has underlined on paper and use this to help him summarize the passage either orally or in writing.

4. Mark should work on developing his composition-writing skills. It might be helpful if his assignments were broken down into specific stages or steps. These might include making notes or listing key ideas, developing a plan and expanding this into an outline, writing a first draft (every other line, in pencil), proofreading and editing, and producing a final copy. He should be encouraged to use introductions, conclusions, and connecting words or phrases.

5. Mark should work on developing effective strategies for problem solving. Using the right method (even in preference to getting the correct answer) should be stressed. Whenever possible, he should be required to articulate in advance his plan for solving a math problem, writing a paragraph, studying for an examination, etc.

6. Mark should receive special help with his spelling. Rules, generalizations, and word families should be stressed. Games and various mnemonic devices might be helpful for reviewing difficult, irregularly spelled words. Mark should be encouraged to look for and recognize spelling mistakes and to see if he can correct them on his own.

7. Mark should have an opportunity to study topics of high motivational interest, in depth and over time. He might read related books or articles, write short essays, and draw pictures or diagrams.

8. Getting Mark more actively involved in his work, making him aware of his own style, and making him more time conscious might reduce his inefficiency and keep him focused. Mark could be given a stopwatch and asked to time various activities in which he is involved. At first, he could practice completing simple assignments within a specified period of time. As his speed increases, longer or more complicated assignments could be tried. Mark might chart his performance on graph paper. In this way, he could see himself performing at increasingly faster rates.

9. Mark would benefit from a structured weight loss program. A behavioral psychologist could be helpful to him. He is obviously motivated to lose weight but will need some consistent structured follow-up.

10. Serious consideration should be given to the use of stimulant medication to help Mark focus more effectively in the classroom. This has been discussed with his parents and will be instituted, in all likelihood, at the start of the coming school year.

11. Mark could benefit from participation in certain activities in which he can become proficient. It is suggested that he master one sport well. His musical and artistic talents also need to be exploited. In all of these enterprises, he needs to be encouraged to focus and specialize. He should be discouraged from quitting or "dabbling." It is important that Mark experience gratification by achieving success in an area which he has explored in depth and over time.

12. Mark's teachers need to be aware of his difficulties with sustained listening. He should be given preferential seating as close to the teacher as possible. There should be some private manner of signaling him when he is obviously "tuned out." In addition, Mark needs to be encouraged to be less impulsive in his approach to tasks. There needs to be more emphasis on advanced planning and organization. Mark also needs to be helped to engage in more self-monitoring or proofreading activity.

13. Dr. Smith would be interested in following Mark's progress over the coming years. Mark should return for a follow-up visit in the fall. At that time, his management can be discussed further and a program of medication and monitoring instituted. Follow-up educational testing should take place in six months. In the meantime, as questions arise, Dr. Smith can be reached during his call hour (7 to 8 A.M.).

*These recommendations pertain to the two children whose formulations were depicted in figure 14-6.

- Many students have learning problems that may not qualify them for services in college. Their difficulties with attention, organization, or language, for example, may not create a discrepancy on IQ and achievement testing that would allow them to be "certified as learning-disabled." The discrepancy formulas, in fact, make little sense in this age group.

- Colleges need to be made aware of the fact that a student can "develop" a learning disorder for the first time during college. An individual may have succeeded in high school but encounter problems when confronted with the unique demands of certain college courses or faculty members.

- Undergraduates with attention deficits appear to have some of their greatest difficulty dealing with time management. There is simply too much time in college. These students may have problems utilizing time effectively. It can be hard for them to allocate time, to stage term papers and other projects, to schedule extracurricular activities, and to arrive at classes on time. Additionally, they may be susceptible to extreme social distractibility, difficulty resisting temptations (e.g., alcohol), hedonism, and problems regulating their sleep patterns.

- Dormitories (or fraternity/sorority houses) can be especially distracting for students with attention deficits. Quieter living arrangements may be needed.

- Some college students with attention deficits can benefit from taking psychostimulants. They should be followed closely and should not be allowed to self-medicate, i.e., to take a pill whenever they think they need it. They should either be on the medication all the time or off it all the time. Otherwise, the medication becomes a way of coping with stressful events or challenges, which is not a good precedent to set for adult life. Clinicians need to be aware of the potential for abuse when medication is prescribed for college students. The drugs should be dispensed with care to prevent their broad distribution on a campus.

- Undergraduates with reading difficulties in college tend to have fewer problems with phonological awareness and decoding than do younger students. However, they often suffer severe difficulties at a semantic level during reading. They are prone to serious deficiencies deriving and retaining sufficient meaning from the new and often technical words they encounter in textbooks and primary sources. They need help in semantic mapping (pp. 183–84) and in maintaining personal dictionaries of difficult but key words in each class they take.

- Many students with learning problems lack the metamemory needed to study for tests. They can benefit from specific forms of assistance aimed at developing a stepwise approach to preparation for examinations. They also need training in note taking and in the use of devices that can help bypass their weaknesses; such equipment includes calculators, laptop computers, personal organizers, and tape recorders).

- Undergraduates with learning disorders desperately need informed advisors or mentors who can guide them through course selection, accommodations (e.g., more time on examinations), the choice of fields of concentration, and possible waivers of requirements. These individuals need to be well versed in learning disorders, and they should be aware of students' individual strengths and affinities. Perhaps more than anything else, advisors in college should be advising undergraduates on how to enhance their strengths and deepen their affinities.

- Colleges need to show some flexibility with respect to required courses. These students may absolutely require certain waivers (such as exemption from a foreign language). However, under all circumstances, students who have received a waiver should have to substitute new requirements that are equally (if not more) rigorous and demanding of time and work output. Again, the preservation of accountability is essential.

- College policy makers need to be aware that many of these students possess minds that are highly specialized (as opposed to "well rounded"). The sooner they can pursue their specialties, the more effective and rewarding their college educations will be.

- Writing difficulties plague many of these undergraduates. They need to become very proficient at word processing. Stepwise approaches to writing need to be taught. The interactions between time management and long-term writing assignments need to be amply demonstrated and practiced.

- Faculties need to be aware that many college students with learning disorders have problems not so much with their basic skills but with the understanding of content, i.e., of ideas, concepts, and processes that are being taught. Students seeking help from faculty or from tutors may need specific assistance in grasping ideas. Such assistance can include diagramming or mapping as well as providing additional examples or prototypes of the ideas. Many of these students can learn best by studying carefully an example of an idea rather than the idea itself. Thus, it might be preferable to learn why the United States is considered a democracy than to study the features of a democracy.

- Students with neurodevelopmental dysfunctions may have problems deriving sufficient meaning from primary sources (original works). They might be more successful if they can first read summaries or overviews of these sources. A student may have problems understanding a treatise by John Stuart Mill without first reading a chapter in a philosophy textbook that summarizes Mill's views, possibly comparing and contrasting him with other thinkers.

- Colleges should offer freshman a course in cognition and learning. The course should be more than a rendering of study skills; it should help students understand how learning works. They should study functions such as memory, attention, problem solving, and language, and learn ways to apply and strengthen these capacities in college course work.

- Students with learning disorders should enter into special written contracts with their schools and/or their individual professors. These contracts should allow for some accommodations while holding students accountable for substantial work output. Alternative assignments and evaluation procedures should be offered. However, in all circumstances these students should be expected to put forth as much work output (if not more) as their classmates.

- College professors must learn about learning disorders. Every university should sponsor workshops to teach their faculty about neurodevelopmental function and dysfunction as it pertains to college students. It has been said that the learning difficulties of college students tend to be "invisible" (Cox and Klas 1996). That is, they are often inapparent to the faculty. With greater education of college professors, fewer students are likely to fall through the cracks and drop out, or experience needless frustration and misunderstanding.

- A student's "readiness for college" is worthy of serious consideration. There are many adolescents who simply are not ready to be undergraduates at age eighteen. Alternative transitional experiences should be explored for them.

The Education of Teachers

This chapter has emphasized the importance of flexibility and sophisticated intervention within regular classrooms. To make this a reality, teachers need excellent training programs so that they may understand the array of neurodevelopmental functions and the roles they play in learning and in academic productivity. At the same time, they must be taught about the phenomenology of neurodevelopmental dysfunction—its observation in the classroom and its optimal management. With grants from the Geraldine R. Dodge Foundation and the federal Department of Education, we established a project called SCHOOLS ATTUNED. In this program, teachers undergo three years of professional development education, during which they learn about the neurodevelopmental constructs and the functions within them. They learn to work with observation tools (*The Views Attuned*), so that they can make systematic observations of children in the classroom, integrate their findings with those of parents, clinicians, and the children themselves, and then formulate regular classroom management plans. The project helps teachers discover the particular neurodevelopmental functions that are keys to success in their particular classrooms. SCHOOLS ATTUNED also includes group demystification activities for students. It makes use of the nonlabeling approach espoused in this book and stresses the management of strengths as well as dysfunctions. The project has clear implications not just for helping children with problematic learning but for the education of all children. SCHOOLS ATTUNED has been ongoing since 1987 and has achieved very positive results. Efforts are now underway to develop curriculum materials for teacher education at a preservice level.

The Role of Professional Organizations

Children with learning disorders and their parents run the risk of intellectual and emotional isolation. These children need to know about others with similar problems. Their parents often need information about learning disorders, services, and legal rights. They also benefit from sharing perspectives and experiences with other parents. Several excellent national organizations foster communication among professionals, among parents and professionals, and among parents. These organizations not only help identify available services but also provide advocacy and disseminate information. Included are The National Center for Learning Disabilities (NCLD), The Association for Children and Adults with Learning Disabilities (ACLD), CHADD (Children and Adults with Attention Deficit Disorders) and the Orton Dyslexia Society. More recently we have established our own nonprofit institute, All Kinds of Minds, to develop and disseminate products to educate and serve parents, teachers, clinicians, and affected children. It is important for professionals and parents to join in supporting and guiding the work of such groups while benefiting from their meetings and publications.

Appendix

A Guide to Tests
Commonly Used
in the Evaluation
of Children with
Learning Disorders

COMMON TERMINOLOGY USED IN DESCRIBING TESTS AND REPORTING RESULTS

Achievement test: a test that measures certain skills or information; usually used to measure performance in school subjects.

Age equivalent: age (years and months) at which a performance would be average relative to the norming sample.

Composite score: a combination of scores usually added together; sometimes scores used in the calculation are weighted to indicate importance.

Criterion-referenced test: a test that measures a person's performance in terms of mastery of a specific skill. Scores reflect what student knows or can do rather than comparing performance to some reference group or normative population.

Diagnostic test: a test used to identify and analyze specific strengths or weaknesses.

Full scale intelligence quotient (FSIQ): a standard score with a mean of 100 and a standard deviation of 15, measuring overall reasoning ability. This is based on a composite of verbal and performance scores but is not an average.

Grade equivalent: grade (years and months) at which a performance would be average relative to the norming sample. Grade equivalents are expressed in years and tenths of years (9 months plus the summer). A grade equivalent of 5.3 means fifth grade, third month.

Grade norms: the test score distribution of a population's performance in a given grade.

Group test: a test administered to more than one individual at a time. Standardized group tests are usually normed and provide percentile ranks, stanines, standard or scaled scores, and grade equivalents.

Independent school norms (ISN): percentile for independent (i.e., private) schools.

Intelligence quotient (IQ): the measure of an individual's cognitive abilities as assessed by performance on standardized tests. It is most frequently expressed as a standard score with a mean of 100 and a standard deviation of 15 or 16. The terms *average* or *normal* tend to be used for scores between 90 and 109.

Individual test: a test administered to one individual at a time.

Local percentile (LP): percentage of students of like grade or age in the community or region scoring below index child.

Mental age (MA): the score that corresponds to the highest year level that a student successfully completes on a test. For example, if in the standardized sample, seven year olds score a 75 on the test, and a ten-year-old student receives a score of 75, his mental age would be recorded as seven years old.

National percentile (NP): percentage of students of like grade or age in the country scoring below index child.

Nonverbal test: a test where no words are used in an item or needed to respond to it.

Norm-referenced test: one in which a person's score is compared to a specific population. The adequacy of the norms depends on the representativeness of the norm sample (factors such as geography, sex, race, socioeconomic status, community size, intelligence, grade, and date), on the size of the sample, and on the relevance of the norms to the purpose of the tests and the individual being tested.

Percentile: a score that represents the percentage of cases in a distribution that fall at or below the individual's score. For example, scoring in the 55th percentile can be interpreted to mean that 55 percent of the population scored below that individual. The score does not reflect the number of correct or incorrect responses.

Performance intelligence quotient (PIQ): a standard score with a mean of 100 and a standard deviation of 15, measuring nonverbal reasoning (reasoning abilities not dependent on language) and most often involving visual-spatial and visual-motor abilities.

Performance test: a test that requires the individual to perform some motor or manual task.

Raw score: the total number of points awarded for responses to test items. This is often the same as the number of items answered correctly; however, some tests include weighted items in which the number of points awarded for a response is determined by the quality of the response, and other tests may subtract points for incorrect responses.

Recall item: an item on a test that requires the individual to supply the answer from memory, such as a fill-in-the-blank or open-ended question.

Recognition item: an item on a test that requires the individual to identify or select the correct answer from a number of choices, such as a multiple-choice question.

Reliability: the extent to which test results are consistent and not subject to random error.

Scaled score: a type of standard score, most often reported for subtests.

Standard deviation: a measure of the variability of scores, it is the square root of the variance. In a normal distribution, two-thirds of the scores are within one standard deviation of the mean.

Standardized test: an individual or group test that measures an individual's performance as compared to a similar population as the individuals taking the test. Standardized tests are usually normed on a specified population, provide percentile ranks, stanines, standard or scaled scores, and grade equivalents, and show evidence of reliability and validity.

Standard scores: transformed raw scores that have the same mean (average score; often designated by *X* or *M*) and standard deviation (the measurement unit of variability in a set of scores; often designated by *s.d.*). For a test with a mean standard score of 100 and a standard deviation of 15, a performance score of 100 would be average, and scores ranging between 85 and 115 would fall within the average range. The term *quotient* is often substituted for *standard score.*

Stanine: a standard score scale that divides performance into sections and indicates an individual's relative performance by assigning it a rating from 1 to 9, with a mean of 5 and standard deviation of 2.

Validity: the extent to which a test measures what it claims to measure.

Verbal intelligence quotient (VIQ): a standard score with a mean of 100 and a standard deviation of 15, measuring verbal reasoning ability (reasoning involving words and language).

Z-scores: scores with a mean of zero and a standard deviation of one. Z-scores reflect how many standard deviations above or below the mean an individual's score is.

The preferred tests cited for each of the following domains represent the opinion of the author based on review of the literature, examination of test manuals and materials, and several years of clinical experience.

GROUP-ADMINISTERED ACHIEVEMENT TESTS

Group achievement tests have different levels for different grades in school. The lower levels tend to assess basic skills (reading, arithmetic, and spelling), while the upper levels may include applied skills (reference skills, math application) and content areas (social studies and sciences). Most skills are assessed through a multiple-choice format. A list of the most commonly used tests follows, along with a table indicating the skills evaluated by each test. All of the tests listed are well normed and have adequate reliability and validity. Scores usually provided are percentile ranks, stanines, standard or scaled scores, and grade equivalents. Most standardized tests listed are machine scorable and may provide elaborate printouts of skills mastered and not mastered. With this feature, they make some claim to be diagnostic and helpful in writing Individual Educational Programs (IEPs); however, group administration and machine scoring do not allow observation and analysis of student performance and methodology. All that can be determined is a general area of weakness.

California Achievement Tests (CAT-5), 1993
Publisher: CTB/Macmillan/McGraw Hill, 20 Ryan Ranch Road, Monterey, CA 93940-5703.
Ages: Grades K to 12

ERB Comprehensive Testing Program III (ERB), 1992
Publisher: Educational Records Bureau, Educational Testing Service, Princeton, NJ 08541.
Ages: Grades 1 to 12

The *ERB* also includes norms for independent (private) schools and, for grades 3.5 to 12, a verbal, quantitative, and total aptitude score.

Iowa Test of Basic Skills (ITBS), 1993
Publisher: Riverside Publishing Company, 8420 Bryn Mawr Avenue, Chicago, IL 60631.
Ages: Grades K to 9

Metropolitan Achievement Tests (MAT-7), 1992
Publisher: Psychological Corp., 555 Academic Court, San Antonio, TX 78204-2498.
Ages: Grades K to 12

SRA Achievement Series (SRA), 1978
Publisher: Science Research Associates, 155 North Wacker Avenue, Chicago, IL 60606.
Ages: Grades K to 12

Stanford Achievement Test Series (STAN-8), 1991
Publisher: Psychological Corp., 555 Academic Court, San Antonio TX 78204-2498.
Ages: Grades K to 9

Test of Achievement and Proficiency (TAP), 1993, an extension into higher grades of the *Iowa Test of Basic Skills*
Publisher: Riverside Publishing Company, 8420 Bryn Mawr Avenue, Chicago, IL 60631.
Ages: Grades 9 to 12

Description of Subtests for Group-Administered Achievement Tests

Reading

Visual Discrimination: matching shapes and letters.

Auditory Discrimination: identifying whether two words or letter sounds are alike or different.

Letters and Sounds: matching upper- and lowercase letters, letter recognition, identifying single letter sounds at the beginning and end of words, and matching sound with letter.

Word Analysis: decoding word meaning using rules governing letter-sound relationships (phonics) and structural elements (prefix, suffix, root words, compound words, contractions, and syllables).

Listening Comprehension: understanding material read aloud by selecting an appropriate picture, word, or sentence.

Vocabulary: understanding the meaning of words by identifying pictures, synonyms, antonyms, selecting an appropriate definition, and using context clues to identify words with multiple meanings. The stimulus may be given orally by the examiner or read by the student.

Reading Comprehension: understanding the meaning of written material—locating the main idea and facts, making inferences, and evaluating perspective and intent.

Words: associating words with pictures.

Sentences: associating sentences with pictures.

Stories/Passages: answering questions (multiple-choice) about various forms of written material (e.g., story, fact, advertisement, poetry).

Spelling

Recognition of the correct spelling of words either in written context (proof-reading) or by selecting one of several possibilities in response to a word dictated by the examiner.

Language

Mechanics: knowledge of rules governing capitalization, punctuation, word usage, sentence structure, and organization of written expression.

Reference Skills: using book elements (index, table of contents, title page), dictionaries, maps, graphs, card catalogs, and other reference materials.

Written Expression: expressing ideas in writing, including letters and themes; organization of ideas, format, and writing mechanics are included in assessing performance.

Mathematics

Concepts: number recognition, counting, sets, place value, basic concepts, and numerical equivalences (e.g., fraction, decimal, percentage).

Computation: addition, subtraction, multiplication, and division with whole numbers, decimals, and fractions; algebra and geometry.

Applications: using number skills to solve word problems and in practical contexts—time, money, and measurement.

Social Studies

Knowledge of basic concepts of political science, geography, sociology, economics, and history.

Science

Understanding facts and basic concepts in the biological and physical sciences and basic skills of scientific inquiry.

SKILLS ASSESSED BY TEST AND GRADE LEVEL

	CAT	ERB	ITBS	MAT	SRA	STAN	TAP
Reading							
Visual Discrimination	K			K–1.5	K–1		
Auditory Discrimination	K		K–2.5	K–1			
Letters and Sounds	K			K–1.5	K–2	K–2	
Word Analysis	1–3	1–3	K–3.5			1.5–7	
Listening Comprehension	K	1–3	K–3.5	K–4	K–2	K–9	
Vocabulary	1–12	3.5–12	K–9	1–9	1–12	1.5–9	
Reading Comprehension	1–12	1–12	X*	K–9	1–12	X*	9–12
Words			K–1			K–3.9	
Sentences			K–3.5			K–1.9	
Stories/Passages			1.7–9			1.5–9	
Spelling	1.5–12	2.5–12	1–9	K–9	2–12	1.5–9	
Language							
Capitalization	1.5–12	2.4–12	1.7–9	1.5–9	2–9	3.5–9	
Punctuation	1.5–12	2.5–12	1.7–9	1.5–9	2–9	3.5–9	
Usage	1.5–12	2.5–12	1.7–9	1.5–9	2–12	3.5–9	
Reference Skills	3–12		1.7–9	K–9	4–12	3.5–9	9–12
Written Expression		3.5–12				3.5–9	9–12
Mathematics							
Concepts	K–12	3.5–9	1.7–9	K–9	K–12	1.5–9	
Computation	1–12	1–12	1.7–9	K–9	1–12	1.5–9	9–12
Application/Problem-Solving	K–12	3.5–12	1.7–9	K–9	4–12	1.5–9	9–12
Social Studies			3–9	1.5–9	4–12	3.5–9	9–12
Science			3–9	1.5–9	4–12	3.5–9	9–12

*X = The method of assessing reading comprehension differs according to age levels and is specified next to Words, Sentences, and Stories/Passages.

INDIVIDUALLY ADMINISTERED TESTS

Unlike group-administered tests, individual testing allows for observation and analysis of the student's performance and methodology.

Reading

Word Recognition

Most standardized individual achievement tests have a word identification subtest, but many provide only a very brief sampling, and often there are tremendous leaps in degree of difficulty—the Woodcock-Johnson is a prime example. Also, with the exception of the Slosson Oral Reading Test–Revised, the lists do not rate words according to grade level of difficulty (grade level performance is determined by the number of words read correctly). Of the standardized tests, the most useful ones are:

Slosson Oral Reading Test–Revised (up to grade 8 or 9)

Diagnostic Achievement Test for Adolescents–2

Wide Range Achievement Test–3 Combined Blue and Tan

Nonstandardized word list possibilities include:

Brigance Inventories

The Dolch list: good for assessing automatic recognition of high-frequency words (many are not phonetic)

Informal Reading Inventories: many provide graded lists of words

The New Reading Teacher's Book of Lists (Prentice Hall): provides several lists that encompass high-frequency sight words and those illustrative of various word analysis skills (phonetic and structural)

Alternative Assessment Techniques for Reading and Writing (Simon and Schuster–Center for Applied Research in Education) also provides extensive lists for assessing sight recognition and word analysis skills

Word Analysis

The Woodcock-Johnson Supplementary Battery and the Woodcock Reading Mastery Tests–Revised have subtests assessing word analysis skills, primarily phonetic.

Other possibilities include:

Brigance Inventories: Early Development, Readiness, Basic Skills

The Roswell Chall Diagnostic Reading Test of Word Analysis Skills (for beginning readers)

The Boder Diagnostic Screening Procedure for Developmental Dyslexia

Alternative Assessment Techniques for Reading and Writing

The New Reading Teacher's Book of Lists

Oral Reading

Standardized:

The Gray Oral Reading Test

The Formal Reading Inventory (oral and silent)

Informal Reading Inventories (most include oral and silent passages):

Alternative Assessment Techniques for Reading and Writing

Analytical Reading Inventory

Ekwall/Shanker Reading Inventory

Qualitative Reading Inventory–2

Steiglitz Informal Reading Inventory

The Qualitative and Steiglitz Reading Inventories provide both narrative and expository passages at each level.

Silent Reading

The reading comprehension subtests of standardized educational achievement batteries all involve silent reading. The response formats differ, however. Furthermore, for most standardized tests (achievement batteries and specific reading tests), the passages tend to be short. There is little evaluation of memory, processing of volume, organization, or selection of salience.

Standardized Achievement Batteries:

Diagnostic Achievement Battery–2: questions from memory

Diagnostic Achievement Test for Adolescents–2: questions from memory

Kaufman Test of Educational Achievement: questions with text

Scholastic Abilities Test for Adults: multiple-choice with text

Wechsler Individual Achievement Test: questions with text

Woodcock-Johnson Psychoeducational Battery: cloze (fill-in-the-blank)

Specific standardized silent reading tests:

Formal Reading Inventory: multiple-choice with text

Gates MacGinitie Reading Tests: (group or individual) multiple-choice with text

Nelson-Denny Reading Tests: multiple-choice with text

Test of Reading Comprehension: multiple-choice with text

Watson-Glaser Critical Thinking Appraisal: (evaluates critical reading comprehension skills) multiple-choice with text

Woodcock Reading Mastery Tests–Revised: cloze (fill-in-the-blank)

Informal Reading Inventories: All involve answering questions from memory and have more than one form.

Analytical Reading Inventory

Ekwall/Shanker Reading Inventory

Qualitative Reading Inventory–2: passages classified narrative or expository; summarization and questions

Steiglitz Informal Reading Inventory: passages classified narrative or expository; summarization and questions

An alternative would be to create an informal inventory using selections from regular class textbooks.

Listening

Listening skills are rarely assessed. However, they are important not only in the classroom but also for determining to what degree a student with reading problems might benefit from tape-recorded lectures and textbooks.

Any reading test or inventory that has multiple forms can be used to assess listening and give a better indication of ability and skill weakness than the few standardized measures that exist:

> Analytical Reading Inventory
> Durrell Analysis of Reading Difficulty
> Ekwall/Shanker Reading Inventory
> Formal Reading Inventory
> Qualitative Reading Inventory
> Spache Diagnostic Reading Scales
> Stieglitz Informal Reading Inventory

Standardized Tests that include listening:
> Diagnostic Achievement Battery–2
> Wechsler Individual Achievement Test

As noted for Silent Reading, passages from classroom texts can be adapted for assessing listening.

Writing

Handwriting:

> Observation. Be especially attentive to fluency, rate of output, and evidence of fatigue.

Copying (sentence from close range/a book and from a distance/the board): There are no formal measures. Have the student copy something from a grade-appropriate book and from a wall chart. Make certain that it is something that the student can read. Rate and efficiency are especially important to note.

Spelling:

> *Recognition:* The Peabody Individual Achievement Test–Revised utilizes a recognition multiple-choice method for assessing spelling.
>
> Informal tasks utilizing dictated words that a student misses can be equally useful in differentiating spelling recognition from retrieval and the effects of memory. The tasks would present several similar versions of a word, some phonetic and some visual approximations but only one correct example (*pepole, poeple, pepel, people, peaple*).

Dictation: The majority of standardized achievement batteries include a spelling dictation subtest that can be used for pattern analysis.

> The Test of Written Spelling–3: a standardized measure of spelling that purports to provide a list of regular (rule-governed words) and a list of irregular "sight" words. Many of the "sight" words are very regular and rule governed, however.

> The Test of Written Language–3: includes a separate spelling subtest.

> Informal diagnostic spelling tests with words selected according to specified rules and phonological elements. An example is the Diagnostic Spelling Test.

Sentence Dictation:

Informal. Sentences from standardized spelling tests can be used. These tests generally present words in the context of a sentence as well as in isolation.

Proofreading and Use of Mechanics:

Standardized–Specifically Delineated:

> Diagnostic Achievement Battery–2

> Scholastic Abilities Test for Adults

> Test of Written Language–3

> Woodcock-Johnson Achievement Scale Supplemental Battery

Standardized-Holistic:

> Test of Written Expression

> Wechsler Individual Achievement Test

> Writing Process Test

Informal Self-Made Measures

Composition:

The methods for evaluating composition skills employed by standardized tests vary significantly in format and specificity. Furthermore, several utilize quantitative bases (i.e., number of words written or number of letters per word) for assessing quality. The quantitative measures also frequently present concrete picture stimuli which guide ideation and organization.

> *Quantitative Measures*

> > Diagnostic Achievement Battery–2

> > Diagnostic Achievement Test for Adolescents–2 (vocabulary)

Scholastic Abilities Test for Adults (vocabulary)

Test of Written Language–3 (vocabulary, number of words written, number of different uses of capitalization and punctuation)

Qualitative Measures

Test of Written Expression

Wechsler Individual Achievement Test

Writing Process Test

Informal Checklists

Alternative Assessment Techniques for Reading and Writing

Evaluating and Improving Written Expression

Note Taking:

Although a writing task, note taking is central to listening and reading comprehension and might more accurately be included under these headings. There are no formal assessment measures. Use passages from reading inventories and regular textbooks. In addition to writing notes, textbook pages can be copied for evaluating underlining skills.

Mathematics

Basic Concepts:

The math applications subtests of many standardized individual achievement batteries:

Diagnostic Achievement Battery–2

Kaufman Test of Educational Achievement

Wechsler Individual Achievement Test

Woodcock-Johnson Psychoeducational Battery Achievement Scale and Supplemental Quantitative Concepts

Specific Mathematics Tests

Brigance Inventories

Key Math Diagnostic Arithmetic Test–Revised

Sequential Assessment of Mathematics Inventories

Stanford Diagnostic Mathematics Test

Test of Early Mathematics Ability

Math Facts:

There are no formal, standardized measures. The Brigance Inventory of Basic Skills provides a selection. Otherwise, create your own and/or observe performance on math computation for excessive reliance on counting strategies. A

word of warning: mastery of addition and subtraction facts receives little emphasis in many schools. Multiplication facts, however, become crucial for efficiency
at more advanced levels.

Written Computation:

Most standardized achievement batteries contain a separate subtest assessing
computation skills. Unfortunately, performance is measured by the number of
items calculated accurately. This procedure may penalize students with attention
problems who commit careless errors while having more advanced knowledge of
procedures, or students with poor fact recall and inaccurate counting strategies.
See listing of standardized achievement batteries at the end of the appendix. Note:
the Peabody Individual Achievement Test–Revised is an exception. It utilizes a
multiple-choice format and does not require actual computation.

Specific Math Tests:

    Brigance Inventories

    Diagnostic Test of Arithmetic Strategies

    Key Math Diagnostic Arithmetic Test–Revised (the basic operations are pre-
        sented by type, not mixed; i.e., there are separate sections for addition,
        subtraction, etc.)

    Sequential Assessment of Mathematics Inventories

    Stanford Diagnostic Mathematics Test–3

    Test of Early Mathematics Ability

Concept Formation:

    Brigance Inventories

    Cognitive Scale

    Scholastic Abilities Test for Adults–Quantitative Reasoning subtest

    The Quantitative Concepts subtest in the Woodcock-Johnson Achievement
        Scale and Quantitative Reasoning subtest in the Cognitive Scale

    Those listed as Specific Math Tests

Application/Word Problems:

    Specific Math Tests listed, except the Diagnostic Test of Arithmetic
        Strategies

    Standardized Achievement Test Batteries listed, except the WRAT

Executive Function

This is largely done via observation, probing, and interview. However, there
are some tests that can provide more structured and, to a degree, norm-referenced

information, particularly with regard to planning, strategy use, and reasoning flexibility.

Diagnostic Test of Arithmetic Strategies

Surveys of Problem-Solving and Educational Skills

The Reasoning subtests (verbal, nonverbal, quantitative) subtests of the Scholastic Abilities Test for Adults

Woodcock-Johnson Psychoeducational Battery–Revised–Cognitive Scale

Writing Process Test

Language

Assessment of language skills is central to evaluation of breakdowns in learning, since learning and school performance require effective processing and production of verbal information, both oral and written. Careful examination of error patterns in reading, listening, written expression, and math word problems will give some indication of weaknesses in language abilities. However, the following tests may be useful in pinpointing and clarifying the nature of language difficulties. All the tests listed are standardized. Most of them are individually administered, at least in part. Tests are listed in alphabetical order with a description of the language components that are measured and the age ranges covered. See also Mercer and Mercer (1993) Teaching Students with Learning Problems, pp. 358–63.

Bankson Language Test–2: (Receptive) Morphology, semantics/vocabulary, syntax, and pragmatics; ages 3–6

Clinical Evaluation of Language Fundamentals–3: (Receptive and Expressive) Semantics/vocabulary, syntax, discourse (story recall), word retrieval, and sentence recall; ages 5–16

Comprehensive Receptive and Expressive Vocabulary Test: Semantics/vocabulary and word retrieval

Detroit Test of Learning Aptitude–3: (Receptive and Expressive) Semantics/vocabulary, morphology, syntax, and discourse (story construction)

Expressive One-Word Picture Vocabulary Test–Revised: (Expressive) Vocabulary and word retrieval

Goldman-Fristoe-Woodcock Test of Auditory Discrimination: (Receptive) Phonology and discrimination of sounds in quiet and noise

Lindamood Auditory Conceptualization Test

Peabody Picture Vocabulary Test: (Receptive) Semantics/vocabulary

Test for Auditory Comprehension of Language–Revised: (Receptive) Semantics and syntax

Test of Adolescent and Adult Language–3: (Receptive and Expressive [oral and written]) Semantics/vocabulary, morphology, syntax, and discourse

Test of Adolescent/Adult Word Finding: (Expressive) Semantics/picture naming, category naming, and syntax/sentence completion

Test of Auditory Perceptual Skills: (Receptive) Phonology/discrimination, sequencing and recall of sounds, semantics, and syntax

Test of Language Competence, Levels 1 and 2: (Receptive and Expressive) Semantics/ambiguous words, figurative language, syntax/sentence formulation, discourse/listening comprehension, and pragmatics/intent

Tests of Language Development–2, Primary and Intermediate: (Receptive and Expressive)

Primary: Phonology/word discrimination and articulation, semantics/picture vocabulary and defining words, morphology, and syntax

Intermediate: Semantics/vocabulary and classification, morphology and syntax/sentence combining, sentence formulation, and grammatic comprehension

Test of Pragmatic Skills: (Expressive) Pragmatics/greeting, informing, answering, naming, requesting, reasoning, rejecting, and closing conversation

Test of Word Finding: (Expressive) Semantics and syntax (see Test of Adolescent/Adult Word Finding)

Token Test: (Receptive) Morphology and syntax

Wepman Auditory Discrimination Test

Word Test–Revised: (Receptive and Expressive) Semantics/synonyms, antonyms, classification, definition, absurdities

TESTS MENTIONED

Standardized Achievement Batteries

Diagnostic Achievement Battery–2 (1990), ages 6–14, Pro-Ed

Diagnostic Achievement Test for Adolescents–2 (1993), ages 3–19, Pro-Ed

Kaufman Test of Educational Achievement (1985), ages 6–18, American Guidance Service

Peabody Individual Achievement Test–Revised (1989), K–18, American Guidance Service

Scholastic Abilities Test for Adults (1991), ages 16 on, Pro-Ed

Wechsler Individual Achievement Test–3 (1992), ages 5–19, Psychological Corp.

Wide Range Achievement Test–3 (1993), ages 5 on, Psychological Corp.

Woodcock-Johnson Psychoeducational Battery–Revised (1989), ages 5 on, Riverside Publishing Co.

The Kaufman-Assessment Battery for Children (1983) has an Achievement Scale (ages 5–12). However, it is not sufficiently comprehensive in assessing basic skills and contains other subtests that are not academically related. Therefore, it is not recommended for purposes of diagnostic assessment.

Informal Educational Batteries

Brigance Diagnostic Comprehensive Inventory of Basic Skills (1983), pre-K–grade 9, Curriculum Associates

Brigance Inventory of Essential Skills (1981), grade 6–adult, Curriculum Associates

Surveys of Problem-Solving and Educational Skills (1987), ages 9–15, Educators Publishing Service

Standardized Reading Tests

Formal Reading Inventory (1986), ages 6–19, Pro-Ed

Gates MacGinitie Reading Tests (1989), grades K–12, Riverside Publishing Co.

Gray Oral Reading Test–D (1991), ages 7–19, Pro-Ed

Nelson-Denny Reading Tests (1993), grades 9–college, Riverside Publishing Co.

Test of Early Reading Ability–2 (1989), ages 3–9, Pro-Ed

Test of Reading Comprehension–Revised (1986), ages 7–17, Pro-Ed

Watson-Glaser Critical Thinking Appraisal (1980), grades high school–college, Psychological Corp.

Woodcock Reading Mastery Tests–Revised (1987), ages 6–adult, American Guidance Service

Informal Reading Inventories and Lists

Alternative Assessment Techniques for Reading and Writing. Wilma Miller (1995), K–12, Center for Applied Research in Education

Analytical Reading Inventory (1991), K–9, Charles E. Merrill/Macmillan

Boder Test of Reading–Spelling Patterns (1982), K–12, Psychological Corp.

Durrell Analysis of Reading Difficulty (1980), K–6, Psychological Corp.

Ekwall/Shanker Reading Inventory–Third Edition (1993), grades 1–9, Allyn & Bacon

Qualitative Reading Inventory–2 (1995), K–8, Harper Collins

Roswell-Chall Diagnostic Reading Test of Word Analysis (1978), grades 1–4, Harvard University

Spache Diagnostic Reading Scales (1981), K–8, CTB/MacGraw-Hill

Stieglitz Informal Reading Inventory (1992), grades 1–9, Allyn & Bacon

The New Reading Teacher's Book of Lists. Fry, Fountoukidis & Polk (1985), K–12, Prentice-Hall

Standardized Tests of Spelling and Written Expression

Test of Early Written Language–2 (1996), ages 3–10, Pro-Ed

Test of Written Expression (1995), ages 6–6–14–11, Pro-Ed

Test of Written Language–3 (1996), ages 7–18, Pro-Ed

Test of Written Spelling–3 (1994), ages 1–18, Pro-Ed

Writing Process Test, ages 8–18 (1992), Riverside Publishing Co.

Standardized Tests of Mathematics

Key Math Diagnostic Arithmetic Test–Revised (1988), grades K–8, American Guidance Service

Sequential Assessment of Mathematics Inventories (1985), grades K–8, Psychological Corp.

Stanford Diagnostic Mathematics Test–3 (1985), grades 1–12, Psychological Corp.

Test of Early Mathematics Ability–2 (1990), ages 3–9, Pro-Ed

Test of Mathematical Abilities–2 (1994), grades 3–12, Pro-Ed

Informal Math Tests

Diagnostic Test of Arithmetic Strategies (1994), grades 1–6, Pro-Ed

Standardized Tests of Language Skills

Bankson Language Test–2 (1990), ages 3–7, Pro-Ed

Clinical Evaluation of Language Fundamentals–3 (1995), ages 5–16, Psychological Corp.

Comprehensive Receptive and Expressive Vocabulary Test (1994), ages 4–18, Pro-Ed

Detroit Tests of Learning Aptitude–3 (1991), ages 6–17, Pro-Ed

Expressive One-Word Picture Vocabulary Test (1983, 1990), ages 2–11 and 12–15, Pro-Ed

Goldman-Fristoe-Woodcock Test of Auditory Discrimination (1970), ages 3–adult, American Guidance Service

Lindamood Auditory Conceptualization Test (1979), ages 4–adult, Riverside Publishing Co.

Peabody Picture Vocabulary Test–3 (1993), ages 2–adult, American Guidance Service

Test for Auditory Comprehension of Language–Revised (1985), ages 3–9, DLM

Test of Adolescent and Adult Language–3 (1994), ages 12–25, Pro-Ed

Test of Adolescent/Adult Word Finding (1990), ages 12–80, Pro-Ed

Test of Auditory Perceptual Skills (1985), ages 4–12, 12–18, Pro-Ed

Test of Language Competence (1988), Level 1 ages 5–9, Level 2 ages 10–18, Psychological Corp.

Tests of Language Development (1988), Primary ages 4–9, Intermediate ages 8–6–13, Pro-Ed

Test of Pragmatic Skills (1986), ages 5–13, Communication Skill Builders

Test of Word Finding (1989), ages 6–6–13, Pro-Ed

Token Test (1978), ages 3–12, Pro-Ed

Wepman Auditory Discrimination Test (1973), ages 4–adult, Language Research Associates

Word Test (1990), ages 7–11, LinguiSystems

Publishers of Tests Mentioned

Allyn and Bacon, Department 894, 160 Gould Street, Needham Heights, MA 02194-2310

American Guidance Service, Inc., 4201 Woodland Road, Circle Pines, MN 55014

Center for Applied Research in Education, West Nyack, NY 10995

Communication Skill Builders, Inc., 3830 E. Bellevue/P.O. Box 42050, Tuscon, AZ 85733

CTB/Macmillan/McGraw Hill, 20 Ryan Ranch Road, Monterey, CA 93940-5703

Curriculum Associates, Inc., 5 Esquire Road, North Billerica, MA 01862

DLM, P.O. Box 4000, One DLM Park, Allen, TX 75002

Educational Records Bureau, Educational Testing Service, Princeton, NJ 08541

Educators Publishing Service, Inc., 31 Smith Place, Cambridge, MA 02138-1089

Harper Collins, P.O. Box 588, Dunmore, PA 18512

Harvard University, Graduate School of Education, Larsen Hall, Appian Way, Cambridge, MA 02138

Language Research Associates, Palm Springs, CA

LinguiSystems, 3100 4th Avenue, P.O. Box 747, East Moline, IL 61244

Merrill/Macmillan, 20 Ryan Ranch Road, Monterey, CA 93940-5703

Prentice-Hall Inc., Englewood Cliffs, NJ 07632

Pro-Ed, 8700 Shoal Creek Boulevard, Austin, TX 78758-6897

Psychological Corporation, 555 Academic Court, San Antonio, TX 78204-2498

Riverside Publishing Company, 8420 Bryn Mawr Avenue, Chicago, IL 60631

Science Research Associates, 155 North Wacker Avenue, Chicago, IL 60606

Slosson Educational Publications, 140 Pine Street, P.O. Box 280, East Aurora, NY 14052

References

Aaron, P.G., and Baker, C. 1991. *Reading Disabilities in College and High School: Diagnosis and Management.* Parkton, Md.: York Press.

Abroms, I.F. 1983. Central nervous system trauma. In M.D. Levine, W.B. Carey, A.C. Crocker, and R.T. Gross (Eds.), *Developmental-Behavioral Pediatrics.* Philadelphia: W.B. Saunders.

Adams, R.D., and Lyon, G. 1982. *Neurology of Hereditary Metabolic Diseases of Children.* New York: McGraw-Hill.

Allard, W.G., Dodd, J.M., and Peralez, E. 1987. Keeping LD students in college. *Academic Therapy* 22:359.

Alley, G., and Deshler, D. 1979. *Teaching the Learning Disabled Adolescent: Strategies and Methods.* Denver: Love Publishing Co.

Anderson, R.C., and Pichert, J.W. 1978. Recall of previously unrecallable information following a shift in perspective. *Journal of Verbal Learning and Verbal Behavior* 17:1.

Anglin, J. 1970. *The Growth of Word Meaning.* Cambridge, Mass.: MIT Press.

Armstrong, F.D., Seidel, J.F., and Swales, T.P. 1993. Pediatric HIV infection: a neuropsychological and educational challenge. *Journal of Learning Disabilities* 26:92.

Asher, S.R. 1983. Social competence and peer status: recent advances and future directions. *Child Development* 54:1427.

Ault, R.L. 1983. *Children's Cognitive Development.* 2d ed. New York: Oxford University Press.

Ayres, A.J. 1972. *Sensory Integration and Learning Disorders.* Los Angeles: Western Psychological Services.

Baddeley, A.D. 1995. The psychology of memory. In A.D. Baddeley, B.A. Wilson, and F.N. Watts (Eds.), *Handbook of Memory Disorders.* New York: John Wiley.

Baghurst, P.A., McMichael, A.J., Tong, S., Wigg, N.R., Vimpani, G.V., and Robertson, E.F. 1995. Exposure to environmental lead and visual-motor integration at age 7 years: the Port Pirie Cohort Study. *Epidemiology* 6:104.

Baker, H., and Leland, B. 1967. *Detroit Tests of Learning Aptitude.* Indianapolis: Bobbs-Merrill Test Division.

Baker, L. 1982. An evaluation of the role of metacognitive deficits in learning disabilities. *Topics in Learning and Learning Disabilities 2:*27.

Bakker, D.J. 1979. Hemispheric differences and reading strategies. *Bulletin of the Orton Society 29:*84.

Bakker, D.J. 1983. Hemispheric specialization and specific reading retardation. In M. Rutter (Ed.), *Developmental Neuropsychiatry.* New York: Guilford Press.

Bakker, D.J. 1994. Dyslexia and the ecological brain. *Journal of Clinical and Experimental Neuropsychology 16:*734.

Barkley, R.A. 1991. Attention deficit hyperactivity disorder. *Psychiatric Annals 21:*725.

Barkley, R.A. 1994. The assessment of attention in children. In G.R. Lyon (Ed.), *Frames of Reference for the Assessment of Learning Disabilities.* Baltimore: Paul H. Brookes.

Barkley, R.A. 1997. Behavioral inhibition, sustained attention, and executive functions: constructing a unifying theory of ADHD. *Psychological Bulletin 121:*65.

Barnard, K.E., and Collar, B.S. 1973. Early diagnosis, interpretation and intervention: a commentary on the nurse's role. *Annals of the New York Academy of Sciences 205:*373.

Barnett, J.C., Sowder, L., and Vos, K.E. 1980. Textbook problems: supplementing and understanding them. In S. Krulik (Ed.), *Problem Solving in School Mathematics.* Reston, Va.: National Council of Teachers of Mathematics.

Barron, R.W. 1980. Visual and phonological strategies in reading and spelling. In U. Frith (Ed.), *Cognitive Processes in Spelling.* London: Academic Press.

Bashir, A.S., Kuban, K.C., Kleinman, S.N., and Scavuzzo, A. 1983. Issues in language disorders: considerations of cause, maintenance, and change. In J. Miller, D.E. Yoder, and R. Schiefelbusch (Eds.), *Contemporary Issues in Language Intervention.* Rockville, Md.: American Speech and Hearing Association.

Bauer, R.H. 1977. Memory processes in children with learning disabilities: evidence for deficient rehearsal. *Journal of Experimental Child Psychology 24:*415.

Bayliss, J., and Livesey, P.J. 1985. Cognitive strategies of children with reading disability and normal readers in visual sequential memory. *Journal of Learning Disabilities 18:*326.

Bell, W.E., and McCormick, W.F. 1981. *Neurological Infections in Children.* 2d ed. Philadelphia: W.B. Saunders.

Bellak, L. (Ed.). 1979. *Psychiatric Aspects of Minimal Brain Dysfunction in Adults.* New York: Grune and Stratton.

Bellinger, D.C. 1995. Interpreting the literature on lead and child development: the neglected role of the "Experimental System." *Neurotoxicology and Teratology 17:*201.

Bellows, B.P. 1980. Running shoes are to jogging as analogies are to creative/-critical thinking. *Journal of Reading* 23:507.

Bender, L.A. 1956. *Psychopathology of Children with Organic Brain Disorders.* Springfield, Ill.: Charles C. Thomas.

Bennett, F.C., Runska, S.H., and Sherman, R. 1980. Middle ear function and learning-disabled children. *Pediatrics* 66:254.

Benton, A.L. 1968. Differential behavioral effects in frontal lobe disease. *Neuropsychologica* 6:53.

Benton, A.L. 1977. Reflections on the Gerstmann Syndrome. *Brain and Language* 4:45.

Berenbaum, S.A., and Denburg, S.D. 1995. Evaluating the empirical support for the role of testosterone in the Geschwind-Behan-Galaburda model of cerebral lateralization: commentary on Bryden, McManus, and Bulman-Fleming. *Brain and Cognition* 27:79.

Berlin, L.J., Blank, M., and Rose, S.A. 1980. The language of instruction: the hidden complexities. *Topics in Language Disorders* 1:47.

Berman, A.L., and Jobes, D.A. 1995. A population perspective: suicide prevention in adolescents (age 12–18). *Suicide and Life-Threatening Behavior* 25:143.

Berndt, R.S. 1983. Phonological coding and written sentence comprehension. *Annals of Dyslexia* 33:64.

Bernstein, N. 1967. *The Coordination and Regulation of Movements.* London: Pergamon Press.

Blachman, B.A. 1984. Language analysis skills and early reading. In G.P. Wallach and K.G. Butler (Eds.), *Language Learning Disabilities in School-Age Children.* Baltimore: Williams and Wilkins.

Blackman, J.A., Levine, M.D., and Markowitz, M. 1986. *Pediatric Extended Examination at Three (PEET).* Cambridge, Mass.: Educators Publishing Service.

Blake, S. 1975. *Teaching Reading Skills Through Social Studies and Science Materials.* Brooklyn: New York City Board of Education.

Bloom, B.S., and Broder, L. 1950. *Problem-Solving Processes of College Students.* Chicago: University of Chicago Press.

Bloom, K.E., and Shuell, T.J. 1981. Effects of massed and distributed practice on the learning and retention of second language vocabulary. *Journal of Educational Research* 74:245.

Boder, E. 1973. Developmental dyslexia: a diagnostic approach based on three atypical reading-spelling patterns. *Developmental Medicine and Child Neurology* 15:661.

Botha-Antou, E., Babyan, J., and Harfouce, J.K. 1968. Intellectual development related to nutritional status. *Journal of Tropical Pediatrics 14*:112.

Bowlby, J. 1960. *Attachment and Loss: I. Attachment.* London: Hogarth Press.

Brainerd, C.J. 1983. Young children's mental arithmetic errors: a working-memory analysis. *Child Development 54*:812.

Brent, D.A. 1995. Risk factors for adolescent suicide and suicidal behavior: mental and substance abuse disorders, family environmental factors, and life stress. *Suicide and Life-Threatening Behavior 25S*:52.

Bresnan, M.J., and Hicks, E.M. 1983. Infections of the central nervous system. In M.D. Levine, W.B. Carey, A.C. Crocker, and R.T. Gross (Eds.), *Developmental-Behavioral Pediatrics.* Philadelphia: W.B. Saunders.

Brier, N. 1995. Predicting antisocial behavior in youngsters displaying poor academic achievement: a review of risk factors. *Developmental and Behavioral Pediatrics 16*:271.

Brooks, R. 1983. Projective techniques in personality assessment. In M.D. Levine, W.B. Carey, A.C. Crocker, and R.T. Gross (Eds.), *Developmental-Behavioral Pediatrics.* Philadelphia: W.B. Saunders.

Brown, A.L. 1976. Semantic integration in children's reconstruction of narrative sequences. *Cognitive Psychology 8*:247.

Brown, A.L., Day, J.D., and Jones, R.S. 1983. The development of plans for summarizing texts. *Child Development 54*:968.

Brown, R. 1973. *A First Language: The Early Stages.* Cambridge, Mass.: Harvard University Press.

Bruininks, R.H. 1978. *Bruininks-Oseretsky Test of Motor Proficiency.* Minneapolis: American Guidance Service.

Bryan, T.H. 1974. Peer popularity of learning disabled children. *Journal of Learning Disabilities 7*:37.

Bryan, T.H. 1978. Social relationships and verbal interactions of learning disabled children. *Journal of Learning Disabilities 11*:59.

Bryan, T.H., Wheeler, R., Felcan, J., and Henek, T. 1976. "Come on dummy": an observational study of children's communications. *Journal of Learning Disabilities 9*:53.

Bryden, M. 1972. Auditory-visual sequential-spatial matching in relation to reading ability. *Child Development 43*:824.

Bryden, M.P., McManus, I.C., and Bulman-Fleming, M.B. 1994. Evaluating the empirical support for the Geschwind-Behan-Galaburda model of cerebral lateralization. *Brain and Cognition 26*:103.

Bryden, M.P., McManus, I.C., and Bulman-Fleming, M.B. 1995. GBG, hormones, and anomalous dominance: a reply to commentaries. *Brain and Cognition 27*:94.

Bulgren, J.A., Schumaker, J.B., and Deshler, D.D. 1994. The effects of a recall enhancement routine on the test performance of secondary students with and without learning disabilities. *Learning Disabilities Research and Practice* 9:2.

Burd, L., Kauffman, D.W., and Kerbeshian, J. 1992. Tourette syndrome and learning disabilities. *Journal of Learning Disabilities* 25:598.

Cain, K.M., and Dweck, C.S. 1995. The relation between motivational patterns and achievement cognitions through the elementary school years. *Merrill-Palmer Quarterly 41*:25.

Campbell, S.B. 1976. Hyperactivity: course and treatment. In A. Davids (Ed.), *Child Personality and Psychopathology: Current Topics,* vol. 3. New York: John Wiley & Sons.

Campbell, S.B., Schleifer, M., and Weiss, G. 1978. Continuities in maternal reports and child behaviors over time in hyperactive and comparison groups. *Journal of Abnormal Child Psychology* 6:33.

Cantwell, D.P. 1979. The "hyperactive" child. *Hospital Practice 14*:65.

Carey, W.B. 1982*a*. Validity of parental assessments of development and behavior. *American Journal of Diseases of Children 136*:97.

Carey, W.B. 1982*b*. Clinical appraisal of temperament. In M. Lewis and L. Taft (Eds.), *Developmental Disabilities: Theory, Assessment, and Intervention.* Jamaica, N.Y.: SP Medical and Scientific Books.

Carey, W.B. 1985. Interactions of temperament and clinical conditions. In M. Wolraich (Ed.), *Advances in Developmental and Behavioral Pediatrics* 6:83.

Carey, W.B., McDevitt, S.C., and Baker, D. 1979. Differentiating minimal brain dysfunction and temperament. *Developmental Medicine and Child Neurology 21*:765.

Carlisle, J. 1982. *Reasoning and Reading.* Cambridge, Mass.: Educators Publishing Service.

Carnegie Council on Adolescent Development. 1995. *Great Transitions: Preparing Adolescents for a New Century.* New York: Carnegie Council on Adolescent Development.

Carroll, J.B. 1962. The prediction of success in intensive foreign language training. In *Training Research and Education.* Pittsburgh: University of Pittsburgh Press.

Carrow, E. 1973. *Test for Auditory Comprehension of Language.* Austin, Tex.: Urban Research Group.

Carte, E., Morrison, D., Sublett, J., Uemura, A., and Setrakian, W. 1984. Sensory integration therapy: a trial of neurodevelopmental therapy for the remediation of learning disabilities. *Journal of Developmental and Behavioral Pediatrics* 5:189.

Cartledge, G., and Milburn, J.F. 1980. *Teaching Social Skills to Children.* New York: Pergamon Press.

Ceci, S.J. 1984. Developmental study of learning disabilities and memory. *Journal of Experimental Child Psychology 38*:352.

Cerezo, M.A., and Frias, D. 1994. Emotional and cognitive adjustment in abused children. *Child Abuse and Neglect 18*:923.

Chall, J.S. 1983. *Stages of Reading Development.* New York: McGraw-Hill.

Chapman, A., ed. 1993. *Making Sense: Teaching Critical Reading Across the Curriculum.* New York: College Entrance Examination Board.

Chess, S. 1979. Developmental theory revisited: findings of longitudinal study. *Canadian Journal of Psychiatry 24*:101.

Chess, S., and Thomas, A. 1983. Dynamics of individual behavioral development. In M.D. Levine, W.B. Carey, A.C. Crocker, and R.T. Gross (Eds.), *Developmental-Behavioral Pediatrics.* Philadelphia: W.B. Saunders.

Chomsky, C. 1969. *The Acquisition of Syntax in Children from 5 to 10.* Cambridge, Mass.: MIT Press.

Chomsky, C. 1970. Reading, writing, and phonology. *Harvard Educational Review 40*:287.

Cicci, R. 1980. Written language disorders. *Bulletin of the Orton Society 30*:240.

Cohen, H., Taft, L.T., Mahadeviah, M., and Birch, H. 1967. Developmental changes in overflow in normal and aberrantly functioning children. *Journal of Pediatrics 71*:39.

Cohen, N.J., Weiss, G., and Minde, K. 1972. Cognitive styles in adolescents previously diagnosed as hyperactive. *Journal of Child Psychology and Psychiatry 13*:203.

Cohn, R. 1968. Developmental dyscalculia. *Pediatric Clinics of North America 15*:651.

Cohn, R. 1971. Arithmetic and learning disabilities. In H.R. Myklebust (Ed.), *Progress in Learning Disabilities*, vol. 2. New York: Grune and Stratton.

Cohn, S.J., and Isaacson, S. 1984. *Expository Writing Skills of Academically Gifted Students (Evaluative Report).* Tempe, Ariz.: Arizona State University.

Coie, J.D., Dodge, K.A., and Coppotelli, H. 1982. Dimensions and types of social status: a cross-age perspective. *Developmental Psychology 18*:557.

Coie, J.D., Dodge, K.A., and Kupersmidt, J.B. 1990. Peer group behavior and social status. In S.R. Asher and J.D. Coie (Eds.), *Peer Rejection in Childhood.* Cambridge: Cambridge University Press.

Compas, B.E., Hinden, B.R., and Gerhardt, C.A. 1995. Adolescent development: pathways and processes of risk and resilience. *Annual Review of Psychology 46*:265.

Cook-Gumperz, J. 1977. Situated instructions: language socialization of school age children. In S. Ervin-Tripp and C. Mitchell-Kernan (Eds.), *Child Discourse*. New York: Academic Press.

Corballis, M.C., and Beale, I.L. 1976. *The Psychology of Left and Right*. Hillsdale, N.J.: Lawrence Erlbaum.

Cott, A. 1971. Orthomolecular approach to the treatment of learning disabilities. *Schizophrenia* 3:95.

Cox, D.H., and Klas, L.D. 1996. Students with learning disabilities in Canadian colleges and universities: a primer for service provision. *Journal of Learning Disabilities* 29:93.

Cravioto, J., and Arrieta, R. 1983. Malnutrition in childhood. In M. Rutter (Ed.), *Developmental Neuropsychiatry*. New York: Guilford Press.

Critchley, M. 1975. Specific developmental dyslexia. In E.H. Lenneberg and E. Lenneberg (Eds.), *Foundations of Language Development: A Multidisciplinary Approach*, vol. 2. New York: Academic Press.

Cronbach, L. 1970. *Essentials of Psychological Testing*. 3d ed. New York: Harper & Row.

Croxen, M.E., and Lytton, H. 1971. Reading disabilities and difficulties in finger localization and right-left discrimination. *Developmental Psychology* 5: 256.

Cruickshank, W.M. 1975. The psychoeducational match. In W.M. Cruickshank and D.P. Hallahan (Eds.), *Perceptual and Learning Disabilities in Children*, vol. 1. Syracuse, N.Y.: Syracuse University Press.

Cummins, J. 1989. A theoretical framework for bilingual special education. *Exceptional Children* 56:111.

Curry, J. 1989. The role of reading instruction in mathematics. In D. Lapp, J. Flood, and N. Farnan (Eds.), *Content Areas Reading and Learning: Instructional Strategies*. Englewood Cliffs, N.J.: Prentice-Hall.

Cziko, G. 1978. Differences in first and second language reading: the use of syntactic, semantic, and discourse constraints. *Canadian Modern Language Review* 34:473.

DeAngelis, E.G. 1983. Recreation, art, music, and dance therapy and adapted physical education. In M.D. Levine, W.B. Carey, A.C. Crocker, and R.T. Gross (Eds.), *Developmental-Behavioral Pediatrics*. Philadelphia: W.B. Saunders.

Delacato, C. 1959. *The Treatment and Prevention of Reading Problems: The Neurological Approach*. Springfield, Ill.: Charles C. Thomas.

Denckla, M.B. 1973. Development of speed in repetitive and successive finger movements in normal children. *Developmental Medicine and Child Neurology 15*:635.

Denckla, M.B. 1978. Minimal brain dysfunction. In *Education and the Brain*. Chicago: The National Society of Education.

Denckla, M.B. 1984. Developmental dyspraxia: the clumsy child. In M.D. Levine and P. Satz (Eds.), *Middle Childhood: Development and Dysfunction*. Baltimore: University Park Press.

Denckla, M.B. 1985. Motor coordination in dyslexic children. In F.H. Duffy and N. Geschwind (Eds.), *Dyslexia: A Neuroscientific Approach to Clinical Evaluation*. Boston: Little, Brown.

Denckla, M.B. 1996. A theory and model of executive function. In G.R. Lyon and N.A. Krasnegor (Eds.), *Attention, Memory, and Executive Functions*. Baltimore: Paul H. Brookes.

Denckla, M.B., and Rudel, R.G. 1976. Rapid "automatized" naming (R.A.N.): dyslexia differentiated from other learning disabilities. *Neuropsychologia 14*:471.

Denckla, M.B., and Rudel, R.G. 1978. Anomalies of motor development in hyperactive boys. *Annals of Neurology 3*:231.

Denckla, M.B., LeMay, M., and Chapman, C.A. 1985. Few CT scan abnormalities found even in neurologically impaired learning disabled children. *Journal of Learning Disabilities 18*:132.

Denney, N.W., and Moulton, P.A. 1976. Conceptual preferences among preschool children. *Developmental Psychology 12*:509.

Deno, S., Marston, D., and Mirkin, P. 1982. Valid measurement procedures for continuous evaluation of written expression. *Exceptional Children 48*: 368.

DeRenzi, E., and Vignolo, L.E. 1962. The token test: a sensitive test to detect receptive disturbances in aphasics. *Brain 85*:556.

Deshler, D.D., Ellis, E.S., and Lenz, B.K. 1996. *Teaching Adolescents with Learning Disabilities: Strategies and Methods*, 2d ed. Denver: Love Publishing Co.

Di Lollo, V., Hanson, D., and McIntyre, J.S. 1983. Initial stages of visual information processing in dyslexia. *Journal of Experimental Psychology: Human Perception Performance 9*:923.

Diagnostic and Statistical Manual of Mental Disorders, Fourth Edition. 1994. Washington, D.C.: American Psychiatric Association.

Diener, C.I., and Dweck, C.S. 1978. An analysis of learned helplessness: continuous changes in performance, strategy, and achievement cognitions following failure. *Journal of Personality and Social Psychology 5*:451.

Dietz, W.H., and Strasburger, V.C. 1991. Children, adolescents, and television. *Current Problems in Pediatrics 21*:8.

Dinklage, K.L. 1971. Inability to learn a foreign language. In G. Blaine and C. McAuther (Eds.), *Emotional Problems of the Student*. New York: Appleton-Century-Crofts.

Dodge, K.A. 1983. Behavioral antecedents of peer social status. *Child Development 54*:1386.

Donahue, M., and Bryan, T. 1984. Communicative skills and peer relations of learning disabled adolescents. *Topics in Language Disorders 4*:10.

Donahue, M., Pearl, R., and Bryan, T. 1983. Conversational skills and modelling in learning disabled boys. *Applied Psycholinguistics 4*:251.

Donlan, D. 1980. Locating main ideas in history textbooks. *Journal of Reading 24*:135.

Dowdall, C., and Colangelo, N. 1982. Underachieving gifted students: review and implications. *Gifted Child Quarterly 26*:179.

Downing, J.A., and Oliver, P. 1974. The child's conception of "a word." *Reading Research Quarterly 9*:568.

Drash, P.W. 1975. Treatment of hyperactivity in the two-year-old. *Pediatric Psychology 3*:17.

Driscoll, M. 1982. *Research Within Reach: Secondary School Mathematics*. Reston, Va.: National Council of Teachers of Mathematics.

Duane, D.D. 1985. Written language underachievement: an overview of the theoretical and practical issues. In F.H. Duffy and N. Geschwind (Eds.), *Dyslexia: A Neuroscientific Approach to Clinical Evaluation*. Boston: Little, Brown.

Duffy, F.H. 1994. The role of quantified electoencephalography in psychological research. In G. Dawson and K.W. Fischer (Eds.), *Human Behavior and the Developing Brain*. New York: Guilford Press.

Duffy, F.H. et al. 1980. Dyslexia: automated diagnosis by computerized classification of brain electrical activity. *Annals of Neurology 7*:412.

Duffy, F.H., and McAnulty, G.B. 1985. Brain electrical activity mapping (BEAM): the search for a physiological signature of dyslexia. In F.H. Duffy and N. Geschwind (Eds.), *Dyslexia: A Neuroscientific Approach to Clinical Evaluation*. Boston: Little, Brown.

Dunn, L.M., and Dunn, L.M. 1981. *Peabody Picture Vocabulary Test—Revised*. Circle Pines, Minn.: American Guidance Service.

Dweck, C.S. 1986. Motivational processes affecting learning. *American Psychologist 41*:1040.

Dweck, C.S. 1989. Motivation. In R. Glaser and A. Lesgold (Eds.), *Foundations for a Psychology of Education*. Hillsdale, N.J.: Lawrence Erlbaum.

Eisenberg, L. 1966. Reading retardation. I. Psychiatric and sociologic aspects. *Pediatrics 37*:352.

Elkind, D. 1976. *Child Development and Education: A Piagetian Prospective.* New York: Oxford University Press.

Emery, R.E., and O'Leary, K.D. 1982. Children's perceptions of marital discord and behavior problems of boys and girls. *Journal of Abnormal Child Psychology 10*:11.

Ernhart, C.B., Landa, B., and Wolf, A.W. 1985. Subclinical lead level and development deficit: re-analyses of data. *Journal of Learning Disabilities 18*:475.

Espenschade, A.S., and Eckert, H.M. 1980. *Motor Development.* 2d ed. Columbus, Ohio: Charles E. Merrill.

Esser, G., Laucht, M., and Schmidt, M.H. 1996. The significance of biological and psychosocial risks for preschool-age behavior problems. In M. Brambring, H. Rauh, and A. Beelman (Eds.), *Early Childhood Intervention: Theory, Evaluation, and Practice.* Berline, N.Y.: de Gruyter.

Faraone, S.V., Biederman, J., and Milberger, S. 1994. An exploratory study of ADHD among second-degree relatives of ADHD children. *Biological Psychiatry 35*:398.

Farnham-Diggory, S., and Simon, H.A. 1975. Retention of visually presented information in children's spelling. *Memory and Cognition 3*:599.

Feagans, L. 1983. Discourse processes in learning disabled children. In J.D. McKinney and L. Feagans (Eds.), *Current Topics in Learning Disabilities.* Norwood, N.J.: Ablex Publishing Corp.

Feingold, B. 1975. *Why Your Child Is Hyperactive.* New York: Random House.

Feingold, C. 1994. Correlates of cognitive development in low-birth-weight infants from low-income families. *Journal of Pediatric Nursing 19*:91.

Ferguson, H.B. 1990. Recent developments in diet theory. In J.G. Simeon and H.B. Ferguson (Eds.), *Treatment Strategies in Child and Adolescent Psychiatry.* New York: Plenum Press.

Feuerstein, R., and Jensen, M.R. May 1980. Instrumental enrichment: theoretical basis, goals, and instruments. *The Educational Forum.*

Feuerstein, R., Rand, Y., Hoffman, M.B., and Miller, R. 1980. *Instrumental Enrichment.* Baltimore: University Park Press.

Filipek, P.A., Kennedy, D.N., and Caviness, V.S. 1992. Neuroimaging in child neuropsychology. In I. Rapin and S.J. Segalowitz (Eds.), *Handbook of Neuropsychology 6.* Amsterdam: Elsevier Science Publishers B.V.

Finucci, J.M., Isaacs, S.D., Whitehouse, C.C., and Childs, B. 1983. Classification of spelling errors and their relationship to reading ability, sex, grade placement, and intelligence. *Brain and Language 20*:340.

Fishel, C.T. 1984. Reading in the content area of English. In M.M. Dupuis (Ed.), *Reading in the Content Areas: Research for Teachers.* Newark, Del.: International Reading Association.

Flavell, J.H. 1982. On cognitive development. *Child Development 53*:1.

Flavell, J.H. 1985. *Cognitive Development.* Englewood Cliffs, N.J.: Prentice-Hall.

Fox, C.L., and Forbing, S.E. 1991. Overlapping symptoms of substance abuse and learning handicaps: implications for educators. *Journal of Learning Disabilities 24*:24.

Frankenburg, W.K. 1983. Infant and preschool developmental screening. In M.D. Levine, W.B. Carey, A.C. Crocker, and R.T. Gross (Eds.), *Developmental-Behavioral Pediatrics.* Philadelphia: W.B. Saunders.

Freud, S. 1965. *New Introductory Lectures on Psychoanalysis.* New York: W.W. Norton.

Freund, L.S., Reiss, A.L., and Abrams, M.T. 1993. Psychiatric disorders associated with fragile x in the young female. *Pediatrics 91*:321.

Frith, U. 1980. Unexpected spelling problems. In U. Frith (Ed.), *Cognitive Processes in Spelling.* London: Academic Press.

Frith, U. 1983. The similarities and differences between reading and spelling problems. In M. Rutter (Ed.), *Developmental Neuropsychiatry.* New York: Guilford Press.

Frostig, M. 1964. *Frostig Developmental Test of Visual Perception.* Palo Alto, Calif.: Consulting Psychologists Press.

Frostig, M., and Maslow, P. 1973. *Learning Problems in the Classroom.* New York: Grune and Stratton.

Fry, M.A., Johnson, C.S., and Muehl, S. 1970. Oral language production in relation to reading achievement. In D.J. Bakker and P. Satz (Eds.), *Specific Reading Disability.* Amsterdam: Rotterdam University Press.

Gaddes, W.H. 1980. *Learning Disabilities and Brain Function.* New York: Springer-Verlag.

Gaddes, W.H., and Edgell, D. 1994. *Learning Disabilities and Brain Function: A Neuropsychological Approach,* 3d ed. New York: Springer-Verlag.

Galaburda, A. 1983. Development dyslexia: current anatomical research. *Annals of Dyslexia 33*:41.

Galin, D., Johnstone, J., Nakell, L., and Herron, J. 1979. Development of the capacity for tactile information transfer between hemispheres in normal children. *Science 204*:1330.

Gallagher, J.J. 1985. *Teaching the Gifted Child.* 3d ed. Newton, Mass.: Allyn and Bacon.

Gallagher, J.J., and Ramey, C.T. (Eds.). 1987. *The Malleability of Children.* Baltimore: Paul H. Brookes.

Gallagher, T., and Darnton, B. 1978. Conversational aspects of language-disordered children; revision behaviors. *Journal of Speech and Hearing Research 21*:118.

Galvin, G.A. 1981. Uses and abuses of the WISC-R with the learnig disabled. *Journal of Learning Disabilities 14*:326.

Gardner, H. 1978. *Developmental Psychology—An Introduction*. Boston: Little, Brown.

Gardner, H. 1983. *Frames of Mind*. New York: Basic Books.

Garfield, J. 1964. Motor impersistence in normal and brain damaged children. *Neurology 14*:623.

Gascon, G.G. 1984. Chronic and recurrent headache in children and adolescents. *Pediatric Clinics of North America 31*:1027.

Gaskins, I.W. 1981. Reading for learning: going beyond basals in the elementary grades. *Reading Teacher 35*:323.

Gerber, A. 1993. *Language-Related Learning Disabilities: Their Nature and Treatment*. Baltimore: Paul H. Brookes.

Gersten, R., and Woodward, J. 1994. The language minority student and special education: issues, trends, and paradoxes. *Exceptional Children 60*:310.

Gerstmann, J. 1940. Syndrome of finger agnosia, disorientation for right and left, agraphia, and acalculia. *Archives of Neurological Psychiatry 44*:398.

Geschwind, N., and Behan, P. 1982. Left-handedness: association with immune disease, migraine, and developmental learning disorder. *Proceedings of the National Academy of Sciences, USA 79*:5097.

Geschwind, N., and Levitsky, W. 1968. Human brain: left-right asymmetries in temporal speech region. *Science 6*:327.

Gesell, A. 1928. *Infancy and Human Growth*. New York: Macmillan.

Getman, G.N. 1985. A commentary on vision training. *Journal of Learning Disabilities 18*:505.

Gibson, E.J. 1971. Perceptual learning and the theory of word perception. *Cognitive Psychology 2*:351.

Ginsburg, H., and Opper, S. 1981. *Piaget's Theory of Intellectual Development: An Introduction*. 2d ed. Englewood Cliffs, N.J.: Prentice-Hall.

Gittelman, R. 1980. The role of psychological tests for differential diagnosis in child psychiatry. *Journal of the American Academy of Child Psychiatry 19*:413.

Glass, A.L., and Perna, J. 1986. The role of syntax in reading disability. *Journal of Learning Disabilities 19*:354.

Golden, G.S. 1984. Controversial therapies. *Pediatric Clinics of North America 31*:459.

Goodman, R., and Stevenson, J. 1989. A twin study of hyperactivity—II: the aeti-ological role of genes, family relationships, and perinatal adversity. *Journal of Child Psychology and Psychiatry 30*:691.

Gopher, D. and Navon, D. 1980. How is performance limited: testing the notion of central capacity. *Acta Psychologica 46*:161.

Gordon, E.W. 1983. Culture and ethnicity. In M.D. Levine, W.B. Carey, A.C. Crocker, and R.T. Gross (Eds.), *Developmental-Behavioral Pediatrics.* Philadelphia: W.B. Saunders.

Gottesman, R.L., Hankin, D., Levinson, W., and Beck, P. 1984. Neurodevelop-mental functioning of good and poor readers in urban schools. *Journal of Developmental and Behavioral Pediatrics 5*:109.

Gottlieb, M.I. 1983. Otitis media. In M.D. Levine, W.B. Carey, A.C. Crocker, and R.T. Gross (Eds.), *Developmental-Behavioral Pediatrics.* Philadelphia: W.B. Saunders.

Graef, J.W. 1983. Environmental toxins. In M.D. Levine, W.B. Carey, A.C. Crocker, and R.T. Gross (Eds.), *Developmental-Behavioral Pediatrics.* Philadelphia: W.B. Saunders.

Graves, D.H. 1983. *Writing: Teachers and Children at Work.* London: Heinemann Educational Books.

Gray, W.S. 1925. *24th Yearbook of the NSSE Part I-Report of the National Com-mittee on Reading.* Bloomington, Ill.: Public School Publishing Co.

Green, W.H. 1995. *Child and Adolescent Psychopharmacology*, 2d ed. Baltimore: Williams and Wilkins.

Greenwald, A.G. 1970. Sensory feedback mechanisms in performance control. *Psychology Review 70*:73.

Gregg, N. 1986. Cohesion: inter and intra sentence errors. *Journal of Learning Disabilities 19*:338.

Grimwood, D., Anderson, V.A., Bond, L., Catroppa, C., Hore, R.L., Keir, E.H., Nolan, T., and Robertson, D.M. 1995. Adverse outcomes of bacterial menin-gitis in school-age survivors. *Pediatrics 95*:646.

Gross, R.T., and Duke, P.M. 1983. Effects of early versus late physical matura-tion on adolescent behavior. In M.D. Levine, W.B. Carey, A.C. Crocker, and R.T. Gross (Eds.), *Developmental-Behavioral Pediatrics.* Philadelphia: W.B. Saunders.

Gualtieri, C.T., Goldin, R.N., and Fahs, J.J. 1983. New developments in pediatric psychopharmacology. *Journal of Developmental and Behavioral Pediatrics 4*:202.

Guillford, J.P. 1967. *The Nature of Human Intelligence.* New York: McGraw-Hill.

Hagerman, R.J., and McBogg, P.M. 1983. *The Fragile X Syndrome.* Dillon, Colo.: Spectra Publications.

Halford, G.S., Maybery, M.T., O'Hare, A.W., and Gratn, P. 1994. The development of memory and processing capacity. *Child Development 65*:1338.

Hall, J. 1988. *Evaluating and Improving Written Expression: A Practical Guide for Teachers*, 2d ed. Boston: Allyn and Bacon.

Hallgren, B. 1950. Specific dyslexia ("congenital word blindness"): a clinical and genetic study. *Acta Psychiatrica et Neurologica Scandinavia,* supplement no. 65.

Hallowell, E.M., and Ratey, J.J. 1994. *Driven to Distraction.* New York: Simon and Schuster.

Hammill, D., and Larsen, S. 1996. *Test of Written Language–3.* Austin, Tex.: Pro-Ed.

Hansen, C.L. 1978. Story retelling with average and learning disabled readers as a measure of reading comprehension. *Learning Disability Quarterly 1*:62.

Harris, A.J., and Sipay, E.R. 1985. *How to Increase Reading Ability.* 8th ed. New York: Longman.

Hart, K.M. 1981. *Children's Understanding of Mathematics: 11–16.* London: John Murray Ltd.

Hasher, L. and Zacks, R.T. 1979. Automatic and effortful processes in memory. *Journal of Experimental Psychology: General 108*:356.

Hauser-Cram, P., Pierson, D.E., Walker, D.K., and Tivnan, T. 1991. *Early Education in the Public Schools.* San Francisco: Jossey Bass.

Hayes, B., and Peters, C. 1989. The role of reading instruction in the social studies classroom. In D. Lapp, J. Flood, and N. Farnan (Eds.), *Content Areas Reading and Learning: Instructional Strategies.* Englewood Cliffs, N.J.: Prentice-Hall.

Healy, A., Hein, H.A., and Rubin, I.L. 1983. Perinatal stresses. In M.D. Levine, W.B. Carey, A.C. Crocker, and R.T. Gross (Eds.), *Developmental-Behavioral Pediatrics.* Philadelphia: W.B. Saunders.

Hechtman, L. 1994. Genetic and neurobiological aspects of attention deficit hyperactive disorder: a review. *Journal of Psychiatric Neuroscience 19*: 193.

Heiskanen, O., and Kaste, M. 1974. Late prognosis of severe brain injury in children. *Developmental Medicine and Child Neurology 16*:11.

Hermann, K. 1959. *Reading Disability: A Medical Study of Word-Blindness and Related Handicaps.* Copenhagen: Munksgaard.

Hier, D.B., Atkins, L., and Perlo, V.P. 1980. Learning disorders and sex chromosome aberrations. *Journal of Mental Deficiency 24*:17.

Hinshaw, S.P. 1992. Externalizing behavior problems and academic under-achievement in childhood and adolescence: causal relationships and underlying mechanisms. *Psychological Bulletin 111*:127.

Hirsh, D.L.O., and Russo, D.C. 1983. Behavior management. In M.D. Levine, W.B. Carey, A.C. Crocker, and R.T. Gross (Eds.), *Developmental-Behavioral Pediatrics*. Philadelphia: W.B. Saunders.

Hiscock, M., and Kinsbourne, M. 1982. Laterality and dyslexia: a critical view. *Annals of Dyslexia 32*:177.

Hoffer, A. 1979. *Geometry, A Model of the Universe*. Menlo Park, Calif.: Addison-Wesley Publishing Co.

Holtzman, N.A., Kronmal, R.A., vanDoorninck, W., Azen, C., and Koch, R. 1986. Effect of age at loss of dietary control on intellectual performance and behavior of children with phenylketonuria. *New England Journal of Medicine 314*:593.

Hooper, S.R., and Willis, W.G. 1989. *Learning Disability Subtyping*. New York: Springer-Verlag, pp. 20–37.

Hooper, S.R., Montgomery, J., Swartz, C., Reed, M., Sandler, A., Watson, T., and Wasileski, T. 1994. Measurement of written expression. In G. Reid Lyon (Ed.), *Frames of Reference for the Assessment of Learning Disabilities: New Views on Measurement Issues*. Baltimore: Paul H. Brookes.

Hoover, J.J. and Patton, J.R. 1995. *Teaching Students with Learning Problems to Use Study Skills*. Austin, Tex.: Pro-Ed.

Howard, B. 1983. Nutrition and development. In M.D. Levine, W.B. Carey, A.C. Crocker, and R.T. Gross (Eds.), *Developmental-Behavioral Pediatrics*. Philadelphia: W.B. Saunders.

Howell, D. 1971. Significance of iron deficiencies: consequences of mild deficiency in children: extent and meaning of iron deficiency in the United States. In *Summary Proceedings of the Workshop of Food and Nutrition Board*. Washington, D.C.: National Academy of Sciences.

Huessy, H.R., Metoyer, M., and Townsend, M. 1974. 8–10 year follow-up of 84 children treated for behavioral disorder in rural Vermont. *Acta Paedopsychiatrica 40*:230.

Hutchings, D.E. 1993. The puzzle of cocaine's effects following maternal use during pregnancy: are there reconcilable differences? *Neurotoxicology and Teratology 15*:281.

Hynd, G.W., Semrud-Clikeman, M., and Lyytinen, H. 1991. Brain imaging in learning disabilities. In J.E. Orzbut and G.W. Hynd (Eds.), *Neuropsychological Foundations of Learning Disabilities: A Handbook of Issues, Methods, and Practice*. San Diego, Calif.: Academic Press, 475.

Isaacson, S. 1988. Effective strategies in written language. In E.L. Meyers, G.A. Vergason, and R.L. Whelan (Eds.), *Effective Instructional Strategies for Exceptional Children.* Denver: Love Publishing Company.

Israel, L. 1984. Word knowledge and word retrieval: phonological and semantic strategies. In G.P. Wallach and K.G. Butler (Eds.), *Language Learning Disabilities in School-Age Children.* Baltimore: Williams and Wilkins.

Jackson, P. 1983. The daily grind. In H. Giroux and D. Purpel (Eds.), *The Hidden Curriculum and Moral Education.* Berkeley, Calif.: McCutchan Publishing Corp.

Jastak, J., and Wilkinson, G. 1984. *Wide Range Achievement Test–Revised.* Wilmington, Del.: Jastak Associates.

Jenkins, M.R., and Culbertson, J.L. 1996. Prenatal exposure to alcohol. In R.L. Adams, O.A. Parsons, J.L. Culbertson, and S.J. Nixon (Eds.), *Neuropsychology for Clinical Practice: Etiology, Assessment, and Treatment of Common Neurological Disorders.* Washington, D.C.: American Psychological Association.

Johnson, B.D. 1973. *Marijuana Users and Drug Subcultures.* New York: John Wiley & Sons.

Johnson, D. 1968. The language continuum. *Bulletin of the Orton Society 28:*1.

Johnson, D., and Myklebust, H. 1967. *Learning Disabilities: Educational Principles and Practices.* New York: Grune and Stratton.

Joseph, J. 1992. *Brain Mechanisms, Attention-Deficit, and Related Mental Disorders.* Springfield, Ill.: Charles C. Thomas.

Kail, R.V. 1979. *The Development of Memory in Children.* San Francisco: W.H. Freeman.

Kamhi, A.G., Catts, H.W., Mauer, D., Apel, K., and Gentry, B.F. 1988. Phonological and spatial processing abilities in language- and reading-impaired children. *Journal of Learning Disabilities 53:*316.

Kane, R.B. 1968. The readability of mathematical English. *Journal of Research in Science Teaching 5:*296.

Kaplan, E., and Goodglass, H. 1975. *The Boston Naming Test.* Experimental Edition.

Karniski, W.M., Levine, M.D., Clarke, S., Palfrey, J.A., and Meltzer, L.J. 1982. A study of neurodevelopmental findings in early adolescent delinquents. *Journal of Adolescent Health Care 3:*151.

Kemme, S.L. 1981. References of speech acts as characteristics of mathematical classroom conversation. *Educational Studies in Mathematics 12:*43.

Kephart, N.C. 1971. *The Slow Learner in the Classroom.* Columbus, Ohio: Charles E. Merrill.

Kessen, W., and Scott, D. 1992. The development of behavior: problems, theories, and findings. In M.D. Levine, W.B. Carey, A.C. Crocker, and R.T. Gross

(Eds.), *Developmental-Behavioral Pediatrics.* 2d ed. Philadelphia: W.B. Saunders.

Kinsbourne, M. 1984. Hyperactivity management: the impact of special diets. In M.D. Levine and P. Satz (Eds.), *Middle Childhood: Development and Dysfunction.* Baltimore: University Park Press.

Kinsbourne, M., and Warrington, E. 1964. The development of finger differentiation. *Quarterly Journal of Experimental Psychology 15*:132.

Kinsbourne, M., and Warrington, E. 1966. Developmental factors in reading and writing backwardness. In J. Money (Ed.), *The Disabled Reader.* Baltimore: Johns Hopkins University Press.

Kirby, J., and Das, J.P. 1978. Information processing and human abilities. *Journal of Educational Psychology 70*:58.

Kirk, S.A., McCarthy, J.J., and Kirk, W.D. 1968. *Illinois Test of Psycholinguistic Abilities.* Champaign, Ill.: University of Illinois Press.

Klaus, M.H., and Kennell, J.H. 1982. *Parent-Infant Bonding.* St. Louis: The C.V. Mosby Company.

Klein-Konigsberg, E. 1984. Semantic integration and language learning disabilities: from research to assessment and intervention. In G.P. Wallach and K.G. Butler (Eds.), *Language Learning Disabilities in School Age Children.* Baltimore: Williams and Wilkins.

Klin, A., Sparrow, S.S., Volkmar, F.R., Cicchetti, D.V., and Rourke, B.P. 1995. Asperger syndrome. In B.P. Rourke (Ed.), *Syndrome of Nonverbal Learning Disabilities: Neurodevelopmental Manifestations.* New York: Guilford Press.

Kohlberg, L. 1963. Development of children's orientation towards a moral order. I. Sequence in the development of moral thought. *Vita Humana 6*:11.

Kraft, M. 1968. The face-hand test. *Developmental Medicine and Child Neurology 10*:214.

Kuczaj, S.A. 1978. Children's judgments of grammatical and ungrammatical irregular past-tense verbs. *Child Development 49*:319.

Kurtz, P.D., Gaudin, J.M., Wodarski, J.S., and Howing, P.T. 1993. Maltreatment and the school-aged child: school performance consequences. *Child Abuse and Neglect 17*:581.

Lee, H., and Barratt, M.S. 1993. Cognitive development of preterm low birth weight children at 5 to 8 years old. *Developmental and Behavioral Pediatrics 14*:242.

Lee, L.L. 1969. *Northwestern Syntax Screening Test.* Evanston, Ill.: Northwestern University Press.

LeMay, M., and Culebras, A. 1972. Human brain morphologic differences in the hemispheres demonstrable by carotid arteriography. *New England Journal of Medicine 287*:168.

Lenz, B.K., Ellis, E.S., and Scanlon, D. 1996. *Teaching Learning Strategies to Adolescents and Adults with Learning Disabilities*. Austin, Tex.: Pro-Ed.

Lerer, R.J., Lerer, M.P., and Artner, J. 1977. The effects of methylphenidate on the handwriting of children with minimal brain dysfunction. *Journal of Pediatrics 91*:127.

Lerner, J.W., Lowenthal, B., and Lerner, S.R. 1995. *Attention Deficit Disorders: Assessment and Teaching*. Pacific Grove, Calif.: Brooks/Cole Publishing.

Leslie, L., and Caldwell, J. 1995. *Qualitative Reasoning Inventory–2*. Laporte, Ind.: Harper Collins.

Levine, M.D. et al. In preparation. *The Survey of Teenage Readiness and Neurodevelopmental Status (STRANDS)*.

Levine, M.D. 1980. *The ANSER System*. Cambridge, Mass.: Educators Publishing Service.

Levine, M.D. 1982*a*. The high prevalence–low severity developmental disorders of school children. In L. Barness (Ed.), *Advances in Pediatrics*. Chicago: Yearbook Publishers.

Levine, M.D. 1982*b*. Encopresis: its potentiation, evaluation, and alleviation. *Pediatric Clinics of North America 29*:315.

Levine, M.D. 1984*a*. *The ANSER System Follow-up Questionnaires*. Cambridge, Mass.: Educators Publishing Service.

Levine, M.D. 1984*b*. Reading disability: do the eyes have it? *Pediatrics 73*:869.

Levine, M.D. 1984*c*. Cumulative neurodevelopmental debts: their impact on productivity in late middle childhood. In M.D. Levine and P. Satz (Eds.), *Middle Childhood: Development and Dysfunction*. Baltimore: University Park Press.

Levine, M.D. 1984*d*. Persistent inattention and unintention. In M.D. Levine and P. Satz (Eds.), *Middle Childhood: Development and Dysfunction*. Baltimore: University Park Press.

Levine, M.D. 1985. *Pediatric Examination of Educational Readiness at Middle Childhood (PEERAMID)*. Cambridge, Mass.: Educators Publishing Service.

Levine, M.D. 1990. *Keeping a Head in School*. Cambridge, Mass.: Educators Publishing Service.

Levine, M.D. 1993. *All Kinds of Minds*. Cambridge, Mass.: Educators Publishing Service.

Levine, M.D. 1994. *Educational Care*. Cambridge, Mass.: Educators Publishing Service.

Levine, M.D. 1996. *The ANSER System (Revised)*. Cambridge, Mass.: Educators Publishing Service.

Levine, M.D. 1997. *The ANSER System Guidelines*. Cambridge, Mass.: Educators Publishing Service.

Levine, M.D., and Rappaport, L. 1983. *Pediatric Early Elementary Examination (PEEX)*. Cambridge, Mass.: Educators Publishing Service.

Levine, M.D., and Rappaport, L. 1984. Recurrent abdominal pain in childhood: the loneliness of the long distance physician. *Pediatric Clinics of North America 31*:969.

Levine, M.D. and Sandler, A. 1996. *The Pediatric Early Elementary Examination (PEEX 2)*. Cambridge, Mass.: Educators Publishing Service.

Levine, M.D. and Sandler, A. 1996. *The Pediatric Examination of Educational Readiness at Middle Childhood (PEERAMID 2)*. Cambridge, Mass.: Educators Publishing Service.

Levine, M.D., and Schneider, E. 1982. *Pediatric Examination of Educational Readiness (PEER)*. Cambridge, Mass.: Educators Publishing Service.

Levine, M.D., and Zallen, B.G. 1984. The learning disorders of adolescence: organic and non-organic failure to strive. *Pediatric Clinics of North America 31*:345.

Levine, M.D., Brooks, R., and Shonkoff, J.P. 1980. *A Pediatric Approach to Learning Disorders*. New York: John Wiley & Sons.

Levine, M.D., Clarke, S., and Ferb, T. 1981. The child as a diagnostic participant: helping students describe their learning disorders. *Journal of Learning Disabilities 14*:527.

Levine, M.D., Karniski, W.M., Clarke, S., et al. 1985. A study of risk factor complexes in early adolescent delinquents. *American Journal of Diseases of Children 139*:50.

Levine, M.D., Oberklaid, F., and Meltzer, L.J. 1981. Developmental output failure—a study of low productivity in school age children. *Pediatrics 67*:18.

Levinson, H.N. 1981. *A Solution to the Riddle Dyslexia*. New York: Springer-Verlag.

Lewis, D.O., Shanok, S.S., and Balla, D.A. 1979. Perinatal difficulties, head trauma, and child abuse in the medical histories of seriously delinquent children. *American Journal of Psychiatry 136*:419.

Lewis, D.O., Shanok, S.S., Pincus, J.H., and Glaser, G.H. 1979. Violent juvenile delinquents: psychiatric, neurological, psychological and abuse factors. *Journal of the American Academy of Child Psychiatry 18*:307.

Liberman, I.Y. 1985. Should so-called modality preferences determine the nature of instruction for children with reading disabilities? In F.H. Duffy and N. Geschwind (Eds.), *Dyslexia—A Neuroscientific Approach to Clinical Evaluation*. Boston: Little, Brown.

Liberman, I.Y., and Shankweiler, D. 1979. Speech, the alphabet, and teaching to read. In L. Resnick and P. Weaver (Eds.), *Theory and Practice of Early Reading*. Hillsdale, N.J.: Lawrence Erlbaum Associates.

Liberman, I.Y., Shankweiler, D., Fischer, F.W., and Carter, B. 1974. Explicit syllable and phoneme segmentation in the young child. *Journal of Experimental Child Psychology 18*:201.

Liberman, I.Y., Shankweiler, D., Liberman, A.W., Fowler, C., and Fischer, F.W. 1977. Phonetic segmentation and recoding in the beginning reader. In A.S. Reber and D. Scarborough (Eds.), *Toward a Psychology of Reading: The Proceedings of the CUNY Conferences*. Hillsdale, N.J.: Lawrence Erlbaum.

Licht, B.G., and Dweck, C.S. 1984. Determinants of academic achievement: the interaction of children's achievement orientations with skill area. *Developmental Psychology 20*:628.

Liles, B., Schulman, M., and Bartlett, S. 1977. Judgments of grammaticality by normal and language-disordered children. *Journal of Speech and Hearing Disorders 42*:199.

Lindamood, P. 1994. Issues in researching the link between phonological awareness, learning disabilities, and spelling. In G. Reid Lyon, (Ed.), *Frames of Reference for the Assessment of Learning Disabilities: New Views on Measurement Issues*. Baltimore: Paul H. Brookes.

Lloyd-Still, J.D., Hurwitz, I., Wolff, P.H., and Shwachmann, H. 1974. Intellectual development after severe malnutrition in infancy. *Pediatrics 54*:306.

Loeber, R., and Dishion, T. 1983. Early predictors of male delinquency. *Psychological Bulletin 94*:68.

Lopez-Reyna, N.A. 1996. The importance of meaningful contexts in bilingual special education: moving to whole language. *Learning Disabilities Research and Practice 11*:120.

Lorsback, T.C., and Gray, J.W. 1986. Item identification speed and memory span performance in learning disabled children. *Contemporary Educational Psychology 11*:68.

Lovell, K., Gray, E.A., and Oliver, D.C. 1964. A further study of cognitive and other disabilities in backward readers of average non-verbal reasoning scores. *British Journal of Educational Psychology 74*:68.

Lucangeli, D., Galderisi, D., and Cornoldi, C. 1995. Specific and general transfer effects following metamemory training. *Learning Disabilities Research and Practice 10*:11.

Lucas, E. 1980. Remediation activities and techniques for spatio-temporal disorders. *Semantic and Pragmatic Language Disorders*. Rockville, Md.: Aspen Systems Corp.

Luria, A. 1980. *Higher Cortical Functions in Man*. New York: Basic Books.

Mackay, R., Barkman, B., and Jordan, B.R. (Eds.). 1979. *Reading in a Second Language*. Rowley, Mass.: Newbury House.

Macoby, E.E., and Jacklin, C.N. 1974. *The Psychology of Sex Differences*. Stanford, Calif.: Stanford University Press.

Mann, L., and Sabatino, D.A. 1985. *Foundations of Cognitive Processing in Remedial and Special Education*. Rockville, Md.: Aspen Publications.

Marland, S. 1972. *Education of the Gifted and Talented*. Report to the Congress of the United States by the U.S. Commission of Education. Washington, D.C.: U.S. Government Printing Office.

Mathison, C., and Lungren, L. 1989. Using computers effectively in content area classes. In D. Lapp, J. Flood, and N. Farnan (Eds.), *Content Areas Reading and Learning: Instructional Strategies*. Englewood Cliffs, N.J.: Prentice-Hall.

Mattis, S. 1978. Dyslexia syndromes: a working hypothesis that works. In A.L. Benton and D. Pearl (Eds.), *Dyslexia: An Appraisal of Current Knowledge*. New York: Oxford University Press.

May, F. 1990. *Reading As Communication*, 3d ed. Columbus, Ohio: Merrill.

Mayes, A.R. 1995. The assessment of memory disorders. In A.D. Baddeley, B.A. Wilson, and F.N. Watts (Eds.), *Handbook of Memory Disorders*. New York: John Wiley.

Mazzocco, M.M.M., Pennington, B.F., and Hagerman, R.J. 1993. The neurocognitive phenotype of female carriers of fragile x: additional evidence for specificity. *Developmental and Behavioral Pediatrics 14*:328.

McCall, R.B. 1981. Nature:nurture and the two realms of development: a proposed integration with respect to mental development. *Child Development 55*:1.

McCarron, L.T. 1976. *McCarron Assessment of Neuromuscular Development*. Texas: McCarron-Dial Systems.

McCauley, E., Ross, J.L., Kushner, H., and Cutler, G. 1995. Self-esteem and behavior in girls with Turner syndrome. *Developmental and Behavioral Pediatrics 16*:82.

McGuire, K.D., and Weisz, J.R. 1982. Social cognition and behavior correlates of preadolescent chumship. *Child Development 53*:1478.

McKee, R.D., and Squire, L.R. 1993. On the development of declarative memory. *Journal of Experimental Psychology: Memory and Cognition 19*:397.

McMichael, A.J., Baghurst, P.A., Vimpani, G.V., Wigg, N.R., Robertson, E.F., and Tong, S. 1994. Tooth lead levels and IQ in school-age children: the Port Pirie Cohort Study. *American Journal of Epidemiology 140*:489.

McNeil, J.D. 1984. *Reading Comprehension: New Directions for Classroom Practice*. Glenview, Ill.: Scott, Foresman and Co.

McTear, M.F., and Conti-Ramsden, G. 1992. *Pragmatic Disability in Children.* San Diego, Calif.: Singular Publishing Group.

Mead, R.G. 1983. *Foreign Languages: Key Links in the Chain of Learning.* Middlebury, Vt.: Northeast Conference on the Teaching of Foreign Languages, Inc.

Meichenbaum, D. 1977. *Cognitive-Behavior Modification.* New York: Plenum Publishing Corp.

Meier, J. 1970. Prevalance and characteristics of learning disabilities in second-grade children. *Journal of Learning Disabilities 4*:6.

Meltzer, L.J. 1984. Cognitive assessment and the diagnosis of learning problems. In M.D. Levine and P. Satz (Eds.), *Middle Childhood: Development and Dysfunction.* Baltimore: University Park Press.

Meltzer, L.J. 1986. *Surveys of Problem-Solving and Educational Skills.* Cambridge, Mass.: Educators Publishing Service.

Meltzer, L. 1996. Strategic learning in children with learning disabilities. *Advances in Learning and Behavioral Disabilities 10B*:181.

Menyuk, P. 1977. *Language and Maturation.* Cambridge, Mass.: MIT Press.

Mercer, C.D., and Mercer, A.R. 1981. *Teaching Students with Learning Problems.* Columbus, Ohio: Charles E. Merrill.

Merzenich, M.M., Jenkins, W.M., Johnston, P., Schreiner, C., Miller, S.L., and Tallal, P. 1996. Temporal processing deficits of language-learning impaired children ameliorated by training. *Science 271*:77.

Miller, L. 1984. Problem solving and language disorders. In G.P. Wallach and K.G. Butler (Eds.), *Language Learning Disabilities in School Children.* Baltimore: Williams and Wilkins.

Miller, P. 1994. Individual differences in children's strategic behavior: utilization deficiencies. *Learning and Individual Differences 6*:285.

Miller, W. 1988. *Reading Teacher's Complete Diagnosis and Correction Manual.* West Nyack, N.Y.: Center for Applied Research in Education.

Millichap, J.G. 1977. *Learning Disabilities and Related Disorders.* Chicago: Year Book Medical Publishers.

Millman, R.B., and Botvin, G.J. 1983. Substance use, abuse, and dependence. In M.D. Levine, W.B. Carey, A.C. Crocker, and R.T. Gross (Eds.), *Developmental-Behavioral Pediatrics.* Philadelphia: W.B. Saunders.

Mirsky, A.F. 1996. Disorders of attention: a neuropsychological perspective. In G.R. Lyon and N.A. Krasnegor (Eds.), *Attention, Memory, and Executive Function.* Baltimore: Paul H. Brookes.

Mirsky, A.F., Anthony, A.J., Duncan, C.C., Ahearn, M.B., and Kellam, S.G. 1991. Analysis of the elements of attention: a neuropsychological approach. *Neuropsychology Review 2*:109.

Moats, L. 1994. Assessment of spelling in learning disabilities research. In G. Reid Lyon, (Ed.), *Frames of Reference for the Assessment of Learning Disabilities: New Views on Measurement Issues*. Baltimore: Paul H. Brookes.

Moats, L.C. 1983. A comparison of the spelling errors of older dyslexic and second-grade normal children. *Annals of Dyslexia 33*:121.

Montgomery, J.W. 1995. Examination of phonological working memory in specifically language-impaired children. *Applied Psycholinguistics 16*:355.

Moore, M.J., Kagan, J., Sahl, M., and Grant, S. 1982. Cognitive profiles in reading disability. *Genetic Psychology Monographs 105*:41.

Morice, R., and Slaghuis, W. 1985. Language performance and reading ability at 8 years of age. *Applied Psycholinguistics 6*:141.

Morris, N.T., and Crump, W.B. 1982. Syntactic and vocabulary development in the written language of learning disabled and non-learning disabled students at four age levels. *Learning Disability Quarterly 5*:163.

Morrison, J.R., and Stewart, M.A. 1973. Evidence for polygenetic inheritance in the hyperactive child syndrome. *American Journal of Child Psychiatry 130*:791.

Myers, J. 1984. *Writing to Learn Across the Curriculum*. Bloomington, Ind.: Phi Delta Kappa Educational Foundation.

Myklebust, H.R. 1965. *Development and Disorders of Written Language*, vol. 1.: *Picture Story Language Test*. New York: Grune and Stratton.

Nagy, W.E., and Anderson, R.C. 1984. How many words are there in the printed school English? *Reading Research Quarterly 19*:304.

Nahrgang, C.L., and Petersen, B.T. 1986. Using writing to learn mathematics. *Mathematics Teacher 79* (6):461.

Needleman, H.L., Gunnoe, C., Leviton, A., Reed, R., Peresie, H., Maher, C., and Barrett, P. 1979. Deficits in psychological and classroom performance in children with elevated dentine lead levels. *New England Journal of Medicine 300*:689.

Nelson, N.W. 1984. Beyond information processing: the language of teachers and textbooks. In G.P. Wallach and K.G. Butler (Eds.), *Language Learning Disabilities in School Age Children*. Baltimore: Williams and Wilkins.

Newcomb, A.F., and Brady, J.E. 1982. Mutuality in boys' friendship relations. *Child Development 53*:392.

Njiokiktjien, C., deSonneville, L., and Vaal, J. 1994. Callosal size in children with learning disabilities. *Behavioural Brain Research 64*:213.

Nolan, E., and Kagan, J. 1978. Psychological factors in the face-hand test. *Archives of Neurology 35*:41.

Oden, S., and Asher, S.R. 1977. Coaching children in social skills for friendship making. *Child Development 48*:495.

Offord, D.R. 1984. Early onset of antisocial behavior. In M.D. Levine and P. Satz (Eds.), *Middle Childhood: Development and Dysfunction.* Baltimore: University Park Press.

Orton, S. 1937. *Reading, Writing, and Speech Problems in Children.* New York: W.W. Norton.

Otero, G.G., and Moeller, C. 1977. *Teaching Reading in the Social Studies: A Global Approach, Skill Series,* vol. 1. Denver: Center for Teaching International Relations, University of Denver.

Owen, F.W. 1978. Dyslexia-genetic aspects. In A.L. Benton and D. Pearl (Eds.), *Dyslexia: An Appraisal of Current Knowledge.* New York: Oxford University Press.

Paine, R.S., and Oppe, T.E. 1966. *Neurological Examination of Children. Clinics in Developmental Medicine, No. 20/21.* London: Heinemann.

Palermo, D.S. 1984. Cognition and language development. In M.D. Levine and P. Satz (Eds.), *Middle Childhood: Development and Dysfunction.* Baltimore: University Park Press.

Palfrey, J.S., Levine, M.D., Walker, D., and Sullivan, M. 1985. The emergence of attention deficits in early childhood. *Journal of Developmental and Behavioral Pediatrics* 6:339.

Paris, S., and Lindauer, B. 1976. The role of inferences in children's comprehension and memory for sentences. *Cognitive Psychology* 8:217.

Pennington, B.F. 1995. Genetics of learning disabilities. *Journal of Child Neurology* 10:s69.

Pennington, B.F., Bender, B., Puck, M., Salbenblatt, J., and Robinson, A. 1982. Learning disabilities in children with sex chromosome anomalies. *Child Development 53*:1182.

Pennington, B.F., Bennetto, L., McAleer, O., and Roberts, R.J. 1996. Executive functions and working memory. In G.R. Lyon and N.A. Krasnegor (Eds.), *Attention, Memory, and Executive Function.* Baltimore: Paul H. Brookes.

Perfetti, C.A. 1985. *Reading Ability.* New York: Oxford University Press.

Peters, J.E., Romine, J.S., and Dykman, R.A. 1975. A special neurological examination of children with learning disabilities. *Developmental Medicine and Child Neurology 17*:63.

Pfeffer, C.R., Solomon, G., Plutchik, R., et al. 1982. Suicidal behavior in latency-age psychiatric inpatients: a replication and cross validation. *Journal of the American Academy of Child Psychiatry 21*:564.

Piaget, J. 1952. *The Origins of Intelligence in Children.* New York: International University Press.

Piaget, J. 1965. *The Child's Conception of Number.* New York: W.W. Norton.

Piaget, J., and Inhelder, B. 1968. *The Psychology of the Child.* New York: Basic Books.

Pirozzolo, F.J., Dunn, K., and Zetusky, W. 1983. Physiological approaches to subtypes of developmental reading disabilities. *Topics in Learning and Learning Disabilities* 3:40.

Polatajko, H.J. 1985. A critical look at vestibular dysfunction in learning-disabled children. *Developmental Medicine and Child Neurology* 27:283.

Politzer, R.L. 1965. *Foreign Language Learning: A Linguistic Introduction.* Englewood Cliffs, N.J.: Prentice-Hall.

Pollit, E., and Leibel, R. 1976. Iron deficiency and behavior. *Journal of Pediatrics* 88:272.

Poplin, M. 1983. Assessing developmental writing abilities. *Topics in Learning and Learning Disabilities* 3:63.

Poteet, J.A. 1980. Informal assessment of written expression. *Learning Disabilities Quarterly* 3:88.

Prechtl, H., and Stemmer, C. 1962. The choreiform syndrome in children. *Developmental Medicine and Child Neurology* 4:119.

Psychological Corporation. 1992. *Wechsler Individual Achievement Test.* Austin, Tex.: Psychological Corporation, Harcourt, Brace, Jovanovich.

Puig-Antich, J., and Rabinovich, H. 1983. Major child and adolescent psychiatric disorders. In M.D. Levine, W.B. Carey, A.C. Crocker, and R.T. Gross (Eds.), *Developmental-Behavioral Pediatrics.* Philadelphia: W.B. Saunders.

Purpel, D., and Ryan, K. 1983. It comes with the territory: the inevitability of moral education in the schools. In H. Giroux and D. Purpel (Eds.), *The Hidden Curriculum and Moral Education.* Berkeley, Calif.: McCutchan Publishing Corp.

Pyle, D.W. 1979. *Intelligence.* London: Routledge and Kegan Paul Ltd.

Quinn, P., and Rapoport, J. 1974. Minor physical anomalies and neurologic status in hyperactive boys. *Pediatrics* 53:742.

Rabin, A.I., and Haworth, M.R. (Eds.). 1960. *Projective Techniques with Children.* New York: Grune and Stratton.

Rachelefsky, G.S., Wo, J., Adelson, J., Mickey, M.R., Spector, S.L., Katz, R.M., Siegel, S.C., and Rohr, A.S. 1986. Behavior abnormalities and poor school performance due to oral theophylline use. *Pediatrics* 78:1133.

Ramey, C.T., Yeates, K.O., and Short, E.J. 1984. The plasticity of intellectual development: insights from preventive intervention. *Child Development* 55:1913.

Rapoport, J.L. 1983. Stimulant drug therapy of hyperactivity: an update. In S. Guze, F. Earls, and J. Barrett (Eds.), *Childhood Psychopathology and Development.* New York: Raven Press.

Rapp, D.J. 1979. *Allergies and Hyperactivity.* New York: Simon & Schuster.

Raskin, L.A., Shaywitz, S.E., Shaywitz, B.A., Anderson, G.M., and Cohen, D.J. 1984. Neurochemical correlates of attention deficit disorder. *Pediatric Clinics of North America 31*:387.

Raven, J.C. 1960. *Guide to the Standard Progressive Matrices.* London: H.K. Lewis.

Rayner, K. 1983. Eye movements, perceptual span, and reading disability. *Annals of Dyslexia 33*:163.

Read, C. 1971. Preschool children's knowledge of English phonology. *Harvard Educational Review 41*:34.

Reichman, J., and Healey, W.C. 1983. Learning disabilities and conductive hearing loss involving otitis media. *Journal of Learning Disabilities 16*:272.

Richards, G.P., Samuels, S.J., Turnure, J., and Ysseldyke, J. 1990. Sustained and selective attention in children with learning disabilities. *Journal of Learning Disabilities 23*:129.

Riesman, D. 1953. *The Lonely Crowd: A Study of the Changing American Character.* New York: Doubleday.

Roberts, J.E., Burchinal, M.R., and Clarke-Klein, S.M. 1995. Otitis media in early childhood and cognitive, academic, and behavior outcomes. *Journal of Pediatric Psychology 20*:645.

Rosner, J., and Simon, D. 1971. The auditory analysis test: an initial report. *Journal of Learning Disabilities 4*:40.

Ross, D.M., and Ross, S.A. 1982. *Hyperactivity—Current Issues, Research and Theory.* 2d ed. New York: John Wiley & Sons.

Ross, L. 1981. The "intuitive scientist" formulation and its developmental implications. In J.H. Flavell and L. Ross, *Social Cognitive Development.* Cambridge: Cambridge University Press.

Roswell, F.G., and Natchez, G. 1977. *Reading Disability: A Human Approach.* New York: Basic Books.

Rourke, B.P. 1995. Introduction: the NLD syndrome and the white matter model. In B.P. Rourke (Ed.), *Syndrome of Nonverbal Learning Disabilities: Neurodevelopmental Manifestations.* New York: Guilford Press.

Rourke, B.P., and Finlayson, M.A.J. 1978. Neuropsychological significance of variations in patterns of academic performance: verbal and visual-spatial abilities. *Journal of Abnormal Child Psychology 6*:121.

Rourke, B.P., and Strang, J.D. 1983. Subtypes of reading and arithmetic disabilities: a neuropsychological analysis. In M. Rutter (Ed.), *Developmental Neuropsychiatry.* New York: Guilford Press.

Rourke, B.P., Del Dotto, J.E., Rourke, S.B., and Casey, J.E. 1990. Nonverbal learning disabilities: the syndrome and a case study. *Journal of School Psychology 28*:361.

Routh, D.K. 1978. Hyperactivity. In R.R. Magrab (Ed.), *Psychological Management of Pediatric Problems,* vol. 2. Baltimore: University Park Press.

Rovet, J.F. 1993. The psychoeducational characteristics of children with Turner syndrome. *Journal of Learning Disabilities 26:*333.

Rubin, D. 1983. *Teaching Reading and Study Skills in Content Areas.* New York: CBS College Publishing.

Rubin, H., and Liberman, I.Y. 1983. Exploring the oral and written language errors made by language disabled children. *Annals of Dyslexia 33:*111.

Rumbaugh, D.M., and Washburn, D.A. 1996. Attention and memory in relation to learning. In G.R. Lyon and N.A. Krasnegor (Eds.), *Attention, Memory, and Executive Function.* Baltimore: Paul H. Brookes.

Rutter, M., Maughan, B., Mortimore, P., Ouston, J., and Smith, A. 1979. *Fifteen Thousand Hours: Secondary Schools and Their Effects on Children.* Cambridge, Mass.: Harvard University Press.

Ryan, E.B. 1978. Metalinguistic development and reading. In F.B. Murray (Ed.), *The Development of the Reading Process.* Newark, Del.: International Reading Association.

Safer, D.J. 1973. A familial factor in minimal brain dysfunction. *Behavioral Genetics 3:*175.

Sanders, A.F. 1983. Towards a model of stress and performance. *Acta Psychologica 53:*61.

Satterfield, J.H. 1973. EEG issues in children with minimal brain dysfunction. *Seminars in Psychiatry 5:*35.

Sattler, J.M. 1974. *Assessment of Children's Intelligence.* Philadelphia: W.B. Saunders.

Schaffer, R. 1977. *Mothering.* Cambridge, Mass.: Harvard University Press.

Schneider, M.B., Friedman, S.B., and Fisher, M. 1995. Stated and unstated reasons for visiting a high school nurse's office. *Journal of Adolescent Health 16:*35.

Schofield, J.W. 1981. Complementary and conflicting identities: images and interaction in an interracial school. In S.R. Asher and J.M. Gottman (Eds.), *The Development of Children's Friendships.* Cambridge: Cambridge University Press.

Schorr, L.B. 1983. Environmental deterrents: poverty, affluence, violence, and television. In M.D. Levine, W.B. Carey, A.C. Crocker, and R.T. Gross (Eds.), *Developmental-Behavioral Pediatrics.* Philadelphia: W.B. Saunders.

Schubert, D.S.P., Wagner, M.E., and Schubert, H.J.P. 1983. Effects of sibling constellations. In M.D. Levine, W.B. Carey, A.C. Crocker, and R.T. Gross (Eds.), *Developmental-Behavioral Pediatrics.* Philadelphia: W.B. Saunders.

Scott, C.M. 1988. Producing complex sentences. *Topics in Language Disorders 8:*44.

Sedita, J. 1989. *Landmark Study Skills Guide*. Prides Crossing, Mass.: Landmark Foundation.

Selman, R.L. 1981. The child as a friendship philosopher. In S.R. Asher and J.M. Gottman (Eds.), *The Development of Children's Friendships*. Cambridge: Cambridge University Press.

Semel, E.M., and Wiig, E.H. 1980. *Clinical Evaluation of Language Functions*. Columbus, Ohio: Charles E. Merrill.

Semrud-Clikeman, M., and Hynd, G.W. 1990. Right hemispheric dysfunction in nonverbal learning disabilities: social, academic, and adaptive functioning in adults and children. *Psychological Bulletin 107*:196.

Sergeant, J. 1996. A theory of attention: an information processing perspective. In G.R. Lyon and N.A. Krasnegor (Eds.), *Attention, Memory, and Executive Function*. Baltimore: Paul H. Brookes.

Shafer, S.Q., O'Connor, P.A., and Stokman, C.J. 1983. Hard thoughts on neurological "soft signs." In M. Rutter (Ed.), *Developmental Neuropsychiatry*. New York: Guilford Press.

Shaffer, D., O'Connor, P.A., Shafer, S.Q., and Prupis, S. 1983. Neurological "soft signs": their origins and significance for behavior. In M. Rutter (Ed.), *Developmental Neuropsychiatry*. New York: Guilford Press.

Shankweiler, D., and Liberman, I. 1972. Misreading: a search of causes. In J.F. Davanagh and I.G. Mattingly (Eds.), *Language by Ear and by Eye: The Relationships Between Speech and Reading*. Cambridge, Mass.: MIT Press.

Shaw, L., Levine, M.D., and Belfer, M. 1982. Developmental double jeopardy: a study of clumsiness and self-esteem in learning disabled children. *Journal of Developmental and Behavioral Pediatrics 4*:191.

Shaywitz, B.A., Cohen, D.J., and Bowers, M.B. 1977. CSF monoamine metabolites in children with minimal brain dysfunction: evidence for alteration of brain dopamine. *Journal of Pediatrics 90*:67.

Shaywitz, B.A., Yager, R.D., and Klopper, J.H. 1976. Selective brain dopamine depletion in developing rats: an experimental model of minimal brain dysfunction. *Science 191*:305.

Shaywitz, S.E., Cohen, D.J., and Shaywitz, B.A. 1980. Behavior and learning difficulties in children of normal intelligence born to alcoholic mothers. *Journal of Pediatrics 96*:978.

Siegel, L.S., and Ryan, E.B. 1989. The development of working memory in normally achieving and subtypes of learning disabled children. *Child Development 60*:973.

Siegler, R.S. 1981. Developmental sequences within and between concepts. *Monographs of the Society for Research in Child Development 46* (2) no. 189.

Sigman, M. 1995. Nutrition and child development: more food for thought. *Current Directions in Psychological Science 4*:52.

Silver, L.B. 1984. *The Misunderstood Child.* New York: McGraw-Hill.

Singer, H.S., Schuerholz, L.J., and Denckla, M.B. 1995. Learning difficulties in children with Tourette syndrome. *Journal of Child Neurology 10*:s58.

Singer, L., Farkas, K., and Kliegman, R. 1992. Childhood medical and behavioral consequences of maternal cocaine use. *Journal of Pediatric Psychology 17*:389.

Smiley, P.A., and Dweck, C.S. 1994. Individual differences in achievement goals among young children. *Child Development 65*:1723.

Smith, D. and Rivers, D. 1991. Mathematics. In B.Y.L. Wong (Ed.), *Learning about Learning Disabilities.* San Diego, Calif.: Academic Press, Inc.

Smith, D.D. 1981. *Teaching the Learning Disabled.* Englewood Cliffs, N.J.: Prentice-Hall.

Snow, J.H., and Hooper, S.R. 1994. *Pediatric Traumatic Brain Injury.* London: Sage Publications.

Snyder, B.R. 1971. *The Hidden Curriculum.* New York: Alfred A. Knopf.

Solan, H.A. 1981. A rationale for the optometric treatment and management of children with learning disabilities. *Journal of Learning Disabilities 14*:568.

Spear, L.C., and Sternberg, R.J. 1986. An information-processing framework for understanding reading disability. In S.J. Ceci (Ed.), *Handbook of Cognitive, Social, and Neuropsychological Aspects of Learning Disabilities.* Hillsdale, N.J.: Lawrence Erlbaum Associates.

Speer, F. 1958. The allergic tension-fatigue syndrome. *Pediatric Clinics of North America 1*:1029.

Stanovich, K.E. 1986. Matthew effects in reading: some consequences of individual differences in the acquisition of literacy. *Reading Research Quarterly 21*:360.

Steeves, K.J. 1983. Memory as a factor in the computational efficiency of dyslexic children with high abstract reasoning ability. *Annals of Dyslexia 33*:141.

Sternberg, R.J. 1985. *Beyond IQ: A Triarchic Theory of Human Intelligence.* Cambridge: Cambridge University Press.

Sternberg, R.J., and Downing, C.J. 1982. The development of higher-order reasoning in adolescence. *Child Development 53*:209.

Stevenson, D.T., and Romney, D.M. 1984. Depression in learning disabled children. *Journal of Learning Disabilities 17*:579.

Still, G.F. 1902. The Coulstonian lectures on some abnormal physical conditions in children. *Lancet 1*:1008.

Stone, L.J., and Church, J. 1968. *Childhood and Adolescence.* 2d ed. New York: Random House.

Storm, G. 1983. Alternative therapies. In M.D. Levine, W.B. Carey, A.C. Crocker, and R.T. Gross (Eds.), *Developmental-Behavioral Pediatrics.* Philadelphia: W.B. Saunders.

Streissguth, A.P., Barr, H.M., Sampson, P.D., and Bookstein, F.L. 1994. Prenatal alcohol and offspring development: the first fourteen years. *Drug and Alcohol Dependence 36*:89.

Svien, K., and Sherlock, D. 1979. Dyscalculia and dyslexia. *Bulletin of the Orton Society 29*:269.

Swanson, H.L. 1983. A study of nonstrategic linguistic coding in visual recall of learning disabled readers. *Journal of Learning Disabilities 16*:209.

Swanson, H.L., and Cooney, J.B. 1996. Learning disabilities and memory. In D.K. Reid, W.P. Hresko, and H.L. Swanson (Eds.), *Cognitive Approaches to Learning Disabilities*, 3d ed. Austin, Tex.: Pro-Ed.

Tallal, P., Sainburg, R.L., and Jernigan, T. 1991. The neuropathology of developmental dysphasia: behavioral, morphological, physiological evidence for a pervasive temporal processing disorder. *Reading and Writing: An Interdisciplinary Journal 3*:363.

Tallal, P., Stark, R.E., and Mellits, E.D. 1985. Identification of language impaired children on the basis of rapid perception and production skills. *Brain and Language 25*:314.

Teasdale, G., et al. 1979. Predicting the outcome of individual patients in the first week after severe head injury. *Acta Neurochiruca* (supplement) *28*:161.

Terman, L. 1954. The discovery and encouragement of exceptional talent. *American Psychologist 9*:224.

Thomas, A., and Chess, S. 1977. *Temperament and Development.* New York: Brunner/Mazel.

Thomas, A., and Chess, S. 1980. *Dynamics of Psychological Development.* New York: Brunner/Mazel.

Thorndike, R., and Hagen, E. 1978. *Cognitive Abilities Test.* Chicago: The Riverside Publishing Co.

Torello, M.W. 1992. EEG and topographic brain mapping. In I. Rapin and S.J. Segalowitz (Eds.), *Handbook of Neuropsychology 6.* Amsterdam: Elsevier Science Publishers B.V.

Torgesen, J.K. 1978. Performance of reading-disabled children on serial memory tasks: a selected review of recent research. *Reading Research Quarterly 14*:57.

Torgesen, J.K. 1982. The learning disabled child as an inactive learner. *Topics in Learning and Learning Disabilities 2*:455.

Torgesen, J.K. 1985. Memory processes in reading disabled children. *Journal of Learning Disabilities 18*:350.

Torrance, E. 1974. *Torrance Tests of Creative Thinking.* Bensenville, Ill.: Scholastic Testing Services.

Touwen, B., and Prechtl, H. 1970. *The Neurological Examination of the Child with Minor Nervous Dysfunction.* Little Clubs Clinics in Developmental Medicine, no. 38. London: Spastics Society.

Tranel, D., Anderson, S.W., and Benton, A.L. 1995. Development of the concept of executive function and its relationship to the frontal lobes. In F. Boller and J. Grafman (Eds.), *Handbook of Neuropsychology*, vol. 9. Amsterdam: Elsevier.

Travis, R., and Kohli, V. 1995. The birth order factor: ordinal position, social strata, and educational achievement. *The Journal of Social Psychology 135*:499.

Vallar, G., and Papagno, C. 1995. Neuropsychological impairments of short-term memory. In A.D. Baddeley, B.A. Wilson, and F.N. Watts (Eds.), *Handbook of Memory Disorders*. New York: John Wiley.

Van Kleeck, A. 1994. Metalinguistic development. In G.E. Wallach and K.G. Butler (Eds.), *Language Learning Disabilities in School Age Children and Adolescents*. New York: Macmillan.

Van Kleeck, A. 1984. Metalinguistic skills: cutting across written language and problem-solving abilities. In G.P. Wallach and K.G. Butler (Eds.), *Language Learning Disabilities in School-Age Children*. Baltimore: Williams and Wilkins.

Vellutino, F.R. 1978. Toward an understanding of dyslexia: psychological factors in specific reading disability. In A.L. Benton and D. Pearl (Eds.), *Dyslexia: An Appraisal of Current Knowledge*. New York: Oxford University Press.

Vellutino, F.R. 1979. *Dyslexia: Theory and Research.* Cambridge, Mass.: MIT Press.

Vellutino, F.R., and Scanlon, D.M. 1986. Linguistic coding and metalinguistic awareness: their relationship to verbal memory and code acquisition in poor and normal readers. In D.B. Yaden and S. Templeton (Eds.), *Metalinguistic Awareness and Beginning Literacy*. Portsmouth, N.H.: Heinemann.

Vellutino, F.R., Steger, J.A., Kaman, M., and DeSetto, L. 1975. Visual form perception in deficient and normal readers as a function of age and orthographic linguistic familiarity. *Cortex 11*:22.

Vogel, S.A. 1975. *Syntactic Abilities in Normal and Dyslexic Children.* Baltimore: University Park Press.

Volger, G.P., DeFries, J.C., and Decker, N. 1984. Family history as an indicator of risk for reading disability. *Journal of Learning Disabilities 17*:616.

Waisbren, S.E., Brown, M.J., de Sonneville, L.M.J., and Levy, H.L. 1994. Review of neuropsychological functioning in treated phenylketonurias: an information processing approach. *Acta Paediatrica Supplement 407*:98.

Waldrop, M.F., Bell, R.Q., McLaughlin, B., and Halverson, C.F. 1978. Newborn minor physical anomalies predict short attention span, peer agression, and impulsivity at age 3. *Science 199*:563.

Walker, D., Greenwood, C., Hart, B., and Carta, J. 1994. Prediction of school outcomes based on early language production and socioeconomic factors. *Child Development 65*:606.

Wallach, G.P. 1984. Later language learning: syntactic structures and strategies. In G.P. Wallach and K.G. Butler, *Language Learning Disabilities in School-Age Children.* Baltimore: Williams and Wilkins.

Wallach, G.P., and Butler, K.G. (Eds.). 1984. *Language Learning Disabilities in School-Age Children.* Baltimore: Williams and Wilkins.

Wallerstein, J.S. 1991. The long-term effects of divorce on children: a review. *Journal of American Academy of Child and Adolescent Psychiatry 30*:349.

Warden, M.R., and Hutchinson, T.A. 1992. *Writing Process Test.* Chicago: Riverside Publishing Company.

Webb, T.E., and Oski, F.A. 1973. Iron deficiency anemia and scholastic achievement in young adolescents. *Journal of Pediatrics 82*:827.

Webster, R.E. 1978. Visual and short-term memory capacity deficits in mathematics disabled students. *Journal of Educational Research 72*:277.

Weidler, S.D. 1984. Reading in the content area of science. In M.M. Dupuis (Ed.), *Reading in the Content Areas: Research for Teachers.* Newark, Del.: International Reading Association.

Weinberg, F. 1982. Overrepresentation of adoptees in children with the attention deficit disorder. *Behavioral Genetics 12*:2.

Weiner, E. 1980. The diagnostic evaluation of writing skills. *Learning Disabilities Quarterly 3*:54.

Weiss, G., Hechtman, L., Perlman, T., Hopkins, J., and Wener, A. 1979. Hyperactive children as young adults: a controlled prospective 10 year follow-up of 75 hyperactive children. *Archives of General Psychiatry 36*:675.

Wender, P.H. 1971. *Minimal Cerebral Dysfunction in Children.* New York: John Wiley & Sons.

Werner, E.E., and Smith, R.S. 1982. *Vulnerable But Invincible.* New York: McGraw-Hill.

Werner, E.E., Bierman, J.M., and French, F.E. 1971. *The Children of Kauai.* Honolulu: University of Hawaii Press.

Werry, J.S., and Sprague, R.L. 1970. Hyperactivity. In C.G. Costello (Ed.), *Symptoms of Psychopathology.* New York: John Wiley & Sons.

Westby, C.E. 1984. The development of narrative language abilities. In G.P. Wallach and K.G. Butler (Eds.), *Language Learning Disabilities in School-Age Children.* Baltimore: Williams and Wilkins.

Wickelgren, W.A. 1979. *Cognitive Psychology.* Englewood Cliffs, N.J.: Prentice-Hall.

Wiig, E., and Secord, W. 1988. *Test of Language Competence.* San Antonio, Tex.: Harcourt Brace Jovanovich–Psychological Corp.

Wiig, E., Semel, E., and Crouse, M. 1973. The use of English morphology in high risk and learning-disabled children. *Journal of Learning Disabilities 6*:457.

Wiig, E.H., and Semel, E.M. 1975. Productive language abilities in learning disabled adolescents. *Journal of Learning Disabilities 8*:578.

Wiig, E.H., and Semel, E.M. 1984. *Language Assessment and Intervention for Learning Disabled Children.* Columbus, Ohio: Charles E. Merrill.

Willerman, L., Broman, S., and Fiedler, M. 1970. Infant development, preschool IQ and social class. *Child Development 41*:69.

Wiseman, D.C. 1982. *A Practical Approach to Adapted Physical Education.* Reading, Mass.: Addison-Wesley Publishing Co.

Wolf, M. 1984. Naming, reading, and the dyslexias: a longitudinal overview. *Annals of Dyslexia 39*:87.

Wolff, P.H. 1982. Theoretical issues in the development of motor skills. In M. Lewis and L.T. Taft (Eds.), *Developmental Disabilities: Theory, Assessment, and Intervention.* Jamaica, N.Y.: Spectrum Publications.

Wolff, P.H., and Hurwitz, I. 1966. The choreiform syndrome. *Developmental Medicine and Child Neurology 8*:160.

Wolraich, M., Milich, R., Stumbo, P., and Schultz, F. 1985. Effects of sucrose ingestion on the behavior of hyperactive boys. *Journal of Pediatrics 106*:675.

Wolraich, M.L., Lindgren, S.D., Stumbo, P.J., Stegink, L.D., Appelbaum, M.I., and Kiritsy, M.C. 1994. Effects of diets high in sucrose or aspartame on the behavior and cognitive performance of children. *The New England Journal of Medicine 330*:301.

Youniss, J., and Volpe, J.A. 1978. A relational analysis of children's friendships. In W. Damon (Ed.), *New Directions for Child Development,* vol. 1. San Francisco: Jossey-Bass.

Zincus, P.W., and Gottlieb, M.I. 1980. Patterns of perceptual and academic deficits related to early chronic otitis media. *Pediatrics 66*:246.

Index

Production controls (*cont.*)
    previewing control, 33–35
    reinforcement control, 40–41
    self-monitoring control, 38–40
    social skills and, 286
    tempo control, 37–38
Production strategies, 572
Professional organizations, 603
Proficiency in math, 416
Progressive Incorporation stage of writing, 351, 358, 359
    sequential organization and, 359
    spatial production and, 358
Projective tests, 555–556
Pronominal growth, 148
Proofs, 413
Proprioceptive feedback, 351, 357, 363, 392
    spelling configuration, 392
    writing production, 363
Propulsion in motor development, 193
Prototype and concepts, 219
"Pseudoreading," 300
Psychoanalytic movement, 6
    Freud, 6
Psycholinguistics, 141
P-type dyslexia, 513

Quantified neurophysiology, 517

Rapid auditory processing deficit, 154
Reactive motor procedures, 78
Reading, 299–346, 304, 432
    defined, 304
Reading comprehension, 327–330
    assessment of, 327–330
    recognizing deficiencies, 329–330
Reading skills, 299–346, 436, 509–513
    assessing, 324–330
    cerebral dominance and, 509–513
    developing, 299–303
    managing, 330–346
    performance variation, 304–323
Reafferent feedback, 188, 193, 205
Reauditorization, 164
Recall, 314, 320
    demands in school, 86
    dysfunctions of, 85–87
    typical findings of students with dysfunctions of recall, 86–87
    writing and, 357, 360
"Reciprocal relationships" (Matthew effects), 543
Recoding, 68, 71
Recognition memory, 83–85
Rehearsal strategies, 68, 129
Reinforcement control, 40–41
    dysfunctions, 41
Rejected children, 273–282, 288
    attention controls and, 282

    awareness of image, 279
    feedback cues, 276–277
    indirect approaches, 276
    recuperative strategies, 279
    relevance, 274–275
    resolution of conflict without aggression, 277
    social memory, 278
    social prediction, 278
    timing and staging, 276
    verbal pragmatic strategies, 277
Resiliency, 493
Response inhibition, 35–36
Reticular activating system, 43
Retrieval memory, 391
    erratic patterns of, 357
    impact on writing skills, 357, 360, 368–369
    mathematics and, 411–412
    motor skills and, 210–211
    word configurations, 387
Ritalin, 520
Rostral dominance, 553
Rote memory, 77, 81, 387, 438, 453
    for foreign language materials, 438
    paired association and, 77, 81
    social studies comprehension and, 453
Rote mimicry, 414
Rourke's nonverbal learning disabilities syndrome, 516
Rule-based learning, 80
Rule development and utilization, 217, 226–228, 247
    troubles with, 227–228
    uses of, 226–227
Rules and regularity, 79–80
    dysfunctions of, 80
    long-term memory and, 79–80
    schemata, 79–80

Saliency determination, 25–27, 35, 42, 320
    distractibility, 26–27
    dysfunctions, 26–27
    incidental learning, 27
    management of poor, 61
    short-term memory and, 69, 70
    significance determination, 27
Satisfaction control, 31–33
    dysfunctions, 31–33
    insatiability, 31–32
Schema, 79–80, 316, 324, 455
Schema theory, 316–318
School-related outcomes, 12
Schools, 287
    role in social development, 287
SCHOOLS ATTUNED project, 602
Science, 454–459
    effects of dysfunction, 457
    management of problems in, 457–459
Segmentation deficits, 155